Praise for *Baseball Between the Numbers*

"If you're a sports iconoclast, one of those folks who believes that the conventional wisdom is usually wrong, a firm believer in the cult of "Moneyball," then this book should be next on your list. The stathead big brains at Baseball Prospectus tackle the articles of baseball dogma and dismantle them one by one. . . . [T]he authors use numbers and cold hard logic to dispute myths you never would've even thought to challenge. It's a must-read for anybody who grew up memorizing statistics on the backs of baseball cards." —Newsweek.com

"*Baseball Between the Numbers: Why Everything You Know About the Game Is Wrong* is this year's baseball book for the fanatic who wants to dominate water cooler and tavern conversations as well as the deadly serious fantasy leagues. . . . Editor Jonah Keri and his experts are smart guys, and to their credit they lay out in the introduction that the ultimate goal of all the 'monster in the closet' numbers is more fun for the fan. Also to their credit, the book is laid out in chapters covering burning baseball questions. . . ." —*Indianapolis Star*

"This is a book about baseball stats and theories for people who . . . don't really like stats." —*San Jose Mercury News*

"This book has the answers. . . ." —CNN.com "Eye on Entertainment"

"I've been told many times that everything I knew about baseball is wrong, but this is the first time anyone ever proved it. And made me enjoy hearing why."

—Allen Barra, author of *Clearing the Bases* and
Brushbacks and Knockdowns

"The best thing about Baseball Prospectus is that its writers not only challenge conventional wisdom, but also supply powerful statistical evidence to support their arguments. *Baseball Between the Numbers* provides fresh insights on classic baseball questions (Is Barry Bonds better than Babe Ruth?) and irreverent ones, too (What if Rickey Henderson had Pete Incaviglia's legs?). Each chapter leaves readers with a greater understanding of the game we all love."

—Ken Rosenthal, Senior Baseball Writer, FOXSports.com

"Freakonomics for statheads. . . . Like [Michael] Lewis, the Baseball Prospectus team can make just about anything interesting. . . . Prodigiously informative, sometimes dense, *Baseball Between the Numbers* is an excellent companion for the long summer ahead."

—*New York Times*

"For years, people have been asking me if there's *one* book that will give them a solid grounding in modern baseball analysis. And for years, I've been forced to admit that no, there wasn't any such book. Until now. *Baseball Between the Numbers* will soon be required reading in every front office with serious aspirations for the World Series."

—Rob Neyer, author of *Rob Neyer's Big Book of Baseball Lineups*

"No one who reads this book can follow baseball the same way again. It's so cutting-edge, your fingers will bleed."

—Alan Schwarz, author of *The Numbers Game*

"[*Baseball Between the Numbers* makes] for great coffee-table referencing for the postseason . . . [with] enough heat to last through the winter, too, if that's what you need."   —Jeff Bathurst, *Philadelphia Enquirer*

"Fascinating new book . . . there is plenty of tasty stuff to chew on."

—*New York Newsday*

"One book that will surely fuel the vicious barroom arguments that make the national pastime so much fun is *Baseball Between the Numbers* by the stat-heads at Baseball Prospectus, a book that brings a meat cleaver to some of the game's most sacred cows. . . . The chapters here—'Is Alex Rodriguez Overpaid?,' 'Do Players Perform Better in Their Contract Years?' . . . puncture cherished myths and suggest that every so often, the old-timers were right."

—*New York Daily News*

"A provocative book that looks at the game in ways not previously imagined . . . these are the people making a huge impact on progressive front offices throughout the game." —*Boston Globe*

"[*Baseball Between the Numbers*], whose authors claim to operate "the top statistical Web site in baseball," attempts to present taxing formulas and equations in a breezy, readable way to address questions that have puzzled fans since Ty Cobb was a boy. Overall, they succeed."
—*San Diego Union-Tribune*

"This is essential reading for all baseball fans, even those who hated math in high school." —*Library Journal*

"For fans in the moderate-to-diehard category, the queries asked and answered within these pages make for surprisingly absorbing, even suspenseful, reading." —*Wall Street Journal*

"The best essays in *Baseball Between the Numbers* . . . present detailed and compelling cases for why the traditional dogmas of baseball hold, just not as well as you might think. . . . [*Baseball Between the Numbers*] will also reveal some fascinating things about the game to anyone from Mr. LaRussa to the guy who despises Mets manager Willie Randolph for batting Mr. Reyes leadoff and owns www.firewillie.com to the lawyer who thinks both of them are nuts." —*New York Sun*

"Always entertaining. . . ." —Scripps Howard, *Sacramento Bee*

"These are people who love baseball; their purpose is not to destroy our enjoyment of it but to provide better understanding. And if you're impatient, you won't have to wait long—it's in an introductory chapter—for the group's answer to the burning question: Who's the better player, Barry Bonds or Babe Ruth? We won't give it away."
—*Roanoke Times*

"While we don't agree that everything we know about the game is wrong, this work presents 29 thought-provoking questions and answers about the game guaranteed to generate animated discussion at ballparks, in living rooms and anywhere else baseball fans gather."
—*New Jersey Times*

"Those truly committed to the study of the inner workings of baseball's numbers call themselves sabermeticians—among them there is a cult-like group who write for *Baseball Prospectus*. A collection of their work appears in *Baseball Between the Numbers: Why Everything You Know About the Game Is Wrong*. The image is one of guys in lab coats and ball caps; there is no aspect of the game too great or too trivial to fall under their analysis."   —*Toronto Star*

"*Baseball Between the Numbers: Why Everything You Know About the Game Is Wrong* by the experts at Baseball Prospectus; edited by Jonah Keri. The reason is simple: Summers are nothing without arguments about baseball. This book is sure to start a few."

—Patrick W. Gavin for nationalreview.com

" . . . [An] interesting book about statistics by the guys from Baseball Prospectus."   —Bill Simmons, The Sports Guy, espn.com

"To get a clear grasp on the scope and depth of the impact of statistical analysis in modern baseball, *Baseball Between the Numbers* is essential reading. . . . This is a book for baseball fans. True fans love their stats and will not be intimidated by samples, variables, means, medians, regressions, correlations, and many other statistical concepts in the book, as each one of them is clearly explained and illustrated with practical applications."   —*Embassy Magazine*

BASEBALL
Between the
NUMBERS

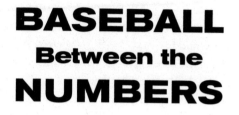

BASEBALL
Between the
NUMBERS

Why Everything You Know

About the Game Is Wrong

BY THE EXPERTS AT
BASEBALL PROSPECTUS

JAMES CLICK ◆ CLAY DAVENPORT

NEIL DEMAUSE ◆ STEVEN GOLDMAN

JONAH KERI ◆ DAYN PERRY

NATE SILVER ◆ KEITH WOOLNER

EDITED BY

JONAH KERI

BASIC
BOOKS

A Member of the Perseus Books Group

New York

Copyright © 2006 by Prospectus Entertainment Ventures LLC

Hardcover published in 2006 by Basic Books
A Member of the Perseus Books Group.
Paperback published in 2007 by Basic Books.

Design by Jane Raese
Text set in 10-point New Aster

Library of Congress Cataloging-in-Publication Data
Baseball between the numbers : why everything you know about the game is wrong / by the Experts at Baseball Prospectus, James Click ... [et al.]., edited by Jonah Keri
    p. cm.
Includes index.
HC: ISBN-13: 978-0-465-00596-3; ISBN-10: 0-465-00596-9
1. Baseball—Statistics. 2. Baseball players—Statistics. I. Click, James.
GV877.B255   2006
796.357021—dc22   2006000118

PBK: ISBN-13: 978-0-465-00547-5; ISBN-10: 0-465-00547-0

10 9 8 7 6 5 4 3

Contents

Preface to the
Paperback Edition

Why Is The American League Better Than The National League?

One of baseball's greatest qualities is its ability to constantly surprise. Every season brings new fodder for discussion, new events that change the way we see the game. That element of surprise and wonder is one of the biggest reasons why we wrote *Baseball Between the Numbers*. The events of 2006 drove us to update the book for 2007, starting with this chapter.

The ink was barely dry on the hardcover before new questions started zooming in. Coors Field was a topic of great debate in the book's last edition, given its Nintendo-like offensive levels. But in 2006, offense at Coors Field dropped dramatically. Rockies pitchers started putting up ERAs that didn't look like model numbers from Boeing. Opposing pitchers no longer suffered night sweats thinking about their next start in Denver. Many attributed the change to the Rockies placing baseballs in humidors before games, deadening fly balls that once soared out of the park. Others gave the Rockies credit for producing a new generation of pitchers, both through the farm system and careful mining of the free-agent market, the trade wire and other sources. Analysts typically look at three-year spans to assess the impact of a ballpark; 2006 could just be a brief anomaly, and Matt Holliday might hit 58 homers in 2007. But one season's results do make us take notice. The baseball world will keep a closer eye on the park in 2007, 2008, and beyond, watching to see which Coors is the real McCoy.

In mere months, "Is Joe Torre a Hall of Fame Manager?" morphed into "Will Joe Torre Have a Job Next Season?" The Yankees got a breakthrough season from young starter Chien-Ming Wang and a bounceback year for Mike Mussina. But the decline of Randy Johnson and other pitching woes had Bombers fans wringing their hands all season. When the Yankees fell in four games in the League Division

Series, many speculated that Torre would take the fall for a sixth straight season without a World Series championship, an eternity in the Bronx. Torre's job in the Yankee dugout has since become more secure. Meanwhile, the characteristics that make one manager a genius and another a bum remained open to debate.

For a brief period after the 2006 season, Alex Rodriguez's job security looked far more tenuous than Torre's. Last year we asked, "Is A-Rod Overpaid?" Using a multitiered system, we found that yes, he was indeed overpaid. The argument has escalated since then. Rodriguez's 2006 season was a strong one by many standards. But a $25 million-a-year contract raises certain expectations. A-Rod saw his numbers drop off significantly from his 2005 MVP levels. Many noted a slip in his defense too. After the 2006 season, people were no longer asking if he was overpaid, but by how much.

As we reflected back on the chapter "Is David Ortiz A Clutch Hitter?" the larger question of whether clutch hitting exists again surfaced. One of A-Rod's biggest shortcomings, his critics claimed, was his constant failures in "clutch situations." These accusations were mostly unfounded. A 1-for–14 performance in the 2006 playoffs is far too small a sample from which to draw any meaningful conclusion. When we look at his body of work over the course of his career, Rodriguez's numbers late in games, with runners in scoring position and in other pivotal instances, don't look much different from his efforts the rest of the time. But perceptions are powerful things, and exceedingly difficult to change. David Ortiz clubbed a few more walk-off hits in 2006. A-Rod failed a few more times. The image of one as folk hero and the other as an overpaid choker grew in the public's mind, fairly or not.

Near the end of the book, we asked "Why Doesn't Billy Beane's Shit Work In The Playoffs?" After multiple attempts, Beane's Oakland A's finally got off the schneid, winning a first-round series. But an unceremonious LCS sweep brought the question back to the fore. We never found out if John Schuerholz's stuff would work in the postseason, as the Braves missed the playoffs for the first time since the 1994 labor stoppage. We did learn that a strong starting rotation and an airtight defense can trump a lineup full of on-base demons come October, as the 2006 Tigers—for a while, anyway—looked like the 2005 White Sox, Version 2.0. Finally, we gained another point in favor of momentum being overrated. A big losing streak and near-collapse right before the postseason may not be as damaging as you'd expect. The 2005

White Sox nearly blew the AL Central to the hard-charging Indians before going on to win it all; the 83-win 2006 Cardinals came even closer to blowing their division, then beat all comers en route to the World Series trophy.

One of the biggest stories of the 2006 season, though, was one we didn't address in the first edition of *Baseball Between the Numbers*: The disparity that's emerged between the American League and the National League. Yes, an NL team, the St. Louis Cardinals, won the 2006 World Series. But other indicators point to the AL being the stronger league. The AL beat the NL in interleague play 154–98 in 2006. That's a staggering .611 winning percentage, the equivalent of a 99-win team. The question naturally arises: Are the American League players, on average, that much better than those in the National League?

The results of interleague play, by themselves, don't answer this question. From a mathematical point of view, whether a game is won or lost is equivalent to whether a coin lands heads or tails, or whether a free throw is hit or missed. In each case, we're dealing with a situation that has only two possible outcomes. These situations are relatively easy to model, using what's called a binomial probability distribution. If the real odds for all the interleague games were 50–50, there would be a .016 percent chance—1 in 6,250—that one side or the other would win 154 (or more) times in 252 tries. Most scientific applications, in order to explain an event as being caused by something other than chance, want to get that number under 5 percent, or one in 20. By that test, the AL certainly looks better than the NL.

Or maybe not. We have a series of procedures at Baseball Prospectus that we use to evaluate how good one league is relative to another. They all work by comparing how player performance changes relative to their league. Suppose you have a group of players who are, collectively, 10 percent better than average in their league. After moving to another league, let's say that same group is now only average. We would then suspect that the second league was about 10 percent harder than the first. Stats go down, league got harder; stats go up, league got easier.

Individual players must be weighted equally in each league. Otherwise, what looks like an upsurge in offense might just be a case where someone like Barry Bonds got twice as many plate appearances. The simplest way to do this is to use the Common Plate Appearance, or CPA. The CPA stat is simply the lesser of the two plate appearance totals. In other words, if Jeff Conine had 432 plate appearances for the

AL Orioles and 107 for the NL Phillies in 2006, the CPA would be 107, the lesser of the two. In the league where the player batted less, the stats stand as they are; but in the other league, they all get multiplied as CPA × PA.

Ideally, you can use a direct approach, testing the players who played in each of the two leagues you are trying to measure. The 2006 season was a particularly good one for this, since there was a relatively large number of players (such as Bobby Abreu, Ron Belliard, Sean Casey, and Aubrey Huff) who switched leagues in midseason. All told, there were 3,360 common plate appearances in 2006, the second-highest total ever; the average for the 10 previous years was 2,053. Going by that approach, the AL comes out as 5.8 percent harder than the NL.

Fortunately for us, we can also use an indirect approach to the problem. We can use a third league as a standard reference point. Let's say that A and B are the leagues we are testing, and C is our reference league. You look at every single player who was in both leagues A and C and check out how their stats changed; then you look at all the players who played in leagues B and C and see how their stats changed. The ratio of the changes is a measure of the difficulty ratio of leagues A and B.

Let's get concrete. For our statistic, we're going to use equivalent runs (EqR) per out. The principal benefit of this measure is that EqR has been corrected for both the average offensive level of the league in question and for park effects (See the Glossary at the end of the book for a definition of EqR). In this case, we want to compare the 2006 AL to the 2006 NL; we're using the 2005 NL as our third league.

All of the players in both the 2005 NL and 2006 NL combined for 61,322 CPA. These players produced .1868 EqR/out in the 2005 NL, and .1779 in the 2006 NL. The ratio here is 1.050.

All of the players from the 2005 NL and 2006 AL combined for 11,223 CPA. They produced .1787 EqR/out in the 2005 NL and .1588 EqR/out in the 2006 AL, for a ratio of 1.125.

The ratio of the ratios is (1.050/1.125), or 0.933. It suggests that the 2006 AL was about 7 percent harder to hit in than the 2006 NL.

Of course, that's just one point. We actually want as many points as we can get, so we do this for every league-season within 25 years. If you're a student of baseball analysis, this may look a lot like the study that analyst Dick Cramer did more than 25 years ago—a study that was originally published in SABR's *1980 Baseball Research Journal*, reprinted in its entirety in Pete Palmer's *The Hidden Game of Baseball* and criticized strongly in Bill James' *Historical Baseball Abstract*. And you would be right, except for one significant difference.

Cramer weighted the comparisons solely by the number of CPA between players. We're doing the same thing here, except that we divide that weight by the number of years of difference between the leagues. That way, leagues with more CPA closer in time—say 2003 compared to 2001, over 1999 compared to 1987—count the most. It also means that we're more confident than Cramer that the player's skill level hasn't changed dramatically over time, although it's still an issue.

Overall, the findings say that the 2006 AL was about 8.6 percent tougher to hit in than the 2006 NL. So conventional wisdom, in this case, had it right. The cases of 21 of the 29 leagues tested, and all of them for the last six years, indicate that the 2006 AL was the harder league.

If the average AL team had an 8.6 percent advantage in runs scored, we would expect the team to win 54 percent of the time, not 50 percent of the time. Go back to the probabilities discussed earlier: Replace a 50 percent coin-flip chance of winning each game with 54 percent, and there is a 1 percent chance that a team would post a record of 154–98 or better. That is a 63-fold increase over our initial guess, but it's still outside the range of probability. We're still missing something.

Of course, we've only been looking at half of the problem—we can dig deeper by doing the same analysis with pitchers as we did with hitters. While we would expect pitchers to behave in more or less the same way as hitters, they wouldn't necessarily be exactly the same. As it turns out, they don't look exactly the same at all; the difficulty trend for pitchers is somewhat steeper than it is for hitting, although the shape is pretty much the same. This may explain why the rules have had to be adjusted periodically to maintain the balance between hitting and pitching, and that those changes—such as lowering the pitcher's mound after pitchers dominated in the late 1960s—have usually been aimed at pumping up the offense. Using the same analysis we used for hitters, we find that the AL pitchers of 2006 were expected to be 4.5 percent better than those in the NL.

A team that scores 8.6 percent more runs and allows 4.5percent less has an expected winning percentage of .564. Plug a .564 winning percentage into a probabilities table and the chance of a 154–98 record goes up to 5.7 percent. That's above the 5 percent threshold generally needed to reject random chance. In other words, the AL was somewhat lucky to have so good a record in 2006. But AL teams could have reasonably expected to beat NL teams, and by a wide margin.

Looking back over the history of interleague play, we can see that this was the least likely result yet given the AL's expected winning percentage. The "favored" league based on difficulty analysis has won the interleague series eight out of 10 times so far (all records from AL point of view):

We can go beyond this. The All-Star Game has been played since 1933 and is a reasonable test of the overall

TABLE X.1   Interleague Play Results, 1997–2006

Year	Expected AL Pct	Actual	Likelihood
2006	.564	.611 (154–98)	.06
2005	.511	.540 (136–116)	.17
2004	.536	.502 (126–125)	.15
2003	.501	.456 (115–137)	.09
2002	.489	.488 (123–129)	.49
2001	.489	.524 (132–120)	.12
2000	.514	.542 (136–115)	.17
1999	.495	.462 (116–135)	.16
1998	.511	.509 (114–110)	.50
1997	.475	.454 (97–117)	.29

talent of the league—or would be, if they played more than one game. We should also add a caveat about how the All-Star Game isn't a full sample of the league, but just the cream of the crop, and thus not necessarily representative of the league strength as a whole. It's easier for an imbalance to occur with 50 players than with several hundred.

With that said, the difficulty test has picked the winner of the All-Star Game 46 out of 75 times. In particular, the difficulty test saw the NL break away from the AL around 1952, with the NL holding a sometimes wide margin as the stronger league every year from 1952 to 1991, with the sole exception of 1972. During those 40 years, the NL won 31 of 43 All-Star Games (ties excluded). The difficulty rating also saw the AL take over as the more difficult league in 1992, with the AL holding that title for most of the 15 years since—the AL has gone 11–3–1 in the All-Star game since then.

Extending this analysis to the World Series is a riskier proposition; just because the league as a whole is weaker does not mean that its best team is, any more than that its best players are. In fact, the simple test of which league is more difficult hasn't done any better at picking World Series winners than flipping a coin, with 51 right and 51 wrong after the Cardinals' win in 2006.

With that established, let's dig deeper. When did the gap between the AL and NL start to emerge? Was there a similar gap before that favoring the NL? Why and how do these gaps emerge in the first place?

The NL of the late 1950s held a bigger edge over the AL than the current AL-over-NL gap, with integration playing a major role. The NL of 1901 also showed a bigger gap, in that case a result of the AL just getting started as a rival major league. The AL quickly reversed that gap in 1902. Once the league demonstrated it wasn't going to fold right away, players were more than willing to leave the despised NL owners behind; MLB labor relations in the 1890s were as hideous as anything in our lifetimes. The AL's sizable gap persisted until 1912. The AL opened another gap in the early 1920s, as stars such as Babe Ruth drove the league to improve, while the NL basically stagnated at 1912 levels. The next big shift occurred after 1925, thanks to the advent of farm systems. Branch Rickey and other NL team operators used player development to their advantage far more than their AL brethren in those early years, allowing the NL to roar back with very rapid growth after 1925.

In the chapter "Batting Practice: Is Barry Bonds Better Than Babe Ruth?" there's a table that shows the ratio of difficulty ratings going back to the 1950s. There's a jump in the gap between NL and AL batters that happens around 1951 and persists until 1990. The usual explanation is that National League teams were more aggressive in implementing racial integration.

We can test this theory through a career MVP score, a measure that tabulates a player's career value to make it easier to compare his contributions to that of another player. Using the 20-year span from 1947, when Jackie Robinson broke the color barrier, to 1967, when the amateur draft started, we can gain some insight into how this progressed. The top-ranked players who would have been prohibited from playing before 1947 were, in order of career value: Willie Mays, Hank Aaron, Ernie Banks, Frank Robinson, Jackie Robinson, Roberto Clemente, Roy Campanella, Minnie Minoso, Juan Marichal, Camilo Pascual, Orlando Cepeda, Larry Doby, Billy Williams, Maury Wills, Vada Pinson, Don Newcombe, Bob Gibson, Jim Gilliam, Luis Aparicio, and Bobby Avila.

Five of the 20—Minoso, Pascual, Doby, Aparicio, and Avila—were AL guys, and they rank 8–10–12–19–20 on this list. Yes, the NL did a lot better in integrating top-flight players onto its rosters (and would continue to pick up difference makers in the early 1960s, with Joe Morgan, Dick Allen, and Fergie Jenkins among the best of those). Until the onset of the draft, black players wanted to "play in Jackie's league" and showed a pretty clear preference to sign with NL teams when they had free opportunity to do so.

In 1991, the tide turned in the AL's favor, a talent gap that still exists today. We ran a program that divided players into groups based on where they went. For instance, the 1991 statistics of players in the American League who also played in the AL in 1992 combined for a .264 Equivalent Average and 9,208 EqR. The 1991 AL stats of players who then played in the NL in 1992 totaled a .244 EqA and 771 EqR (see the Glossary at the back of the book for a definition of EqA). That ratio, 771 EqR moving to the other league over the 9,208 who stayed, is 8.4 percent, one of the smaller totals of the last 20 years. If we do the exact same thing for players in the 1991 NL and break them up based on where they went the next year, then 7,909 EqR stayed put, and 999 moved to the AL— 12.6 percent. That difference, a little over four percentage points in the AL's favor, is the largest change in either direction in the last 20 years, and part of a sustained AL advantage from the mid-1980s to mid-1990s, as shown in Table X.2. A positive number suggests a net talent flow to the AL. Note the increase in player movement after 1995 and the see-sawing back and forth since 1997.

TABLE X.2 Forward One Year, Ratio of Switching EqR to staying EqR, 1985–2005

Year	AL	NL	AL Advantage
1985	4.7	4.3	-0.4
1986	8.8	11.1	2.3
1987	8.5	12.4	3.9
1988	11.1	13.5	2.4
1989	8.7	9.2	0.5
1990	10.8	11.4	0.6
1991	8.4	12.6	4.2
1992	13.9	15.5	1.6
1993	7.4	10.1	2.7
1994	8.3	11.7	3.4
1995	17.2	19.1	1.9
1996	17.5	19.3	1.8
1997	21.3	19.1	-2.2
1998	13.1	12.4	-0.7
1999	15.8	18.1	2.3
2000	12.0	10.9	-1.1
2001	15.1	15.8	0.7
2002	17.1	13.5	-3.6
2003	20.5	24.4	3.9
2004	20.9	18.1	-2.8
2005	20.5	22.0	1.5

We went through a 10-year stretch where the AL took more talent from the NL than it gave back.

We don't have an analogue as clean as EqR with which to test pitchers. Instead, we used Runs Above Replacement level (RAR), based on a replacement value of a 6.00 ERA. That is, ERAs below 6.00 would yield positive RAR figures, while ERAs above 6.00 would yield negative results, as shown in Table X.3. Again, positive in the third column means

TABLE X.3   One Year Forward, Ratio
of RAR, Switching Pitchers to Staying
Pitchers, 1985–2005

Year	AL	NL	AL Advantage
1985	10.2	8.5	-1.7
1986	14.8	15.1	0.3
1987	7.5	12.8	5.3
1988	14.4	16.1	1.7
1989	3.9	10.5	6.6
1990	8.0	7.9	-0.1
1991	12.3	12.8	0.5
1992	11.1	17.6	6.5
1993	8.4	15.0	6.6
1994	7.2	17.0	9.8
1995	13.4	12.7	-0.7
1996	11.3	17.8	6.5
1997	21.0	12.9	-8.1
1998	13.1	9.5	-3.6
1999	8.4	13.1	4.7
2000	18.1	8.1	-10.0
2001	11.3	13.1	1.8
2002	10.0	12.0	2.0
2003	13.4	22.0	8.6
2004	20.9	19.7	-1.2
2005	18.7	17.3	-1.4

a net flow of talent from the NL to the AL:

Again, there were some wild oscillations in recent years, like a big gain for the NL in 2000–2001. Of pitchers with 20+ RAR in 2000, the NL lost Rick Reed, Steve Parris, Pat Hentgen, Chris Holt, and Rob Bell, five pitchers. But it gained Mac Suzuki, Albie Lopez, James Baldwin, Kevin Appier, Steve Trachsel, Jeff Fassero, Tomo Ohka, Steve Karsay, Justin Speier, Mike Fyhrie, Rick White, Jose Santiago, Mike Trombley, and Kent Bottenfield, 14 pitchers. The 2003 season saw a reverse swing. The AL lost six 20+ RAR pitchers in Roger Clemens, David Wells, John Thomson, Andy Pettitte, Victor Zambrano, and Andy Hawkins. But it gained 15 such pitchers: Kevin Brown, Javier Vazquez, Curt Schilling, Miguel Batista, Mark Redman, Octavio Dotel, Paul Quantrill, Joe Nathan, Ron Villone, Terry Adams, Gil Heredia, Ugueth Urbina, Justin Speier, Sidney Ponson, and Jeff D'Amico. The top four pitchers gained were better in 2003 than any of the ones lost.

Why did this happen? Several pitchers migrated to the two teams with the most aggressive recent approach to player acquisition and the biggest recent payrolls, the Yankees and the Red Sox (the Mets later moved into this echelon too). The spillover effect of the Yanks' and Red Sox's aggressiveness was a keeping-up-with-the-Joneses effect, with other AL teams becoming more aggressive in chasing free-agent talent. In the AL East in particular, the perceived need for pitching has grown to massive proportions; think of the $105 million the Blue Jays shelled out after the 2005 season to ink A. J. Burnett and B. J. Ryan in an effort to chase down the front-running Yankees and Red Sox.

Of course, free agency and trades aren't the only ways a team can stock its roster. A team's age can also make a big impact. A club full of up-and-coming 25-year-olds will often click better than a roster bogged down with late–30s talent on their last legs. Indeed, an interesting pattern has emerged: The AL has become younger than the NL. Weighting players by plate appearances or innings pitched, the AL used to be older, but no longer. This trend is more pronounced for batters than pitchers; but for both sets of players, starting around 1982 (five years after the 1977 expansion), the NL was predominantly younger than the AL. That trend has reversed itself, with the AL the younger league in seven of the last eight years, as shown in Tables X.4 and X.5.

Another way to attack this discussion is to look at contributions from players who were rookies in the past three years in each league. This helps gauge the influx of top young talent in the AL vs. the NL. Since the leagues have varied in size—the AL now has two fewer teams than the NL, but it wasn't always that way—we looked at average contribution per recent rookie. The result: There was no clear pattern on the position player side.

But on the pitching side, the AL has been getting slightly more production out of "recent rookie" pitchers than the NL has for a couple of decades. Starting with the advent of divisional play in 1969, the NL had more productive near-rookie hurlers for six out of seven years. Over the next 31 years (starting in

TABLE X.4   Batter Age, 1960–2006 (weighted by PA)

Year	AL Age	NL Age	Diff (Diff < 0 means AL is younger)
1960	28.50	27.85	0.647
1961	28.18	27.55	0.626
1962	27.80	27.89	−0.086
1963	27.69	27.43	0.257
1964	27.40	27.21	0.189
1965	27.21	27.33	−0.120
1966	27.09	27.24	−0.148
1967	27.09	27.46	−0.371
1968	27.17	27.85	−0.681
1969	27.18	27.45	−0.266
1970	27.53	27.58	−0.044
1971	27.70	27.50	0.199
1972	27.81	27.20	0.603
1973	27.99	27.30	0.691
1974	27.67	27.12	0.554
1975	27.52	27.17	0.352
1976	27.49	27.61	−0.122
1977	27.45	27.44	0.006
1978	27.51	27.84	−0.337
1979	27.80	28.32	−0.519
1980	28.03	28.49	−0.457
1981	28.74	28.39	0.350
1982	28.83	28.51	0.325
1983	28.87	28.47	0.407
1984	28.77	28.49	0.280
1985	29.03	28.70	0.333
1986	28.90	28.50	0.400
1987	28.39	28.17	0.216
1988	28.55	28.02	0.533
1989	28.56	28.34	0.220

(continues)

TABLE X.4 (continued)

Year	AL Age	NL Age	Diff (Diff < 0 means AL is younger)
1990	28.59	28.29	0.296
1991	28.53	28.37	0.161
1992	28.58	28.15	0.424
1993	28.86	27.96	0.894
1994	29.12	28.28	0.838
1995	29.06	28.25	0.801
1996	28.95	28.80	0.145
1997	29.10	28.78	0.324
1998	29.32	28.54	0.785
1999	28.88	28.90	−0.016
2000	29.12	29.11	0.012
2001	29.02	29.23	−0.207
2002	28.82	29.43	−0.612
2003	28.69	29.52	−0.827
2004	29.20	29.37	−0.167
2005	28.80	29.39	−0.588
2006	28.72	29.16	−0.434

TABLE X.5   Pitcher Age, 1960–2006 (weighted by IP)

Year	AL Age	NL Age	Diff
1960	27.86	27.37	0.482
1961	27.68	27.35	0.336
1962	27.66	27.80	−0.142
1963	27.63	28.31	−0.674
1965	26.91	28.37	−1.465
1966	26.79	27.74	−0.953
1967	26.81	27.34	−0.524
1968	26.82	27.29	−0.473
1969	26.95	26.90	0.055
1970	27.11	26.94	0.174
1971	26.93	27.26	−0.332
1972	27.24	27.05	0.188
1973	27.68	27.29	0.395
1974	28.07	27.25	0.817

(continues)

1976), only five times have the NL's young hurlers been better, on average, than their AL counterparts. That could mean that the AL has been getting slightly better pitching for a long time, allowing the overall quality of the league to rise, eventually catching and passing the NL.

One possible explanation for this advantage among AL younger pitchers might be the impact of the designated hitter rule. The advent of the DH rule coincides almost exactly with the AL's newfound edge in quality young pitching. It's possible that the DH rule has allowed AL pitchers to focus and specialize on pitching more than NL pitchers have. That could in turn make those AL pitchers a bit better at pitching than NL ones, since they don't have other demands on their skills, such as hitting and bunting. Table X.6 shows the gap.

One caveat to this rookie and near-rookie analysis: Rookie performance is often something of a counterfactual indicator. Good rookie performances, especially spread over the depth of a class, tend to indicate that the quality of the league they were joining was unusually low, not that the rookies themselves were

TABLE X.5 (continued)

Year	AL Age	NL Age	Diff
1975	28.07	27.11	0.968
1976	27.59	27.48	0.103
1977	27.40	27.42	-0.016
1978	27.20	28.00	-0.804
1979	27.41	28.24	-0.829
1980	27.72	28.35	-0.632
1981	27.88	28.78	-0.896
1982	28.30	28.68	-0.380
1983	28.56	28.47	0.085
1984	28.43	28.10	0.322
1985	28.43	28.21	0.220
1986	28.13	28.33	-0.196
1987	28.51	28.17	0.335
1988	28.44	28.48	-0.034
1989	28.50	28.73	-0.232
1990	28.40	28.33	0.070
1991	28.42	27.99	0.426
1992	28.78	28.12	0.654
1993	28.57	28.07	0.495
1994	28.93	27.97	0.964
1995	28.60	27.68	0.926
1996	28.21	28.22	-0.007
1997	28.71	27.88	0.826
1998	29.12	28.21	0.912
1999	28.90	28.38	0.521
2000	28.71	28.59	0.114
2001	28.30	28.71	-0.420
2002	28.56	28.58	-0.027
2003	28.53	28.45	0.079
2004	28.69	29.00	-0.304
2005	28.83	28.94	-0.111
2006	28.30	28.68	-0.377

better than average. Thus, it could be that AL rookies during the time frame examined were better, but that's not absolutely certain.

So what lessons can we take away from the AL's rise to supremacy? Does anything need to be done to level the playing field between the two leagues? *Can anything be done?* Or is 2006 just an extreme example of a natural cycle that happens whenever any set of sports teams is split into leagues or conferences?

The reason for the current imbalance is fundamentally different from old reasons, which generally relied on a big event (such as the AL's beginnings as a major league or integration) creating an imbalance and then holding that imbalance for a decade or more. Volatility, in the form of turnover in players, has increased dramatically since 1990. Getting rid of interleague play could drive the NL to be a little more aggressive in the free-agent market, since it currently causes more NL teams to have sub-par records. If NL teams become less willing to lose their own players and more willing to acquire talent from other teams, that should drive the gap between the two leagues back toward equilibrium.

Since interleague play is not going away any time soon, perhaps NL fans' best hope for parity is some equivalent to the Yankees that will

TABLE X.6 AL Near-Rookie Pitchers vs. NL Near-Rookie Pitchers, 1969–2006 (AL/NL Columns Are # of Near-Rookie Pitchers in Each League)

Year	AL	AL IP	AL VORP	NL	NL IP	NL VORP	Diff	AL Rate	NL Rate	Diff
1969	93	6295.0	395.5	99	7342.0	575.1	-179.6	4.25	5.81	-1.556
1970	102	6722.0	456.8	95	7298.7	634.4	-177.6	4.48	6.68	-2.200
1971	90	6256.7	428.7	86	5903.7	284.4	144.3	4.76	3.31	1.456
1972	89	6256.7	143.5	76	5921.0	274.2	-130.7	1.61	3.61	-1.995
1973	81	5862.3	380.4	80	5868.3	457.0	-76.7	4.70	5.71	-1.017
1974	73	4974.3	284.8	100	7479.7	537.4	-252.6	3.90	5.37	-1.473
1975	88	5987.7	496.4	93	7374.7	613.6	-117.2	5.64	6.60	-0.957
1976	73	6063.7	402.1	91	6159.7	354.9	47.2	5.51	3.90	1.609
1977	105	7853.7	822.6	92	7106.0	564.6	258.0	7.83	6.14	1.697
1978	103	8298.7	740.9	94	6297.0	354.8	386.1	7.19	3.77	3.419
1979	121	9024.3	903.6	89	6074.7	520.2	383.4	7.47	5.85	1.622
1980	95	7417.0	754.4	82	5811.0	388.2	366.2	7.94	4.73	3.207
1981	89	4553.3	447.4	78	3958.7	232.7	214.7	5.03	2.98	2.044
1982	95	6083.7	579.4	84	6657.0	548.4	30.9	6.10	6.53	-0.430
1983	101	7064.7	633.8	96	7256.0	696.6	-62.8	6.28	7.26	-0.981
1984	108	8287.0	745.3	97	6844.7	503.4	241.9	6.90	5.19	1.712
1985	120	8424.3	796.0	95	6695.7	524.7	271.2	6.63	5.52	1.109
1986	111	8535.3	955.8	96	6456.3	618.7	337.1	8.61	6.45	2.166
1987	109	7430.3	764.1	99	6348.0	543.2	220.9	7.01	5.49	1.523
1988	128	8152.0	737.3	100	6153.3	383.3	354.1	5.76	3.83	1.928
1989	130	7866.7	677.7	96	5245.0	322.4	355.4	5.21	3.36	1.855

(continues)

TABLE X.6 (continued)

Year	AL	AL IP	AL VORP	NL	NL IP	NL VORP	Diff	AL Rate	NL Rate	Diff
1990	136	7854.3	709.2	109	5675.7	506.3	202.9	5.21	4.64	0.570
1991	145	8330.7	639.0	112	6992.3	561.4	77.5	4.41	5.01	-0.606
1992	111	6809.7	701.6	104	6772.0	278.7	422.9	6.32	2.68	3.641
1993	139	7335.7	709.9	138	8249.3	594.2	115.8	5.11	4.31	0.802
1994	110	4319.0	514.0	130	6426.0	599.8	-85.8	4.67	4.61	0.059
1995	158	6396.7	565.5	172	8548.7	911.0	-345.5	3.58	5.30	-1.717
1996	162	8175.7	953.9	148	8015.7	605.7	348.2	5.89	4.09	1.796
1997	147	8243.0	750.2	161	8692.0	846.4	-96.2	5.10	5.26	-0.154
1998	133	7623.0	858.5	171	9623.3	655.3	203.1	6.45	3.83	2.622
1999	160	7756.0	1018.6	154	8458.7	802.5	216.2	6.37	5.21	1.156
2000	157	7636.0	852.5	160	8273.0	783.1	69.4	5.43	4.89	0.536
2001	149	8591.7	997.7	151	8180.7	914.6	83.1	6.70	6.06	0.639
2002	158	8612.7	943.5	168	9098.3	688.1	255.4	5.97	4.10	1.876
2003	156	8614.0	870.3	170	9087.3	766.6	103.7	5.58	4.51	1.069
2004	163	7541.7	872.8	167	8274.7	577.8	295.0	5.35	3.46	1.895
2005	141	7275.3	795.9	158	7477.0	747.6	48.3	5.64	4.73	0.913
2006	175	8037.7	1103.4	179	8993.0	1077.1	26.2	6.30	6.02	0.288

make all the other teams compete harder to keep up. The NL has never had such a team; its closest recent equivalent to a dynasty, the Atlanta Braves, won fourteen straight division titles but only one world championship in that span. The Mets have recently been spending money—and developing top young talent through their farm system—as if they aim to dominate the league for some time. If they succeed at this, then the Braves, Cardinals, Dodgers, and anyone else with World Series hopes will have to become that much better to have a chance of making it. That way, too, we could see a return to parity.

Preface

In ballparks and on message boards, in bars and by the water cooler, great baseball debates rage. Who's the best player of all time? Why'd they pay that guy so much money? What's the deal with steroids, anyway? Fans are divided among thirty different teams, but they all seem to love a good argument.

The people charged with resolving these debates have plenty of opinions to share—and plenty of decibels with which to share them. Too often, however, those opinions don't get you closer to the truth. The ex-jock who raves about a player's character often ignores that same player's complete inability to help his team on the field. Yet for years, we fans lapped up everything the ex-jock said. After all, he'd played the game. His experience hanging in the clubhouse, taking the field in front of fifty thousand fans and standing in against a 95-mph fastball, must have given him knowledge others didn't have.

That's all changed. The last few decades have brought about a revolution for baseball fans. A great equalizer has emerged that has put everyone on an even footing. It turns out you don't need to stare a batter down from the pitcher's mound or take him out on a slide into second to know if he can play. If you know how to think properly about the statistical side of baseball, you can have insights that elude even some professionals. Learning to use numbers in a productive way has opened the door for a new generation of informed fans, a group that doesn't require insider knowledge to get the goods on their favorite team.

The use of numbers in the game dates back more than a century—to Henry Chadwick, a baseball enthusiast who produced the first box scores in the nineteenth century. Chadwick's record-keeping stoked a growing interest in numbers that would eventually spread to baseball operators. When Branch Rickey rose to the equivalent of today's general manager role with the 1920s St. Louis Cardinals, he brought with him a strong understanding of the role of numbers in team building.

After the 1942 season, Rickey took over as GM of the Brooklyn Dodgers. Seeking help with number crunching to gain a competitive edge, Rickey turned to Allan Roth. In his years working under Rickey, Roth uncovered a wealth of new information. Suddenly the Dodgers could look at a player's batting average in every count, or weigh his performance against left- and right-handed pitchers. Roth may have been the first of his kind, a team statistician charged with both compiling and analyzing numbers. When the Dodgers enjoyed the most successful era in their history, it seemed as if more Roths would soon spring up everywhere. But the influence of numerical analysis on the game remained minimal. Though researchers like Earnshaw Cook worked to advance baseball research into new areas, it remained the province of outsiders, with fans and teams both slow to accept the benefits of applied numbers.

It took Bill James and his series of *Baseball Abstract* books in the 1970s and '80s to pull numbers into the limelight. James advocated the use of "sabermetrics" (a take-off on the Society of American Baseball Research, or SABR) as a way of learning more about the game. His sharp writing style, combined with recent discoveries of how the game worked, created a new generation of curious, knowledgeable fans. The revolution spread rapidly from there. *The Hidden Game of Baseball* by John Thorn and Pete Palmer and *The Diamond Appraised* by Craig Wright and Tom House were seminal books that tackled new sabermetric ideas and analyzed some older ones in greater detail.

In 1996, Baseball Prospectus grabbed the baton. Much like James, Baseball Prospectus began as a group of young, inquisitive fans with no particular connections, armed only with brainpower and writing skill. The growth of the group over the years, combined with the explosion in database capabilities and the Internet, has helped us become a leader in the field, with some of the most powerful analytic tools in the business. At the same time, we recognize our place within the much larger revolution. Today there's a whole new way of thinking about baseball that extends from the bleachers to every major league front office.

All of which leads us to this book. Within these pages the authors pose twenty-nine provocative questions, meant to stir up those debates we love so much. But the answers to those questions aren't the main goal of this book. In a sense, we don't really care whether Barry Bonds is a better player than Babe Ruth. More important than the particular answers is how we arrived at them. When we ask, "Is Barry Bonds Better Than Babe Ruth?" we must figure out the best way to evaluate one player versus another. It's not enough to say, "I saw Barry Bonds play at SBC Park. He hit a ball so hard, it sank one of those boats in McCovey Cove. He's awesome!" Well, Bonds has indeed enjoyed an awesome career. And the condition of some of those dinghies in McCovey Cove is pretty suspect.

But to arrive at an answer that expands our knowledge of the game, we need to ask the right smaller questions within the framework of the bigger question. How much credit should Bonds get for his base-stealing? How did the ballparks each man played in affect his production? How do we account for Ruth playing in a vastly different era, before the huge advances made in medical technology and training regimens, and before integration? We use numbers as a framework to delve into these answers. But it's the process of learning to think critically about the game that defines this book, and in a broader sense defines our experiences as avid fans of the game. It's the baseball *between* the numbers that we seek.

We put this book together because we love baseball, and we want to see it grow and succeed. That we approach the game with an analytical eye and a critical keyboard doesn't diminish the joy we've derived from baseball—it enhances it. Reading *Baseball Between the Numbers* will make you a smarter fan of the game, able to look at any bunt situation, any pitching change or 3-run homer, and understand its implications. But it will also heighten your enjoyment of the game. The next time you're at the park arguing a manager's decision, you'll be well armed for the debate. Better yet, you'll have a lot more fun.

—*Jonah Keri*
Seattle, Washington

Pay No Attention to the
Glowing, Orange-Eyed Satan-Dog
Behind the Closet Door

In his 1981 novel *Cujo,* Stephen King, perhaps to add a touch of the implausible to the narrative, included an opening chapter in which the soul of a serial killer was reincarnated as a canine demon haunting a young boy's closet: "Low to the ground it was, with huge shoulders bulking above its cocked head, its eyes amber-glowing pits—a thing that might have been half man, half wolf."

King dropped the serial killer/hell-pooch after five pages and never returned to it. The "amber-glowing pits" were a red (or amber) herring seemingly intended to gull thrill-seeking readers into thinking they were about to be titillated by a terrifying tale of the supernatural. When what they actually had in their hands was a plausibly real-world story about a rabid St. Bernard.

Baseball Between the Numbers comes with its own red herring, and it's right there in the title. Our monster in the closet is Numbers: those squiggly symbols that you seriously contemplate only when trying to guess the correct tip at the end of a meal. Otherwise you may not have thought about math since you last faced that spinster algebra teacher with the misaligned teeth who sewed her own clothing and glared balefully whenever you dropped your pencil. Government surveys suggest that nine out of ten Americans don't like numbers, don't understand them, and would be favorably inclined toward replacing channel designations for television stations with a system of pictographs.

Fortunately, you need be only mildly conversant with numbers to enjoy this book. The operative word here is "Between" rather than "Numbers." In this book we're *around* the numbers, *beyond* the numbers, and quietly tiptoeing *past* the numbers but not necessarily *through* the numbers. Imagine Druids cavorting at Stonehenge, and you'll get the idea. They danced in the spaces where the big blocks were not. They didn't run right at them (or, if they did, it's no surprise that their religion died out).

That being said, Baseball Prospectus does have a well-earned reputation for concocting new baseball statistics with acronyms that are either jazzy or obscure, depending on your point of view. These "advanced" statistics are really just the old statistics (hits, home runs, walks, all of your Topps cards favorites) remixed for greater clarity. If you haven't run into them before, either at our Web site, www.baseball prospectus.com, or during your local baseball broadcast (for the BP meme has begun to penetrate the yolk of mass media), there is an extensive glossary in the back of the book. The glossary covers not only some of the funky-lettered acronyms you'll see in this book but also broader concepts such as "regression to the mean" and "Mendoza Line." We explain all of these concepts in the book, but not necessarily every time they're used. Feel free to consult the glossary if you find yourself stuck at any point.

For now, though, get to know these three items and you'll be fine:

- The "slash stats," typically rendered as (for example) .281/.405/ .518. They stand for batting average, on-base percentage, and slugging average. In 1941, Ted Williams batted .406/.553/.735, one of the best seasons in history. In 2005, Corey Patterson of the Chicago Cubs hit .215/.251/.348, which is about as bad a season as a player can have.
- VORP stands for Value Over Replacement Player. VORP is an all-in-one statistic, which means that it takes all of a player's disparate offensive contributions and sums them up in one handy figure. In this case, VORP is meant to answer the question, "How many runs did a given player generate over the worst acceptable major leaguer a team could find at his position?" (We call that barely adequate fellow a "replacement-level" player.) In 2005, the major league VORP leader was Derrek Lee of the Cubs, with 105.9. Corey Patterson was last among full-time players at –10.6, meaning he gave his team about 10.6 fewer runs than it would have gotten from a good Triple-A player. Ten VORP equals roughly 1 win for the team, so Lee was worth nearly 11 wins more to the Cubs than a replacement-level player. Patterson canceled out one of those wins with his sub-replacement-level performance. There's also VORP for pitchers, which depicts how many runs the pitcher in question saved beyond what a replacement-level pitcher would have been able to do. In 2005, Roger Clemens led Major League Baseball at 80.6; Jose Lima of the Kansas City Royals was last at –30.8. VORP does not consider defense.

◆ Equivalent Average, or EqA, is another all-in-one statistic. This time, a player's total offensive output is taken, adjusted for league and park, and expressed on a scale that looks very much like batting average. For example, a .260 EqA is about average, same as a .260 batting average; .300 is very good; .190 is horribly bad. Among full-time players, the 2005 EqA leader was Alex Rodriguez of the Yankees, at .350. Derrek Lee was a close second at .347. The trailers were Corey Patterson at .209 and Cristian Guzman with .204. Like VORP, EqA doesn't consider defense.

That's all you need to know. So fear no numbers. They are a path to understanding, a door to a room, not the room itself. In fact, we only put the word "Numbers" in the title because we wanted to limit our audience to a crowd of intrepid, enlightened risk-takers who would not be dissuaded by a word that would send the majority of their contemporaries screaming for the exits. *Baseball Between the Numbers* is *Cujo* in reverse. Whereas that book had an intriguing opening followed by 250 torturous pages about a sick puppy, we restricted the difficult stuff to a single word on the title page, after which it's all special effects and stunning revelations.

Now close the closet door and enjoy the rest of the book.

Batting Practice

Is Barry Bonds Better Than Babe Ruth?

NATE SILVER

There are few irrefutable truths in baseball. Pretty much anything, from David Ortiz's clutch hitting (Chapter 1-2) to the viability of pitch counts (Chapter 2-3), is fodder for a lively barroom argument. That's why we wrote this book. We believe some of these questions have "right" answers, while the answers to others will remain tantalizingly uncertain, to be debated long after the bartender has begun picking up the chairs and you're scrounging for pocket change to tip the cabbie on your way home. All of these questions deserve to be asked, and few are simple to resolve.

That's why it's so remarkable that until recently there could be no serious debate about perhaps the most important question of all: Who is the best baseball player of all time? With the possible exception of Ted Williams's name in a Boston tavern, any answer other than Babe Ruth would have gotten you laughed out of the room. In the summer of 2002, a group of nineteen members of the Society for American Baseball Research (SABR) conducted a *Survivor*-like contest in which the one hundred best baseball players in history were voted out, one player at a time, until just one remained. Sabermetricians—the name is derived from the SABR acronym—are a contrarian lot who rarely agree on much. But when the final vote came down to Ruth and Honus Wagner, Ruth didn't just win—he won unanimously.

However, that was before Barry Bonds had really shown us what he could do. Bonds had long been a great player. Through the year 2000, he hit 494 home runs, won three MVP awards, and appeared in the All-Star game nine times. But Bonds would be turning thirty-six in the 2001 season, had become increasingly vulnerable to injuries, and could no longer steal bases or race after fly balls as he used to. All signs pointed to a steady, if slow, decline.

Instead, between 2001 and 2004, Bonds won four consecutive MVP awards, two batting crowns and a home-run title, and broke the single-season records for home runs, on-base percentage, slugging average, and walks. He hit 209 home runs during that stretch—equaling Ruth's total between 1927 and 1930, the best period of his career—with a .349 batting average. His on-base percentage for those four seasons was .556, higher than Ruth's mark in his single best season (.545 in 1923). His slugging average was .809, a figure Ruth topped just twice in his career. It was the most impressive run of sustained success that a baseball player had ever recorded, and possibly the most complete display of dominance in any American sport.

Can we now call Barry Bonds the best player of all-time? Is he even better than the Bambino?

That depends on how you choose to settle the argument. Is the benchmark how good the player was relative to his league? Or do we want a grander scale: How good was the player relative to all baseball players throughout history? Most people start (and end) by looking at the players' raw batting statistics, as in Table BP.1. That standard would seem to favor Ruth.

TABLE BP.1 Babe Ruth and Barry Bonds, Career Statistics

	G	AB	R	H	2B	3B	HR
Ruth	2,503	8,399	2,173	2,873	506	136	714
Bonds (through 2005)	2,730	9,140	2,078	2,742	564	77	708

	RBI	SB	BB	SO	BA	OBP	SLG
Ruth	2,213	123	2,062	1,330	0.342	0.474	0.690
Bonds (through 2005)	1,853	506	2,311	1,434	0.3	0.442	0.611

Bonds has a small edge in doubles and bases on balls and a large edge in stolen bases. He's closing in on Ruth in two other key categories (runs scored and home runs) and may surpass him on both fronts in the next couple seasons. On the other hand, Ruth has an insurmountable edge in batting average and probably in runs batted in.

Those of you who are familiar with Baseball Prospectus know that we are most concerned with the last two categories in the table: on-base percentage (OBP) and slugging average (SLG). We'll discuss the relative merits of offensive statistics in more detail in Chapter 1-1, but the reason we place the most emphasis on these two particular stats is simple: They have the strongest statistical relationship with run scoring. OBP and SLG represent the two essential components of creating offense—getting on base and hitting for power. Teams that are best in these two areas score the most runs and win the most games. Ruth has a large edge in OBP and an even larger edge in SLG. In terms of the stats that help win ball games, he appears to be the better player.

But as any baseball fan over the age of fourteen knows, the level of offense in baseball has varied greatly over time. In the 1968 American League, for example, pitching dominated the game. The mound was high, the strike zone was large, and the designated hitter was but a flicker in George F. Will's nightmares. The average AL batter hit .230 that year, and Carl Yastrzemski's .301 handily won the batting crown. By contrast, the *average* hitter in the 1930 National League (NL) hit .303; Yastrzemski's .301 would have ranked thirty-fourth among qualifying hitters.

It's not as though every batter in the 1968 AL suddenly forgot how to hit, or that every pitcher in the 1930 NL threw underhand. When Yastrzemski hit .301 in 1968, he was certainly a better hitter than the Pirates' Adam Comrosky, who hit .313 in 1930, or the Phillies' Pinky Whitney (.342 in '30), or the Boston Braves' Lance Richbourg (.304 in '30). The reasons these forgettable players hit for higher averages than Yastrzemski are environmental, outside their immediate control. Factors such as the size of the strike zone, the height of the pitching mound, the dimensions of the ballparks, and the potency of the baseballs make a tremendous difference in offensive statistics.

Both Bonds and Ruth—especially the latter—played most of their careers in environments that were very favorable to offense. But these eras were not without their differences. The 1920s and 1930s of Ruth's time featured a lively baseball but also large ballparks with distant fences and fielders who were far less skilled than today's. The result was extremely high batting averages and on-base percentages but home-run totals that would today be considered moderate. When Ruth hit 59 home runs in 1921, no other hitter hit more than 24.

Recent seasons have been just the opposite. The game is now dominated by power hitting and power pitching, with both home-run and strikeout rates at all-time highs. But batting averages have remained relatively stagnant. When Bonds hit .370 to win the batting crown in 2002, that was good enough to lead the league by some 32 points.

Any comparison of Ruth and Bonds needs to take these environmental factors into account. If we want to judge which of the two players was better relative to his league, we first need to place them on a level playing field. Suppose Ruth and Bonds had both spent their entire careers in a neutral park in the 1985 American League—an environment that rates as almost exactly average by historical standards. What would their hitting statistics look like?

We should also consider the characteristics of the players' home parks. Bonds has played in difficult ballparks, particularly since coming to the Giants as a free agent in 1993. Both Candlestick Park and SBC Park, with their cool air and ocean breezes, depress batting average and home-run output. Despite being called "The House That Ruth Built," Yankee Stadium has never been a particularly favorable offensive ballpark, either in Ruth's time or today. Although a player playing for the Yankees can expect to see his home-run output improve slightly, the park has tended to depress singles, doubles, and triples with its cozy dimensions down the lines and large center field. The lifetime park factors for Ruth and Bonds are listed in Table BP.2. The park factors are structured so that 100 represents an average ballpark. Numbers above 100 are favorable to hitters, while numbers below 100 favor pitchers. (We'll delve into park factors in more detail in Chapter 8-2.)

TABLE BP.2 Lifetime Park Factors for Babe Ruth and Barry Bonds

	Singles	Doubles	Triples	HR	BB	Runs
Ruth	97.1	93.7	92.4	105.5	99.8	94.9
Bonds	98.9	98.9	98.6	95.5	99.9	96.7

The process of neutralizing the biasing effects of these environmental factors is known as "normalization." The mechanics behind normalization are somewhat involved. We've prepared an extensive set of notes to accompany this text (see the Notes section at the end of the book) and encourage you to browse through them if you're interested in the gory details. But the basic idea is this: We figure out how much better a player was relative to his league and translate that onto a level playing field. For example, suppose a player in the offense-happy 1930 National League hits for a .320 batting average, after adjusting for park effects. This figure is good enough to rate as better than three-quarters of his counterparts. What would a player need to hit in a neutral environment such as the 1985 AL to be better than three-quarters of his counterparts? Something much lower than .320, since the offensive environment was much less favorable—a batting average of about .280 would do the trick. So this player's .320 batting average, translated to the 1985 AL, becomes .280.

Table BP.3 presents the normalized AVG, OBP, and SLG for Ruth and Bonds. For the time being, we'll restrict our study to the meaty portions of the players' careers, when they were between twenty-one and thirty-nine years old.

TABLE BP.3 Babe Ruth and Barry Bonds Normalized AVG, OBP, and SLG

Babe Ruth		Actual			Normalized		
Year	Age	AVG	OBP	SLG	AVG	OBP	SLG
1916	21	.272	.320	.419	.274	.320	.522
1917	22	.325	.382	.472	.315	.379	.578
1918	23	.300	.407	.555	.296	.399	.711
1919	24	.322	.451	.657	.312	.441	.787
1920	25	.376	.528	.847	.323	.481	.747
1921	26	.378	.506	.846	.328	.462	.766
1922	27	.315	.429	.672	.279	.394	.610
1923	28	.393	.540	.764	.349	.479	.702
1924	29	.378	.509	.739	.338	.469	.714
1925	30	.290	.390	.543	.254	.348	.489
1926	31	.372	.510	.737	.338	.476	.723
1927	32	.356	.481	.772	.316	.436	.711
1928	33	.323	.459	.709	.294	.425	.666
1929	34	.345	.424	.697	.309	.390	.635
1930	35	.359	.487	.732	.316	.444	.629
1931	36	.373	.488	.700	.343	.447	.666
1932	37	.341	.483	.661	.322	.459	.626
1933	38	.301	.438	.582	.288	.416	.579
1934	39	.288	.443	.537	.269	.414	.510
Career (ages 21–39)		.344	.471	.694	.312	.436	.664

Barry Bonds		Actual			Normalized		
Year	Age	AVG	OBP	SLG	AVG	OBP	SLG
1986	21	.223	.330	.416	.218	.322	.421
1987	22	.261	.329	.492	.253	.318	.469
1988	23	.283	.368	.491	.291	.380	.525
1989	24	.248	.351	.426	.259	.358	.461
1990	25	.301	.406	.565	.302	.404	.588
1991	26	.292	.410	.514	.299	.412	.553
1992	27	.311	.456	.624	.312	.454	.671
1993	28	.336	.458	.677	.327	.446	.664
1994	29	.312	.426	.647	.301	.413	.592

(continues)

TABLE BP.3 (continued)

Babe Ruth		Actual			Normalized		
Year	Age	BA	OBP	SLG	BA	OBP	SLG
1995	30	.294	.431	.577	.284	.418	.546
1996	31	.308	.461	.615	.299	.447	.579
1997	32	.291	.446	.585	.283	.426	.547
1998	33	.303	.438	.609	.297	.418	.564
1999	34	.262	.389	.617	.252	.368	.556
2000	35	.306	.440	.688	.305	.415	.638
2001	36	.328	.515	.863	.338	.505	.816
2002	37	.370	.582	.799	.385	.570	.821
2003	38	.341	.529	.749	.341	.512	.719
2004	39	.362	.609	.812	.357	.582	.763
Career (ages 21–39)		.300	.443	.611	.299	.432	.599

Each player loses some ground relative to his actual statistics, since the 1985 AL represents an average offensive environment, while both Ruth and Bonds played in above-average offensive environments. But the statistics confirm that Ruth was the superior hitter relative to his time. Although normalization diminishes his advantage in AVG and OBP, he retains his substantial lead in SLG. Ultimately, the fact that Ruth hit so many more home runs than his counterparts is significant. Ruth hit 714 homers over the course of his career, which spanned the years 1914 to 1935. His next-closest competitor, teammate Lou Gehrig, hit just 378 over the same period.

That sort of dominance would seem to be immutable. However, this argument can almost as easily cut the other way. Perhaps Ruth's supremacy reflects the inferiority of his competition as much as the superiority of his skills.

You'll often hear old-timers declare that baseball was a tougher game twenty, forty, or sixty years ago—an argument that can be hard to rebut. The reason is that baseball is a zero-sum confrontation between batters and pitchers. If batters are better than they used to be, it won't show up in their statistics if the pitchers they're facing are also tougher.

It might help to briefly divert our attention to another sport, in which there is a more absolute standard of achievement. Table BP.4 provides the gold medal–winning times in the men's 100-meter freestyle swimming competition each time that event has been held in the Summer Olympics.

TABLE BP.4 Gold Medal–Winning Times,
Men's Olympic 100–Meter Freestyle
Swimming

Year	Swimmer, Country	Time (sec)
1896	Alfréd Hajós, HUN	82.2
1906	Charles Daniels, USA	73.4
1908	Charles Daniels, USA	65.6
1912	Duke Kahanamoku, USA	63.4
1920	Duke Kahanamoku, USA	60.4
1924	Johnny Weissmuller, USA	59.0
1928	Johnny Weissmuller, USA	58.6
1932	Yasuji Miyazaki, JPN	58.2
1936	Ferenc Csik, HUN	57.6
1948	Wally Ris, USA	57.3
1952	Clarke Scholes, USA	57.4
1956	Jon Henricks, AUS	55.4
1960	John Devitt, AUS	55.2
1964	Don Schollander, USA	53.4
1968	Michael Wenden, AUS	52.2
1972	Mark Spitz, USA	51.2
1976	Jim Montgomery, USA	50.0
1980	Jorg Woithe, E. Ger	50.4
1984	Rowdy Gaines, USA	49.8
1988	Matt Biondi, USA	48.6
1992	Aleksandr Popov, UT	49.0
1996	Aleksandr Popov, RUS	48.7
2000	Pieter van den Hoogenband, NED	48.3
2004	Pieter van den Hoogenband, NED	48.2

The 100-meter freestyle is about the simplest of all possible athletic competitions: Jump in the pool and swim as fast as you can. Yet the winning time decreased by more than 40 percent in the one hundred years between 1896 and 1996. When the 100-meter freestyle is held today in high school girls' regional swimming meets, it is generally won by a girl who swims the distance in just under 60 seconds. That time would have won the *men's Olympic competition* in 1920, or any year before it.

The same phenomenon holds in just about every Olympic sport. Athletes are bigger, better, faster, and stronger than they used to be. It would be naïve to deny that the same phenomenon exists in baseball. Rather, the steady increase in the skill level at which baseball and other sports are contested is the result of two elements that are just about as inevitable as death and taxes.

The first of these elements is technology. In the broad sense, technology includes events such as the development of baseball bats with a larger sweet spot and more ergonomic gloves. But it also includes the vast improvements in nutrition, training methods, and sports medicine that have been made over the past century. Consider:

- The average baseball player today is about an inch and a half taller than he was fifty years ago, a reflection of improved nutrition during childhood and adolescence.
- In 1964, about 4 percent of major league at-bats were made by players aged thirty-five or older. In 2004, about 14 percent of major league at-bats were made by players aged thirty-five or older.

Baseball players are playing longer and remaining effective longer because of vast improvements in training methods.

◆ In 2005, there were at least twenty-two pitchers on major league Opening Day rosters who had successfully undergone Tommy John surgery, a procedure that was invented in 1974 (and only perfected much later). That represents about 6 percent of all active major league pitchers, including stars such as John Smoltz and Eric Gagne. Thirty-five years ago, these pitchers' careers would have been over, their roster spots filled by inferior alternatives.

Technological improvements also extend off the field. The development of the farm system—which began with Branch Rickey in the 1930s but didn't really take hold until after World War II—significantly improved the ability of baseball teams to identify the best players and train them appropriately. More recently, the introduction of statistical analysis into baseball front offices has made the competition tougher, since a major goal of sabermetrics is to improve talent evaluation.

But perhaps the more important factor behind baseball's progress is population growth. The U.S. population has roughly doubled from Babe Ruth's time to today. That fact disguises an ugly truth: There were no black major leaguers until Jackie Robinson joined the Dodgers in 1947. Babe Ruth didn't have to face fastballs from Satchel Paige or Bullet Joe Rogan or compete with Josh Gibson for home-run titles. If it weren't for integration, we wouldn't even be talking about Barry Bonds.

Integration also opened the door for players from Latin America and, more recently, from Asia. Foreign-born players now make up close to 30 percent of major league rosters. Table BP.5 documents the geographic progress of the sport. We consider baseball to have "opened" to a country in the first season in which there are at least five active major leaguers from that nation.

The resulting effect on baseball's population is seen in Figure

TABLE BP.5 Introduction of Countries Represented in Major League Baseball, by Year

Canada	1902
Cuba	1913
Mexico	1954
Puerto Rico	1954
Dominican Republic	1960
Panama	1964
Venezuela	1967
Australia	1993
Japan	1997
South Korea	2002

BP.1. In Babe Ruth's time, baseball drew from an effective population of about 110 million people—white Americans along with a handful of Canadians and light-skinned Cubans. Now baseball selects the best players from a pool of nearly 700 million. The difference is more than enough to offset the expansion in the number of baseball clubs and the competition from other sports. In 1930, there were about 300,000 people per major league baseball player. In 2005, there are closer to 900,000 people per baseball player.

FIGURE BP.1 Total pool of available MLB player candidates

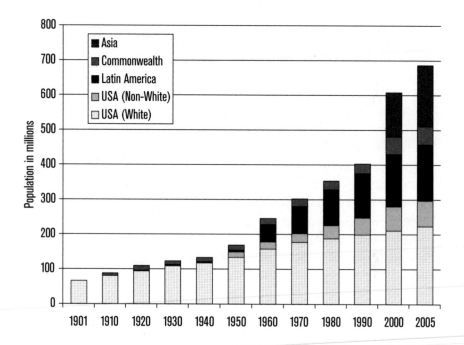

It is helpful to keep these facts in mind when debating back-in-the-day types. But it is also possible, if we are creative enough, to use the sport's statistics to get an objective read on the increasing degree of difficulty.

Let's start with a transparent example. In 1943, with war raging abroad and the United States sharply increasing its military commitment to the Allies, there were 29 hitters in the American League who received at least 500 at-bats. Six of these players went off to serve the country the next season, while the other 23 remained in the major leagues. Table BP.6 shows what happened to the batting average of the players who remained.

Of the 23 hitters who remained in the big leagues, 17 improved their batting averages, in most cases by a significant margin. The average improvement was 18 points. The reason, of course, is that it wasn't just hitters who were going off to fight. Many pitchers were drafted too, and that made the going much easier for those hitters who stayed at home.

We can generalize this process to other seasons by comparing the performance of players in a particular league from one season to the next. If these players tend to do better as a group, as they did in 1944, we can infer that the competition weakened. If they tend to do worse, we can infer that the competition was tougher.

The statistic that we'll use to track the changes is Equivalent Average (EqA). EqA has three distinguishing features:

TABLE BP.6 Batting Averages, Pre- and Post–World War II Draft

Player	1943 AVG	1944 AVG
Lou Boudreau	.286	.327
George Case	.294	.250
Doc Cramer	.300	.292
Bobby Doerr	.270	.325
Nick Etten	.271	.293
Don Gutteridge	.273	.245
Irv Hall	.256	.268
Pinky Higgins	.277	.297
Oris Hockett	.276	.289
Joe Hoover	.243	.236
Joe Kuhel	.213	.278
Chet Laabs	.250	.234
Tony Lupien	.255	.283
Ray Mack	.220	.232
Wally Moses	.245	.280
Dick Siebert	.251	.306
Stan Spence	.267	.316
Vern Stephens	.289	.293
Jim Tabor	.242	.285
Thurman Tucker	.235	.287
Dick Wakefield	.316	.355
Jo-Jo White	.248	.221
Rudy York	.271	.276
Average	**.263**	**.281**

- ◆ It accounts for all significant components of offensive performance, including base stealing. But it places the most emphasis on the events that most influence run scoring, such as getting on base and hitting for power.
- ◆ It is a normalized statistic that places hitters on a level playing field relative to their park and league environment. Carl Yastrzemski's EqA in 1968, when he hit .301/.426/.495 (AVG/OBP/SLG) in a very difficult offensive environment, was .340. Lefty O'Doul's EqA in 1930, when he hit .383/.453/.604 in a ridiculously easy environment, was .324.
- ◆ It operates on the same scale as batting average. A .260 EqA is considered average, just as a .260 batting average would be considered average. A .300 EqA is very good, and an EqA above .350

is world-class. The best EqA of all time belongs to Barry Bonds, who posted a .455 EqA in 2004. This is similar to the best batting average in history, Hugh Duffy's .440 in 1894.

EqA was developed by Baseball Prospectus's Clay Davenport as part of his system of Davenport Translations (DTs). The DTs were originally designed to translate the performance of minor league players to their major league equivalents. For example, we might look at a group of players in the Triple-A International League who posted a .290 EqA on average. The next season, when those players advanced to the majors, they averaged a .270 EqA. The ratio of these two figures, .290 and .270, gives us a sense of how much more difficult the majors are than Triple-A. (Chapter 7-2 contains much more on evaluating minor league performance.)

The DT system can just as easily be used to compare two major leagues rather than a major and a minor league. For example, returning to our study of the wartime American League, the EqAs of players who remained in the league from 1943 to 1944 improved by about 5 percent. Thus, we can conclude that the 1944 AL was about 5 percent easier than the 1943 AL. Figure BP.2 extends this system of comparison across baseball's history. The figure is calibrated so that the 1975 AL is assigned a difficulty rating of 1.0. Any league more difficult than the 1975 AL has a difficulty rating higher than 1.0, and any league easier than the 1975 AL has a difficulty rating less than 1.0.

We see a few blips along the way. League difficulty dipped during World War II, then picked up again after the war ended. There is a sharp increase in difficulty in the 1900 National League, when the league contracted from twelve teams to eight, but an even sharper decrease in the early 1900s after the American League was established with eight teams of its own, bringing the total number of major league clubs to sixteen. The NL was notably stronger than the AL during a long period stretching from the mid-1950s to the mid-1980s. Not coincidentally, it won 24 of 28 All-Star games between 1960 and 1985.

But the basic trend is unmistakable: the competition has grown steadily tougher. The differences in difficulty may be almost undetectable between any two consecutive seasons, but they become quite significant over time. Recall that the difficulty factors are derived by comparing EqAs from one season to the next. We can also extrapolate them to compare players across eras. In 1941, Ted Williams became the last player to hit .400. He also posted a .417 EqA in a league that

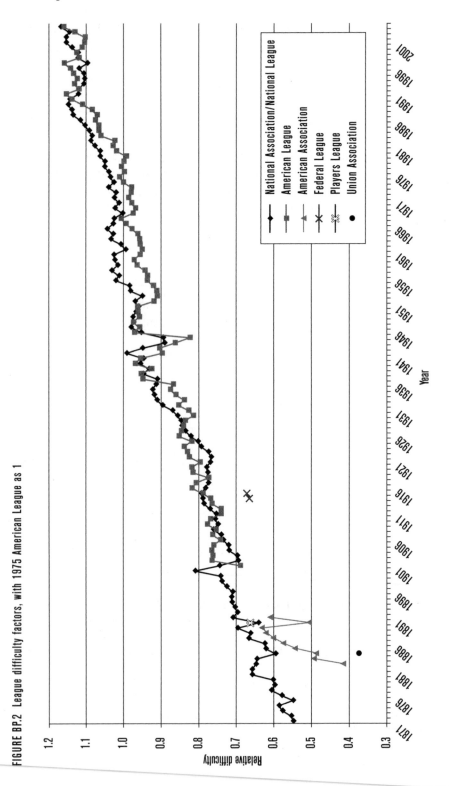

FIGURE BP.2 League difficulty factors, with 1975 American League as 1

had a difficulty rating of .969. By comparison, the 2005 AL has a difficulty rating of 1.159. Translated into the 2005 AL, Williams's EqA would be:

$$.417 \times \frac{.969}{1.159} = .349$$

We might call this procedure the Baseball Time Machine. It gives us a sense of what might happen if Williams were cryogenically frozen before the 1941 season and transported to 2005, competing against modern players but not allowed to take advantage of modern technology. By this standard, Williams would still be one of the best players in the league; a .349 EqA is about what Alex Rodriguez and Albert Pujols posted in 2005. But it's very unlikely that Williams would hit .400.

The Time Machine's effects are more noticeable as we transport players from further back in history. Honus Wagner had a .354 EqA in the 1908 National League, an outstanding figure for a shortstop. But his league had a difficulty rating of just .760. Translated into today's terms . . .

$$.354 \times \frac{.760}{1.159} = .232$$

. . . we come up with a .232 EqA. That would qualify Wagner as a good-field, no-hit shortstop, along the lines of Neifi Perez or Adam Everett. All of this might seem blasphemous, but imagine Honus Wagner, a player who had never even heard of a slider, his hands choked up high on his 40-ounce Louisville Slugger, trying to hit against Pedro Martinez or Johan Santana.

What does this mean for Babe Ruth? Let's put Ruth into our Time Machine and transport him exactly seventy years forward so that he comes up as a rookie in 1984 and finishes his career in 2005. The resulting effect on Ruth's EqA is seen in Table BP.7.

TABLE BP.7 Babe Ruth's EqA, Adjusted for Time Machine Effect

Original League	AB	EqA, Relative to League	Difficulty	Trransported to	Difficulty	Difficulty Ratio	Time Machine EqA
1914 AL	10	.196	0.768	1984 AL	1.060	0.724	.142
1915 AL	92	.337	0.788	1985 AL	1.066	0.740	.249
1916 AL	136	.281	0.818	1986 AL	1.066	0.768	.216
1917 AL	123	.318	0.806	1987 AL	1.074	0.751	.239

(continues)

TABLE BP.7 (continued)

Original League	AB	EqA, Relative to League	Difficulty	Trransported to	Difficulty	Difficulty Ratio	Time Machine EqA
1918 AL	317	.347	0.773	1988 AL	1.070	0.722	.251
1919 AL	432	.377	0.815	1989 AL	1.083	0.753	.284
1920 AL	458	.413	0.818	1990 AL	1.110	0.737	.305
1921 AL	540	.399	0.796	1991 AL	1.138	0.699	.279
1922 AL	406	.346	0.825	1992 AL	1.153	0.716	.248
1923 AL	522	.404	0.83	1993 AL	1.120	0.741	.299
1924 AL	529	.387	0.839	1994 AL	1.131	0.741	.287
1925 AL	359	.305	0.818	1995 AL	1.124	0.728	.222
1926 AL	495	.397	0.852	1996 AL	1.134	0.751	.298
1927 AL	540	.386	0.846	1997 AL	1.142	0.741	.286
1928 AL	536	.375	0.84	1998 AL	1.158	0.725	.272
1929 AL	499	.358	0.835	1999 AL	1.119	0.746	.267
1930 AL	518	.382	0.814	2000 AL	1.125	0.723	.276
1931 AL	534	.394	0.822	2001 AL	1.111	0.740	.292
1932 AL	457	.382	0.853	2002 AL	1.104	0.772	.295
1933 AL	459	.352	0.838	2003 AL	1.102	0.760	.267
1934 AL	365	.339	0.861	2004 AL	1.130	0.761	.258
1935 NL	72	.295	0.922	2005 NL	1.167	0.790	.233
Career		**.373**					**.274**

Ruth's career EqA would be .274. He probably would have made the All-Star team a couple of times, with an EqA in his best seasons approaching .300. But he'd be remembered as merely a good player and certainly wouldn't be a credible candidate for the Hall of Fame. In modern terms, Ruth might be Tino Martinez (career .274 EqA) or Raul Mondesi (.278). By the Time Machine standard, Barry Bonds is not only better than Babe Ruth—he runs circles around him.

The Time Machine standard, however, is not entirely fair to Ruth. Previously, we described two reasons for the increasing difficulty of the game. The first is the increased size of baseball's player pool, particularly as a result of integration from 1947 onward. Ruth doesn't bear any direct responsibility for the moratorium on black players, but it is right to downgrade his statistics for playing in a whites-only universe. If Ruth had to hit against the best black and Latino pitchers of his time, as modern hitters do, his numbers would not have been as good.

On the other hand, Ruth also suffers under the Time Machine standard because he doesn't get to reap the benefits of new technology. If Ruth were playing today, his nutritionist would take notice of his penchant for red meat and put him on the Atkins Diet, keeping his muscles strong but subtracting the excess weight that hampered him toward the end of his career. Perhaps the Yankees' team psychologist would detect that Ruth's periodically heavy drinking was the result of clinical depression and compel him to turn to Prozac rather than the bottle. Perhaps he would have been able to DH instead of playing the field, extending his career by a couple of seasons.

We can also think of things the other way around: What if Barry Bonds had somehow overcome the color barrier and were playing in the 1930s? Bonds severely damaged his elbow during the 1999 season, suffering from bone spurs and a damaged triceps tendon. He also had bad knees for most of his thirties. The most productive portion of Bonds's career has come in spite of these injuries. Without access to modern medicine, his career might have ended much sooner.

Our solution to this problem is to eschew the Time Machine in favor of something more moderate: the Timeline Adjustment. Let's take another look at the graph of league difficulty factors. We can draw a trend line on the graph representing the typical increase in difficulty since World War II, as in Figure BP.3.

The end of World War II brought a confluence of events that combined to sharply increase baseball's difficulty level over a short period: the integration of blacks, the expansion of the game into Latin America, and the widespread acceptance of the farm system. These events went beyond the ordinary, inevitable, and highly linear increase in difficulty that we see in other seasons. As a result, essentially all of the data points before World War II fall below the trend line. To make the Timeline Adjustment, we compare players not against an absolute standard of quality but against the relative standard of quality represented by the trend line. Honus Wagner's .354 EqA in 1908, for example, is adjusted downward not to .232, as under the Time Machine standard, but only to .344.

Let's look at a concrete example of the Timeline Adjustment in action. Table BP.8 is our best guess at what Babe Ruth's career would have looked like if he had come up as a rookie alongside Roger Clemens with the Boston Red Sox in 1984. These statistics adjust for league difficulty factors, as determined by the Timeline Adjustment, as well as for the characteristics of the leagues and ballparks that the modern-day Ruth would have played in.

As we can see, the Timeline Adjustment is relatively gentle, confirming that Ruth was a tremendously valuable baseball player. In particular, the Timeline Adjustment reiterates Ruth's superiority in the

FIGURE BP.3 League difficulty factors, with timeline adjustment

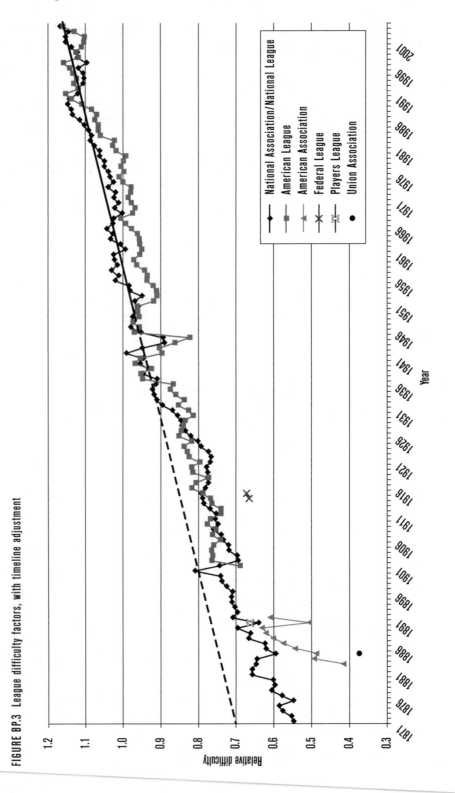

TABLE BP.8 Estimate of Babe Ruth's Career, if He Started in 1984

Age	Year	Team	AB	R	H	2B	3B	HR	RBI	BB	SO	SB	AVG	OBP	SLG
19	1984	BOS-A	11	1	2	1	0	0	2	0	6	0	.182	.182	.273
20	1985	BOS-A	95	18	27	4	0	11	24	8	32	0	.284	.340	.674
21	1986	BOS-A	140	22	36	3	0	10	20	10	34	0	.257	.307	.493
22	1987	BOS-A	128	18	39	3	0	11	17	12	29	0	.305	.364	.586
23	1988	BOS-A	399	70	108	19	0	42	94	66	126	3	.271	.377	.634
24	1989	BOS-A	488	115	146	28	2	52	134	109	107	3	.299	.433	.684
25	1990	NY-A	464	131	156	26	3	57	120	146	141	17	.336	.497	.774
26	1991	NY-A	544	142	172	37	6	60	142	137	151	20	.316	.457	.737
27	1992	NY-A	411	77	107	17	0	39	83	82	143	1	.260	.385	.586
28	1993	NY-A	534	138	181	37	4	56	125	166	164	21	.339	.498	.738
29	1994	NY-A	386	95	127	17	1	45	84	100	118	7	.329	.470	.728
30	1995	NY-A	325	48	80	8	0	26	53	51	125	1	.246	.352	.511
31	1996	NY-A	520	144	180	23	1	64	155	145	152	11	.346	.492	.763
32	1997	NY-A	559	142	181	25	1	70	150	135	187	4	.324	.455	.748
33	1998	NY-A	554	150	162	25	1	64	134	136	173	2	.292	.435	.688
34	1999	NY-A	509	115	160	23	1	56	147	73	117	3	.314	.405	.694
35	2000	NY-A	525	133	172	24	2	56	139	137	103	12	.328	.468	.701
36	2001	NY-A	536	135	187	25	0	59	149	115	93	6	.349	.465	.726
37	2002	NY-A	459	109	150	17	0	48	125	115	110	2	.327	.465	.678
38	2003	NY-A	473	93	136	17	0	46	100	101	159	6	.288	.416	.615
39	2004	NY-A	382	77	105	14	0	34	83	92	110	1	.275	.420	.579
40	2005	ATL-N	67	13	12	1	0	7	12	20	41	0	.179	.368	.507
Career			8,509	1,986	2,626	394	22	913	2,092	1,956	2,421	120	.309	.441	.682

power department. The system projects that, taking advantage of to-day's small ballparks and normalized to a 162-game season, he would have broken Roger Maris's record by hitting 64 homers in 1996, then topped his own mark with 70 home runs in 1997. For his career, Ruth would have hit 913 home runs, leaping past Hank Aaron at about the midpoint of the 2001 season. However, not all the adjustments are so favorable. Ruth would have hit for a .309 batting average—some 33 points lower than his actual total—and would have struck out 2,421 times, more than any other hitter in history except Reggie Jackson.

We can perform the same analysis for Barry Bonds (Table BP.9). What if Bonds had played for the Pirates and Giants starting in 1916 instead of 1986? Bonds's career would have closely resembled that of Ted Williams. He would have won four batting titles, topped the .400 mark in 1932, and earned renown for almost never striking out. He'd still have drawn plenty of walks and posted some incredible on-base percentages. His home-run output, however, would have dropped con-siderably. Although Bonds would be an excellent power hitter for his time (and would have won four National League home-run titles to go with his batting crowns), his career total of 444 would have paled in comparison to Ruth's 714.

These experiments help to reveal how conventional statistics can be misleading. If the real, twenty-first-century Barry Bonds, already holding the single-season home-run record, goes on to surpass the lifetime home-run totals of Ruth and Hank Aaron, he will no doubt be hailed as the best power hitter of all time. But in fact, although Bonds's power is impressive, his home-run totals are partly the prod-uct of an era in which home runs are relatively easy to come by. Bonds's most important and differentiating skill is his ability to get on base. Ruth, conversely, was a power hitter first and foremost.

So which player was better? Bonds, with his superior on-base skills, or Ruth, with his superior power? The verdict using our Timeline Ad-justment is so close that we need a couple of additional concepts to break the tie.

The most important of these concepts is replacement level. Re-placement level is so vital to understanding player value that we've de-voted an entire chapter to it (Chapter 5-1), but it deserves at least a preliminary explanation here. Sabermetricians define replacement level in a couple of different ways. It is either:

◆ The worst level of performance that a player can sustain while maintaining his job in Major League Baseball, or

TABLE BP.9 Estimate of Barry Bonds's Career, if He Started in 1916

Age	Year	Team	AB	R	H	2B	3B	HR	RBI	BB	SO	SB	AVG	OBP	SLG
21	1916	PIT-N	363	58	85	24	7	5	33	46	59	33	.234	.324	.380
22	1917	PIT-N	483	81	130	23	16	6	38	37	49	36	.269	.325	.420
23	1918	PIT-N	382	76	118	22	10	7	36	47	32	20	.309	.387	.474
24	1919	PIT-N	455	80	131	25	11	6	41	60	39	34	.288	.372	.431
25	1920	PIT-N	464	97	166	37	9	18	102	71	38	49	.358	.446	.593
26	1921	PIT-N	463	101	172	31	13	16	123	81	29	39	.371	.469	.598
27	1922	PIT-N	430	132	160	35	11	30	120	113	29	36	.372	.507	.714
28	1923	NY-N	491	133	190	38	10	34	123	110	34	25	.387	.501	.713
29	1924	NY-N	499	119	176	31	3	36	105	83	25	39	.353	.451	.643
30	1925	NY-N	519	125	177	33	18	23	116	112	38	29	.341	.461	.607
31	1926	NY-N	464	108	157	31	9	21	115	124	30	35	.338	.479	.580
32	1927	NY-N	487	119	158	28	11	22	92	116	37	34	.324	.459	.563
33	1928	NY-N	498	112	164	36	14	20	112	112	38	33	.329	.457	.578
34	1929	NY-N	323	93	99	25	5	24	82	60	27	14	.307	.418	.638
35	1930	NY-N	449	140	161	34	10	37	110	91	35	10	.359	.469	.726
36	1931	NY-N	444	117	162	43	7	47	127	149	44	11	.365	.529	.811
37	1932	NY-N	397	118	159	34	6	36	109	156	23	7	.401	.574	.788
38	1933	NY-N	370	93	135	27	2	25	70	111	27	5	.365	.518	.651
39	1934	NY-N	360	121	137	27	6	28	90	188	21	5	.381	.597	.722
40	1935	NY-N	29	6	10	2	0	3	7	5	3	0	.345	.441	.724
Career			8,370	2,029	2,847	586	178	444	1,751	1,872	657	494	.340	.464	.612

◆ The level of performance that can be obtained by an MLB club for little or no marginal cost, such as a player who can be found on the waiver wire or a Triple-A veteran who would be paid the minimum salary.

These definitions are really the same. A major league team doesn't have much incentive to keep a player in the lineup if a better player can be found for little or no cost. More to the point, a major league team doesn't have much incentive to *pay* a player if an equal or better player can be found for free.

Replacement level stems from the fact that the talent distribution in baseball is asymmetrical. Figure BP.4 presents a histogram of the EqAs for all players in American professional baseball (MLB plus the affiliated minor leagues) in 2004. Recall that a .260 EqA is defined as a major league–average performance. A replacement-level performance is somewhat worse than this: about .230. Historically, players who can't maintain an EqA of at least .230 will not keep their major league jobs.

FIGURE BP.4 EqAs of all players in MLB and affiliated leagues, 2004

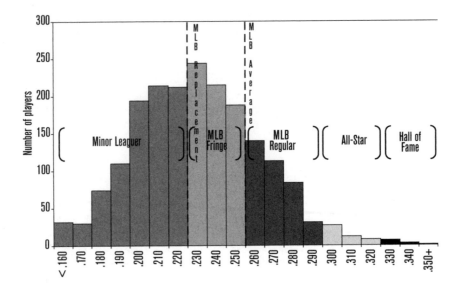

The key thing to notice is that there are many more below-average players than above-average ones. Players on the major league fringe— with an EqA better than .230 but worse than the league average of .260—are still worth something because major league talent is a scarce commodity. Jose Vizcaino, a player with a lifetime EqA of .237, has played in seventeen major league seasons and has made almost $25 million in his career. Of course, there are also many fewer All-Star-caliber players than there are major league regulars and many fewer Hall-of-Famers than there are All-Stars. But the point at which we start crediting players with providing value to their clubs is the replacement-level threshold.

In 1997, for example, Barry Bonds posted a .348 EqA in 690 plate appearances. EqA is a "rate statistic." It has a companion "counting" statistic, equivalent runs (EqR), that estimates how many runs a player has produced for his club. In 1997, Bonds produced 139 EqR for the Giants. However, we don't credit Bonds with all of these runs because even a player from Triple-A would have been capable of making some contribution—he certainly wouldn't have struck out in all of his at-bats. More specifically, we estimate that a replacement-level player would have produced about 49 runs, given the same amount of playing time that Bonds had. Bonds's contribution above replacement level is his 139 EqR, less the 49 runs that the replacement-level player would have produced, for a net total of 90 runs. We call this amount his Batting Runs Above Replacement (BRAR).

Table BP.10 provides the career BRAR data for our two contestants. (All the statistics listed in Table BP.10 and for the rest of the chapter incorporate the Timeline Adjustment.) Ruth rates as the slightly more productive player on a rate basis: His EqA is .364, against Bonds's .354. But by the end of the 2005 season, Bonds had about 1,000 more plate appearances than Ruth, roughly two additional seasons' worth of playing time. This is enough to give him the superior BRAR by a margin of 59 runs. Bonds has provided more value with his bat than any other player in baseball history, Babe Ruth included.

TABLE BP.10 Career Batting Runs Above Replacement, Babe Ruth and Barry Bonds

	Babe Ruth (1914–1935)				Barry Bonds (1986–2005)			
Age	PA	EqA	EqR	BRAR	PA	EqA	EqR	BRAR
19	10	.187	1	0				
20	103	.328	20	12				
21	150	.276	21	8	484	.279	68	26
22	142	.312	24	13	611	.282	89	36
23	380	.335	74	45	614	.312	109	58
24	542	.369	124	86	679	.299	110	53

(continues)

TABLE BP.10 (continued)

Age	Babe Ruth (1914–1935)				Barry Bonds (1986–2005)			
	PA	EqA	EqR	BRAR	PA	EqA	EqR	BRAR
25	616	.405	159	121	621	.341	129	81
26	693	.387	164	120	634	.337	128	79
27	495	.339	96	59	612	.371	143	100
28	699	.396	168	125	674	.371	158	110
29	681	.381	156	112	474	.345	99	63
30	426	.296	63	30	635	.339	124	77
31	652	.391	158	116	675	.360	144	97
32	691	.379	163	116	690	.348	139	90
33	684	.367	153	105	697	.344	140	89
34	587	.349	124	80	434	.327	82	48
35	676	.369	150	104	607	.359	132	89
36	663	.381	152	109	664	.424	190	149
37	589	.374	129	91	612	.449	174	142
38	575	.342	111	70	550	.410	139	107
39	471	.332	83	50	617	.454	168	138
40	92	.295	14	6	52	.341	11	7
Career	10,617	.364	2,307	1,577	11,636	.354	2,477	1,636

Why has Bonds accumulated more playing time than Ruth? Each player came to the majors early, stayed late, and remained healthy more often than not. But Ruth played in an era where teams played 154 games a season, instead of the 162 played in Bonds's day. More importantly, Ruth spent the early part of his career as a pitcher; his first appearance in the outfield came in 1918, his fourth full season in the big leagues.

Ruth was an excellent pitcher, in fact, and we'll give him credit for his performance in a moment. But first let's look at another important facet of the game: fielding. There is little doubt that Bonds was an outstanding defensive player, at least until his first knee surgery in 1999. He won eight Gold Gloves between 1990 and 1998, a remarkable feat since left fielders are rarely awarded Gold Gloves.

Ruth played in an era before Gold Gloves and probably wouldn't have won one anyway. But he was no slouch in the field. Earle Combs, Ruth's partner in center field, described how Ruth's "eyesight, good teaching, and perfect coordination made him a natural." Dixie Walker, who came up with Ruth's Yankees and later went across town to play for the Brooklyn Dodgers, praised Ruth's "wonderful coordination."

Ruth also had a strong arm and routinely placed near the top of the league in outfield assists.

Certainly, Ruth's defense declined later in his career, after he had gained weight. In 1932, when Ruth was thirty-seven, columnist Westbrook Pegler, flaunting prose that would get him banned from any contemporary press box, described him as a "fat, elderly party who must wear corsets to avoid immodest jiggling, and cannot waddle for fly balls, nor stoop for grounders." But over his career, Ruth did more good than harm with his glove.

We keep track of Fielding Runs Above Replacement (FRAR), just as we do BRAR. The trick to coming up with good defensive statistics is to recognize that a player's defensive contributions are worthwhile only insofar as they help his team. If a team is adept at turning batted balls in play into outs, that means it has a number of above-average fielders. (A deeper exposition of fielding statistics is provided in Chapter 3-2.) Although there are some notable exceptions, FRAR usually dovetails with anecdotal and observational data about a player's contributions in the field. The five best lifetime scores under our FRAR system belong to Ozzie Smith (765), Cal Ripken (708), Rabbit Maranville (677), Honus Wagner (635), and Bill Mazeroski (633), great fielders by reputation.

All of those players were middle infielders. Playing in a corner outfield spot isn't nearly as hard as playing a position such as shortstop or second base. It's relatively easy to find a competent outfielder, so teams tend to concentrate on offense from those positions. Consequently, corner outfielders don't score as high under our FRAR system as players at more difficult positions. Still, a run saved is as good as a run earned, and it's certainly a bonus to have a left fielder as good as Bonds was in his defensive prime. The lifetime FRAR numbers for Bonds and Ruth are in Table BP.11, along with the related statistic, Fielding Funs Above Average (FRAA).

TABLE BP.11 Career FRAR and FRAA, Babe Ruth and Barry Bonds

Age	Babe Ruth (1914–1935)			Barry Bonds (1986–2005)		
	G	FRAR	FRAA	G	FRAR	FRAA
19	5	0	0			
20	42	4	3			
21	67	4	2	113	24	9
22	52	6	4	150	28	13

(continues)

TABLE BP.11 (continued)

Age	Babe Ruth (1914–1935)			Barry Bonds (1986–2005)		
	G	FRAR	FRAA	G	FRAR	FRAA
23	95	10	2	144	12	0
24	130	17	7	159	25	12
25	142	21	9	151	31	17
26	152	24	9	153	29	16
27	110	18	9	140	21	8
28	152	32	18	159	16	2
29	153	17	3	112	14	5
30	98	9	1	144	13	0
31	152	7	-6	158	12	-2
32	151	19	7	159	16	2
33	154	2	-11	156	27	13
34	135	7	-3	102	13	4
35	145	3	-9	143	18	6
36	145	4	-6	153	4	-9
37	133	10	0	143	2	-10
38	137	6	-3	130	15	4
39	125	4	-3	147	10	-1
40	28	1	-1	14	0	-1
Career	2,503	225	31	2,730	330	89

Our statistics are consistent with the popular perceptions of the players' respective fielding abilities. Ruth rates as an above-average fielder in his twenties and a below-average one in his thirties. Bonds was a truly outstanding defensive player early in his career. Anything over 25 FRAR or 10 FRAA would be considered an excellent season for a corner outfielder, and Bonds met each of those standards on five occasions. His defense had declined by the time he left Pittsburgh for San Francisco, and his last couple of Gold Gloves were awarded more on reputation than on sustained excellence. But he was clearly a superior defensive outfielder to Ruth, widening his overall lead with a 105-run edge in FRAR.

The most critical defensive position of all, of course, is the pitcher. Ruth pitched in 163 games in his career, almost all of them while he was still in Boston, compiling a 94-46 record and a 2.28 earned run average (ERA). These statistics exaggerate Ruth's prowess somewhat, since he did his pitching in the deadball era, when league ERAs were around 2.75. Still, he was considerably above average as a pitcher and certainly far better than replacement level.

We list Ruth's Pitching Runs Above Replacement (PRAR) numbers in Table BP.12, as well as his Normalized Run Average (NRA). NRA is a parallel statistic to EqA, accounting for a pitcher's run-prevention skill after adjustments for league, park, and timeline. NRA operates on the same scale as modern-day ERAs; an NRA of 4.50 is considered average.

Ruth pitched quite well. Just as importantly, he pitched quite *often*, finishing third in the American League in innings pitched in 1916 and second in 1917. All told, Ruth's pitching provided 262 runs' worth of value to his clubs. That's small beans compared to his contributions with his bat, but it is just enough to make up the difference in the race with Bonds, as we see in Figure BP.5.

TABLE BP.12 Career Pitching Runs Above Replacement, Babe Ruth

Year	Age	IP	ERA	NRA	PRAR
1914	19	23.0	3.91	6.14	0
1915	20	217.2	2.44	4.22	40
1916	21	323.2	1.75	3.31	94
1917	22	326.1	2.01	3.68	78
1918	23	166.1	2.22	4.11	34
1919	24	133.1	2.97	4.82	20
1920	25	4.0	4.50	8.92	-2
1921	26	9.0	9.00	9.59	-5
1930	35	9.0	3.00	3.90	3
1933	38	9.0	5.00	5.30	2
Career		**1,221.1**	**2.28**	**3.95**	**262**

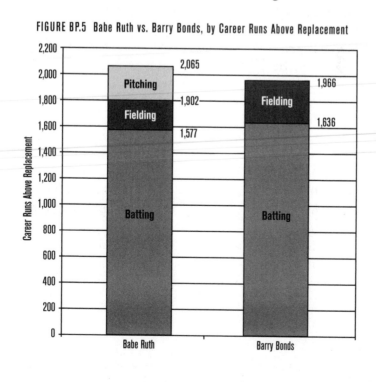

FIGURE BP.5 Babe Ruth vs. Barry Bonds, by Career Runs Above Replacement

Our statistics give about a 100-run lifetime advantage to Babe Ruth, considering his batting, pitching, and fielding and accounting fairly for his era. That is certainly close enough that Bonds could make up the difference with good seasons in 2006 and 2007. Although the world will be watching Bonds chase down Hank Aaron's career home-run total, a few of us will also be watching him battle time and Babe Ruth for the title of best baseball player in history.

It is also close enough that the answer could change depending on one's assumptions:

- We haven't talked much about baserunning, a department in which Bonds has been far superior to Ruth. Although BRAR accounts for stolen bases and caught stealing, it doesn't look at such things as taking the extra base on another player's hit. While baserunning effects tend to be minimal, they may help Bonds close the gap somewhat. (Chapter 4-1 discusses baserunning in detail.)
- We also haven't uttered the s-word. Is there some way to estimate how much difference steroids have made in Bonds's performance, if he's used them? (See Chapter 9-1.)
- Nor have we talked about postseason play. Ruth's statistics in his ten World Series were even more impressive than his performances during the regular season. Do certain players have an ability to rise to the occasion when it matters the most? (See Chapter 1-2 for more on this topic.)

I risk sounding like one of those old L. Ron Hubbard commercials, but you'll find the answers to all of these pressing questions within the book. Let's thank Barry Bonds for forcing the argument—and let the debates begin.

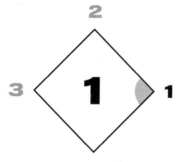

What's the Matter with RBI?

. . . and Other Traditional Statistics

JONAH KERI

Hitters at all levels, from Little League to the big leagues, pride themselves on getting runs batted in (RBI). Most Valuable Player awards often hinge on how many a player can rack up. Those hitters who get a lot receive praise for their determination and confidence under pressure, as if they dwelled on a higher moral plane than the rest of the world. If home runs stand in our minds for strength, and batting average denotes aggressiveness and cunning, RBI stand for character, clutch performances under duress, and the willingness to share your success with the team. Who could possibly question the value of character?

Baseball analysts have been skeptical of the RBI statistic for decades, arguing that it does not accurately reflect a player's worth. RBI rely so heavily on context and opportunity that even a fringe player can amass 100 in a season. As we explore in Chapter 1-2, they're not a reliable indicator of ability to perform in clutch situations. Statistical levels supposedly indicative of the game's elite can in fact be reached by average or even below-average players, given the right circumstances.

Many of baseball's seminal statistics, the kind you've seen on the back of baseball cards since you shoved your 1978 Willie Randolph Topps #359 between the spokes of your ten-speed, neither properly illustrate a player's production nor provide a reliable guide to his future. Even baseball's Triple Crown statistics—batting average, home runs, and RBI—can distort what a player really brings to the table.

For that reason, baseball researchers have spent decades crafting and perfecting more sophisticated statistical measures. These truth-seekers aim to connect hitting to wins. If you've read Michael Lewis's *Moneyball*, Baseball Prospectus's annual book, or a similar text, you've likely come across an array of alphabet-soup stats. Those numbers are designed to uncover which players—and which actions—do the most to win ballgames. Later chapters in this book—including Chapter 5-1 on replacement level—go into detail on how those calculations are made. In this chapter, we'll get the discussion rolling.

◆

Of the three Triple Crown stats, RBI may be the most flawed. In their groundbreaking book *The Hidden Game of Baseball*, John Thorn and Pete Palmer reveal that the debate over the stat's usefulness began well before *Moneyball*, Bill James, or even Branch Rickey:

> Another stat which was "sent back to the minors" before settling in for good in 1920 was the RBI. Introduced by a Buffalo newspaper in 1879, the stat was picked up the following year by the Chicago Tribune, which in the words of Preston D. Orem, "proudly presented the 'Runs Batted In' record of the Chicago players for the season, showing Anson and Kelly in the lead." Readers were unimpressed. Objections were that the men who led off, Dalrymple and Gore, did not have the same opportunities to knock in runs. The paper actually wound up almost apologizing for the computation.

Even 125 years ago, baseball fans understood how context-dependent a stat RBI was. First, they recognized that leadoff hitters were at a disadvantage when it came to RBI opportunities. In his first plate appearance, a leadoff man can hope to drive only himself in with a home run. For the rest of the game, leadoff hitters must follow the dregs of the lineup—the Punch-and-Judy types batting in the #8 and #9 slots. In the National League, that means following pitchers, most of whom struggle to hit their weight. While there are exceptions, most teams tend to follow something resembling an optimal lineup, with players who get on base more frequently batting toward the top of the batting order. The result is that middle-of-the-order hitters, whatever their ability, usually have the most RBI chances.

The intersection of batting order and RBI opportunities becomes obvious when the runners on first, second, and third base during each of a player's plate appearances throughout the season are added together to show the sum of his RBI opportunities. In 2005, just one of the twenty-five hitters with the most RBI opportunities, Boston Red Sox #2 hitter Edgar Renteria, batted higher than third. The Red Sox led the majors in on-base percentage; even their eighth and ninth hitters were more adept at reaching base than the typical hitters for those spots. Renteria, though having a poor offensive year himself, was granted an inordinate number of chances to hit with runners on base.

That last point highlights another factor that plays a huge role in a player's RBI total—the sheer number of plate appearances he accumulates in a season. While a leadoff hitter and a #9 hitter may both find their RBI chances restricted by the mediocre batters hitting in front of them, the leadoff man will gain more chances simply by having more times at bat. Roughly speaking, for every lineup spot a player moves up, he gains eighteen plate appearances over a full season. Thus, when the Yankees briefly toyed with the idea of putting the speedy but punchless Tony Womack in the leadoff spot in 2005, they were giving their worst hitter more chances to squelch potential rallies.

Other trends emerge from the RBI Opportunities Report as well. In 2005 many sportswriters supported Atlanta Braves center fielder Andruw Jones for the National League Most Valuable Player award. The numbers Jones put up over the course of the season (51 home runs and 128 RBI) were doubly impressive, they argued, given the many rookies and no-names around him in the Braves lineup. The theory doesn't hold water, as Jones headed the list of National League hitters with the most RBI opportunities. In fact, when it came to total RBI per runner on base, Jones trailed fellow MVP candidates Albert Pujols and Carlos Delgado by a wide margin. He was also behind Garrett Atkins, Felipe Lopez, and that vaunted clutch hitter David Eckstein. Still, Jones's RBI total dwarfed that of Eckstein and company—not just because of his 51 homers but also because of his greater number of RBI chances.

While RBI aren't indicative of a player's greatness, great players tend to accrue them in high numbers—legitimate superstars like Alex Rodriguez, Manny Ramirez, Pujols, and others. There is a simple reason: Most managers have a pretty good idea who their best players are, so a Ramirez or Pujols is likely to bat in the middle of his team's lineup. That way the player's true ability combines with greater opportunity to produce RBI numbers. It's a key distinction: Albert Pujols isn't a great player because he gets a lot of RBI. Rather, he gets a lot of RBI because he's a great player who gets a lot of RBI opportunities.

Opportunity alone can often bring big RBI totals for lesser players. Take Joe Carter. In his sixteen-year career, Carter totaled 1,387 RBI, good for fifty-second place all-time at the end of the 2005 season. He topped 100 RBI seven times, good for nine top-10 finishes, including a league-leading 121 in 1986 and two second-place results in 1992 and 1994. Those gaudy RBI totals, spiced with Carter's famous World Series–winning homer in 1993, persuaded nineteen voters to cast Hall of Fame ballots for him in 2004. While he fell short of getting the 5 percent vote total needed to stay on the ballot, Carter's career still made an impression, at least on some voters. They didn't have the full picture. Later on we'll look at some of the information those voters were lacking.

◆

RBI isn't the only baseball-card stat that misstates a player's value. Other counting statistics—runs scored, hits, even home runs—do the same, and for similar reasons: playing time and context.

A leadoff hitter is likely to lead his team in hits simply by coming to the plate more often than anyone else. In 2004 Cesar Izturis had 193 hits, and Manny Ramirez had 175. That didn't make Izturis better than Ramirez—Ramirez's far higher extra-base hit and walk totals more than negated Izturis's edge in hits.

Perhaps few would have been tempted to exchange Ramirez for Izturis on the basis of their hits totals, but surely some would have looked at Craig Biggio's 24 homers in 2004 and concluded that he was more valuable than Mark Loretta, who had only 16. If so, they'd have been mistaken. Loretta topped Biggio in batting average, on-base percentage, slugging average, singles, and walks, all while playing in a much tougher hitter's environment at PETCO Park than Biggio had at Minute Maid Park. Home runs alone not only don't provide a complete picture—they can actually distort assessments of a player's value to his team.

Batting average can also paint a misleading picture, though in different ways. Where counting stats largely depend on playing time, a player can earn the top batting average in the league just by going 1-for-1 for the season. In 1998 Shane Spencer played twenty-seven late-season games for the Yankees, hitting a robust .373 in 67 at-bats.

Already twenty-six years old and lacking the minor league track record to back up his outburst, Spencer never developed into a major league regular, managing just a .262 average, with a .326 on-base percentage and middling power for a corner outfielder. In December 2004, unable to find a big-league job, he signed with the Japanese League Hanshin Tigers.

At least Spencer brought some power along with this lofty batting average, socking 10 homers in those 67 at-bats—an impressive feat, even granting the small sample size. Again, a .300 batting average seen in isolation reveals almost nothing about a player. Does he bring power with his high batting average? If so, does that power show up in the form of homers or doubles? How often does he get on base? Has he developed a keen batting eye and drawn a lot of walks? With so many questions left unanswered, batting average needs companion statistics to better describe a player's contribution to his team. There are other numbers that are better storytellers than RBI, home runs, or batting average.

On-base percentage (OBP) shows how often a player reached base via hit, walk, or hit by pitch; among traditional offensive statistics, it's the most important. Of the major team sports, baseball is the only one that doesn't run on the whims of a clock. Rather, the game's "clock" is outs: Every time a player makes an out, he's brought his team 1/27 of the way closer to ending a nine-inning game. The higher a player's OBP, the less often he's cost his team an out at the plate and the more he's prolonged innings and created more runs, which leads to more wins. A player with a .400 OBP is getting on base in 40 percent of his plate appearances and making outs 60 percent of the time. A player with a .300 OBP is getting on base 30 percent of the time and making outs 70 percent of the time.

Slugging average (SLG) measures a player's power, though not perfectly. Calculated by dividing total bases by at-bats, SLG places the highest value on a home run, followed by a triple, double, and single. A player who goes 1-for-4 with a double earns a SLG of .500, as in 2 total bases divided by 4 at-bats equals .500.

More and more, publications, TV broadcasts, and even stadium Jumbotrons are presenting batting average (AVG) together with on-base percentage and slugging average to give fans a better grasp of a player's performance. The key statistics presented for a player were once given as .300-30-100, signifying a .300 average, 30 home runs, and 100 RBI; now a player's line may look like this: .300/.400/.500, where .300 is the player's AVG, .400 is his OBP, and .500 is his SLG.

Other statistics can be derived from this trio. OPS is the sum of a player's on-base percentage and slugging average, producing a quick-and-easy number that is less context-dependent and more representative of a player's broader skill set—including extra-base power and the ability to draw walks—than is apparent from AVG-HR-RBI. Derrek Lee led major league regulars with a 1.080 OPS in 2005; Cristian Guzman finished last at .569. Isolated Slugging (ISO) is the player's slugging average minus his batting average. This expresses how much true power he has by focusing solely on his extra-base hits.

Of the three Triple Crown statistics, batting average provides the least important information. This is no surprise given the stat's origin. Developed in the 1870s, during the game's infancy, batting average became the most popular stat. A traditional over-the-fence home run, common today, was virtually nonexistent then, as batters slapped at a dead ball that was not nearly as tightly wound and had likely been in play for hours by the late innings, black with chewing tobacco. Pitchers were instructed to serve the ball over the plate and let batters make contact. Batting average, a decent measure of the ability to hit 'em where they ain't, became the most closely watched statistic of the time. The modern game now focuses far more on walks and extra-base hits; batting average cannot speak to these things.

Because baseball has been played over a long time under varying conditions, including widely disparate physical environments, neither trinity—batting average, homers, and RBI; batting average, on-base percentage, and slugging average—paints a definitive picture. A .300 batting average, 30 homers, and 100 RBI or a .300/.400/.500 AVG/OBP/SLG line compiled in 2005 in Colorado carries vastly different weight than the same line achieved in Washington, D.C., in 1965. Different eras in baseball history and the unique configurations of ballparks have brought about big changes in offensive production over the history of the game.

A player's position must also be taken into account. Shortstops and catchers shoulder the heaviest defensive responsibilities on the diamond. Most teams have difficulty finding players who are skillful enough defensively to play these positions while also making a large offensive contribution. Conversely, first basemen and left fielders face fewer demands on the field; players whose primary skill is offense can cover those positions competently, even if they provide limited defensive skill. Thus, what would be a weak offensive season for a first baseman might be a strong one for a shortstop. It's necessary, then, not only to consider a player's productivity given the limitations of his position but also to adjust a shortstop's offense in light of his position if you want to gain a fair understanding of his contribution.

The necessity of comparing players across positions creates a sizable problem, not unlike a United Nations meeting in which all the translators have called in sick. Which position and era, if any, should serve as the baseline for translating performances into a common standard? What's a good batting average? What's a good on-base percentage? Home runs? SLG? RBI? OPS? Until players can be normalized to one common standard in which neither the ballpark, the era they played in, nor the positions they manned makes a difference, there's no good answer to these questions. Fortunately, as discussed in Chapter 5-1 ("Why Is Mario Mendoza So Important?"), baseball researchers have invented metrics that allow players to be compared across different eras, parks, and positions:

- **Equivalent Average (EqA),** developed by Baseball Prospectus's Clay Davenport, combines all major aspects of offense into a single measure while adjusting for park and league difficulty as well as incorporating team pitching and a player's baserunning. EqA uses roughly the same scale as batting average. A good player will put up a .300 EqA, an average player roughly .260, and a poor player in the low .200s.
- **Value Over Replacement Player (VORP),** developed by Baseball Prospectus's Keith Woolner, shows the number of runs a player contributes beyond what a replacement-level player (defined as a fringe major leaguer readily available off the waiver wire) at the same position would contribute if given the same percentage of team plate appearances.
- **MLVr** is a rate-based version of **Marginal Lineup Value (MLV)**, a measure of offensive production created by David Tate and further developed by Keith Woolner. MLV estimates the additional number of runs a given player will contribute to a lineup of average offensive performers. MLVr is approximately equal to MLV per game; the league average MLVr is 0 (0.000). Derrek Lee led major league regulars with a .532 MLVr in 2005; Cristian Guzman finished last at −.270. In 2004 Barry Bonds put up an otherworldly MLVr of .928. Albert Pujols produced a .535 MLVr, Ichiro Suzuki .287 in his record-breaking season for total hits.

As Chapter 5-2 ("Is Alex Rodriguez Overpaid?") explains, these improved measures permit a meaningful discussion of a player's monetary value. By comparing how much a player contributes versus a journeyman who can be had for the league-minimum salary, teams can apply more meaningful analysis and less guesswork to what have become multimillion-dollar decisions. Better decisions by management put better talent on the field.

The new measures also allow us to defrock "RBI man" Joe Carter, despite those 1,387 career RBI. Playing during one of the best offensive eras in major league history, Carter managed an anemic .306 on-base percentage, an atrocious figure for a corner outfielder of his vintage. He did hit 396 career home runs and posted fairly robust .464 career slugging average and .205 isolated slugging (.464 career SLG − .259 career AVG) figures.

To merit the kind of accolades he received during his career, though, Carter would have had to post strong numbers across the board, not just strong Triple Crown stats. Table 1-1.1 compares his career totals to someone we'll call Player X.

TABLE 1-1.1 Joe Carter vs. Player X

	AVG	OBP	SLG	ISO	HR	RBI	VORP	MLVr	EqA
Joe Carter	.259	.306	.464	.205	396	1,387	243.2	.048	.263
Player X	.236	.302	.478	.242	442	1,220	222.4	.080	.274

Player X trailed Carter by a fair margin in batting average and RBI. But he also posted a nearly identical OBP, slightly higher SLG and isolated slugging figures, and more career home runs. The advanced numbers tip the scale toward Player X. Despite accumulating 1,745 more at-bats, Carter's total value over replacement level is nearly identical to Player X's. Looking at MLVr and EqA, two stats that strip out playing time and focus solely on production, Player X holds a solid edge over Carter. Player X's career spanned nearly all of the 1970s and about half of the 1980s—a much tougher era for hitters than Carter's. Adjust for those different eras and Player X would appear to be Carter's match or superior nearly across the board.

Still, the gap in RBI needs to be reconciled. While Player X, like Carter, enjoyed a sixteen-year major league career, he amassed 1,745 fewer at-bats. More playing time naturally means more chances to knock in runs. How did Carter get that much more playing time over the same number of seasons? Despite his prodigious power, Player X batted lower in his team's lineup, on average, than Carter. While both players batted in the cleanup spot more than anywhere else during their careers (4,616 times for Player X, 4,150 times for Carter), Carter batted third or higher in the order 3,887 times in his career, compared to just 270 for Player X.

Player X also played in 248 fewer games. This was partly a testament to Carter's durability (140 or more games per year played 11 times, versus 5 for Player X) and partly due to Carter getting penciled into the lineup more often, given that he lacked Player X's ability to drive his manager, the fans, and the media crazy. Player X did this by racking up 1,816 strikeouts in his career—the ninth-highest all-time total, including leading the league in punchouts three times.

Studies have shown that a player who strikes out a lot isn't hurting his team by any significant margin versus a player who strikes out far less, assuming their other statistics are the same. Although a strikeout can't advance a runner the way a "productive" groundout or flyout can, a batter who doesn't make contact also can't ground into a double play. The benefit of the occasional runner advancement is canceled out by the cost of the double plays, making the strikeout, on average, no worse than other kinds of batting outs. But try telling that to a manager who's just watched his hitter swing and miss twelve times in a game. The bias against high-strikeout hitters remains alive and well, facts be damned.

Today Joe Carter is regarded by many as one of the best clutch hitters in baseball history, due largely to inflated RBI chances and one shining World Series moment. Player X is regarded by many as one of baseball's bad jokes, a flashy player but ultimately a loser, despite career offensive numbers that are arguably better than Carter's, after adjusting for career timelines. Player X is Dave Kingman.

Worst and Best 100-RBI Seasons

When a player notches 100 RBI in a season, it's usually assumed that he performed well. But a 100-RBI season doesn't always come with healthy numbers in other categories. A few players have actually driven in a hundred runs while having seasons that were demonstrably poor.

In 2004 Tony Batista made history of sorts in the Montreal Expos' last season before their move to Washington, D.C. Batting behind strong on-base threats Brad Wilkerson (.374 OBP) and Jose Vidro (.367 OBP), Batista amassed 103 RBI. But his .272 OBP was so far below league norms that Batista actually put up a negative VORP for the season, −1.1. In other words, the Expos would actually have done better to pick up a fringe replacement-level talent than to give Batista the 600-

plus plate appearances he received that year, from a strictly offensive standpoint (VORP does not account for defense).

Only one other player in the last three decades has combined a 100-RBI season with a negative VORP. That's our old friend Joe Carter.

Table 1-1.2 is a list of the fifty worst 100-RBI seasons since 1972 (as far back as Baseball Prospectus's database goes for these parameters). The players are ranked by RBI per VORP + 10, the 10 added to account for the negative figures by Carter and Batista. The player's OBP and SLG figures are also included to shed further light on their seasons. Note the last column, RBI per out, as well; as mentioned earlier, outs are baseball's most precious commodity. Many of the players below squandered far too many outs during their 100-RBI campaigns. Carter appears here five times, meaning that five of his seven 100-RBI seasons were offensively mediocre. Eric Karros, another overrated, overpaid player, ranks second with three appearances.

TABLE 1-1.2 Worst 100-RBI Seasons Since 1972

Player	Year	PA	OBP	SLG	RBI	VORP	RBI per VORP	RBI per Out
Joe Carter	1997	668	.284	.399	102	−2.4	13.48	.218
Tony Batista	2004	603	.272	.450	103	−1.1	11.56	.239
Tony Armas	1983	613	.254	.453	107	6.9	6.33	.239
Joe Carter	1990	697	.290	.391	115	8.9	6.08	.241
Ruben Sierra	1993	692	.288	.390	101	10.3	4.98	.210
Sammy Sosa	1997	694	.300	.480	119	14.8	4.80	.249
Rico Brogna	1998	624	.319	.446	104	11.8	4.77	.246
Joe Carter	1996	682	.306	.475	107	13.0	4.64	.231
Richie Sexson	1999	525	.305	.514	116	17.2	4.27	.322
Eric Karros	2000	663	.321	.459	106	15.3	4.19	.240
Derek Bell	1996	684	.311	.418	113	18.4	3.98	.246
Jeff King	1997	647	.340	.451	112	19.0	3.86	.269
Ruben Sierra	1987	696	.302	.470	109	18.3	3.85	.227
George Bell	1992	670	.294	.418	112	19.6	3.78	.241
Glenn Wilson	1985	650	.311	.424	102	17.7	3.68	.236
Garret Anderson	2001	704	.314	.478	123	24.8	3.53	.261
Vinny Castilla	1999	674	.331	.478	102	19.2	3.49	.231
Torii Hunter	2003	642	.312	.451	102	19.8	3.43	.239
Andres Galarraga	1995	604	.331	.511	106	21.4	3.38	.272
Butch Hobson	1977	637	.295	.489	112	24.2	3.27	.253
Gary Gaetti	1987	628	.303	.485	109	23.6	3.24	.256
Bill Buckner	1986	681	.311	.421	102	21.5	3.24	.224
Willie McGee	1987	652	.311	.434	105	22.5	3.23	.239

(continues)

TABLE 1-1.2 (continued)

Player	Year	PA	OBP	SLG	RBI	VORP	RBI per VORP	RBI per Out
Jeromy Burnitz	1998	691	.339	.499	125	28.7	3.23	.275
Rico Brogna	1999	679	.336	.454	102	21.6	3.23	.228
Brian Jordan	1999	645	.346	.465	115	25.8	3.22	.278
Chili Davis	1993	645	.327	.440	112	26.2	3.10	.260
Kevin Young	1998	657	.327	.481	108	25.5	3.04	.249
Eric Karros	1996	670	.316	.479	111	26.6	3.03	.246
Jim Presley	1986	660	.302	.463	107	25.5	3.02	.237
Joe Carter	1987	629	.304	.480	106	25.9	2.95	.250
Andre Dawson	1991	596	.302	.488	104	25.3	2.94	.257
Danny Tartabull	1996	541	.340	.487	101	24.5	2.92	.289
Eric Karros	1997	700	.329	.459	104	25.7	2.91	.226
Rafael Palmeiro	1997	692	.329	.485	110	28.0	2.89	.238
George Hendrick	1982	569	.322	.450	104	25.9	2.89	.277
Joe Carter	1994	483	.317	.524	103	25.9	2.87	.320
Paul O'Neill	1999	675	.353	.459	110	28.9	2.83	.256
Tino Martinez	1999	665	.341	.458	105	27.2	2.82	.241
Jose Canseco	1998	658	.318	.518	107	28.2	2.80	.243
Ben Ogilvie	1982	677	.326	.453	102	26.7	2.78	.229
Albert Belle	2000	622	.342	.474	103	27.3	2.76	.256
Jay Gibbons	2003	682	.330	.457	101	26.7	2.75	.224
Jermaine Dye	2001	675	.345	.467	106	29.3	2.69	.244
Andruw Jones	2001	693	.312	.461	104	28.7	2.69	.223
Tony Perez	1980	635	.320	.467	105	29.8	2.64	.251
J. T. Snow	1995	606	.350	.465	102	29.3	2.59	.264
Carl Yastrzemski	1976	636	.357	.432	102	29.9	2.56	.253
Dan Ford	1979	628	.331	.464	101	29.6	2.55	.246

Now, here's the flip side. Table 1-1.3 is a list of the fifty players with the most valuable 100-RBI seasons since 1972, sorted by lowest RBI-per-VORP ratios (minimum 400 plate appearances). Sorting by lowest RBI per VORP puts the spotlight on VORP, which measures a player's contribution in terms of runs—and hence wins—contributed to his team, rather than on RBI, where context and opportunity can often be as important, or more, than ability. VORP here serves as a proxy for wins, thus highlighting players who contributed the highest number of wins to their teams during their 100-RBI campaigns. Remember, the goal of this chapter was to better connect hitting to wins, which VORP does better than RBI. It's no surprise that Barry Bonds, the best MLB hitter in the time frame covered (since 1972), sports three of the four most valuable 100-RBI seasons of the last thirty-three years as well as six of the top seventeen.

TABLE 1-1.3 Best 100-RBI Seasons Since 1972

Player	Year	PA	OBP	SLG	RBI	VORP	RBI per VORP	RBI per Out
Barry Bonds	2004	617	.609	.812	101	142.0	0.711	.432
Barry Bonds	2002	612	.582	.799	110	147.4	0.746	.437
Derek Jeter	1999	739	.438	.552	102	118.0	0.864	.250
Barry Bonds	2001	664	.515	.863	137	154.1	0.889	.427
Chipper Jones	1999	701	.441	.633	110	114.6	0.960	.284
Rod Carew	1977	694	.449	.570	100	101.5	0.985	.267
Derrek Lee	2005	691	.418	.662	107	106.0	1.010	.271
Alan Trammell	1987	668	.402	.551	105	103.2	1.018	.271
Alex Rodriguez	1996	677	.414	.631	123	119.9	1.026	.315
Robin Yount	1982	704	.379	.578	114	110.3	1.033	.270
John Olerud	1993	679	.473	.599	107	102.7	1.042	.302
Frank Thomas	1994	517	.487	.729	101	96.8	1.044	.388
Jason Giambi	2001	671	.477	.660	120	114.2	1.051	.346
Barry Bonds	1997	690	.446	.585	101	95.8	1.054	.271
Barry Bonds	1992	612	.456	.624	103	96.1	1.072	.310
Nomar Garciaparra	1999	595	.418	.603	104	97.0	1.072	.309
Barry Bonds	1993	674	.457	.678	123	113.0	1.088	.338
Chipper Jones	2001	677	.427	.605	102	92.6	1.101	.270
Edgar Martinez	1995	639	.479	.628	113	102.4	1.103	.348
George Brett	1985	665	.436	.585	112	101.3	1.106	.304
Cal Ripken Jr.	1991	717	.374	.566	114	102.5	1.112	.267
Mark McGwire	1996	548	.467	.730	113	101.1	1.117	.387
Joe Morgan	1976	599	.444	.576	111	99.3	1.118	.345
Roberto Alomar	2001	677	.415	.541	100	88.9	1.125	.254
Mike Piazza	1997	633	.431	.638	124	109.9	1.128	.356
Barry Bonds	2000	607	.440	.688	106	93.8	1.130	.317
Ken Griffey Jr.	1993	691	.408	.617	109	95.1	1.146	.270
Albert Pujols	2003	685	.439	.667	124	108.2	1.146	.328
Albert Belle	1994	480	.438	.714	101	87.5	1.155	.387
Brady Anderson	1996	687	.396	.637	110	95.3	1.155	.266
Todd Helton	2003	703	.458	.630	117	99.9	1.171	.312
Don Mattingly	1986	742	.394	.573	113	95.8	1.180	.260
Darin Erstad	2000	747	.409	.541	100	84.7	1.181	.230
Cal Ripken Jr.	1983	726	.371	.517	102	86.1	1.185	.230
Albert Pujols	2005	700	.430	.609	117	98.7	1.185	.298
Edgar Martinez	1996	634	.464	.595	103	86.7	1.188	.313
Alex Rodriguez	2000	672	.420	.606	132	111.1	1.188	.347
Albert Pujols	2004	692	.415	.657	123	103.5	1.189	.315

(continues)

TABLE 1-1.3 (continued)

Player	Year	PA	OBP	SLG	RBI	VORP	RBI per VORP	RBI per Out
Frank Thomas	1991	701	.453	.553	109	91.4	1.193	.291
George Brett	1980	515	.454	.664	118	98.8	1.195	.429
Carlos Delgado	2000	711	.470	.664	137	114.3	1.198	.369
Brian Giles	2002	644	.450	.622	103	85.4	1.207	.293
Alex Rodriguez	2001	732	.399	.622	135	111.6	1.210	.314
Jeff Kent	2000	695	.424	.596	125	102.4	1.221	.319
Larry Walker	1997	664	.452	.720	130	106.3	1.223	.365
Alex Rodriguez	2003	715	.396	.600	118	96.3	1.225	.278
Jim Thome	2002	613	.445	.677	118	95.4	1.237	.354
Jason Bay	2005	707	.402	.559	101	81.7	1.237	.243
Robin Yount	1989	690	.384	.511	103	83.2	1.238	.246
Edgar Martinez	1997	678	.456	.554	108	87.2	1.238	.297

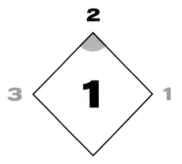

Is David Ortiz a Clutch Hitter?

NATE SILVER

Ask fans to recall the most memorable events they have seen on a base-ball field. Depending on their age and rooting interests, the list is likely to include some of the following: Carlton Fisk's twelfth-inning blast off the Green Monster foul pole in the 1975 World Series, a gimpy Kirk Gibson's pinch-hit homer off Dennis Eckersley in the 1988 World Se-ries, Joe Carter's three-run homer in the bottom of the ninth to give the Blue Jays the 1993 championship, and Aaron Boone's left-field blast in the 2003 ALCS to extend the Red Sox' misery by one last season.

What these events have in common is that they were big clutch hits—more specifically, big clutch home runs. The reason these big hits make such an impression is that they're so unlikely: Even the best hitters struggle to get a base hit in more than three out of ten at-bats, with home runs making up only a small fraction of those. Pitchers, on the other hand, are expected to get the out, and fielders are expected to make the play. Clutch-pitching performances are not often remem-bered; even the last out of a no-hitter can be strangely anticlimactic. Fielding plays are remembered, but typically only if they're miscues—such as the ball between Bill Buckner's legs in the 1986 World Series. But a hitter who salvages a victory with a clutch home run attains a mythological status. He has made the impossible possible.

It's that characteristic that might explain why so much is made of the clutch hitter. At various times, hitters such as Carter, Gibson, Reggie Jackson, and Tony Perez have been touted as top clutch hitters. In the 2004 playoffs, David Ortiz slugged five home runs and hit .400 in fourteen games, including key hits such as the game-winning homer in Game 4 of the ALCS. But it was the 2005 regular season that cemented Ortiz's reputation. In that season, he totaled 148 RBI and hit .352 with runners in scoring position. Perhaps most impressive, he blasted twenty home runs that either tied the game or put the Red Sox ahead. In September 2005, Red Sox owner John Henry presented a plaque to Ortiz with the following inscription:

DAVID ORTIZ

#34

THE GREATEST CLUTCH HITTER IN THE

HISTORY OF THE BOSTON RED SOX

The Red Sox have been on both sides of a disproportionate number of clutch hits, so this is no small praise. Some readers, however, might find a bit of irony in its source. The Red Sox organization, from Henry on down, takes pride in following the tenets of sabermetric analysis, and clutch hitting is a dubious concept in the minds of most sabermetricians, contrary to baseball's popular wisdom. Sabermetricians have conducted dozens, if not hundreds, of studies on clutch hitting, going back to Dick Cramer's work in the 1977 *Baseball Research Journal*. All of them have come to the same conclusion: Clutch-hitting ability either doesn't exist at all or is so rare that it is hardly worth worrying about.

Most of these studies have applied a similar technique to evaluate the issue of clutch hitting. Situations are broken down into two groups: "clutch" situations (for instance, late in a close game) and everything else. Summary batting statistics—whether traditional ones such as batting average or modern ones such as on-base percentage plus slugging average (OPS) or runs created—are then compared across the two situations. Regardless of the way the situations are defined or the batting statistics are used, this technique has found little evidence of clutch-hitting ability. Hitters who rate as good clutch hitters in one season have no disposition to rate as good clutch hitters in the next one.

While there's no doubt that clutch hitting is far less important than a lot of baseball people would have you believe, there are a couple of problems with the way that sabermetricians have attacked the clutch-hitting question in these studies. First, the division between "clutch" and ordinary situations is arbitrary and may be misleading. One popular definition of an important plate appearance is a close and late situation: "In the 7th inning or later with the batting team either ahead by one run, tied or with the potential tying run at least on deck." This would define, for example, a situation in which the home team is batting with the bases empty, down by two runs, with two outs in the bottom of the ninth, as a clutch situation. But that isn't a tremendously important at-bat—the game is probably already lost at that point. Over the past decade, home teams facing this situation went on to win the game less than 1 percent of the time. However, home teams down by just *one* run with two outs and the bases empty in the bottom of the ninth didn't fare much better, winning the game just 2.3 percent of the time. Thus, even if the batter in the down-two situation hit a home run to close the deficit to one, he would improve his team's winning chances by only about 1 percent. By comparison, a home run to lead off the game in the top of the *first* inning improves a team's winning chances by about 9 percent—yet it would never be called a clutch hit.

It would help the discussion if we could define situations along a spectrum of importance, or "clutchness." Some of these situations are obvious—two outs in the bottom of the ninth inning with the go-ahead run at home plate is a clutch situation. Others are subtler— what we might call "hidden-clutch" situations. Leading off the inning is a hidden-clutch situation, since making the first out of the inning is more than twice as costly as making the last out of the inning. Another example is when a team hits with one out and a runner on third base. It's critical to score the runner from third base with one out in the inning, since the runner can score on a sacrifice fly, groundout, or suicide squeeze with one out, but not with two. If the batter strikes out, pops up, or hits a liner or groundout too sharply, the runner can't advance, considerably reducing his team's run expectation.

A related problem with this type of clutch-hitting evaluation follows the assumption that it's good enough to compare the same batting statistic across different situations. Even relatively sophisticated offensive metrics like runs created assume that the value of a given offensive event is static; a double, say, is worth 0.7 runs. While that might be an excellent estimate of the average value of a double over the long run, it does not account for the fact that hitting situations are highly dynamic and that the value of different plays changes dynamically with them. For example:

- With the bases empty, a walk is every bit as good as a single. This is not the case with runners on base.

- ◆ In a tie game in the bottom of the ninth with a runner on third base, a single is every bit as good as a home run.
- ◆ If the home team is batting in the bottom of the ninth down by two runs with nobody on, a walk is virtually as good as a home run.
- ◆ With a runner on first base and less than two outs, a strikeout is preferable to a groundout.

Table 1-2.1 provides some further examples of this phenomenon, based on a complete record of major league play-by-play data between 1996 and 2005. Any situation in a baseball game can be described by four key elements: the inning, the number of outs, the score, and the number of bases occupied. We can look back at the play-by-play record to determine how often the batting team went on to win the game when a situation defined in terms of these four elements occurred. For example, the visiting team won about 17 percent of the time when it got the leadoff hitter on in the eighth inning while down by two runs (situation E in the table). However, if the next hitter hits a home run, the visiting team finds itself in a much more favorable situation: top of the eighth inning, no outs, tie game, bases empty. The visiting team went on to win the game about 48 percent of the time when this new situation occurred, meaning that the home run improved its probability of winning the game by about 31 percent.

Note the degree to which the *relative* value of batting events changes in different contexts, as described in Table 1-2.1. In some cases, a home run is worth about the same amount as a single; in other cases, it's worth five times as much. The value of different types of hits changes dramatically given different game situations.

Imagine you had a hitter who was able to change his approach, however slightly, to fit the game situation. The hitter could decide to "swing for contact," in which case he'd hit five more singles than he usually does per 100 plate appearances, but two fewer home runs. The hitter can't change himself completely—he can't go from being Rob Deer to Tony Gwynn. But he can change the probabilities just a little bit by tinkering with his swing plane or pitch selection.

Roughly speaking, this is a fair trade: Two home runs are about equal in value to five singles in the long run. But a hitter who tended to hit home runs *when home runs were relatively more valuable* and singles *when singles were relatively more valuable* would give his team an advantage. If such a hitter was able to "swing for contact" in situation F, for example—a situation in which any kind of hit would do—

TABLE 1-2.1 Clutch Situations, by Win Probability

	Situation				Win Probability (%) (Batting Team)	Impact on Win Probability (%)			
	Inning	Outs	Score	Bases		Single	HR	Walk	Strikeout
A	Top first	0	tied	empty	46.5	4.6	8.8	4.6	-2.3
B	Top third	1	down by 1	first, second	41.8	8.9	26.3	6.6	-4.3
C	Bottom fifth	2	ahead by 1	second, third	70.3	17.3	21.9	5.1	-2.9
D	Top sixth	2	empty	tied	54.7	3.3	17.7	3.3	-1.8
E	Top eighth	0	down by 2	first	17.4	10.3	30.5	6.8	-5.6
F	Bottom ninth	1	tied	second	72.5	19.5	27.5	0.3	-12.6
G	Bottom ninth	1	down by 2	empty	4.1	4.6	5.1	4.6	-3.7

Note: A single is assumed to advance a runner from first to third base 50 percent of the time and score a runner from second base 60 percent of the time.

he'd produce an extra 0.43 wins for his team over those 100 plate appearances. That isn't a large advantage, but baseball is a game that is won by exploiting small advantages over the long haul. Certainly clutch hitting may exist in the classic sense of the term. A lot of what we think of as clutch hitting may really be *situational hitting.*

◆

In *Baseball Prospectus 2005,* Keith Woolner developed a rigorous framework for estimating the probability of a team going on to victory at any point in a given game. The model takes advantage of the sort of data described in Table 1-2.1, the historical probability of victory based on the game situation: the inning, number of outs, score, and number of bases occupied. However, it generalizes the historical data to smooth over issues related to small sample sizes as well as to account for different run-scoring environments. The value of runs and of the hits and walks that produce those runs are different when a good offensive club is playing at Coors Field than when a bad one is playing at PETCO Park.

The model allows us to estimate with a high degree of accuracy the number of wins that a player contributed to his team by comparing a team's win expectation before and immediately after a given batting event occurs. Table 1-2.2, taken from the ninth inning of the Giants-Nationals game played on Sept. 20, 2005, provides an example of the procedure in action.

Clutch situations are naturally associated with larger swings in a team's win expectation. Hits are relatively more beneficial and outs are relatively more costly when the game is on the line. In this particular game, Moises Alou hit a three-run homer in the top of the ninth with two outs and the Giants trailing. That is about as clutch as home runs get: It improved the Giants' chances of winning the game from 14 percent to 93 percent, a 79 percent increase. Alou thus gets credit for that 79 percent, or .79 of a win. On the other hand, Brad Wilkerson's flyout to end the game was especially devastating, as the Nationals had managed to close the gap to one run and had two runners on base. Wilkerson is "credited" with −.16 wins for his failure to deliver, since his out reduced the Nationals' chances of winning from 16 percent to nothing. By adding up the win expectation increases over all of a player's plate appearances in a given year, we can arrive at an estimate of the total number of wins that the player's hitting contributed in a particular season, which I will call the player's Win Expectancy (WinEx).

TABLE 1-2.2 Win Expectation, Nationals-Giants Game, September 20, 2005

	Top of Ninth: Giants Batting					*Win Expectation (%)*		
Batter	*Inning*	*Outs*	*Score*	*Bases*	*Result*	*Before*	*After*	*Change*
Winn	Top 9th	0	Nats 2-1 (–1)	empty	groundout	15.3	8.4	–6.8
Alfonzo	Top 9th	1	Nats 2-1 (–1)	empty	walk	8.4	16.9	8.5
Vizquel	Top 9th	1	Nats 2-1 (–1)	1B	flyout	16.9	7.4	–9.6
Bonds	Top 9th	1	Nats 2-1 (–1)	1B	walk	7.4	14.3	7.0
Alou	Top 9th	2	Nats 2-1 (–1)	1B, 2B	home run	14.3	92.9	78.6
Durham	Top 9th	2	Giants 4-2 (+2)	empty	flyout	92.9	92.6	–0.3

	Bottom of 9th: Nationals Batting					*Win Expectation (%)*		
Batter	*Inning*	*Outs*	*Score*	*Bases*	*Result*	*Before*	*After*	*Change*
Wilson	Bot 9th	0	Giants 4-2 (–2)	empty	groundout	7.4	3.9	–3.6
Castilla	Bot 9th	1	Giants 4-2 (–2)	empty	double	3.9	11.2	7.3
Schneider	Bot 9th	1	Giants 4-2 (–2)	2B	walk	11.2	19.0	7.8
Church	Bot 9th	1	Giants 4-2 (–2)	1B, 2B	walk	19.0	31.6	12.6
Zimmerman	Bot 9th	1	Giants 4-2 (–2)	loaded	sac fly	31.6	16.5	–15.0
Wilkerson	Bot 9th	2	Giants 4-3 (–1)	1B, 2B	flyout	16.5	0.0	–16.5

This is not a new method. On the contrary, determining win expectancy in this fashion is one of the oldest tricks in the sabermetric playbook, with its roots in the work of E. G. and H. D. Mills in 1970 and a great number of imitations thereafter. However, Win Expectancy provides a compelling framework for evaluating the clutch hitting question because it works around the problems that I described before. The WinEx method defines the importance of different situations along a spectrum rather than placing them in either/or categories. Moreover, the model is dynamic. Different types of hits are valued differently in different situations, depending on the actual contribution they make in terms of winning the game.

The next few tables provide some sense of what WinEx numbers look like. Table 1-2.3 contains a list of the WinEx "MVPs" in each league since 1972. Tables 1-2.4 and 1-2.5 highlight the best and worst WinEx performances over the same period. Note that because WinEx evaluates a hitter's performance based on an implicit comparison to how other hitters performed in the same situations, an average hitter should have a WinEx score of zero.

These lists don't contain many surprises. The players with the highest WinEx scores are overwhelmingly among the best hitters of the

TABLE 1-2.3 WinEx MVPs, 1972–2005

Year	American League	WinEx	National League	WinEx
1972	**Dick Allen**[a]	+6.85	Billy Williams	+6.02
1973	Dave May	+5.29	Willie Stargell	+5.75
1974	**Jeff Burroughs**	+5.31	Willie McCovey	+4.56
1975	Rod Carew	+4.53	Steve Garvey	+5.19
			Ted Simmons	+5.19
1976	Reggie Jackson	+4.80	Rusty Staub	+6.09
1977	Ken Singleton	+5.49	**George Foster**	+4.70
1978	**Jim Rice**	+5.31	**Dave Parker**	+5.77
1979	Sixto Lezcano	+5.03	Dave Winfield	+7.95
1980	**George Brett**	+5.33	Jack Clark	+5.27
			Mike Schmidt	+5.27
1981	Dwight Evans	+4.76	**Mike Schmidt**	+5.27
1982	Eddie Murray	+4.96	Leon Durham	+5.26
1983	Wade Boggs	+6.93	Dale Murphy	+4.76
1984	Eddie Murray	+7.17	Tony Gwynn	+6.95
1985	George Brett	+5.94	**Dale Murphy**	+6.76
1986	Wade Boggs	+5.81	Glenn Davis	+4.60
1987	Dwight Evans	+4.10	Jack Clark	+5.17
1988	Cal Ripken	+4.82	Andres Galarraga	+5.62
1989	Lou Whitaker	+5.02	Will Clark	+7.03
1990	**Rickey Henderson**	+4.60	**Barry Bonds**	+4.24
1991	Jose Canseco	+4.92	Barry Bonds	+6.13
1992	**Frank Thomas**	+6.25	Gary Sheffield	+5.92
1993	**Frank Thomas**	+5.99	**Barry Bonds**	+6.44
1994	Frank Thomas	+4.32	Fred McGriff	+4.86
1995	Edgar Martinez	+7.10	Barry Bonds	+7.42
1996	Mark McGwire	+5.52	Barry Bonds	+7.46
1997	Frank Thomas	+7.14	Tony Gwynn	+6.77
1998	Albert Belle	+4.19	Mark McGwire	+8.90
1999	Derek Jeter	+4.96	Vladimir Guerrero	+6.00
2000	Carlos Delgado	+6.67	Todd Helton	+8.06
2001	Jason Giambi	+7.51	**Barry Bonds**	+11.12
2002	Jim Thome	+6.52	**Barry Bonds**	+9.60
2003	Carlos Delgado	+5.40	**Barry Bonds**	+7.57
2004	Gary Sheffield	+4.27	**Barry Bonds**	+11.17
2005	David Ortiz	+7.31	Carlos Delgado	+5.91

[a]Boldface indicates a player who won his league's MVP award in that season.

past three decades, while the players with the lowest WinEx scores are among the worst. Barry Bonds's dominance is particularly well highlighted here, while Mario Mendoza, of the "Mendoza Line" (described in detail in Chapter 5-1), makes an appearance on the worst seasons list. In some sense, WinEx suffices on its own to answer the question of who the best clutch hitters are: They're usually just the best hitters, period.

Nevertheless, people are generally thinking about something different when they describe clutch hitting. When Tony Perez was the subject of some intense campaigning a few years ago on behalf of his candidacy for the Hall of Fame, a good number of his contemporaries brought up the subject of his clutch hitting. "He's the best clutch hitter I've ever seen," said his manager in Cincinnati, Sparky Anderson. The reason we heard this argument so frequently is that Perez needed a little something extra to get him into Cooperstown. Perez's most comparable players, according to his conventional batting statistics, are Harold Baines, Dave Parker, and Andre Dawson. All three are fine players but also short of Hall of Fame caliber. The argument Perez's advocates were making was that his conventional batting statistics didn't do him justice. He had a tendency to get the right hits at the right times above and be-

TABLE 1-2.4 Twenty Best and Ten Worst WinEx Seasons Since 1972

Best WinEx Seasons			
	Player	Year	WinEx
1	Barry Bonds	2004	+11.17
2	Barry Bonds	2001	+11.12
3	Barry Bonds	2002	+9.60
4	Mark McGwire	1998	+8.90
5	Todd Helton	2000	+8.06
6	Dave Winfield	1979	+7.96
7	Barry Bonds	2003	+7.57
8	Jason Giambi	2001	+7.51
9	Barry Bonds	1996	+7.46
10	Barry Bonds	1995	+7.42
11	David Ortiz	2005	+7.31
12	Eddie Murray	1984	+7.17
13	Frank Thomas	1997	+7.14
14	Edgar Martinez	1995	+7.10
15	Will Clark	1989	+7.03
16	Tony Gwynn	1984	+6.95
17	Wade Boggs	1983	+6.93
18	Brian Giles	2002	+6.93
19	Lance Berkman	2001	+6.89
20	Dick Allen	1972	+6.85

Worst WinEx Seasons			
	Player	Year	WinEx
1	Neifi Perez	2002	−5.83
2	Gary Disarcina	1997	−4.83
3	Brad Ausmus	2001	−4.31
4	Roy Smalley	1977	−4.28
5	Rennie Stennett	1979	−4.28
6	Mario Mendoza	1979	−4.27
7	Roger Metzger	1972	−4.15
8	Mike Felder	1993	−4.12
9	Randy Hundley	1972	−4.05
10	George Wright	1985	−4.04

TABLE 1-2.5 Twenty Best and Ten Worst Career WinEx Totals, 1972–2005

Best Career WinEx Totals

	Player	WinEx
1	Barry Bonds	102.65
2	Gary Sheffield	57.01
3	Tony Gwynn	53.75
4	Frank Thomas	51.96
5	Jeff Bagwell	51.10
6	George Brett	50.92
7	Mark McGwire	49.58
8	Eddie Murray	48.61
9	Mike Schmidt	48.61
10	Fred McGriff	46.79
11	Rickey Henderson	45.35
12	Larry Walker	44.59
13	Ken Griffey Jr.	43.01
14	Will Clark	41.17
15	Edgar Martinez	40.51
16	Dave Winfield	40.02
17	Mike Piazza	39.97
18	Chipper Jones	38.95
19	Vladimir Guerrero	38.62
20	Rafael Palmeiro	38.28

Worst Career WinEx Totals

	Player	WinEx
1	Larry Bowa	-27.80
2	Royce Clayton	-27.15
3	Ozzie Guillen	-23.07
4	Neifi Perez	-22.99
5	Doug Flynn	-22.88
6	Alfredo Griffin	-22.73
7	Bob Boone	-21.82
8	Tim Foli	-20.45
9	Rey Sanchez	-20.28
10	Rey Ordonez	-18.09

yond those statistics, they claimed. That was what should set Perez above Parker, Baines, or Gil Hodges, and that was why he should be in the Hall.

The Perez quandary raises an important question: Are there hitters who are more valuable than their regular statistics would suggest because of their tendency to hit in the clutch? We've already settled on the Win Expectancy model as the way to account for clutch situations. But we also need some point of comparison for regular offensive statistics. Fortunately, sabermetricians are very good at working with regular offensive statistics and translating them into the number of runs and wins they produce over the long run. As our point of departure, we'll use a variation of Marginal Lineup Value (MLV), a member of the Value over Replacement Player family of statistics that were introduced in Chapter 1-1. Let's walk through the process:

Step 1. Estimate a player's MLV. One of the nice things about MLV is its elegance: It allows us to estimate, with a high degree of accuracy, the number of runs that a player produces based solely on his batting average, slugging average, and on-base percentage. Ordinarily, MLV operates by comparing the number of runs that a lineup of nine average hitters would score against the number of runs that the same lineup would score if we replaced one of those average hitters with a specific player. Like WinEx, MLV is structured so that an average player has an MLV of zero.

I use a modified version of MLV here. Rather than placing a player in an average, hypothetical lineup, I placed the player in the lineup of his actual team. (The 2005 version of Vladimir Guerrero, for example, is placed on the 2005 Angels.) I then compare the number of runs that MLV estimates the Angels would score with Guerrero in the lineup versus the number of runs the same lineup would score with Guerrero replaced by an average hitter. In this case, the formula estimates that the Angels would score 737 runs with Guerrero and 700 without him, for a marginal contribution of 37 runs. We'll call this figure MLVRuns.

Step 2. Translate MLV into wins. All runs are not created equal—a run is more valuable in a low-scoring environment than a high-scoring one. The WinEx method, which adjusts for run-scoring context, is naturally inclined to reflect this difference, so it's important to have it reflected in our comparison statistic too. This can be accounted for by translating MLV into wins through a variation of the Bill James Pythagorean Formula, which estimates a team's winning percentage given the number of runs it scores and allows. Sticking with our example from before, the 2005 Angels scored 760 runs and allowed 643, which the Pythagorean formula suggests is worth 93.4 wins over a 162-game schedule. However, we determined through MLV that without Guerrero in the lineup, the Angels would have scored 37 fewer runs, or 723. A team that scored 723 runs and allowed 643 would be expected to win 89.7 games. The difference between the two figures provides an estimate of the number of wins that the player produced. Here, Guerrero is estimated to be worth about 3.7 additional wins to the 2005 Angels. We'll call this figure MLVWins.

Step 3. Account for "Leverage." Certain players can expect to have a disproportionate number of their at-bats occur in clutch situations. A cleanup hitter or a hitter on a team that played in a lot of close games might have more than his fair share of clutch opportunities. If the player took advantage of such opportunities, it would have a favorable effect on his WinEx.

We have a statistic called "Leverage," developed as part of our Win Expectancy model, which is designed to account for exactly this effect. Leverage is structured so that the first plate appearance of the game is given a score of 1.00. Subsequent plate appearances are given comparative scores in consideration of the relative importance that scoring one additional run would have on the outcome of the game. We can average the Leverage scores from a hitter's individual plate appearances over the course of a year to see how many clutch situations he faced during the season.

For the most part, Leverage scores don't vary all that much from hitter to hitter and stay close to the 1.00 benchmark, as important plate appearances and those in blowouts balance out. In 2005, for example, the range of Leverage scores among regular hitters was between 0.92 (Jay Gibbons) and 1.21 (Joe Mauer); the range becomes even narrower if we look at a player's entire career. We do have the statistic in our toolbox, however, to account for its effect on WinEx.

Step 4. Predict WinEx and determine clutch rating. It turns out that we can do a reasonably good job of predicting WinEx by accounting for the three factors we've just described: a hitter's MLVRuns produced, his MLVWins produced, and his Leverage factor. If these three factors are placed into a regression analysis, the model can explain about 70 percent of WinEx. Put differently, about 70 percent of "clutch hitting" can be explained by a hitter's conventional batting statistics, his run-scoring environment, and his opportunity. The remaining 30 percent is luck—and clutch-hitting ability, if it exists.

We'll call the prediction from our regression model Leveraged MLV Wins (LMLVW). LMLVW accounts for just about everything you might want, except how the hitter performed in clutch situations specifically. Therefore, we can evaluate a hitter's clutch performance by means of this equation:

$$\text{Clutch} = \text{WinEx} - \text{LMLVW}$$

"Clutch" is measured in wins. Hitters with positive clutch scores contributed additional wins to their teams as a result of their clutch hitting, above and beyond what would be predicted by their batting statistics, Leverage, and run-scoring environment. In 2005, for example, David Ortiz had an LMLVW of 3.7; that's what we'd have expected his WinEx to be, given average luck and clutch-hitting prowess. Instead, Ortiz had a WinEx of 7.3, for a clutch score of 3.6. That means Ortiz added nearly four extra wins to the Red Sox' total as a result of his timely hitting. If Ortiz hadn't hit so well in the clutch, the Red Sox would likely have lost the Wild Card to the Cleveland Indians.

Ortiz's season was an outlier, a year out of proportion with the rest of his career that he's unlikely to repeat. Table 1-2.6 lists the twenty best and ten worst clutch scores since 1972, with Ortiz's 2005 in fifth place.

When a player has a season that extreme, it's generally fairly easy to tell. In 2002, for example, Randy Winn, then with the Tampa Bay Devil

26

TABLE 1-2.6 Twenty Best and Ten Worst Clutch Scores Since 1972

Best Clutch Scores

	Player	Year	WinEx	LMLVW	Clutch
1	Tim Foli	1972	+1.17	-2.63	+3.80
2	Mark Grace	1999	+5.56	+1.79	+3.77
3	Randy Winn	2002	+4.86	+1.10	+3.76
4	Todd Helton	2000	+8.06	+4.41	+3.65
5	David Ortiz	2005	+7.31	+3.68	+3.63
6	Eric Young	1998	+4.15	+0.59	+3.56
7	Bruce Bochte	1980	+5.32	+1.76	+3.56
8	Tony Gwynn	1984	+6.95	+3.44	+3.51
9	Larry Walker	2002	+6.60	+3.17	+3.43
10	Dante Bichette	1993	+4.51	+1.09	+3.42
11	Scott Podsednik	2004	+1.56	-1.84	+3.40
12	Kirby Puckett	1985	+2.58	-0.78	+3.36
13	Dante Bichette	1996	+4.26	+0.90	+3.36
14	Darrell Evans	1977	+4.06	+0.73	+3.33
15	Rusty Staub	1976	+6.09	+2.79	+3.30
16	Troy O'Leary	1996	+2.69	-0.59	+3.28
17	Wade Boggs	1983	+6.93	+3.73	+3.20
18	Toby Harrah	1972	+3.04	-0.15	+3.19
19	Rick Cerone	1979	+1.69	-1.48	+3.17
20	Mike Hargrove	1979	+4.57	+1.43	+3.14

Worst Clutch Scores

	Player	Year	WinEx	LMLVW	Clutch
1	Bill Mueller	2003	-1.72	+2.11	-3.83
2	Joey Cora	1996	-3.91	-0.41	-3.50
3	Lee May	1972	-0.82	+2.66	-3.48
4	Chris Sabo	1991	-0.43	+3.03	-3.46
5	J. T. Snow	1998	-3.04	+0.38	-3.42
6	Benito Santiago	1988	-3.73	-0.47	-3.26
7	Don Baylor	1973	-2.19	+1.04	-3.23
8	Paul Molitor	1983	-2.46	+0.74	-3.20
9	Al Oliver	1974	-0.48	+2.67	-3.15
10	Rafael Palmeiro	1991	+0.45	+3.52	-3.07

Rays, hit .298/.360/.461 (AVG/OBP/SLG) overall. However, he hit .316/.385/.519 with runners in scoring position and .368/.414/.581 in close and late games. He also hit .325/.383/.571 when leading off the inning, one of those hidden-clutch situations that I discussed before. All told, he had a highly "clutch" season. On the other hand, there's Bill Mueller's 2003. Mueller hit .326/.398/.540 overall, but just .237/.326/.342 in close and late situations, killing many rallies for the Red Sox.

These sorts of lists are fun to look at, but they are no proof of clutch-hitting skill. By virtue of luck alone, some players are going to rank at the top of the list and others at the bottom each season. The question is whether the same players do well in their clutch rating year after year. Table 1-2.7, for example, shows David Ortiz's clutch scores for each of his big league seasons.

Ortiz does well by the clutch metric, but most of the damage was limited to just two seasons, 2000 and 2005. Take those two years away, and his lifetime clutch rating is essentially zero. He didn't rate as a clutch hitter in 2004—at least not during the regular season—or in 2002. It isn't a bad track record, but if clutch hitting really exists, one would expect more consistency out of the "greatest clutch hitter in the history of the Boston Red Sox." Tony Gwynn, one of the greatest batting-average hitters of all time, didn't have any seasons where he hit .240.

TABLE 1-2.7 David Ortiz's Year-by-Year Clutch Scores

Year	PA	Clutch
1997	51	-0.33
1998	326	+0.23
1999	25	-0.07
2000	478	+1.48
2001	347	+0.61
2002	466	-0.28
2003	509	+0.21
2004	669	-0.32
2005	713	+3.63
Total	3,584	+5.16

Table 1-2.8 provides the lifetime clutch scores for twenty-five players who are "famous" clutch hitters, either by virtue of a well-remembered hit or two or by general reputation. The list was compiled from the suggestions of Baseball Prospectus authors before I ran any of the numbers. Players are rated both by their lifetime clutch scores from 1972 to 2005, and by their clutch score per 650 plate appearances (about equal to a full season's worth of playing time).

There are a few players like Leyritz, Guerrero, and Brett who acquit themselves well. But in general, there is little relationship between perception and performance when it comes to clutch hitting. Players

TABLE 1-2.8 Clutch Rating, 25 "Famous" Clutch Hitters

Player	PA	Career	Per 650 PA
Jim Leyritz	2,961	+6.78	+1.49
David Ortiz	3,584	+5.16	+0.94
Aaron Boone	3,440	+3.92	+0.74
Vladimir Guerrero	5,490	+6.10	+0.72
George Brett	11,624	+7.63	+0.43
Eddie Murray	12,817	+7.12	+0.36
Edgar Martinez	8,672	+2.73	+0.20
Joe Carter	9,154	+2.43	+0.17
Miguel Tejada	5,396	+1.25	+0.15
Ichiro Suzuki	3,692	+0.59	+0.10
Willie Stargell	4,330	+0.39	+0.06
Kirk Gibson	6,656	+0.55	+0.05
Carl Yastrzemski	6,696	+0.35	+0.03
Pete Rose	9,649	−0.05	+0.00
Paul Molitor	12,160	−0.68	−0.04
Reggie Jackson	8,834	−1.02	−0.08
Paul O'Neill	8,329	−1.10	−0.09
Don Mattingly	7,721	−1.06	−0.09
Steve Garvey	9,114	−1.97	−0.14
Juan Gonzalez	7,155	−1.97	−0.18
Tony Perez	6,865	−2.20	−0.21
Derek Jeter	6,996	−2.39	−0.22
Carlton Fisk	9,799	−3.56	−0.24
Manny Ramirez	7,225	−3.54	−0.32
Jim Rice	9,058	−6.67	−0.48

such as Reggie Jackson, Tony Perez, and Derek Jeter have actually performed a bit worse than the norm in clutch situations, at least in the regular season. To be fair, a reputation for clutch hitting is often formed in the postseason, or in particularly important games down the stretch. Our ratings do not account for postseason performance at all, or for the relative importance of various regular-season games. On the other hand, branding someone as a clutch hitter because he gets a handful of fortuitous hits is specious at best. To the extent that clutch hitting actually exists as a repeatable skill, it should appear consistently throughout a player's career.

It's time, finally, to tackle the clutch-hitting question more systematically. One good way to test whether clutch-hitting skill exists is to break a player's career into halves, with even seasons (1998, 2000) on one side and odd seasons (1991, 1993) on the other. Figure 1-2.1 presents a scatterplot of clutch rating per 650 PA for the 292 players who had at least 2,500 PA in each half of their careers since 1972, with even seasons on the horizontal axis and odd seasons on the vertical. If clutch-hitting skill exists, we'll see a linear pattern, with the data points arranging themselves diagonally from the bottom left of the graph across to the top right. If it doesn't exist, we'll instead see just a random blob of dots.

FIGURE 1-2.1 Clutch wins per 650 PA

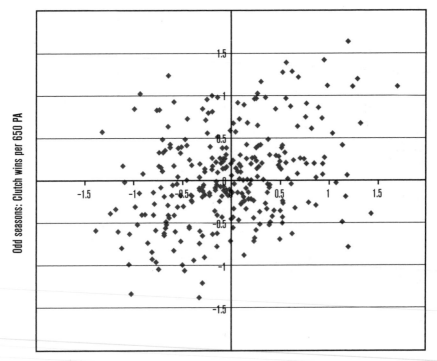

Even seasons: Clutch wins per 650 PA

What we have is much closer to the random smattering than the straight line. Still, there is some pattern to the data; players with good clutch ratings in the odd halves of their careers have some tendency to have good clutch ratings in the even halves. Mathematically speaking, the correlation in clutch rating between the two career halves is about .33, where a correlation of 0 would represent complete randomness and a correlation of 1 a perfect linear relationship. Another way to look at this is via the R-squared statistic, a product of regression analysis that describes how much of a dependent variable can be explained by independent variables. Regressing clutch ratings in even seasons against clutch ratings in odd seasons results in an R-squared of .10. Simply put, it suggests that 10 percent of clutch-hitting performance can be explained by skill, with the remaining 90 percent a matter of luck. That's a much higher skill quotient than other studies have identified. But to paraphrase Bill James, the observation that clutch-hitting performance is random is more true than false.

Nevertheless, it's worth seeing what we can make out of the skill element that does exist. Is there any pattern to which sort of players do better in clutch situations? Or do you know a clutch hitter only once you've seen him succeed in those situations many times over? Tables 1-2.9 and 1-2.10 present the best and worst hitters in terms of clutch performance since 1972, as ranked by lifetime clutch rating and clutch rating per 650 PA (minimum 5,000 PA).

TABLE 1-2.9 Twenty-five Best and Twenty-five Worst Clutch Ratings, 1972–2005

	Best Career Clutch Ratings			
	Player	*PA*	*Career*	*Per 650 PA*
1	Mark Grace	9,290	+13.68	+0.96
2	Toby Harrah	8,337	+13.46	+1.05
3	Jason Kendall	5,958	+12.96	+1.41
4	Kent Hrbek	7,137	+12.83	+1.17
5	Matt Lawton	5,541	+12.10	+1.42
6	Darrell Evans	10,352	+11.81	+0.74
7	Scott Fletcher	5,976	+11.43	+1.24
8	Jeromy Burnitz	6,237	+11.26	+1.17
9	Kirby Puckett	7,831	+11.06	+0.92
10	Harold Baines	11,092	+10.73	+0.63
11	Tony Gwynn	10,232	+9.83	+0.62
12	Dante Bichette	6,855	+9.23	+0.88
13	Bruce Bochte	5,994	+9.11	+0.99
14	Jose Vidro	4,242	+9.09	+1.39
15	Rickey Henderson	13,346	+8.86	+0.43
16	Bobby Higginson	5,660	+8.80	+1.01
17	Orlando Merced	4,530	+8.74	+1.25
18	Jose Cruz Sr.	4,437	+8.73	+1.28
19	Darrin Erstad	5,673	+8.58	+0.98
20	Rusty Staub	5,861	+8.48	+0.94
21	Leroy Stanton	2,856	+8.37	+1.91
22	Mike Sweeney	4,733	+8.20	+1.13
23	Randy Winn	4,093	+8.07	+1.28

(continues)

TABLE 1-2.9 (continued)

	Player	PA	Career	Per 650 PA
	Best Career Clutch Ratings			
24	Larry Walker	8,025	+7.93	+0.64
25	Von Hayes	6,052	+7.85	+0.84

	Player	PA	Career	Per 650 PA
	Worst Career Clutch Ratings			
1	Royce Clayton	7,446	−13.56	−1.18
2	Larry Parrish	7,797	−12.17	−1.01
3	Don Baylor	9,376	−11.96	−0.83
4	Chet Lemon	7,872	−11.62	−0.96
5	Joey Cora	4,279	−10.38	−1.58
6	Bob Boone	8,148	−10.35	−0.83
7	Larry Bowa	7,830	−10.27	−0.85
8	Ron Cey	8,342	−10.13	−0.79
9	Gary Carter	9,019	−9.68	−0.70
10	Mike Schmidt	10,062	−9.61	−0.62
11	Richard Hidalgo	3,927	−9.24	−1.53
12	Bill Mueller	4,760	−9.09	−1.24
13	Cesar Geronimo	4,091	−8.86	−1.41
14	Benito Santiago	7,515	−8.77	−0.76
15	Larry Herndon	5,316	−8.77	−1.07
16	Rick Dempsey	5,378	−8.30	−1.00
17	Tony Pena	7,073	−8.30	−0.76
18	Davey Lopes	7,340	−8.21	−0.73
19	Ivan Rodriguez	7,740	−8.18	−0.69
20	Rennie Stennett	4,645	−8.05	−1.13
21	Carney Lansford	7,905	−7.98	−0.66
22	Brad Ausmus	5,774	−7.95	−0.89
23	Rich Aurilia	4,866	−7.88	−1.05
24	Marvin Benard	2,945	−7.80	−1.72
25	Scott Brosius	4,356	−7.70	−1.15

Mark Grace rates as the best clutch hitter of the past three decades according to our metrics, producing between 13 and 14 more wins as a result of his clutch hitting than his regular batting statistics would indicate. This makes a certain amount of sense. Grace had a reputation for being a very smart hitter, and there are some references to his clutch ability in the historical literature. Other names will come as

TABLE 1-2.10 Twenty-five Best and Twenty-five Worst Clutch/PA Ratings, 1972–2005

	Best Clutch/PA Ratings			
	Player	*PA*	*Career*	*Per 650 PA*
1	Matt Lawton	5,541	+12.10	+1.42
2	Jason Kendall	5,958	+12.96	+1.41
3	Scott Fletcher	5,976	+11.43	+1.24
4	Jeromy Burnitz	6,237	+11.26	+1.17
5	Kent Hrbek	7,137	+12.83	+1.17
6	Toby Harrah	8,337	+13.46	+1.05
7	Bobby Higginson	5,660	+8.80	+1.01
8	Bruce Bochte	5,994	+9.11	+0.99
9	Darrin Erstad	5,673	+8.58	+0.98
10	Mark Grace	9,290	+13.68	+0.96
11	Rusty Staub	5,861	+8.48	+0.94
12	Kirby Puckett	7,831	+11.06	+0.92
13	Dante Bichette	6,855	+9.23	+0.88
14	Von Hayes	6,052	+7.85	+0.84
15	Willie Montanez	5,696	+7.34	+0.84
16	Todd Helton	5,424	+6.63	+0.79
17	Hubie Brooks	6,476	+7.47	+0.75
18	Ben Ogilvie	6,560	+7.51	+0.74
19	Darrell Evans	10,352	+11.81	+0.74
20	Jeff Burroughs	6,231	+7.08	+0.74
21	Cliff Floyd	5,064	+5.68	+0.73
22	Vladimir Guerrero	5,490	+6.10	+0.72
23	Mike Hargrove	6,693	+7.23	+0.70
24	Mike Greeenwell	5,166	+5.53	+0.70
25	Carlos Delgado	6,634	+6.88	+0.67

	Worst Clutch/PA Ratings			
	Player	*PA*	*Career*	*Per 650 PA*
1	Royce Clayton	7,446	−13.56	−1.18
2	Larry Herndon	5,316	−8.77	−1.07
3	Larry Parrish	7,797	−12.17	−1.01
4	Rick Dempsey	5,378	−8.30	−1.00
5	Chet Lemon	7,872	−11.62	−0.96
6	Brad Ausmus	5,774	−7.95	−0.89
7	Howard Johnson	5,715	−7.61	−0.87
8	Jeffrey Leonard	5,476	−7.27	−0.86
9	Rick Burleson	5,717	−7.59	−0.86
10	Larry Bowa	7,830	−10.27	−0.85
11	Neifi Perez	5,123	−6.70	−0.85

(continues)

TABLE 1-2.10 (continued)

	Player	PA	Career	Per 650 PA
	Worst Clutch/PA Ratings			
12	Don Baylor	9,376	−11.96	−0.83
13	Bob Boone	8,148	−10.35	−0.83
14	Ron Cey	8,342	−10.13	−0.79
15	Johnny Bench	6,093	−7.37	−0.79
16	Tony Pena	7,073	−8.30	−0.76
17	Benito Santiago	7,515	−8.77	−0.76
18	Davey Lopes	7,340	−8.21	−0.73
19	Tony Armas	5,502	−6.09	−0.72
20	Cecil Fielder	5,939	−6.56	−0.72
21	Gary Carter	9,019	−9.68	−0.70
22	Ivan Rodriguez	7,740	−8.18	−0.69
23	Javy Lopez	5,429	−5.62	−0.67
24	Enos Cabell	6,304	−6.51	−0.67
25	Greg Gagne	6,207	−6.38	−0.67

surprises. Matt Lawton? Toby Harrah? Jason Kendall? One thing that these relatively obscure players have in common with Grace is that they had excellent plate discipline—they drew walks often and struck out rarely. Meanwhile, on the "choke" side of the ledger, we have lots of players like Royce Clayton, Jeffrey Leonard, and Tony Armas who had notably poor plate discipline. The pattern isn't absolute: Hubie Brooks, who couldn't take a walk to save his career, rates as a good clutch hitter, while Davey Lopes, who had a fine batting eye, rates as a poor one.

But there is something there. I ran a correlation of various career hitting statistics, adjusted for league and park effects, against clutch rating per PA for players with at least 5,000 sampled plate appearances. Two of these statistics had a statistically significant relationship with clutch performance: walk rate and strikeout rate. Players who walk often and strike out rarely indeed tend to do well in the clutch. We can combine those two statistics into something I call batting eye: two times unintentional walk rate minus strikeout rate. The correlation between batting-eye and clutch rating is .29, which is not overwhelming but enough to be interesting.

What we may be seeing here is the effect of smart situational hitting. As you'll recall, a player who had the ability to adjust his hitting approach in different situations—slapping a single or blasting a home run as the situation required—would provide some small but discernible benefit to his club. This difference would be reflected in his WinEx but not in his conventional batting statistics. What sort of hitter might be most capable of making those adjustments? Presumably one who has some plan at the plate. A right-handed hitter hoping to drive a ball to right field to score a key run from second would love to see a fastball on the outside portion of the plate, but he needs to have the patience to wait for that pitch and the skill to hit it once it comes. Conversely, an undisciplined right-handed hitter who spends most of his time battling to stay alive is at the mercy of the pitcher, who surely will be trying do to everything but give him that outside fastball.

This advantage provides another incentive for teams to acquire disciplined hitters who control the strike zone and control the at-bat. Not only do those players tend to post great OBPs, but they may be better able to take advantage of clutch situations as well.

That said, apart from the bonus effects of plate discipline that I've just described, it's probably folly for a club to go looking for clutch hitters—the ability just isn't important enough in the bigger scheme of things. Suppose I wanted to predict a hitter's WinEx—how many wins his bat actually provides to his club, accounting for the effects of clutch hitting. I can do a reasonably good job by using his regular hitting statistics, adjusted for his Leverage and run-scoring environment (his LMLVW). This is enough to explain 70 percent of the player's WinEx.

But suppose I also take the player's clutch-hitting history into account—that is, his clutch scores over his previous three seasons. Does this increase the explanatory power of my model? It does, but only in the slightest way; instead of explaining 70 percent of WinEx, the model now explains 71 percent or 72 percent of WinEx. So one way to look at it is as follows: Producing wins at the plate is about 70 percent a matter of overall hitting ability, 27 percent dumb luck, and perhaps 3 percent clutch skill. It's your choice what you want to do with that 3 percent.

It's your choice what you want to do with that 2 percent. Clutch-hitting ability exists, more than previous research would indicate. It's about on the order of something like baserunning ability (see Chapter 4-1). Sometimes baserunning can make the difference between success and failure. Sometimes a hitter like David Ortiz gets a bunch of big hits down the stretch, and it makes the difference in a pennant race. Usually, though, it's the big three that prevail: Pitch the ball, catch the ball, and most of all hit the ball.

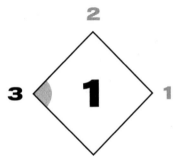

Was Billy Martin Crazy?

JAMES CLICK

On Sunday morning, August 13, 1972, the Detroit Tigers had dropped into second place, a game behind the Baltimore Orioles in the AL East. After holding off the Orioles for months, the Tigers were in a free fall with just 3 wins in their last 13 games. Only the Orioles' mediocre 7-7 record over the previous two weeks was keeping the Tigers from falling further behind.

Billy Martin, in his second year at the helm of the Tigers, decided desperate times called for desperate measures. Instead of the customary impassioned speech to the team or deftly organized "players-only" meeting, Martin decided to shake things up on the field. He wrote down the names of his starters on slips of paper, put them into a hat, and filled out his lineup card by pulling out the names at random. Whether because of the lineup changes or something else, the Tigers won the first game of their doubleheader with the Indians, 3-2. Then, using their traditional lineup for the nightcap, they got crushed, 9-2.

Picking a lineup is one of baseball's most scrutinized decisions. Players often discuss feeling more comfortable in one lineup spot or another. Whether a player bats seventh or fifth can cause major controversy on sports radio and talk shows. Managers move players around the lineup in attempts to increase the team's run scoring, both by getting better players more plate appearances and by supposedly protecting the big bats in the lineup.

Martin's challenge to one of baseball's most visible strategies thus raises an important question: Just how important is batting order in determining a team's success? There have been many attempts at an answer. In his 1988 *Bill James Baseball Abstract,* Bill James wrote that the key to scoring in any individual inning is getting the first batter on base. After noticing that teams scored the most runs in the first inning, the fewest in the second, and about equal amounts in each subsequent inning, he posited that a player with a low on-base percentage should bat in the third spot in the lineup, since that spot is the least likely to lead off the second inning. After that, which spot bats first in any given inning is largely out of the manager's hands.

James's theory was logical, but he lacked a useful method to test it. With the increased popularity of personal computers, other baseball fanatics took up the task, building models that could be used to test theories about lineups. In an article originally appearing at Baseball Prospectus.com, we explored this problem in more depth using a custom program called Baseball Lineup Order Optimization Program (BLOOP). BLOOP is essentially a very fast version of the Strat-O-Matic baseball simulation game. Instead of rolling dice to determine what happens in a given at-bat, the computer generates a random number, based on ranges inputted for each player. For example, for a player with a .300 batting average, if the computer generates a random number (always from 0 to 1) that falls between 0 and .3, the player gets a hit. BLOOP allows us to attack the basic questions of lineups. How much does lineup order affect team scoring? Where is the ideal place to bat sluggers? Should a team's best hitters be bunched together or spread out?

In BLOOP, each player is assigned a range of probabilities for different events, for instance a single, double, triple, home run, walk/hit by pitch (HBP), or strikeout. Here is a basic example: Joe Smith—single: .232 (23.2 percent); double: .035; triple: .012; home run: .002; walk/HBP: .069; strikeout: .010. The sum of the first five outcomes (.350) corresponds to Smith's on-base percentage (OBP). In any at-bat, if the random number generated by the program is less than .350, he reaches base. If the number falls between 0 and .232 (his probability of a single), he is credited with a single. If the number falls between .233 and .267 (the sum of the probability of a single and a double), he gets a double, and so on. The program then adjusts the game situation accordingly and moves on to the next batter. By specifying the types of hits a player makes, as well as incorporating walks and HBPs, we get a more detailed list of results that better reflects the player's true abilities.

Using **BLOOP**, we played tens of thousands of seasons with different lineups and reached a few basic conclusions.

First, using a lineup of players similar to a typical major league team, the difference between the most optimal (lineups ordered by descending **OBP** or slugging average [SLG]) and least optimal batting orders (for example, lineups where the pitcher bats leadoff and the best players bat at the bottom of the order) was 26 runs, a similar finding to several other previous studies on batting order. Although 26 runs (about 2.5 wins in the standings) may seem like a big difference, that's the gap between the *most* and *least* optimal lineups; few managers ever reach these extremes. The standard baseball lineup actually comes fairly close to achieving optimal results based on our simulation. Changing a lineup from the industry standard to our ideal model typically nets at most 10 runs over a whole season, or about 1 win. This small range of available improvement means that minor changes to the lineup for brief periods of time have virtually no discernible effect on run scoring.

In most cases, switching two hitters in the lineup will gain or lose teams only a handful of runs over the course of an entire season, to say nothing of a week or a month. In extreme cases, it gains a bit more. For example, the 2004 Giants typically batted Barry Bonds in the fourth spot in the lineup. BLOOP found that if the Giants moved Bonds to the third spot, they gained about 7 runs, mostly because Bonds saw about 18 more plate appearances (PA) per season. Moving him from third to second netted another 18 PA and an additional 2 runs; from second to first yielded 1 more run on average. All told, that's 10 runs the Giants sacrificed by batting Bonds fourth instead of leadoff, or about 1 win in the standings. Moving other batters into more optimal positions gets the Giants up to about a win and a half, nearly all of their final 2-game deficit to the Dodgers that year. Similarly, if the 2005 Yankees had for some reason led off with Tony Womack all year and batted Derek Jeter ninth, they would have given Womack about 144 PA that should have gone to Jeter, costing the Yanks as much as 14 runs over the course of the season.

Second, a team's best hitters should bat sequentially. Lineups in which a team's three best hitters batted with either one or two average batters between them fell 8 runs short of the lineup in which the top batters batted in three sequential spots.

Third and most obvious, **OBP** is the most important variable—more important than SLG or AVG. Given any group of nine hitters, the batting order that scores the most runs is the one ranked in order of descending OBP. Give the hitters who make the fewest outs the most chances to bat, and you'll score more runs.

For a follow-up article, we fed BLOOP a more varied group of players in an effort to discern the optimal interplay between on-base percentage and slugging average, given that managers are almost always dealing with players superior in one metric but inferior in the other. Using Wily Mo Pena (a .259/.316/.527 hitter in 2004, indicating a low OBP and high SLG) and Luis Castillo (.291/.373/.348 in '04, high OBP, low SLG) as samples, BLOOP found that lineups featuring Castillo in the leadoff spot scored 2 to 3 runs more than those without him there. Pena's OBP was bad enough that batting him leadoff instead of Castillo would cost a team 3 to 4 runs, but a lineup batting Pena second or lower scores nearly as many runs as a lineup batting Castillo second. While baseball's best hitters—those who are strong in both OBP and SLG—should be batted as high in the lineup as possible, teams that are forced to choose between OBP and SLG are generally following a highly optimal model, using on-base fiends up top and big sluggers toward the middle. OBP is generally about twice as important as SLG when considering lineup order—identical lineups sorted by descending and ascending OBP show double the difference in runs scored to the same lineup sorted by SLG. Players such as Tony Womack or Jose Reyes, who display little of either skill, should not bat near the top.

While a program such as BLOOP allows us to test theories of lineup order, it is forced to make several assumptions. It excludes stolen bases, assumes all batters are league-average baserunners (both in taking the extra base and grounding into double plays), and doesn't adjust batter performance based on external factors such as the opposing pitcher or ballpark. Adding these features to BLOOP would allow us to test a few more theories about lineups, but we would once again be working in the absence of actual game data. Because teams vary from the traditional lineup structure so infrequently, there is very little real-life data to use in testing batting orders. Despite this lack of variety, some questions about the lineup can be answered with actual data.

BLOOP's final assumption—that batter performance is largely independent of outside factors—begs one of the lineup's most essential questions: Can one hitter "protect" another? The theory of protection was put to the ultimate test by the San Francisco Giants from 2001 to 2004. Provided a lineup of Bonds and seven hitters who (with rare exceptions such as 37-homer hitter Rich Aurilia in 2001) were either league average or worse, managers Dusty Baker and Felipe Alou faced the daily chore of somehow forcing the opposing pitcher to pitch to Bonds rather than walking him (see Table 1-3.1).

TABLE 1-3.1 Barry Bonds's Performance and Following Batters, 2001–2004

Year	Batter	PA	UBB	IBB	AB/HR	Next Batter
2001	Barry Bonds	664	143	34	6.52	Jeff Kent
2002	Barry Bonds	612	130	68	8.76	Jeff Kent/Benito Santiago
2003	Barry Bonds	550	87	61	8.67	Edgardo Alfonzo/Benito Santiago
2004	Barry Bonds	617	112	120	8.29	Edgardo Alfonzo/Pedro Feliz

In 2001 and 2002, the primary batter behind Bonds was Jeff Kent, who hit .298/.369/.507 and .313/.368/.565 in those two seasons. In 2001, teams intentionally walked Bonds only 34 times, even though he hit home runs at a staggering rate, once every 6.5 at-bats. But in 2002, they increasingly began pitching around him. With the team 4.5 games behind the Dodgers on June 27, the Giants swapped Kent and Bonds in the order, batting Kent third and Bonds in the cleanup spot. This didn't work. Before the switch, Bonds walked in 93 of his 293 PAs (63 unintentional walks [UBB], 30 intentional [IBB]), hitting a home run every 7.8 ABs. After the switch, he walked in 87 of 268 PAs (52 unintentional walks, 35 intentional walks), hitting a home run every 11.1 ABs. After the Giants moved Bonds to the cleanup spot, his walk rate increased slightly, his intentional walk rate increased significantly, and his home-run rate plunged, possibly because he was seeing significantly fewer hittable pitches.

With Bonds still batting cleanup in 2003, the trend continued, though teams pitched to Bonds a little more, walking him "only" 148 times. But in 2004, the situation spiraled out of control: he walked in 37.6 percent of his plate appearances. Even if Bonds never swung his bat all year, he still would have had the highest OBP on his team and the seventeenth highest in the NL. His 120 intentional passes were more than all but three other players' *total* walks on the season. Teams had quit pitching to Barry Bonds.

Who could blame them? Averaging the hitters who followed Bonds in 2004 and weighting for playing time, the composite batter mustered a .288/.346/.450 line. Whom would you rather pitch to: the man hitting .362 and slugging .812 with the bases empty or a slightly above-average hitter with a man on first? Nearly 40 percent of the time, NL pitchers chose the latter. It would also be easy to blame batters in front of Bonds—the rest of the Giants' lineup managed only a meager .264/.330/.411 line—for providing the opposition with more "walk-friendly" situations. If Bonds consistently came to the plate with more men on base and fewer outs, the opposing pitcher would likely be less inclined to give him a free pass for fear of prolonging a rally or encouraging a big inning. But breaking down Bonds's plate appearances by baserunners and outs, Figure 1-3.1 shows that he came to the plate almost exactly as often as the average league batter in each situation.

FIGURE 1-3.1 Percentage of PA by baserunner/out situation for Barry Bonds and average MLB batters, 2004

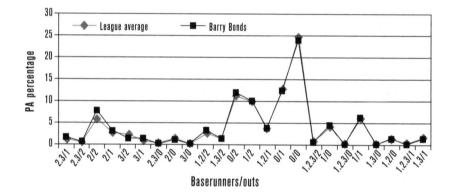

So Bonds did not encounter a disproportionate number of "walk-friendly" situations. (The chart is ordered by league-wide walk rate in the situation from left to right.) If he were coming to the plate when teams were more likely to walk any batter, he would see a significant number of his plate appearances coming toward the left side of the graph. (Actually, to get as many walks as Bonds did purely from the baserunner/out situation, he would have had to come to bat with runners on second and third and one out for 126 percent of the time—which is, of course, impossible.) Instead, teams chose to walk Bonds, because in their estimation the likelihood of the Giants' scoring was lower if they put him on and pitched to the next man.

Bonds's predicament shows the theory of protection in a nutshell. The following batter doesn't have to be as good as the man he's protecting. But the difference between the two must be small enough that the presence of an additional baserunner increases the likely number of runs scored more than pitching to the inferior batter decreases them. In 2004, the Giants could send up no such batter to follow Bonds.

There are two main aspects of protection that must be considered: (1) if batters see better pitches to hit if they are protected, and (2) if they see any pitches to hit at all. The first is largely a performance question; the second is a decision made by pitchers and managers. Thus, the analysis of these two aspects differs. The first question can be answered by looking at the data, while the second asks us to analyze a conscious decision made by the opposition.

Whether batters see better pitches would seem to be very easy to answer on the surface: We simply break down batting performance data by the next batter. Breaking Bonds's playing time into PAs in front of three classes of subsequent batters, we see that he batted .404/.644/.981 in front of "poor" batters, .571/.824/1.571 in front of "average" batters, and .342/.598/.778 in front of "good" batters. However, there are several problems with these numbers. First, the sample sizes of "poor" and especially "average" batters are very small—only 87 and 17 PAs, respectively. Second, batting-order changes are not random. While players may fall into one of the offensive categories overall, they may be moved around the order based on whether the opposing pitcher is right- or left-handed, or perhaps a hitting style that better fits a particular park. Bonds may appear to do worse when better batters are behind him, but that may be because the better batters are behind him when left-handed pitchers are on the mound, or when the Giants are in pitcher-friendly Dodger Stadium instead of Coors Field.

But on a larger scale, this study can reveal whether batter performance changes as the quality of the following batter changes. Using all batters in the league gives us a large enough sample that other changes in environment will not skew the results. The results are in Table 1-3.2. In this case, we find a nice, steady upward trend as the quality of the following batter increases, supporting the theory that batters hit better when the player behind them in the lineup is better.

TABLE 1-3.2 Batting Performance by Following Batter Quality, 2004

Year	Next	AVG	OBP	SLG	BB	IBB
2004	Low	.257	.324	.404	.082	.010
2004	Med-low	.259	.327	.417	.083	.006
2004	Med	.268	.335	.429	.085	.008
2004	Med-high	.271	.342	.435	.090	.007
2004	High	.273	.346	.450	.091	.005

Case closed, right? But there's one major problem: Teams tend to group their batters by their ability; the worst hitters bat lowest in the lineup, and the best bat toward the top or the middle. Players who bat in front of high-quality batters are thus more likely to be high-quality batters themselves; it isn't the guy behind them that's particularly notable, but rather those hitters' overall ability that creates the illusion of lineup protection.

To correct for this problem, rather than looking at the raw numbers that batters put up, broken down by who's batting behind them, we can compare those raw numbers to what we would expect the batters to do based on their season numbers. The results of this study are in Table 1-3.3. Suddenly, rather than a smooth progression as subsequent batter quality increases, the numbers come very close to zero. Batting performance *does not change significantly* with the quality of the following batter, and it does not change in any meaningful manner as batter quality trends upward or downward.

TABLE 1-3.3 Relative Batting Performance by Following Batter Quality, 2004

Year	MLVR Class	AVG	OBP	SLG	BB	IBB
2004	Low	.001	.006	.002	.004	.003
2004	Med-low	−.003	.001	−.003	.000	−.001
2004	Med	−.001	.000	−.002	−.002	−.001
2004	Med-high	.004	.008	.002	.001	.000
2004	High	−.005	−.003	−.010	−.003	−.002

What does this mean if you're the pitcher, or the pitcher's manager? Do you pitch to the star hitter, or pitch around him and deal with the next guy? League run expectation charts—which show the average number of runs scored in an inning for every baserunner/out situation—show that walking a batter *always* increases run expectation. For instance, in 2004, walking a batter with the bases empty increased run scoring by .3880, .2630, and .1325 runs with 0, 1, and 2 outs, respectively. But protection isn't about the league average; it's about the elite batters and the specific quality of the following batter. To answer the question, then, we need to see how various batters affect run expectations.

This is difficult because the traditional metrics used to measure batting performance—the kind we see on the back of a baseball card—don't say much about performance in specific baserunner/out situations. For instance, take two hypothetical players who have the exact same stats, except that one hits 20 doubles, zero triples, and 20 home runs and the other hits zero doubles or home runs but 40 triples. The two players would have exactly the same AVG/OBP/SLG but would alter the run expectations in different ways. The first batter would end up on second half the time and score half the time, while the second batter would always end up on third. As Palmer and Thorn pointed out in *The Hidden Game of Baseball,* a home run is not worth two doubles, and a triple is not worth three singles. So although our two batters have the same AVG/OBP/SLG, they contribute to run scoring in different ways. Instead, we must look at various batters' more specific outcomes—singles rate (1B/PA), doubles rate, etc.—and see how they correlate to traditional metrics and changes in run expectation tables.

First, let's look at a simple example. Rangers first baseman Mark Teixeira leads off an inning, giving the Rangers a run expectation of .5379 runs if they were a league-average offense. However, when we input Teixeira's averages, the run expectancy increases to .5556, meaning if the Rangers followed Teixeira with an average lineup, they could expect to score .5556 runs in the inning. If, instead, the opposing team chooses to walk Teixeira and the average lineup follows, the run expectancy increases to .9259. But if the next batter makes an out after Teixeira reaches first, the run expectancy falls back to .5496, lower than the .5556 with Teixeira leading off. Thus, if the man behind Teixeira is guaranteed to make an out, the opposing team reduces the expected runs the Rangers would score by walking Teixeira—the Rangers failed to protect him. Of course, no major league player is an automatic out, but we can use this method to find situations in which protection fails. In this case, note that the difference between the two batters would have to be very close to Teixeira's actual line on the season to force the opposition to pitch to him, because the run expectancy with him leading off the inning (.5556) is almost exactly the same as when he's on first and the next batter makes an out (.5496). Even if the batter behind Teixeira is hitting just .100, the opposition is still better off pitching to Teixeira.

Expanding the same analysis to all players who notched at least 300 PA in 2004, Figure 1-3.2 shows how the run expectations for the two situations in question shake out.

The large bump at the left is the number of players whose run expectation falls into that range with the bases empty; the bump at the right is the same, but with a man on first. If there were any place where these two areas overlapped, it would be in lineup combinations

FIGURE 1-3.2 Run expectations for regulars before and after a walk—bases empty, none out

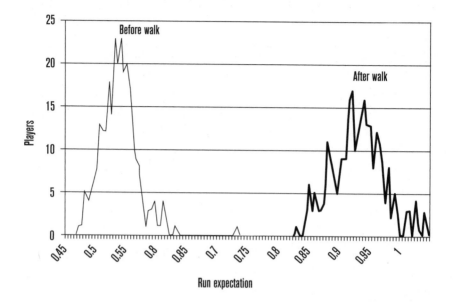

in which the opposing team would be better served by walking the initial batter and pitching to the next man. In this case, no such situations existed among all regulars in 2004. Even Chad Moeller—who hit a brutal .208/.261/.303 as the Brewers' catcher—could "protect" Bonds with the bases empty. It's still unlikely that teams would pitch to Bonds in that situation, but the numbers say they should.

In other situations, things can change dramatically. Looking at the same data, but with runners on second and third and two outs, Figure 1-3.3 shows that things look very different.

The curve on the left is the run expectation before a walk with men on second and third with two out. The curve on the right is the run expectation after a walk to load the bases. The area where these two curves overlap is where existing combinations of batters fail to protect each other. In this situation, there are quite a few instances among regulars in which the opposing team would do well to walk the initial batter and pitch to the next man. (Note the small bump around .8 for the first series. This outlier is Bonds, a player so dominant that well over 75 percent of the league's regulars can't protect him adequately in this situation.)

These situations are few and far between. With men on second and third and two out, the second batter has to be on the order of 60 points worse in AVG, 95 points worse in OBP, and over 175 points

FIGURE 1-3.3 Run expectations for regulars before and after a walk—second and third, two outs

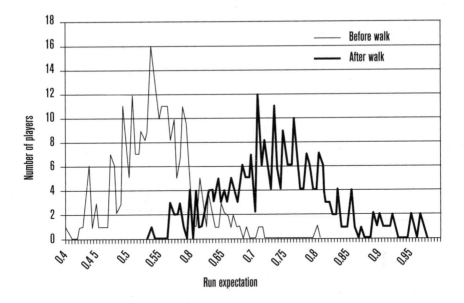

worse in SLG to make it advantageous for the opposing team to walk
the initial batter. Except for players hitting in front of the pitcher, such
disparities are seldom found between two batters in consecutive spots
in the batting order. It can be very difficult for a team to find someone
to protect a player like Bonds. In 2004, standouts such as Miguel Tejada, Chipper Jones, and Ichiro Suzuki would have fallen short of the
performance needed to justify pitching to Bonds in this situation.

Out of all twenty-four baserunner-out situations, only half have
protection failure thresholds that occurred between any two regular
batters in 2004. For these twelve, for an intentional walk to have a
positive run expectancy for the pitcher, the differences between the
performance of the two batters can be found in Table 1-3.4. For example, with a runner on third and two outs, the pitching team would decrease its opponents' run expectation by walking any batter who was
more than .028/.051/.085 better than the following batter. This is by
far the most common situation in which an intentional walk is a viable strategy. Other situations, such as first and third with one out,
have such an enormous run expectaton gap that they occur only when
one of the league's worst batters is hitting behind Barry Bonds. From
the PA% column—the percentage of plate appearances in which each
situation arises—it becomes obvious that protection is likely to break
down very rarely indeed.

TABLE 1-3.4 Required Differences Between Consecutive Batters for an IBB to Benefit the Pitching Team, as Measured by Run Expectancy

Situation	Outs	AVG	OBP	SLG	PA%
3rd	2	.028	.051	.085	2.4
2nd & 3rd	2	.060	.095	.178	0.7
2nd	2	.043	.090	.196	5.9
1st & 3rd	2	.071	.122	.234	1.4
1st	2	.066	.137	.274	10.0
3rd	1	.078	.254	.331	1.1
1st & 2nd	2	.094	.270	.418	2.7
2nd	1	.095	.300	.447	2.9
2nd & 3rd	1	.101	.283	.456	1.2
2nd & 3rd	0	.125	.314	.465	0.4
3rd	0	.147	.319	.480	0.2
1st & 3rd	1	.120	.322	.484	1.8

Protection is overrated. There's no evidence that having a superior batter behind another batter provides the initial batter with better pitches to hit; if it does, those batters see no improvement in performance as a result. Additionally, it's very rare that a situation arises in which run expectation drops after the pitching team walks the batter at the plate. Therefore, if the pitching team does walk a batter because it would rather pitch to the following man, it is *almost always making a mistake* by opening the door for a big inning. The situation changes late in close games as the importance of a single run begins to trump that of many runs, but even in those situations, the difference between the two batters would have to be extreme.

In short, most of the hand-wringing and scrutiny of batting orders is for naught. Batting order simply does not make that much difference. Managers tinkering with lineups so rarely shun convention that most of their changes would affect their teams' output by only a few runs over the course of a season. Sorting a lineup in descending order of OBP yields the most runs, but players with high SLG can offset a low OBP as early as third in the lineup. The conventional lineup's most egregious flaw is that it costs the game's best players about 18 PA per lineup spot per season. If Barry Bonds led off instead of hitting fourth, he would see about 54 more PA per year, adding perhaps 10 runs to the Giants' offensive output. Teams without a player of Bonds's caliber could gain about 10 runs (1 win) a year by routinely batting their players in order of descending OBP. Furthermore, managers worrying about protecting their best hitters need not fret. Situations in which the pitcher would gain by walking the initial batter to pitch to the following man are so rare that employing an optimal lineup order would eliminate nearly all of them. Intentionally walking any batter in a correctly ordered lineup is nearly always a bad decision.

So was Billy Martin crazy? Not, at least, with regard to his batting order. He understood that who is in the lineup is much more important than where they bat. Were it not that the conventional wisdom has become self-fulfilling prophecy—batting order is important because everybody *thinks* it's important—Martin could have pulled his lineups out of a hat all year long and hardly lost a game in the standings.

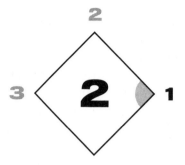

Why Are Pitchers So Unpredictable?

KEITH WOOLNER AND DAYN PERRY

In 1973, Tom Seaver worked 28 more innings than he did the previous season and lowered his ERA by almost a full run. His win total dropped by 2. In 1998, Roger Clemens won the AL Cy Young Award. The following year, he endured the worst season of his career. Also in 1998, Tom Glavine won the NL Cy Young on the strength of his 20 wins and 2.47 ERA. In 1999, Glavine won just 14 games as his ERA ballooned to 4.12. Again in 1998, Randy Johnson went 9-10 with a 4.33 ERA for Seattle. After a midseason trade to Houston, he went 10-1 with a 1.28 ERA the rest of the year.

These anecdotal facts all point to one statement that statistically inclined analysts and mainstream observers can agree upon: Pitching is hard to predict. Much harder, in fact, than hitting.

There are two reasons for this phenomenon. First, while the margin for error to be successful in pitching is small, the act of pitching is itself physically demanding and subject to degradation. Second, we use flawed statistics to measure pitching performance that make the pitcher responsible for factors beyond his own performance.

The Demands of Pitching

The act of pitching is an exercise in minutiae. Seemingly minor factors can drastically influence a pitcher's performance: where he stands on the rubber, how high he holds his elbow, what he does with his glove hand during the delivery, how much he rotates his hips, the placement of his fingers on the ball, the action of his pivot foot, the placement of his landing foot, his follow-through, the stillness of his head during delivery. An intricate web of interrelated and overlapping actions must align for a pitcher to deliver a successful pitch.

But being able to deliver a variety of types of pitches with different velocities to any location around the plate is only part of the challenge. The pitcher has to do all those things over and over again, consistently and repeatedly. Furthermore, he must do all of it without giving cues to the hitter, injuring himself, or losing his ability to deceive. A breakdown in any part of the flow can lead to ineffectiveness and failure. Famed Yankees hurler Don Larsen met with success only after adopting a no-windup delivery. Future Hall-of-Famer Randy Johnson didn't truly dominate opponents until Nolan Ryan helped him make some mechanical tweaks. Legendary Braves (now Orioles) pitching coach Leo Mazzone has rescued countless careers by making minor in-game adjustments and altering off-day throwing patterns.

Yet despite the razor-thin margins of error, the act of overhand pitching is itself an unnatural one. It is a destructive process, exacting a fierce toll on the shoulder and elbow. Rare is the hurler who has a career of significant length and doesn't undergo at least one major surgical procedure. Even those injuries that don't sideline the pitcher for an extended period of time or subject him to the surgeon's knife can hinder his performance. Nagging cases of tendonitis or "tired arm syndrome" usually mean less effectiveness on the mound—though the time off gained may help the pitcher's arm rest and recuperate in the process. Given the precision demanded by pitching, the ability of opposing hitters to crush weak pitches, and the risk of injury inherent in the physical act of throwing a baseball, it's little wonder that it's difficult to predict what the future holds for any given pitcher.

Won-Lost Record

Then there are the statistics we use to evaluate pitcher performance. The primary goal of a pitcher is to win games for his team. To many fans, then, the primary way to measure a starting pitcher's success is his won-lost record. Any pitcher worth his salt should win more than he loses, and a 20-win season is the hallmark of excellence.

Except that there are two parts to winning a game: having your team score runs and preventing your opponent from doing so. In theory, pitchers can affect only half the equation by preventing runs. But since defense makes up a significant portion of run prevention, pitchers actually influence a fair bit less than half the equation. Pitchers in the National League may get a plate appearance or two toward scoring runs, but their general ineptitude at the plate means the burden lies mainly on their teammates; AL pitchers don't even get to bat, thanks to the designated hitter rule.

Pitchers need run-scoring help from their teammates to win games. But there are wide differences between the amounts of run support that pitchers receive, even on the same team. For example, Jeremy Bonderman and Nate Robertson were teammates on the 2005 Tigers. Bonderman threw 189 innings in 29 starts, posting an ERA of 4.57, while Robertson threw 196.7 innings in 32 starts, with a slightly better ERA of 4.48. But their run-support levels were vastly different. Bonderman received an average of 5.67 runs of support, while Robertson suffered through just 3.66 runs of support per 9 innings. The result? Bonderman posted a winning record of 14-13, while Robertson was 9 games below .500 at 7-16.

Furthermore, starting pitchers don't throw complete games as they did one hundred years ago. It's rare for a pitcher to finish even 20 percent of his games. Other pitchers from the bullpen will finish what he starts, and his team's chance to win or lose a game often rides on the fortunes of those relievers. Relievers can preserve a lead the starter gave them or blow the opportunity to close out the win. They can rescue a pitcher who leaves with runners on base in a tight game, or allow those runs to score, hanging the loss on the now-departed starter. A reliever can also come in with his team trailing and hang in there long enough for the bats to rally, bailing out the starter from a deserved loss. With the outcome of the game and the eventual awarding of wins and losses so dependent on factors other than the pitcher's own performance, won-lost record and winning percentage cannot act as credible measures of pitcher performance.

Earned Run Average

Baseball long ago recognized the problem of relying solely on won-lost record, though the traditionalists still refer to it more than they should. To eliminate some of the confounding effects of the pitcher's supporting offense, earned run average was created to measure a pitcher's own run-prevention abilities in isolation. This was an improvement. A good pitcher on a bad-hitting team might have a terrible W-L record while still sporting a low ERA. Among the most famous examples of this occurred in 1987, when Nolan Ryan led the NL with a 2.76 ERA yet was credited with just an 8-16 W-L record.

Tracking ERA lessens the problem of teammate reliance but does not eliminate it. True, the impact of a pitcher's offense is eliminated, but there is still a dependency on the bullpen, as a pitcher can leave the game with runners on base. If the next reliever does a good job and strands those runners, the starting pitcher escapes with no further damage to his ERA. But if the reliever allows them to score, all the resulting runs from those inherited runners are charged to the previous pitcher, even though he's not entirely to blame.

Treating all runs the same has its problems too—within a game all runs are not created equal. Giving up an eleventh run is not as damaging as giving up a fourth run, because once you've given up 10 you've already probably lost the game. Yet ERA treats all runs equally. One bad outing out of ten can have disproportionate effects on a pitcher's ERA, even if he pitched brilliantly the other nine times out. A pitcher who throws nine 7 IP, 2 R games and one 3 IP, 10 R game will have a winning percentage implied by his ERA (based on the Pythagorean formula) of about .574, about 20 points lower than an average team's actual expected winning percentage of .594. The negative effect of the one blown game is overstated in his ERA and taints his overall record.

Support Neutral Statistics

To address the "runs are not created equal" problem, Baseball Prospectus created the Support Neutral family of statistics. Unlike position players, starting pitchers participate in few games but are involved in almost every defensive play of those games for as deep into the game as they go. A pitcher's performance is a continuous chain of batters faced, with the results of one plate appearance directly setting up the circumstances of the next one. The pitcher is more responsible for the game situation than anyone else on the field at the time; the allocation of credit or blame should reflect that fact. But at the same time, no matter how well or poorly he performs in this game, the pitcher can create at most one win or one loss. Were he to allow 20 runs to score, his ERA would skyrocket, yet only one loss would be recorded in the standings.

The Support Neutral statistics are designed to address both this one-game reality and the fact that offensive and bullpen run support vary widely and are outside a pitcher's immediate control. The most elementary member of this family is the Support-Neutral Win (SNW):

Given how many innings the pitcher threw, the number of runs scored before he was removed, and any runners still on base when he was removed, what is the probability that an average-hitting team with an average bullpen would win the game? The Support-Neutral name comes from the fact that we are removing, or neutralizing, the variability of having different levels of run support and bullpen support. An average-hitting team might win games where the starter went 7 innings and allowed no runs 85 percent of the time and thus would be worth 0.85 SNW. A Support-Neutral Loss (SNL) is the reverse—the chance of an average team losing given that effort by the starting pitching. That 7 IP, 0 R start would be worth 0.15 SNL. Over the course of a season, a pitcher's Support-Neutral Won-Lost (SNWL) record is simply the sum of SNW and SNL in each start. This gives a truer indication of how well a pitcher performed, without the distortions of offensive and bullpen support. The deeper into a game a pitcher goes and the fewer runs he allows, the greater portion of a SNW he will earn.

Support-Neutral Value Added (SNVA) measures how far a pitcher performed above an average (.500) pitcher. In our 1-game 0.85 SNW example, his SNVA is $0.85 - 0.50 = 0.35$ SNVA. There are further extensions for comparing pitchers not to average but to replacement level and for adjusting probabilities based on how strong the opposing hitters were. The most comprehensive statistic in the Support-Neutral family is Support-Neutral Lineup-adjusted Value Added Above Replacement (SNLVAR). In 2005 Roger Clemens led the majors with a 9.4 SNLVAR, meaning he pitched well enough to add 9.4 wins to an average team above what a fringe, replacement-level pitcher would have done against the same batters (see Chapter 5-1 for more on replacement level).

ERA Redux

Let's return to earned run average and another of the goals behind it. ERA attempts to isolate the effect of the fielders behind a pitcher from his own performance, as runs are charged to the pitcher only if they are "earned"—that is, if they did not score due to the result of a fielder's error. Although noble in intent, the concept of earned versus unearned runs is faulty. Error rates have fallen dramatically over the decades, and fielding percentages are at or near all-time highs. The defensive differences among fielders in the modern game are more the result of range and positioning than whether they are error-prone. A fly ball that Andruw Jones effortlessly glides over to catch will fall into the gap for an easy double if Bernie Williams is patrolling center field.

Errors and fielding percentage do not adequately capture the differences in the quality of fielders behind a pitcher. Thus, using errors to differentiate between runs that are the pitcher's fault and those that are the fielders' fault is unsound.

Run Average

Run Average (RA) is often used instead of ERA to eliminate the misleading distinction between earned runs and unearned runs. This seems like a step backward, not even attempting to separate pitcher performance from fielder performance. However, if we recognize that what is being measured is really the performance of the whole defense (pitching plus fielding), then it makes more sense. Run prevention is run prevention, and it doesn't matter whether a run is earned or unearned for determining wins and losses. As we will see, there are better ways of separating pitcher and fielder performance than using an incomplete and skewed method such as ERA.

Both ERA and RA have a problem related to the clustering of batting events. More runs score when hits and walks are clustered together than if they are scattered evenly throughout a game. This is because, except for a home run, the offense needs a sequence of batting successes to bring a run across the plate. Two pitchers with the same hit, extra-base, and walk totals allowed can end up with different numbers of runs, based on how those hits and walk happen to be distributed. But that's mostly random, as pitchers don't exhibit significant control over when they give up hits and walks.

Peripheral ERA

To overcome the clustering problem, we can use a pitcher's "peripherals"—the basic rates at which he gives up hits, walks, strikeouts, and home runs—to put together an "expected" ERA or RA. This is called Peripheral ERA (PERA). (ERA is traditionally used instead of RA in the name, though the concept is equally applicable to either version.) PERA essentially adjusts the clustering in a pitcher's record to that of an average pitcher. A pitcher who gave up unusually large numbers of runs given his peripherals will see that high clustering reduced, while a pitcher who happened to scatter his hits and walks will see the effect of a more typical amount of clustering in his PERA.

PERA synthesizes a pitcher's peripheral rates into something recognizable and interpretable to the average fan—the ERA he deserved. PERA, which uses just hit rate, walk rate, home-run rate, and strikeout rate, is a better predictor of ERA in the following season than ERA is.

It is a truer reflection of how the pitcher performed. In computing PERA, one of the peripherals is the rate of hits given up. But other than home runs, hits result from balls batted into the field of play. Fielding these batted balls almost always involves other fielders, and thus the defensive performances of a pitcher's teammates are reflected in his hit rate too. We touched on this subject earlier in dismissing the concept of an earned run because it does not properly account for the influence of teammates' defensive range. Even a pitcher's peripheral rates, specifically hit rate, are not a sufficiently pure indication of a pitcher's performance.

Defense-Independent Pitching Statistics

So how can you separate pitching from fielding? For batted balls that stay on the field, the entire event flows from the ball leaving the pitcher's hand, coming off the hitter's bat, and landing in a fielder's glove. It's an interconnected series of acts that takes place in mere seconds, without the break in the action that separates one inning, one plate appearance, or even one pitch from another. For years, teasing out the relationship between how pitchers and fielders interact seemed impossible until a radical theory proposed by Voros McCracken took the baseball analysis world by storm in the early 2000s.

McCracken demonstrated that what happens to a ball that the hitter puts into play has little to do with the pitcher who threw it. Measuring how often a ball in play went for a hit, a statistic dubbed batting average on balls in play (BABIP), can show how well the pitcher and fielders performed as a unit at their primary defensive responsibility: turning batted balls into outs. By comparing pitchers who were teammates—and thus were working with the same defense from year to year—it was possible to estimate how much of an effect the pitcher has on BABIP and how much of BABIP was the fielder's responsibility.

The results were shocking. There seemed to be no relationship between the quality of a pitcher and his BABIP. The best pitchers in the league were almost as likely to have a high BABIP as the worst. For example, in 2005, perennial Cy Young candidate Roy Oswalt had a .310 BABIP. Lowly Devil Ray Doug Waechter had a .308. Gopher-ball generator Eric Milton posted a .317, front-line starter John Lackey a .328. The mediocre Scott Elarton had a .274 BABIP, while budding star Jake Peavy had a .281.

Furthermore, these were not mere one-year flukes. Good and bad pitchers appeared scattered through the list of BABIP leaders and laggards season after season. Also, there was no consistency in a pitcher ranking high or low over time. The same pitcher might top the list one year and be near the bottom the next. The same pitchers would see their BABIP bounce up and down to a frightening degree. The inevitable conclusion McCracken reached was that pitchers had a surprisingly small influence on whether batted balls in play became hits or outs—so small, in fact, that it could be virtually ignored as a first approximation. If the ball stayed in play, what happened to it was almost entirely the purview of the fielders, not the pitcher. And while team fielding was relatively consistent across entire seasons, the defensive support given to individual pitchers on a team varied widely and randomly, leading to the chaotic BABIP results for pitchers.

To say this result was counterintuitive or hard to believe is an understatement. A ball hit off Pedro Martinez was virtually no different from one hit off Jose Lima (excluding ones hit over the fences)? After McCracken presented his results in a variety of forums, including the Baseball Prospectus Web site, his conclusions were scrutinized thoroughly and were largely confirmed. Unfortunately, the popularized version of what he found was that "pitchers have no effect on balls in play." Though that's a succinct way to put it, it's not quite correct—the statement needlessly sparked a controversy in the baseball press when highlighted in Michael Lewis's book *Moneyball*. Distortions and sensationalism aside, the essence of the results—that pitchers have a very small influence on BABIP and that such an influence is dwarfed by variations in defensive support from year to year—proved to be true and is now well accepted in the analysis community. BABIP can now be found even on mainstream sports Web sites such as ESPN's.

From this research, a new pitching measurement arose. Defense-independent pitching statistics (DIPS) are a further attempt to eliminate the fielder's effect on the pitcher's performance. By removing all the outcomes that routinely involve another fielder, non-strikeout outs, and non-home-run hits, we are left with just strikeouts, walks (and hit by pitches), and home runs. Much like Peripheral ERA, DIPS ERA estimates what a pitcher's ERA should have been with an average defense behind him given only his strikeout, walk, and home-run rates. But DIPS ERA is "purer" than PERA, as it eliminates the randomness of BABIP from its evaluation. (See Chapter 3-1 for more on DIPS.)

Component Pitching Rates

Of course DIPS ERA itself is a synthesis of more fundamental components: strikeout rate, walk rate, and home-run rate. In terms of outcomes over which the pitcher has the most influence, these three rates can be considered the basis of pitcher performance. It's the clearest look at the pitcher and the events in the game he can control, without the distorting effects of his fielders, offensive support, and clustering of hits.

Actually, we're not quite done yet—there's another slight improvement we can make. There are some external factors involved with a pitcher's home-run rate too. Pitchers seem to be able to influence whether the ball is hit on the ground or in the air. But how far the ball is hit, or whether it lands in play versus going over the wall, depends a lot on other factors. Prevailing weather conditions and winds, the configuration of the park, the power of the batter at the plate, and other events make home-run rate more variable from year to year than simply looking at a pitcher's overall groundball and flyball tendencies. This aspect differs from the statistics we've looked at up to now in that it doesn't reflect an actual game outcome—outs, hits, walks, runs, and wins—but rather a flavor or type associated with some of those events. A groundball single is not different from a flyball single. A run is worth the same whether it scores on a sacrifice fly or on a ground-out to second. But in terms of understanding how well a pitcher has performed, it's a useful distinction to make, so we'll substitute groundball percentage in place of home-run rate.

These three component statistics—strikeout rate, walk rate, and groundball percentage—reflect important abilities that are fundamental to a pitcher's job: the ability to find the strike zone, to make hitters miss the ball, and to keep the balls that batters don't miss on the ground. At this level, none of these are dependent on the offensive or defensive performance of his teammates—the pitcher bears these responsibilities. They are also the most reliable and consistent pitching statistics from year to year. In fact, these component statistics are as reliable as batting statistics.

Reliability of Pitching Statistics

Traditional measures of pitching performance don't provide an accurate picture. A pitcher can deliver the same quality of performance in one year as he did in a previous season, but if he's had worse defenders playing behind him, didn't get offensive run support, or just plain got unlucky on the timing of giving up hits, those traditional numbers aren't going to look the same. You have to look deeper to see that the pitcher hasn't changed. Instead, his environment has.

Another way to illustrate the point is to look at the year-to-year stability of the different pitching statistics. More specifically, we can look at the correlation between the value of a statistic in one year and the value of the same statistic in the following year. Correlations range from –1 to +1. The closer the value is to +1, the more stable and predictable the stat is from year-to-year. Correlations near zero indicate that there is no consistency from year-to-year. Correlations near –1 indicate that the values flip-flop—high value in the first year strongly suggests a low value in the second year. Table 2-1.1 looks at every pitcher from 1972 to 2004 who faced at least 500 batters in consecutive seasons and computes the correlation from year-to-year in various pitching statistics that we've examined in this chapter.

TABLE 2-1.1 Year-to-Year Correlation in Pitching Statistics

Statistic	Year-to-Year Correlation
Winning percentage	.204
Batting average on balls in play (BABIP)	.272
ERA	.380
Home runs per batter faced	.470
Hits allowed per batter faced	.499
Walks per batter faced	.676
Strikeouts per batter faced	.790
Groundball percentage	.807

Measures such as walks, strikeouts, and groundball percentage that reflect skills attributable to the pitcher show up as highly correlated and thus consistent and sustainable from year to year. On the other hand, measures that have a lot of other factors that affect them, such as winning percentage and BABIP, have very low correlations. The highest correlations on the list are comparable to the predictability we see in batting statistics such as on-base percentage (OBP) and slugging average (SLG), which measure a batter's performance independent of his teammates.

Pitchers are unpredictable in that they're more likely to get injured or fatigued than any other player on the diamond. But when it comes to measuring a pitcher's performance by the numbers, only flawed, context-dependent measures such as wins and ERA make them unpredictable. Use the right measures, and pitching performance becomes much less enigmatic. At Baseball Prospectus, we use a variety of statistics such as Support-Neutral Value Added, Peripheral ERA, and component pitching rates that progressively peel away the layers of the onion to inform our analyses, improve our predictions, and understand how pitchers are truly performing. By using better tools, you can gain a better understanding of a pitcher's value—and a better shot at predicting what he'll do in the future.

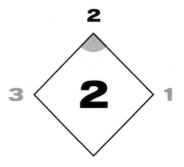

Are Teams Letting Their Closers Go to Waste?

KEITH WOOLNER

As noted in Chapter 2-3, complete games have been on the decline for over a hundred years. This trend has naturally heightened the emphasis on relief pitchers. Today, the closer is as high-profile a pitcher as any on a team. Stars like Mariano Rivera, Billy Wagner, Trevor Hoffman, and Eric Gagne are well known to even casual fans, and 40-save seasons are not uncommon. But are these pitchers really best used as closers? Is protecting a 3-run lead in the ninth inning the best use of a relief ace? Or are there other practical strategies that can help a team win more over the course of a season? How do we evaluate the contribution of relief pitchers?

The closer is a relatively recent phenomenon in baseball. The earliest recognized relief "ace" is probably Firpo Marberry. Pitching from 1923 to 1936, Marberry was the first pitcher to make 50 relief appearances in a season as well as the first to earn 20 saves in a season and 100 saves in a career (retroactively applying the save definition first adopted in 1969).

In the 1950s, Ellis Kinder was a proto–Dennis Eckersley, complete with a 20-win season; stints with teams in Boston, St. Louis, and Chicago; a conversion from starter to relief; multiple seasons leading the league in saves; a time as the oldest player in the league; and a drinking problem. There was knuckleballer Hoyt Wilhelm, the first pitcher with 200 career saves and the first Hall-of-Famer to be elected primarily as a reliever. Elroy Face posted an 18-1 record in relief in 1959, the highest single-season winning percentage in major league history. Lindy McDaniel, Stu Miller, and Dick Radatz were three of the best relievers of the 1960s.

Mike Marshall was the first reliever to win the Cy Young Award, paving the way for Sparky Lyle, Bruce Sutter, Rollie Fingers, Willie Hernandez, Steve Bedrosian, Mark Davis, Dennis Eckersley, and Eric Gagne. Goose Gossage and Rollie Fingers started on the road toward Hall of Fame–caliber careers in the 1970s as well.

The birth of the modern closer can be traced back to Bruce Sutter. He is the first reliever who came in to start the ninth in about 20 percent of his appearances during his career, followed a couple of years later by Dan Quisenberry. Sutter's success (he won the Cy Young Award in 1979) set off a trend of other relievers used mostly to start the ninth, such as Dave Smith, Jeff Reardon, Lee Smith, and Dave Righetti. Except for one lone season by Clay Carroll in 1972, no pitcher made one-third of his season's appearances at the beginning of the ninth until Rollie Fingers in 1982. John Franco became the first relief ace to be used more than half the time in that situation in 1987. Lee Smith was the first to top the 75 percent mark, with 80.5 percent in 1994. By 2002, Eddie Guardado was on the verge of 90 percent start-the-ninth usage with 89.7 percent (exactly matched by Mike MacDougal in 2003). Which brings us to the present, where most closers are reserved exclusively for ninth-inning use, and the accumulation of saves is seen as the mark of a good closer.

Game Context and Decision Making

Closers and relief aces, generally, are affected more by managerial game-time decisions than any other player. Even pinch-hitting specialists generally get a few starts. A manager selects his starting lineup and pitcher in advance, with some idea of who the opposing pitcher is and who needs a day off. But decisions about relievers are based on the unique trajectory of the game as it unfolds. An ace reliever is a weapon that can be saved until a key game situation to maximize the impact on winning. Indeed, the value of a relief ace lies in the ability to use him strategically when an inning or two of work will have a disproportionate effect on the outcome of the game.

It's easy to see what the situation is today, but you don't know what kind of game you will face tomorrow. It could be a nail-biter or a

TABLE 2-2.1 Closer Appearances in the Ninth, None on, None Out

Year	Games Pitched	Percentage Appearances in Ninth Inning, No Outs, None On
1972	50.9	15.8
1973	55.5	9.9
1974	59.5	8.8
1975	53.8	11.3
1976	57.7	10.8
1977	60.7	10.8
1978	58.0	11.8
1979	57.2	13.6
1980	62.6	13.4
1981	42.2	13.9
1982	61.3	13.2
1983	59.8	14.0
1984	60.4	18.1
1985	61.0	19.8
1986	60.4	23.1
1987	57.1	22.2
1988	57.5	27.0
1989	59.5	32.4
1990	58.5	37.9
1991	59.8	38.6
1992	60.7	43.6
1993	59.5	51.4
1994	41.3	52.8
1995	53.4	56.9
1996	62.8	54.1
1997	64.0	55.8
1998	62.3	58.1
1999	64.3	59.4
2000	63.3	58.9
2001	63.5	63.7
2002	64.3	68.2
2003	59.2	62.4
2004	61.5	65.0

blowout. Furthermore, the decisions you make today have an impact on what options are available to you tomorrow—pitchers can't pitch every day (Mike Marshall possibly excepted). A manager's job is to assess the current situation and decide: "Is this situation important enough for me to deploy one of my most valuable resources, or should I save him for another day?"

In recent decades, the decision making has become almost automatic. Your best pitcher is saved for games where the team is leading by 3 runs or less entering the ninth inning. This is vastly different from how ace relievers were used in the past. Three-inning saves were once common, and Rollie Fingers or Goose Gossage would be called upon whenever the game threatened to get out of hand.

We can see this vividly in Table 2-2.1. In each season, take each team's leader in saves and look at when he was brought into games. The percentage of games where the closer comes in to start the ninth has soared to almost two-thirds of all these pitchers' appearances.

Reliever ERA, Win Expectation, and Leverage

Since relievers pitch only partial games, and in particular because they often come in partway through an inning, ERA is a remarkably poor way to evaluate their performance. Runs scored by runners already on base when they enter the game are charged not to the reliever but to the preceding pitcher. Yet one of the primary roles of an ace reliever is to stop a rally—that is, to prevent inherited runners from scoring—as well as to prevent additional runs. Furthermore, a reliever may pitch to just one or two batters before being removed himself—perhaps to gain a platoon advantage, whether righty versus righty or lefty versus lefty. That reliever may bequeath to his successor not only his own runners, but also those belonging to the pitcher before him. The relievers following him will determine whether he gets charged with these runs.

A fairer way of assigning responsibility for runs is to charge a pitcher with the expected number of runs that would result from runners who are still on base when he exits the game and to credit the incoming reliever with the higher degree of difficulty he faces in preventing runs. This, of course, can be done for starting pitchers as well, charging them with the average number of expected runs for any runners still on base when they leave the game, regardless of whether the bullpen performs exceptionally well or poorly.

The expected-runs matrix, popularized in *The Hidden Game of Baseball* by John Thorn and Pete Palmer, expresses the expected number of runs that would score in the remainder of an inning, given the number of outs and the baserunner situation (Table 2-2.2).

TABLE 2-2.2 Expected Runs Matrix for Different Base-Out Situations

Outs	---	1--	-2-	12-	--3	1-3	-23	123
0	0.454	0.783	1.068	1.380	1.277	1.639	1.946	2.254
1	0.249	0.478	0.699	0.888	0.897	1.088	1.371	1.546
2	0.095	0.209	0.348	0.457	0.382	0.494	0.661	0.798

In *Baseball Prospectus 2005*, we introduced a mathematical framework that extends this idea, allowing us to compute the run-scoring distribution for any point in the game and any offensive environment. For example, with runners on second and third with two outs in the fifth inning, a team that averages 0.5 runs per inning might have a 15 percent chance of scoring exactly 2 more runs through the rest of the game. The expected-runs matrix, at best, tells us only the run expectation, not the probability of scoring each number of runs. This framework takes what Thorn and Palmer did empirically and turns it into a more flexible analytical tool for answering questions about the likelihood of different game outcomes, including how to assign credit or blame more fairly to relievers.

When a pitcher leaves a game, instead of waiting to see whether any baserunners left on base come around to score, we will instead charge that pitcher with the expected number of runs that would score in that situation, minus those with the bases empty with the same number of outs. Similarly, when a reliever enters the game with runners on base, and fewer runs score than expected, we will credit him with preventing the expected runs from scoring. This both rewards exceptional performance with inherited runners and deals fairly with runners a pitcher has left on base. His performance is unaffected by pitchers who follow.

For example, Tom Gordon relieves Mike Mussina in the eighth inning with runners on first and third, nobody out. Gordon gives up a sacrifice fly, allowing a run to score, but otherwise shuts down the opposing lineup for the rest of the inning. He then leaves the game, making way for Mariano Rivera in the ninth.

When Mussina was pulled, he left a situation where 1.8367 runs were expected to score, based on 2005 average offense. If Mussina had departed with no runners still on base and none out, the expected runs for an average team that inning would have been 0.5172. The expected runs in the situation that Mussina left was 1.8367, meaning that the runners he bequeathed to Gordon have an expected value of 1.8367 – 0.5172 = 1.3195 runs. These extra runs, which represent what an average bullpen would have allowed, are charged to Mussina no matter what Gordon does with the runners.

Gordon, on the other hand, enters the game in a tough situation. An average pitcher would be expected to allow 1.8367 runs to score during the remainder of the inning. Of that total, 1.3195 are due to the runners on base that Gordon has inherited from Mussina. He actually allowed 1 run to score. Thus, he actually prevented runs that "should" have scored from crossing the plate. We credit him with 1 run allowed minus 1.3195 runs expected due to inherited runners = –0.3195 runs for that appearance. That's right—negative runs. It's possible for a reliever to give up fewer than zero runs in this system. It sounds strange at first, but it makes sense—if a reliever comes into a situation where runs are expected to score and none do, he's done something more than the usual job of not allowing any runs—hence, negative runs!

Using this fairer system of allocating responsibility for runs, we can compute a couple of new statistics. The first is Fair Run Average (FRA)—this is much like earned run average, but instead of looking at earned runs, we look at all runs, including the values of runners left on when a pitcher leaves a game, and inherited runs prevented. The number can be viewed just like ERA, but it more properly reflects a reliever's contribution.

The next stat to look at is Adjusted Runs Prevented (ARP), which is the additional number of runs that an average pitcher would have allowed to score, given the same appearances, innings, and inherited runners. FRA and ARP are related—FRA is a rate statistic, showing runs allowed per inning, and ARP is a cumulative statistic, showing total runs prevented (Table 2-2.3).

TABLE 2-2.3 Top Relievers, 1960–2004, by ARP

Name	Played	IP	SV	ARP
Rich Gossage	1972–1994	1,552.3	309	276.1
Rollie Fingers	1968–1985	1,364.7	321	263.0
Mariano Rivera	1995–2004	678.3	336	241.1
Jesse Orosco	1979–2003	1,277.0	144	222.4
Lee Smith	1980–1997	1,252.3	478	196.5
Dennis Eckersley	1975–1998	793.3	389	194.9
Trevor Hoffman	1993–2004	764.7	393	191.8
Tom Henke	1982–1995	789.7	311	188.1
Keith Foulke	1997–2004	623.0	175	185.0
Mike Jackson	1986–2004	1,154.7	142	175.6
Kent Tekulve	1974–1989	1,334.0	175	172.2
Dan Quisenberry	1979–1990	1,043.3	244	170.7
Hoyt Wilhelm	1960–1972	1,002.7	142	167.3
Armando Benitez	1994–2004	654.0	244	166.4
Sparky Lyle	1967–1982	1,286.0	214	159.5
Jeff Reardon	1979–1994	1,132.3	367	158.7
Mark Eichhorn	1982–1996	847.7	32	154.0
Tug McGraw	1965–1984	1,204.0	169	152.5
Troy Percival	1995–2004	585.7	316	150.9

In addition to the problem of inherited runners, relievers have gotten short shrift from the sabermetric community because they pitch relatively few innings. Given a starting pitcher who throws 200 innings and a closer who throws 60 with the same ERA (say, 3.00), a sabermetric measure such as runs prevented compared to average would give the starter 33 runs prevented and the closer only 10.

The difference, of course, is that the starter pitches every five days, and the game he throws could be close or could be a laugher. The closer, by virtue of the way the manager uses him, almost always comes in during a late-game situation, where keeping an extra run off the board has a much greater impact. The sabermetric community recognizes these high-leverage innings, but there have been only sporadic and unsatisfactory attempts at quantifying such leverage and how it affects a pitcher's contribution. Let's try to do that here.

At any point during a game, we can estimate the probability of a team's winning from the current score, inning, number of outs, runners on base, and relative strengths of each team. To measure the true value of a reliever, we can look at his team's chance of winning when he enters the game, then again when he leaves the game or the game ends. The difference between them could be attributed to the reliever's performance.

For example, Francisco Rodriguez enters the game with the Angels clinging to a 2-1 lead in the seventh inning, with none out and the bases loaded. Despite the lead, the situation is dire, and the probability of the Angels' winning is only about 39 percent. But suppose K-Rod gets two strikeouts and a groundout, finishing the inning with no runs scored. The probability of an Angels win has now risen to 79 percent. Rodriguez is removed from the game and is credited for 40 percent of a win, or 0.4 wins, regardless of the actual outcome of the game, because what happens from then on is not under his control. Rodriguez's 0.4 wins are dubbed as his Expected Wins, but abbreviated as WX, from the Win Expectancy Framework.

However, that's not entirely satisfactory in all circumstances. A reliever who pitches in more than one inning will have his team come to bat for at least a half-inning. The change in probability could have resulted from his team's scoring additional runs rather than the pitcher's getting out of a jam or preventing runs from scoring.

For example, Keith Foulke enters in the top of the eighth inning with runners on second and third and two outs, the Red Sox down by a run. The Sox have a 25 percent chance of winning the game given average offense and pitching. Foulke gets out of the jam, and the Red Sox rally with 4 runs in the bottom of the eighth. In the ninth, Foulke gets one out, then walks two men before getting pulled. The chance of Boston's winning is 92 percent when he exits. But a substantial part of that increased probability comes from the extra runs scored while Foulke has been the Boston pitcher, not from his own efforts. To assess his contribution, we have to assume that we don't know anything about how the Red Sox bats will perform while Foulke is in the game, and just consider how well he pitched. In fact, Foulke's getting out of a jam in the eighth was almost completely offset by his setting up a jam in the ninth. The win expectation based only on Foulke's pitching is 26 percent—just 1 percent better than when he entered the game. The other 66 percent gain came from the 4 runs scored.

Given this Win Expectancy framework, we now have a way of measuring how crucial a run is at any point in the game. A leadoff home run in a game between equally matched teams raises the probability of winning from 50 percent to 59.8 percent. A homer to lead off the eighth in a tie game raises the probability of winning from 50 percent to 74.9 percent. One run is thus valued differently depending on the game situation—9.8 percent in the first case, 24.9 percent in the second. We can express how much more valuable the run in the second case is as a ratio of the two: 24.9 percent/9.8 percent = 2.54. Because of the situation, the eighth-inning HR was worth 2.54 times as much as the first-inning HR. This ratio is called Leverage and captures exactly the question of how much more important runs are in certain situations. The concept of Leverage, and more importantly a tangible means to measure it, proves invaluable in understanding closer usage patterns.

The most important situations in a game often occur well before the ninth inning. For games whose highest-leverage situation is above the median for all games, the most critical situation is likely to occur in the ninth inning only 40 percent of the time. Fully 60 percent of all highly leveraged situations occur in innings six, seven, and eight.

In deciding to use his ace reliever, the manager has to make a trade-off between the value of the current game situation and the likelihood of needing the reliever for an even more important situation in the next day or three. Although some relievers can be used on consecutive days, the risk of fatigue and ineffectiveness grows without occasional rest. A manager can't know for sure what the near future holds, but he has to make decisions today that will affect his options in the days to come.

To answer this, we need to know something about what the highest Leverage during a game is likely to be. By examining every plate appearance for each game from 2000 through 2004, we can construct a chart showing the probability of the highest game Leverage reaching a certain level (Table 2-2.4).

A Simple Model of Closer Usage Strategy

Let's consider a simple model for closer usage. Suppose we have an ace reliever who is capable of pitching one inning every other day but can't pitch on consecutive days. In other words, he can be used today or tomorrow, but not both. During any given game where there's another game the following day, and the reliever didn't pitch yesterday, the manager must consider whether to use him to win today's game or

TABLE 2-2.4 Situational Leverage Using 2005 Average Offense

		Run Differential[a]										
Inning	Runners	-5	-4	-3	-2	-1	0	1	2	3	4	5
6.0	---	0.20	0.34	0.55	0.84	1.23	1.66	1.66	1.23	0.84	0.55	0.34
	--3	0.13	0.23	0.38	0.60	0.91	1.30	1.62	1.55	1.17	0.81	0.53
	-2-	0.16	0.26	0.43	0.68	1.01	1.40	1.60	1.41	1.07	0.74	0.49
	-23	0.11	0.18	0.30	0.49	0.75	1.08	1.39	1.49	1.33	1.02	0.72
	1--	0.18	0.30	0.48	0.75	1.10	1.51	1.59	1.29	0.97	0.67	0.44
	1-3	0.12	0.20	0.33	0.53	0.81	1.16	1.48	1.49	1.23	0.93	0.65
	12-	0.14	0.24	0.39	0.61	0.91	1.28	1.46	1.35	1.13	0.86	0.60
	123	0.10	0.17	0.28	0.44	0.68	1.00	1.29	1.39	1.28	1.07	0.82
6.3	---	0.22	0.36	0.59	0.91	1.31	1.75	1.69	1.17	0.77	0.47	0.28
	--3	0.16	0.27	0.44	0.70	1.04	1.46	1.69	1.47	1.04	0.68	0.43
	-2-	0.19	0.31	0.51	0.79	1.16	1.58	1.65	1.31	0.92	0.61	0.38
	-23	0.14	0.24	0.39	0.62	0.92	1.30	1.52	1.44	1.16	0.84	0.56
	1--	0.20	0.34	0.54	0.84	1.22	1.65	1.64	1.23	0.86	0.56	0.35
	1-3	0.15	0.26	0.42	0.66	0.99	1.38	1.60	1.42	1.08	0.76	0.50
	12-	0.18	0.30	0.48	0.75	1.10	1.50	1.57	1.28	0.98	0.69	0.45
	123	0.14	0.23	0.38	0.60	0.90	1.26	1.46	1.37	1.13	0.87	0.62
6.7	---	0.23	0.38	0.62	0.95	1.37	1.82	1.71	1.12	0.70	0.42	0.24
	--3	0.21	0.35	0.56	0.87	1.26	1.71	1.70	1.24	0.81	0.50	0.30
	-2-	0.21	0.35	0.57	0.88	1.28	1.72	1.70	1.21	0.80	0.49	0.29
	-23	0.20	0.33	0.53	0.83	1.20	1.62	1.61	1.23	0.90	0.59	0.37
	1--	0.22	0.37	0.60	0.92	1.32	1.77	1.69	1.15	0.76	0.46	0.27
	1-3	0.20	0.34	0.55	0.85	1.23	1.66	1.66	1.23	0.85	0.55	0.34
	12-	0.21	0.35	0.56	0.86	1.25	1.68	1.66	1.20	0.83	0.54	0.33
	123	0.19	0.32	0.51	0.79	1.15	1.56	1.58	1.22	0.92	0.64	0.42
7.0	---	0.15	0.26	0.46	0.78	1.26	1.99	1.99	1.26	0.78	0.46	0.26
	--3	0.09	0.17	0.30	0.52	0.87	1.39	1.94	1.81	1.20	0.76	0.45
	-2-	0.11	0.20	0.35	0.61	0.99	1.58	1.90	1.58	1.08	0.69	0.42
	-23	0.07	0.13	0.24	0.41	0.70	1.13	1.57	1.72	1.47	1.03	0.67
	1--	0.13	0.23	0.41	0.69	1.12	1.77	1.88	1.38	0.96	0.62	0.37
	1-3	0.08	0.15	0.26	0.46	0.76	1.23	1.73	1.72	1.30	0.93	0.60
	12-	0.10	0.18	0.32	0.55	0.90	1.44	1.70	1.49	1.19	0.86	0.56
	123	0.07	0.12	0.22	0.38	0.64	1.04	1.45	1.57	1.39	1.12	0.82
7.3	---	0.16	0.29	0.50	0.85	1.36	2.14	2.04	1.16	0.68	0.38	0.21
	--3	0.11	0.21	0.36	0.63	1.03	1.64	2.04	1.67	1.02	0.61	0.34
	-2-	0.13	0.24	0.43	0.73	1.17	1.86	1.98	1.40	0.89	0.53	0.30
	-23	0.10	0.18	0.32	0.55	0.90	1.44	1.77	1.62	1.23	0.81	0.50
	1--	0.15	0.26	0.46	0.78	1.25	1.98	1.97	1.26	0.81	0.48	0.27
	1-3	0.11	0.19	0.35	0.59	0.97	1.55	1.90	1.59	1.09	0.72	0.43

(continues)

TABLE 2-2.4 (continued)

		Run Differential[a]										
Inning	*Runners*	*-5*	*-4*	*-3*	*-2*	*-1*	*0*	*1*	*2*	*3*	*4*	*5*
	12-	0.13	0.23	0.40	0.69	1.11	1.76	1.86	1.35	0.97	0.65	0.39
	123	0.10	0.17	0.31	0.53	0.88	1.40	1.70	1.51	1.18	0.87	0.59
7.7	---	0.17	0.30	0.53	0.90	1.43	2.25	2.07	1.07	0.59	0.32	0.17
	--3	0.15	0.27	0.48	0.81	1.30	2.05	2.06	1.27	0.73	0.41	0.22
	-2-	0.15	0.28	0.49	0.82	1.32	2.09	2.05	1.23	0.71	0.40	0.21
	-23	0.14	0.26	0.45	0.77	1.23	1.95	1.91	1.26	0.88	0.52	0.30
	1--	0.16	0.29	0.51	0.86	1.38	2.17	2.03	1.13	0.67	0.37	0.20
	1-3	0.15	0.26	0.46	0.79	1.27	2.00	2.00	1.26	0.79	0.47	0.26
	12-	0.15	0.27	0.47	0.80	1.29	2.04	1.99	1.21	0.77	0.46	0.26
	123	0.14	0.25	0.43	0.73	1.18	1.87	1.86	1.25	0.89	0.59	0.37
8.0	---	0.09	0.18	0.34	0.65	1.21	2.53	2.53	1.21	0.65	0.34	0.18
	--3	0.05	0.11	0.21	0.40	0.76	1.47	2.43	2.19	1.16	0.65	0.34
	-2-	0.07	0.13	0.25	0.48	0.90	1.83	2.37	1.78	1.04	0.59	0.32
	-23	0.04	0.08	0.16	0.31	0.59	1.16	1.81	2.05	1.64	1.01	0.59
	1--	0.08	0.15	0.30	0.56	1.05	2.18	2.34	1.42	0.91	0.53	0.29
	1-3	0.05	0.09	0.18	0.35	0.66	1.27	2.12	2.05	1.34	0.90	0.52
	12-	0.06	0.12	0.23	0.44	0.81	1.66	2.05	1.63	1.23	0.84	0.49
	123	0.04	0.07	0.15	0.28	0.54	1.06	1.68	1.83	1.52	1.16	0.80
8.3	---	0.10	0.19	0.37	0.71	1.31	2.77	2.61	1.02	0.51	0.25	0.12
	--3	0.07	0.13	0.26	0.50	0.93	1.86	2.60	1.93	0.90	0.47	0.23
	-2-	0.08	0.16	0.31	0.60	1.10	2.29	2.51	1.44	0.78	0.41	0.21
	-23	0.06	0.11	0.22	0.43	0.81	1.63	2.15	1.85	1.28	0.74	0.41
	1--	0.09	0.18	0.34	0.65	1.20	2.52	2.48	1.20	0.71	0.37	0.19
	1-3	0.06	0.13	0.25	0.47	0.88	1.77	2.38	1.81	1.04	0.64	0.34
	12-	0.08	0.15	0.29	0.56	1.04	2.17	2.31	1.36	0.93	0.58	0.31
	123	0.06	0.11	0.22	0.42	0.79	1.60	2.06	1.68	1.20	0.84	0.54
8.7	---	0.10	0.21	0.40	0.76	1.39	2.96	2.65	0.86	0.40	0.18	0.08
	--3	0.09	0.18	0.35	0.67	1.24	2.61	2.64	1.22	0.56	0.27	0.13
	-2-	0.09	0.19	0.36	0.69	1.27	2.67	2.62	1.14	0.55	0.26	0.12
	-23	0.09	0.17	0.34	0.64	1.18	2.49	2.37	1.20	0.83	0.41	0.20
	1--	0.10	0.20	0.38	0.73	1.34	2.83	2.59	0.96	0.51	0.24	0.11
	1-3	0.09	0.18	0.34	0.65	1.21	2.54	2.53	1.19	0.66	0.37	0.18
	12-	0.09	0.18	0.35	0.67	1.24	2.61	2.52	1.11	0.64	0.35	0.17
	123	0.08	0.16	0.32	0.61	1.12	2.36	2.32	1.20	0.83	0.51	0.30
9.0	---	0.04	0.08	0.18	0.41	0.91	3.44	3.44	0.91	0.41	0.18	0.08
	--3	0.02	0.05	0.10	0.23	0.51	1.46	3.26	2.79	0.94	0.45	0.20
	-2-	0.03	0.06	0.13	0.29	0.64	2.17	3.16	2.02	0.88	0.43	0.19
	-23	0.02	0.03	0.08	0.17	0.39	1.15	2.17	2.55	1.86	0.91	0.46

(continues)

TABLE 2-2.4 (continued)

Inning	Runners	\-5	\-4	\-3	\-2	\-1	0	1	2	3	4	5
						Run Differential[a]						
	1--	0.03	0.07	0.16	0.35	0.77	2.85	3.11	1.31	0.79	0.39	0.18
	1-3	0.02	0.04	0.09	0.19	0.43	1.24	2.75	2.56	1.28	0.81	0.40
	12-	0.02	0.05	0.12	0.26	0.58	2.01	2.63	1.75	1.24	0.79	0.39
	123	0.01	0.03	0.07	0.16	0.35	1.04	2.03	2.20	1.63	1.19	0.77
9.3	---	0.04	0.09	0.20	0.45	1.00	3.87	3.57	0.55	0.22	0.09	0.03
	--3	0.03	0.06	0.13	0.29	0.65	2.13	3.56	2.29	0.59	0.25	0.10
	-2-	0.03	0.07	0.16	0.37	0.81	2.99	3.40	1.36	0.56	0.24	0.10
	-23	0.02	0.05	0.11	0.25	0.56	1.89	2.74	2.16	1.30	0.59	0.28
	1--	0.04	0.08	0.18	0.40	0.90	3.44	3.34	0.89	0.51	0.21	0.09
	1-3	0.03	0.06	0.13	0.28	0.62	2.07	3.19	2.06	0.86	0.50	0.21
	12-	0.03	0.07	0.16	0.35	0.77	2.86	3.06	1.21	0.82	0.49	0.20
	123	0.02	0.05	0.11	0.25	0.56	1.89	2.66	1.87	1.16	0.79	0.47
9.7	---	0.04	0.10	0.22	0.48	1.07	4.21	3.66	0.24	0.08	0.03	0.01
	--3	0.04	0.08	0.19	0.42	0.94	3.53	3.63	0.93	0.25	0.08	0.03
	-2-	0.04	0.09	0.19	0.43	0.96	3.67	3.60	0.78	0.25	0.09	0.03
	-23	0.04	0.08	0.18	0.40	0.89	3.42	3.12	0.88	0.75	0.25	0.09
	1--	0.04	0.09	0.21	0.46	1.02	3.99	3.54	0.43	0.24	0.08	0.02
	1-3	0.04	0.08	0.18	0.41	0.91	3.45	3.45	0.87	0.42	0.23	0.07
	12-	0.04	0.08	0.19	0.42	0.93	3.59	3.43	0.72	0.41	0.22	0.07
	123	0.03	0.08	0.17	0.38	0.84	3.22	3.07	0.90	0.71	0.41	0.22

[a]Run differential is determined from the perspective of the pitching team, that is, run differential = pitching team's score minus batting team's score.

save him for tomorrow. Of course, if the following day is an off day, then the pitcher can be used without restriction—but the manager still wants to save him for the key situation. Under the presumption that he is significantly better than other bullpen alternatives, the manager wants to maximize both the leverage of the pitcher's appearances and the frequency to maximize the impact on the team's winning percentage.

The most basic decision is whether to use the reliever today or tomorrow. Regardless of what happens today, the manager cannot predict how the game will go tomorrow. How high should the Leverage be in the first game to make it worth bringing in the pitcher instead of waiting for the second game?

If the Leverage in the first game ever exceeds the median maximum Leverage, then the chances are less than 50 percent that the next game will see a plate appearance with a Leverage as high. In other words, we should plan to use the ace reliever in the first game once the situation exceeds median maximum Leverage. Over the span 2000 to 2004, the median maximum Leverage was 1.66. Once the game situation has a Leverage exceeding 1.66—meaning a situation where allowing a run to score has 66 percent more impact on the likelihood of winning than it did at the start of the game—it becomes one where we should consider bringing the ace into the game.

But if we bring in the ace as soon as we cross this threshold, he will almost always be pitching in situations close to a 1.66 Leverage, which is not how some actual closers are used. The highest-leveraged closers in any given season tend to enter in situations with an average Leverage of 2.0 to 2.1. Just because we have the green light to bring in the ace doesn't mean we jump at that opportunity. We can still bide our time, letting the Leverage of the situation increase. What we need to know is when we have probably reached the near-maximum Leverage situation for that game. If it's the ninth inning and we haven't opted to use the reliever, we would bring him in at that point, provided the Leverage still exceeded 1.66.

Again, we can look at the historical data to tell us what to expect. The median maximum Leverage prior to the ninth inning for games that meet the minimum threshold requirement is 2.32. That's a confusing statement, so let's spell it out more thoroughly—once a game reaches a point where the Leverage exceeds 1.66, half the time it will go on to a situation with Leverage exceeding 2.32 before the game reaches the ninth inning. Therefore, once we go "on alert" by realizing the game is tight enough to warrant using the relief ace, we should look for a point where the Leverage is at least 2.32 and bring the ace in then. If we reach the ninth inning without having such a situation, we can use the ace then, if we're still above the critical threshold of 1.66.

This simplified model of how a closer can be used can be summed in two rules:

1. Through the eighth inning, if the situational Leverage ever exceeds 2.32, bring in the relief ace.
2. If the ace hasn't been used by the start of the ninth, and the Leverage at the start of the ninth is 1.66 or greater, bring in the relief ace.

Of course, that's an overly simplistic model of closer usage. Most relievers can pitch at least two days in a row, and they need some level of regular work to stay sharp. So we'll try a more complicated, realistic model:

1. A relief ace can be used on two consecutive days at most.
2. One day of rest returns the ace to full strength.
3. A relief ace needs regular work, so if more than five days have elapsed since his last appearance, he will be brought in to work the ninth, regardless of the situation.

The decision for the manager is now more complicated, as he must consider not only one day of history and one day of upcoming games but two days and the future. We can follow a similar procedure to the case above to find the critical threshold levels for bringing in a reliever before the ninth inning, or to start the ninth inning. We'll spare the gory mathematical detail and summarize the results in Table 2-2.5.

For example the code NP indicates that the pitcher pitched one day ago but did not pitch two days ago. The code G- indicates a game the following day, and it doesn't matter whether there's a game two days from now.

TABLE 2-2.5 Manager Decisions Based on Leverage

Previous 2 Days	Next 2 Days	Leverage Pre-9th	Leverage 9th
NP	0-	1.66	1.00
NP	G-	2.55	1.66
-N	GG	2.00	1.28
-N	0-	1.66	1.00
-N	GO	2.55	1.66
PP	–	not available to pitch	

Notes: Previous days: P = did pitch, N = did not pitch; Next days: G = game scheduled, 0 = off day (no game). A dash indicates that the value for that day doesn't matter (both pitch/no pitch or game/no game are applicable).

In the second row, NP/G- means the pitcher appeared yesterday but not two days ago and therefore is available to pitch. But if we use him today, that's two consecutive appearances, and he would be unavailable for tomorrow's scheduled game. This would force a day of rest tomorrow, and thus it would not matter—for the purpose of deciding whether to use him today—whether there's a game two days from now. In this circumstance, we should wait for a situation with a Leverage of 2.55 to bring in the reliever earlier than the ninth inning. If we reach the ninth inning and the Leverage is still above 1.66, then we should bring him in.

Even this model is still simpler than real life, where a manager might consider using a closer three days in a row (especially if some of the outings were short), having him pitch more or less than one in-

ning or giving him more than one day of rest following a long string of
outings. But it starts to capture some of the usage patterns that an ace
reliever might typically face.

We know, from Baseball Prospectus's Win Expectancy reliever stats,
how many runs prevented (ARP) and Expected Wins (WX) each reliever contributed to his team. Table 2-2.6 shows the pitchers with the
top WXRL (Expected Wins added over a replacement-level pitcher's
performance), from 1960 to 2004.

TABLE 2-2.6 Top Relievers, 1960–2004, by WXRL

Name	Played	IP	SV	ARP	WX	WXRL
Rich Gossage	1972–1994	1,552.3	309	276.1	29.66	54.16
Trevor Hoffman	1993–2004	764.7	393	191.8	28.95	49.98
Mariano Rivera	1995–2004	678.3	336	241.1	31.79	48.55
Lee Smith	1980–1997	1,252.3	478	196.5	19.67	47.47
John Franco	1984–2004	1,230.7	424	147.8	18.74	45.34
Rollie Fingers	1968–1985	1,364.7	321	263.0	19.62	43.16
Randy Myers	1985–1998	814.3	347	147.7	19.90	38.99
Troy Percival	1995–2004	585.7	316	150.9	21.83	38.26
Armando Benitez	1994–2004	654.0	244	166.4	22.49	37.75
Tug McGraw	1965–1984	1,204.0	169	152.5	20.27	37.70
Tom Henke	1982–1995	789.7	311	188.1	20.81	36.90
John Wetteland	1989–2000	683.0	330	147.8	18.24	35.35
Keith Foulke	1997–2004	623.0	175	185.0	22.17	34.86
Dennis Eckersley	1975–1998	793.3	389	194.9	17.36	34.79
Mike Jackson	1986–2004	1,154.7	142	175.6	16.29	34.03
Dan Quisenberry	1979–1990	1,043.3	244	170.7	17.96	33.99
Jesse Orosco	1979–2003	1,277.0	144	222.4	14.73	33.56
Bruce Sutter	1977–1988	958.7	290	123.4	11.85	33.32
Hoyt Wilhelm	1960–1972	1,002.7	142	167.3	17.29	33.17
Doug Jones	1982–2000	1,097.3	303	147.6	13.61	33.15
Robb Nen	1993–2002	697.0	314	128.7	14.73	31.98
Billy Wagner	1995–2004	552.7	246	139.1	18.07	31.63
Jeff Reardon	1979–1994	1,132.3	367	158.7	10.55	31.46

Given those reliever measures, how much would such an ace reliever usage strategy actually help a team? Although it's impossible to
replay a season with different decisions fully explored, we can make
some educated guesses. We can look at the sequence of events in every
game the team played and construct an alternate universe where we
get to decide when to bring in our relief ace based on the Leverage

rules we have defined. Knowing that the definition of Leverage is the ratio of the value of a run in that situation to an average run, we can multiply the Leverage of the situations faced by the number of runs prevented to get the total impact of those runs on winning. Using the well-established sabermetric principle that 10 marginal runs is roughly equal to 1 win in the standings, we can convert those highly leveraged runs to wins and compare that total to the actual wins added.

Using this approach, we estimated how much this new strategy could help teams win. We took the saves leaders from every team over 2000 to 2004 who had an above-average run-prevention total and looked up their actual usage, leverage, and expected wins added. We then ran through the complete play-by-play for every team's season and made decisions inning by inning about whether to bring in the reliever, based on the leverage rules of our new proposed strategy and the constraints against pitching three days in a row. We then estimated the number of wins he would have added in the new usage strategy. The comparison of the actual usage number and the estimated new usage numbers are given in Table 2-2.7.

TABLE 2-2.7 Comparison of Actual and Estimated Usage Numbers

Category	Actual	New Strategy
No. of appearances	62.4 games	58.6 games
Average leverage	1.68	2.26
Average wins added	1.89 wins	3.49 wins
Average team improvement		1.60 wins
Maximum team improvement		4.54 wins
Percentage of teams with more wins added		77

Just by reconsidering how relief aces are brought into the game, over three-quarters of teams would win more games than they do now. The average team would add about 1.6 wins, which is about the same as replacing Rick White with Jason Isringhausen (using their 2005 stats). In the best case, a team could add more than 4.5 wins, which is comparable to replacing Brad Halsey with Barry Zito. We're not even changing the total workload of the closer all that much—we're actually shaving a few games off his season totals. Are there any teams that would turn down a few extra wins for free?

Are teams wasting their closers? Not completely, but they aren't getting as much out of them as they could, and it's costing them wins.

This is one area where the refinement of strategy has actually taken us away from the optimal usage pattern. During the "stopper" era of the 1970s, it was common to see a relief ace such as Rollie Fingers or Goose Gossage come in as early as the sixth inning to halt a nascent rally. That was the smart way to go. Focusing on situational leverage, rather than the accumulation of easy ninth-inning saves, is the best way to get the most out of a relief ace.

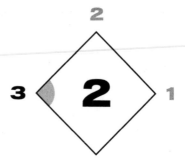

Five Starters or Four?

On Pitching and Stamina

KEITH WOOLNER

I expect the real reason baseball will eventually return to the four-man rotation will be the simplest of all: It helps win games. The five-man rotation is not on that evolutionary path; it's a digression, a dead-end alley. Just as baseball once believed that walking a lot of batters was better than throwing a home-run pitch, we are now chasing an illusion that our pitchers work better on four days' rest and that the five-man rotation significantly improves their future.
—Craig Wright, *The Diamond Appraised,* 1989

If it were an owl, it'd be on the endangered species list. If it were in Manhattan, it'd be an affordable apartment. If it were a baseball player, it'd be a left-handed third baseman.

We're talking about the complete game. Long ago it was a fixture in the big leagues. Today it is nearly nonexistent. Pitchers haven't finished even half of the games they've started since before the Harding administration, and in recent years the number of complete games in the majors has been vanishingly small. The demise of the complete game is almost, well, complete. Why?

Pitchers have been throwing fewer and fewer complete games ever since the day in 1893 when the mound was moved back to 60 feet, 6 inches.

FIGURE 2-3.1 Complete game percentage

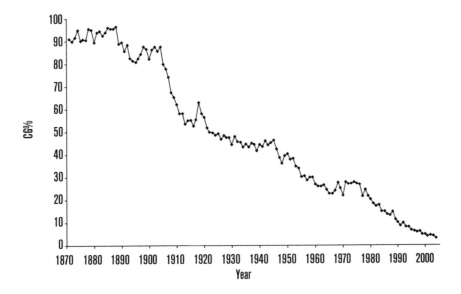

In 2004, the percentage of complete games dropped below 4 percent for the first time—meaning the starting pitcher finished less than one game in twenty-five (Table 2-3.1).

Furthermore, pitcher specialization is on the rise, which will surprise no one who has ever tuned in to a Tony LaRussa three-and-a-half-hour, five-pitching-change special. Not only are starters going fewer innings, but it's taking more relievers to get through the rest of the game (Fig. 2-3.2).

So are modern pitchers just less durable than their predecessors? Are they incapable of shouldering the workloads that men like Charles Radbourne, Jack Chesbro, and Walter Johnson could handle?

TABLE 2-3.1 Starts Resulting in Complete Games over the Past One Hundred Years

Year	Games Started	Complete Games	Complete Games as Percent of Starts
1904	2,496	2,186	87.6
1914	3,758	2,067	55.0
1924	2,462	1,198	48.7
1934	2,446	1,061	43.4
1944	2,484	1,123	45.2
1954	2,472	840	34.0
1964	3,252	797	24.5
1974	3,890	1,089	28.0
1984	4,210	632	15.0
1994	3,200	255	8.0
2004	4,854	150	3.1

FIGURE 2-3.2 Pitchers used per game

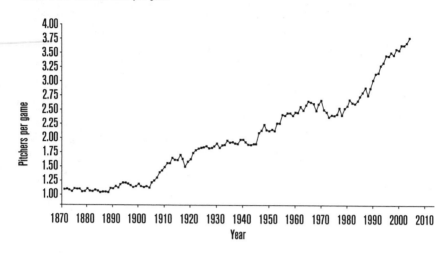

There is anecdotal evidence that pitchers in the past did not use maximum exertion on every pitch. With the deadball era suppressing offense in the early twentieth century and teams mostly carrying defense-first options at positions such as second base and catcher, pitchers like the legendary Christy Mathewson could pace themselves, letting up at nonessential moments of the game. In his book *Pitching in a Pinch,* Mathewson described his methods for staying fresh:

> I have always been against a twirler pitching himself out, when there is no necessity for it, as so many youngsters do. They burn them through for eight innings and then, when the pinch comes, something is lacking. . . . Some pitchers will put all that they have on each ball. This is foolish for two reasons.
>
> In the first place, it exhausts the man physically and, when the pinch comes, he has not the strength to last it out. But second and more important, it shows the batters everything he has, which is senseless. A man should always hold something in reserve, a surprise to spring when things get tight. If a pitcher has displayed his whole assortment to the batters in the early part of the game and has used all his speed and his fastest breaking curve, then, when the crisis comes he hasn't anything to fall back on.

With middle infielders often smacking 20, 30, or more homers in a season, and even the worst modern-day hitters still more dangerous than their forefathers, pitchers have to exert more effort with each batter. After six, seven, or eight innings, today's pitchers often find themselves with higher pitch totals and more fatigued arms than Mathewson and his contemporaries would experience when they'd go the distance.

One of the earliest analyses of historical trends in pitcher usage was the landmark 1989 book *The Diamond Appraised* by Craig Wright and Tom House. The authors looked at pitchers of various ages and their workloads and discovered that young pitchers who pitched to a high number of batters per game seemed to get hurt more often. This was the beginning of the modern movement to monitor pitch counts.

In the mid-1990s, Baseball Prospectus's Rany Jazayerli was one of the first researchers to try to organize and codify what the mishmash of evidence on pitch counts was telling us; he summed it up in his principle of pitcher fatigue: *Throwing is not dangerous to a pitcher's arm. Throwing while tired is dangerous to a pitcher's arm.*

In *Baseball Prospectus 2001*, we showed evidence that even the starting pitchers who regularly work deep into games do decline in performance, as a group, after throwing a high number of pitches. We compared how they pitched in the weeks before such a game to how they pitched in the three weeks after. We found that pitchers throw fewer innings per start, strike out fewer batters, and allow more hits and walks in the starts following the high-pitch outing. We rolled these factors into a formula called pitcher abuse points (PAP):

$$PAP = (\text{no. of pitches} - 100)^3 \quad \text{for no. of pitches} > 100$$
$$PAP = 0 \quad \text{for no. of pitches} \leq 100$$

Through this formula, we can see that as pitch counts grow, they quickly produce unwieldy numbers (Table 2-3.2).

To help manage this numbers explosion, we break starts down into five categories of risk (Table 2-3.3).

As the pitch counts increase, we've observed corresponding declines in the weeks following a long start. The reduction in quality may not seem big, but if a

TABLE 2-3.2 Pitcher Abuse Points, by Number of Pitches Thrown

No. Pitches	PAP
95	0
100	0
105	125
110	1,000
115	3,375
120	8,000
125	15,625
130	27,000
140	64,000

TABLE 2-3.3 Pitcher Abuse Points, Five Risk Factor Categories

Category	Pitch Count Range	% Change in in RA	% Change in Batters Faced	Risk of Short-Term Decline
I	0–100	0.47	1.10	Smallest risk
II	101–109	1.62	1.13	Minimal risk
III	110–121	2.31	–1.11	Moderate risk
IV	122–132	2.95	–2.01	Significant risk
V	133+	4.08	–3.82	High risk

staff is regularly asked to go too deep into a game, it may spend much of the season at less than optimum performance levels, costing the team runs and multiple wins. In this respect, PAP is more about the manager and how he handles a staff than about any particular pitcher.

But aren't pitchers paid to pitch? How does having them pitch less help the team?

If you cut a pitcher's workload by an inning per start over 30 starts, say from 240 innings pitched to 210 IP, and in doing so you reduce his runs allowed by half a run, to 4.00 from 4.50, are you better off as a team? To analyze this dilemma, let's look at a pitcher through the prism of Value Over Replacement Player. VORP measures the number of runs a pitcher prevents from scoring, above what a replacement-level pitcher—a Triple-A lifer or a fringe player—would be expected to prevent. Because VORP rewards both production and increased playing time, a pitcher would need to show a substantial improvement in production to override the 30 innings he's now being forced not to throw.

Not *that* substantial, though. Using $(6.50 - RA) \times (IP/9)$ as an estimate of a pitcher's VORP:

$$(6.50 - 4.50) \times (240/9) = 2.00 \times 26.67 = 53.3 \text{ VORP}$$
$$(6.50 - 4.00) \times (210/9) = 2.50 \times 23.33 = 58.3 \text{ VORP}$$

If this pitcher's workload is reduced by 30 innings, his team actually *gains* about 5 runs, or half a win, over a full season, assuming his pitching less often cuts half a run off his run average (ERA minus the impact of errors, see Chapter 2-1 for more on RA). But this assumption doesn't always hold: Sometimes the gain in RA does not offset the loss of innings pitched. Suppose that instead of half a run the pitcher only improved by a tenth of a run in RA (0.10).

$$(6.50 - 4.50) \times (240/9) = 2.00 \times 26.67 = 53.3 \text{ VORP}$$
$$(6.50 - 4.40) \times (210/9) = 2.10 \times 23.33 = 49.0 \text{ VORP}$$

At this point, it looks as if the team is probably better off pushing the starter for those extra 30 innings, depending on the quality of the bullpen. There is a break-even point between a pitcher's lost innings and his increased effectiveness. Fortunately for major league managers, the innings lopped off the ends of pitchers' totals would occur late in games, with the skipper typically coming out in the seventh, eighth, or ninth inning to bring in a fresh reliever. The manager has the luxury of knowing whether he is in a tight contest or a blowout. Judiciously removing pitchers earlier in games where those extra innings are not high leverage—that is, the game is not close—thus helps keep the staff fresh for when its pitchers really need to bear down.

And then there's the risk of injury—whether or not the pitcher is around to throw those innings we'd like him to pitch. Once again we return to the principle of pitcher fatigue: *Throwing is not dangerous to a pitcher's arm. Throwing while tired is dangerous to a pitcher's arm.*

Just as certain kinds of workloads create a risk of ineffectiveness in the short term, they can also create a higher risk of injury. As another part of the study in *Baseball Prospectus 2001*, we compiled a list of pitchers who had gotten injured as well as healthy pitchers of similar age and total career workload. When we compared the injured pitcher to his healthy counterparts, we found that the injured pitcher tended to have accumulated more PAP over his career. In other words, given two starting pitchers who have thrown a similar number of pitches in their careers, the one who pitched more high-pitch-count games was at greater risk of injury.

We capture this occurrence in a metric called stress, which is simply PAP divided by total pitch count. Stress usually ranges from zero to 100, although a few exceptional cases of stress levels above 100 have happened. To see the relationship between stress and injury, we took all the pitchers analyzed, ranked them in order of stress, and looked at a moving average of the percentage of pitchers who were injured around a given stress level (Fig. 2-3.3).

The trend shows a sharply increased risk of injury as stress levels climb from zero to 30 or so, followed by a tapering off but still largely increasing risk. There are very few pitchers in the region above 80 stress, so an outlier like Livan Hernandez or Randy Johnson can have a distorting effect on the overall results because there are so few comparable pitchers to examine.

FIGURE 2-3.3 Average injury rate as a function of stress of workload (50-point forward averaging)

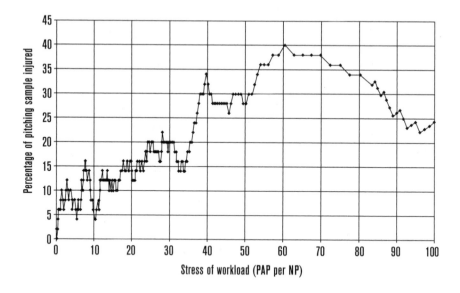

One important lesson from the PAP research is that not all pitchers have the same injury risk. What we're looking at is the aggregate result of pitchers with differing capabilities, physiques, and endurance. Livan Hernandez may be able to throw 130 or more pitches without ill effects, while Pedro Martinez may suffer when asked to go more than 90; this could be due to body type or any number of different factors. PAP and stress give us a general indication of how pitchers, as a group, respond to different workloads. They are a useful baseline from which to work, but they do not directly incorporate additional knowledge about a player's physical capabilities. There's still much research to be done to help us determine each specific pitcher's capacity and threshold. Biomechanical studies by people like Dr. Glenn Fleisig at the American Sports Medicine Institute could one day bridge the gap.

But there are right and wrong ways to protect pitchers' careers. If we accept that high pitch counts increase the risk of pitcher injury, does it not follow that starting on three days' rest is more dangerous than starting on four days' rest?

No, it doesn't. The risk from high pitch counts comes from the pitcher being fatigued. The standard five-man rotation in use today typically gives starting pitchers four days between starts. A generation ago, four-man rotations that gave pitchers three days of rest were more common. One advantage of the four-man rotation is that it gets your best pitchers more starts. As the five-man rotation has taken hold, the starter who gets 36 or more starts has become as rare as a complete game (Table 2-3.4).

In the past twelve years combined, there have been fewer pitchers with 36 starts in a season than in any individual season between 1969 and 1980. Starts that used to go to the number 1, 2, and 3 pitchers are now going to lesser arms. Contrast the distribution of starts between 1974 and 2004 shown in Table 2-3.5.

Compared to thirty years ago, teams in 2004 are giving more starts to swingmen, emergency starters, and failed experiments. Their top three pitchers are accounting for roughly twelve fewer starts today than three decades ago. Twenty-first-century teams have taken 8 percent of the season away from their best arms and given it to replacement-level players.

The original thesis of this chapter was that a fatigued pitcher sometimes loses his mechanics, which in turn causes strain on his arm and creates the risk of injury. Teams can mitigate that risk by ensuring that a pitcher does not spend an undue amount of time pitching while fatigued, and giving him enough rest between outings to fully recuperate. Since we're so concerned with preserving pitchers' health by providing better rest, doesn't it stand to reason that the performance of pitchers on four days of rest would justify the lost innings?

No, it doesn't. There's no medical evidence that four days of rest are better than three for allowing the pitcher's body to recover. Further-

TABLE 2-3.4 Pitchers with 36 or More Starts in a Season, 1969–2004

Year	Pitchers with 36+ Starts
1969	23
1970	23
1971	28
1972	19
1973	31
1974	33
1975	21
1976	18
1977	17
1978	16
1979	14
1980	14
1981	0 (strike year)
1982	12
1983	9
1984	5
1985	13
1986	10
1987	11
1988	4
1989	6
1990	2
1991	4
1992	2
1993	5
1994	0 (strike year)
1995	0 (strike year)
1996	2
1997	0
1998	1
1999	0
2000	0
2001	0
2002	1
2003	2
2004	0

TABLE 2-3.5 Distribution of Starts per Rotation Slot, 1974–2004

| | | | | Totals[a] | | |
Slot	1974	2004	Diff	1974	2004	Diff
1	37.8	33.2	−4.6	37.8	33.2	−4.6
2	36.0	30.9	−5.1	73.8	64.0	−9.7
3	29.9	27.0	−2.9	103.7	91.1	−12.6
4	22.4	23.0	0.7	126.0	114.1	−11.9
5	16.1	18.0	2.0	142.1	132.1	−10.0
6+	20.0	29.7	9.7	162.0	161.8	−0.3

[a]In the row starting with 2 under Totals, for example, the figures given refer to the #1 and #2 starters combined; the row starting with 3 refers to #1, #2, and #3 starters combined, and so on.

more, relief pitchers, even long relievers, don't get four days of rest before they're considered available again.

Since 1972, 175 pitchers have tossed 408 seasons with at least 8 starts on both three and four days of rest. Weighting each pitcher's season (so that pitchers who routinely threw on three days of rest—usually the best pitchers—are not overrepresented) shows that this group actually did *better* in most important categories on three days of rest than on four days of rest:

- Winning percentage was 0.014 higher (.539 vs. .525, a 2.60 percent improvement).
- ERA was 2.4 percent lower, 3.54 versus 3.62.
- RA, which includes unearned runs, was 2.2 percent lower, 3.93 versus 4.01.
- Strikeout rate (−0.44 percent) and walk rate (+0.7 percent) were each slightly worse.
- Home runs per inning was 4.1 percent lower.
- Opposing batters hit .254/.306/.269 against these pitchers on three days of rest; they hit .254/.305/.274 on four days of rest—virtually identical.
- These pitchers threw just as deep into the game (6.90 innings on three days versus 6.86 innings on four days—a tiny difference).

The only category in which there was even as much as a 3 percent difference between the two sets of performances was in home runs per inning—and that was a 4 percent difference in favor of *three* rest days. But rather than trumpet these small differences as proof that pitchers actually perform better on three days' rest, let's simply conclude that there's no evidence to suggest that starting on three days' rest hurt these pitchers' performance.

But perhaps we're focusing on the wrong group of pitchers. We're looking at a group that started a minimum of sixteen times, whose managers asked them to do so at least eight times on three days' rest. Perhaps the pitchers who weren't counted on to start on short rest did noticeably worse. Back to the data.

There have been 879 pitchers who were asked to start between one and eight games on three days' rest while making at least one other start on four days' rest. Comparing their performances on three versus four days of rest (again weighting them to prevent overrepresentation), we do find that such pitchers do slightly worse on three days' rest. Vindication for common wisdom? Hardly. The difference in every category is still less than 3 percent.

- ◆ ERA was 4.47 on three days' rest vs. 4.38 on four days' rest.
- ◆ RA was 4.84 versus 4.70.
- ◆ Hits, walks, strikeouts, and home runs were all less than 2 percent different.
- ◆ Opponents hit .269/.324/.408 on three days of rest versus .267/.321/.406 on four days of rest.

Even pitchers who rarely threw on three days of rest achieved a level of performance very similar to what they achieved when they were given "full" rest.

Another possible objection to the four-man rotation is that pitchers will tire more over the course of a season—that their performance in September will suffer more than their performance in April and May would. This is also false. We looked at all pitchers who started at least 30 games who made more than half their starts on either three days' rest or four days' rest. We then compared how they performed through the entire season until Aug. 31 to how they performed in regular-season games in September and October (Table 2-3.6).

Pitchers in a four-man rotation actually reduced their RA and ERA slightly more than pitchers in a five-man rotation did. For the most part, the differences between the September performances of the two groups are slight. Five-man rotations did better in strikeouts, while four-man rotations were much better in preventing home runs. There's no indication that pitchers suffered disproportionately late in the season when pitching in a four-man rotation.

TABLE 2-3.6 Performance on Three Days' vs. Four Days' Rest in September and October Compared to the Rest of the Season[a]

Rest	RA	ERA	H/IP	BB/IP	SO/IP	HR/IP	AVG	OBP	SLG
3 days	97.8	93.6	100.5	99.3	101.9	98.6	100.2	99.9	98.6
4 days	98.4	101.0	98.9	100.6	105.3	108.0	99.3	100.2	99.4

[a]100 means the same performance as before Aug. 31; numbers above and below 100 mean higher or lower than before Aug. 31.

But wait, you say; you can't expect pitchers who've grown up and pitched all their careers in five-man rotations to suddenly make the switch to a four-man rotation. The changes in their preparation, routines, and demands on their bodies are simply too difficult to accommodate. The truth is that we expect pitchers to make even greater changes every year and rarely give it a second thought. They are frequently taken out of the rotation and moved to the bullpen, or vice versa. Most minor league pitching prospects progress through the system as starters, particularly early in their careers. Even if their organization had projected them as relief pitchers in the majors, the players worked regularly in the starting rotation to ensure a consistent usage pattern.

Starting and relieving have very different requirements. Starters know when they are expected to pitch, and do so until they tire or lose effectiveness. Relievers work in shorter outings but often have only minutes of warning before they are called upon to pitch. They may work several days in a row or be left in the pen for a week or more, but they're still expected to be sharp when needed. Yet pitchers switch roles all the time.

Eric Gagne, Tom Gordon, Miguel Batista, Dave Righetti, Jeff Russell, LaTroy Hawkins, and Tim Wakefield all converted from starter to reliever in a season or less and found success. Derek Lowe, Kelvin Escobar, Bob Stanley, and Billy Swift moved from being closers to pitching in the starting rotation. John Smoltz has done it both ways, converting from a Cy Young–caliber starter to a dominating reliever and then back to a very successful starter a few years later. Pitchers can clearly adapt to much bigger changes in their usage patterns than a four-man rotation would require.

On the other hand, consider what a team can gain by abandoning the five-man rotation. Using some comparisons between the pitcher usage in the early 1970s and the early 2000s to estimate what a four-man rotation would look like, we can make some educated guesses.

- Thirteen starts currently being given to fifth starters or worse are instead made by the top three starters.
- About 10 runs are saved by a combination of the better RA of the top three starters and by the extra innings they pitch, taking innings away from the shallow end of the bullpen.
- The bullpen has to throw fewer innings, reducing the wear and tear on those pitchers who don't have the luxury of a predictable schedule.
- The manager has an extra roster spot to spend as he sees fit. That could be a position player, such as a platoon partner, a defensive replacement, or a pinch-hitting specialist, or an extra pitcher to further spread the work around in the bullpen.

In our scenario, the direct benefits in run prevention and needing fewer bullpen innings amount to about one and a half wins in the standings. The strategic benefit of having an extra roster spot could potentially be as great, but let's be conservative and say that the best use of that roster spot is worth 5 runs, or about another half win. A 20-run or two-game swing obtained solely by better usage of players already on a team is a gigantic advantage—akin to replacing Endy Chavez's bat with Andruw Jones's in 2004.

But with the four-man rotation comes the responsibility to vigilantly monitor pitch counts and fatigue levels. Consider the 1995 Kansas City Royals, perhaps the most recent team to try a four-man rotation for an extended period. Manager Bob Boone stuck with a four-man rotation of Kevin Appier, Mark Gubicza, Tom Gordon, and Chris Haney for most of the first half of the season. The experiment looked successful at first; at the end of June, Appier was a Cy Young candidate with an 11-3 record and a 2.30 ERA. Haney (2.82 ERA), Gubicza (3.38 ERA), and Gordon (4.02 ERA) were also more than respectable.

Then the wheels came off. The best ERA managed by any of the four after July 1, Gubicza's 4.02, equaled the worst any of them had posted prior to that point. Gordon's ERA rose over half a run to 4.66. Haney started only three more games with a bloated 9.22 ERA before being lost for the season. Perhaps most disappointingly for Royals fans, staff ace Appier had a 4-7 record and a 5.79 ERA the rest of the way, including a stint on the disabled list with shoulder tendonitis.

Do pitch counts give us any insight into what happened? Mark Gubicza, the Royals' most consistent starter throughout the year, was also one of the best handled, topping out at a single start of 120 pitches and two of 119, but otherwise routinely throwing 100 to 115 pitches per game. Chris Haney was handled even more carefully, never throwing more than 109 pitches, before succumbing to a herniated disc in his back. He's a good example of how tracking pitch counts, while a useful tool for reducing injuries, cannot completely prevent them.

Tom Gordon was worked considerably harder. He pitched three category-IV starts (significant risk of decline) in the span of a month, starting with a complete game, 1-run effort in 124 pitches on June 16. The stretch culminated in a 131-pitch outing in which Gordon surrendered 4 runs in less than seven innings on July 18. His stress factor (PAP per pitch thrown) for the season as of July 18 was 43, his ERA 3.83. Gordon's ERA from June 16 to July 18 was a solid 3.02—but his stress was a high 65. He put up a 5.11 ERA over the rest of the season.

Appier fared even worse. Beginning on May 13, his pitch counts were 132, 131, 112, 123, 125, 109, 122, 141, and 133. That streak of two category-V and five category-IV starts in a span of nine appearances took its toll. His stress factor for the year after the 133-pitch start was a staggering 145. His ERA stood at 2.20, but it would swell to 5.38 over the rest of the season, despite his throwing 7.1 shutout innings in just 98 pitches in his next start. Following that effort, he managed only one decent start in the next six, including giving up 10 runs in 3.2 innings, 6 runs in 2 innings, and 7 runs in 6 innings before landing on the disabled list with shoulder tendonitis. Appier was kept on a much shorter leash after he returned, topping 115 pitches only once during the rest of the season. But the damage was done. Kevin Appier's 1995 season, and the Royals' season generally, is an example of how *not* to run a four-man rotation. You can run your starters out there every fourth day, but don't expect them to go all nine innings if you want them to thrive for the full season.

The complete game is a relic of another era because we know more about why pitchers get hurt. Throwing while tired is particularly dangerous to a pitcher's arm. We've seen this both by looking at the risk of arm injury and by observing declines in pitcher performance following high-pitch-count games. But this doesn't mean that starting pitchers are doomed to become forever more fragile. By pulling starters more aggressively as their pitch counts and fatigue levels rise, and shifting to a four-man rotation to give them adequate but not excessive rest, we can keep pitchers healthy and effective, see a return of the 275-inning season (which the majors haven't seen since Reagan was in office), and improve teams' roster management as well.

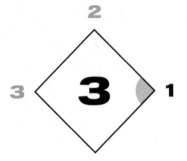

When Does a Pitcher Earn
an Earned Run?

DAYN PERRY

Even a highly experienced scout may find it very difficult to tell if a player is any good. At any given moment, the player may look like Alex Rodriguez and Willie Mays combined, but his true worth is in all his moments, not just one. Unless you have an eidetic memory, even a month's worth of game action gets reduced to a handful of impressions. The statistical record provides a shorthand version of what a player did over that span, which can then be compared to memory.

Even then, it's not always clear which statistic to use. Many people still believe that wins are the measure of a pitcher's effectiveness. Since the Cy Young Award was first given out in 1956, fifty-five of eighty-eight recipients have led their league in wins. Thirty-one of those led *only* in wins, not in earned run average or strikeouts, two other traditional measures of a pitcher's dominance. From this it can be inferred that for many observers, wins carry more information about a pitcher's ability than any other statistic.

Yet a win is credited to a pitcher based on a set of criteria that is indifferent to his actual performance. (See Chapter 2-1 for more on pitching statistics.) If he's a starting pitcher, all a win signifies is that he pitched at least 5 innings and left with a lead that the team preserved. It takes no notice of whether he gave up zero runs or 15.

Won-lost records have more to do with run support, bullpen support, quality of opposition, and blind luck than with pitching excellence. When Hall-of-Famer Nolan Ryan won the National League earned run average title in 1987 but posted an 8-16 record for the season, it was mostly because the Houston Astros lineup couldn't score any runs for him. The Astros averaged only 3.38 runs in games Ryan started (for the entire year, the team averaged 4.0 runs per contest), and in exactly half of his 34 starts they scored 2 or fewer runs. Under such conditions, Ryan could do everything in his power to accumulate wins and still fail.

Earned run average is a better guide than won-lost record, but it too is subject to distortions that lessen its accuracy. First, ERA, which is designed to isolate the pitcher's performance from the defense's performance, absolves the pitcher of responsibility for what occurs after a fielding error, not charging him with runs that result from a misplay by the defense (the "earned" in "earned run average"). In this, ERA does not go far enough, protecting the pitcher's record if a fielder bobbles a ball or has it go through his legs but failing to absolve him for runs that result from the more subtle defensive lapses of fielders who never reach the ball in the first place. The pitcher whose defense bungles the routine play is forgiven, but one who plays on a team with generally poor fielding range is not. After all, an error can't be committed on a ball that the defender doesn't get to.

Moreover, the scoring of errors is highly subjective; what is an error to one official scorer may be a hit to another. And what about those weak pop-ups that fall between two perplexed fielders? According to the way the earned-run rule is interpreted, pitchers are to blame for those too. Baseball Prospectus's Michael Wolverton satirized the twisted logic behind the earned-run rule:

I've done it! I've solved the problem of removing the corrupting influence of fielding on pitchers' runs allowed. We simply pay a sportswriter to sit in the press box, munch Cheetos, and decide which safeties would have been outs with normal fielding effort. Whenever one of these "errors" occurs, we reconstruct the inning—not the game, mind you, just the inning—pretending as if the error never happened. Count up the runs that would have scored in this hypothetical reconstructed inning, and you have a revised run total for the pitcher. Things get a lot more complicated for relievers and team totals, and we'll broaden the "plays that should have been made" definition a little bit, but you get the idea.

ERA sounds plainly ridiculous in those terms. Still, it's the rule we have. Following the 2002 season, venerable lefty Tom Glavine parted ways with the Atlanta Braves and signed a lucrative free agent contract with the New York Mets. At various points in his career, Glavine showed pronounced fly-ball tendencies, and in Atlanta that was to his advantage with a peerless fly-chaser like Andruw Jones behind him. In Queens, however, the center fielders in Glavine's first year included such forgettable names as Jeff Duncan, Tsuyoshi Shinjo, and Raul Gonzalez. In right were lethal doses of Jeromy Burnitz and Roger Cedeño. That was a tremendous drop-off in outfield defense, and Glavine paid for it.

Despite logging peripheral statistics (strikeout rate, home-run rate, walk rate) that weren't out of step with the rest of his career, Glavine put up an ERA of 4.52, his worst such mark since his first full major league season in 1988. Mets center fielders that season actually posted an above-league average fielding percentage, which means they weren't committing an inordinate number of errors. But in fielding range, they simply couldn't compare to the great Andruw Jones. All those balls that Duncan and company didn't reach counted against Glavine's ERA. Many of those would've been tracked down for outs had Glavine still been pitching in Atlanta.

As for the overly forgiving nature of ERA, consider Texas Rangers knuckleballer Charlie Hough, who in 1987 logged a solid ERA of 3.79 while the American League as a whole posted an ERA of 4.46. This would seem to suggest that Hough was a comfortably above-average pitcher that season. In fact, Hough allowed 39 unearned runs, which is the highest single-season unearned run total of the post–World War II era. Hough allowed 5.02 runs per game in 1987, while AL pitchers as a group allowed only 4.90 runs per game. On that basis, Hough was squarely below average.

Crystallizing this divide was Hough's outing against the Detroit Tigers on Aug. 30, 1987, when he worked 7 innings, struck out 6, and allowed no earned runs. Certifiable gem? Not even close. Hough also allowed 7 unearned runs, and the Rangers lost 7-0. Here's how the Tigers' half of the fifth inning went:

- ◆ Tom Brookens hit a foul pop-out to first;
- ◆ Lou Whitaker struck out but reached first on a passed ball;
- ◆ Whitaker stole second and advanced to third on a passed ball;
- ◆ Bill Madlock was hit by a pitch;
- ◆ Darrell Evans grounded to first, scoring Whitaker and moving Madlock to second;

- ◆ Alan Trammell hit a two-run home run; and
- ◆ Matt Nokes grounded out.

None of the 3 runs in the frame were considered earned, including Trammell's long ball. Hough had avoided responsibility for those runs by throwing a couple of passed balls that were deemed to be catcher Geno Petralli's fault. This was overly generous to the pitcher: Knuckleballers deliver an inordinate number of throws that are difficult for the catcher to handle. Whether an individual offering is a wild pitch or a passed ball is often an entirely subjective decision. Regardless of how the official scorer sorts things out, wildness is a native weakness of the knuckleballer, and it's this weakness that makes Hough's disastrous outing look stellar in the box scores.

Run Average, which makes no arbitrary distinctions between "earned" and "unearned" runs, is a far better statistic, and in the absence of more advanced metrics, it should always be used in lieu of ERA. RA avoids many of the pitfalls of ERA, but it still doesn't reliably tell us which runs are the pitcher's fault and which aren't.

To take an analogy from chemistry, runs are more like molecules than atoms. They're compounds made up of singles, doubles, triples, home runs, walks, errors, stolen bases, baserunning, sacrifices, balks, hit batsmen, strikes, balls, fouls into the stands, and so on. To evaluate how a pitcher is doing his job, we need to focus on how well he masters the game at the atomic level.

The statistical community has done an outstanding job of divining the best ways to evaluate offensive performance, but with pitchers in particular and run prevention in general, sorting out who should be credited (or blamed) for each run element has been more difficult. In *Baseball Prospectus 2000*, we wrote that "pitching and defense are so intertwined that they seem impossible to separate." Key word: "seem." A "eureka" moment of sorts came a few years ago when researcher Voros McCracken stumbled upon something that set the baseball world on its ear and is still hotly debated. In a 2001 article that appeared at BaseballProspectus.com, McCracken posited that "there is little if any difference among major-league pitchers in their ability to prevent hits on balls hit in the field of play." In other words, contrary to common sense and decades upon decades of received wisdom, pitchers have exceedingly limited and unpredictable control over the fate of balls once they're in play.

This is, at first, a strongly counterintuitive notion—good pitchers don't allow hits. According to McCracken, this is still true: Good pitchers *don't* allow hits—the defense does. Pitchers exert almost total control over walks, strikeouts, and home runs (with the rare exception involving something like Jose Canseco's coconut), and they mostly hold sway over whether a batted ball is on the ground or in the air. The defense plays a significant (but not absolute) role in almost everything else—runs, earned runs, innings, hits allowed, sacrifice hits, and sacrifice flies.

McCracken began his journey of discovery by focusing on what pitchers themselves could control, and he called his resulting metrics Defense-Independent Pitching Statistics (DIPS). For a very long time, it was assumed that pitchers had a significant degree of influence over whether a batted, non-home-run ball was an out or a hit. McCracken's research indicated that this might not be the case. After all, in a hypothetical world where all defenders have exceptional range, sure-handedness, and flawless positioning, *every* fair ball that stays in the park should be an out. So it's hardly an outrageous proposition to say that defense—or even luck—has a great deal more influence on a pitcher's performance than was previously thought.

McCracken was led to his stunning conclusion by several findings:

- The pitchers who were the best at preventing hits on balls in play one year were often the worst the next year. The incomparable Greg Maddux in 1998 had one of the best batting averages on balls in play (BABIP), but in 1999 he had one of the worst, although many other key indicators remained similar.
- A pitcher's hits per balls in play could more accurately be predicted from the rate of the rest of the pitching staff than from the pitcher's own previous rates.
- The range of career rates of hits per balls in play for pitchers with a significant number of innings was about the same as the range that would be expected from random chance. The vast majority of pitchers with a significant number of career innings have BABIPs between .280 and .290.
- When adjusted for environmental advantages (the designated hitter rule, park effects, league, etc.) the BABIP range became even smaller.

Subsequent research by Baseball Prospectus's Keith Woolner and Clay Davenport and Tom Tippett of Diamond Mind Baseball revealed several problems with McCracken's work:

- The single year's worth of data that McCracken drew on in his initial study wasn't adequate to support his conclusions;

- ◆ Some specialized pitchers—knuckleballers like Tim Wakefield, control artists like Ferguson Jenkins, and soft-tossing lefties like Jamie Moyer—*do* demonstrate a consistent ability to limit hits on balls in play;
- ◆ Major league pitchers are manifestly better at preventing hits on balls in play than minor league pitchers who never made it to the highest level;
- ◆ Inducing infield pop-ups has proved to be a repeatable skill among major league pitchers; and
- ◆ Pitchers do have a great degree of control over whether a ball is hit on the ground or in the air, and those two categories of batted balls vary greatly in how often they go for base hits.

In the final analysis, though, McCracken's general observation still stands, leaving a truth that, retrospectively speaking, should've been obvious from the get-go: It's not that pitchers have *no* control over what becomes of a ball in play but that they have less control in that respect than they do over walks, strikeouts, and home runs.

So what *does* determine the fate of a ball in play? Researchers Erik Allen, Arvin Hsu, and Tango Tiger ran a series of regression analyses, which are computations that predict the average of one random variable based on the measures of other random variables on pitchers with at least 700 balls in play in a given season. They arrived at the following breakdowns on what determines the fate of a batted ball:

Luck	44 percent
Pitcher	28 percent
Defense	17 percent
Park	11 percent

The most powerful determinant is blind luck, followed by the pitcher, and then by defense and the tendencies of the ballpark. While these findings conflict with McCracken's, they still embody a sea change in the way we think about pitchers. When the bat hits the ball, and the ball stays in the park, luck, rather than the pitcher's ability, usually holds sway.

ERA tends to fluctuate fairly significantly from year to year, but DIPS statistics show more consistency. To demonstrate this, let's take a snapshot look at how these measures carry over from year to year. Table 3-1.1 has four sections showing the top-ten 2004 major league rankings for pitcher wins, ERA, RA, and DIPS ERA. In parentheses next to each pitcher's entry are his 2005 wins, ERA, RA, and DIPS ERA, along with his 2005 ranking (provided he logged enough innings to qualify in 2005).

As you can see, only one pitcher with a top-ten ranking in wins in 2004 also finished in the top ten in 2005. Three carry over for ERA, three for RA; but five—exactly half the list—carry over for DIPS ERA. Pitchers tend to perform more consistently in DIPS ERA because it does a better job of isolating their core skills.

This means that by looking at a pitcher's DIPS indicators and by evaluating his home park and the defense, we can come up with a reasonably accurate forecast of his performance. Needless to say, these improved forecasting abilities have value to fans, writers, fantasy players, and executives alike. There's a great deal of inaccuracy in ERA, but much less when a pitcher's performance is viewed through the prism of DIPS. By homing in on what pitchers themselves control and by sensibly evaluating the external factors, we can better predict how they'll fare in successive seasons.

On another level, with DIPS, McCracken was trying to isolate pitching from defense, something of which ERA does a manifestly poor job. His work has

TABLE 3-1.1 Pitching Measures from Year to Year

2004 Pitcher's Rank, Wins (2005 Wins and Rank)

1. Curt Schilling, 21 (8, 101st)
2. Johan Santana, 20 (16, 11th)
4. Roger Clemens, 18 (13, 39th)
4. Bartolo Colon, 18 (21, 2nd)
4. Carl Pavano, 18 (4, 200th)
4. Kenny Rogers, 18 (14, 24th)
4. Jason Schmidt, 18 (12, 54th)
8. Mark Mulder, 17 (16, 11th)
9. Six tied with 16

2004 ERA Rank (2005 ERA and Rank)

1. Jake Peavy, 2.27 (2.88, 8th)
2. Randy Johnson, 2.60 (3.79, 40th)
3. Johan Santana, 2.61 (2.87, 6th)
4. Ben Sheets, 2.70 (3.33, did not qualify)
5. Carlos Zambrano, 2.75 (3.26, 14th)
6. Roger Clemens, 2.98 (1.87, 1st)
6. Oliver Perez, 2.98 (5.85, did not qualify)
8. Carl Pavano, 3.00 (4.77, did not qualify)
9. Jason Schmidt, 3.20 (4.40, 64th)
10. Al Leiter, 3.21 (6.13, did not qualify)

2004 Runs per Game Rank (2005 RA and Rank)

1. Jake Peavy, 2.65 (3.10, 7th)
2. Johan Santana, 2.72 (2.99, 4th)
3. Carlos Zambrano, 3.13 (3.55, 13th)
4. Roger Clemens, 3.19 (2.17, 1st)
5. Randy Johnson, 3.22 (4.07, 35th)
6. Ben Sheets, 3.23 (3.79, did not qualify)
7. Carl Pavano, 3.24 (5.94, did not qualify)
8. Oliver Perez, 3.26 (5.94, did not qualify)
9. Curt Schilling, 3.34 (5.69, did not qualify)
10. Jason Schmidt, 3.36 (4.71, 64th)

2004 DIPS ERA Rank (2005 DIPS ERA and Rank)

1. Randy Johnson, 2.36 (3.78, 8)
2. Ben Sheets, 2.77 (3.71, did not qualify)
3. Johan Santana, 2.95 (2.89, 1)

(continues)

forced us to reevaluate what we think we know about those two elements of run prevention. ERA is a relic and is best treated as such; Run Average is a far superior measure. DIPS is better still. Researchers have continued to dig deeper, developing gauges such as Baseball Prospectus' Support-Neutral statistics (see Chapter 2-1). But despite all the available measures, we still haven't developed an ideal way to analyze a pitcher's actual contribution to his team's success.

TABLE 3-1.1 (continued)

2004 DIPS ERA Rank (2005 DIPS ERA and Rank)

4. Jason Schmidt, 2.99 (3.95, 29)
5. Curt Schilling, 3.16 (4.09, did not qualify)
6. Roger Clemens, 3.21 (3.02, 2)
7. Jake Peavy, 3.25 (3.06, 3)
8. Roy Oswalt, 3.28 (3.33, 8)
9. Jaret Wright, 3.41 (6.74, did not qualify)
10. Oliver Perez, 3.50 (5.80, did not qualify)

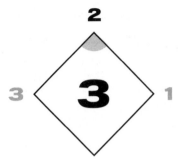

Did Derek Jeter Deserve
the Gold Glove?

JAMES CLICK

There is nothing on earth anybody can do with fielding.
—Branch Rickey

Depending on whom you talk to, Derek Jeter is either among the best defensive players in the game today or one of the worst. Fans, scouts, and commentators lavish praise on the Yankees shortstop for his exciting plays in the field: throws to first while leaping backward into left field, running headlong into the stands to catch a foul pop-up, or his famous flip to Jorge Posada to nab Jeremy Giambi at home plate. Jeter is one of the game's great entertainers, constantly displaying the utmost limits of his effort and talent. But performance analysts, citing various metrics showing that Jeter has often cost the Yankees some 20 runs a year compared with the average shortstop, are less enthralled.

As in many other great baseball debates, the numbers challenge our visual impressions. Which should we believe? Toronto's general manager, J. P. Ricciardi—former assistant GM to Oakland's Billy Beane—summed things up in a Q&A with Baseball Prospectus's Jonah Keri in 2004: "By watching [Jeter] play, I know I want the ball hit to him. Maybe that's the scout part of me. Defense is probably the one area where I disregard the numbers. A lot of people that aren't around the game, that's where the arguments come from. They don't see players play every day. If you don't see that every day, you're not going to get the full picture. Certain guys make plays every day."

Both sides of the argument are problematic. Commonly used defensive statistics—the building blocks of any metric or measure of performance—are terribly and perhaps irrevocably flawed. The mainstream measure of defensive performance—the error—is a judgment call by the game's official scorer, who is guided only by his gut and a vague reference in the rules to "ordinary effort." Most of the time, he is correct. But consider a player who reached third but was given a double instead of a triple because the ball took a bad hop on the fielder. Or a pop-up that lands safely among three players, any one of whom could have called the others off and taken it. In these and countless other situations, the official statistics are not an objective reflection of what's happening on the field. These discrepancies are the primary reason that standard defensive statistics cannot be used to determine quality of defensive performance—the same play on the same field can be seen differently by different scorers depending on their interpretation of the word "ordinary." A home run is a home run, but an error is not always an error.

But throwing out the numbers completely is just as bad. Human memory is one of the worst data-collection devices in the world. In *How We Know What Isn't So*, Thomas Gilovich noted the many problems with human perception and analysis of everyday events. We find nonexistent patterns in random data, extrapolate from too little information, weight events that confirm our preconceptions vastly more than those that disagree with them, and eagerly accept secondhand information as fact. This is not to say that our eyes lie to us all the time, but there are inherent biases when people trust only their eyes.

Watching baseball is no different. You could spend a year watching two shortstops, both of whom fielded the exact same number of balls, threw the same number of guys out, and made the same number of errors. If one did it with flair—diving for balls, charging hard, and barehanding a dribbler—and the other did not, you would almost certainly rate the flashy player as the superior fielder. We all tend to remember special events, such as difficult plays and plays that we didn't expect to be made. But while spectacular effort is a joy to watch, it should not be confused with results.

The first step to evaluating defense is to acquire meaningful information. Just as we cannot use a statistic like errors because it isn't consistently applied to identical situations, we cannot rely on our visual interpretations because they too are inconsistent, weighing identically efficient plays differently based on the apparent difficulty of the fielder's maneuvers.

To a large extent, this means we must throw errors out of the equation when measuring defense. Bill James recognized this when he introduced range factor and defensive efficiency; the former is a measure of how many balls a player fielded per game (using assists and put-outs), and the latter is a measure of the percentage of balls in play a team defense turned into outs. The crucial component to these two metrics is not the performance of the defense once a defender has the ball but rather the act of getting to the ball in the first place. A player cannot make an error on a ball he doesn't reach. In effect, errors are the same as hits as far as the defense is concerned; they are simply balls on which the defense failed to make the play.

Though stats like range factor were advancements over fielding percentage, they still rested on the assumption that, over a season, most players at similar positions had the same number of fielding opportunities. Anyone who's watched Carl Yastrzemski, Manny Ramirez, or any other left fielders in Fenway knows that that's not the case. To correct for these inequalities—no one really expected Yaz to scale the Green Monster to field balls that would be easy outs in any other park—several new fielding metrics have been created to better estimate the number of chances presented to each fielder.

At Baseball Prospectus, Clay Davenport's Fielding Runs (FR) uses five adjustments to each fielder's situation to better estimate his total chances: park factor, total balls in play allowed, groundball/flyball tendencies, pitcher handedness, and men on base. By adjusting each fielder's total chances, FR avoids punishing players like Yastrzemski or Ramirez for failing to scale the wall or shortstops for working with high-strikeout pitching staffs who don't give them as many chances. Individual defensive performance can then be converted into estimated runs saved or lost by each fielder. FR provides a handy way to compare historical player performance, particularly for players who played before play-by-play data were available.

For the first eight seasons of his career, Jeter did not do well when measured by FR. Table 3-2.1 shows his defensive stats. A "Rate" of 100 represents an average shortstop. Jeter's Rate of 88 in his rookie season means he cost the Yankees 12 percent more runs per 100 games than an average shortstop would. FRAA is Fielding Runs Above Average, and FRAR is Fielding Runs Above

Replacement. These stats measure the total runs a player was worth over the season compared to either an average fielder (FRAA) or a theoretical replacement-level fielder—a waiver acquisition or a Triple-A player (FRAR). In 1996, Jeter was 18 runs worse than the average shortstop but 14 runs better than a replacement-level shortstop. His major league rank in Rate among all shortstops who played at least 81 games at the position is listed in the final column.

TABLE 3-2.1 Derek Jeter Defensive Stats, 1996–2004

Year	Rate	FRAA	FRAR	Rank
1996	88	−18	14	23 of 26
1997	89	−17	15	24 of 26
1998	95	−7	23	19 of 29
1999	90	−15	17	20 of 24
2000	88	−17	12	26 of 28
2001	85	−22	8	24 of 26
2002	89	−17	14	26 of 28
2003	80	−23	1	25 of 26
2004	98	−3	27	13 of 26
2005	104	6	37	9 of 27

By these measures, Jeter performed well below the average major league shortstop from 1996 through 2004, costing the Yankees a total of 140 runs, or about 1.5 games per season. He did arrest that trend in 2005, adding 6 runs to the Yankees' ledger with his glove.

But 2005 aside, the reason Jeter has hurt his team defensively is that he doesn't get to many balls and is not spectacularly efficient with those he does get to. There was even a popular joke that new fans initially thought Jeter's first name was "Pastadiving" since the phrase "Past a diving Jeter" was uttered so often during broadcasts. He's consistently near the bottom of the league in chances, put-outs, and assists. Many of his flashy plays would be routine for a better defensive shortstop like Miguel Tejada or Rafael Furcal.

When Jeter won the Gold Glove in 2004, he posted the best defensive numbers of his career to that point, jumping from a Rate of 80 to 98 and from 23 runs below average to 3. He still didn't deserve the Gold Glove—the Orioles' Tejada posted the league's best fielding numbers—but he showed an impressive jump from his established career levels. Searching for the reasons for this remarkable turnaround, Clay Davenport could find no single change that clearly explained it. Instead, Jeter's numbers—put-outs, assists, double plays, all relative to chances and league average—were up across the board, vaulting him from objectively terrible to merely below average.

How unprecedented was this sudden jump in defensive performance? At first it does not look like such a great leap. Since 1901, there have been 180 instances, about two per year, of a regular shortstop improving his Rate by 18 or more runs from one season to the next.

But Jeter's improvement was not a correction for a bad year; by 2004, he had had eight years to establish himself as one of the game's worst defensive shortstops. The list of shortstops with at least eight years in the majors who improved on their established career Rate by more than 10 runs amounts to just eleven men, shown in Table 3-2.2.

TABLE 3-2.2 Sudden Defensive Improvements at Shortstop

Player	Year	Rate	Established	Jump
Derek Jeter	2004	98	88.0	10.0
Greg Gagne	1996	114	101.4	12.6
Greg Gagne	1993	109	98.9	10.1
Dick Schofield	1992	113	101.4	11.6
Bert Campaneris	1977	115	104.3	10.7
Bert Campaneris	1973	120	102.4	17.6
Dick Groat	1963	117	103.7	13.3
Rabbit Maranville	1928	118	107.3	10.7
Dave Bancroft	1925	118	104.6	13.4
Roger Peckinpaugh	1924	121	103.5	17.5
George McBride	1916	119	106.7	12.3
Honus Wagner	1912	120	107.4	12.6
Monte Cross	1903	107	95.3	11.7

The difference between Jeter and the others is that nearly all of the other ten were above-average fielders. Greg Gagne in 1993 and Monte Cross in 1903 were the only ones with below-average numbers before their jump. No shortstop as bad as Jeter had a career year with the glove like he did in 2004. Only Johnnie LeMaster in 1984 and Pat Meares in 2000 were even close. Jeter improved his defense even more in 2005, recording the first above-average season in his ten-year career.

So how did a thirty-year-old shortstop with a long track record of terrible defense suddenly post consecutive seasons of roughly league-average defense? One answer is that Jeter isn't the best shortstop on his own team. When the Yankees acquired Alex Rodriguez before the 2004 season, they launched a debate about who should play shortstop. Should it be the incumbent, the Yankee captain and beloved super-star? Or should it be the two-time Gold Glove winner and reigning AL MVP? Rodriguez held all the hardware, but he settled the debate almost before it began. The Yankees were Jeter's team, he said, and he volunteered to move to third base. But was this the best decision for the Yankees?

In the spring of 2004, Joe Sheehan of Baseball Prospectus advocated moving Jeter to center field, where his athleticism would mitigate his flaws—"slow reaction time and poor footwork." Incumbent center fielder Bernie Williams had been deteriorating defensively for a few seasons—things got so bad the next spring that the Yankees briefly moved second baseman Tony Womack to left and Hideki Matsui to center—and with Rodriguez on the scene, the move appeared to make sense. This idea, as well as others floated during the brief public debate, revolved around Bill James's idea of a defensive spectrum. In its original version, moving from left to right in order of increasing difficulty, the spectrum looked like this:

1B—LF—RF—3B—CF—2B—SS—C

James determined the spectrum both from observation and from the tendencies of players to change positions later in their careers as their defense eroded. The Astros' Craig Biggio is a good example: He originally came up as a catcher, then moved to second and then outfield after the Astros signed Jeff Kent. Likewise, the Cardinals' Albert Pujols moved from left to first when he was hampered by injuries. The Orioles' Cal Ripken Jr. shifted from short to third late in his career (after going the opposite way in his rookie season). Pete Rose regressed from second to third to first. Many prospects start out at shortstop but move to other positions as they advance up the organizational ladder.

Though it's a handy guide to the relative difficulty of defensive positions, the spectrum does not estimate how a player would perform defensively if moved to another spot on the diamond. Players who saw significant time at more than one position in a single season can give an idea of how well any player would do at a different defensive position. This method will likely downplay the difference between positions because teams will use only versatile defensive players at more than one position. The method doesn't consider any hypothetical performances—we don't know how Willie Mays would have worked out at shortstop or Johnny Bench in center—but players who did play multiple positions in one season give us an idea of what we could expect of others making similar transitions.

The Orioles have bounced Melvin Mora all over the diamond. In 2002, he played at least ten games in left field, in center field, and at shortstop, where he posted Rates of 110, 108, and 99, respectively. These numbers fit with the defensive spectrum: Mora was better in left than in center and better in center than at short. In 2003, he played left, right, and short, with Rates of 111, 92, and 90. These numbers again slide down James's defensive spectrum as expected. The difference between left field and right field is larger than anticipated, but there are bound to be a few fluky seasons here and there, especially when dealing with small sample sizes.

The results of comparing the various performances can be found in Table 3-2.3. (Catchers have been excluded, as catching is distinctly different from the other positions.)

TABLE 3-2.3 Comparative Defensive Performances

		From Position						
		1B	LF	RF	3B	CF	2B	SS
To Position	1B	0.0						
	LF	-0.1	0.0					
	RF	0.6	-0.4	0.0				
	3B	-1.7	-2.4	-4.5	0.0			
	CF	0.8	-0.6	-0.2	4.4	0.0		
	2B	-1.5	-1.5	-3.7	-1.1	-1.8	0.0	
	SS	-3.2	-4.8	-6.0	-1.9	-4.6	-1.6	0.0

The vertical columns are the position from which the player moved, and the horizontal rows are the new position. The numbers show change, in runs per year, in going from the old position to the new. For example, a player moving from left field, the second column, to third, the fourth row, would be estimated to be 2.4 runs worse at third than he was in left. (The reverse transition—moving from third to left—is not shown because it is simply the negative of the displayed value: in this case, the player would be approximately 2.4 runs better in left.) While many positions fit our preconceptions—players moving from shortstop perform better at any other position—there are some inconsistencies with James's original theory and within the chart itself. For example, players moving from left field perform slightly worse if they move to right field (−0.4) but slightly better if they move to first (0.1, the inverse of moving from first to left). But players moving from first to right perform better in right (0.6), seemingly indicating that if a player were to move from left to first to right, he would do better than if he simply moved from left to right. This is nonsense, but it shows that players who have played both first base and a corner outfield position have not performed consistently better at either position.

There is one correction to James's original scale: Third and center should be switched. Players who played both third and center were 4.4

runs better in center than at third, one of the largest differences on the chart. Other than that, the spectrum falls into place as James originally drew it up.

Using Table 3-2.3, teams could begin to break free of the constraints of positional thinking. If a team needs a new right fielder, its managers don't have to search their farm system or the free-agent market for players with experience playing right field. Instead, teams can speculate how many runs various players already on their team would gain or cost them if moved to right field. Suddenly, the number of available options increases dramatically. If a team needs an outfielder, but there are only infielders available on the free-agent market, it could sign one of the quality infielders and train an incumbent to play outfield. Using the defensive spectrum, the team would be able to better project the costs and benefits of that move as compared to signing a poorer-quality player with outfield experience.

Getting back to the Yankees in spring 2004, it's possible to estimate their ideal defensive alignment. From 2001 to 2003, Jeter averaged a Rate of 85, Rodriguez 102, and Williams 95. With Rodriguez at third, we estimate he would gain 1.9 FR, raising his Rate to about 104; the three positions would average a Rate of 94.7. Moving Jeter to center would raise his Rate to about 90 (85 + 4.6), with Rodriguez playing shortstop at 102 and Williams at DH. Then, if the Yankees could find a third baseman with a Rate of 92 or better, they would come out ahead. From 2001 to 2003, twenty-six players totaled 92 or better at third in at least a full season of playing time. Based on information available at the time, moving Jeter to center and bringing in a defender like Ty Wigginton (99.5 Rate), Vinny Castilla (97.5), or Shea Hillenbrand (97.5) would have saved 5 to 7 more runs than moving Rodriguez to third—roughly 1 in the standings, if things broke right.

While the Yanks would likely have benefited slightly from moving Jeter to center, his sudden defensive improvement made the argument null. Could they have known he would improve? Did they think the presence of a great fielder like Rodriguez to Jeter's right would allow the shortstop to field a few more grounders up the middle? Considering Jeter's continued improvement in the 2005 season, it seems like a plausible theory. But as Table 3-2.4 shows, Rodriguez does not appear to be significantly better at third than Jeter's previous partners there.

Rodriguez's Rates of 102 and 95 in 2004 and 2005, respectively, were significantly worse than the combination of Robin Ventura and Aaron Boone in 2003 and than Scott Brosius's four years of quality defense from 1998 to 2001. Expanding to other teams, there is no correlation between changes in the performance of third basemen and shortstops.

TABLE 3-2.4 Primary Yankees Third Basemen, 1996–2004

Player	Year	Games	Rate	FRAR	FRAA
Wade Boggs	1996	115.4	100	14	0
Charlie Hayes	1997	89.0	96	8	-3
Wade Boggs	1997	67.4	103	11	2
Scott Brosius	1998	146.0	108	31	12
Scott Brosius	1999	129.5	110	30	13
Scott Brosius	2000	130.0	111	31	15
Scott Brosius	2001	119.4	102	18	2
Robin Ventura	2002	125.2	100	16	0
Robin Ventura	2003	74.3	106	14	5
Aaron Boone	2003	51.5	107	10	4
Alex Rodriguez	2004	153.1	102	23	3
Alex Rodriguez	2005	156.8	95	12	-8

A new third baseman on a team doesn't have a predictable effect on the performance of the incumbent shortstop. There is no evidence that Rodriguez's presence caused Jeter's defensive improvement.

These issues raise one final aspect of measuring defense in baseball: the interaction between teammates. Fielding, unlike hitting, is inherently a team activity. The nine players ideally act as one unit. While defense primarily involves the range of the individual fielders, it also involves their choices once they've reached the ball. The combination of skill and choice could cause FR to give too much credit to a player like Jeter and too little to Rodriguez if the two fielders have chosen to let Jeter field many balls that either man could field equally well. If this is the case, FR—or any defensive metric—may be misinterpreting this choice as a change in the skill of one or both. From the perspective of the players, the end result—an out—is the same, but from the perspective of individual defensive statistics, the end result is different.

All available individual defensive statistics have problems. Understanding what those problems are allows us to use the available information as best we can without overstating our conclusions. In the case of Derek Jeter's radical improvement as measured by FR, it's possible that FR is overlooking a choice in the Yankees infield, but it's also possible that Jeter simply had a great year or two with the glove. Or perhaps A-Rod has helped him work on his technique. Regardless of the reason, Jeter's transformation is no illusion; he vaulted from the depths of the shortstop position to become a league-average defender in 2004 and 2005. Did he deserve the Gold Glove? Not according to the numbers. But he deserves credit for a drastic improvement in his defensive performance.

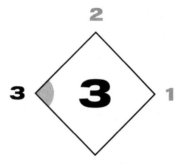

Is Mike Matheny
a Catching Genius?

KEITH WOOLNER

On December 13, 2004, the San Francisco Giants signed catcher Mike Matheny to a three-year, $9 million contract. What made this signing so remarkable was that the Giants already had a good catcher on their roster in A. J. Pierzynski. Pierzynski was younger, a better hitter in 2004, and a better hitter over his career. In fact, Pierzynski's worst seasons in batting average, on-base percentage, and slugging average were as good as Matheny's best. Pierzynski already had a year of experience working with the Giants' pitchers. He was arbitration-eligible, meaning the Giants could have ensured his return for at least a season by offering him salary arbitration. Since a player rarely gets full market value through salary arbitration, the Giants could have secured their 2005 catcher at a better price than if they had ventured into the free-agent market.

Yet the Giants signed Matheny anyway because there were other considerations besides money, or even hitting. As Mike Bauman put it on MLB.com, Pierzynski "was not, to put it mildly, a particular favorite of the pitching staff." Putting it less mildly, the Giants had a rebellion on their hands.

The pitchers were convinced that they could not work with Pierzynski behind the plate. Now, the Giants staff was not exactly Tom Seaver, Juan Marichal, and Bob Gibson, and no catcher in the world would have made them so. But the team did the expedient thing and chose to believe them. The Giants' decision to swap Pierzynski for Matheny starkly illustrates the belief that catchers make an immense defensive contribution. Though personality issues played a role, the team essentially chose Matheny's defense over Pierzynski's offense.

A catcher can influence a pitcher's performance in at least ten ways:

1. He can study the opposing batters and call for the right pitches in the right sequence.
2. He can use his glove and body to frame incoming pitches to subtly influence the umpire to call more strikes.
3. He can be attuned to what a pitcher wants to throw, or what pitches he is throwing well, and keep his pitcher comfortable.
4. He can control the tempo of the game, calling pitches quickly when a pitcher is in a groove or slowing things down by heading out to the mound for a quick meeting.
5. He can monitor a pitcher's emotional state and use leadership and psychological skills to help a pitcher maintain his focus.
6. He can be skilled at blocking balls in the dirt so that the pitcher is not afraid to throw a low pitch with runners on base.
7. He can watch for signs of fatigue and work with the manager to decide to make a pitching change before the game gets out of hand.
8. He can engage in conversation or actions to distract the batter while staying within the rules of the game. A distracted batter is less likely to get a hit.
9. He can remain aware of the game situation and call for an unexpected pitch for the situation, gaining the element of surprise.
10. He can prevent opposing baserunners from stealing, either by throwing them out or keeping them from trying to steal at all.

This last item is the most obvious and therefore most celebrated aspect of the catcher's job. A major factor in a catcher's defensive reputation is how he controls base-stealing. Ivan Rodriguez would be legendary for his ability to throw runners out from his knees even if he called the worst game in the business. However, catchers have another major responsibility besides controlling the running game, and that is working with pitchers. The first nine items on the list all have to do with the catcher's handling of the pitcher. It is here that the subtler, more powerful influences of a veteran catcher are said to appear.

Ultimately, these influences should show up as pitchers' being more effective. They should give up fewer hits, walks, and runs when working with a good "game caller" and more if paired with a poor one. One of the first attempts to prove this theory statistically came in the book by Craig Wright and Tom House, *The Diamond Appraised*. Wright looked at a catcher's ERA (CERA)—that is, the ERA allowed by pitchers when that catcher was in the game—and compared catchers on the same team to determine whether each one was good or bad at handling pitchers. He was careful to take into account the fact that some pitchers have personal catchers, and thus some catchers get to work with better pitchers more often.

Wright concluded that there were significant differences in catcher game-calling ability, and that those differences were reflected in their CERAs. Good defensive catchers posted significantly better CERAs than their teammates. Wright cited six-time Gold Glove winner Jim Sundberg as being overrated defensively because his CERA was regularly worse than any other Rangers catcher. Gino Petralli was singled out as one of the worst catchers by CERA, largely because of his mechanical flaws in receiving pitches. The best catcher by CERA, according to Wright, was Doug "Eyechart" Gwosdz, who posted spectacular CERAs backing up Terry Kennedy with the Padres in the early 1980s. Catcher ERA became a fairly well-accepted, if esoteric, statistic by which to measure catcher game-calling.

But Wright's findings were flawed. The results cited were based on limited, anecdotal evidence. Wright had not presented a comprehensive analysis that showed that CERA had any predictive value or measured any intrinsic skill of a catcher. In fact, the differences among catchers appear to be random and don't appear to correlate with any actual defensive ability. In *Baseball Prospectus 1999*, a study looked at every qualifying pitcher-catcher battery over a seventeen-year span and compared how the pitcher did with the given catcher, versus all other catchers on the team. Diving even deeper than just analyzing runs given up, the study looked at every plate appearance, examining the specific number of hits, walks, and extra-base hits given up. This is akin to looking at a pitcher's batting average, on-base percentage, and slugging average allowed and seeing if they varied according to who was catching at the time.

They did vary, but randomly. There was no trend of catchers who performed well in one year performing well again the next year. Contrast this with what we see with batters hitting home runs, or pitchers getting strikeouts. Good home-run hitters like Adam Dunn or Albert

Pujols generally remain good from year to year. That didn't happen with the catchers' opposing batter statistics. Catchers who posted excellent game-calling results one year were just as likely to be at the bottom of the pile the following year as the worst catchers. It's akin to saying that Johan Santana and Kirk Rueter were each equally likely to lead the league in strikeouts. This lack of consistency, and the fact that the results for all catchers closely matched what we'd expect if the game-calling was perfectly random in effect, suggested there is no such thing as game-calling skill, or at the very least that it was eluding detection.

Several follow-up studies were done, both at Baseball Prospectus and elsewhere, in an effort to find proof that some catchers have a portable pitcher-handling skill—that some, by their mere presence, improve a pitching staff. No statistical evidence for a significant pitcher-handling or game-calling ability—such as would reduce the number of runs the opposition puts on the scoreboard—has been found.

But what about other possible effects? Do some catchers improve their pitcher's efficiency, helping him get through more batters with the same number of pitches, or get more borderline strike calls, thus giving the pitcher the advantage of favorable counts? In the Baseball Prospectus database, we identified 3,361 instances where a pitcher worked with two different catchers for at least 100 plate appearances on the same team in the same season. Table 3-3.1 shows some examples.

Our analysis showed that catchers did not show any consistent ability to influence average pitches per batter. In looking for year-to-year trends, we found that there was at best the faintest relationship between catcher performance in consecutive years. When Mike Lieberthal worked with Robert Person, for example, Person averaged more than half a pitch more per batter than when he was throwing to Gary Bennett, as

TABLE 3-3.1 Examples of Pitcher-Catcher Combinations, 2000

Year	Team	Pitcher	Catcher 1	PA1	AVG_PITCH1	SD_PITCH1	Catcher 2	PA2	AVG_PITCH2	SD_PITCH2
2000	ANA	Kent Bottenfield	Ben Molina	221	3.855	1.803	Matt Walbeck	350	3.911	1.868
2000	PHI	Robert Person	Mike Lieberthal	502	4.255	1.999	Gary Bennett	164	3.744	1.872

Notes: PAn = number of plate appearances (batters faced) by the pitcher with catcher n
AVG_PITCHn = average number of pitches per plate appearance with catcher n
SD_PITCHn = standard deviation of pitches per plate appearance with catcher n

shown in Table 3-3.1. But the very next year, their positions were reversed, with Person throwing 0.15 more pitches per batter with Bennett catching than with Lieberthal.

One surprise was that the range of results within a season was much wider than would be expected by chance. If you look at enough pairs of catchers, you'd expect some big differences through random luck alone. But there were more pairs of catchers with big differences than the math tells us there should be. Is this an indication of some true ability? Or are there other factors at work? We will come back to this question later in the chapter.

There are some other places we can look for a catcher's defensive ability. A catcher who frames pitches well should get more borderline calls. A higher percentage of pitches that are taken should be called strikes for a good framing catcher. Once again, nothing indicating any "framing" ability shows up.

Another way a catcher might help a pitcher is with his location within the strike zone. If pitches are spotted better, batters should have a harder time putting them into play. Can a catcher help a pitcher make batters swing and miss? Yet again, nothing in the statistical record supports the idea of this being an actual catcher ability. We did, once again, observe an unusually large range of performances between pairs of catchers. Though there was no year-to-year consistency, there were more extreme differences between some catchers than would be expected if everything was left to chance.

One of the simplifying assumptions we made in our analyses is that the mix of batters seen by each catcher is more or less the same. But this is not necessarily so. Because pitchers, particularly starting pitchers, play in relatively few games compared to everyday players, the mix of opposing teams that they face is more variable. A pitcher may get 30 starts; one catcher may have caught 10 of the starts and the other 20. The starting lineups in each of those 10 starts will probably get three to five plate appearances in each game. The opposing batters in those 10 games are thus overrepresented in that catcher's sample. If a handful of those opponents are free-swinging teams, it will artificially drive up the differences between catchers, not because the catchers themselves are skillfully making them miss but by the luck of the draw and the repetitive nature of how plate appearances are distributed in a game.

This factor affects all of the studies that rely on comparing two catchers working with one pitcher. The small number of games any starting pitcher appears in, compounded by dividing that number across two catchers and then facing the same nine opposing batters for most of the game, creates more variability in batter characteristics than our simple model of more or less league-average opposing batters can accommodate.

We've considered four possible ways that good game-calling catchers might distinguish themselves from poor ones in the statistical record. For each of them, we'll check how Mike Matheny, whose defensive exploits formed the basis for this chapter, measures up. There are three instances where a pitcher worked with Matheny and another catcher for at least 100 batters in two consecutive years. In 1996–1997, Matheny and Jesse Levis caught both Mike Fetters and Scott Karl. In 2000 and 2001, Matheny and Eli Marrero both worked with Andy Benes.

1. Good game-callers would help pitchers allow fewer hits, walks, and extra-base hits, and thus fewer runs than poor ones. This does not seem to be the case. A. J. Pierzynski might not have been his pitchers' best friend, but neither should he shoulder the blame for less-than-stellar pitching. As for Matheny, his battery-mate Mike Fetters was better at preventing runs with Jesse Levis in 1996 but better with Matheny in 1997. Scott Karl posted better performances with Matheny in 1997 but virtually identical performances with Matheny and Levis the year before. Andy Benes pitched slightly better with Matheny than with Eli Marrero catching him in 2000 but substantially better with Matheny behind the dish in 2001.

2. Catchers who read their pitchers well might help pitchers be more efficient, lowering the average number of pitches needed per batter. The research showed a wider-than-expected variation between catchers but no consistent effect from year to year, and the wider variation can be explained by imperfect assumptions about the characteristics of opposing batters. Matheny was better than Levis when working with Karl in both 1996 and 1997. He merely equaled Levis's performance when working with Fetters in 1996 and fared worse than Levis in 1997. When Benes pitched to both Matheny and Marrero in 2000 and 2001, he fared better with Marrero than with Matheny.

3. Catchers who frame pitches well might get more strike calls from the umpire by framing borderline pitches. Again, we see no evidence that certain catchers produce more called strikes than others. Matheny was worse than Marrero in called strike percentage

in both 2000 and 2001 with Benes. He was better than Levis in 1996–1997 with Karl but worse than Levis with Fetters in the same two years.

4. Some catchers might help with a pitcher's location, inducing more missed or fouled pitches when the batter swings. Though the variation between catcher pairs was larger than expected, no discernible year-to-year trend distinguished itself for catchers. Matheny and Levis were comparable working with Fetters in 1996. Matheny was better in 1997, but Levis posted better numbers than Matheny in both years when working with Karl. Matheny was better than Marrero with Benes in 2000, but Marrero was better in 2001.

One of the most controversial results from the sabermetric community is the lack of evidence supporting big differences in catcher defensive ability, other than differences in controlling the running games. Professionals within the game insist that catchers make a gigantic difference and that the question is simply beyond the capability of statistics to find. However, the further we look into catcher performance, the fewer places the elusive realm of catcher influence has to hide. There is no objective evidence that the catchers considered to be the best at their craft actually improve pitcher efficiency, increase strike rates, induce more misses and fouls, or do anything else to reduce batters' offensive output. If the professionals are right and the best game-callers are having some effect that statistics can't measure, we still have to ask how much offensive production a team could responsibly give up to obtain such an undetectable improvement.

Quotations on Catcher Duties Through the Years

Brawn and Brain, A. J. Bushong, catcher, Brooklyn Baseball Club, compiled by Arthur F. Aldridge (John B. Alden Publishers, 1889).

"No position to my mind is so high or so powerful as that of catcher."

"It is a good point or an advantage, for the pitcher is thus relieved somewhat of a share of the responsibility if a ball that is asked for is hit. He consoles himself with the thought that it wasn't all his fault, and so can perhaps do his work better."

"Each then understands the other in a variety of ways, knows his weak and strong points, and in the end must work together successfully."

Baseball, the Fans' Game, Mickey Cochrane (New York: Funk and Wagnalls, 1939).

"One of the major requirements of a catcher is to install confidence in the pitchers he is receiving. They must have absolute faith in his judgment and his ability to catch every pitch" (p. 40).

"Pitchers are funny persons and must be cajoled, badgered, and conned along like babies, big bad wolves, or little sisters with injured feelings."

"A catcher who asks a pitcher if he needs help must have some doubts. . . . He gets to know the speeds of a pitcher's stuff better than the pitcher himself."

Baseball: How to Become a Player, John Montgomery Ward (Cleveland, OH: SABR, 1993; reprint of The Athletic Publishing Company, 1888).

"There are some cases in which a steady intelligent catcher is of more worth to a team than even the pitcher, because such a man will make pitchers of almost any kind of material."

Baseball: Individual Play and Team Strategy, John W. (Jack) Coombs, baseball coach, Duke University (New York: Prentice-Hall, 1945).

"I consider it very important for the catcher to warm up the pitcher who has been selected for the game. . . . So doing gives the catcher an opportunity to judge properly the speed, the curve, and the control which the pitcher has on any kind of ball that he might pitch."

New Thinking Fan's Guide to Baseball, rev. ed., Leonard Koppett (Toronto: SportClassic Books, 2004).

"Then there is the matter of 'handling the pitcher.' This has nothing to do with fielding skill, but with psychology, rapport, intelligent calling of pitches, pacing, even personality. It's important, but it's largely subjective."

"Joe Garagiola . . . stresses the inanity of some pseudo-expert reactions. Talk that a catcher 'called a great game' is just as silly as blaming 'a bad call' for the home run that was hit. The pitcher is doing the throwing and the responsibility is his. Great pitchers make brilliant catchers, and poor pitchers make dumb ones."

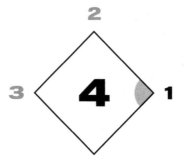

What if Rickey Henderson Had Pete Incaviglia's Legs?

JAMES CLICK

In the early 1980s, Oakland A's leadoff man Rickey Henderson would often start the game with a walk or single, quickly steal second, steal third, and then score on a hit or sacrifice fly before the home team's fans could grab a dog and a beer and find their seats. Henderson wreaked so much havoc on the basepaths that A's radio man Bill King, needing a name for his frequent romps around the diamond, coined the term "Rickey Runs." In a twenty-five-year major league career, Henderson swiped 1,406 bases, 468 more than the second-place man, Lou Brock. His 130 steals in 1982 alone launched the stolen base back into baseball's consciousness.

On the other end of the spectrum was Pete Incaviglia, who over the course of his career reduced baseball to a simple game between pitcher and batter. More often than those of nearly any other player of his era, his at-bats ended either in a whiff or a slow trot around the bases, leaving defense completely out of the equation. But Incaviglia—a power prospect so highly touted that he skipped the minor leagues entirely— never hit 30 home runs after his rookie season. Given his good but not great power, everyone focused on his terrible defense and high strike-out rates. John Kruk said, "I'm not an athlete, I'm a ballplayer," but Incaviglia embodied the idea. A Rickey Henderson he wasn't.

There was no greater honor in the 1980s than membership in the "30-30 Club": players who stole at least 30 bases and hit at least 30 home runs in the same season. In the 1980s, unlike now, power wasn't enough—you had to have speed to be among the game's elite. As offense increased through the 1990s, the stolen base fell out of vogue. One additional base was no longer worth the risk of an additional out. After all, if the next batter hit a home run—as, it seemed, nearly everyone could by the late '90s—it didn't matter if the baserunner was on first, second, or third. Teams quickly grew to understand a concept that had been espoused by many of baseball's original statistical researchers: It didn't matter how many bases you stole but how good you were at it.

In his record-setting 1982 season, Henderson was caught stealing 42 times, a success rate of 76 percent. Nearly a quarter of the time when he made a break for it, he left the A's in a worse situation. John Thorn and Pete Palmer addressed this issue in their seminal book *The Hidden Game of Baseball,* using what would later be called a "Run Expectation Table." Digging back through play-by-play data from 1961 to 1977, they calculated the number of runs an average team scored in the remainder of an inning after a given baserunner-out situation. For example, with a man on first and no one out, teams scored an average of .783 runs in the rest of the inning; with a runner on second and no one out, 1.068; with no one on and one out, .249. By looking at all situations like these where teams typically attempted a stolen base, Thorn and Palmer showed that no matter how many bases players stole, if they were successful less than 63 percent of the time, they were costing their team runs.

The run-expectation tables from 1982 show that Henderson added an extra 22.2 runs to the A's offense with his 130 steals. But the 42 times he was caught cost the team 20.6 runs, meaning that for all that running, the A's gained a total of 1.6 runs for the season. In his first season, Incaviglia stole three bases and was caught twice. He cost his team about half a run. Because Henderson got caught so often, the difference between his base-stealing performance in 1982 and Incaviglia's in 1986 added up to about 2 runs.

How is this possible? If Henderson was stealing bases at a record-setting pace, with a 76 percent success rate in an era when the break-even rate was only 63 percent, why was he contributing only an extra 2 runs on the season? The 63 percent break-even point was calculated based on the offensive numbers from 1961 to 1977, but the 1960s were one of baseball's lowest-scoring eras. The 1990s and 2000s have seen some of the highest run-scoring totals of all time. Typically, as the run-scoring environment increases, the value of the stolen base declines, the cost of being caught rises, and thus the break-even point for stolen base success rises.

In Figure 4-1.1—the average break-even rates for stealing second base from 1982 to 2004—you can see that, despite odd spikes in 1982 and 1985, the break-even point rose steadily for much of this period, peaking around 78 percent in 2000. It has since come down a bit, to around 73 percent—still a much higher figure than in the 1960s and 1970s.

FIGURE 4-1.1 SB break-even rate, 1982–2004

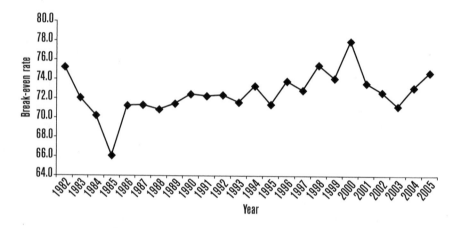

Along with the break-even rate, the value of the stolen base changes depending on the offensive levels, both of the season and of the individual team and ballpark. A general valuation of stolen bases can be derived from the same expected-runs table used to determine the break-even rate (see Table 4-1.1).

In 2004, teams with a runner on first and no one out averaged .9259 runs over the rest of the inning. (Compare that to the .783 used by Palmer and Thorn in their study and you can see how radically the offensive environment has changed.) A runner on second with no one out yielded

TABLE 4-1.1 Expected Runs, 2004

	No Outs	1 Out	2 Outs
Empty	0.5379	0.2866	0.1135
1st	0.9259	0.5496	0.2460
2nd	1.1596	0.7104	0.3359
1st & 2nd	1.4669	0.9577	0.4605
3rd	1.4535	0.9722	0.3623
1st & 3rd	1.8540	1.2236	0.5219
2nd & 3rd	2.1343	1.4717	0.6179
Loaded	2.2548	1.5946	0.8082

1.1596 runs, a gain of .2337. The gain decreases as outs increase—a successful steal of second with two outs nets only .0899 runs—and the cost of getting caught stealing can be extremely high, depending on the situation. For example, a runner caught attempting to steal second with two outs costs his team the .2460 runs they would have been expected to score in the rest of the inning. But a runner caught trying to steal third with no one out costs his team .8730 runs, more than three times as much.

Weighting the situations in which bases were stolen in 2004 by the value of those bases to the average team, a stolen base was worth an average of .1593 runs. Getting caught cost teams .3687 runs. The Brewers' Scott Podsednik—who led the majors in SB in 2004 with 70—gave his team an added 11.2 runs on the bases but gave back 4.8 by getting caught 13 times, for a net gain of 6.4 runs. That total was barely more than that of Carlos Beltran, who stole 28 fewer bases in '04. But Beltran swiped those 42 in 45 attempts, giving his team an added 5.6 runs. Marlins center fielder Juan Pierre was third in the majors with 45 stolen bases. Because he was caught 24 times, though, Pierre actually *cost* the Marlins 1.7 runs on the basepaths. The stolen base may be exciting, but even the best base-stealers in the game are producing only marginal gains for their teams in the recent offensively dominated era. (Going by the formula of 10 runs equaling 1 win, no player in all of MLB added so much as a single win through base-stealing alone.) Stolen-base totals still garner a lot of attention, as teams like to point out how they play "Smallball" or emphasize the running game. But very little attention is paid to the number of times those same runners are thrown out and the damage those outs can do.

Another supposed advantage of the stolen base, as any announcer will tell you, is that base-stealers distract the pitcher, alter the positioning of the opposing team, put pressure on the defense, and do everything but part the defense like the Red Sea for the batters behind them. Such theories do stem from logical observations of the action on the field. With a man on first, pitchers throw over to first, requiring the first baseman to play much closer to the bag and the batter than he normally would. The shortstop and second baseman may play closer to second in anticipation of a throw from the catcher, or they may break toward the bag on a hit-and-run, allowing a few extra singles to dribble past. But the idea of putting pressure on the defense isn't based on simply any runner on first; only players who are threats to steal supposedly have that effect. Thus, the stolen base creates scoring opportunities by its mere threat. That's the theory, anyway.

To test this theory, we can start by breaking runners on first in steal situations into five groups based on the frequency of their stolen-base attempts. Then we compare the performance of the batters behind them to their expected performance given their overall stat lines. (It's crucial to adjust for the expected performance of the subsequent batters, as base-stealers tend to be in the highest spots in the lineup so that a disproportionate number of subsequent batters will be #3, #4, and #5 hitters.)

In 2004, batters who came to the plate with the top 20 percent of base-stealers on base—as determined by their stolen-base attempts rate—saw their on-base average plus slugging average (OPS) increase by 34 points over expected performance. On the other hand, batters coming to the plate with the slowest runners on first saw an increase of just 4 points. Over the past five years, batters at the plate with baserunners most likely to steal on first improved their OPS by an average of 24 points, the next group by 27, then 17, 20, and 13 for the slowest. So it's true that runners on first who are more likely to steal improved the performance of the batter at the plate, but the difference between the most and least aggressive base stealers is marginal: about 11 points of OPS, with data points bouncing around among the five groups of base-stealers. Even adding the minor and inconsistent improvement in subsequent batter performance, base-stealers rarely contribute to a team's offensive performance in amounts that merit the attention they receive. The stolen base is a useful weapon but also an overrated one.

Beyond Base-Stealing

Stolen bases are only part of the skill of baserunning. No less important are the extra bases taken when the ball is in play. Swiping a bag from under the nose of the defense may be more glamorous, but going from first to third or scoring from second on a single counts for just as much as stealing third or home. Until recently, efforts to assess the hidden values of baserunning were hampered by a lack of statistical information. Stolen bases and times caught stealing have been tracked in box scores for decades, but nowhere is there a record of players taking the extra base.

With the arrival of newly available play-by-play data, those hidden advances can now be counted and analyzed. In an essay in *Baseball Prospectus 2005*, I tackled this question in detail using a similar technique to the one used to evaluate stolen bases. A runner taking an extra base was awarded the difference between the expected runs of the resultant base-out situation and that of the base-out situation if he had only taken the next base. For example, in 2004 a runner on first with no one out who advanced to third on a single was granted the expected runs from runners on first and third with no one out (1.8540) minus the expected runs from runners on first and second (1.4669) to equal 0.3871 runs. Note that taking the extra base on a single with no one out gains a team more than 1.5 times as many runs as stealing second with no one out (0.2337). Stolen bases may get the glory in the box score, but sneaking in a few extra bases when the ball is in play is where the real money is.

Both stolen bases and baserunning in general are subject to outside factors. Stealing a base when Pudge Rodriguez is behind the plate, for instance, is quite different than when Mike Piazza is calling the pitches. Players who can steal against the best defenders should thus be credited slightly more than those who may cherry-pick opportunities against the game's weaker-armed backstops. When taking the extra base, however, things are a little different, as runners very rarely attempt to take the extra base on the same fielder more than once in a season. While it's possible that certain baserunners run against a collective group of stronger-armed fielders such as Ichiro Suzuki or Andruw Jones, the varying defenses faced by baserunners are very close to league average and thus are not counted in the adjustments. We also considered the possibility that certain batters advance runners an extra base more than others due to some special hitting skill. It certainly appears easier to take the extra base on a David Ortiz smash single off the Green Monster than a Johnny Damon infield single. In fact, we found no such effect: Baserunners showed no consistent benefit or detriment from the batters at the plate behind them.

Two factors that were found to have a consistent effect on baserunning numbers are the number of outs and the ballpark. In all situations, baserunners showed a sharply higher attempt rate when there were two outs than when there was one or none. The reason is simple: Baserunners "run on contact" when there are two outs, since there is nothing to lose if the ball is caught or the batter is thrown out. Those extra few steps allow them to take the extra base much more often. Baserunning park factors are, like all other park factors, a result of the fact that baseball is played in a variety of unique environments. Certain ballparks—most notably Coors Field and Fenway Park—have large or irregular areas where it can take outfielders a few extra moments to retrieve the ball, giving a baserunner more time to attempt an extra base. Just as Rockies hitters should not be unduly credited for their prodigious home-run totals, we have to adjust for baserunners who take advantage of particular environments.

Using these adjustments, we compared each runner's season to the league average, seeing how many more or fewer bases he took than the average baserunner, given his park factor and the number of outs when he was on base. Then we matched each extra base to the average run value of that base (from the expected-runs table). The runner's total runs were then compared to the league average, yielding a metric called Equivalent Base Runs (EqBR). In 2004, the runner notching the highest total was Rockies rookie outfielder Matt Holliday (5.0 EqBR) with the Braves' Rafael Furcal (4.9) and the Blue Jays' Vernon Wells (4.5) close behind. The three worst runners were Mike Piazza (–4.7), A. J. Pierzynski (–4.4), and Bill Mueller (–4.2).

Looking at seasons beginning in 1972—the first season for which the necessary play-by-play data are available—the best season on the basepaths was Rod Carew's 1977, in which he attempted to take the extra base a staggering 74.3 percent of the time, with a 98.2 percent success rate. That year the league-average runner attempted the extra base 46.2 percent of the time, with a 91.6 percent success rate, meaning Carew obliterated the competition. Yet despite such historic baserunning skill, Carew racked up just 9.3 EqBR—several runs more than Scott Podsednik's 2004 base-stealing was worth but still short of adding even 1 win in the standings. The worst season since 1972 was Mark McGwire's 1999, when he amassed a total of –9.7 EqBR (McGwire's offensive value lay elsewhere).

Like stolen bases, then, the difference between the best and worst baserunners is significantly smaller than between the best and worst hitters in the league. In Rickey Henderson's 1982 season—the one in which he stole 130 bases—he managed an additional 4.1 runs on the basepaths as measured by EqBR. Despite his plodding style, Pete Incaviglia was actually a decent baserunner in his 1986 rookie season, netting 1.8 EqBR. For his career, Henderson totaled 54 EqBR, the second-highest total since 1972, trailing only Robin Yount. Yount was certainly not as fast as Henderson but was better at not getting thrown out. Incaviglia totaled 4.5 EqBR for his much shorter career. Henderson averaged, per season, fewer than 3 runs on the basepaths more than Incaviglia.

But there's more to baserunning than stealing or taking the extra base on someone else's hit. It takes in other common occurrences such as turning doubles into triples, turning groundouts into singles, and breaking up or beating out a double play. The first of these falls neatly into the kind of analysis already performed on stolen bases and general baserunning situations. Most of the time, the trajectory and distance of a hit on which a player achieves a triple are very similar to those of a double. Baseball researcher Cyril Morong—attempting to discern EqBR estimates for years prior to 1972—found a decent correlation between EqBR and 2B/3B ratio relative to league average. The correlation suggests that the skill needed to turn a double into a triple is the same as that needed to take the extra base when already on base.

While we could analyze triples according to EqBR, they are already accounted for by basic offensive measures like slugging average, since the batter is already at the plate. Adding runs to a player's value by counting triples in a baserunning score would be counting them twice. What should be factored in are times in which a batter was thrown out trying to take an extra base. In 2004, batters were thrown out 303 times stretching for the extra base, or about 10 times per team. These situations are exactly like a batter caught stealing but are not counted in the box score; instead the batter is credited with the last base he reached safely. When evaluating baserunning and player value, these rare situations should be counted, whereas the times a player successfully "turned a double into a triple" (or a single into a double) are already being counted.

One place where baserunning skill may be overlooked is in a player's ability to avoid grounding into double plays (GIDP). Baseball Prospectus tracks double-play rates for batters against the league average. For example, in 2004, Bobby Abreu led the major leagues, notching a mere 8 GIDP in 149 opportunities, a net DP of –11.05 (in 149 opportunities, a league-average batter would have grounded into 19.05 DP). It's tempting to say that a player of Abreu's quality would naturally lead the league because he gets on base so often that his high OBP would reduce his number of GIDP. But Aramis Ramirez, who hit .318/.373/.578 in 2004, was the league's worst culprit, netting an extra 16.30 GIDP. Furthermore, the correlation of a player's DP percentage (the number of times he grounds into a double play per opportunity) from year to year is extremely low, indicating that much of a player's skill at avoiding the double play is luck. In addition, an individual player accumulates so few double-play opportunities that the difference between the player who does the best job of avoiding twin killings and the worst double-play dodger is small. Smooth out all the year-to-year fluctuations in double-play records over entire careers, and very few players show markedly better ability in this department.

Anyone who's seen many catchers lumber down to first knows that beating out the double plays can't be entirely random. Yet the lack of any year-to-year consistency assures us that it is. This conclusion is difficult to swallow, given how rarely you'll see a Mike Piazza or Jim Thome beat out a potential double play. The most likely reason is that defenses play to the batter. If Ichiro is up, fielders play closer to the plate, knowing they will have to field the ball quickly to catch him. With slower runners up, they can afford to play back and field more balls. While this strategy prevents more grounders from getting to the outfield, it means the ball must be hit that much harder to permit a double play. That's only one of several possible explanations, but the fact remains that there appears to be little consistent skill to avoiding the double play for most players.

Breaking up the double play by sliding hard into second is a skill that's even more lost in the randomness of small sample sizes. A baserunner who sacrifices his body in an effort to disrupt the relay throw to first is generally praised for "doing the little things." While that's certainly to be applauded, it's not a skill that returns any consistent or significant results over the league-average runner at the major league level. That's not to say that runners shouldn't attempt to break up the double play—even if the chance is slight, it's worth the risk— but rather that the difference between the best and worst players in the game in this category is hard to detect.

When you add together net stolen bases, EqBR, and the performance of subsequent batters when a stolen-base threat is on first, it's clear that even the most extreme baserunners—the Hendersons and the Incaviglias—are seldom more than 15–20 runs apart in any given season. While this is not a trivial difference, the gap applies only to the extremes; the vast majority of ballplayers are, in any given season, within 10 runs of each other in all baserunning aspects.

The effect of team speed, though, can be substantially bigger. A team with speed up and down the lineup—for example, the Cardinals teams of the 1980s—could gain 2 or even 3 wins from baserunning, a significant total in a tight pennant race. This assumes all else being equal, though—that the speedy players in question contribute equally in all other areas: power, defense, and so forth. Given every team's budget, it also assumes that these players cost the same as comparable but slower players. In the case of, say, Vince Coleman, you had a player who did little to help a team except run fast, while also playing in an era where someone with his skill set was overvalued and thus overpaid. The team-speed concept worked better for the 2003 Florida

Marlins, a team that featured players such as Juan Pierre and Luis Castillo, who added good on-base ability and defense to their speed while playing in an era where their talents were underrated—thus making them all the more valuable to their World Series–winning team. Such cases, though, remain rare.

We could simply estimate that the best baserunners generate about 1 additional win a year and leave it at that, and we wouldn't be far off. But not all extra bases are equal. Some—like Dave Roberts's steal of second against Mariano Rivera in Game 4 of the 2004 ALCS, which allowed the Red Sox to tie the game, triggering their improbable series comeback—are clearly more important than others. Some are so inconsequential that baseball defined a new stat just to avoid having to count them as true stolen bases: defensive indifference (DI). DI is awarded to players who "steal" a base when the opposing team makes absolutely no effort to prevent them from doing so. DI usually rears its head in blowouts or when a team is up by 2 or more runs with 2 outs in the ninth; the runner currently on base is insignificant to the outcome of the game, so the difference between a runner on first and a runner on second isn't worth the defense's effort to prevent.

Win-Expectation Framework

Roberts's steal and the existence of DI raise the issue that the best way to evaluate stolen bases and baserunning may be to use a win-expectation framework instead of a run-expectation framework. Just as with run expectations, each situation is given an average likelihood of a win rather than an expected number of runs. Take Roberts's situation, down by 1 in the bottom of the ninth with a man on first and no one out; in 2004, the home team managed to win in that situation a mere 20.4 percent of the time. But with a man on second and no one out, the home team won 36.7 percent of the time, an enormous jump of 16.3 percent. (By comparison, if Roberts had pulled the same trick in the bottom of the first, he would have increased the Red Sox's win expectation by only 7.4 percent.) While baserunners don't know the exact win expectation of various situations, they certainly understand that Roberts's situation is both higher-risk and higher-reward than stealing a base in the first inning.

The major issue presented by win expectation as opposed to run expectation is sample size. In any one year, there are certain situations that almost never arise. For example, in 2004, no visiting team ever found itself in a tie game with no one out in the fourth inning with men on second and third. How do we know what a team's odds are of

winning the game if that situation never arose? To combat this problem, Keith Woolner developed a theoretical framework for Win Expectancy. Instead of taking the raw values from actual games,
Woolner's formula estimates the win expectation of a situation based
on the run-expectation table, the offensive averages of the two teams,
the typical number of runs scored in an inning by those offenses, and
other adjustments. This construct not only creates values for every
possible situation but is also adjusted for the two teams involved.

Using Woolner's framework, we can answer a few outstanding
questions about baserunning. First, we can establish new break-even
success rates for various situations. Figure 4-1.2 shows the break-even
success rate, by inning, for a runner on first with no one out in a tie
game. The home team's break-even point is consistently lower because
it has an extra half-inning in which to score. Therefore, the extra out
from being caught stealing does not represent as significant a loss as it
does for the visiting team. Interestingly, the trend is exponential, not
linear: The difference between the first and fifth innings is not nearly
as large as that between the fifth and ninth. Roberts's steal carried a
lower required success rate than if he'd tried it earlier in the game.
Baserunners don't have to be quite as good to attempt a steal if the
game is close in the late innings.

FIGURE 4-1.2 SB break-even success rates by inning

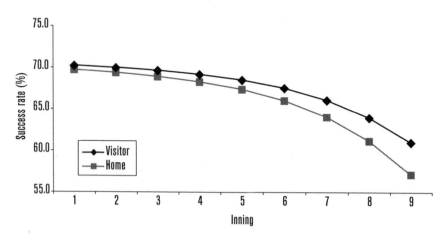

Figure 4-1.3 shows how much a successful steal of second with no
one out increases a team's win expectation by inning. Again, we see
that Roberts's steal (though it came with the Sox down by 1, not tied)

FIGURE 4-1.3 SB value by inning

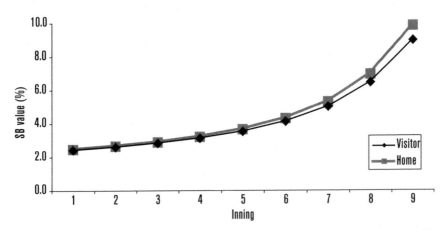

was worth more than four times as much as a similar steal in the first inning.

If we look at the break-even points for the same situation, but instead of changing the inning change the run differential, we get the results shown in Figure 4-1.4. In this case, once again the visitor is required to be more successful than the home team at every stage, but rather than the exponential curve in Figure 4-1.2, this graph shows a more linear trend, though certainly with some curvature. Like increasing innings, an increasing lead (or decreasing deficit) continually pushes the break-even point for stolen bases down. Roberts needed to

FIGURE 4-1.4 SB break-even success rates by run differential

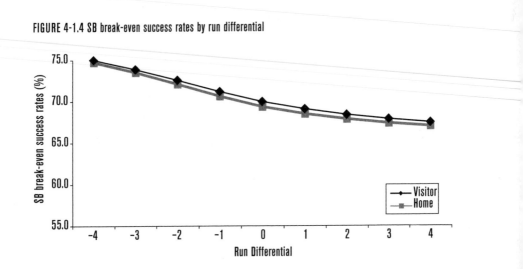

be more sure of his success than if the game was tied but less so than if his team were down by 2.

In Figure 4-1.5, we can see the changing value of the stolen base in Win Expectancy for different run-differential situations. The stolen base is most valuable to a home team down by 1 run—the very situation in which Roberts's theft occurred.

FIGURE 4-1.5 SB value by run differential

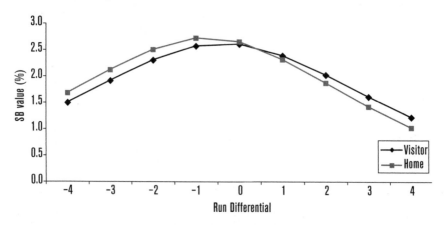

Finally, we can look at a team's own scoring tendencies. Teams that score more runs per game are less likely to encourage stolen bases, especially if they're stacked with power hitters. The Win-Expectancy framework provides an estimate for the changing break-even success rates and values for different run-scoring teams and environments. These estimates are shown in Figures 4-1.6 and 4-1.7. (The extremely

FIGURE 4-1.6 SB break-even success rate by team R/G

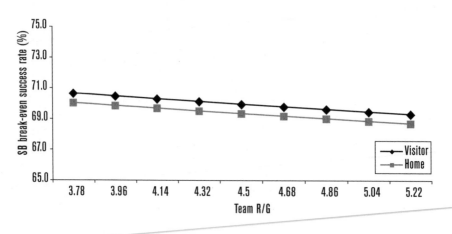

FIGURE 4-1.7 SB value by team R/G

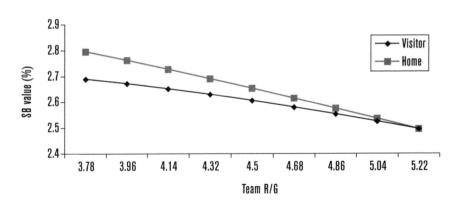

linear trend is more a result of the theoretical framework employed than of some divination about a natural tendency of baseball.) The most important difference between these estimates and the previous four is that the range in the first four is vastly larger.

The decision to steal should be driven more by the inning and the run differential than by the team's run-scoring potential. Extra bases may feel more important in lower-run-scoring environments, but actually the difference is quite small. A team averaging just under 3.8 runs per game sees an increase in win expectation by 2.8 percent with a successful stolen base, while a team that scores over 5.2 runs per game gains 2.5 percent. Certainly the stolen base is somewhat more important to the lower-scoring team (0.3 percent), but even between vast differences in team run-scoring averages, the benefit of a stolen base remains fairly constant. (The last four studies assume a tie game, second inning, the first inning where the visiting team could be either behind or ahead. As noted earlier, the value of the stolen base increases as the game goes on.)

Combine all these analyses and we can see that when Roberts found himself as the pinch runner that October night, he was in one of the best situations in which to attempt a stolen base. It was very late in the game; his team was at home, down by 1; and although the Sox were a high-powered offensive team, that fact didn't matter much. The situation was as high-risk as it was high-reward: If Roberts had been caught, Boston's season would assuredly have ended. But few successful thefts have been as valuable.

Baserunning is a complex and understudied issue, but applications such as Win-Expectancy frameworks can illuminate many previously unanswered questions. We can confirm the long-held notion that stolen bases and extra bases are worth exponentially more in the later innings, especially in close games. More importantly, the game situation—inning and run differential—is more significant than the team's scoring tendencies when it comes to attempting the extra base. The vast majority of baserunners contributes, or subtracts, a very small amount from a team's overall winning percentage, but with the very best runners, the threat of the steal has shown a slight but consistent ability to improve the performance of the following batters. But there are still questions to be answered. For example, who are baseball's best decision makers? Which players are adept at recognizing both when they can take the extra base without risk and when the situation calls for accepting additional risk for the increased reward? Who runs their team out of games the most often?

So what if Rickey Henderson had Pete Incaviglia's legs? The game would certainly be less exciting, but Henderson's value would hardly be different. In a typical season, the difference between a great baserunner and a terrible one is significantly smaller than between the best and worst hitters in the league. If Henderson hadn't stolen a single base in 1982, the A's would have lost about 2 runs on the season, or about one-fifth of a game. If he'd been only as good as Incaviglia on the basepaths over his career, he would have contributed about 5 fewer wins in 25 seasons. Henderson was fun to watch, and his excellent on-base skills rank him among the best players of all time. But the first rule of baserunning is "don't get caught," advice Henderson disobeyed more than 700 times. Taking the extra base is good, but getting on base, not getting thrown out, and eventually scoring is better.

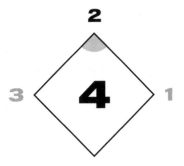

When Is One Run
Worth More Than Two?

JAMES CLICK

During the last week of the 2005 season, the Cleveland Indians were on the verge of completing a remarkable turnaround to their season. A little more than a month into the season, the Indians were 12-18 and 11.5 games behind the Chicago White Sox in the AL Central. But after four amazing months of baseball, the Indians closed the White Sox' lead to two games by September 28 and sat tied with the Boston Red Sox and New York Yankees for the lead in the AL Wild-Card race. With two games remaining against the lowly Tampa Bay Devil Rays and a weekend series against the White Sox, the Indians were in a good position to win either the division or the Wild Card and advance to the postseason.

That day's game against the Devil Rays was a surprising pitching duel. Tampa pitcher Seth McClung—who would finish the season with a 6.59 ERA—had shut out Cleveland on 3 hits through 7 innings. Down 1-0, the Indians led off the bottom of the eighth with a double to left by Ben Broussard, bringing up Aaron Boone. Manager Eric Wedge called for the sacrifice, and Boone squared around to bunt. If Boone could get the runner to third, Broussard could score on a sacrifice fly or a well-placed groundball and tie the game; the Indians could then hope to score the winning run in the ninth or extra innings.

That logic ignored the pivotal question: Would a sacrifice bunt be a good idea in this situation?

This dilemma cuts to the heart of baseball strategy, limiting the potential for many runs in exchange for the increased likelihood of a single run. Tactics like stolen bases, sacrifice bunts, and squeeze bunts all dovetail with that mind-set. From the pitching team's perspective, playing the infield in and issuing intentional walks provide tradeoffs. With the infield in, you're hoping for an out at the plate, but your fielders are less likely to field a sharp groundball. An intentional walk may set up a double play, but you're also raising the other team's run expectation by putting an extra runner on base. Whether they understand the exact percentages or not, teams are willing to sacrifice additional runs to get that single run across the plate.

These strategies are employed far too often. Much of the time, performance analysts describe such strategies as "antiquated" or "unsuitable for the modern run environment." Earlier research was largely based on run-expectation tables popularized by John Thorn and Pete Palmer in *The Hidden Game of Baseball*. The table shows the average number of runs scored in the remainder of an inning given a particular number of outs and baserunners' positions. Thorn and Palmer determined that in *every* situation, a team employing a 1-run strategy—sacrificing or otherwise moving the runner over, intentional walks, and all—reduced its chances of scoring. This analysis mirrored the work done by George Lindsey in his article "An Investigation of Strategies in Baseball" and Earnshaw Cook in *Percentage Baseball*.

These conclusions have not changed in the twenty years since Thorn and Palmer published their book. In 2005, a team with a runner on second base and no one out scored an average of 1.14 runs in the inning. With a runner on third and one out, teams scored .98 runs per inning, a decrease of .16 runs. Given those numbers, Wedge would be, on average, costing the Indians about a sixth of a run by asking Boone to sacrifice Broussard to third.

There are two main problems with relying on these tables. First, they only project the average number of runs scored, as opposed to the likelihood of scoring at least 1 run. Second, they only address league-average batters. While they do tell us that using an average batter on an average team to move a runner over reduces the number of runs a team can be expected to score, that's generally accepted. Teams that employ these strategies often understand that they are reducing their chance of scoring many runs for the chance of scoring at least 1 run.

When the game is tied in the bottom of the ninth, the game ends the instant the first runner for the home team touches the plate, and all subsequent runs are irrelevant. The home team has zero incentive to play for more than 1 run, so its strategy should be to score at least 1, not an average number of runs. Instead of displaying the average number of runs scored, Table 4-2.1 shows the percentage of the time that at least one run scored, a more essential piece of information in this situation.

TABLE 4-2.1 2005 Scoring Expectation (percent)

Runners	0 Out	1 Out	2 Outs
Empty	28.0	16.5	7.1
1st	41.7	27.2	12.7
2nd	62.5	41.0	22.9
3rd	82.7	66.1	25.4
1st & 2nd	61.6	41.4	22.8
1st & 3rd	84.6	64.5	26.8
2nd & 3rd	86.1	67.4	26.6
Loaded	85.6	65.4	30.7

As in run-expectation tables, the probability of scoring goes down as outs increase. However, this table reveals that there are several situations in which teams would be well advised to employ 1-run strategies. For example, having runners on first and second with no one out yields at least 1 run 61.6 percent of the time. But if those runners are sacrificed to second and third, the scoring probability rises to 67.4 percent. Likewise, with zero or one out and men on second and third, the pitcher would reduce the chances of the opponent scoring by 0.5 percent and 2.0 percent, respectively, when he intentionally walks the next man. In the Indians' situation, sacrificing Broussard to third would have increased their scoring probability from 62.5 to 66.1 percent. So on average, sacrificing in this situation makes sense. But note that sacrificing a man from first to second *never* increases the likelihood of scoring at least 1 run on average. If teams are to successfully employ sacrifices to increase their chances of scoring, the sacrifice must send a runner to third base with fewer than two outs. (Of course, this assumes a 100 percent success rate with the sacrifice attempt. The real success rate is often considerably lower, depending on the situation.)

Scoring expectation versus run expectation answers only half the question; the discussion still relies on league-average numbers rather than data from specific run-scoring environments. Intuitively, sacrificing appears to be a much worse idea in a high-run-scoring environment like Coors Field than in a low-run-scoring environment like RFK Stadium. Even former Dodgers general manager Paul DePodesta—one of the poster boys for recent statistical analysis advances in baseball—acknowledged that the run-scoring environment is a key variable in the decision to sacrifice: "If I play my home games in Coors Field, I'm probably not going to be doing a whole lot of bunting.

If I play my home games in PETCO Park or Dodger Stadium, it's probably going to be a more valuable tool."

Teams sacrifice because they want to increase the likelihood that the runner will make it into a better scoring position. In a park like Coors, where players have much higher on-base percentages and slugging averages than elsewhere, it's much more likely that the batter can advance the runner while getting on base himself. In RFK, batters have a much more difficult time reaching base. So if the chances for a successful sacrifice are the same in both parks, the sacrifice in Washington—instead of letting the batter swing away—would increase the likelihood that the runner reaches second or third more than the same choice would in Colorado.

To quantify this difference, lower- and higher-scoring environments can be compared to see how the difference in scoring expectation changes. However, some parks with similar run-scoring environments suppress or encourage run scoring in different ways. For example, Table 4-2.2 shows the park factors for Dodger Stadium and Kauffman Stadium.

TABLE 4-2.2 Component Park Factors, 2004

Park	Year	Runs	H	2B	3B	HR	BB
Kauffman Stadium	2004	95	98	96	143	71	98
Dodger Stadium	2004	95	97	77	61	103	86

Dodger Stadium and Kauffman Stadium had overall park factors of 95 in 2004, meaning they suppressed offense by about 5 percent compared to the league average. But their component park factors are extremely different: While Kauffman Stadium increased triples and suppressed home runs, Dodger Stadium suppressed doubles, triples, and walks while actually encouraging home runs. As a result, run- and scoring-expectation tables from similar run environments cannot be relied upon to assess the strategic decisions made in those parks.

A more robust tool is Win Expectancy, developed by Keith Woolner in *Baseball Prospectus 2005* and discussed in detail in several chapters in this book. This framework provides the probability that a team will win a game based on the scoring expectations for the team and the opponent as well as the inning, the number of outs, and the baserunners. For example, a home team that averages 4.5 runs per game has a 41.1 percent chance of winning a game when it begins the bottom of the fifth inning down by 1 run against an opponent who scores 4.5 runs per game. Win

Expectancy can calculate the probability of a team winning the game in any situation and can therefore test the efficacy of various strategies.

Back to the Indians' dilemma: In 2005, down by 1 in the bottom of the eighth with a man on second and no one out, Cleveland would be expected to win the game 49.6 percent of the time. (This figure is slightly higher than the average team because the Indians were a better offensive team than the Devil Rays were.) With a man on third and one out, the probability drops to 46.8 percent, meaning the Indians would have cost themselves a 2.8 percent chance of winning the game if they had successfully sacrificed. Considering that Win Expectancy is significantly more robust than the run- and scoring-expectation tables and takes into account many more specific factors facing the Indians, it is a much better tool to answer the specific question here.

Figure 4-2.1 shows the change in the Indians' Win Expectancy if they chose to sacrifice with a man on first and no one out in various innings and run differentials.

FIGURE 4-2.1 Changes in Win Expectancy after sacrificing, man on first, no out

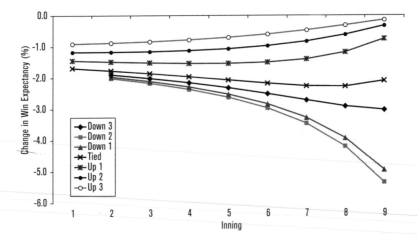

First note that in every situation, Win Expectancy goes down when a team successfully sacrifices a man from first to second with no one out. Second, it's significantly *worse* to do so when down by 1 or 2 runs than when down by 3, largely because the win expectation is so low when a team is down by 3 that there just isn't much to be lost by sacrificing. More important, the *worst* time to sacrifice is when a team is down in a close game, even when that deficit is only 1 run.

Of course, teams don't sacrifice only with a man on first and no outs. Figure 4-2.2 shows the same information as the previous figure but considers when there is a man on second and no one out rather than a man on first.

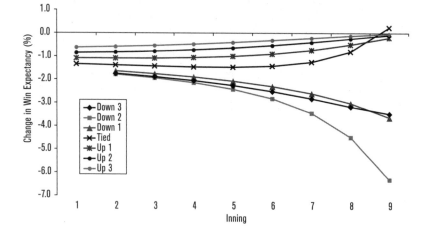

FIGURE 4-2.2 Changes in Win Expectancy after sacrificing, man on second, none out

As before, sacrificing is almost always a bad idea, but in this case there is one situation in which a successful sacrifice increases a team's chances to win the game: in a tie game in the ninth inning. It's crucial that the game be tied: If the team sacrifices when behind by 1 run, then instead of increasing the chance of winning, it decreases the win expectation by 3.6 percent. Additionally, the run differential matters very little in the early innings, but as the game progresses, the score becomes increasingly important.

While Win Expectancy sheds light on how the score, the inning, and the overall run environment affect the decision to sacrifice, it still overlooks two key elements: the success rate of the attempted sacrifice and the particular batters involved. In the preceding analysis, the sacrifice was assumed to be successful 100 percent of the time, but many teams cite "making the defense work" as another reason to attempt a sacrifice. Bill James noted recently that even he "would certainly signal a bunt with a good bunter against a poor defensive third baseman" because there are more possible outcomes of a sacrifice bunt than the simple successful advance of a baserunner. If the opponent fails to field the ball cleanly or commits an error often enough, that failure may turn the decision to sacrifice from a costly play into a beneficial one, overall.

A series of articles at Baseball Prospectus titled "Taking One for the Team: When Does It Make Sense to Sacrifice?" covered both of these factors. To determine when sacrifices increased a team's chances to score—both multiple runs and a single run—the articles created a model similar to Win Expectancy. Whereas Win Expectancy determines a team's chances to win the game, this approach was on a much smaller level—like microeconomics to Win Expectancy's macroeconomics. It analyzed a team's run-scoring chances based on the probability of a successful sacrifice, the batter at the plate, and the batter on deck.

The first adjustment over methods we've explored so far is to take into account what actually happens on the field when a batter attempts a sacrifice, the "probability of a successful sacrifice" mentioned before. While there are a multitude of possible outcomes in each situation, four of them make up over 99 percent of all possible outcomes: a successful sacrifice, the runner advancing as well as the batter reaching base, the lead runner being cut down trying to advance, or a double play. In Table 4-2.3, the percentage in which each of these four outcomes occurred when teams attempted to sacrifice is displayed.

TABLE 4-2.3 Sacrifice Bunt Outcomes, 2000–2005

Situation	Sacrifice	Success[a]	Failure	GIDP
First, 0 out	72.9	13.6	11.2	2.0
First, 1 out	71.6	10.6	14.4	3.2
Second, 0 out	69.5	18.6	11.4	0.5
First and second, 0 out	67.0	17.1	13.4	2.2

[a]For the purposes of this table, the "Success" column includes any instances in which the runner scored on the play as well as instances in which the batter was not put out by the defense.

In Table 4-2.3, any situation in which the expected result of the sacrifice occurred—for example, a runner on first advanced to second while the batter was retired—is counted in the "Sacrifice" column. The "Success" column includes results better for the offense than the successful sacrifice; "Failure" includes those worse (for example, when the lead runner is thrown out); and "GIDP" includes all double plays, a result that is similar to "Failure" but to a much greater extent. From this, it's easy to see that sacrifices are more successful than expected—the desired result of "putting pressure on the defense"— almost exactly as often as they are distinctly unsuccessful. As a result, adjusting for the specific outcome of the sacrifice attempt doesn't change the results of the analysis to any great extent.

The other primary adjustment made in "Taking One for the Team" was the quality of the batter at the plate and the batter on deck. The results of the at-bats of actual major league hitters were simulated and compared to the results if the same hitters sacrificed with the success rates described above. By comparing the expected run scoring both before and after a successful sacrifice (and the following at-bat) to the expected scoring if the batter swung away, "thresholds" of batting performance were determined. Any hitter batting below certain thresholds would benefit his team by sacrificing; any hitter above them would be costing his team a chance to score at least 1 run. The results are listed in Table 4-2.4.

TABLE 4-2.4 Batter Thresholds for Sacrifices

Situation	Goal	AVG	OBP	SLG
Man on first, 0 out	1+ runs	.191[a]	.206	.182
First, 1 out	1+ runs	.195	.221	.178
Second, 0 out	1+ runs	.249	.305	.363
First & second, 0 out	1+ runs	.218	.253	.266
First, 0 out	1 run	.177	.192	.153
First, 1 out	1 run	.199	.224	.174
Second, 0 out	1 run	.277	.350	.451
First & second, 0 out	1 run	.206	.235	.263

[a]While it's clearly impossible for a hitter to have a higher AVG than SLG, these impossibilities occasionally arise because the threshold for each metric was computed independently.

With a runner on second and no one out, needing just a single run, the Indians would increase their likelihood of scoring those runs by attempting to sacrifice only if the batter at the plate was hitting below .277/.350/.451. The batter due up (Boone) was hitting .243/.299/.378 that season, so calling for a sacrifice would, going strictly by this test, increase the Indians' chances of scoring at least 1 run. The batter on deck may alter the numbers. Sacrificing is most beneficial when the batter on deck is a singles or doubles hitter; if the batter due up after Boone were among the most extreme singles hitters in the league, the thresholds in Table 4-2.4 would rise by about 10–15 points per metric. This adjustment rarely changes the overall conclusion, but can make a slight difference in specific cases.

Generally, having pitchers sacrifice in the National League is the correct strategy, especially considering the likelihood of their batting in front of a singles hitter. However, some pitchers who have the ability to hit above the established thresholds—such as the Marlins' Dontrelle Willis—should not sacrifice. It makes sense for non-pitchers to sacrifice only with a runner on second and no outs, only with a very small percentage of batters, and only when teams need one run. Win Expectancy and the sacrifice model show that nearly every time a team employs a non-pitcher in a sacrifice, it is reducing a chance not only to score many runs but also to score even a single run. The sacrifice is not always a bad idea, but it's vastly overused.

Unlike other 1-run strategies, sacrifices purposely trade one of a team's 27 outs for the increased likelihood of scoring a run. Other strategies are not so cut-and-dried. Stolen bases (covered in depth in Chapter 4-1) attempt to gain the benefit of a sacrifice (the extra base) without the out and are thus much more valuable when successful. The intentional walk (discussed in Chapter 1-3 on lineup construction) almost always increases the likelihood that a team will score both many runs and a single run, despite the increased likelihood of the double play.

Besides those obvious attempts, there are other, more subtle changes teams can make in an attempt to trade many runs for a single run. These smaller adjustments—situational hitting, for example—can be nearly impossible to measure. We cannot know if a batter was actively attempting to hit a single rather than a home run (or vice versa) just by looking at the data. Thus, we cannot determine whether a team was playing for 1 run or for many. Rather than attempting to quantify those instances, it's important to understand which situations warrant playing for 1 run rather than for many runs.

To reach this understanding, Nate Silver introduced One-Run Value Yield (ORVY) at Baseball Prospectus. ORVY is a measure of the relative value of scoring a single run to the value of scoring a second run, as measured by Win Expectancy. Take the Indians' situation again: Coming into the eighth inning down by 1, the Indians have a 32.7 percent chance to win the game. If the Indians fail to score in the inning, their win expectation drops to 17.6 percent. If they score 1 run, it rises to 51.4 percent. In this case, scoring 1 run in the eighth inning is worth an 18.7 percent chance of winning the game. If they score 2 runs to take the lead, their win expectation jumps all the way to 83.7 percent; that second run is worth 32.3 percent (83.7 – 51.4 percent). By taking the ratio of those two increases (18.7/32.3), ORVY estimates that the first run is worth 58 percent as much as the second run.

ORVY only compares 2 runs to 1; while it is very informative, batters may be choosing between scoring a single run and several more runs. To account for this scenario, we can create two hypothetical teams who differ only by their run-scoring distributions. One team scores runs at the league-average distribution, while the other has a high propensity to score a single run in an inning but a drastically reduced probability of scoring more than 1. Their specific distributions are shown in Table 4-2.5.

TABLE 4-2.5 Hypothetical Run-Scoring Probabilities (percent)

Team	Runs							
	0	1	2	3	4	5	6	7
League Average	72.0	15.0	7.0	3.3	1.5	0.7	0.3	0.1
1 Run	56.8	37.6	4.3	0.7	0.4	0.2	0.0	0.0

In 72 percent of its innings, the League Average team will not score any runs; 15 percent of the time, that team will score 1 run; 7 percent of the time, the team will score 2 runs, and so forth. (Innings in which teams score more than 7 runs happen so infrequently that they are not considered here.) These two teams will score exactly the same number of runs in a season, but they will do so in dramatically different fashions. Comparing the two teams' Win Expectancy in different situations reveals which team is better equipped to win games in various situations. Figures 4-2.3 and 4-2.4 show the difference in each team's win expectation in various situations.

These charts reveal several key differences between the two teams. First, until the sixth inning, the difference between the two teams is

FIGURE 4-2.3 Home team change in Win Expectancy when playing for one run by inning and run differential

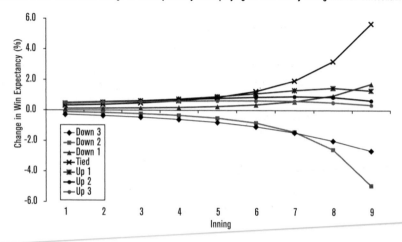

FIGURE 4-2.4 Visiting team change in Win Expectancy when playing for one run by inning and run differential

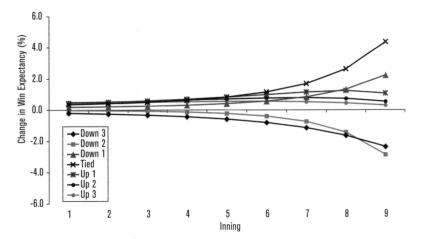

less than 1 percent. There's little reason for a team to change its offensive approach until at least the sixth. Second, the 1-Run team has a greater disparity than the League Average team when it is the visitor; it's more important for a visiting team to understand what kind of inning they need than the home team. Third, the 1-Run team has a higher Win Expectancy than the League Average team in every situation except when it's down by more than one run. This is a key point made by ORVY and emphasized here: Once teams have fallen behind by 2 or more runs, they must play for the big inning. But when trailing by 1, tied, *or leading by any number of runs*, it's beneficial to play for 1 run. The 1-Run team shows a diminishing advantage as the lead increases, so it's possible that when the lead reaches 4 or 5 runs, the League Average team will again show an advantage. But most of the time, the 1-Run team is going to come out ahead.

At the start of this chapter, we showed that sacrifices were demonstrably a bad idea even when a team was down by a single run, a conclusion that may seem to contradict this finding that a team should play for 1 run when down by 1. But remember that in most cases, sacrifices decrease the likelihood of scoring even a single run. Playing for 1 run is a good idea when down by 1, but sacrificing is not a good way to achieve that goal. Instead, other tactics to score a single run—stolen-base attempts with highly favorable odds and situational hitting, for example—are necessary; giving away outs is not.

So with Aaron Boone coming to the plate in the Indians' pivotal game against the Devil Rays, would it be beneficial for Wedge to call for a sacrifice? Primarily, he must consider the hitters involved: Boone, as we've seen, was well below the requisite threshold for a beneficial sacrifice attempt in that situation. Furthermore, the Indians were down by 1 run as the home team; in that situation, the 1-Run team had a 2.0 percent higher Win Expectancy than the League Average team. In this case, even when considering the probability that the sacrifice will not work, attempting to bunt Broussard to third increases the Indians' odds both of scoring at least 1 run and of winning the game.

Sometimes going with the odds can backfire, though. In this game, Boone failed to get the bunt down and the Indians failed to score in the inning. In the ninth, Coco Crisp led off the inning with a single. Once again, Wedge made the right call, this time by letting Jhonny Peralta—a much better hitter than Boone, or most other players in 2005 for that matter—swing away. Once again, the strategy failed: Peralta grounded into a double play, and the Indians went on to lose the game and failed to make the postseason. In the long run, Wedge's decisions were correct, but that's small comfort to a team that failed to execute when the season swung in the balance.

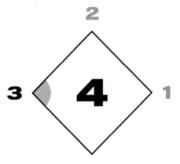

Is Joe Torre a
Hall of Fame Manager?

JAMES CLICK

A baseball manager is a necessary evil.
—Sparky Anderson

After a 20-27 start to the 1995 season, the St. Louis Cardinals felt they needed a change; on June 16 they fired their manager, fifty-four-year-old former National League MVP Joe Torre. In parts of six seasons, Torre's Cardinals had amassed a 351-354 record and failed to reach the playoffs. The results of Torre's two previous managerial stints were vastly different: He had steered the Mets—a team filled with objectively terrible players—to a 286-420 record from 1977 to 1981, but he had skippered the Braves to a 257-229 record in three seasons, winning one division title. All told, in fourteen seasons his teams won 894 games, lost 1,003 (a .471 winning percentage), and won just the lone division title and zero postseason games. At that point, the performance of teams managed by Torre based on winning percentage and postseason success ranked him just below Pat Corrales and Lee Fohl.

That November, the New York Yankees hired him as their new skipper. Their previous manager, Buck Showalter, had done an admirable job in the Bronx, totaling 313 wins and 268 losses in four years, a .539 winning percentage. He also had the team in first place when the labor crisis ended the 1994 season, and the team's 1995 Wild-Card win represented its first time in the postseason since 1981. But the team's loss in the American League Divisional Series was largely blamed on Showalter and his use of closer John Wetteland. Showalter's contract was up that fall, and when the manager rejected the team's initial contract offer, Yankees owner George Steinbrenner—whose support of Showalter was so lacking that he publicly applauded opposing manager Lou Piniella's work in the ALDS—quickly took the negotiating tactic as a resignation and hired Torre. Never one to stick with a decision for long, Steinbrenner reportedly met with Showalter to arrange for his return "if Torre faltered in early 1996," a move that would have reduced Torre's role to that of "very well-paid and very perturbed adviser."

The 1996 New York Yankees were not loaded with superstars. They returned the same outfield from the 1995 squad—Gerald Williams, Bernie Williams, and Paul O'Neill (Tim Raines might have displaced Gerald Williams at the outset had it not been for an injury)—as well as third baseman Wade Boggs and designated hitter Ruben Sierra. Some homegrown prospects offered hope, led by rookie shortstop Derek Jeter. Still, only Bernie Williams and O'Neill brought any power to the lineup, and it showed. The Yanks finished the year second in the league in batting average but only ninth in runs scored. On the mound, only twenty-three-year-old Andy Pettitte and the aging David Cone and Jimmy Key returned, returned, joined by Kenny Rogers and the remnants of Dwight Gooden. Wetteland headed the bullpen, joined by twenty-six-year-old Mariano Rivera, who the Yankees hoped would do better in relief than he had in the rotation. This last was a parting gift from Showalter, who had turned to Rivera in the ALDS when Wetteland had faltered and received shockingly dominant performances.

The young talent and able veterans jelled faster than expected, and the Yankees won a weak division by four games. Again facing mediocre competition, they dispatched the Rangers in the ALDS and then got another break when their divisional rival, the Orioles, upset the juggernaut Indians. The Yanks and a young fan named Jeffrey Maier downed the O's in the ALCS 4-1. In the first two games of the World Series, the Atlanta Braves demolished the Yanks by a combined score of 16-1, and the Bombers' run appeared to be over. But New York stormed back to win four straight against one of the greatest rotations of all time. Over the next four seasons, the Yankees won the World Series three more times, reestablishing the franchise as the face of baseball and transforming Joe Torre from a managerial retread into a god.

But how much of the Yankees' success belongs to Torre? "Players win games; managers lose them" goes the axiom, but even that assumes that managers have some influence over the outcome of the games. What exactly does a manager do? More important, what results of managerial influence can we measure?

In-Game Strategic Decisions

The key to winning is pitching, fundamentals,
and three-run homers.
   —Earl Weaver

Over the last few chapters, the areas of clear managerial influence— the bullpen, lineup, and 1-run strategies—have been discussed at length. Recapping that analysis is not necessary, but it's important to remember that modern managers make these strategic decisions within strict limits. Virtually all of them follow the same ground rules. The best reliever pitches to start the ninth inning only with the team leading by between one and three runs; the best two hitters bat third and fourth in the lineup; and so on. Because of this lack of variation, there is only a small difference between even the best and worst managers in terms of applied strategic decisions.

Regardless, baseball is a game of inches, and those small differences are worth exploring. One way to analyze managerial decisions is to view some of the typical decisions attributed to the manager—sacrifice hits, stolen bases, and intentional walks—through Keith Woolner's concept of Win Expectancy, discussed in earlier chapters. However, performing analysis using the Win-Expectancy framework still overlooks much of the reason the manager is hired: to use the available personnel as best he can. The Win-Expectancy framework adjusts for the offensive levels of both teams and the game situation, but it does not take into account the individual players involved. As discussed in Chapter 4-2, the skill set of the player involved in many 1-run strategies is at least as important as the game situation. For example, in 2004, Jeter bunted 23 times while batting .292/.352/.471 (AVG/OBP/SLG) with 23 home runs; if he had swung away during those plate appearances, he would have notched approximately 6 more hits—including another HR—and two walks. A player of Jeter's offensive qualifications should rarely, if ever, bunt, and instances when players of Jeter's ilk square around should certainly be counted against managers more than when a player like Cristian Guzman (.219/.260/.314 in 2005) does.

This example brings to light another point against viewing managerial performance through the Win Expectancy framework: Sometimes it's not the manager who initiates 1-run strategies. Managers are often said to give certain players "the green light" when on the basepaths, or players may square around to bunt without a signal from the bench. Because we have no clear way of knowing whether the manager did or did not call for the strategy used on the field, analyzing managers by the results of those decisions would be erroneous.

As such, the results of any managerial Win-Expectancy analysis must be taken with a grain of salt (Tables 4-3.1–4-3.4). It's likely that, on a macro level, the results are indicative of managerial decisions, but the primary conclusion to be taken from this analysis is that nearly every manager costs his team wins through overuse of these strategies. Only six times in thirty-three years has any manager used sacrifice attempts, stolen base attempts, and intentional walks to increase his team's win expectation over an entire season. Even the best managers cost their team more than a game per season by employing these tactics. At worst, they can cost a team nearly six games in a single season (as Roger Craig did for the 1987 Giants). Again, it's possible that some managers, based on the players involved, call for these 1-run strategies at better times than others. But on the whole, they are still used far too often.

TABLE 4-3.1 Best Manager Seasons by Strategic Decisions, 1972–2004

Manager	Year	Team	SH	SBA	IBB	Wins
Dick Williams	1983	SDN	52	240	52	0.63
Sparky Anderson	1975	CIN	25	199	63	0.58
Felipe Alou	1993	MON	43	270	38	0.53
Dick Howser	1983	KCA	29	225	23	0.52
Bobby Cox	1981	ATL	39	135	31	0.22
Dick Williams	1980	MON	33	307	42	0.10
Chuck Tanner	1976	OAK	57	448	34	0.00
Jim Frey	1980	KCA	32	225	47	−0.07
Walter Alston	1975	LAN	55	184	20	−0.10
Chuck Tanner	1972	CHA	35	147	29	−0.11
Sparky Anderson	1976	CIN	17	256	56	−0.12
Bill Virdon	1980	HOU	42	266	26	−0.13
Joe Torre	1981	NYN	31	143	35	−0.28
Whitey Herzog	1988	SLN	52	282	90	−0.37
Lou Piniella	2003	TBA	30	180	36	−0.39
Tony LaRussa	1983	CHA	49	212	32	−0.41
Lou Piniella	1986	NYA	35	185	25	−0.41
Felipe Alou	1994	MON	11	167	28	−0.41
Bill Virdon	1983	MON	25	181	50	−0.42
Lou Piniella	2001	SEA	40	205	28	−0.44

TABLE 4-3.2 Worst Manager Seasons by Strategic Decisions, 1972–2004

Manager	Year	Team	SH	SBA	IBB	Wins
Roger Craig	1987	SFN	22	220	86	-5.92
Frank Robinson	1975	CLE	62	190	78	-5.68
Jim Marshall	1976	CHN	43	147	60	-4.74
Gene Mauch	1973	MON	81	138	74	-4.65
Ken Aspromonte	1972	CLE	42	99	93	-4.34
Frank Robinson	1983	SFN	32	218	95	-4.28
Sparky Anderson	1993	DET	31	159	92	-4.17
Butch Hobson	1992	BOS	55	91	56	-4.13
Lloyd McClendon	2001	PIT	28	161	72	-4.12
Lou Piniella	1993	SEA	63	154	56	-4.09
Joe Torre	1978	NYN	38	175	94	-4.03
Frank Robinson	2002	MON	68	180	80	-4.03
Don Baylor	1993	COL	37	230	66	-4.00
Ken Aspromonte	1974	CLE	52	142	67	-4.00
Lloyd McClendon	2002	PIT	39	127	93	-3.96
Bobby Mattick	1980	TOR	60	138	57	-3.92
Tom Trebelhorn	1994	CHN	25	117	35	-3.92
Buck Rodgers	1986	MON	31	280	60	-3.92
Joe Torre	1992	SLN	34	321	46	-3.90
Bobby Valentine	1986	TEX	28	184	37	-3.88

TABLE 4-3.3 Best Managers, 1972–2004, by Wins/Season (minimum five seasons)

Manager	Seasons	SH	SBA	IBB	Wins	Wins/Season
Dick Howser	5	193	864	136	-5.23	-1.05
Bill Virdon	9	362	1,698	360	-9.87	-1.10
Dick Williams	12	526	2,412	483	-14.42	-1.20
Cito Gaston	6	187	872	221	-7.68	-1.28
Davey Johnson	12	346	2,091	406	-16.38	-1.36
Terry Francona	5	117	666	153	-7.03	-1.41
Jim Fregosi	11	435	1,537	357	-16.48	-1.50
Felipe Alou	10	334	1,369	356	-16.00	-1.60
Earl Weaver	12	570	1,693	429	-21.12	-1.76
Larry Dierker	5	116	935	114	-8.97	-1.79

TABLE 4-3.4 Worst Managers, 1972–2004, by Wins/Season (minimum five seasons)

Manager	Seasons	SH	SBA	IBB	Wins	Wins/Season
Frank Robinson	10	497	1,640	662	−32.03	−3.20
Roger Craig	9	433	1,643	649	−27.94	−3.10
Bobby Valentine	12	465	1,839	552	−36.26	−3.02
Gene Mauch	12	1,097	1,820	466	−34.72	−2.89
Darrell Johnson	5	341	793	216	−13.16	−2.63
Pat Corrales	6	306	1,056	285	−15.79	−2.63
Jim Riggleman	7	198	913	404	−18.26	−2.61
Buck Rodgers	7	213	1,833	409	−17.98	−2.57
Don Zimmer	8	294	1,070	465	−20.52	−2.56
Danny Ozark	6	215	1,028	376	−14.93	−2.49

Outplaying Projected Records

A manager's job is simple. For 162 games, you try not to screw up all the smart stuff your organization did last December.
    —Earl Weaver

The manager's true influence on a team is revealed more by his ability to get the most out of his players than by his in-game decisions. This charge manifests itself primarily in lineup order, playing-time distribution, timing, and bullpen usage. It's possible that over the long haul, some managers squeeze a little more out of their teams than expected.

One of the main contributions Bill James made to the study of baseball was the connection between a team's run differential and its winning percentage, a formula he called the "Pythagorean Formula" because of its similarity to the geometric equation. By comparing this estimated winning percentage with a team's actual winning percentage, we can see if a team squandered wins along the way or played above its expected level. For example, the New York Mets and Florida Marlins both finished the 2005 season 83-79, indicating that the teams were evenly matched. They scored almost identical numbers of runs on the season, 719 for New York and 717 for Florida. But the Mets allowed 95 fewer runs, 637 to 732. Based on their runs scored and runs allowed, we can see that the Marlins won a few more games than they would be expected to, the Mets 9 to 10 fewer. Analysts have tried to explain the discrepancy between run differential and wins by pointing to things like the quality of the bullpen and the run environment, but maybe it has something to do with the manager.

To that end, rather than seeing how teams do compared to their expected "Pythagorean" record, the same can be done with managers. First, though, we have to know whether the relationship between a manager's actual won-lost record and his Pythagorean won-lost record is random. If it is, crediting managers for exceeding their Pythagorean won-lost record would be like crediting someone for flipping a coin on heads more often than tails: There is no skill involved.

To accomplish this, a statistical tool called the coefficient of determination—R-squared, commonly—is useful. Like other statistics in previous chapters, the manager's ability to exceed his team's Pythagorean record is compared across seasons. If he has a consistent, repeatable ability to affect his team's actual won-lost record when compared to his Pythagorean won-lost record, R-squared should be closer to 1 (a perfect correlation) than zero (total randomness).

Unfortunately, after sampling well over 1,000 seasons, R-squared is 0.002. A manager's previous season has essentially zero correlation with his current season with regard to exceeding his Pythagorean won-lost record. Similarly, when we compare larger sample sizes— sets of even- or odd-numbered years to simulate randomly selected career halves—R-squared remains near total randomness (0.030). Like teams as a whole, managers show no ability to outperform the number of runs their teams score and allow. Although some managers have managed to outplay their run differential for a while, there is no evidence that any manager can do so consistently.

Playing-Time Distribution

Leo [Durocher] would play a convicted rapist
if he could turn the double play.
    —Jim Bouton

Outplaying a projected record based on individual team stats may still overlook the possibility that some managers do a better job of getting the most out of their resources by controlling their players' playing time. If managers don't play the right players in the right places, their teams will not win as many games as expected based on the talent on hand. Managers often take flack in the press for benching certain players or calling on certain relievers—perhaps none more than Cubs manager Dusty Baker, who's known for battling the media when his decisions are questioned. But when Baker insists on batting Jerry Hairston Jr. (.261/.334/.371) and Neifi Perez (.274/.300/.383) in the first two spots in the lineup, as he did in 2005, it's hard not to side with the critics.

On the other hand, so many pieces of information go into player usage that it's nearly impossible to determine whether the manager truly made a bad choice. For example, Table 4-3.5 shows the Cubs' total plate appearances for 2005 alongside their Marginal Lineup Value Rate (MLVr). MLVr is a measure of how many runs a player contributed to an average team per game based on his AVG, OBP, and SLG, adjusted for the player's home park. An MLVr of zero means a player was a league-average contributor on offense. Derrek Lee's .532 MLVr—indicating that he added just over a half a run a game—was the highest in the majors in 2005 among qualified players. Corey Patterson netted a –.255 MLVr, second-worst in the majors, ahead of only Guzman.

The "Team Rank" column shows where each player ranked on the Cubs in MLVr. The fact that Lee is first in both MLVr and PA means that the Cubs did give the most playing time to their best player (and that Lee stayed healthy all season). But three of the top five players in PA ranked eighth or lower in MLVr, suggesting that many of the team's weaker hitters saw too much playing time. While it's easy to criticize Baker for playing Perez in lieu of better hitters like Ronny Cedeño, drawing the same conclusions on a large-scale basis is nearly impossible. The table overlooks a variety of factors:

Defense. MLVr considers only offensive batting performance, excluding stolen bases. While Cedeno hit better in 2005 than Perez, it's possible that Perez made up for the difference in the field. In fact, Baseball Prospectus's defensive measure "Rate" gives Perez a 15-run edge in 2005, meaning that Cedeno's .108 advantage in MLVr—about

TABLE 4-3.5 Cubs' Marginal Lineup Value Rate

Batter	PA	MLVr	Team Rank
Derrek Lee	691	.532	1
Jeromy Burnitz	671	.012	8
Neifi Perez	609	-.097	13
Aramis Ramirez	506	.287	2
Corey Patterson	483	-.255	17
Michael Barrett	477	.121	5
Todd Walker	433	.153	4
Jerry Hairston	430	-.059	11
Todd Hollandsworth	290	-.089	12
Nomar Garciaparra	247	.048	6
Jose Macias	190	-.244	16
Henry Blanco	178	-.128	14
Matt Murton	160	.278	3
Jason Dubois	152	-.001	10
Ronny Cedeno	89	.011	9
Carlos Zambrano	84	.019	7
Matt Lawton	83	-.231	15
Greg Maddux	83	-.632	18

10.8 runs per 100 games—is completely negated by Perez's defense. Further, teams often play specific defenders behind particular pitchers to maximize their usefulness. Playing Pokey Reese behind Derek Lowe—as the Red Sox did in 2004—makes a great deal more sense than playing him behind Curt Schilling.

True offensive ability. While Matt Murton had the third-best season on the Cubs in terms of MLVr, he might not continue to perform at that level in extended playing time. The sample size involved with players at the top of the list reduces the error inherent in many of the stats used in baseball. But for players farther down the list, there is very little confidence in the predictive value of past performance.

Platoons. Managers may limit certain batters to situations in which they are more likely to succeed. The most obvious example is when players are platooned, playing only against pitchers of the opposite handedness or in situations that favor their particular skill set. If managers are successfully platooning, some players may appear to be better than they would be in full-time duty.

Injuries. The Cubs suffered their share of injuries in 2005. Some fans blame the downfall of Kerry Wood and other Cubs pitchers on Baker's tendency to overwork them—but no similar reasoning applies to batters. Obviously, any manager would rather play Nomar Garciaparra and Aramis Ramirez than lesser replacements, but both players missed time due to injury; the manager should not be punished for not playing an injured player.

Limited information on other options. It's possible that a manager insisted on playing a washed-up veteran instead of an impressive prospect in the high minor leagues, but without minor league statistics, the prospect would be overlooked. The fact that the manager or front-office personnel chose to continue with a worse option would not be found in the data. The decision may also be based in service-time issues. Teams may choose to keep a younger, better player in Triple-A to prevent him from reaching free agency at a younger age. The Oakland Athletics have been noted for doing this; the Tampa Bay Devil Rays kept hot prospect B. J. Upton in Triple-A Durham throughout the 2005 season because he would make little difference that year to the struggling major league club.

Trades. Giving 83 plate appearances to Matt Lawton and 290 to Todd Hollandsworth may look bad, but neither player spent the full season with the Cubs. Because players come and go from team rosters during the season as a result of trades and other transactions, we cannot judge managerial decisions by comparing player ranks in offensive performance on the team. Acquiring a top-notch free agent midseason (as the Cardinals did with Larry Walker in 2004) shouldn't be a reason to punish the manager for not playing Walker while he was on the Rockies. With service-time data largely unavailable, it's impossible to tell if teams were actively benching a player or if he had been traded to another team. It's possible to estimate a player's availability based on his stats with other organizations during the same season, but accuracy of that estimation is highly suspect.

Other decision makers. Some modern managers more closely resemble middle managers than major decision makers. Front-office personnel may dictate how the team is run. If the general manager demands that Perez hit at the top of the lineup, it would be wrong to criticize Baker for choosing to play him there. Unless we know who's really calling the shots, we can't evaluate the manager with any accuracy.

Most of the time, it's still up to the manager to play the right players, but so many issues are involved that discerning when a manager is making a poor choice is impossibly difficult. Several of the issues listed here could be eliminated with currently available information, but many more would still remain. For now, analyzing managerial performance based on playing-time distribution will have to be left to the future.

Playing-Time Distribution: An Alternative Approach

I'd yank my own son if it was the right move.
　—Eddie Stanky

While it appears that the mitigating factors involved in distribution of playing time make analysis of that aspect of managerial decisions untenable on a macro level, an alternative approach may yield a few results. If we assume that the manager's job—particularly early in the season—is to determine which batters fit into what roles, and that he uses the early part of the season to separate the wheat from the chaff, it may be possible to identify managers whose teams show consistent improvement in team batting performance over the course of a season. Obviously, many of the same factors listed above cloud any analysis of this methodology, but we still may be able to find some confirmation of managerial influence in this regard.

To do so, each season has been broken into three roughly equal sections—all games through May 31, June and July, and any games after Aug. 1—and within each section, the team's batting performance is assessed through MLVr. Because MLVr is a league-adjusted stat, each section of the season will be compared to the rest of the league only in that section. (This methodology should remove any problems such as changes in offensive levels based on the weather.) Once each team's MLVr is calculated for each of the three seasonal sections, we can compare late-season batter performance to the early season. The results are shown in Figures 4-3.1 and 4-3.2.

FIGURE 4-3.1 Early-season batter improvement by managerial experience, 1972–2005

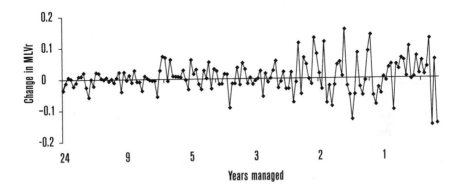

FIGURE 4-3.2 Late-season batter improvement by managerial experience, 1972–2005

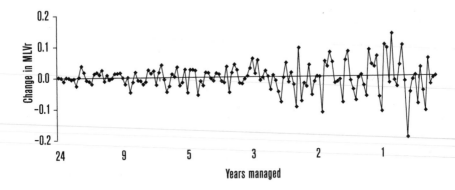

These results are ordered by managerial experience from left to right. For example, the first data point is Tony LaRussa, next is Sparky Anderson, then Bobby Cox, Joe Torre, Tommy Lasorda, and so on. Looking at these results, there are two main points to be discerned. First, the data are extremely random; while there are nearly as many managers above zero as below, changes in MLVr over the course of a season show virtually no correlation to the same manager in subsequent seasons. Second, there doesn't appear to be any advantage held by more experienced managers. The smaller variance in the left side of both graphs is because managers with more experience have a greater sample size of seasons and therefore trend heavily toward zero. The more seasons a skipper is in charge, the more his team's changes in MLVr over a season regress toward zero; this trend indicates that no managers consistently improve team batting performance over the course of a season.

Substitutions

All I do is write their names on the lineup card and let them play. It's not a tough job. I haven't misspelled one name yet.
—Harvey Kuenn

Aside from total playing-time distribution and in-game strategic decisions, the other easily measured area of managerial influence is substitutions. Pinch hitters, relief pitchers, and defensive replacements all clearly fall under the purview of the manager. By measuring how players perform in these situations, it may be possible to determine whether certain managers are better at managing their bench and bullpen than others.

Analyzing the performance of pinch hitters leaves open the question of whether or not the manager was actually selecting the best option off the bench. Analysis of those decisions goes beyond our current data capabilities—in particular, injury information not reported on the official disabled list is completely unavailable—but we can still analyze the performance of pinch hitters. Of course, if a team's pinch hitters consistently perform above the league average, that may not be a result of the manager putting them in advantageous situations but rather of the team doing a good job of selecting bench players. Instead, by comparing the performance of batters as pinch hitters to their overall season performance, we may find that some managers display a talent for consistently using batters in situations in which they're more likely to succeed.

Over the past 34 seasons as measured by OPS (OBP plus SLG), pinch hitters have hit 30 points worse when pinch-hitting than when playing the field. There are many possible reasons for this—pinch hitters may often be countered with superior relievers or players may benefit from an extended warm-up period unavailable when pinch-hitting—but whatever the reason, it seems unlikely that all managers select their pinch hitters badly. Even when adjusting for the overall depreciation of skills when pinch-hitting, no managers show a consistent ability to select pinch hitters from year to year. In fact, the correlation in adjusted pinch-hitter performance (that is, how the hitters hit compared to their season averages and adjusted for the overall difficulty of pinch-hitting) from season to season is so close to zero (.001) as to be completely random. While we cannot say whether managers select good or bad options from the bench, it's clear that no manager has shown the talent to put his pinch hitters in a situation to succeed more than any other manager.

On the flip side of pinch hitters are relief pitchers. While no team uses its bullpen as best it could (see Chapter 2-2), there may be some managers who separate themselves from the pack by employing their given resources better than most. To determine if this is the case, two tools are highly useful: Fair Run Average (FRA) and Leverage. FRA is just like ERA except that it corrects for inherited and bequeathed runners, a particularly useful update when it comes to relievers. For example, if a pitcher leaves the game with a man on first and 2 outs and the following reliever allows a home run, ERA would credit that first run to the pitcher who had already left. By contrast, FRA attributes some of the credit to each pitcher since one was responsible for putting him on base and the other for letting him score. Leverage is just what it sounds like: a measure of how important a situation is as measured by the impact of 1 additional run on a team's chances of winning the game.

Combining these two metrics allows us to determine who each team's best reliever was in a given season and which relievers were used in the most important situations. For example, in 2005, the Oakland Athletics' best reliever (minimum 30 IP) was rookie Huston Street, who posted a 1.48 FRA (compared to his 1.72 ERA). However, Street's Leverage of 1.19 (league average is 1.00) was second on the team to Justin Duchscherer, indicating that the Duchscherer was used in the most important situations throughout the season. Duchscherer's 3.39 FRA ranked him fourth on the A's, behind Street, Ricardo Rincon, and Kiko Calero. By using his fourth-best reliever in the most important situations, A's manager Ken Macha misappropriated his resources. By comparing other managers in this regard, it may be possible to determine whether some managers show a consistent ability to manage their bullpen better than the rest of the league.

It quickly becomes clear from the numbers that there is virtually no consistency from year to year in this regard. Some managers—such as Billy Martin—have shown an ability to utilize their relievers more effectively than other managers—Bobby Cox and Roger Craig are very low on the list. But year-to-year consistency is absent, as are any kind of larger trends. Furthermore, most managers fall within a very small range of values, an expected result considering the near complete absence of bullpen innovation in modern baseball. Regardless of the reason, once again no managers have separated themselves from the pack with regard to any measurable influence.

Finally, there is the matter of defensive substitutions. Late in games, typically when a team has a small lead, managers will often remove superior hitters for superior defenders, sacrificing some small chance that the big sluggers will reach the plate one more time for the increased assurance of preventing a tying run. Usually these changes are made only when it's obvious that the slugger will not come to bat again unless the game goes into extra innings or the leading team sends quite a few men to the plate in the late innings. As such, there is little to no risk in removing him from the lineup. But just how much of a difference do those defensive substitutions make?

Typically, the league's best defenders are about 10 to 15 runs above average per 100 games (as measured by Rate), while the worst are somewhere on the flip side of that total. Of course, those are only the most extreme cases. For the most part, teams see a difference of 5–10 runs at most between backups and starters. While managers would obviously do well to play a superior defender if they were certain that that player's spot in the order would not come up again, the advantage provided by those substitutions is almost too small to measure.

Improving Individual Batter Performance

The workout is optional.
Whoever doesn't come gets optioned.
   —Bobby Valentine

One final possible influence of the manager is in the performance of the players themselves. Individual coaches are usually in charge of teaching technique to the players, but the manager chooses his coaches and makes sure their authority is respected. By comparing the performance of players under a particular manager with their performance elsewhere, we may find that certain managers positively influence player performance. Performing this analysis is tricky because so many factors influence player performance; many of these factors—for instance, the individual coaches employed—are unavailable and cannot be removed from the analysis. Other factors—such as the park and the player's age—are known and can be removed. Park factors are easily employed to remove the influence of the home stadium, but adjusting for age is more difficult.

Players typically peak between the ages of twenty-six and twenty-nine. An evaluation of the performance of players under a manager may be skewed if he happens to manage a particularly old or young team. If his team is older, the manager may appear to be negatively influencing player performance because the players are simply aging. Conversely, a manager of a young team may appear to do the same because his players hit their peak seasons after they leave his care. Fortunately for this study, most managers deal with players within a very small average age range. Among the 456 managers tested, 436 acquired players between ages twenty-six and twenty-nine on average, and nearly as many parted ways with them in those same ranges.

As before, we would be remiss to analyze managerial influence on batter performance without first confirming that there is a distinguishable skill involved. To that end, we can compare artificial subsets of the data to each other to see if there is any correlation. Manager-player relationships can be broken into two groups based on the first letter of the player's last name and then correlated. If managers show a consistent ability to improve player performance, the two groups should show a high correlation. But if a manager does a great job with players whose names start with A through M and less so with the N-through-Z's, we know that his apparent ability is a matter of chance. No manager's influence (one assumes) depends on where a player lands in the alphabet.

Using the R-squared test as we did before, we find that the correlation between the two groups is almost exactly zero: 0.003. There is no connection between change in batter performance and the manager among the 456 managers studied.

Conclusions and Future Analysis

Managing is getting paid for home runs someone else hits.
    —Casey Stengel

In the end, we may be forced to concede that the evaluation of managers is one area of analysis in which the numbers cannot provide any useful insight. Through a slew of different analytical techniques, no evidence of managerial influence has been found. We have seen that most managers overuse strategies like sacrifice bunts, stolen bases, and intentional walks, but it's unclear if they are the instigators or if the personnel involved escape the analysis of the Win Expectancy framework. Managers show no consistent ability to exceed their team's projected record based on runs scored and runs allowed. There is, as yet, no viable way to evaluate on a macro level how a manager distributes playing time, nor does there appear to be any consistent ability to improve a team's batting performance over the course of the season. The use of either pinch hitters or relief pitchers does not reveal any skippers who show an ability to deploy their available resources better than others, and the benefit of late-inning defensive replacements is so small that attempting to find superior managers in that regard is nearly impossible. Finally, managers show no consistent ability to improve batter performance.

The singular problem with statistical analysis of managerial ability is that there are too many factors in play that are not measured by any available numbers. Not only do individual managerial decisions take into account a wide variety of factors—the individual players involved, unreported injuries or fatigue, the particular aspects of the park or weather, other available options—but the very choices normally attributed to the manager may not be his decision or influence at all. Perhaps another coach on staff provided some additional information to aid in the decision-making process. The front office may mandate in-game strategies, pitch counts, or playing-time distribution. We can neither quantify the decision-making process faced by the manager nor conclusively attribute any individual decision to him.

The analysis of managers may instead be best undertaken through a more historical approach, as opposed to an analytic tack. While this methodology is filled with nearly as many pitfalls as the ones already undertaken, it does allow many more factors to be explored. For example, we can convincingly attribute Dusty Baker's playing-time distributions to him because he frequently discusses his reasoning with the media. He makes it very clear why he plays certain players and why he does not. Thus, when he refuses to play players such as Corey Patterson, we can analyze that particular decision and determine how much Baker gained or cost his team by making those decisions.

However, this analysis would also lead to reliance on a great deal of hearsay. Torre is often cited as providing a calming influence on his players and shielding them from the machinations of a fickle ownership group. But can we quantify the benefits of that calmness? Do we know how well the 1996 Yankees would have played under Showalter? Is Torre's reputed calmness simply a hindsight justification of the team's sudden improvement and march to the championship?

Why did those traits fail him in three previous managerial jobs? Perhaps this particular ability was not a necessary asset in those positions. Could it be that a manager is a bullet with some team's name on it, highly effective when deployed with that team, which matches his strengths, and useless at all other times?

In Torre's case, this may be true. He is seemingly the first of fourteen managers who have worked for George Steinbrenner to understand that the owner's tempestuousness and impulsivity is a fact of life that the manager tacitly accepts when he agrees to manage the team. Indeed, prior to Torre, Steinbrenner's influence on the team was often credited for its poor results. The most famous of these blowups may have been in 1985, when Steinbrenner, furious with the team for losing 3 straight to the division-leading Blue Jays in a pennant race, called Dave Winfield "Mr. May"—a turn on the postseason heroics of Reggie Jackson—and publicly ripped the team. The Yankees then immediately dropped another 5 games in a row. After the streak, the Yanks were 6.5 games out with just over two weeks to play; even an 11-3 kick to finish the season couldn't overtake the Jays.

For the most part, Torre has played the role of shield better than his predecessors. Whether or not his quiet resolve has enjoyed a lucky propinquity to a team that would have done well anyway, the players seem to believe in him, and when it comes to confidence, a placebo effect is almost as good as the real thing.

Baseball is a human industry with human employees. It's impossible to say how much a team's performance is helped by a positive work environment. While performance analysts scoff at the notion of clubhouse harmony, it's silly to say that team morale doesn't exist simply because it's difficult to measure. Managers have long been credited with setting a tone for their teams. Heywood Broun once said of John McGraw, "He could take kids out of the coal mines and out of the wheat fields and make them walk and talk and chatter and play ball with the look of eagles." Joe McCarthy of the Yankees, responding to an atmosphere of permissiveness that had been a constant distraction to his predecessor, Miller Huggins, famously told his players, "You're a Yankee. Act like one." Though the word "Yankee" had no previous positive connotation of professional comportment, McCarthy proceeded to redefine it that way. It is in that realm—keeping players happy and fostering a positive atmosphere—that we must look for a manager's influence, because there is little evidence that he consistently affects the game on the field.

Particular managers may make it easier for teams to sign and re-tain players, while others make it harder. Cliff Floyd, to take a well-known example, would probably not have moved from the Marlins to the Mets while Bobby Valentine was in New York. Managers may earn their salaries by bringing in better players and making them want to stay. But other than that, it's difficult to see direct managerial influence on a team's performance.

As long as managers' contributions remain shrouded in mystery, should Joe Torre—or Bobby Cox, or Tony LaRussa—be given a ticket to Cooperstown? When deciding whether to vote to put a skipper into the Hall of Fame, sportswriters nearly always focus on the manager's reputation and the number of championships he's won. Torre's four World Series championships and his highly public position as manager of a Yankees dynasty will almost certainly get him in. But in terms of actually contributing wins on the field, the influence of managers remains clouded by auxiliary factors, hidden somewhere beneath the numbers.

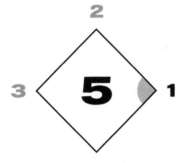

Why Is Mario Mendoza
So Important?

KEITH WOOLNER

Mario Mendoza wasn't the kind of player you'd expect to achieve immortality. He played nine seasons, from 1974 to 1982, topping 200 plate appearances just three times. He never played in a World Series or was named to an All-Star team. He was regarded as a good defensive shortstop but never won a Gold Glove. The only category where he ever cracked the top ten in the league was sacrifice hits. Of the three teams he played for (Pittsburgh 1974–1978, Seattle 1979–1980, Texas 1981–1982), only one finished in first place (the '74 Pirates, Mendoza's rookie year), and three finished with 95 or more losses. He played some second base and third, and even pitched in one game (giving up 3 hits, 2 walks, a homer, and 3 earned runs in 2 innings in his sole appearance in 1977). In over 1,300 career at-bats, he hit only 4 home runs; showed unremarkable speed, patience, or even gap power; and never hit above .245 in any season.

Simply put, Mendoza was not a good player. Actually, "not good" is understating the case. He ranks as one of the worst hitters in the history of Major League Baseball. That offensive ineptitude became his lasting claim to fame: It gave rise to the term "Mendoza Line," meaning a .200 batting average. Hit above the Mendoza Line, the theory goes, and you've achieved the minimum tolerable level of offense a player must produce to hang around the fringes of a major league roster.

The term's origins are murky. Former major leaguers George Brett, Bruce Bochy, and Tom Paciorek have all been credited with coining it. Some claim it refers to an entirely different Mendoza. The line's location is also subject to debate: It's customarily set at a .200 batting average, but Mendoza's career average was actually .215. Yet regardless of the line's origins or precise definition, its implication is huge. If you are a major league batter and your production is on the wrong side of the Mendoza Line (or indeed anywhere near it), your job is in jeopardy. (Mendoza's .245 career on-base percentage was well below the .300 OBP mark sometimes seen as the Mendoza Line for that stat; though there's no widely recognized Mendoza Line for slugging average, his .262 career SLG would surely fall well below it).

Why does the Mendoza Line represent such a boundary? A lot of athletes aspire to play major league baseball—more athletes than MLB can ever absorb, no matter how much it expands. With more aspirants than positions, teams have the luxury of taking only the best from the crowds of minor leaguers and journeymen on the outside looking in. They will never have to settle for less than some level of expected offense when they can easily find a few dozen players capable of producing at least that much and ready to sign on at a moment's notice. When a team suddenly loses a player and has to fill a hole in its roster, this pool of talent is waiting to replace the lost player at minimal cost. This "replacement level" of cheap and readily available offense is embodied by Mario Mendoza and his eponymous line. Replacement level is an important concept for roster construction and player valuation that goes far beyond the flippant invocation of his name.

The Problem with Raw Statistics

Why do we need a concept like replacement level? Can't you just look at a player's stats and tell how good he is?

You may have some intuition regarding how good a player is by inspecting his stats alone. If you see someone bat .320 with 120 RBI, you know you're looking at a good hitter. But that's because you have internalized some notion about what a "good" batting average is and how many RBI a cleanup hitter should get. There's context in your value judgments.

Also, raw statistics like HR and RBI are highly dependent on playing time. If a player has 10 HR and 30 RBI, you might not be impressed if you assumed he was a full-time player. If you find out he did that in 150 at-bats, your perspective changes—he's "on pace" for 40 HR and 120 RBI in 600 at-bats. You need to consider both the amount of playing time a player gets and the rate of production to get a full picture of his contribution.

Furthermore, "good" varies according to what the rest of the league does. If the league's overall batting average is .245, like the 1963 National League, .280 is possibly an All-Star level of hitting. In the 1999 American League, when the league average was .275, a .280 average barely gets noticed. You need to know the environment in which the raw stats were produced to figure out how valuable they were.

Different positions have differing offensive expectations. A shortstop's defensive responsibilities are huge, and there are very few players, even at the top of the talent pool, who are capable of fielding the position well. The number of potentially great hitters is thus reduced proportionally. This is why we see shortstops perennially hitting worse than first basemen (Miguel Tejada, Derek Jeter, and former star shortstops Alex Rodriguez and Nomar Garciaparra notwithstanding). A hitter of Mendoza's caliber could never have had a nine-year major league career playing, say, right field. While it's difficult to quantify exactly how much harder it is to play shortstop than right field, some consideration must be given to a position's defensive requirements.

The Problem with Average-Based Metrics

Raw statistical totals and averages cannot, by themselves, give us a fair picture of a player's contribution. To help address some of these issues, statistical measures such as Normalized Production (PRO+) and Batting Runs (both the creations of Pete Palmer), as well as Runs Created Above Average (RCAA, created by Lee Sinins) have come upon the scene. All involve comparing a player's statistics to the league average and expressing them as either a percentage above or below average (PRO+) or a number of runs above or below average (Batting Runs and RCAA). A player with a 130 PRO+, for instance, has produced at a rate 30 percent above league average. In the case of Batting Runs, where players can have negative values, one with –10 has produced 10 *fewer* runs than an average hitter with the same number of plate appearances. Zero Batting Runs means exactly league average, whether the batter had 100 or 600 PA.

But there's a problem with this approach. Since all the players who secure jobs are at or above replacement level, then their average performance must be higher than replacement level. A player with average performance is actually playing at a level few others can match.

There will always be a significant number of players in the majors who are below average, and untold thousands below replacement level. Average performance is hard to find.

Measures that use average production as the basis of comparison will thus incorrectly account for the value of playing time for average players. To see why, Table 5-1.1 compares two players on otherwise identical teams. (We're using Equivalent Average [EqA], a Baseball Prospectus statistic, as the metric for offensive performance in this example because it aggregates all major aspects of offense into a single measure. EqA uses roughly the same scale as batting average, so you can assume that a good EqA looks like a good batting average and vice versa.)

TABLE 5-1.1 Comparison of Two Players on Otherwise Identical Teams, by Equivalent Average

Name	PA	EqA
Joe Average	600	.260
Flash Fragile	100	.320

Joe Average produces at the league-average rate of .260, steady and reliable but not an All-Star. If he's healthy enough to play, Flash Fragile hits like an MVP. But as you can see from his few plate appearances, that's a big "if."

Let's say for simplicity that 600 plate appearances per season are needed from each position. Joe can play the entire season for his team. Flash, on the other hand, accounts for just one-sixth of the playing time needed. What will his team do the rest of the time?

Now, suppose Flash's team did not know about his fragility at the start of the season. If they expected him to play all or most of the season, his replacement is likely a cheap utility player kept on the bench to pinch-run or for late-inning defense. But now Flash's team may be forced to use that utility player, or find some fringe major leaguer waiting for the phone to ring, or perhaps call up a player from Triple-A to fill in. That's the best the team can do without sacrificing more resources (including future value in the form of prospects) to fill Flash's lost playing time.

Let's say that Bill Backup becomes the starter when Flash gets hurt. Bill is a fringe player drawing a modest salary. If he were significantly better than fringe level, he would likely have a starting job somewhere else. Based on what we know about bench players, we expect about a .230 EqA from Bill; since EqA runs along roughly the same scale as batting average, Bill's a .230 hitter no matter how you slice it. When you look over the course of the entire season, Table 5-1.2 shows how the team with Joe Average does, compared to the Flash-and-Bill combination. Joe's team got more overall production, a .260 EqA, from his position, whereas Flash and Bill's team managed just a .245 EqA because of Flash's lack of durability and Bill's weak bat.

From the replacement-level perspective, Joe's performance well exceeds the combined contributions of Flash and Bill. Since we've assumed Bill is a typical replacement-level player, his contribution is zero; that is, he gives a team nothing above replacement level. This means that Joe's value must be more than Flash's.

TABLE 5-1.2 Comparison of Average, Everyday Player vs. Combined Performance of Above-Average Player Who Gets Injured and His Backup, by Equivalent Average

Name	PA	EqA
Joe Average	600	.260
Flash Fragile	100	.320
Bill Backup	500	.230
Flash + Bill Total	600	.245

Let's switch to some names that are more familiar. In 2003, Ken Griffey Jr. amassed an on-base percentage of .368 and a slugging average of .566 while playing center field for the Cincinnati Reds. But due to injuries, Griffey played in just 53 games and had only 201 plate appearances. The same year, Padres center fielder Mark Kotsay batted .266, with an OBP of .342 and a SLG of .384, albeit in a tougher hitter's park in San Diego. He put up those numbers over 542 plate appearances, while Griffey missed two-thirds of the season. Thus, while Kotsay trailed Griffey in rate categories like OBP, SLG, and even home runs (13 for Griffey, 7 for Kotsay), Kotsay's ability to put up league-average numbers on a regular basis was worth more to the Padres than Griffey's excellent but infrequent contributions were to the Reds. (We'll discuss how much more a little later.)

Comparison to average does not completely capture what we think of as value because players who are average are quite rare. When a major league–average player puts up 600 plate appearances of league-average performance, that's rarer still. Using a replacement-level approach rewards players for durability as well as performance above the free-talent level.

The Definition of Replacement Level

Replacement level is the expected level of performance a major league team will receive from one or more of the best available players who can be obtained with minimal expenditure of team resources to substitute for a suddenly unavailable starting player at the same position.

Each of those qualifiers is important—let's run through them.

Expected level of performance. Even if you have perfect information when the decision is made, a player may hit better or worse than his projection over a small number of plate appearances. Replacement level is based on what you expected from the potential replacements using the best information you had available, not what he does in his 50 PA. You'd need a much larger sample of performance to know the player's true ability.

One or more of the best available players. When you replace a starting player's performance, you can do so with a platoon, with an offense/defense tandem arrangement, or by moving a player from somewhere else and putting the replacement in that player's position. The flexibility in filling the gap is not limited to one player, and what we're interested in is the overall effect on the team's production.

Minimal expenditure. If you're the New York Yankees, you're better able to take on another team's albatross contract. Thus, you can get a player who's better than replacement level. That said, while spending a lot of money, or top prospects, to acquire a better talent to "replace" a lost player is a viable strategy, it doesn't represent "freely available talent"—the kind any team could pick up in a pinch.

Suddenly unavailable. Given the benefit of long-term planning, a team can invest its scouting and developmental resources into grooming players at a particular position. A replacement player is what you settle for when you're caught unprepared.

Given all that, it's worth asking: If replacement-level talent is freely available, why do we see players performing below that level? There are several possibilities:

- *Improper evaluation/bad information.* Our definition of replacement level assumes that general managers make the best decision their information allows. If they have faulty information—an error in a player's age, a mistake in reading the radar gun, transposing stats in a scouting report—they may end up with a much worse player than expected.
- *Suboptimal decision making.* There are plenty of examples of teams keeping a highly paid player, even if his performance stinks, when they should cut bait. Teams should be able to acknowledge sunk costs and move on, but they often can't. It's tough for many GMs and managers to admit they're wrong. It's even tougher to explain to owners how the $20 million you spent on a player is long gone and the investment cannot be recouped.
- *Strategic reasons other than short-term win maximization.* Sometimes a team will call up a prospect "who has nothing left to prove in the minors" and play him even if he's overmatched for a

while. If the team is not in contention, the long-term benefits of developing the player may outweigh his short-term performance.

◆ *Injury.* A player hampered by an injury, or playing while recovering from one, may play poorly for a while even if he is normally able to perform above replacement level, especially if the player has kept his injury a secret for fear of losing his job.

◆ *Alternative beliefs about replacement level.* A GM who has not identified which low-cost players are actually out there may form misguided beliefs about scarcity and thus overrate the low-level talent already on hand.

◆ *Defensive performance.* Thus far, we've talked about replacement level mostly in terms of offense. But a player's total value includes defensive play. An exceptional defender may be a below-replacement-level hitter and still have a positive impact. The classic example is Hall of Fame shortstop Ozzie Smith, who in his early years was a terrible hitter (over his first four full seasons, he averaged .231 AVG/.295 OBP/.278 SLG in more than 2,200 at-bats) but whose glove kept his job for him.

◆ *Sample size/statistical noise.* This is the stathead's favorite explanation for any event not predicted. Given a handful of plate appearances, there can be enormous variance in observed performance around a true level of ability. You can't judge a player, veteran or rookie, by 50 plate appearances. Too many random events can occur in such a small sample of playing time.

Replacement-Level Formulas

So how do we find out what replacement level is? Baseball Prospectus's approach is to look at the collective performance of backup players—those who have actually filled in for regulars—and see how their performance compares to the average for their positions. For each year, we look at each team and see which player amassed the most plate appearances at each position. For example, the player with the most PA at catcher for the Red Sox, then the Yankees, then the Orioles, and so on; then the player with the most PA at first base for the Red Sox, Yankees, etc. These players are identified as the regular players for that season. Each remaining player is assigned to a position based on where he played most frequently. For instance, a bench player with 30 games at third base and 10 in the outfield would be considered a 3B. The batting statistics of all of the backup players at a given position are added up and compared to the league average for that position. This process is repeated for every position and every season. Over the long haul, regular players account for about 80 percent of all plate appearances, with backup players picking up the remaining 20 percent.

When you chart the results of this process (Fig. 5-1.1), a remarkable relationship emerges. The collective performance of all non-regular players hovers around 80 percent of the average offensive level for the position (expressed as Runs Created per 27 outs, or RC/27). The only minor exceptions are at catcher, arguably the position with the highest defensive demands, at which backups produce at about 85 percent of average; and first base, the least demanding defensive position, which sees backups hit at about 75 percent of the regulars' average.

Determining Replacement Level from AVG/OBP/SLG and OPS

Most fans don't automatically think of a more advanced stat such as RC/27 when considering offense. Batting average (AVG) has been king for a long time, and more recently on-base percentage (OBP) and slugging average (SLG) have been added to form a "trio" of rate stats that capture a player's performance concisely. Fortunately, there's a way to estimate replacement-level in terms of this trio of rate stats. For a position with a replacement level of R percent (R = 80 percent for most positions), subtract P points from the position's average AVG/OBP/SLG, using the following formula:

$$P = (0.1073 - 0.11 \times R) \times \sqrt[3]{\left(\frac{25 \times OBP \times SLG}{1 - AVG} \right)}$$

Let's simplify the math with an example. Suppose we want to find replacement level for left field, where the league-average LF hits .270/.340/.430, which is about 5.0 RC/27. Left field is an 80 percent replacement-level position, so we plug R = 80 percent into the formula above, and find that P is equal to 33 points. Left field in this hypothetical league would have a replacement level of .237/.307/.397, which is 33 points below the position's average AVG, OBP, and SLG.

Table 5-1.3 shows the actual replacement levels for every non-pitcher position in 2005. Remember that these levels are for 2005 only and don't apply to other years, since baseball changes. Thus, replacement levels in 1968—when pitching dominated the landscape—would be much lower for hitters and higher for pitchers.

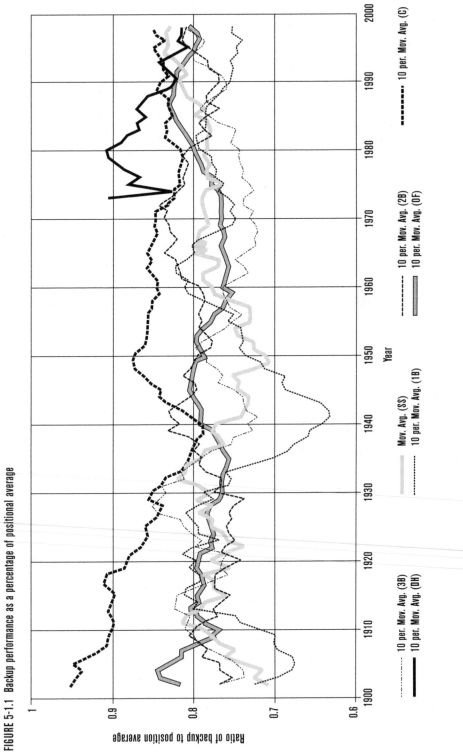

FIGURE 5-1.1 Backup performance as a percentage of positional average

TABLE 5-1.3 Replacement Level for All Non-Pitcher Positions, 2005

Year	League	POS	Position Average			Replacement Level		
			AVG	OBP	SLG	AVG	OBP	SLG
2005	AL	C	.257	.313	.392	.234	.291	.370
2005	AL	1B	.271	.343	.458	.228	.300	.415
2005	AL	2B	.271	.323	.413	.240	.291	.382
2005	AL	3B	.266	.329	.427	.234	.297	.395
2005	AL	SS	.276	.331	.412	.244	.299	.380
2005	AL	LF	.278	.333	.436	.246	.301	.404
2005	AL	CF	.268	.322	.407	.237	.291	.376
2005	AL	RF	.270	.332	.451	.237	.299	.419
2005	AL	DH	.259	.337	.440	.226	.304	.408
2005	NL	C	.250	.314	.388	.228	.291	.365
2005	NL	1B	.280	.361	.483	.236	.317	.438
2005	NL	2B	.276	.338	.414	.244	.306	.382
2005	NL	3B	.274	.344	.442	.241	.311	.409
2005	NL	SS	.264	.313	.378	.234	.283	.348
2005	NL	LF	.272	.348	.457	.238	.314	.423
2005	NL	CF	.275	.340	.437	.242	.307	.405
2005	NL	RF	.269	.346	.456	.235	.312	.423
2005	NL	DH	.249	.331	.383	.218	.300	.352

Pitchers

To figure out replacement level for pitching, we need to divide pitch-ers into starters and relievers. These two categories of pitchers face such different demands that we must think of them as different "posi-tions." Starting pitchers need the endurance to go at least six innings, but they have the advantage of a regular schedule. Relievers may be called upon at any time but rarely throw more than a couple of in-nings. Since the requirements for endurance and flexibility are so different, it makes sense to treat them as having two different replace-ment levels.

Starting Pitching Replacement Value

For starting pitchers, let's stick with the modern period that is most familiar to us. The five-man rotation has been established for some time, so we'll treat each spot in the rotation as a separate "position."

In every season during the five-man rotation era—started during the late 1960s—the percentage of starts by the five most frequent starters on each team has ranged from 78 percent to 85 percent, averaging just over 80 percent, similar to the percentage seen in position players' playing time. This means that a typical team dips into the replacement pool for about 30 starts a year—nearly the equivalent of a full-time starter.

Interestingly, to cover 80 percent of the total starts in the league, taking the same number of pitchers from each team, we have to select the five pitchers with the most starts per team in every season since 1901, decades before the establishment of the five-man rotation. This represents the league average for all those years. It's not clear why—perhaps because more frequent usage brought more injuries to pitchers, or because training techniques and nutrition were more primitive. In any case, because the percentage of starts is so consistent, we've used a five-man rotation as the baseline for the entire data set, even for decades we think of as dominated by four-man or three-man rotations. What has changed over time is the distribution in starts among the five pitchers. In earlier eras, the top three pitchers received a larger fraction of the 80 percent than the #4 or #5 pitchers (see Chapter 2-3 for more on four-man vs. five-man rotations).

When we look at the remaining 20 percent of starts—those not made by any of a team's top five starters—and compare their collective performance to the league average, we get the following formula:

$$\text{Replacement-level RA} = 1.37 \times \text{League RA} - 0.66$$

. . . where RA is Run Average, like the familiar ERA except that it includes all runs allowed. This formula does a credible job of estimating replacement level throughout the modern era, as shown in Figure 5-1.2.

Relief Pitching Replacement Value

To find relief pitcher replacement level, we list all relievers on a team in descending order of their relief innings pitched. Then we take as many relievers on the list as necessary to reach 80 percent of all relief innings thrown by that team. The remaining 20 percent of innings go to the least used relievers, who constitute the replacement pool.

Overall, replacement relief pitchers do a little better than replacement starting pitchers, averaging about two-tenths of a run better in RA. This finding reinforces our belief that relief pitchers are those who were not made starters because of their limited endurance. The pool of potential relievers is larger because pitchers with lower

FIGURE 5-1.2 Starting pitching replacement-level RA vs. league-average starting RA, 1978–2000

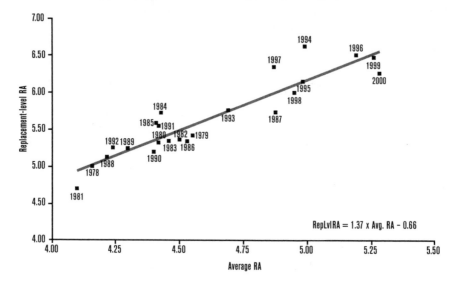

endurance are not automatically eliminated; thus, pitchers who are better on a per-inning basis can find work in the bullpen.

Deriving the formula for replacement-level RA for relievers as a function of league average RA (Fig. 5-1.3) gives us:

$$\text{Replacement-level relief RA} = 1.70 \times \text{League RA} - 2.27$$

FIGURE 5-1.3 Relief pitcher replacement-level RA vs. league-average relief RA, 1978–2000

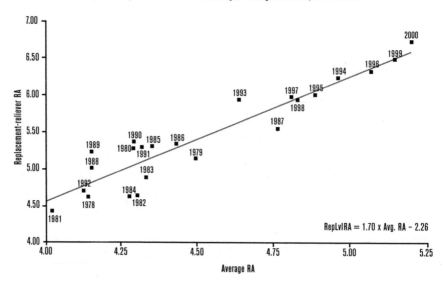

For 2005, the league replacement levels for starting pitching and relief pitching using these formulas are in Table 5-1.4. The caveats made earlier about how replacement level changes in different eras apply here as well.

TABLE 5-1.4 League Replacement Levels for Starting Pitching and Relief Pitching, 2005, by Run Average

League	League-Average RA	Starting Rep.-Level RA	Relief Rep.-Level RA
AL	4.74	5.83	5.78
NL	4.57	5.61	5.50

Putting It All Together: VORP

One of Baseball Prospectus's most popular statistics, Value Over Replacement Player (VORP), uses replacement level (as the name suggests) to measure the performance of players. Rather than compare a player to the average performance of the league, or even the average at his position, VORP lets us compare him to the replacement level at the position he plays. This method credits players whose performance level is not available to all teams (if you're average, then by definition someone is below you) and properly values that scarcity.

VORP simply measures in runs the value a player contributes to his team above what a replacement-level player would likely produce. For every 10 runs of VORP, the player is adding roughly 1 win to his team's ledger above what a replacement-level player would contribute. Thus, a player with a negative VORP is performing *worse* than what we might expect from a freely available warm body. A player with a VORP of 100, on the other hand, is breathing rarefied air and should be considered a strong MVP candidate.

Replacement-level concepts permeate Baseball Prospectus's approach to player evaluation. BP's Win Expectancy report adjusts for replacement level for relief pitchers. The Support Neutral Value Added does the same for starting pitchers. The PECOTA system (Player Empirical Comparison and Optimization Test Algorithm), the tool Baseball Prospectus uses every year to predict player performance, includes a projection of each player's VORP as well. In sum, comparison to replacement level instead of average properly captures the dilemmas real baseball teams face when acquiring or developing talent.

And in an era when bench players are paid like CEOs, those dilemmas usually involve money. When we set the zero level for measurement at replacement level instead of at average, certain economic realities emerge.

- ◆ Players who are above replacement level but below average will be recognized as having made a positive contribution to their teams, and that contribution increases with more playing time, rather than decreasing as in an average-based value system.
- ◆ For two players who are both performing at the league average, the one with more playing time will be credited as having more value. The positive value of durability is reflected in replacement-level metrics such as VORP.
- ◆ Value measurements will more closely approximate the tradeoffs that team management faces in making roster decisions.

Replacement level is thus an important concept in understanding the economics of the game and in particular why unremarkable talent has been overvalued.

Let's simplify things for a moment and pretend that a player's value is completely determined by home runs. Suppose a reliable 50-homers-a-year first baseman is worth $20 million on the open market. How much is a 25-HR hitter worth? If you guessed $10 million, read on.

To find replacement level at first base, we can use the same technique described earlier—remove the top thirty first basemen by plate appearances and compute the performance of the remaining group. In doing so, we get a player who, if given 500 at-bats' worth of playing time, would look like this:

AB	H	2B	3B	HR	BB	AVG	OBP	SLG
500	109	15	3	17	39	.218	.276	.362

That's roughly the 2005 performance of Jose Offerman, extrapolated to 500 at-bats. Offerman, not coincidentally, had a Value Over Replacement Player of near zero.

If a replacement-level first baseman, easy to find and making well under a million dollars per year, can hit 17 homers in a season, then we can say that a 17-homer first baseman is not very valuable. It's the homers beyond 17 that separate good players from bad (keeping in mind our simplified model, where homers are everything).

So, rather than saying our $20 million slugger hit 50 homers, we might say that he hit 33 homers above replacement level. Assuming a generous replacement-level cost of $1 million, the extra 33 homers are how he earns the other $19 million. Each home run above replacement level is thus worth 19/33 = $575,757.

Our 25-homer player hit only 8 homers above replacement level. At $575,757 each, those 8 homers are worth $4,606,055 beyond the replacement-level salary of $1 million, making his total market salary about $5.6 million. If you, as a GM, signed him for $10 million, you overvalued his production by 78 percent!

Not surprisingly, it's the middle-of-the-market players who tend to be most overvalued. Recently, however, there have been indications that teams are getting smarter about replacement level. No longer are #3 starters pulling down eight-figure annual salaries; run-of-the-mill outfielders are seeing their salaries fall below the $5-million-a-year level. Despite an uptick in the price of pitching in the 2005 off-season, this appears to be the start of a long-term trend of better valuation rather than a one-time market correction. The new breed of general manager, such as Billy Beane of the Oakland A's, has recognized the inefficiencies in the market caused by not understanding replacement level; shrewd GMs considered more old-school due to their increased focus on scouting—such as the Atlanta Braves' John Schuerholz—have done the same. Though salaries ticked back up in the 2005 off-season, that increased recognition of replacement level remains largely intact.

Replacement level is just as important in fantasy baseball. Knowing the easily available talent level and deriving value judgments from that level keep GMs and fantasy players alike from overpaying for the middle of the market while still properly valuing durability.

Baseball analysts often say that a replacement-level player has "no value" as a simple shorthand. But keep in mind that value is relative. Even Mario Mendoza, the patron saint of replacement level, was a better ballplayer than 99.9 percent of the people on the planet and in his prime would certainly have kicked my sorry ass on the ballfield. It's only because we're comparing players to the universe of major league–caliber talent that we can say a Mendoza or an Offerman "has no value." So let's honor the Mendoza Line. While a player on the line won't help a team win the World Series, he still represents a level of talent and performance that most of us watching the games from our living rooms could never attain.

From Mario Mendoza to Babe Ruth

Bill James invented Similarity Scores as a fun way to compare two players' career batting lines and determine how much they resemble each other. Higher scores indicate more similarity between the two players, and perfect similarity is 1,000.

Computing Similarity Scores involves taking the difference between the two players' totals in a variety of statistical categories and converting them to a point total to subtract from 1,000. This can be rather complicated. However, Sean Forman's excellent Web site www.baseball-reference .com provides the top-ten most similar batters for every player in major league history, sparing us the need to slog through the math ourselves.

One amusing diversion that can kill your productivity at work is to play a version of the famous "Six Degrees of Kevin Bacon" movie-connection game, but with similar players. Pick a starting player and an ending player. Choose any of the ten most similar batters listed on the Baseball-Reference.com page for that player. Then look up that player's page and consult the list of ten players most similar to him. Repeat the process until you get to the ending player.

For example, suppose I want to connect Jim Rice to John Olerud.

Jim Rice's #10 most similar batter is Chili Davis.

Chili Davis's #9 most similar batter is Steve Garvey

Steve Garvey's #9 most similar batter is John Olerud.

Babe Ruth is the consensus pick for the best player of all time, having posted the greatest career offensive numbers in history. Mario Mendoza, while perhaps not the worst player ever to don a uniform, has come to epitomize offensive futility. Is it possible to link Mendoza to the Babe?

It turns out that although it is possible, it takes a while to get there. One such chain, containing forty-six players, is shown below. This isn't necessarily the shortest chain, but it shows it can be done. If you find a shorter link, drop us a line at BaseballProspectus.com.

Mario Mendoza
Rick Auerbach (#6, 955)
John Boccabella (#9, 954)
Kiko Garcia (#10, 948)
Neal Ball (#10, 954)
Mike Phillips (#9, 954)
Roberto Pena (#6, 932)
Chuck Hiller (#7, 959)
Bobby Young (#7, 965)
Danny Murtaugh (#3, 958)
Dave Chalk (#9, 952)
Denny Doyle (#6, 954)
Jose Lind (#4, 956)
Johnny Rawlings (#1, 964)

Doug Flynn (#10, 936)
Tommy Thevenow (#3, 926)
Davy Force (#3, 937)
Otto Knabe (#8, 911)
Ted Sizemore (#6, 923)
Bobby Richardson (#2, 943)
Felix Millan (#7, 937)
Hughie Critz (#9, 922)
Bill Hallman (#5, 920)
Joe Quinn (#6, 911)
Kid Gleason (#1, 922)
Tony Taylor (#4, 870)
Bill Mazeroski (#9, 865)
Toby Harrah (#10, 843)
Sal Bando (#4, 854)
Ron Cey (#2, 897)
Matt Williams (#4, 879)
Frank Howard (#5, 865)
Norm Cash (#3, 911)
Jack Clark (#6, 900)
Fred Lynn (#9, 891)
Reggie Smith (#1, 960)
Dick Allen (#8, 898)
Chuck Klein (#9, 867)
Johnny Mize (#6, 865)
Duke Snider (#6, 853)
Ken Griffey (#5, 880)
Sammy Sosa (#3, 875)
Mickey Mantle (#5, 840)
Jimmie Foxx (#7, 807)
Ted Williams (#2, 864)
Babe Ruth (#6, 728)

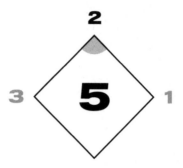

Is Alex Rodriguez Overpaid?

NATE SILVER

On Dec. 10, 2000, Alex Rodriguez agreed to a ten-year contract with the Texas Rangers that guaranteed him $252 million in salary. Rodriguez's salary outstripped the $250 million that Rangers owner Tom Hicks had paid for the Texas franchise itself when he purchased it prior to the 1997 season and the $191 million it cost to construct Rodriguez's new home, the Ballpark in Arlington. It represents the largest contract given to an individual athlete in sports history.

It also assured that Rodriguez would be associated forever with his hefty contract. Seattle Mariners fans, who had seen the shortstop propel their once moribund franchise to three playoff appearances in his first six big-league seasons, cried treason. Talking heads rushed to the airwaves and the editorial desk to decry the deal, pointing out that it promised Rodriguez more than $500 per pitch.

There was little debating that Rodriguez, just twenty-five at the time he signed the contract, was one of the most talented free agents in the history of the sport. But his new contract seemed beyond the pale. Could a baseball player possibly be worth that much? For many people, the answer is a simple "of course not." It can be pointed out, for example, that Rodriguez's yearly take of $25 million could pay the annual salaries of 530 Dallas-area elementary school teachers, or 660 Fort Worth firefighters.

For better or for worse, however, our economy goes about assigning salaries based roughly on the value of the output that a worker is able to produce—what an economist calls his marginal revenue product. In Rodriguez's case, the output is entertainment. It's fun to watch a baseball game, and millions of people are willing to invest their precious time and money in order to do so. It's particularly fun to watch a baseball game involving a competitive local team, and there's ample evidence that people are willing to pay a fair bit more to watch a good team play than a poor one. Rodriguez produces value because he's a supremely talented baseball player who makes his team more competitive and more fun to watch.

But just how much value are we talking about? Could it be as much as $252 million worth?

To start with, we should think about the different sorts of ways that a baseball team can make money. This problem is more difficult than it otherwise might be because baseball teams do not publicly disclose their financials—they are generally operated either as small, privately owned trusts or holding companies or as part of large conglomerates like Time Warner (Braves) or Anheuser-Busch (Cardinals), for which the baseball club is just one tiny part of a huge business. One exception is the Cleveland Indians, who filed financial disclosures with the Securities and Exchange Commission (SEC) over periods from 1998 to 2000 as part of a small public offering. The disclosures revealed precisely how much revenue the Indians received from various sources as well as the costs of operating the club.

The Indians reported income from eight primary sources (revenue recorded in the Indians' American League championship season of 1997 is included in parentheses):

- Ticket sales ($49 million)
- Local radio and television ($17 million)
- Merchandise sales ($17 million)
- Major League Baseball Central Fund ($16 million)
- Concessions and catering ($14 million)
- Postseason revenue ($13 million)
- Private-suite and club-seat rental ($9 million)
- Revenue sharing ($7 million loss provision)

Of these eight sources of revenue, seven are materially dependent on the Indians' success on the field. If the Indians are a good team, more people will attend their games, and consume peanuts, Cracker Jack, and beer while they're there. Similarly, more people will buy Chief Wahoo hats and other Indians paraphernalia when the team fosters local pride. Networks will be willing to pay more to broadcast Indians games because they can anticipate higher ratings and attendant increases in advertising revenue when the team is playing well, and luxury boxes will become a hot property among Cleveland's wealthiest individuals and corporations. Postseason revenue, of course, can be obtained only if the team is good enough to reach the playoffs in the first place.

The Indians' revenue-sharing figure is also tied to the quality of the ballclub, although in an inverse way. If the Indians are a better team, they will generate more local revenue but must pay out more in revenue sharing as a result (specifically, 34 percent of their locally generated revenue under baseball's present Collective Bargaining Agreement, which went into effect in 2003; in 1997, baseball's cut was 20 percent). The only source of revenue that *isn't* tied to the Indians' on-field performance is that received from the Major League Central Fund, the Indians' share of Major League Baseball's national television deal. This revenue is divided equally among MLB's thirty member franchises, without regard to how the individual teams perform.

Let's look at each of these sources of revenue in more detail.

Ticket Sales

Major League Baseball teams play eighty-one home games during the regular season and receive the largest share of their income from the ticket sales associated with these games. We can estimate revenue associated with these ticket sales by combining attendance figures, which are reported publicly, and ticket price information, which has been collected annually since 1993 by Team Marketing Report. In 2004, for example, the Yankees sold 3.78 million seats, at an average ticket price of $27.34, for gate receipts of about $103 million. The Expos, on the other hand, sold fewer than 750,000 tickets in spite of charging just $10.82 per seat, for gate receipts of about $8 million.

There are several factors that might potentially affect gate receipts, which broadly can be classified into three categories: team quality, stadium quality, and market quality. Our immediate concern is with differences in attendance revenue that result from differences in team quality, but we must also evaluate the other two factors. Some of the reason that the Yankees outdrew the Expos is because they were a much better ballclub, but some of it was also because New York is a much bigger market than Montreal and because Yankee Stadium is a much nicer place to watch a ballgame than (now-retired) Stade Olympique.

We can accomplish this evaluation by means of a regression analysis, which is designed to isolate and quantify the impact of several independent variables (for example, games won or market size) on one dependent variable (in this case, home attendance revenue in 2005 U.S. dollars). Specifically, I looked at all major league teams over the period 1997–2004, accounting for the following independent variables:

Team Quality Variables
   1. Number of games won in current season
   2. Number of games won in previous season
   3. Playoff appearance in current season
   4. Playoff appearance in previous season
   5. Number of winning seasons in past ten years
   6. Number of playoff appearance in past ten years

These measures should be largely self-explanatory. The first four are concerned with a team's success in the near term, while the latter two evaluate its success over the medium term. Both the current and the previous season's performance need to be considered carefully since many baseball tickets are purchased in advance—if the White Sox win a lot of games in 2006, more people will buy 2007 season tickets as a result.

Stadium Quality Variables
   1. Seating capacity
   2. Stadium quality rating
   3. Honeymoon effect

Although seating capacity should be familiar, the other two metrics require an introduction. Stadium quality rating is a numeric measure of the aesthetic experience associated with watching a ballgame at a particular park. These ratings were obtained from a 2003 series of articles compiled by ESPN.com, which assigned ratings from 0 to 100 to each of the then-existing major league ballparks based on factors such as seat comfort, concessions items, and interior and exterior beauty. The lowest-rated park was Olympic Stadium, which received a score of 49, and the highest was PNC Park in Pittsburgh, which received a score of 95.

The honeymoon effect is a well-documented phenomenon; a team can expect to receive a temporary boost in attendance as a result of opening a new stadium. Because so many teams opened new stadiums over the period 1997–2004, it is important to account specifically for this effect. The honeymoon effect is thought to last for approximately three seasons, so the honeymoon effect variable was set at 3 in the first year that a team opened a new ballpark, 2 in the second year after it opened the ballpark, 1 in the third year, and 0 thereafter.

Market Quality Variables
  1. Market size
  2. Per-capita income

Market size is based on an evaluation conducted by baseball researcher Mike Jones, who evaluated the top-fifty Nielsen TV markets (plus Toronto and Montreal) in order to determine the relative size of each baseball team's potential audience. Jones made educated guesses to assign markets outside the immediate metropolitan areas that the thirty teams occupy (for example, most of Providence, Rhode Island, was assigned to the Boston Red Sox) as well as to divide up those markets that more than one team occupies (for example, the Cubs were assigned a 70 percent share of Chicago and the White Sox 60 percent, providing for some number of Chicagoans who are fans of both clubs).

Per-capita income was determined based on 2001 Bureau of Economic Analysis estimates.

Results
The regression analysis revealed that seven of these variables had a statistically significant impact on attendance revenue. In declining order of statistical significance, these variables were:

  1. Stadium quality rating
  2. Market size
  3. Honeymoon effect
  4. Games won in previous season
  5. Playoff appearances in past ten years
  6. Games won in current season
  7. Per-capita income

Before proceeding, we should discuss the four variables that did not make the cut. Stadium capacity made no meaningful difference. A team like the Red Sox that has a small stadium can still capture increased demand by increasing ticket prices—Red Sox tickets, in fact, more than doubled in price between 1997 and 2004.

Playoff appearances in the current and previous seasons, and number of winning seasons in the past ten years, also had no statistically significant effect after other, similar variables were accounted for. It appears that, in the near term, fans are able to adjust their behavior more precisely according to small changes in team quality (e.g., they prefer a team that wins 79 games to a team that wins 75), but over the longer term, they are more concerned with the team being competitive enough to reach the playoffs.

Now for the variables that did drive attendance revenue.

Stadium Quality

Some analysts have speculated that stadium quality is overrated in determining attendance. The argument goes that the novelty effect quickly wears off and that fans are ultimately more concerned with the quality of the ballclub. My analysis suggests that stadium quality makes a tremendous difference. A state-of-the-art facility that scores an 85 in the ESPN ratings is associated with about $19 million in additional gate revenue per season as compared with an outmoded ballpark that scores a 60. ESPN's ratings weren't compiled in a vacuum—ESPN was unlikely to give a low rating to a stadium that sold out night after night or a high rating to one that was empty, regardless of the reasons why. Still, many other factors went into the study, and stadiums often sell out specifically because of their quality. As such, we'll let this finding stand.

Honeymoon Effect

The honeymoon effect is evaluated as producing a bump of about $17 million in revenue, spread out over the first three years in which a new ballpark is open. This figure, combined with the stadium quality effect, suggests that upgrading to a new ballpark is potentially a highly profitable endeavor.

Market Size

As anticipated, market size makes a significant difference in gate receipts. The largest market under this method, that belonging to the New York Yankees, is evaluated as providing about $28.5 million in additional gate receipts per season as compared with the smallest market, belonging to the Kansas City Royals.

Per-Capita Income

Per-capita income, although statistically significant at the 90 percent level, makes relatively little difference once market size is accounted for. The wealthiest market, San Francisco/Oakland, is evaluated as providing about $7 million in additional gate receipts versus the poorest domestic market, Tampa Bay. In spite of price increases in recent years, baseball tickets are still relatively affordable and should probably not be considered a luxury good.

Team Quality Measures

While market quality and stadium quality are important determinants of a team's gate receipts, its on-field quality probably makes the largest difference. Specifically, the model suggests the following:

◆ Winning an additional game translates to about $700,000 in additional gate receipts, before accounting for any effects of playoff appearances. This impact is distributed as about $300,000 in the current season—mostly as the result of improved walk-up ticket sales—plus about $400,000 in the season that immediately follows—mostly as the result of improved season ticket sales.

◆ In addition, a team realizes slightly more than $1.9 million in additional ticket revenue *per season* for *each* playoff appearance in the past ten seasons. This implies that an additional playoff appearance is worth about $14.9 million in present value.

These two measures, when combined, provide for a realistic portrayal of the behavior of baseball fans toward their local team. Fans are responsive to somewhat small changes in team quality over the near term, even if these changes do not result in a playoff appearance. The Detroit Tigers, for example, recognized about $27 million in gate receipts in 2003, a year in which they went 43-119, nearly breaking the all-time record for losses, but $34 million in gate receipts in 2004, when they went 72-90, still far back from the playoff hunt but notably more lively.

Over the longer term, however, fans want a more tangible measure of success, and this success comes in the form of pennants and postseason appearances. One buzzword used by fans and baseball executives alike is "competitive." A good working definition of "competitive" might be "being involved in a certain number of pennant races, and winning those pennant races at least some of the time." Those teams that have really suffered at the box office in recent seasons, like the Pirates and Tigers, are those that are long removed from any pennant-race memories.

We'll revisit this bifurcated model of team success—accounting for wins and playoff appearances separately—in a moment. In the meantime, it might be worthwhile to focus on just one-half of the team quality equation—number of games won. Looking at games won is helpful because we've been able to develop some reasonably reliable measures of the number of games that an individual player season is worth. We can say, for example, that Alex Rodriguez was worth about 11 wins in 2002, 10 wins in 2003, and 8 wins in 2004, as compared with a replacement-level player at his position who would have made the league-minimum salary. Thus, we can compare Rodriguez's salary against the economic value of the extra wins that he produces for his ballclub in order to determine whether or not he's overpaid. We'll call this the Linear Model of Player Valuation since it assumes that the revenue growth associated with additional wins takes the form of a straight line—the seventieth game won in a season, which has no impact on a team's playoff hopes, is assumed to be just as important as the ninetieth game won, which very probably does.

Importantly, if we take playoff appearances out of the regression equation, the revenue associated with a regular season win increases, since a win then represents not only value in itself but also a proxy for the improved probability of reaching the playoffs. Specifically, an additional win turns out to be worth about $880,000 under this model, rather than $700,000.

Our next task is to figure out how an additional win affects the other sources of team revenue, above and beyond gate receipts. Figure 5-2.1 shows the Linear Model of Player Valuation.

FIGURE 5-2.1 Linear Model of Player Valuation

1 additional win =

$880,000 in gate receipts +
_____ in concessions revenue +
_____ in luxury-suite and club-seat revenue +
_____ in postseason revenue +
_____ in merchandise revenue +
_____ in local media broadcast revenue –
_____ in revenue-sharing payments =

_____ total

Concessions

Concessions revenue—consisting primarily of food, alcoholic and nonalcoholic beverages, and parking—can be treated as a "multiplier" on gate receipts. That is, since a fan needs to have bought a game ticket in order to purchase concessions items, we might say that for every X dollars the fan spends on tickets, he'll spend an additional Y dollars on food, beer, and parking.

We can get a sense of this multiplier by looking at the concessions revenue reported by the Cleveland Indians in their public financial statements. Between the 1996 and 1997 seasons, the Indians reported an average of $14.4 million in concessions and catering revenue versus $47.5 million in ticket sales, a ratio of about 30 percent.

Although we can't confirm this figure against data for other baseball teams, we can cross-check it against data in a related industry: movie theaters. Loews Cineplex, a large, publicly traded chain of movie theaters, reported profits on concessions items as averaging a little more than $38 million per year from 1998 to 2002—for a total of about $191 million—versus profits on ticket sales of $621 million. This implies a multiplier of 31 percent, very similar to what we estimated for the Indians. Movie theaters are not a perfect economic match for baseball stadiums—movie tickets cost less than baseball tickets, and movie theaters do not generally sell beer or charge for parking. But the Loews data provide some confirmatory evidence that the 30 percent figure is reasonable. A 30 percent multiplier implies $267,000 in concessions revenue for each additional game won, above and beyond the cost of the tickets themselves.

Luxury Suites and Club Seats

Another important source of stadium-related revenue comes from the sale of luxury suites and club seats. These premium items, which have become omnipresent at modern sports venues, are generally rented by large corporations or wealthy individuals for one season at a time. Their profitability is one of the primary motivations for building new sports stadiums, as older facilities, such as the Metrodome in Minneapolis, may not have adequate numbers of luxury boxes and club seats available.

Unfortunately, the economics of luxury suites and club seats are ambiguous. Teams do not report revenue information for luxury suites and club boxes, nor do they publicly disclose the price associated with renting such facilities (the price is high enough that the rental fees are probably subject to negotiation). Nor is it clear whether luxury-suite and club-seat revenue is as sensitive to team quality as are regular gate receipts.

We do have a couple of data points, however, that should allow us to make a reasonable approximation of the scope of luxury-suite revenue. Turning again to the Cleveland Indians' public financial disclosures, we find that the Indians reported an average of $7.9 million in luxury-suite and club-seat revenue between 1996 and 1997, as compared with an average $47.5 million in gate receipts, a ratio of about 16.5 percent.

There are also data on luxury suites and club seats available at the industry Web site sportsvenues.com. SportsVenues reports that:

◆ MLB stadiums have an average of seventy-seven luxury suites, with a median price of $133,829, implying average luxury-suite revenue of just over $10 million per season per team.

◆ In addition, MLB stadiums have an average of 3,983 club seats, with a median price of $3,985, implying average club-seat revenue of about $16 million per season per team.

Thus, SportsVenues concludes that major league teams record an average of about $26 million in revenue per season from luxury boxes and club seats. This is compared with an average of about $52 million in gate receipts, for a ratio of about 50 percent.

The SportsVenues figures may be somewhat too generous; a few stadiums still lack much in the way of luxury suites or club seats, and a certain percentage of these probably go unsold. On the other hand, the Indians' figure may be too low for other teams. Cleveland is home to relatively few large corporations. Moreover, the luxury-box concept is a relatively new one, and it may have grown in currency since 1997. If we split the difference between the Indians and SportsVenues estimates, we come up with a ratio between luxury-suite/club-seat and regular attendance revenue of about 33 percent.

This doesn't resolve the question of how responsive luxury-suite and club-seat revenue is to changes in team quality. Luxury suites and club seats are bought before the season begins; you're stuck footing the bill even if the team stinks. In addition, corporations may have incentives for purchasing luxury suites and club boxes other than seeing a good ballgame—entertaining clients, say, or providing a perk to executives. It seems probable that luxury-suite revenue is at least slightly less responsive to team quality than ordinary seats are. A reasonable guess is that we should reduce the 33 percent multiplier by about one-third to reflect for these factors. This suggests that, for every additional $1.00 a team receives in gate receipts as a result of an improvement in team quality, it will also receive an additional $0.22 in luxury box revenue. One additional win, then, would be worth about $196,000 in additional luxury-suite and club-seat revenue.

Postseason

As we've described, a team receives a long-term benefit to its regular-season attendance as a result of reaching the postseason. In addition, making the playoffs brings the bonus of getting to play some number of additional home games in front of a packed house at higher-than-normal ticket prices.

In the 2001 financials it presented to Congress, Major League Baseball reported that its teams had received a total of $45.5 million in postseason revenue in a season in which 35 postseason games were played. This implies that the host of a postseason game made about $1.3 million in additional income in 2001, or $1.4 million in 2005 dollars.

How many home games does a typical postseason team get to play? Since 1995, the first year that baseball introduced the Wild Card, there have been an average of 33 postseason games per season, divided among the eight teams that reach the playoffs. This works out to an average of 4.1 home games per combatant, for about $5.8 million in additional income per postseason appearance.

If we were working with a model that differentiated between regular-season wins and playoff appearances, we could leave it at that: A team makes an extra $5.8 million from playoff gate receipts if it reaches the postseason and nothing if it doesn't. However, we're still working with the Linear Model, which evaluates everything in terms of regular-season wins. One way to translate postseason appearances back into regular-season wins is to run a regression of regular-season wins on playoff appearances. If we do this over the period 1996–2004, we find that each win is "worth" about one-fortieth of a playoff appearance. This number flows from the fact that the typical range of regular-season win totals runs about 40-wide between 60 and 100 wins; a team that wins 60 games will never make the playoffs, whereas a team that wins 100 almost certainly will.

Thus, we divide the $5.8 million in revenue by 40 and come up with a figure of $154,000. This represents the "bonus" that an additional regular-season win provides by improving the probability that a team will reach the postseason and host additional home games as a result.

Merchandise

Although sales of team-branded sports paraphernalia are big business, MLB clubs have only limited opportunities to capitalize on these sales directly. In particular, after the establishment of Major League Baseball Properties in 1966, MLB is responsible for marketing team-branded merchandise at a national level, such as in major chain stores or on the Internet. The revenue received from these sales is distributed equally to the thirty teams. Therefore, although a successful season can trigger a major upswing in merchandise sales, teams do not realize all of these profits.

Teams are permitted, however, to operate club-owned retail stores within a two hundred–mile radius of their home field, including within the ballpark itself, and capture the revenue associated with these sales. Such club-operated stores are the source of the merchandise income that the Indians reported on their financial statements. Specifically, the Indians reported average profits of slightly less than $4 million per year on merchandise sales between 1996 and 1997, or about 8 percent of their gate receipts over the same period.

A substantial number of these merchandise sales take place in the ballpark itself, meaning they operate as a multiplier on gate receipts, much like concessions revenue do. In the absence of reliable data points to the contrary, we will apply the Indians' 8 percent multiplier to merchandise sales at team-operated stores. An additional win, then, is worth about $70,000 in extra caps, jerseys, and foam fingers sold.

Local Media

Excluding ticket sales, the most important source of local revenue is selling TV and radio rights within the home market. The amount earned by teams in exchange for licensing their games for broadcast can vary greatly depending on market size and team quality. In 2003, for example, the Yankees earned more than $60 million for their local broadcast rights, while the Expos earned nothing.

Data on broadcast rights fees is notoriously hard to come by, and may be subject to manipulation. Fortunately, with the help of colleague Andy Gefen, I was able to gather reliable data on local media deals for the years 1998, 1999, 2000, 2001, and 2003, as reported in an industry publication, *Broadcasting & Cable* magazine. I performed a regression analysis on these local media revenues similar to the one I conducted for gate receipts. The independent variables I initially considered in the regression analysis were:

1. Average number of games won in previous three seasons
2. Playoff appearance in previous season
3. Number of winning seasons in past ten years
4. Number of playoff appearances in past ten years
5. Market size
6. Per-capita income
7. Superstation dummy

Most of these variables are exactly the same as those included in the attendance revenue analysis. The exceptions are the first and the last variables. After some experimentation, average number of games won in the *previous three seasons* proved to be more reliable than other direct measures of wins. "Superstation dummy" is a special variable created to apply to the cases of the Cubs and the Braves, which own their own national cable stations (WGN and TBS, respectively) and broadcast many of their teams' games to a national audience on these stations. The Cubs and Braves can expect to receive extra media revenue from these stations above and beyond what could normally be achieved based on team quality and local market characteristics.

The regression found that the vast bulk of differences in local broadcast revenue can be explained by evaluating just three variables: market size, number of playoff appearances in the past ten seasons, and Superstation dummy. Having a Superstation makes a huge difference to the Cubs and Braves, to the tune of about $35 million extra in broadcast revenue per season.

Market size is also a highly significant predictor of local media revenue. The annual difference in expected local broadcast revenue between the largest and smallest local markets—those belonging to the New York Yankees and Kansas City Royals, respectively—was evaluated at about $30 million, or about $1.88 per additional citizen.

Playoff appearances are the final key factor in local media deals. One additional playoff appearance is estimated to produce an increase of $1.8 million in media rights fees per season for each of the next ten seasons, or a total of about $14 million in present-day value. Interestingly, none of the variables related to number of games won were found to be significant once playoff appearances had been accounted for. That is, while both wins and playoff appearances have an independent impact on gate receipts, broadcast revenue appears to be driven by playoff appearances alone. There are a couple of reasonable explanations for this phenomenon. First, media rights deals involve longer-term arrangements than the purchase of tickets, either explicitly in the form of a multiyear contract or implicitly because baseball games can become an important part of a local network's brand and programming schedule. Therefore, broadcasters are especially interested in tangible evidence of a team's longer-term competitiveness in the form of playoff appearances.

Second, in an era of three hundred–channel cable lineups, consumers have lots of choice as to what to do with their TV-watching time, generally including several baseball games on a given evening. Although a citizen of Detroit might find some aesthetic pleasure in taking in a "meaningless" Tigers-Royals game in person at Comerica Park, there is less to be gained from watching it on TV, particularly when he could watch Red Sox–Yankees or Iron Chef instead.

The Linear Model is limited in scope to number of games won. If the playoff appearances variable is removed, the number of wins does not become statistically significant in its place. The regression finds that an additional win is worth about $244,000 in additional local broadcast rights in 2005 dollars once playoff appearances are removed.

Revenue Sharing

Figure 5-2.2 shows the Linear Model of Player Valuation with most of the variables filled in. We find that among additional gate receipts, concessions revenue, luxury-suite rentals, postseason revenue, merchandise sales, and local broadcast revenue, an additional win adds about $1,812,000 to a team's top line.

FIGURE 5-2.2 Linear Model of Player Valuation including variables

> *1 additional win =*
>
> $880,000 in gate receipts +
> $267,000 in concessions revenue +
> $196,000 in luxury-suite and club-seat revenue +
> $154,000 in postseason revenue +
> $ 70,000 in merchandise revenue +
> $244,000 in local media broadcast revenue –
>
> _____ in revenue-sharing payments =
>
> _____ total

We have yet to account for the detrimental impact of revenue sharing on a winning team's finances. Under the revenue-sharing rules encoded in baseball's current Collective Bargaining Agreement, teams must contribute 34 percent of their locally earned revenue—including all of the revenue sources described in this analysis—to a central fund that is then redistributed evenly among the thirty MLB clubs. Teams earning greater-than-average local revenue, therefore, lose money as a result of revenue sharing, while teams earning below-average local revenue gain from it.

There is a second form of revenue sharing consisting of payments into and out of the Central Fund. Under this "split pool" system, additional moneys are taken from those teams with above-average local revenue and given to the teams with below-average local revenue. Paradoxically, this causes the tax rate on revenue generation to be higher for poorer clubs than for richer ones. Economist Andrew Zimbalist estimates that in 2005, the Yankees will contribute a total of 39 percent of their locally generated revenue to the revenue-sharing pool and the Royals 47 percent. We will use the average of these—43 percent—in our model.

The local revenue streams affected by revenue sharing are exactly those that are included in our model, so we simply subtract 43 percent. Specifically, revenue-sharing payments of 43 percent on revenue of $1,812,000—our estimate of the gross amount earned from an additional win—work out to $779,000. Thus, the *net* increase in profits from winning an additional game is just slightly more than $1 million under our Linear Model (Fig. 5-2.3).

FIGURE 5-2.3 Linear Model of Player Valuation including revenue sharing

> *1 additional win =*
>
> $880,000 in gate receipts +
> $267,000 in concessions revenue +
> $196,000 in luxury-suite and club-seat revenue +
> $154,000 in postseason revenue +
> $ 70,000 in merchandise revenue +
> $244,000 in local media broadcast revenue –
> $616,000 in revenue-sharing payments =
>
> $1,196,000 total

With this estimate in hand, we can say, for example, that a player who produces 5 additional wins for his team is worth about $5.2 million, or a player who produces 8 additional wins for his team is worth about $8.3 million. Alex Rodriguez, by this standard, is in fact grossly overpaid. Rodriguez's best season according to our Wins Above Replacement Player (WARP) statistic was 2000, when he produced 12.4 extra wins for the Mariners. The Linear Model estimates that these wins were worth about $12.8 million in extra revenue, a healthy figure but no match for the $25 million or so that Rodriguez is paid annually. In fact, at this salary level, even Babe Ruth would be overpaid. Our WARP system regards Ruth's best season as 1923, when he produced 18.1 wins for the Yankees. Ruth's season would be worth "only" $19.3 million according to the Linear Model.

Market-Price Model

Perhaps we shouldn't be picking on Rodriguez. Lots of baseball players are paid handsomely, and the vast majority of them can't hold a candle to A-Rod. Another important question to ask is whether Rodriguez is overpaid relative to other baseball players. And if the answer is *no,* then what are we to make of the implication that *all* baseball players are overpaid?

The key to this other kind of salary assessment is figuring out what teams are *willing to pay* for an additional win. In theory, this amount should be no higher than the additional revenue that a win produces; you wouldn't pay a player $6 million if you expect him to earn you only $5 million.

To evaluate this problem, I performed an analysis of the winter 2005 free-agent market. Prior to the 2005 season, sixty-two free agents were signed to contracts with a lifetime value of at least $2.5 million. I examined both the input (salaries after adjusting for various economic factors) and the output (expected production in terms of wins) linked with each of these contracts. The total number of wins projected for the sixty-two free agents over the guaranteed years of their new contracts was 612, while the net cost of salaries guaranteed to these players was $1.08 billion. Dividing the latter number by the former nets us this conclusion: Teams are willing to pay about $1.75 million per additional win.

We said before that a win contributes about $1 million to a team's bottom line in 2005 dollars. However, prior to the 2005 season, teams were willing to pay about $1.75 million for a win, or almost 50 percent more. How to account for this discrepancy? Are baseball teams, which are run by wealthy individuals and wealthy corporations that have made billions of dollars over their lifetimes, incapable of performing a rational cost-benefit analysis?

That is not entirely a rhetorical question, and later we will discuss an important characteristic of the free-agent market that tends to encourage "irrational" behavior. However, there are also some reasons to suspect that major league teams are in fact making correct decisions in awarding player salaries of this magnitude.

Two-Tiered Model

Until now, we've been assuming a linear relationship between team wins and local revenue earned. But our regression equations have also shown that baseball teams can expect a substantial nonlinear bump in revenue as a result of making the postseason. Let's go back through our sources of local revenue, this time accounting separately for regular-season wins and playoff appearances. We'll call this the Two-Tiered Model of Player Valuation.

- *Regular-season gate receipts.* If both regular-season wins and playoff appearances are accounted for, then we find that each additional win is worth $705,000 in gate receipts, and each additional playoff appearance is worth about $14.9 million.
- *Concessions.* We have treated concessions revenue as a 30 percent multiplier on gate receipts. Therefore, the value of an additional win in terms of concession revenue is about $214,000, and an additional playoff appearance $4.5 million.
- *Luxury suites and club seats.* Although data on luxury-suite and club-box revenue is somewhat lacking, our best estimate was that 22 cents in luxury-box and club-seat revenue is received for each marginal dollar in gate receipts as a result of improved team performance. This implies that an additional win is worth about $157,000 in this category, and a playoff appearance $3.3 million.

◆ *Postseason gate receipts.* Direct postseason revenue in the form of additional home playoff dates is estimated at $5.8 million. This figure can obviously be assigned entirely to the playoff appearance column.

◆ *Merchandise.* Merchandise sales at team-operated stores can be treated much like concessions items; we estimate 8 cents in merchandise sales for each $1 increase in attendance revenue. This results in an estimate of $56,000 in additional merchandise revenue per regular-season win and $1.2 million per playoff appearance.

◆ *Local broadcast rights.* Our regression model found that a playoff appearance results in a present value increase of about $14.1 million in local broadcast rights. After playoff appearances have been accounted for, additional regular-season wins have no material impact on broadcast fees.

◆ *Revenue sharing.* The 43 percent tax is applied to top-line locally generated revenue, regardless of whether this revenue is generated as the result of regular-season performance, playoff appearances, or something else. This implies a revenue-sharing payment of $487,000 per regular-season win and $18.8 million per playoff appearance.

These results are summarized in Table 5-2.1. Our Two-Tiered Model finds that, after all categories of revenue are accounted for and revenue-sharing payments are deducted, an additional regular-season win is worth about $650,000 and a playoff appearance $25 million.

TABLE 5-2.1 Two-Tiered Model of Player Valuation

Revenue Category	Additional Regular-Season Win	Additional Playoff Appearance
Regular-season gate receipts	$705,000	$14,869,000
Concessions	$214,000	$4,514,000
Luxury suites and club seats	$157,000	$3,314,000
Postseason gate receipts	$0	$5,797,000
Merchandise	$56,000	$1,182,000
Local broadcast rights	$0	$14,093,000
Revenue-sharing payments (34%)	($385,000)	($14,881,000)
Total	$747,000	$28,887,000

This Two-Tiered Model would work well if we wanted to look backward and guess how much money a certain team had made. We'd expect a team that won 93 games and made the playoffs, for example, to have made about $30 million more than a team that won 85 games and missed the playoffs.

For planning purposes, however, the Two-Tiered Model is less useful, since a team can't know in advance whether it will make the playoffs. We can estimate with some reasonable degree of certainty, however, the probability of a playoff appearance given a particular number of wins. Between 1996 (the first full season with the Wild-Card system in place) and 2005, the team with the most number of wins that *didn't* make the playoffs was the 1999 Cincinnati Reds, which won 96 games but lost the division race to the 97-win Houston Astros and a one-game playoff for the Wild Card to the New York Mets. Conversely, the team with the fewest number of wins that reached the playoffs was the 2005 San Diego Padres, which won the NL West with an 82-80 record. The Pirates finished second in the division that season with a 79-83 record, meaning that 80 wins would have sufficed for Houston to win. So we might say that a team that wins fewer than 80 games has essentially no chance of reaching the playoffs, while a team that wins more than 96 games is just about guaranteed to reach the playoffs.

These probabilities can be estimated more explicitly by the means of a logistic regression, which is similar to a linear regression but operates on dependent variables like reaching the playoffs that represent an all-or-nothing proposition. Figure 5-2.4 presents the results of this analysis, which estimates the probability of reaching the playoffs based on the number of regular-season wins:

FIGURE 5-2.4 Logistic regression analysis

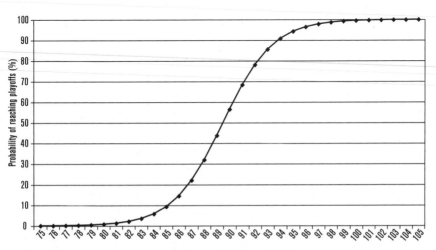

Regular-season wins (162-game season)

Evaluating the individual data points from this graph, we find for example that:

- ◆ A team that wins exactly 80 games has a 0.8 percent chance of making the playoffs;
- ◆ A team that wins exactly 85 games has a 9.3 percent chance of making the playoffs;
- ◆ A team that wins exactly 90 games has a 56.5 percent chance of making the playoffs;
- ◆ A team that wins exactly 95 games has a 94.3 percent chance of making the playoffs; and,
- ◆ A team that wins exactly 100 games has a 99.5 percent chance of making the playoffs.

The most sensitive part of the graph—what we'll call the *sweet spot*—is between about 86 and 93 wins. Winning 90 games rather than 89, for example, improves a team's chances of making the playoffs by about 13 percent. We can look at a couple of other presentations that help to illustrate what a profound impact the sweet spot can have on optimal team behavior. Figure 5-2.5 estimates the amount of local revenue that a team can expect to have, starting with a baseline of $25 million at 60 wins and attributing additional monies both directly based on increasing regular-season wins and indirectly based on the improved probability of reaching the playoffs.

FIGURE 5-2.5 Expected local revenue

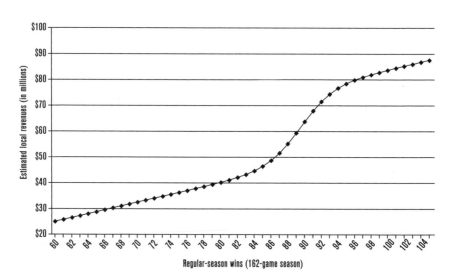

As we can see, revenue takes a sharp turn upward at about 85 wins, when the sweet spot kicks in, but slows down again at about 95 wins, when additional wins become superfluous. We can further extrapolate the marginal economic value of winning one additional game, as in Figure 5-2.6.

FIGURE 5-2.6   Marginal economic value of 1 additional win

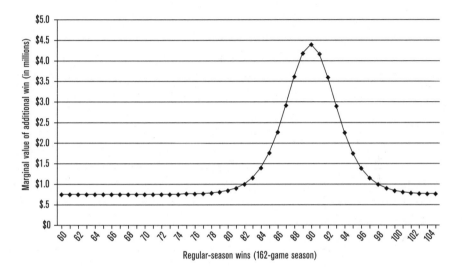

The seventieth win or the one hundred fifth win, which have no discernible impact on a team's playoff chances, are worth only about $747,000. But the ninetieth game won, right at the peak of the sweet spot, is worth nearly $4.4 million all on its own.

Needless to say, this could have a profound impact on the price a team is willing to pay to a free agent. Imagine, for example, that three teams—the Royals, Mets, and Cardinals—are considering signing a certain free agent. All these teams agree that the player will be worth 6 additional wins. The Royals, however, expect to win 65 games if they *don't* sign the free agent, the Mets 85 games, and the Cardinals 95 games. The teams reach the following conclusions:

◆ Royals: The free agent, who allows them to win 71 games rather than 65, is worth about $4.1 million ($590,000 per win).
◆ Mets: The free agent, who allows them to win 91 games rather than 85, is worth about $17 million ($2.8 million per win).
◆ Cardinals: The free agent, who allows them to win 101 games rather than 95, is worth about $4.8 million ($800,000 per win).

Guess which team is going to wind up with the player?

The Winner's Curse

The problem of differing evaluations of a free agent's value, whether they are based on rational factors such as the playoff sweet spot or irrational ones such as inability to properly estimate a player's value, is amplified by a phenomenon known as the Winner's Curse. As described at a popular Web site:

> The Winner's curse . . . occurs in common value auctions with incomplete information. In such an auction, the goods being sold have a similar value for all bidders, but players are uncertain of this value when they bid. Each player independently estimates the value of the good before bidding.
>
> The winner of an auction is, of course, the bidder who submits the highest bid. When each bidder is estimating the good's value and bidding accordingly, that will probably be the bidder whose estimate was largest. If we assume that on average the bidders are estimating accurately, then the person whose bid is highest has almost certainly overestimated the good's value. Thus, a bidder who wins after bidding what he thought the good was worth has almost certainly overpaid.

A free agent has certain advantages when it comes to negotiating his new contract. He can solicit bids from any number of the thirty MLB clubs, all of which are well aware of his availability on the market but which will have different assessments of his value. He can compare and contrast these bids and select the best offer, while the teams themselves may have limited ability to compare figures with one another out of fear of triggering claims of collusion.

Nor is it the case that a large number of bidders are required to trigger the Winner's Curse. I ran a simulation that attempts to represent the conditions of the free-agent market, shown in Figure 5-2.7. The simulation assumed that the average bid for a given free agent is $5 million, but the estimates of his value made by different teams ranged randomly between $2.5 million and $7.5 million. I then tracked the average *highest* bid and the average *second*-highest bid over thousands of trials given various numbers of teams bidding on the player.

The simulation reveals that even a relatively small number of bidders can produce a dramatic uptick in the contract that the player is able to achieve. With just three of the thirty MLB teams bidding, for example,

FIGURE 5-2.7 Results of Winner's Curse simulation

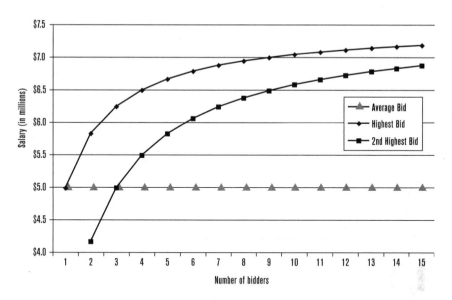

the player will receive an average *highest* bid of $6.25 million versus a theoretical maximum of $7.5 million. With five bidders, his take increases to nearly $6.7 million, and with seven bidders, $6.9 million.

The Winner's Curse has traditionally been associated with inefficient bids in an auction setting as a result of imperfect information. I don't mean to deemphasize too strongly the notion that baseball teams are capable of behaving inefficiently. Indeed, one of the central themes of this book is that baseball teams have a long history of behaving inefficiently. Determining what to bid on a free agent is essentially a valuation exercise, and any valuation exercise is highly sensitive to the assumptions that go into it. Making an incorrect assumption about how many wins a player is likely to be worth to the club, how much a win is worth in terms of profits, or both, could lead to a radical overpayment.

Nevertheless, because of the playoff sweet spot, much the same consequences can emerge even if teams *are* behaving efficiently. Baseball teams intuitively open their wallets when they feel that they are on the verge of making the playoffs, hoping to find the player who will push them over the top. This is, in fact, an economically valid way of thinking; a playoff appearance carries with it a large financial benefit. Still, because of the Winner's Curse, if just one of the teams bidding on a player is near the playoff sweet spot, the player should wind up doing very well.

There are probably also other sorts of sweet spots apart from the playoff push. An owner looking to sign a new long-term local TV deal, sell his team for a high valuation, or sway public support for a new ballpark might reap some extra benefit from a good season and might be willing to pay more for free-agent talent as a result. Rangers owner Tom Hicks made such a sweet-spot argument when he signed Alex Rodriguez, claiming that he hoped the deal would trigger a real estate boom around the Ballpark at Arlington.

What's more, the value of a successful season varies naturally from team to team. Some economists have found, for example, that the value of an additional win is greater in a larger market than a smaller one. Intuitively, it would seem reasonable that a win is worth more to the New York Mets, which play in an aging facility in a competitive division in a large, two-team market, than it is to the San Diego Padres. Finally, there may be signaling effects associated with signing free agents. If the Mariners sign Adrian Beltre, and five hundred fans buy season-ticket packages the next day as a result, then they receive some benefit from this signing even if Beltre breaks his leg on the first day of the season. All of these factors tend to increase the differentiation in what one team is willing to pay to a player versus another, and will therefore increase the salary for the player, who will eagerly accept the highest bid.

Returning to Rodriguez

There are valid economic reasons that baseball salaries are as high as they are: Players who help their teams to win games provide lots of profit for their owners, particularly if their contribution results in a playoff appearance. Nevertheless, Alex Rodriguez's $252 million contract overshot the mark by a considerable margin. In Table 5-2.2, we have estimated Rodriguez's value over the first five years of his contract using the three methodologies described in this chapter: the Linear Model, which estimates a player's value by establishing a value per additional win (about $1 million); the Market-Price Model, which uses an evaluation of the most recent free-agent market to establish what teams are willing to pay for an additional win (about $1.75 million); and the Two-Tiered Model, which gives more credit to wins that result in a material increase in the likelihood of a playoff appearance. The table also provides Rodriguez's salary in each of these seasons (including signing bonus payments). All figures are adjusted for inflation to 2005 dollars, and adjusted to reflect the revenue-sharing plan in place during a given season.

TABLE 5-2.2 Rodriguez's Value over the First Five Years of His Contract

Year	Salary	WARP	Linear Model	Market-Price Model	Two-Tiered Model
2001	$24,840,000	11.6	$18,157,000	$22,101,000	$11,341,000
2002	$24,610,000	10.8	$16,748,000	$20,386,000	$10,461,000
2003	$24,150,000	9.8	$12,303,000	$18,153,000	$7,685,000
2004	$23,690,000	7.9	$9,729,000	$14,355,000	$10,114,000
2005	$25,000,000	10.2	$12,199,000	$16,555,000	$32,361,000
Total	$122,290,000	50.3	$69,136,000	$91,550,000	$71,962,000

Each of these methodologies evaluates Rodriguez as overpaid by a dramatic margin. The most favorable valuation is that obtained by the Market-Price Model, which estimates that replacing the 50 wins Rodriguez generated for his clubs between 2001 and 2004 would have cost about $92 million in the free-agent market. This is no match for the more than $122 million that he has received in salary and signing bonuses during this period.

The Two-Tiered Model is no more kind to Rodriguez, as it recognizes that Rodriguez has made little contribution to pennant races since signing his new contract. Even with Rodriguez's contribution, the Rangers finished last in their division in each season between 2001 and 2003, and well out of the Wild-Card race, making it hard for them to earn additional revenue. Rodriguez was traded to the Yankees before the 2004 season and helped the club to a division title, but the Yankees would likely have made the playoffs even without him. Finally, in 2005, Rodriguez provided a 10-win season to the Yankees that might well have made a critical difference; the Yankees finished in a dead heat with the Red Sox atop the AL East, and just two games ahead of the Indians in the Wild-Card race. The Two-Tiered Model credits Rodriguez with generating $32.4 million in value in 2005, but this is barely enough to pay off his salary, let alone the debt he accumulated in the first four years of his contract.

What's remarkable is that Rodriguez has been overpaid even though his on-the-field contributions have been everything his employers might have expected from him and then some. Rodriguez won the AL MVP in 2003, a year in which he also broke his own record for most home runs hit by a shortstop. He received Gold Glove Awards in 2002 and 2003 and appeared in the All-Star game in each of the first five years of his new deal, while missing fewer than ten games due to injury. If Rodriguez had been injured or his performance had declined unexpectedly, both of which happened to ex–Red Sox shortstop Nomar Garciaparra, the evaluation would have been much harsher.

In fairness to Rodriguez and Tom Hicks, the year 2000 was a unique economic time; the NASDAQ hit its all-time high on March 10, 2000, nine months to the day before Rodriguez's record-breaking deal was signed. Also, in fairness to Hicks, the new revenue-sharing plan wasn't yet in place, so the marginal tax on revenue per win was much lower. The tax rate was 20 percent, and distributions were done on the 75 percent straight pool/25 percent split pool formula. As such, the overall marginal tax rate would have been around 25 percent, which would have made for a higher valuation of Rodriguez. We raised Rodriguez's value for 2001 and 2002 to adjust for this. But Hicks would have expected that the old system was going to remain in place forever. Thus, he would have been projecting higher dollar values for the entire length of the contract.

Several other enormous deals were signed that winter, including a $160 million contract with Manny Ramirez, $121 million to Mike Hampton, $55 million to Darren Dreifort, and $51 million to Denny Neagle, each of which have turned out to be similarly problematic investments. Nevertheless, Rodriguez's contract is best characterized by the phrase "irrational exuberance," and his employers will be paying the price of that exuberance for years to come.

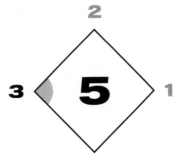

Do Players Perform Better in Contract Years?

DAYN PERRY

It's a familiar refrain among fans and mainstream sportswriters: Players perform better in their "walk years," the seasons that precede entry into the free-agent market. Players are aware, the theory goes, that a big walk year will increase their value on the open market and thus fatten their wallets. Free-agent contracts now run as high as nine figures, and major league ballplayers know they have a limited career window. It makes sense that they'll employ a little extra focus and time—in the batting cages, on the mound, or in the gym—during that walk season. Their performance that year could mean the difference between a set-for-life contract and one that simply tables the same pressures for a few years. Players have every self-interested economic reason under the sun to be at their best when free agency looms.

Take the conspicuous example of Adrian Beltre. In 1994, the Los Angeles Dodgers, pursuing one of the most hotly coveted talents ever to come out of the Dominican Republic, signed Beltre to what they believed was an allowable contract. A few years later, Beltre's agent Scott Boras discovered that his client had been signed at the age of sixteen—too young according to the rules of Major League Baseball. As a result, Boras agitated to have Beltre declared a free agent. Eventually, MLB Commissioner Bud Selig ruled that Beltre would remain

Dodgers property but that the organization had to suspend its scouting operations in the Dominican Republic for a full year. The Players' Association filed a grievance on behalf of Beltre, again seeking free agency for him. The union dropped its claim after the Dodgers inked Beltre to a lucrative three-year contract.

A major league regular by the age of nineteen, Beltre possessed a broad base of skills that led the Dodgers to believe he was a future star. At age twenty-one, he batted .290, drew 56 walks, and tallied 52 extra-base hits in 138 games. But his production cratered from 2001 to 2003, and the word "bust" began to be bandied about. Beltre's aggregate on-base percentage over those three seasons barely topped .300, the Mendoza Line equivalent under which hitters don't deserve a roster spot, barring huge power or other hidden talents. (See Chapter 5-1 for more on the Mendoza Line.) His best slugging average during that period was .426, a serviceable figure for a third baseman but hardly the stuff of superstars.

In 2004, however, Beltre broke out: He posted a batting line of .334 batting average/.388 on-base percentage/.629 slugging average, blasting 48 homers and flashing Gold Glove–level defense. Coincidentally—skeptics would say conveniently—the 2004 season was also his walk year. Beltre opted for free agency; executives and observers around the league pondered whether it was wise to pay him based on his 2004 performance. On the one hand, his numbers that season were wildly out of step with the rest of his career. On the other hand, many in the game had long predicted great things for Beltre—perhaps he was finally realizing his vast potential.

Dodgers general manager Paul DePodesta, who had been weaned on Billy Beane's cold-eyed, frugal approach in Oakland, took a pass. The Seattle Mariners didn't, lavishing Beltre with a five-year, $64 million contract. Coupled with the arrival of fellow highly paid free agent Richie Sexson, Beltre was supposed to restore winning baseball to the Pacific Northwest. But while Sexson had a big year, Beltre and the Mariners didn't. The team went 69-93; Beltre flailed to the tune of .256/.304/.414. That was even worse than his cumulative pre-2004 numbers—if it hadn't been for a midseason hot streak, it could have been even uglier.

The cynical explanation is that Beltre, out of brazen selfishness, willfully ramped up his production in 2004 to inflate his market value. Then, once he'd grabbed his multiyear, guaranteed contract, he indolently regressed to form. The less cynical explanation is that, as a matter of happenstance, Beltre's career year and his walk year occurred at the same time.

In any isolated case where a player experiences a walk-year spike, there's no way to answer the questions of motive and causation. A quandary we *can* tackle, though, is whether players tend to perform better in walk years than they do in seasons preceding or following their entry into the free-agent market. To do this we'll use a Baseball Prospectus statistic called Wins Above Replacement Player (WARP). Similar to Value Over Replacement Player (VORP—introduced in Chapter 1-1), WARP measures the number of wins—rather than runs—a player contributes above what a fringe Triple-A veteran would produce, while also accounting for defense. Using WARP, we'll compare the walk years of 212 prominent free agents from 1976 to 2000 with their immediate pre- and postwalk seasons.

In Table 5-3.1, column "WY" will be the average WARP for all the aforementioned players in their walk years; "WY – 1" will be the average WARP for all players in the seasons immediately preceding their walk years; and "WY + 1" will be the average WARP in the seasons immediately following their walk years.

TABLE 5-3.1 Average WARP, 1976–2000, Top Free Agents

	WY	WY - 1	WY + 1
Average WARP	5.56	5.08	5.08

Based on these results, it does appear that players experience a cumulative performance spike in their walk years—a 9.4 percent uptick in WARP, to be specific. Of course, before we draw any firm conclusions from these data, there's the matter of age to con-

TABLE 5-3.2 Average Age, 1976–2000, Top Free Agents

	WY	WY - 1	WY + 1
Average age	31.0	30.0	32.0

sider. Using the same pool of 212 players, let's look at the average age for players in their walk years, before their walk years, and after their walk years (Table 5-3.2).

These 212 players average thirty years of age in their prewalk seasons, thirty-one in their walk seasons, and thirty-two in their postwalk seasons. Studies by Bill James and other researchers show that a player most often hits his peak between ages twenty-five and twenty-nine. That makes the walk year in this study further removed from prime territory than the prewalk year. In other words, age doesn't explain away the walk-years' performance discrepancy.

Let's take a closer look. Table 5-3.3 shows the percentages of players who peaked in WY, WY − 1, or WY + 1.

TABLE 5-3.3 Percent of Players Peaking in Walk Year, Before, or After, 1976–2000, Top Free Agents

	WY	WY − 1	WY + 1
Players peaking	37.7% (80)	34.0% (72)	28.3% (60)

According to this table, players: (1) perform better in their walk years, (2) do so at an age that doesn't lend itself to peaking, and (3) perform better in their walk years than they do in their pre- or postwalk seasons. Whether this phenomenon is a function of accident, unconscious design, or willful self-interest is impossible to say, but the trend is manifest. Of course, WARP is a measure that's dependent, to some extent, on playing time. It's possible to put up better rate numbers (e.g., AVG, OBP, SLG, ERA) than another player but to have a less valuable season because of a playing-time deficit. After all, a player who slugs .550 in 250 plate appearances is less valuable than one who hits .510 in 600 plate appearances. WARP and statistics like it reflect this fact. As such, it's possible that players, rather than actually performing at a higher level during walk years, merely soldier on, playing through minor injuries and fatigue that might have sidelined them in other seasons. Table 5-3.4 explores whether that's the case for these 212 players.

TABLE 5-3.4 Average Games Played/Pitched in Walk Year, Before, or After, 1976–2000, Top Free Agents

	WY	WY − 1	WY + 1
Average games played/pitched	89.2	82.9	84.4

Indeed, players do play or pitch in more games in their walk years, by a margin of 6.3 over their prewalk seasons and 4.8 over postwalk seasons. The bump in playing time explains away part of the walk-year WARP advantage, but, in light of what we learned about average age and the degree of the WARP edge, it's not enough to nullify the trend completely.

If anything, these data should make organizations even more cautious on the free-agent market. Baseball's economic structure is such that players don't become free agents until after six seasons of major league service. Often, this means they hit the open market after their prime seasons are behind them. Also to be considered are the corollary costs of signing a prominent free agent. If a player has been offered salary arbitration by his former team and is a free agent ranked by the Elias Sports Bureau that year, then the team that signs him must forfeit—depending on the player's rankings—one or two high draft picks to his former team. A team that regularly fritters away compensatory draft picks will inevitably thin out its farm system. Doing so, of course, exacts a cost down the road. Signing free agents who have been offered arbitration is even more costly than the contract years and dollars would lead you to believe. The upshot is that organizations had better be darn sure they've got the right guy.

Regardless of what a player has done in the past, teams need a dispassionate evaluation of what that player will do in coming seasons. This means taking into account not only the player's age but also the context of his previous performances.

In the winter of 1999, the Tampa Bay Devil Rays, going into only their third season of existence and seeking to make a splash on the free-agent market, signed outfielder Greg Vaughn to a four-year, $34 million whale of a contract. What the Rays saw was a player who'd tallied 95 home runs in the previous two seasons. What they should've seen was a 34-year-old player who was slow of foot, defensively challenged, and burdened with "old player" baseball skills—power and walks, and little else. The result was one of several D-Ray free-agency disasters.

In Vaughn's first season in Tampa, he posted a line of .254/.365/.499, roughly even with his .245/.347/.535 performance the previous season; but his homer total plunged, from 45 in 1999 to 28 in 2000. The next season, Vaughn hit .233/.333/.433 with just 24 homers; his .433 SLG was the worst showing among all regular designated hitters that season. The following year, Vaughn, making a career-high $8.75 million, reached new depths. Injuries limited him to only 69 games. Mercifully so, given Vaughn's horrific .163/.286/.315 performance—numbers that, on a per–plate appearance basis, made him one of the worst hitters in all of baseball that season. In spring training 2002, Vaughn scuffled once again, and the Rays cut him, eating the $9.25 million he was owed that season. After a brief 22-game dalliance with the Colorado Rockies in 2003, Vaughn was out of baseball for good.

The most precipitous drop from walk year to the season immediately following was experienced by Nick Esasky. In 1983, Esasky replaced an aging Johnny Bench as the third baseman for the Cincinnati Reds. In 1985, he enjoyed a breakout season of sorts, hitting 21 homers in 125 games of action. In December 1988, the Reds dealt Esasky to the Boston Red Sox as part of a five-player trade. Fenway Park is a great environment for right-handed power hitters, and accordingly, Esasky thrived in his lone season in Boston. For the 1989 season, Esasky, by then a full-time first baseman, slugged .500, totaled more than 60 extra-base hits, and drew 66 walks. On the seeming strength of that season, the Atlanta Braves and then-GM Bobby Cox signed the twenty-nine-year-old Esasky to a three-year contract worth $5.6 million, just before his thirtieth birthday.

Once you adjust for the tendencies of Fenway, in what was then a more moderate era for offense, Esasky's work in 1989 was unimpressive considering the higher offensive bar for first basemen. On the road that season, Esasky hit .253/.331/.459; at Fenway, he hit .300/.379/.541. In fact, Esasky, in the context of park and league, had never been anything special with the bat. However, in failing to leaven his numbers in Boston, the Braves and Cox overvalued Esasky.

What happened, however, no amount of statistical correction could predict. Not long after Opening Day in 1990, Esasky developed an inner-ear infection that eventually resulted in a debilitating case of vertigo. Esasky's malady caused him unrelenting dizziness, which obviously wouldn't allow him to play baseball. The 9 games he played for the Braves in April were the final 9 games of his career. An insurance policy covered the remainder of his contract. On the WARP front, Esasky went from a walk-year mark of 7.2 to a 1990 WARP of –0.4.

You can make a compelling case that no multiyear, high-dollar free-agent contract tendered to a first baseman has turned out to be a wise decision. That's mostly because first basemen, as a species, don't tend to be athletic and don't tend to age well. The Angels were so smitten with Mo Vaughn's résumé—which included the 1995 MVP Award and a 1998 walk year that saw him hit .337/402/.591 with 40 homers—that they signed him to a massive six-year, $80 million contract. The Angels, like so many other teams hungry for a slugging first baseman, were willing to overlook Vaughn's age (he turned thirty-one during the off-season in which he signed the deal); his huge, cumbersome physique; and his decidedly old-player skills. After a respectable but injury-shortened 1999 in which he hit .298/.353/.508, Vaughn's numbers dropped further the next season. Dumped on the Mets in exchange for Kevin Appier's albatross contract, Vaughn slipped to .259/.349/.456 in 2002—a solid result for a low-priced shortstop but a catastrophe for a first baseman making more than $17 million that year. Vaughn played just 27 games in 2003, then succumbed to injury and never played again; he pocketed $34.3 million for the 2003 and 2004 seasons.

The list of disastrous free-agent first-baseman contracts runs on and on. The five-year, $85 million contract extension the Astros gave Jeff Bagwell after the 2001 season also became a boondoggle when age and a degenerating right shoulder curtailed Bagwell's production, then forced him to miss huge chunks of time. On the Astros' 2005 playoff roster more out of ceremony than anything else, Bagwell will cost the Astros nearly $20 million in 2006, with little hope of returning to everyday duty, let alone his old elite level of performance. Jim Thome and Jason Giambi—also barrel-chested slugging first basemen on the wrong side of thirty—looked like they might be exceptions to the free-agent first-baseman trap early in their megadeals with the Phillies and Yankees. Injuries and other ailments have all but assured a nasty ending for both. Though Carlos Delgado fared well in year one of his four-year, $52 million contract, it's hard to like his odds of sustained stardom as he turns thirty-four, thirty-five, and thirty-six over the next three seasons. At the time of this writing, several teams were engaging in a veritable death match in an effort to sign playoff hero Paul Konerko to a long-term deal. With five- and six-year deals and huge dollars being bandied about, it's not hard to picture Konerko becoming a big financial burden as he moves well into his thirties, declining over the life of such a deal. Given teams' reluctance to learn these lessons, you can already squint and see some team throwing away tens of millions too much on 2005 Rookie of the Year Ryan Howard in the winter of 2011.

Not all high-dollar free-agent contracts culminate so grimly, though—if they did, even the most Steinbrennian urges would be set aside in the name of restraint. In the winter of 1992, Barry Bonds was one of the most feverishly pursued free agents in history. He was coming off a season in which he hit .311/.456/.624, swatted 75 extra-base hits, drew 127 walks, swiped 39 bags, claimed his third straight Gold Glove in left, and won his second MVP Award for the division-winning Pittsburgh Pirates. In terms of WARP, Bonds's 1992 season was the best of his career to that point, a league-leading mark of 12.9.

After being courted by the usual deep-coffered suspects, Bonds signed a six-year, $43.75 million contract—the richest in baseball history at that time—with the San Francisco Giants, his hometown team and the club that had originally drafted him in 1982. (Rather than sign then, Bonds accepted a baseball scholarship to Arizona State; coming out of college, he was drafted by the Pirates with the sixth overall pick of the 1985 draft.)

Over the next twelve seasons as a Giant, Bonds would become the first player in history to steal 500 bases and hit 500 homers—after becoming the first player in history to steal 400 bases and hit 400 homers. He would also win *five* more MVP trophies; lead his team to Game 7 of the World Series; and, as of the end of the 2005 season, tally 708 career home runs.

The Giants did several things right in signing Bonds. First, they got a player who, at age twenty-eight, was young relative to other six-year free agents. Second, they got a player whose skills—an ability to hit for average, broad-based power indicators, speed on the bases, high walk totals in tandem with low strikeout totals, and excellence with the glove—figured to hold up over time and augured a promising aging curve. Third, they signed a player who, in every sense of the word, was an elite performer. Even with modest age-related decline, Bonds would still be among the best in the game. It just so happened that his finest seasons were yet to come. In four of the next twelve seasons, Bonds would beat his former career-high VORP; only twice over that span did he dip below the 10-WARP mark.

In the case of Adrian Beltre, the age was right, but the established record of performance wasn't. In the cases of Greg Vaughn and Mo Vaughn, each had been a consistent high-level performer, but both were old, with old-player skills. In Bonds's case, all signs pointed to success. By knowing the age at which players begin to decline, keeping a player's recent performance in context, valuing skills that tend to be maintained over time, and being aware that the walk-year performance spike is often a genuine phenomenon, organizations can make better decisions on the free-agent market. Ignore any of those factors, and teams will make costly missteps.

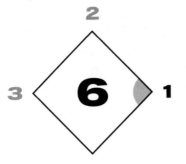

Do High Salaries
Lead to High Ticket Prices?

NEIL DEMAUSE

Ask baseball fans what peeves them most about the modern game, and most will say, "The players get paid too damn much money." In a poll at the start of the 2005 season, the Associated Press asked Americans what they felt was baseball's "biggest problem." Coming in at number one, with 33 percent of the votes, was player salaries—and this mere weeks after the sensational congressional hearings into steroid use in baseball.

Probe a bit further, and many will say that their biggest objection to the $15-million-a-year player is that fans feel the pinch at the ticket window. (The cost of attending games, in fact, finished a close third in the AP poll, right behind steroids.) It's a common refrain, especially during labor disputes: Baseball players make too much money and are making the games unaffordable.

The link between ticket prices and player salaries made headlines in 2000 when the Cincinnati Reds, on the verge of trading their star shortstop Barry Larkin to the New York Mets, instead reversed course and signed him to a three-year, $27 million contract extension. In announcing the move to the public, Reds CEO John Allen made clear that while the popular Larkin would now almost certainly finish his career in Cincinnati (he would ultimately retire a Red at age forty in

2004), there would be consequences: "We may do something nobody else has ever done. We've got to generate the revenues to pay for this."

The "something" Allen spoke of soon became clear: an unprecedented midseason hike in ticket prices to Reds games, setting off a bitter public squabble over greed, big contracts, and Larkin's aging bat. The deal was proof, critics said, of what fans had long feared: When teams hand out megabucks contracts, they pass along their costs to fans at the box office.

Or do they?

For the first three-quarters of the twentieth century, player salaries remained relatively low as owners used baseball's reserve clause to force players to sign for whatever management was offering, unless they wanted to take up a career selling vacuum cleaners. (When home-run champ Ralph Kiner asked the Pirates for a raise in the 1950s, GM Branch Rickey famously snapped, "We finished last with you, we can finish last without you." Kiner would later organize one of the first fledgling players' unions.) With the nineteenth-century reserve clause tying players to their teams for life, players had only one negotiating option: Hold out and hope that your owner blinked before your next mortgage payment came due.

As a result, major league salaries remained remarkably low by modern standards through the first two-thirds of the twentieth century. In 1970, they averaged less than $30,000 a year. That works out to about $150,000 in today's dollars—a good living, but hardly an extravagant one for players whose big-league careers averaged only a few years in length.

Then came arbitrator Peter Seitz's decision in the Andy Messersmith case, which ruled that players could play out the "option year" in their contracts and become free agents, eligible to sign with any team. The owners promptly fired Seitz, but the genie was out of the bottle. The sudden free market in players sent salaries soaring, revealing the extent to which players had been underpaid in previous decades.

Since 1976, the first year of free agency, the average major league salary has skyrocketed from $51,501 to a once unthinkable $2,632,655. Even accounting for inflation, that's a 1,395 percent increase. The average baseball player now makes about sixty times what the median U.S. family does. To put it another way, if the median U.S. household had seen its income rise at the same rate as big-league ballplayers, the average family would now be raking in nearly $650,000 a year.

Ticket prices have also leaped, if less dramatically. In 1976, the average baseball ticket would have set you back $3.45. By 2005, it had risen to $19.82. While much of that rise was due to inflation—$3.45 in 1976 had the buying power of $11.80 in 2005 dollars—even after accounting for inflation, that's still an increase of 67.5 percent.

Let's take a closer look at the relationship between ticket prices and player salaries over the past three decades (Fig. 6-1.1). Both salaries and ticket prices have gone up, true, but in anything but lockstep. In fact, in the first dozen years of free agency, as salaries more than tripled, ticket prices actually went *down* in inflation-adjusted dollars. It's only been since 1990 that ticket prices have begun an upward march to match salaries, with a notable reversal in both following the 1994 strike.

FIGURE 6-1.1 Relationship between ticket prices and player salaries

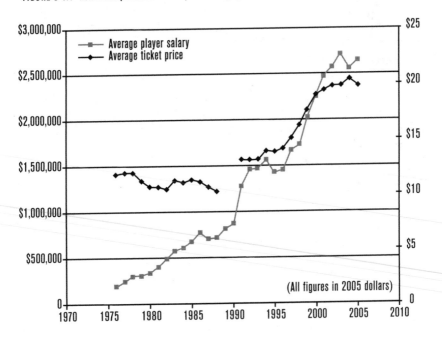

So what's going on here? If owners are being forced to pay through the nose for their players, why *wouldn't* they pass along the costs to the ticket-buying public?

Economists have an answer for that. Baseball owners, like any business owners, are assumed to act as rational price-setters. ("Rational" here just means selecting the price that makes them the most money. It has nothing to do with making sensible decisions about, say, signing Eric Milton.) As such, they look at market research on how much fans are willing to pay to see games and then pick a price point for tickets that maximizes revenue, that price point being one where, if they tacked on another 10 cents, they anticipate losing more from fans staying home than they'd gain in additional dimes.

When costs of doing business go up, they can affect prices—witness, for example, debates in recent years over the impact of high oil prices on food and other goods that must be shipped by truck or plane. But it's not always that simple. Let's say, for example, you're building an automobile. If the price of steering wheels goes up, you might rationally boost car prices to compensate, figuring that you'd rather have a bigger profit margin on fewer sales than sell more cars but make less money on each one.

Steering wheels, though, are a *marginal cost:* If you sell fewer cars, you have to buy fewer steering wheels to put in them. Player salaries, on the other hand, are a *fixed cost:* If you sell only ten thousand tickets for Tuesday night's game, that doesn't mean you can employ fewer outfielders. The price point you select for your tickets, then, shouldn't change: If you're already charging the price that will bring in the most money, then raising ticket prices in response to increased player costs would be foolish. Conversely, if you think you *can* get away with charging more for tickets, you'd be foolish not to do so, regardless of what you're paying your players.

(Of course, there is another factor at work here: If paying through the nose for players improves your team, that will likely increase demand for tickets and allow you to raise prices. But that's not "passing along" payroll costs, it's just the natural increased demand you get with a winning ballclub—whether it's thanks to big-money free-agent signings or to a bunch of stud rookies earning the minimum.)

As James Quirk and Rod Fort wrote in their 1992 sports business treatise *Pay Dirt,* "Nobody has to force an owner to raise ticket prices if he or she is fielding a successful team with lots of popular support and a sold-out stadium. Put another way, even if player costs did not rise, one would expect that ticket prices and TV contract values would rise in the face of increasing fan demand. On the other hand, if the team already is having trouble selling tickets, only sheer folly would dictate raising ticket prices."

This, apparently, is what was happening in the early free-agent era. Salaries were skyrocketing, but interest in baseball remained fairly low by modern standards. Team owners thus concluded that fans were already paying all they were willing to pay to see Reggie Jackson, regardless of how much he was being paid. Instead, owners just ate the new payroll costs, taking it out of their own profits.

Around 1990, all this changed. Ticket prices showed little correlation with payroll in the late 1970s and 1980s, but since 1991, the two have been closely synchronized: For twenty-four of the thirty major league teams, ticket prices and payroll since 1991 are highly correlated.

What changed? As it turns out, something did happen around 1990—on June 5, 1989, to be precise—that caused baseball teams' revenue to begin a sharp upward spike. That's the day Toronto's SkyDome opened to the public. Whereas previous new stadiums had focused primarily on increasing capacity, SkyDome put its architecture squarely where the money was, featuring 161 luxury suites and unprecedented vast concessions concourses. (The two SkyDome elements that drew the most comment, after the retractable roof, were the $7 hot dog and the hotel beyond right field where guests could watch the Jays play from their rooms—and, infamously, fans could occasionally watch the guests play from their seats.) Baltimore's Camden Yards may have started the "retro" trend of modern steel-and-brick stadiums, but SkyDome was the first modern "mallpark."

Within two years, the Jays became the first team in history to crack the four-million mark in attendance. Suddenly every baseball bean counter began calculating how to replicate the marvel of the north. "You take the suites, the signage, throw the media on top," marveled Mariners owner Jeff Smulyan after a visit to the brand-new SkyDome, "and you have an economic juggernaut." Neither baseball nor its ticket prices would ever be the same.

In the stadium mania that followed in the wake of SkyDome and its brethren, team execs discovered that fans would pay unprecedented prices to gawk at the new retractable roofs and sample the garlic fries. (See Chapter 6-2, "Are New Stadiums a Good Deal?" for more on this topic.) Here, for example, is a list of the twenty biggest single-season ticket increases since 1991 (bold signifies first year of a new stadium):

1. **Det** **2000** **103.0 percent**
2. **SF** **2000** **75.2 percent**
3. **Pit** **2001** **65.3 percent**
4. **Phi** **2004** **51.3 percent**
5. **Hou** **2000** **50.6 percent**
6. Cin 2001 43.5 percent
7. **Mil** **2001** **39.2 percent**

8.	Cle	1994	38.6 percent
9.	Tex	1994	35.2 percent
10.	Ana	2003	35.5 percent
11.	Col	1995	34.3 percent
12.	SD	2004	31.9 percent
13.	ChW	2001	31.0 percent
14.	Atl	1997	31.5 percent
15.	Bal	1997	29.5 percent
16.	StL	1997	28.4 percent
17.	Sea	1999	27.2 percent
18.	TB	2001	25.0 percent
19.	NYY	1997	25.9 percent
20.	Oak	2001	24.0 percent

Eight of the top-ten single-season price hikes—and ten of the top twelve, and eleven of the top fourteen—came when a team was moving into new digs. (The number-one team without a new stadium is the 2001 Cincinnati Reds, who likely sought a way to defray some of the dollars being paid to fan favorite Ken Griffey Jr. with the star center fielder entering his second season with the club.) And the '99 Mariners might have been in the upper echelon had Safeco Field not opened in July, meaning their numbers were watered down with half a season at the Kingdome; ticket prices rose another 23.3 percent in the Mariners' first full season at Safeco in 2000.

The result was an unprecedented boon for baseball owners, whose revenue soared from $1.35 billion in 1990 to $4.27 billion in 2004. Players benefited as well. For while rising player salaries may not drive up ticket prices, the reverse is not necessarily true. More ticket revenue means more money in the pockets of owners, money that quickly found its way into the pockets of the Barry Bondses and Alex Rodriguezes (not to mention the Pat Meareses and Derek Bells) of the baseball world. Even more importantly, more expensive tickets make the rewards of spending on players much greater: If A-Rod puts an extra half-million fannies in the seats each season, you can afford to spend more on him if those fannies are sitting in $30 seats as opposed to $10 ones.

That said, we can't pin all the blame for ticket-price hikes on new stadiums: The twelve teams that did not move into new homes raised ticket prices by an average of nearly 50 percent, after inflation, between 1991 and 2005. Clearly something else had changed. Fans became more willing—or more able—to pay higher prices to attend a baseball game.

The easy explanation is simply that "demand for baseball rose." Unless you're a particularly literal-minded economist, though, that doesn't explain much. For that matter, recent decades have seen the steady decline of baseball's popularity compared to other sports: By 2001 a mere 12 percent of adults called baseball their favorite sport, a distant third to football and basketball.

Yet interest in sports overall—or at least *spending* on sports—has gone through the roof. As University of Chicago sports economist Allen Sanderson notes, this has driven up revenue, and ticket prices, across the board: "Ticket prices have also gone up rather dramatically at big-time college football and basketball programs, and salaries haven't changed at all."

Some of this, certainly, was the result of the 1990s economic boom, which put more money in the pockets of the affluent fans who are increasingly sports' target demographic. "Certainly people in the upper half of the income distribution the last twenty years have done quite well," said Sanderson. "Those in the lower ranks have not, but those are not the ones that are going to sporting events."

This flood of money into the upper echelons of U.S. society was unprecedented in recent memory: While the median U.S. household gained $3,400 in yearly after-tax income from 1979 to 1997, the average household in the top 1 percent of the population made a whopping $414,000 more each year. Compounding the effect were the massive income-tax cuts put in place during the 1980s, when the top tax bracket fell from 70 percent to 35 percent, leaving wealthy fans with refund checks that were handy for buying up all those new luxury suites and club seats.

The result is that grandstands are now markedly more exclusive: The only demographic segment to attend more games in the '90s than the '80s was households earning more than $50,000 a year. In the late 1990s, economists John Siegfried and Tim Peterson spent fifteen months poring over consumer-price-index surveys to determine the income levels of buyers of tickets to sporting events and found that the average ticket buyer's income was nearly twice the national average. And, notes Siegfried, since the survey excluded corporate buyers and luxury-suite holders, the true figure was likely even higher.

In effect, lower-income fans were being squeezed out by the big spenders, for whom dropping $75 to watch a ballgame from a padded seat with waiter service was suddenly not unreasonable. Sanderson describes this process as "trading up." He explains, "Just as we trade up from Sears or Penney's to Nordstrom's, we're trading up in that we want to see a game, but we want to see a game while eating a better brat." Another way to look at it is that when they design their new stadiums, the teams themselves are "trading up" from bleacher bums to the well-heeled.

In another industry, this increase in high-end demand would lead to an increase in supply—as it apparently did in, for example, the movie business, where competition from new theaters and the home video market left movie ticket prices rising no faster than inflation throughout the 1990s. Of course, that doesn't work in the closed world of baseball: You can open another two hundred Nordstrom's, but you can't add two hundred teams to the AL East.

The same can be said, incidentally, for those other hallmarks of modern baseball, the $7 beer and high cable-subscription rates. Just like ticket prices, these are unaffected by fixed costs like player salaries—fans aren't more willing to open their wallets at the concessions stand just because the third baseman got a raise—but do reflect the sport's monopoly status: If you want to watch baseball on TV or guzzle watery Bud at the ballpark, there's only one game in town. So when fans' wallets are newly abulge, prices can be expected to rise accordingly.

So if you're angry about those $30 nosebleed tickets, better to blame Ronald Reagan or the nation's ongoing love affair with garlic fries and cupholders than player salaries. After all, look what happened in the wake of the Reds' Larkin fiasco. The team held off on price hikes until the end of the season, then jacked them up by 43.5 percent the following off-season—only to see attendance plummet from 2,577,371 to 1,879,757, wiping out any potential gains in revenue.

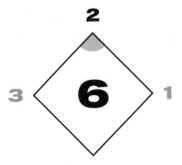

Are New Stadiums a Good Deal?

NEIL DEMAUSE

"It's about a baseball stadium," read the glossy brochure. "And it's about a City." A new stadium, it continued, "will pump new life into our community, will support 1,500 permanent jobs and 3,000 construction jobs, will encourage other businesses to locate in a rejuvenated downtown area," and "will help restore pride in the city and encourage new retail shopping downtown and a new sense of community purpose." Moreover, since the public would own the new ballpark, "the city will have the ability to add more police officers on the street to cut crime and increase services to neighborhoods. . . . With a new downtown stadium, everybody wins." The city was Detroit, the year 1996. The brochure, put together by a pro-stadium group calling itself Detroiters for Jobs & Development, was sent to registered voters in advance of a referendum to repeal a ban on public tax subsidies for stadium construction that had been passed just four years earlier.

Publications like these—usually slickly produced, often with the help of professional public relations firms or political campaign managers—are common sights in cities debating whether to spend public money to help build new homes for their sports teams. A new stadium, it is promised, is a win-win for both the franchise and the public: The team will thrive on the field and at the bank, the city will reap untold economic riches and a redeveloped downtown, and fans will enjoy a better ballpark experience.

The counterargument is equally familiar by now: Whenever new stadiums have been built, the promised lavish economic benefits have failed to materialize. Publicly financed ballparks make teams richer and cities poorer.

The modern stadium boom began in 1989 with the opening of Toronto's SkyDome. With its food courts, retractable roof, and luxury seating, it set the standard for state-of-the-art baseball palaces—at a cost to Ontario taxpayers of $600 million Canadian. Between 1990 and 2006, baseball has added eighteen new major-league stadiums, at a cost of $5.6 billion. Officially, just under two-thirds of that total—$3.6 billion or so—was public money (Table 6-2.1). But in the murky world of stadium finance, the numbers paraded before the public are seldom what they seem.

TABLE 6.2-1 Stadium Construction and Costs

Team	Stadium	Opened	Total Cost	Public Cost
Arizona	Bank One Ballpark	1998	$355 million	$270 million
Atlanta	Turner Field	1997	$444 million	$209 million
Baltimore	Oriole Park at Camden Yards	1992	$235 million	$226 million
Chicago (AL)	(new) Comiskey Park	1991	$150 million	$150 million
Cincinnati	Great American Ballpark	2003	$361 million	$300 million
Cleveland	Jacobs Field	1994	$173 million	$152 million
Colorado	Coors Field	1995	$215 million	$161 million
Detroit	Comerica Park	2000	$290 million	$145 million
Houston	Minute Maid Park	2000	$266 million	$180 million
Milwaukee	Miller Park	2001	$414 million	$324 million
Philadelphia	Citizens Bank Park	2004	$458 million	$231 million
Pittsburgh	PNC Park	2001	$233 million	$193 million
St. Louis	Busch Stadium	2006	$402 million	$127 million
San Diego	PETCO Park	2004	$449 million	$303 million
San Francisco	Pacific Bell Park	2000	$306 million	$15 million
Seattle	Safeco Field	1999	$517 million	$393 million
Tampa Bay	Tropicana Field	1990 (renovated 1998)	$150 million	$136 million
Texas	The Ballpark at Arlington	1994	$191 million	$153 million
Total (1990–2006)			$5.609 billion	$3.668 billion

Source: League of Fans (www.leagueoffans.org)

This flood of new facilities has changed the face of baseball. Within a single generation, baseball has almost obliterated both the prewar ballparks that once dominated the landscape and the multipurpose "concrete donuts" that followed them. The result has been an undeniable windfall for team owners and, as we saw in Chapter 6-1, for their players. The Baltimore Orioles, for example, were a low-revenue team when Eli Jacobs bought them for $70 million in 1989, when Camden Yards was under construction. Just four years later, Jacobs resold the Orioles for $173 million, after seeing annual revenue soar by $23 million thanks to the new park. Jacobs's profit was thus over $100 million. For the Maryland public, which paid for Camden Yards through a state-sponsored sports lottery, the return was very different.

Over the past decade and a half, independent economists have been busily critiquing both the rise of the taxpayer-funded stadium and the claims regarding its benefits for the public. Some of these names have become familiar: Andrew Zimbalist, Mark Rosentraub, Roger Noll, Allen Sanderson, Robert Baade, Rod Fort, Dennis Coates, Tim Chapin, and so on. In fact, it's now become boilerplate for newspaper reporters to write in their articles that "economists say stadiums provide few economic benefits"—usually then following with team claims that those ivory-tower economists are full of hooey.

So what do the economic studies actually say, and how damaging are they to stadium boosters' claims?

Probably the most-cited stadium study—at least the most ambitious—was conducted by Robert Baade, an economist at Lake Forest College in Illinois. To see whether new stadiums really created economic benefits for their hometowns, he studied thirty years' worth of data from forty-eight cities, noting when a new facility appeared and whether it represented a new team or just a relocation from an older building elsewhere in town. After controlling for other economic indicators, he posed the question: When a city builds a new stadium, what happens to its residents' per-capita income?

The result: Among the thirty cities with new stadiums or arenas, twenty-seven showed no measurable changes to resident income at all. In the other three, per-capita income appeared to *drop* as a result of the new sports facility. Concluded Baade: "Professional sports teams generally have no significant impact on a metropolitan economy [and do] not appear to create a flow of public funds generated by new economic growth. Far from generating new revenues out of which other public projects can be funded, sports 'investments' appear to be an economically unsound use of a community's scarce financial resources."

Baade's study has since been repeated by other economists. It has been conducted on other sets of cities (for example, major and minor league stadiums in the state of California) with similar results. But these findings don't prove that stadiums don't have a positive economic impact. Rather, they show that if they do have an impact, it's too small to measure with a coarse-grained indicator like per-capita income. So let's look at some other measures of economic impact, starting with job creation.

Proponents everywhere tout the thousands of jobs to be created by stadium projects. But the government "creates jobs" when it spends money on just about anything—including John Maynard Keynes's famous suggestion of burying money in bottles and paying people to dig it up again. So how do stadiums compare to other public works in terms of job creation?

Comerica Park, according to official figures, was slated to cost Michigan taxpayers $145 million. Even if the 1,500 permanent jobs promised came to pass—and were full time, not jobs as seasonal hot-dog vendors and the like—that would amount to about $100,000 in public expense per job created. Many stadiums boasted considerably higher cost-per-job figures: The Arizona Diamondbacks projected that Bank One Ballpark would create 340 full-time-equivalent jobs from a public expenditure of $240 million ($705,000 per job); one Minnesota Twins stadium plan promised 168 jobs at a cost of $310 million (almost $2 million per job).

In terms of bang for the public buck, figures like these are somewhere on the far side of dismal. For example, both the U.S. Department of Housing and Urban Development and the Small Business Administration require that projects they fund come in at no more than $35,000 per job. Well-designed economic development programs, say planning experts, typically come in at a cost-per-job ratio of less than $10,000; a study by the state of Maine found that job-training programs in that state cost just $2,300 per new job.

Another way to evaluate the public's return on investment is to look at cash flow. In 1998, Johns Hopkins economists Bruce Hamilton and Peter Kahn conducted a study of how much money Camden Yards was costing the state of Maryland, versus how much new tax revenue it was bringing in. Their conclusion: Economic benefits amounted to about $3 million a year, while costs averaged $14 million—a net annual loss of $11 million. This figure was measured during Camden Yards' "honeymoon" period, when sold-out games (and Cal Ripken at-bats) were still commonplace.

Hamilton and Kahn's study appeared in *Sports, Jobs & Taxes*, a 1998 anthology from the Brookings Institution. The publication included a who's who of sports economists, tackling the question of what sports stadiums do for—or *to*—local economies. As editors Roger Noll and Andrew Zimbalist wrote at the time: "In every case, the conclusions are the same. A new sports facility has an extremely small (perhaps even negative) effect on overall economic activity and employment. No recent facility appears to have earned anything approaching a reasonable return on investment. No recent facility has been self-financing in terms of its impact on net tax revenues."

How can this be? New stadiums have drawn millions of additional fans. Don't all those dollars provide some boost to their local economy?

Actually, no. As it turns out, not all consumer spending is created equal. Stadium spending fails as an economic engine in two ways: It isn't new spending, and it doesn't stay at home.

The first factor is called the *substitution effect*. The argument goes like this: By and large, residents of a city have a certain amount of disposable income to spend on entertainment, whether that be sporting events, movie tickets, or a night out at a bowling alley. If a baseball stadium draws three million fans, that's three million people who otherwise might have spent money elsewhere that night. Even tourists, unless they came to town specifically to see a baseball game, provide no net gain if their Yankees tickets are substituting for, say, an afternoon at the Museum of Modern Art.

One of the headaches of economics (and baseball analysis, for that matter) is that you can't do controlled experiments. You can't rewind the clock to see how a given city would have fared without its new stadiums. Fortunately, with baseball we have the next best thing: the 1994 labor stoppage. The sport shut down in early August of that year, wiping out the rest of the season and thus its economic benefits.

Shortly after the strike began, Canada's CBC News reported "a grand slam for some businesses" such as theaters and "dramatic increases in rentals at the video store." One comedy club manager quipped, "We really feel it would be in the best interest of entertainment in Toronto if the hockey players sat out the whole season too." Several studies failed to find any sign of lost tax revenue thanks to the loss of baseball; economist John Zipp reported that "the strike had little, if any, economic impact on host cities. Retail trade appeared to be almost completely unaffected by the strike." The obvious conclusion: People were spending the same money, just on different things.

The second factor in reducing any positive impact from stadiums is *leakage*. When you spend money at a bowling alley, most of the money goes to local residents who work as pinsetters, shoe-rental clerks, and the like; even the owner probably lives nearby. This creates what's called a *multiplier effect,* where every dollar you spend gets re-spent locally by all these local workers.

At a baseball stadium, much less of your consumer dollar recirculates in the local economy. Some of your cost in attending a Yankees game goes to pay the beer vendor or the groundskeepers, but the lion's share goes to George Steinbrenner and his players, none of whom are likely to spend it on cans of tuna fish at a Bronx bodega. In a study of the Mariners' impact on the nearby Pioneer Square district of Seattle, Baade found that "the stadium may have served as little more than an economic conduit through which spending on Kingdome events passed from one set of non-resident hands to another."

Add it all up, and you get a situation that soaks up public money with minimal public return. As University of Chicago sports economist Allen Sanderson, himself a diehard White Sox fan, has said: "If you want to inject money into the local economy, it would be better to drop it from a helicopter than invest in a new ballpark."

So if stadiums don't boost cities' bottom lines, what do they provide? Some of the additional arguments put forth by stadium proponents include:

Preventing a move. Virtually every team seeking a new stadium drops hints that it will skip town if its demands aren't met, or allows local political leaders to make the threat for it. Yet franchise relocations in baseball are rare—the Expos' decampment for Washington, DC, in 2005 was the first such move in thirty-three years. This is less a function of baseball's commitment to "stability," as Bud Selig might have you think, than a result of its financial structure: MLB relies far more on local TV revenue than other sports. So where an NFL team owner can safely move from big-market Houston to relatively tiny Memphis, knowing that he'll still be entitled to a share of the league's lucrative national TV contract, a baseball owner doing the same would take a huge hit to the wallet. As MLB discovered while trying to unload the Expos, the supply of untapped large baseball markets is next to exhausted.

Not that this has stopped teams from using move threats to extract stadium deals from their hometowns. Sometimes, in fact, pro-stadium politicians have even suggested bogus move threats to team owners as a means of jump-starting stadium negotiations: Both the Chicago White Sox' rumored move to Tampa Bay in the 1980s and the Minnesota Twins' dalliance with North Carolina in the late 1990s turned out to have been ideas hatched in the Illinois and Minnesota governors' offices.

Winning baseball. One of the most common pro-stadium arguments is that the additional revenue streams from a new park will make the team "competitive," especially if the team isn't saddled with much construction debt. For every team that found winning ways in a new home, though (the Cleveland Indians are usually the poster child in such examples), there's another team, such as the Pirates, that moved into its new home and then promptly sank deeper into the cellar. Which is the truth?

Table 6-2.2 is a list of every team that has moved into a new stadium since 1991 (the Rockies are excluded, since they played only two seasons in their original park). The list also includes the teams' average winning percentages in the final five seasons of their old parks and in the first five seasons (if they've played that many) in their new ones. The overall averages: a .486 winning percentage before the move, .520 afterward. It appears that a new ballpark is worth about 5.5 wins a year.

TABLE 6-2.2 Teams Moving to New Parks Since 1991, with Winning Percentage in Final Five Years in Old Park, First Five in New Park

Team	Previous Five	Next Five	Change
Cleveland	.443	.595	+.152
Baltimore	.434	.534	+.100
San Diego	.443	.537	+.094
San Francisco	.504	.586	+.082
Seattle	.508	.583	+.075
Chicago (White Sox)	.474	.543	+.069
Philadelphia	.487	.531	+.044
Detroit	.412	.443	+.030
Texas	.511	.509	−.002
Atlanta	.612	.608	−.004
Pittsburgh	.455	.435	−.020
Houston	.556	.528	−.028
Cincinnati	.495	.448	−.048
Milwaukee	.469	.401	−.069
Total	.486	.520	+.034

In economic terms, this actually makes sense. One thing new stadiums do, as we saw in Chapter 6-1, is increase the marginal return on spending to improve your team. In simple terms, a team is more likely to sign a Barry Bonds—or, to use the actual example of Cleveland, give long-term contracts to Jim Thome and Kenny Lofton—if it knows the people turning out to watch him are paying $25 per ticket instead of $15.

Of course, a $500 million stadium is an awfully expensive way to pick up five and a half games in the standings. (As Nate Silver has estimated in Chapter 5-2, each extra win is worth an average of $1.1 million to a team, with the benefit going up the closer a team gets to playoff contention.) This was noted in 2000 by Minnesota state representative Phyllis Kahn, who proposed that instead of buying the Twins a new stadium, the state just chip in $2 million a year toward Brad Radke's contract.

A better place to see a game. It's hard to argue with success, and baseball fans have poured into new stadiums in record numbers, at least when the gates first open. But it's equally hard to argue with geometry, and measurements have found that what fans are getting for their money isn't necessarily a better seat from which to watch the game. New stadiums are invariably described by designers as "intimate." But while most feature a smaller foul territory, which brings the first-row seats closer to the action, the need for roomy club seats and luxury suites has pushed upper decks skyward.

The result, according to Seattle-based stadium consultant John Pastier, is that new parks' upper decks—the cheap seats that most noncorporate fans must settle for—are invariably farther from the field than the top decks in the old parks they replaced, even when the new stadium's seating capacity is smaller. In the most infamous example, when the White Sox replaced the 52,000-seat Comiskey Park with a 44,000-seat new stadium of the same name in 1991, fans were alarmed to discover that the first row of the new upper deck was farther from the field than the last row in the old park.

Still, the claims of "intimacy" roll on unchallenged. Perhaps the most unintentionally amusing example of this came in the summer of 1999, when the Boston Red Sox owners were stumping for a new stadium to replace Fenway Park. The new park, explained a ubiquitous TV ad, would place fans "closer to the field, but not to the fans next to you." How team architects would manage this feat of non-Euclidean engineering was left unexplained.

Urban renewal. While the substitution effect generally precludes using a stadium to bring new money into a city, economists do admit that it can move spending from one part of a metropolitan area to another. Even here, though, economic studies have found that the "revitalization" effects of new stadiums are largely overblown.

One flaw in the theory of baseball stadiums becoming a neighborhood "catalyst" is that since they're rarely used for anything other than their teams' home games, they're dark some 284 days a year. (Arenas, which can book a full schedule of basketball, hockey, and concerts, are better, but even then the transient crowds are often less than useful for encouraging new businesses.) In 2000, six years after Cleveland's downtown Gateway complex opened, the Cleveland *Plain Dealer* examined the impact of Jacobs Field and the Gund Arena on the surrounding neighborhood: "The streets are often empty on nights when there are no sporting events or shows. Some popular restaurants and bars have not survived." The shopping district on nearby Euclid Avenue had deteriorated into "a retail no-man's land" and was seeking a $292 million trolley project to spur development.

Studies of other "revitalized" stadium districts found similarly shallow results. When Robert Baade looked at Seattle's Pioneer Square area, he found that some restaurants and bars had opened immediately adjacent to the Kingdome, but "three or four blocks walking distance from the stadium was sufficient to eliminate most of the positive economic impact cited by bars a block or less away." In downtown Baltimore, economists Hamilton and Kahn found that hotel receipts rose throughout the 1980s as the Baltimore harborfront was built up, but once Camden Yards opened, the trend flattened out.

Intangibles. These benefits, usually summed up as the "civic pride" that comes from rooting for a pro sports team, are the hardest to evaluate. As "intangibles," they're by definition impossible to measure.

Not that that's stopped some people from trying. Economics professor Bruce Johnson of Kentucky's Centre College took the survey methodology that environmental economists use to put a dollar value on intangible commodities—clean air, unspoiled wilderness—to gauge how much residents of Pittsburgh, Jacksonville, and Lexington would spend to keep or attract a local team. The answer: Between $23 and $48 million, far short of what teams usually demand in stadium subsidies. Johnson told a local newspaper that he had anticipated "really big numbers," but it turned out that "nobody was willing to pay anywhere near what cities were routinely spending on stadiums and arenas."

In fact, one of the dirty little secrets of the stadium game is that while new buildings are promoted as cash cows, when public subsidies are discounted, they seldom even pay for their own construction and operation costs. (Camden Yards, according to Hamilton and

Kahn, was producing $23 million a year in new revenue for the Orioles during its early boom years, but $20 million of that came in the form of state subsidies.) Given the skyrocketing cost of building new stadiums (PETCO Park, for example, cost more than double what the new Comiskey Park or Jacobs Field cost, even accounting for inflation), this makes sense: A $500 million stadium needs to bring in $35 million a year *more* than the old place to turn a profit. It's little wonder, then, that one seldom sees team owners exclusively invest private money to build pro sports facilities. They're generally bad investments.

The counterexample invariably raised is the San Francisco Giants and their Pacific Bell (now AT&T) Park. Built after four consecutive attempts at public funding were rejected at the ballot box in the late 1980s and early '90s, Pac Bell was funded almost entirely by Giants ownership, earning plaudits for breaking the cycle of public stadium finance. But San Francisco in the late 1990s was hardly a typical environment for building a baseball stadium. With the booming tech economy having left many Bay Area residents and businesses with money to burn, the Giants were able to sell fifteen thousand "charter seat licenses" (more commonly known as personal seat licenses, or PSLs) to fans seeking prime season-ticket locations, raising about $70 million. Pacific Bell paid a then-high $50 million for naming rights. Even ticket prices 75 percent higher than at the Giants' old home at Candlestick Park proved no deterrent to nightly sellouts.

Furthermore, Pac Bell's "private financing" turns out to have been not so private after all. While the Giants paid the full $306 million construction cost, they received both free land and tax breaks from the city. In all, according to Rutgers stadium-lease expert Judith Grant Long, the public ended up subsidizing about 14 percent of Pac Bell's cost. (Long's figures show that on average, the typical stadium project costs about 40 percent more than the "official" figures, thanks to unreported costs like free land, property-tax breaks, and public operations and maintenance costs.)

Finally, while the Giants have been a success so far at Pac Bell, it's still early in the new park's life cycle: By the time the stadium bonds are paid off, Barry Bonds will be almost sixty years old, and nightly sellouts could be a thing of the past. (The Toronto SkyDome, remember, was a four-million-fans-a-year juggernaut in its first few seasons; by year ten, it had filed for bankruptcy, and the Jays were threatening to move out.) With the Giants on the hook for $18 million a year in construction debt until the year 2020, and lifetime PSLs already sold, the jury is still out on whether the team will ultimately turn a profit on its new park.

The short honeymoon of new stadiums is by now an established fact. Open the gates to a new park, and curiosity-seekers will pour in— for a time. Provide some winning teams, and you can stretch out the good times for a few more years. But by year eight, the new fans will slip away no matter what, and attendance will swiftly fall back toward what it was in the team's old home (Figure 6-2.1).

FIGURE 6-2.1 Stadium honeymoon

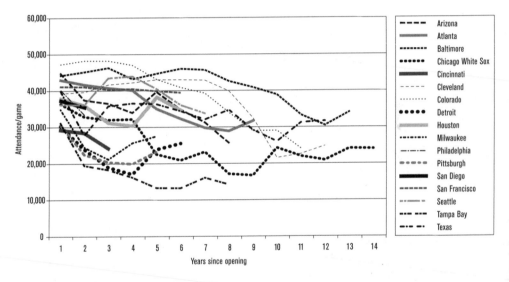

All of the lines in Figure 6-2.1 slope downward after the first few years. But there's more: Look at the four lines that start at the bottom of the pack, then immediately plunge to around twenty thousand fans per game or lower. These are Detroit's Comerica Park, Milwaukee's Miller Park, Pittsburgh's PNC Park, and Tampa Bay's Tropicana Field. A mix of domes and open-air stadiums, in small to medium-large markets, these parks have two things in common: All host teams have been out of contention for a generation (or were never contenders), and all opened late in the stadium game, when fans were less likely to make a cross-country pilgrimage to visit the latest in new "retro" parks. Numbers like these have led many to suggest that baseball is suffering from "stadium fatigue," where the initial attendance bump has grown weaker and the honeymoon shorter. Teams are no longer breaking new ground, merely keeping up with the Joneses.

So does all this mean that new stadiums should never be built? Of course not. But it does mean that if subsidies were removed from the equation, it would usually make more sense for teams to look at other options—renovation, for example, or less grandiose designs that keep costs in line with projected revenue—than to leap to build the next Camden Yards. Of the new ballparks that have mushroomed across America in recent years, not one was built because it was a good business proposition. They were built because team owners saw them as a good way to obtain public cash.

Despite being a bad deal, public subsidies have shown no sign of going away, nor have new stadium demands—the benefits to teams are just too great. Since 2002, team owners have been willing to put up a bit more of their own money, thanks to a new MLB rule—installed, it is rumored, at the behest of George Steinbrenner—that allows teams to deduct stadium expenses from their income for the purposes of revenue sharing, a bookkeeping gimmick that effectively allows teams to pass along 40 percent of their construction expenses to their rival ballclubs.

Of course, this had also led to an acceleration of the trend cited by Long, in that teams are increasingly seeking subsidies that don't show up either in the newspaper or on their revenue-sharing statements: property-tax breaks, free land, and the like. In 2001, for example, New York Mayor Rudy Giuliani proposed building twin stadiums for the Mets and Yankees, of which half the cost, $400 million apiece, would be paid by the city. The plan was swiftly dismissed by his successor, Michael Bloomberg, on the ground that the city couldn't afford it.

Four years later, Bloomberg proudly announced plans to build the new Mets and Yanks stadiums entirely with private money. But an analysis of the costs of land, infrastructure, and forgone tax and lease revenue (neither team would pay rent or property taxes) revealed that the taxpayer cost was still about $400 million apiece—almost double what Camden Yards had cost the Maryland public in 1991, even after adjusting for inflation.

The forms of the subsidies may change, but new stadiums are still mostly about one thing: boosting team profits by separating taxpayers from their money.

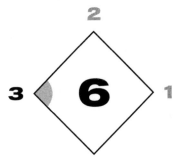

Does Baseball Need
a Salary Cap?

NEIL DEMAUSE

Perhaps no two words in baseball generate as much controversy and emotion as "salary cap." ("Designated hitter" might be a close second.) Depending on whom you ask, a salary cap would either save the game, destroy the players' union, provide hope for small-market fans, pervert the free market, or create a tangle of red tape that would turn every trade deadline into a battle of wits among dueling "capologists." Whenever owners and players have to negotiate a new collective bargaining agreement—the next tussle is scheduled for after the 2006 season—discussion of a cap is sure to follow. Mere mention of the c-word usually throws a giant wrench into labor talks and raises fans' fears of another 1994.

The concept of a cap sounds simple enough. Every team, whether the Yankees or the Devil Rays, is given an annual salary budget, and no team is allowed to exceed it. But as actually practiced by pro sports leagues, salary caps come in a million flavors: hard caps and soft caps, franchise-player exemptions, and luxury taxes. Each tweak to the system runs headlong into the economics of unintended consequences.

Before we can determine whether a salary cap would fix baseball, we have to decide just what it is about baseball that we want to fix. Taxes and caps have been suggested to cure various ills, including payroll inflation, high ticket prices, and competitive imbalance. Let's take them one at a time.

Reducing Player Salaries

As economists like to point out, if you want less of something, you should put a tax on it—and player salaries are no exception. Reduce the ability of the richest teams to bid up the price of players and salaries are sure to fall.

How this plays out depends on the type of tax in place. A salary cap—which should more properly be called a "payroll cap," since it says nothing about individual player salaries, only overall team payrolls—is the simplest to envision. Once teams have reached the magic payroll number, they are forbidden to spend more. This reduces salaries in two ways: Teams that are over the cap are taken out of the bidding for free agents (or for pricey trade targets), giving available players fewer options and reducing bidding pressure, and teams that are just below the cap will resist blowing their budget on a single player. This is precisely why the players' union has always fought bitterly and successfully against a hard cap.

Instead, baseball now has two modified cap-type mechanisms: the luxury tax and revenue sharing. The luxury tax, instituted in the 2002 collective bargaining agreement after a brief trial run in the late 1990s, is essentially a soft cap. Teams can bust their league-appointed budget, but at the cost of being taxed—"fined" might be a better word—for the excess amount. The tax starts at 22.5 percent and increases for repeat offenders. As a three-time recidivist, the Yankees paid a 40 percent tax on their excess spending in 2005. (Thanks to the oddities of collective bargaining, first-time violators received a bye in 2006.)

It's easy to see how a 40 percent tax would be a drag on spending. Coughing up $20 million a year for a superstar player is one thing, but adding another $8 million in payments to the league could make the deal untenable. Imagine how you would react if you had to pay a 40 percent surcharge for every gallon of gas you bought over the first ten. Filling up would become a thing of the past.

The main reason the luxury tax hasn't led to a crash in player salaries is that it very rarely comes into play. The tax threshold started at $117 million in 2003, rising in steps to $136.5 million in 2006. In its first three years, it was paid only six times, half of those by the Yankees. (The luxury tax, in fact, is widely known as the "screw the Yankees tax.") This is why the players' union didn't consider it worth striking over: While putting the reins on George Steinbrenner's checkbook may have been distasteful, it left the rest of the league free from constraints, and perhaps, with the Yankees brought down to earth a bit, more willing to spend. If the owners' original proposal—a 50 percent tax on all spending over $84 million per team—had been enacted, it would have hit ten teams in 2005 and sent shock waves through baseball's salary structure.

Baseball's other main income-redistribution scheme is revenue sharing, which has existed in one form or another for decades (counting such ancient innovations as giving a portion of ticket receipts to the visiting team). In this general form, revenue sharing is a less obvious means of keeping down salaries, but it's a means toward that end nonetheless. To see why, think about players as cost-conscious owners do—not as heroes to cheer from the grandstand but as business investments.

Let's say you're Texas Rangers owner Tom Hicks in the winter of 2000–2001, and you're deciding whether to sign Alex Rodriguez to a record $25-million-a-year contract. Certainly, you're going to look at A-Rod's stats: just twenty-five years old with 189 home runs and a batting title under his belt. But when figuring out how much to pay him, you'll also consider his *value:* How many more tickets will he sell; how much will he increase advertising revenue on your team's broadcasts; how many more souvenir jerseys will fans buy; how much will he increase the value of the franchise? If the answer isn't "more than $25 million a year," then paying A-Rod that much would be foolish—unless you're willing to lose money in pursuit of a World Series ring.

Add in revenue sharing and the picture changes greatly. The current system is complicated, but it can be summed up in a simple rule: Every team in the league, rich or poor, gets to keep about 60 cents on every new dollar it earns. For high-revenue teams, this percentage comes from having to write bigger checks to the league the more money they make; for the low-revenue ones, it's in receiving *smaller* checks from the league as revenue increases.

Go back to Hicks's dilemma. Now he doesn't need to ensure that Rodriguez brings in $25 million a year to pay his own way. Rather, A-Rod needs to increase revenue by *$41.7 million* a year ($25 million = 60 percent of $41.7 million). Suddenly his potential dollar value to a team has plummeted. That's even more true for teams at the bottom of the barrel, who are subject to a higher tax rate. (Chapter 5-2, "Is Alex Rodriguez Overpaid?" explores this topic in more detail.)

It's easy to see, then, why the players' union has fought bitterly against revenue sharing, considering it a thinly disguised way to transfer money from players' pockets to owners'. It's also easy to see why owners love it, Steinbrenner notwithstanding. But to see what revenue sharing means to fans, who presumably don't care which millionaire is getting their hard-earned money, we need to look at the proposed *effects* of cutting player salaries.

Lowering Ticket Prices

The theory here is that reducing the amount of money teams spend on players will reduce the amount of income they need and thus allow them to lower ticket prices—or at least not increase them quite so fast.

If you've been skipping around in this book, here's where you should go back and read Chapter 6-1 on the link between team payroll and ticket prices. In a nutshell, there is no such link. Or rather, while increased ticket prices do seem to drive up payroll, increased payroll decidedly *doesn't* drive up ticket prices. So don't expect your favorite team to offer cheaper seats just because they failed to sign Carlos Beltran.

Yet this isn't entirely true. If the Yankees hadn't been afraid of the luxury tax and had signed Beltran, they would have been a better team: Despite his disappointing 2005 season, Beltran was still markedly better than the likes of Bernie Williams and Tony Womack, who contributed next to nothing as the Yankees' center fielders. This could in turn have increased demand for tickets—yes, even beyond the four million fans the Yankees drew in 2005—and allowed them to raise ticket prices. On the other hand, the distribution of talent is a zero-sum game: When Beltran didn't sign with the Yankees, he did sign with the Mets, driving up demand for *their* tickets and thus their ability to raise prices. Such are the hazards of revenue redistribution. If it makes your team more competitive, you'll be asked to pay for it at the box office.

Competitive Balance

Arguments about salary caps and revenue sharing always come down to competitive balance. When owners were pushing a cap in the run-up to the 2002 labor wars, they made sure to sell it as a means to restore, in Bud Selig's famous words, the fans' "hope and faith" that their team could have a shot at a pennant. "Perhaps 12 of 30 Major League teams have any possibility of reaching postseason play, and fewer still have a realistic hope of winning a pennant," Padres owner John Moores wrote in the *Wall Street Journal* shortly after his team had, ironically, reached the World Series. "Unless baseball changes the way it does business, it risks seeing its fans drift away, tired of their teams' futility."

Of course, in any given year, most teams won't come close to making the playoffs. A more significant measure is whether poor revenue potential is locking teams out of pennant races for years at a time. The numbers here are less clear: Since the expanded playoffs began in 1995, twenty-two of the thirty big-league teams have reached the postseason at least once; two of the remaining eight, the Phillies and Blue Jays, had just met in the final World Series under the old setup. Compare that to baseball's "golden age," when the Phillies once went thirty years without finishing higher than fourth while teams like the St. Louis Browns and Washington Senators rarely even sniffed a pennant race.

That said, the Yankees are one of two teams never to have missed the postseason under the current system (the Braves are the other). If we chart postseason appearances against average team revenue (see Table 6-3.1), we find that the two are correlated at a coefficient of determination (R-squared) of .51—which is to say that a little more than half of getting to the postseason is determined by team revenue.

Of course, there's a problem here. High revenue may help lead to the postseason, but postseason appearances increase revenue as well. Not only are playoff tickets a lucrative item, but a winning team typically sees regular-season sales soar. Table 6-3.1 could as easily be telling us that half of *team revenue* can be explained by *who gets to the postseason*, which isn't quite what we were after.

To avoid this dilemma, let's instead

TABLE 6-3.1 Postseason Appearances and Average Team Revenue, 1995–2005

Team	Playoff Appearances	Avg Revenue, 1995–2004 (millions)
Yankees	11	$187.54
Braves	11	134.38
Red Sox	6	131.83
Indians	6	129.09
Mets	2	127.96
Orioles	2	125.72
Dodgers	3	122.63
Diamondbacks	3	121.13
Mariners	4	119.03
Rockies	1	115.44
Rangers	3	113.33
Cubs	2	113.19
Giants	4	106.50
Cardinals	6	104.73
Astros	6	100.18
Devil Rays	0	92.36
Angels	3	91.27
White Sox	2	91.08
Tigers	0	84.56
Phillies	0	83.87
Padres	3	82.64
Blue Jays	0	81.42
Athletics	4	75.13
Marlins	2	74.89
Reds	1	74.55
Brewers	0	72.39
Pirates	0	72.08
Royals	0	69.07
Twins	3	63.36
Expos	0	55.13

TABLE 6-3.2 Playoff Appearances and
Market Size, 1995–2005

Team	Playoff Appearances	Market Size (100=league average)
Yankees	11	262
Mets	2	244
Dodgers	3	175
Red Sox	6	155
Angels	3	147
Phillies	0	130
Orioles	2	124
Mariners	4	112
Cubs	2	105
Rangers	3	103
Braves	11	102
Blue Jays	0	96
Tigers	0	95
Marlins	2	95
White Sox	2	90
Devil Rays	0	87
Astros	6	86
Giants	4	84
Indians	6	84
Expos	0	78
Twins	3	69
Reds	0	69
D-Backs	3	64
A's	4	61
Rockies	1	59
Cardinals	6	56
Pirates	0	54
Padres	3	45
Brewers	0	39
Royals	0	38

compare postseason appearances not with revenue but with TV market size (Table 6-3.2). Beyond the obvious—you really don't want to play in the tiniest markets, or in Canada—the correlation between market size and playoff appearances is extremely weak. What explains the Cardinals' or the Indians' success, or the Phillies' lack of it? The correlation coefficient has dropped to a mere .11—market size accounts for 11 percent of the cause—meaning anyone who's tempted to place bets on division winners based solely on TV market size is kidding himself.

Regardless of how big a problem you consider competitive balance to be, there's still the question of how it would be affected by a salary cap. As we've seen, a hard cap is an effective way to stop high-revenue teams from spending as much money as they'd like—and even a "soft cap" like the luxury tax can help put on the brakes. But what if your team isn't near the cap? You have no reason to spend more on players: If that new left fielder wasn't worth $10 million a year to you before, you're certainly not going to think he is now. In fact, you might now be willing to pay *less* for him. Since the big spenders over the cap are out of the running, there are fewer teams eligible to bid on his services, meaning you have a better shot at lowballing him on salary. Even if it lowers salaries across the board, a soft cap doesn't eliminate the hierarchy of revenues. The teams that can afford to pay the most in luxury taxes will still have their pick of players.

There are only two ways, then, that a spending cap could conceivably improve baseball's balance. One, if the big-spending teams were brought somewhat down to earth, it might increase the number of teams in contention and thus increase the number of teams willing to invest in high-priced talent to get them over the hump. It's a bit early to tell if there's any evidence of this happening since 2002, but if so, the impact is minimal. In any case, it would still do nothing to promote spending among second-division teams.

The other possibility is that if you depress salaries far enough, you eventually get to the point where no teams are priced out of the market for any player—even the Kansas City Royals could fit Barry Bonds into their budget at $100,000 a year. Of course, long before you arrived at that point, you'd have Don Fehr leading a picket line around your house while Gene Orza dropped tear-gas grenades down your chimney. It's not exactly a workable solution to competitive-balance issues.

The usual union-friendly suggestion for forcing lower-echelon teams to spend on payroll is a "salary floor," a minimum team payroll to match the maximum imposed by a cap. (The NBA and NHL currently have payroll floors in place.) While this would certainly encourage spending, it might not be the kind of spending you want. It's arguably more effective for rebuilding baseball teams to throw money into scouting and player development in the short term, then invest in payroll only when they have players worth spending on. Any system that would encourage irrational spending sprees such as the Devil Rays' run a few years ago on Greg Vaughn, Vinny Castilla, and their ilk wouldn't be helping matters.

Outsiders' Proposals

So much for the owners' ideas. Can baseball outsiders do any better? There's been no shortage of suggestions for better mousetraps. In 2002, Baseball Prospectus's Doug Pappas suggested a simple progressive revenue-sharing rate, where teams would keep all their revenue up to 80 percent of the league average, then pay a graduated rate scaling up to 75 percent for revenue over double the league average. Most alternative suggestions, though, have focused on taxing market size rather than revenue. The idea here is that unlike revenue—a gauge of both market size and front-office savvy—market size is a measure of differing *opportunity* to make money. The Yankees will always have an advantage over the Devil Rays by virtue of being in New York, even if the Rays hire the ghost of Branch Rickey as general manager and the Yanks hire an entire front office of Syd Thrift clones.

One such revenue-sharing plan, devised by Baseball Prospectus's Keith Woolner, would impose a "market size" tax on payroll, starting at zero for the smallest markets, then scaling up to about 9 percent for the top teams. On the subsidy side, the bottom 40 percent of teams would earn payments based on total wins and improvement in wins over the previous year, plus additional bonuses for making the playoffs or being one of the top teams among small-market clubs. In his book *May the Best Team Win*, sports economist Andrew Zimbalist proposed an even simpler system: Calculate a theoretical baseline revenue for each team based on how much they'd be expected to earn in a season with a .500 record, then tax them on that, regardless of their actual income.

Of course, these plans have their difficulties: Woolner's is still a payroll tax and so would create a drag on payrolls. Zimbalist's would be a nightmare to calibrate, as every new stadium or shift in metro population would move the "average season" baseline. And with untested systems like these, there's always the risk of creating unforeseen negative effects, such as (under Woolner's system) teams losing games intentionally to boost the next season's "win improvement" numbers.

For that matter, there are plenty of ways to encourage competitive balance that have nothing to do with revenue. The player-compensation draft for free-agent losses—the one memorable for making Tom Seaver White Sox property—was one short-lived mechanism, as was the never-adopted suggestion that all foreign players be subject to the player draft, thus preventing wealthy teams from grabbing the best Latin American talent with big signing bonuses. For that matter, if "hope and faith" for every team is the goal, you could give a twenty-game head start in the standings to any team stuck in a below-average TV market. Or you could pick teams by lot and hand the trophy to the first name out of the hat. But at a certain point, this sort of "balance" defeats the purpose.

This is why as many fans hate the salary cap as yearn for it. The more complex the arrangement you devise to level the playing field, the more it feels like the winners are those who can game the system.

Ultimately, baseball requires as many losers as winners. Short of four or five World Series a year, some franchises are bound to go for generations without winning the big prize. "Hope and faith" is a nice idea and a great public relations slogan. But the cure shouldn't be worse than the disease.

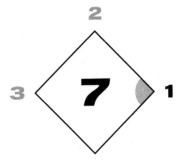

What Happened
to Todd Van Poppel?

DAYN PERRY

For Oakland, the story starts with veteran slugger Dave Parker, whose contract with the A's ran out in 1989. Parker had put up rather paltry numbers that season for a corner outfielder/DH type, and he was in his late thirties. The decision from Oakland's perspective wasn't difficult, but Parker's cachet as a veteran performer created a market for him. The Brewers accommodated Parker nicely and in the process forfeited a pair of compensatory draft picks to the A's. In the June draft of 1990, the A's would spend their glut of draft picks—four of the first thirty-six selections—on a quartet of promising hurlers who would come to be called (prematurely, as it turned out) the "Four Aces." The Four Aces were Kirk Dressendorfer, Don Peters, Dave Zancanaro, and Todd Van Poppel, the last a fireballing Texan long on promise and press clippings.

The fourteenth overall pick, Van Poppel was widely hailed as the most gifted high school pitcher ever. It's a historical imperative that any Texan under nineteen with a good fastball will be crowned "the next Nolan Ryan," and so Van Poppel was. That thirteen teams passed on him that year shouldn't suggest any divided enthusiasm; most teams simply doubted they could sign him. (He had a baseball scholarship waiting for him at the University of Texas).

But the A's bit and, after protracted negotiations, wound up signing Van Poppel to a $1.2 million major league contract. To this day, he and Josh Beckett of the Marlins are the only two pitchers to be signed to major league contracts straight out of high school. The consequence of a major league contract tendered to a newly drafted player is that the player must be added to the major league roster within three years or be exposed to waivers. In the case of a college-trained draftee, that's not all that risky; in the case of raw prep pitcher, it presents both parties with an unrealistic timetable.

Sure enough, Van Poppel, despite dubious command of his curveball, made his major league debut at age nineteen, after only thirty-two games in the minors (and on the "strength" of a stint in Double-A in which he walked 90 batters in 132.1 innings). Whether he was mishandled or was never hardwired for long-term success cannot be known; what's beyond dispute is that he was a colossal disappointment. Van Poppel's stuff was tremendous, but his control was terrible, and he was never able to cultivate a reliable off-speed pitch. He floundered for a decade before finally meeting with a modicum of success as a middle reliever with the Cubs. By the time he retired following the 2004 season, he had a 5.58 career ERA, had logged a 40-52 record with six different organizations and had been waived twice and released three times.

The other three aces fared even worse. Peters and Zancanaro never reached the majors, and Dressendorfer logged only seven games at that level. Still, it was Van Poppel who became, to many observers, the exemplar of squandered promise. His story and its cautionary elements raise the question: What's the wisest way for a team to spend a draft pick?

More than any other sport, baseball's amateur draft entails a huge amount of uncertainty. Even the shrewdest teams have been known to throw away millions of dollars on players who never panned out. So should teams focus on high school talents, who can range from a Todd Van Poppel to future Hall-of-Famer Greg Maddux? Or is it wiser to focus on college-trained ballplayers, whose realized promise ranges from who-dat Antone Williamson to all-time great Barry Bonds?

For a long time the debate was defined by received wisdom on both sides. The statistically inclined camp held that college draftees were manifestly superior, while traditionalists and scouts believed that drafting eighteen-year-olds with imposing tools better allowed an organization to craft a future superstar. Each side trotted out study after study and anecdote upon anecdote to buttress its position, but never to its opponents' satisfaction.

So which is the better strategy—focusing on high school talents or stockpiling the system with college-trained ballplayers? The answer is somewhat fluid: Different eras, for whatever reason, yield different results. That said, Rany Jazayerli, in a 2005 series of articles on Baseball Prospectus.com, has done the most definitive research to date, scrutinizing every draft from 1984 through 1999. Specifically, Jazayerli examined the top one hundred selections from each of those drafts. After he eliminated players who failed to sign with the team that drafted them, that still left 1,526 players in the study pool, of whom 752 (49.3 percent) made the majors. To measure the quality of the draftees, Jazayerli used each player's Wins Above Replacement Player (WARP) rating, a Baseball Prospectus metric that measures, in wins, what a player provides over a readily available "replacement-level" player for the first fifteen years of his major league career.

Here's some of what Jazayerli discovered:

Point 1: The greatest difference in value between consecutive draft positions is between the first and second picks. Top overall picks, on average, logged a fifteen-year WARP of around 46. Second overall picks, meanwhile, posted WARPs of about 31, or less than the average of the third and fourth overall picks.

Point 2: There's very little difference in value between second-round and third-round draft picks. Picks 41–65 (roughly speaking, the second round of the draft) on average tallied a fifteen-year WARP of 4.51, while picks 66–90 (roughly speaking, the third round of the draft) logged an average WARP of 4.56—a negligible difference.

Point 3: College-trained players are about 50 percent more likely to reach the major leagues than high school players at equivalent draft positions. This advantage has remained constant over time. Broken down into eras, Table 7-1.1 shows how collegians and high schoolers compare in terms of percentage of draftees reaching the majors.

While upside can be debated, college talents are far safer bets to reach the highest level. This is because they've already survived a winnowing process from having played college

TABLE 7-1.1 Percent of High School and College Players Reaching Major Leagues

Group	Era	Percent Reaching Major Leagues
High school	1984–1991	41
High school	1992–1999	39
College	1984–1991	60
College	1992–1999	57

ball in the first place. In the case of pitchers, they've also made it through the critical ages of eighteen through twenty, when many career-altering injuries occur.

Point 4: In a year where there's a widely coveted superstar talent available in the high school ranks, it's perfectly acceptable to use the top overall pick to get him.

You don't need to look far to find elite prep performers justifying their overall No. 1 selection: Jeff Burroughs in 1969, Harold Baines in 1977, Darryl Strawberry in 1980, Ken Griffey Jr. in 1987, Chipper Jones in 1990, Joe Mauer in 2001. Spending the top overall pick on a gifted high school hitter has paid off time and again.

Point 5: Through the first one hundred picks of the draft, not only are college players about 50 percent more likely to reach the major leagues than high school players drafted in the same slot, but they also provide approximately 55 percent more value over the course of their careers. This advantage persists at every point *after the No. 1 pick.* From 1992 to 1999, however, the edge enjoyed by college talents slowly degrades until the two groups are almost equal, with the college set retaining a narrow and perhaps statistically questionable advantage.

Point 6: The value of high school players relative to their college counterparts has increased over time, even though teams were more likely to use top draft picks on high school players in the 1990s than in the 1980s. For instance, from 1984 to 1991, college draftees held an average fifteen-year WARP advantage of 11.15 to 6.08. However, from 1992 to 1999, that WARP advantage declined to just 6.33 to 5.22.

Point 7: Although the collegiate edge nearly evaporated in the 1990s, college-trained hitters remain easily the most valuable draft pick on average, enjoying a substantial edge over every other type of pick throughout the duration of the study. No matter how you massage the data, college hitters come out ahead of every other group—college pitchers, high school hitters, high school pitchers—usually by a wide margin. Table 7-1.2 shows the numbers.

Point 8: High school pitchers remain the riskiest selections in the first round. This is mostly because, unlike college hurlers, they haven't made it through the "injury nexus." Pitchers in their late teens and early twenties are part of that nexus, often suffering career-altering or -ending injuries to their elbows and shoulders. But the gap between success rates for high school and college pitcher draftees is much smaller than it once was. No longer is it a grave error—going strictly by the percentages—to draft a high-school hurler in the first round.

However, it's still not a great idea to spend the top overall pick on a high school arm. Only twice since the June draft was instituted in 1965 has a team selected a prep-trained pitcher first overall. In 1973, the Rangers took David Clyde, who logged only 416 innings in his major league career, and in 1990 the Yankees did it with Brien Taylor, a hurler from East Carteret High School in rural North Carolina.

TABLE 7-1.2 Average WARP for College and High School Hitters in the Major Leagues

Group	Era	Avg. WARP
College hitters	1984–1991	9.53
College hitters	1992–1999	8.53
College pitchers	1984–1991	7.63
College pitchers	1992–1999	5.26
High school hitters	1984–1991	4.31
High school hitters	1992–1999	5.00
High school pitchers	1984–1991	3.43
High school pitchers	1992–1999	4.52

At the time, Taylor was considered one of the brightest pitching prospects ever to enter the draft. He came from a modest background, a trailer home in the small burg of Beaufort. His father was a mason, and his mother worked shelling crabs. Given Taylor's blend of talent and financial need, the Yankees may have figured they'd nab a major steal at the top of the draft. It was not to be.

The Bombers' late offer of an $850,000 signing bonus, which was more than the previous two number-one picks—Ben McDonald and Chipper Jones—had received *combined*, was flatly refused. Advising Taylor and his parents (or, some would say, pulling the strings) was the agent Scott Boras. Boras wasn't yet the uberagent he would become, but he was about to help Taylor shatter the perception of an amateur having limited bargaining power.

For the Yankees, that wasn't the worst part of the story. Brien Taylor, the man seemingly destined to save what was then a languishing Yankees franchise, the man whose eventual $1.55 million signing bonus so shocked the nation that *60 Minutes* ran an entire segment about it, never pitched an inning in the major leagues.

After making his minor league debut, Taylor told the media, "In high school nobody ever got on base, so I've got some adjusting to do." He had some early success in the low minors, but in a bar fight following the '93 season, an acquaintance of Taylor's hurled him down on his pitching shoulder, effectively ending his career. Some within the Yankees organization believed the assailant knew exactly what he was doing. The injury cost Taylor the entire '94 season, and a series of abortive comeback attempts yielded 111 innings, 184 walks, and an 11.27 ERA. He never made it past Double-A.

In selecting Taylor, a young and unpolished yet deeply gifted long-term project, the Yankees in 1991 passed on a litany of other first-rounders, including Manny Ramirez, Cliff Floyd, Shawn Green, Dmitri Young, Scott Hatteberg, Aaron Sele, Joey Hamilton, and Shawn Estes.

Hindsight is often an odious indulgence, but it's worth asking whether the Yankees should have known better than to slather a king's ransom on an untested eighteen-year-old. While there's not much of a direct cautionary tale to be found in Taylor's travails (other than the hazards of underage pub-crawling), the prevailing lesson still applies: eighteen-year-olds, the pro-athlete mentality, and sudden cash windfalls are often a volatile mix.

Were the Yankees stupid to choose Taylor, or merely unlucky? The stakes of the amateur draft are very high. Rash, uninformed decisions can cost a team millions, and not only in bonus payments. When a league rival has Manny Ramirez swatting 40 homers a year while you're mourning the sad case of Brien Taylor, the botched opportunity is all the more painful.

Point 9: With the exception of those chosen in the first round, high school pitchers are about as valuable as high school hitters.

Point 10: College pitchers are, generally speaking, not significantly more valuable than either high school pitchers or hitters, regardless of which round they're selected in.

Oakland general manager Billy Beane, who was in the lower rungs of the organization back when Van Poppel was drafted, took away some valuable lessons from that fiasco. Not only did he develop an affinity for college hurlers, but he also came to prefer the pitchers who demonstrated impressive athleticism—something Van Poppel plainly didn't.

Tim Hudson was undersized for a right-hander, but he was a tremendously gifted athlete (he was also Auburn's best hitter and best defensive outfielder during his final collegiate season). Mark Mulder was tall and strong—the preferred build for a pitcher—but he was also graceful and quick. All the focus on Oakland's preference for college talents overlooks the fact that the team has homed in on a prototype in recent years—the athlete who also puts up the numbers.

And there you have it. The "stathead" preference for college hitters is justified, but the disdain for high school draftees is largely without basis. Most notably, there's nothing wrong with taking an elite prep talent with the top overall pick. Pitchers from any source tend to be worse investments than position players. And no case better illustrates the risk of investing in high school pitching than Van Poppel's.

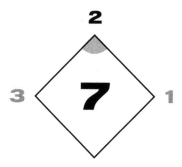

Is There Such a Thing as a Quadruple-A Player?

CLAY DAVENPORT

In 1996, Mike Berry, a player in the Orioles system, had a big year in the minors. He hit .361 with 44 doubles, drew 99 walks, scored 109 runs, and drove in 113. Have you ever heard of Mike Berry? Probably not. Given his failure to ever make the big leagues, skeptics would call him a Quadruple-A player—one who can hit in the minor leagues but not the majors. The question is: Does such a player exist?

Yes, he does. Any time you're dealing with people, there are going to be some who are unable to handle a transition, in this case the transition between the minor and major leagues.

That said, the vast majority of players who acquire the Quadruple-A label don't really deserve it. Most are players who never should have been expected to perform well in the major leagues. Some put up big numbers only after repeating the same level multiple times, feasting on prospects five, even ten years younger. Others put up superficially impressive numbers in favorable offensive environments—a 30–home run season in the thin air of Colorado Springs is far less impressive than the same feat in pitcher-friendly Myrtle Beach. Still others never hit all that well in the first place—a .300 batting average doesn't mean much without ample walks and extra-base hits to back it up. The broader lesson is this: You simply can't look at minor league performance the same way you look at major league numbers—at least not until you consider context.

In his *Baseball Abstract* books of the 1980s, sabermetric pioneer Bill James attacked the prevailing notion that minor league statistics were meaningless, that there was no relationship between the way a player hit in the minors and how he would later hit in the majors. He was able to show that the reason people thought that minor league numbers were meaningless was because they failed to consider context. People were trying to read minor league numbers in exactly the same way they read major league numbers.

James developed something he called the Major League Equivalencies, or MLEs. By a series of steps, anyone could turn a set of minor league numbers into a set of equivalent major league numbers. MLEs accounted for the difference between runs per game in a minor league environment and runs per game in the equivalent major league environment. James used the player's parent club as the guide: A Red Sox farmhand would get an MLE tuned to Fenway Park, Dodger farmhands got adjusted to Dodger Stadium, and so on. In other words, he took the original statistics and used the contextual difference to change them. James changed each statistic separately: He had one factor to adjust for singles, another to adjust for doubles, another for triples, and so on.

A few years later, I was working on a project to figure out what a player like Ty Cobb would have hit in the modern game—if he'd be able to dominate modern competition the same way he had dominated his early-twentieth-century peers. We may look at Cobb today and see him as a player who hit for a high batting average, with little power and great base-stealing ability, ideally suited to the leadoff role. After adjusting for the context of the deadball era, though, we see that Cobb was also one of the best power hitters of his day. It's just that power levels were so low overall—thanks to a baseball with little more bounce than an overripe grapefruit—that you had to look very carefully, using the right adjustments, to notice.

To further refine James's work, I applied Equivalent Average, a system that rated a player's total offensive value, adjusted for league and park. EqA's final numbers look like a batting average, which makes it easy to recognize them as good, bad, or in between. Honus Wagner produced an EqA of .341 in 1907. We knew the overall shape of his offense: He derived 40 percent of his value from singles (an average player from 1907 got 53 percent), 19 percent from doubles (average was 12 percent), 9 percent from triples (7 percent), 5 percent from homers (2 percent), 13 percent from walks (19 percent), and 15 percent from steals (7 percent). I then used a series of ratios comparing just about every statistic to every other statistic, to come up with a rating of how well Wagner performed relative to the league. To convert Wagner's stats from 1907 to 1987, I started with the .341 EqA. The equations to generate EqA can be run backward to a certain point, which allowed me to figure out how many total bases would come from singles, extra-base hits, walks, and steals to equal a .341 EqA in 1987 terms. It took 371 bases to get a .341 EqA in 1907; it would require 520 in 1987.

That part was pretty easy. The hard part was fitting Wagner's 1907 ratios onto a 1987 set of statistics, a task similar to mounting a 1907 Model T body onto a 1987 Mustang frame. It is mathematically impossible to make all of the ratios match up with each other and still generate the right total value at the end. The program I wrote starts with a league-average line and changes one factor at a time, such as adding one single. It then computes all the ratios again. The process continues until it can't make any more improvements. I called the final products Translations; they later became known as Davenport Translations, or DTs.

It didn't take long to realize that this procedure, designed to work across different eras and environments, would also work very well across different leagues—all you had to do was build in a measure to change the target EqA. If a player hit for a .341 EqA in the Double-A Eastern League, we would run the translation exactly the same way we did for Honus Wagner, except we would downgrade the EqA based on how much players typically lose when going from Double-A to Triple-A and Triple-A to the majors. In this case, it would be somewhere around .275.

The DT system is still basically the same today as it was when it was created nineteen years ago, although some of the internal details have changed over time. Those changes account for other variables such as player age when setting the target EqA. One big difference between DTs and MLEs was the decision to put all minor league players on the same scale, rather than the thirty separate scales that would come from translating each of them into their parent team's home park.

The Good, the Bad, and the Maybe

There are basically three types of players in the minors: The ones who are clearly good enough to play in the majors, the ones who are clearly not good enough to play in the majors, and a whole bunch in between who may or may not be good enough. The tools used to evaluate players, either by stats or by scouting, aren't perfect. Neither is the definition of how good you have to be to make the major leagues. The talent level that defines the difference between the majors and the minors isn't a line—it's a big fuzzy cloud, a fog bank that divides the players who clearly reside on one side or the other. The players themselves are not robots that always perform at exactly one level; rather, they have a range of outcomes superimposed on the cloud.

Players within the cloud are more or less interchangeable, and there are a lot more of them than there are major league jobs available. These are the players who bounce up and down between the majors and minors, depending on a host of circumstances besides their own ability. Whether or not someone else got hurt, who's been on a hot streak—the smallest happenings can make all the difference. Figure 7-2.1 gives you some idea of how thin the margins are for major league hopefuls, with so many players vying for jobs and MLB offering so few.

FIGURE 7-2.1 Margins for major league hopefuls

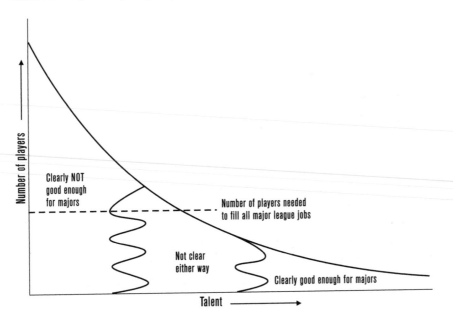

The judgment that a player can hit in the minors but couldn't in the majors is rarely true. There are three common reasons why a player could look that way. If you knew the key factors to look for, though, your perspective would likely change. The first one is a form of selection bias: the lucky player.

There is a common problem that affects any system that involves promotions from level to level with professional baseball. Players are not robots. They have a basic skill and talent level—sometimes they play above their talent level (a "hot streak"), and sometimes they play below it (a "cold streak"). However, despite all of the blustering among major league general managers about not paying attention to statistics, they do read the numbers. When something goes wrong and they need to grab a guy from Triple-A, GMs are far more likely to take the guy who's hitting .330 than the one who's hitting .230, even if both of them are .280 career hitters. The player who is playing over his head is much more likely to get called up than a player who is just being his regular self, or struggling.

The effect of that decision is that when the hot streak wears off and the player goes back to being his usual self, it's going to look like he can't handle the major leagues. Which, in this case, is true; the team erred in thinking he was ever major league caliber. He wasn't "ready" because he wasn't good enough in the first place.

Most people don't have a good understanding of just how variable statistics are, even when you are dealing with robots. We did a little experiment where we took 100 players and gave each of them 500 at-bats. We used the computer to give all 100 players a 27 percent chance of getting a hit on every at-bat, so that theoretically each of them should have a .270 batting average. We then let the computer spit out random numbers between 0 and 1,000; if the random number was 270 or less, we called it a hit; otherwise it was an out. We let the program run through 1,000 theoretical seasons.

In every one of those 1,000 years, there was at least one player whose batting average came out at .302 or better. Half the time, the league had at least one player who hit .320 or better. In the most extreme case, there was a player who hit .362. Even though each player's "true" ability was to hit .270, somebody always wound up hitting at least 32 points above that, and usually someone hit 50 points better.

If you go to fewer at-bats, the range gets even wider. After 100 at-bats, there's a fifty-fifty chance that one of these 100 .270 hitters will be hitting .390, just by luck. After 200 at-bats, there's a fifty-fifty chance for at least one .350 hitter.

Think about that: After 200 at-bats—what a full-time minor league player would have around the end of May—one out of every 100 minor leaguers is going to be hitting 80 points above his real average.

There are about 400 regular players in Double-A and Triple-A, which means you're likely to have about four players in early June who look like they've made a huge improvement in their game but who have just gotten lucky.

When a player has that sort of luck in the major leagues, we call it a fluke season. Of course, many fluke seasons are seen as something more sinister, whether it was the allegations of Brady Anderson using steroids in his 1996 season or Norm Cash using a corked bat in 1961. There have been plenty of fluke seasons in major league history, and there is no reason to suppose that they aren't just as common in the minors. Mike Berry's huge 1996 campaign could be one of them. He spent eight years in the minors, posting a .295 batting average (with no full-season batting average above .314), .385 on-base percentage, and .458 slugging average. Yet in 1996 he posted a tremendous line of .361/.473/.562.

Now, consider that real-life players face a wide range of scenarios that simulated players don't, and you have an even muddier situation. Players battle through injuries. They face good pitchers one night, bad pitchers the next. They give themselves up by making an out with a man on second and nobody out. They play day games after night games, in parks with bad lights or bad umpires. All of these elements affect how well they'll hit at any given time. Combine those possibilities with random bursts of luck, and a lot of players get promoted to the majors who aren't as good as they look.

There is a phrase, originally from a logician named Alfred Korzybski, that the map is not the territory. Similarly, we can say here that the statistics are not the player. A player has certain skills and attributes that he brings to the baseball diamond. They include how fast he can run, how far he can hit a baseball, whether his swing is level or an uppercut, how often he swings and misses, how well he can recognize a curveball or a slider, and his ability to recognize each particular pitcher's habits and know which pitch is coming. Those skills are his and his alone.

How those skills get turned into statistics depends on a lot more than just the player. Obviously, those you play against are going to make a big difference in your statistics. It is not at all unusual for players taken in the amateur draft to come out of high school with batting averages of .500, .600, or even .700, ridiculous numbers that come from totally outclassing their competition. Likewise, there are pitchers taken in the draft with ERAs under 0.50 (in 2005, the Cubs drafted a pitcher who threw 63 innings in high school with zero earned runs). In high school, most of these hitters and pitchers never met. But once they turn pro and get to face each other, their performances come down to earth in a hurry.

Luck of the Environment

This brings us to the second reason for players to look better than they really are, a completely different kind of luck. Namely, minor league players have essentially zero control over where they get to play, and some are lucky enough to play in very favorable hitting environments. Baseball parks are gloriously unstandardized, and the differences between them can dramatically change the way the game is played. The first thing most people think of—the distance to the outfield fences—is just one of the factors that determine how friendly a park is for hitters. How much foul territory is there, for instance? Lots of foul ground means more foul pop-ups caught, instead of the batter getting another chance to hit when the ball goes into the stands. How does the wind blow through the stadium? How good are the lights? What about the hitter's background? How's the humidity? And hey, what about altitude?

The 1993 expansion that put a major league team in Denver made everyone aware of just how big a difference it makes to play in thin air. It isn't just that the ball travels farther at altitude; the thin air changes the way the ball and air interact in lots of other ways. A typical ball, hit hard with an undercut, has a lot of backspin. At sea level, that backspin creates a little bit of lift that tends to keep the ball in the air longer, almost holding it up for outfielders. In Denver, that lift doesn't happen, with the end result that the ball not only goes farther (because of reduced drag) but also lands sooner (because of reduced lift). The same interactions that create lift also create the curve on a curveball. Thus, when curveballs don't break as much, as is the case at Coors Field, they hang there, waiting to get clobbered. Those same forces are also responsible for balls slicing or hooking when they're hit down the line, meaning they don't hook as much and are more likely to stay fair, turning into a double instead of a do-over. (For more on park effects, check out Chapter 8-2.)

As much as major league parks vary, there's even more variety in the minor leagues. The majors have thirty different parks; the minors have about two hundred. Coors Field is the only major league stadium at significant altitude; in the minors, the entire Pioneer League and half of the misnamed Pacific Coast League qualifies. Leagues are, in many ways, the sum of their parks. When all of the parks are small or elevated, you get the offense-friendly Pioneer and California Leagues, which get another offensive boost with the drier climate of the West. The eastern part of the country, more humid and closer to sea level, tends to produce pitcher's leagues like the Florida State League.

All of this may seem pretty obvious when you step back and think about it, but most people don't step back and think about it. People don't typically consider the context of the league when they talk about a player's stats because they usually don't know it. Most references don't tell you what the league totals are, and even if they did, they don't tell you how all the parks rate. The difference between a pitcher's park in a low-offense league and a hitter's park in a high-offense league can easily be more than 2 runs a game. Over the course of a season, that's a huge swing. A player who scores or drives in 80 runs in a 4-runs-per-game environment has done just as much, relatively speaking, as a player who drives in 120 runs in a 6-runs environment. It's about the same as the difference between hitting .275 and hitting .325.

What's "Normal"?

The trouble is that we don't think in relative terms. We have a built-in sense of what is "normal," one not necessarily derived from present-day baseball. People who grew up in the '60s find it easy to believe that 300 innings pitched and sub-3.00 ERAs are "normal"; kids from the '90s aren't going to be impressed by 40 home runs when they saw three different players hit 60. We see a number, like a .323 batting average, and we immediately think, "That's good," when the fact is that we know very little until we know what a typical player in that league and that park would hit. Baseball is relative; it doesn't matter how few or how many runs you score, as long as it's more than the other team.

The minor leagues have a wider range of "normal" than the majors. When Mike Berry had his big year, he was playing in a league (California) that scored 5.85 runs per game and a park (High Desert) that boosted run scoring by about 30 percent. He was essentially playing in a 7-runs-per-game setting. When you scale his .361 average, 109 runs, and 113 RBI down to a typical major league setting of about 4.5 runs per game, we're talking about only 70 runs, 73 RBI, and a .303 batting average (remarkably similar to his typical minor league season). A lot of the hitters who supposedly hit so well in the minors did so only because they were lucky enough to play somewhere that made their numbers look good.

Still, random variation and high offensive environments aren't the only ways for a minor leaguer to post superficially good statistics. There is another factor, one that's just as important as the statistics when evaluating a minor league player: age.

Baseball is not a purely athletic event; it is a combination of athleticism and experience. As such, the peak age for a baseball player isn't in his early twenties, as it is for "pure" athletic events like sprinting and swimming, but rather in his mid- to late twenties. That's time enough for players to learn the game and improve, but not so much that the physical effects of aging start to drag them down.

Usually, when we talk about the age of minor leaguers, we're focusing on young players. A player who can play Triple-A ball at the age of twenty-one and still has six to eight years of expected improvement ahead of him is clearly a better prospect than another player, equally skilled, who's already twenty-five. The latter player, with only two to four years of anticipated growth assuming a typical pattern of improvement, isn't likely to match the younger player. Yet there is something more involved that affects the statistics of older players.

A player who is older than the average player in his league appears to have an advantage. Why that is so isn't clear. It could be an advantage of experience, such as being better able to anticipate what kind of pitch will be thrown. Or it could be that emotional maturity makes him a steadier player throughout the season. Whatever it is, though, it seems to disappear when the player is promoted to the majors and has to play against people his own age.

If you were to look at two players hitting .300, one who is the correct age for his league and one who is too old, you could divide them up like this:

Young player: skill .300, experience .000
Old player: skill .270, experience .030

When these players get promoted, the experience will drop to zero for both of them, and the young player will end up outhitting the old player. Skill translates to the majors better than experience.

Remember Mike Berry? He turned twenty-six in August 1996, toward the end of that big season in the High-A California League. The average age in the California League is about twenty-two and a half. Berry never made the big leagues. Many of his younger leaguemates, despite lesser stats, eventually did.

Top Minor League Hitters of 2005, as Measured by EqA (minimum 200 minor league plate appearances)

Rank	Name	Age	EqA	Parent Club	Context (1,000 = 5 runs per game)
1	Ryan Howard	25	.346	Phillies	975
2	Chris Snelling	23	.326	Mariners	980
3	Marcus Thames	28	.320	Tigers	927
4	Jeremy Hermida	21	.316	Marlins	909
5	Todd Linden	25	.310	Giants	989
6	Rickie Weeks	22	.308	Brewers	1,011
7	Chris Shelton	25	.303	Tigers	927
8	Ross Gload	29	.302	White Sox	1,015
9	Brad Eldred	24	.301	Pirates	951
10	Justin Huber	22	.300	Royals	1,012
11	Carlos Pena	27	.296	Tigers	927
12	Matt Murton	23	.296	Cubs	933
13	Marshall McDougall	26	.294	Rangers	1,102
14	Conor Jackson	23	.293	Diamondbacks	1,178
15	Adrian Gonzalez	23	.291	Rangers	1,102
16	Edwin Encarnacion	22	.291	Reds	948
17	Brandon Jones	21	.290	Braves	903
18	Jeff Keppinger	25	.289	Mets	903
19	Matt Diaz	27	.288	Royals	1,070
20	Russell Martin	22	.288	Dodgers	861
21	Shane Victorino	24	.288	Phillies	975
22	Chris Denorfia	24	.287	Reds	969
23	Curtis Granderson	24	.287	Tigers	927
24	B. J. Upton	20	.286	Devil Rays	965
25	Chip Ambres	25	.286	Royals	1,022
26	Ronny Cedeno	22	.286	Cubs	1,137
27	Ben Johnson	24	.285	Padres	1,022
28	Josh Willingham	26	.285	Marlins	1,189
29	Brandon Sing	24	.284	Cubs	911
30	Chris Young	21	.284	White Sox	927
31	Dan Johnson	25	.284	A's	1,030
32	Corey Hart	23	.283	Brewers	1,011
33	Howie Kendrick	21	.283	Angels	1,094
34	Justin Ruggiano	23	.283	Dodgers	947
35	Matt Watson	26	.283	A's	1,030
36	Prince Fielder	21	.283	Brewers	1,011

(continues)

Top Minor League Hitters (continued)

Rank	Name	Age	EqA	Parent Club	Context (1,000 = 5 runs per game)
37	Rick Short	32	.283	Nationals	1,008
38	Andy Phillips	28	.282	Yankees	961
39	Jarrod Saltalamacchia	20	.282	Braves	959
40	Andy Marte	21	.281	Braves	1,012
41	Chase Lambin	25	.281	Mets	952
42	Hunter Pence	22	.281	Astros	970
43	Kevin Kouzmanoff	23	.281	Indians	980
44	Kevin Orie	32	.281	Nationals	1,008
45	Ryan Mulhern	24	.281	Indians	944
46	Jason Bartlett	25	.280	Twins	1,007
47	Mike Jacobs	24	.280	Mets	1,008
48	Wes Bankston	21	.280	Devil Rays	960
49	Andy Laroche	21	.278	Dodgers	934
50	Daric Barton	19	.278	A's	1,056
51	Ryan Zimmerman	20	.278	Nationals	951
52	Delmon Young	19	.277	Devil Rays	931
53	Eddy Martinez-Esteve	21	.277	Giants	1,044
54	Ryan Shealy	25	.277	Rockies	1,057
55	Joe Dillon	29	.276	Marlins	1,201
56	Ronny Paulino	24	.276	Pirates	946
57	Brian Daubach	33	.275	Mets	903
58	Felix Pie	20	.275	Cubs	911
59	Nick Markakis	21	.275	Orioles	954
60	Rashad Eldridge	23	.275	Rangers	1,085
61	Ryan Spilborghs	25	.275	Rockies	1,036

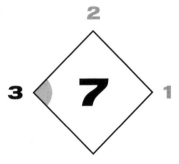

Why Was Kevin Maas a Bust?

NATE SILVER

It's hard to remember such a time, but in the summer of 1990, the Yankees were the laughingstock of baseball. On July 24, the Yankees lost to the Texas Rangers to drop their record to a league-worst 34-59, and their star first baseman played in his last game of the season until mid-September. Three days later, Don Mattingly would be placed on the disabled list with a chronically sore back. Mattingly wasn't playing like a star—his average had dropped below .250 and he hadn't hit a home run in almost two months—but he was the most popular player on the club, and one of the few reasons to watch a team that was on pace to lose 100 games for the first time since 1912.

Into the breach stepped Kevin Maas, a twenty-second-round pick from the University of California who'd worked his way up the Yankees' minor league ladder one rung at a time. Maas was hardly a complete ballplayer. He had battled a knee injury in the minor leagues, was a lumbering baserunner, had sub-par instincts at first base, and had struck out in more than 20 percent of his professional plate appearances. He was already twenty-five years old, an advanced age for a player who hoped to have a substantial major league career. But Maas could do two things well: hit the ball a long way, and draw walks. When he was called up to the Yankees in late June, his batting average at Triple-A Columbus was an uninspiring .284—but his on-base percentage was an excellent .393, his slugging average .582. He was exactly the sort of player whose skill set Baseball Prospectus would have been touting had BP been around back then.

Maas had already made something of an impression when Mattingly went down. Working his way into the lineup as the designated hitter, he hit 6 home runs in his first 51 big-league at-bats, including one that produced the Yankees' only run in that July 24 loss to the Rangers. Now the starting first baseman, he would hit another home run the next day, giving him homers in three consecutive games; in his next six games, he hit 3 more. That added up to 10 in just 77 at-bats, making Maas the fastest player in baseball history to reach 10 home runs.

The name of Wally Pipp began to be murmured around the Yankee Stadium press box. Maas kept on hitting through August, leading the Yankees to their only winning month of the year; he was the fastest player in history to reach 13 home runs, and the fastest to reach 15, before finishing the year with 21 in spite of having played less than half the schedule. He had become a symbol of hope for what was then considered a failing franchise. "If Maas isn't the real thing," wrote one columnist, "then the others hardly matter." Mattingly compared Maas to Will Clark, the National League's All-Star first baseman.

Maas began the 1991 season as the Yankees' starting DH, filling in at first base when Mattingly's back needed a day off. He started the year well enough, managing 8 home runs by Memorial Day, but went into a horrendous slump just before the All-Star break, hitting .154 between July and August as pitchers started to exploit the holes in his swing. The Yankees, short on personnel and on their way to their third straight losing season, kept playing him. His average dipped as low as .209 before recovering in the season's last three weeks to finish at .220. The damage was mitigated somewhat by Maas's solid home-run and walk totals: 23 and 83, respectively. But his season was hardly worthy of the next Will Clark, let alone Lou Gehrig.

Maas lost his starting gig in 1992, stuck between Mattingly, who had managed to stay healthy, free agent Danny Tartabull, and the up-and-coming Bernie Williams. He hit 11 home runs in half a season's worth of at-bats, but his plate discipline suffered as he struggled for respect and playing time, sending his OBP down to an unacceptable .305. The next year wasn't any better; Paul O'Neill had been added to the mix, Mattingly looked rejuvenated, and the Yankees, contenders for a good chunk of the season, could no longer afford to waste time on projects. Maas hit just .205 in limited playing time, receiving just 5 at-bats after the All-Star break before being dispatched back to the Yankees' Triple-A affiliate in Columbus.

The next spring the Yankees released him. Maas would receive just 57 more at-bats and hit 1 home run in the remainder of his major league career. Nobody had much use for a slow-footed, aging designated hitter with more strikeouts than base hits.

◆

The story back then was that nobody could have seen it coming. Nobody could have predicted Maas's fast rise from obscurity or his equally fast fade into oblivion. With better analytical tools at our disposal, we know nowadays that the first part of that story is wrong: Maas's minor league numbers suggested that he was a good prospect, particularly in the critical OBP and SLG departments. Nobody could have guessed that he'd hit like Reggie Jackson for three months, but he deserved a chance, especially as the Yankees in those years were wasting playing time on immortals like Steve Balboni and Oscar Azocar.

By the same token, nobody could have guessed that Maas's big-league career, after such a promising start, would derail as quickly as it did. But there are some reasons to think that, while he could have been a solid contributor for a few years, Maas wasn't destined for a particularly long or glorious career. In the 1987 *Baseball Abstract*, Bill James introduced the notion of "old player's skills." As position players age, James explained, they tend to lose speed and batting average while drawing somewhat more walks and relying more on their ability to hit for power. Speed and batting average are thus "young player's skills," while drawing walks and hitting home runs are "old player's skills." James contended that *young* players whose value mainly consisted of "old player's skills" would decline prematurely; once those skills atrophied, the player would have nothing left to fall back upon.

James had ceased publishing the *Abstracts* by the time Maas reached the big leagues, but Maas could have been a poster boy for his theory. Maas's strengths exactly matched James's profile of "old player's skills," while he was weakest in the "young player's skills." What was more, he played an easy defensive position (and didn't play it well), he frequently struck out, and his knees were balky, all traits we'd typically associate with an aging player.

We can test James's theory by looking at the career paths of players who meet his "old player's skills" criterion. I ran a database search among players who had 300 plate appearances or more in their age-twenty-five season, meaning that they had established themselves as regulars, or at least platoon players. This database incorporates adjustments for park and league difficulty and includes all major league players since World War II. I looked for players who, in their age-twenty-five seasons:

- ◆ Had an unintentional walk rate that ranked in the *top quartile* of qualifying players.
- ◆ Had a speed score that placed in the *lowest quartile* among qualifying players.
- ◆ Had isolated power that ranked in the *top half* among qualifying players.
- ◆ Had a batting average that ranked in the *lower half* among qualifying players.

The twenty-six players who met these criteria are:

1. Bob Bailey
2. Jeff Burroughs
3. Ron Cey
4. Tony Clark
5. Darnell Coles
6. Clay Dalrymple
7. Mike Epstein
8. Tommy Glaviano
9. Willie Greene
10. Ralph Kiner
11. Dick Kokos
12. Kevin Maas
13. Mark McGwire
14. Denis Menke
15. Eric Munson
16. Dan Pasqua
17. Bob Robertson
18. Gary Roenicke
19. Pat Seerey
20. Bill Serena
21. Roy Smalley
22. Chris Speier
23. John Stearns
24. Fernando Tatis
25. Tim Teufel
26. Robin Ventura

Among this list, Ralph Kiner is a Hall-of-Famer, Mark McGwire will be, and Ron Cey and Robin Ventura had distinguished careers. But most of the other names are players like Maas, Jeff Burroughs, and Fernando Tatis, whose careers ended prematurely, or are hardly recognizable at all.

I then compared these players' performance from age twenty-six onward against a control group of post–World War II players who also had 300 PA in their age-twenty-five seasons but did not meet the other criteria for "old player's skills." The measure I used to evaluate the players was Equivalent Runs (EqR). As it happens, the "old player's skills" group was almost exactly as valuable as the control group in their age-twenty-six season—the "old player's skills" players produced an average of 66.6 runs, the control group 68.2. But just as James anticipated, a performance gap soon emerged. By age twenty-nine, the "old player's skills" group produced an average of 43.7 runs, compared with 55.1 for the control group. At age thirty-two, the "old" players produced 29.6 runs and the control group 38.4. As seen in Figure 7-3.1, the "old player's skills" players performed below the control group's level at every age, generally by about 10 runs per season.

FIGURE 7-3.1 "Old player's skills" vs. control group performance, by Equivalent Runs

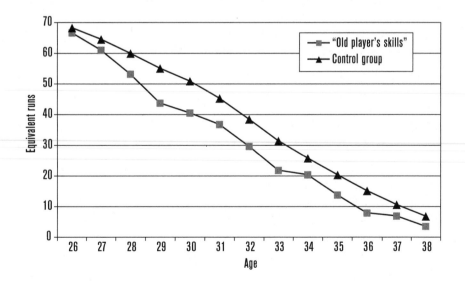

A question needs to be posed. If we can identify one group of players who age differently from the norm, can we find others? For example, do speedy, slap-hitting second basemen age well?

These were exactly the sorts of questions that led me to develop PECOTA, a system for projecting players' career paths based on the careers of comparable players from the past. PECOTA identifies comparable players based both on statistical measures of performance like walk rate and isolated power and other important variables like position, body size, and handedness. Albert Pujols, for example, gets compared to Eddie Murray and Hank Aaron, and Johnny Damon to Kenny Lofton and Andy Van Slyke; Maas would be compared to Dan Pasqua and Dick Kokos. The key idea behind PECOTA is that different types of players age differently.

We'll get into more about how PECOTA selects these comparables in a moment. In the meantime, let's consider how a traditional projection system operates. A projection system usually applies a two-step process:

1. Establish a player's "baseline" level of performance, based on a weighted average of his performance over the past several seasons, while accounting for some regression to the mean.
2. Adjust the prediction based on a player's age, adding something to the projection of a young player and subtracting something from that of an older player.

As long as the weighted averaging and age adjustments are done reasonably, such a system can provide some competent projections. "Competent" may not be good enough, however, for general managers who are looking to stake tens of millions of dollars on the fate of a single ballplayer. PECOTA applies the same basic process: It establishes a baseline forecast, then tweaks it based on the player's age. But it also makes a number of adjustments that make its forecasts materially more accurate.

Baseline Projection

To attain this accuracy, PECOTA does two critical things. The first is to recognize that all statistics are not equally reliable. We can evaluate the reliability of a given statistic by looking at its correlation coefficient. Simply put, the higher the correlation coefficient, the greater the relationship between two variables; variables that have a perfect linear relationship have a correlation coefficient of 1, while variables that have a perfect *inverse* relationship have a correlation coefficient of –1. For example, "percentage of body fat" would have a strong positive correlation with "number of Big Macs consumed" but a strong negative correlation with "number of miles jogged." Meanwhile, variables that are independent of each other will have correlations close to zero, indicating no statistical relationship. If you throw two dice, for example, the correlation coefficient between the numbers that come up on each die will approach zero, since you're dealing entirely with random chance.

We can also use a correlation coefficient to get an idea of how consistent a statistic is over time. For instance, my weight today has a high correlation with my weight yesterday and tomorrow. But if I wake up every morning and roll a fair die, the number I get on Tuesday has no correlation with the number I get on Wednesday. This is the type of correlation that PECOTA applies to offensive statistics in order to determine how much predictive value they have. Table 7-3.1 shows the correlation coefficients for some key offensive statistics across consecutive seasons.

TABLE 7-3.1 Correlation Coefficients Across Consecutive Seasons

Batting average	0.43
Isolated power	0.76
Walk rate	0.76
Strikeout rate	0.83
Stolen bases	0.81

For the most part, these are high correlation coefficients; offensive statistics are fairly reliable. The exception is batting average, which is subject to a much greater degree of randomness. This makes intuitive sense. Watch any baseball game, and you're likely to see some bloop base hits—a ball deflects off the pitcher's glove or lands just out of the reach of the right fielder, who got a late jump on the ball. On the other hand, unless the game is at Coors Field, you're not likely to see many bloop home runs.

The implication is that when you're making predictions, you should expect batting average to see more regression to the mean—performance moving away from extremes toward a set baseline—than most statistics. Players whose value consists mostly of batting average are likely to see their performances decline in the next season. Conversely, although the phenomenon is not perfectly symmetrical, players who perform poorly in batting average but well in other categories are good candidates to show some improvement.

Table 7-3.2, for example, shows the performance of National League batting champions from 1960 to 1979 in the year after they won the batting crown. A few of these players, most notably Pete Rose and Roberto Clemente, were able to turn in strong performances year after year. For the most part, however, the players exhibited a significant decline. Nineteen of the twenty players saw their batting averages drop in their next season, and eight failed to break .300. The mean batting-average decline was 37 points. Perhaps the most important characteristic of a good baseline projection is that it helps us differentiate skill from luck; these players were fine hitters, but they weren't quite as good as their league-leading averages suggest.

TABLE 7-3.2 Performance of 1960–1979 National League Batting Champions

Year	Player	AVG Year of Championship	AVG Next Season
1960	Dick Groat	.325	.275
1961	Roberto Clemente	.351	.312
1962	Tommy Davis	.346	.326
1963	Tommy Davis	.326	.275
1964	Roberto Clemente	.339	.329
1965	Roberto Clemente	.329	.317
1966	Matty Alou	.342	.338
1967	Roberto Clemente	.357	.291
1968	Pete Rose	.335	.348
1969	Pete Rose	.348	.316
1970	Rico Carty	.366	.277
1971	Joe Torre	.363	.289
1972	Billy Williams	.333	.288
1973	Pete Rose	.338	.284
1974	Ralph Garr	.353	.278
1975	Bill Madlock	.354	.339
1976	Bill Madlock	.339	.302
1977	Dave Parker	.338	.334
1978	Dave Parker	.334	.310
1979	Keith Hernandez	.344	.321
	Average	**.343**	**.307**

The other key factor that PECOTA considers is that some statistics have important predictive relationships with other statistics. One such relationship is between strikeouts and batting average. There is an element of luck involved once a ball is put in play—what kind of jump an outfielder gets on the ball, whether it takes a bad hop when the third baseman is trying to field it—that has little to do with the batter's skill. On the other hand, if a player does not put the ball into play at all, he has no chance of getting a hit. Thus, a player who has a mediocre batting average but a low strikeout rate has a good chance of seeing his average improve, while a player with the same batting average but a high strikeout rate might expect his problems to continue.

Table 7-3.3 contains the results of another database search. This time, I looked for players who hit between .250 and .260 in a season in which they qualified for the batting title but struck out in fewer than 6 percent of their plate appearances. Twenty-one of 22 players saw their batting average improve in the next season, with an average improvement of almost 30 points.

TABLE 7-3.3 Change in Batting Average Among Low-Strikeout Hitters

Player	Year	AVG	Strikeouts[a]	AVG Next Season
Luis Aparicio	1959	.257	40	.277
Buddy Bell	1972	.255	29	.268
Wade Boggs	1992	.259	31	.302
Horace Clarke	1970	.251	35	.250
Billy Cox	1950	.257	24	.279
Nellie Fox	1961	.251	12	.267
Granny Hamner	1951	.255	32	.275
Tommy Helms	1971	.258	33	.259
Tommy Helms	1972	.259	27	.287
Gregg Jefferies	1997	.256	27	.301
Ted Kluszewski	1951	.259	33	.320
Johnny Lipon	1949	.251	24	.293
Whitey Lockman	1954	.251	31	.273
Peanuts Lowrey	1946	.257	22	.281
Felix Millan	1972	.257	28	.290
Vic Power	1954	.255	19	.319
Vic Power	1957	.259	21	.312
Bobby Richardson	1960	.252	19	.261
Phil Rizzuto	1948	.252	24	.275
Ozzie Smith	1990	.254	33	.285
Gary Sutherland	1974	.254	37	.258
Eddie Waitkus	1951	.257	22	.289
Average		**.255**		**.283**

[a]Striking out in less than 6 percent of plate appearances.

There are all sorts of relationships like this in the data, all of which are accounted for by PECOTA. Often the relationships are symbiotic. For example, doubles and home runs are both indicators of power-hitting ability and serve to predict one another. A player who hits a lot of doubles in a season but relatively few home runs will tend to hit more homers (but fewer doubles) in his next season, and vice versa. Another such relationship is between walk rate and isolated power. Taking a lot of walks is an indication of working deep into the count, where batters tend to hit for most of their power; a player with a good walk rate but middling power numbers is a good candidate to see his home-run output improve the following season. Conversely, a player who hits a lot of homers can expect pitchers to work him more carefully in the next season, and thus to see his walk rate increase.

Career Path Adjustment

However intricate it might be, the baseline projection is just half the battle; it's reasonable to expect a young player to improve his performance and an older player to deteriorate. Bill James did the first serious study of the career paths of offensive players. For the *1982 Baseball Abstract*, James evaluated thousands of baseball players throughout the game's history and counted the ages at which they turned in their best offensive performances. James found that the greatest number of players peaked at age twenty-seven by this measure, with many others peaking at ages twenty-six and twenty-eight.

Thus the "Age-Twenty-Seven Peak" theory was born. James's theory was considered somewhat revolutionary at the time—conventional wisdom had held that ballplayers peaked later, sometime between the ages of twenty-eight and thirty-two. Since players are not eligible to sign free-agent contracts until they've accumulated six years of MLB service time (which typically occurs sometime between the age of twenty-eight and thirty) James's research had significant implications for teams that were trying to determine how to bid on free agents. Signing a twenty-nine-year-old to a three-year contract based on his performance in his past couple of seasons could lead to his being overvalued; most likely his peak had already come and gone.

Later researchers, including Baseball Prospectus's own Keith Woolner, have attempted to duplicate James's method and have confirmed his findings. I prefer to ask a slightly different question: I want to determine the extent to which a player improves or declines at a given age. It might be that the average, say, thirty-four-year-old produces 10 percent fewer runs than he did when he was thirty-three.

Specifically, I looked at the average number of Equivalent Runs produced by all post–World War II hitters at a given age, and compared it to the average number of Equivalent Runs produced by those players in their next season. The results are seen in Table 7-3.4.

We find, for example, that the typical twenty-five-year-old improves on his previous season's performance by about 8 percent, while the typical thirty-four-year-old sees his performance decline by 10 percent. The typical twenty-seven-year-old turns in a performance just slightly worse (by about 1 percent) than he had in his age-twenty-six season. Thus we might put the peak at age twenty-six rather than twenty-seven.

These figures can be better understood by extrapolating them into a career path. Assume for example that a player puts up 50 EqR in his rookie season, at age twenty, improves that figure by 26.9 percent in his age-twenty-one season as predicted by our model, 15.1 percent in his age-twenty-two season, and so forth. We can track his career path as shown in Figure 7-3.2.

A typical hitter can expect to experience rapid improvement through age twenty-three and continued steady improvement through age twenty-six. He will then typically see his performance plateau between ages twenty-six and twenty-nine; note that the graph is somewhat asymmetrical, and that

TABLE 7-3.4 Equivalent Runs Produced by Post–World War II Hitters

Age	Mean Change in EqR (%)[a]
21	26.9
22	15.1
23	16.4
24	6.1
25	8.2
26	4.0
27	−1.1
28	−2.5
29	−3.1
30	−4.6
31	−5.9
32	−8.0
33	−8.1
34	−10.2
35	−11.1
36	−11.6
37	−13.0
38	−19.3

[a]Runs produced at given age, compared to average number of Equivalent Runs produced by those players in their previous season.

FIGURE 7-3.2 Average player's career path, by Equivalent Runs

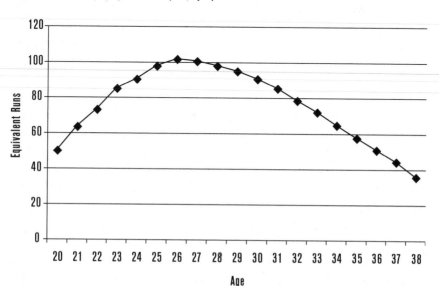

players do not decline after reaching their peak as rapidly as they improved on their way up. Still, aging typically begins to take its toll once the player enters his thirties, with performance declining by a slightly greater margin in each subsequent year. By the time he hits thirty-four, the player can expect to lose more than 10 percent of his value every season.

This is a useful finding, and many projection systems apply their career path adjustments based on an identical analysis. They form a baseline projection for a twenty-five-year-old, tweak it upward by 8 percent to reflect the improvement he can expect due to his age, and call it a day. The problem is that these projection systems can't account for the Kevin Maas problem—the fact that different types of players age on different schedules. The "average" career path is an abstraction, the sum of many thousands of wildly divergent individual paths.

Imagine, for example, that we are looking at the career paths of three hypothetical players: Eddie Early, who has his best year at age twenty-three, Len Latebloom, who does his best work at thirty-one, and Pete Peaky, who is very valuable between the ages of twenty-four and twenty-nine but not before or afterward. There are plenty of real-life players with career paths very much like these; Eddie Early is a reasonable approximation of Kevin Maas or Bob Horner; Len Latebloom resembles Jeff Kent or Jim Edmonds; Pete Peaky looks like Albert Belle or Kevin Mitchell. The "average" career path of these three players looks nice and smooth but does a poor job of forecasting any one of their actual careers. The "average" twenty-seven-year-old, for example, is at the peak of his abilities and doesn't notice much change in his performance from the year before. But a Len Latebloom type of player is still improving dramatically, while an Eddie Early is already well into his decline—as shown in Figure 7-3.3.

PECOTA's solution is to model career paths according to an analysis of similar players at a given age. We might find, for example, that while the "average" player improved his performance by 4 percent between ages twenty-five and twenty-six, the typical Kevin Maas–type player saw his performance *decline* by 3 percent. This is why I describe the process as a "career path adjustment" rather than an "age adjustment."

PECOTA's analysis of comparable players is based on a variation of yet another Bill James invention—Similarity Scores. James introduced Similarity Scores in the 1986 *Baseball Abstract*. Players start with a "perfect" score of 1,000, and points are subtracted for each

FIGURE 7-3.3 Career paths of three different types of players, by Equivalent Runs

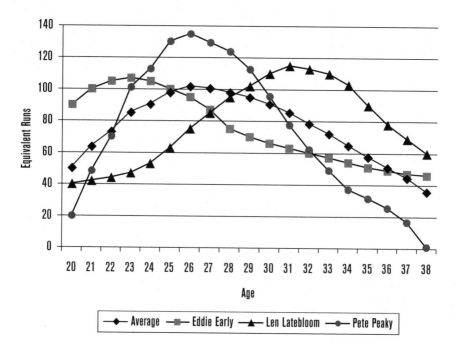

meaningful difference between two compared players; one point is subtracted, say, for each difference of 2 home runs. Similarity Scores are most frequently used by sabermetricians to assess a player's qualifications for the Hall of Fame. If we're looking at a player and find that most players with similar statistics are in Cooperstown, we have a good (though not ironclad) argument that the player we're evaluating deserves to be there too.

PECOTA's Similarity Scores involve a number of differences from James's version. Some are trivial—for one, a perfect score starts at 100 rather than 1,000—while others are more meaningful. For instance, PECOTA's Similarity Scores are adjusted for park and era, while James's are not. The most important difference, however, is that PECOTA's Similarity Scores are meant to be applied *prospectively* rather than *retrospectively*. For the purpose of forming projections, we aren't concerned about how a player performed in the past. We want to see how he can be expected to perform in the future.

This leads to some differences in the weight assigned to particular player characteristics. Sabermetricians are fond of making the point, for example, that base-stealing is an overrated skill. It's a nice bonus to be able to steal a bag, but not nearly as valuable to a team as getting on base or hitting for power. Appropriately, James doesn't assign a lot of emphasis to stolen bases in his Similarity Scores. But it turns out that stolen bases, and other speed-related metrics like triples, are relatively important in predicting how a player is going to do in the future. A player's body type (that is, his height and weight) is also useful for projecting his future: Bigger, stronger hitters age more favorably. On the other hand, body type obviously wouldn't matter if you were attempting to determine a player's fitness for the Hall of Fame.

Here are the factors we used in PECOTA's similarity scores for position players, in descending order of importance:

- Isolated power
- Walk rate
- Batting average
- Playing time
- Defensive position
- Speed score
- Career length
- Weight in pounds
- Strikeout rate
- Handedness (lefty, righty, switch-hitter)
- Height in inches
- Defensive ability

The big things, like hitting for power, hitting for contact, and drawing walks, are given the most emphasis by the system, but the little things that differentiate players are considered too. It is rarely possible, of course, to match any two players on every one of these factors, but with almost eighteen thousand major league player seasons in its database, PECOTA usually provides some pretty good compromises. Tony Gwynn, for example, is not a perfect match for Ichiro Suzuki: The players have different body types, and Gwynn had lost much of his speed by age thirty. But Gwynn ought to tell us a lot more about how Ichiro is going to age than a completely dissimilar player like Mark McGwire.

The Importance of Balance

The "old player's skills" profile represented by Kevin Maas is but one of an almost infinite number of player typologies we might construct. Nevertheless, a couple of underlying themes are common to many different typologies. The most important of these is that players who do several different things well tend to age better than players who do just one or two things well.

For example, let's look at the aging patterns of players with respect to their performance in two particularly important dimensions: speed and power, as measured by speed score and isolated power, respectively. We'll split these players into three different categories based on their performances in their age-twenty-five seasons:

1. *Speed Only* players had speed scores that ranked in the top quartile of the league but isolated power that ranked in the bottom quartile of the league.
2. *Power Only* players had isolated power that ranked in the top quartile of the league but speed scores that ranked in the bottom quartile of the league.
3. *Speed + Power* players had both speed scores and isolated power that ranked in the top third of their league.

It's no big surprise that the players who did both things well tended to be more valuable. The Speed + Power players averaged 97.8 Equivalent Runs in their age-twenty-six peak season, the Power Only players 75.6 EqR, and the Speed Only players 63.8 EqR. But despite being more valuable to begin with, the Speed + Power players also retained more of their value as they aged, as seen in Figure 7-3.4.

FIGURE 7-3.4 Aging patterns of players with speed and power skills

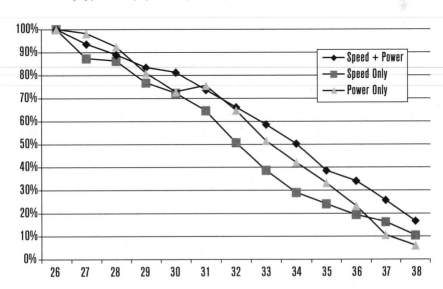

At age thirty, for example, the Speed + Power players produced 81 percent as many runs as they did at age twenty-six, compared with 73 percent for the Power Only group and 72 percent for the Speed Only group. The pattern persisted for just about every age level; while all three groups declined significantly as they aged, the balanced players declined relatively less.

You may sometimes hear it claimed that speedy hitters age well—speed is, after all, a "young player's skill." But players who possess speed without any other above-average skills tend to see their careers end relatively early. Vince Coleman and Brian Hunter lost their jobs in the everyday lineup by the time they were twenty-nine and Omar Moreno's last useful year came at twenty-eight. Once such a player loses a step or two, he'll steal bases less effectively, won't be able to leg out as many base hits, won't reach as many balls in the field, and will quickly assume a spot on the bench.

Other skills combinations behave similarly. Figure 7-3.5 shows the same analysis applied to the combination of batting average and isolated power. Players who hit for both contact and power age much better than players who have just one of these skills.

FIGURE 7-3.5 Aging patterns of players with batting average and power skills

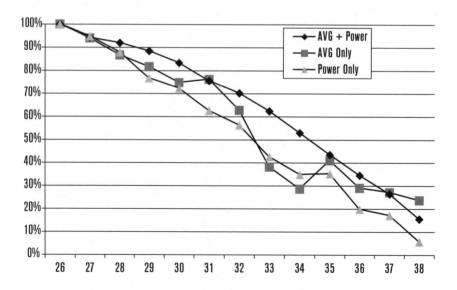

The same holds true for the interaction between power and batting eye and between batting average and batting eye, as seen in Figures 7-3.6 and 7-3.7.

FIGURE 7-3.6 Aging patterns of players with batting eye and power skills

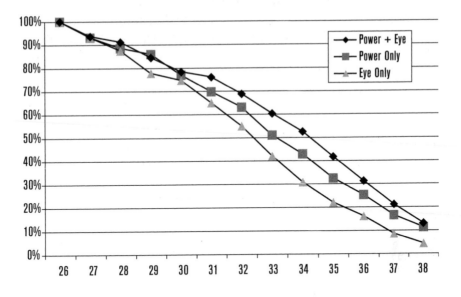

FIGURE 7-3.7 Aging patterns of players with batting average and batting eye skills

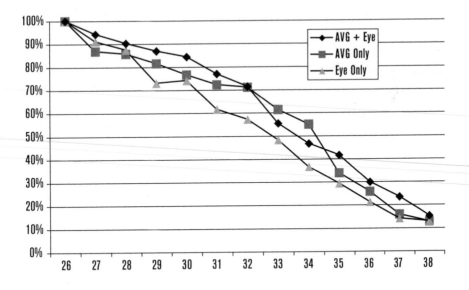

Why do these multifaceted players age so much better than their counterparts? I suspect it has to do with what I call the Double A's—adaptability and athleticism. Adaptability is the notion that a player can compensate by improving some skills while others are declining.

George Brett was certainly an "adaptable" player: He won his first batting title at age twenty-three and his last one at age thirty-seven. Table 7-3.5 breaks Brett's numbers down into the first and second halves of his career and provides a good indication of how he managed this:

TABLE 7-3.5 George Brett's Performance per 650 PA

	AB	R	H	2B	3B	HR	RBI
Before age 29	592	91	189	37	12	14	86
Age 29+	569	87	168	37	5	20	92
	BB	K	SB	CS	AVG	OBP	SLG
Before age 29	48	37	17	9	.318	.367	.496
Age 29+	70	60	7	3	.295	.371	.482

Brett ran reasonably well early in his career, averaging 12 triples and 17 steals per 650 PA before age twenty-nine and legging out his share of base hits. Like Vladimir Guerrero today, he swung early and often, taking advantage of his tremendous reflexes; he walked relatively rarely and almost never struck out. But as injuries and age took their toll on Brett's raw skills, he found ways to adapt. He began to work deeper into counts, striking out more often and collecting fewer base hits but considerably improving his walk rate and home-run output. He shifted from third base, where he was a fine defensive player in his prime, to first base and eventually to DH. He scored fewer runs but knocked in more. Brett became a different player but remained an incredibly effective one.

Not just any player, of course, could have managed this. The diversity of skills that Brett displayed early in his career shows that he was tremendously athletic. He was a high school quarterback with good baseball bloodlines, his brother Ken toiling as a major league pitcher for fourteen seasons. The ability to drive pitches in many different parts of the strike zone, for example, was an asset to Brett later in his career, allowing him to take pitches and work the count without getting himself into trouble. What distinguishes Brett and other great players is not that they have one or two highly refined skills but that they have a real aptitude for the sport and the ability to refine their game over time.

The problem with players like Kevin Maas, on the other hand, isn't so much that they don't have the "right" skills as that they don't have a diverse enough portfolio of skills. When Vince Coleman loses his foot speed or Kevin Maas loses his bat speed, they have little else to fall back upon. Maas, to be fair, drew his share of walks, but this was offset by his high strikeout rate: Working deep into counts can be dangerous once you can no longer catch up with a 3-2 fastball.

This is not to suggest that baseball teams should give up on players like Kevin Maas. A skills profile that tends to peak early is a risk when you're looking to sign a thirty-year-old free agent to a multiyear deal, but it's potentially a good thing when you're drafting an amateur. Players like Maas tend to mature quickly, providing plenty of value in their mid-twenties before they become eligible for free agency. And while these players might not have tremendously long careers, few of them go into the tank as fast as Maas did.

Either way, the key is to move beyond the simple notion that a player is going to do this year pretty much what he did last year. Every baseball club, whether consciously or not, is in the business of forecasting, insofar as it needs to determine which players to keep and which to discard, and how much to pay those it retains. Forecasting techniques that recognize that different types of players progress through their careers differently provide a head start to smart baseball decisions.

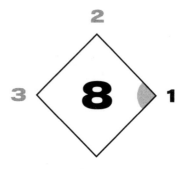

Can a Team Have Too Much Pitching?

STEVEN GOLDMAN

This could easily be the shortest chapter in the book.

Q: Can you have too much pitching?

A: No.

But wait—the above exchange represents a vast oversimplification of the question, or more accurately questions, for our title interrogative is a blanket for several distinct inquiries:

- Does pitching have a greater impact on winning than hitting does?
- Does a team that has vastly more pitching than hitting talent prosper as much as one that has an even mix of pitching and hitting, or one that that has more hitting than pitching?
- Should a team with average hitting and pitching add pitching if it expects to get better?
- Does the simple accumulation of pitchers beyond immediate need offer teams a special benefit?

In a state of nature in which all baseball resources are freely available, a team could never have too much pitching. A team with a great pitching core—say, the 2005 Houston Astros—could augment Roger

Clemens, Roy Oswalt, Andy Pettitte, and closer Brad Lidge with Johan Santana, Dontrelle Willis, and Mariano Rivera. This would help the team not only because the staff would be dominant but also because pitchers are easily injured; the all-time leader in days spent on the disabled list is Bret Saberhagen, the two-time Cy Young Award winner, with 1,016, or roughly six and a quarter full seasons. Saberhagen merely leads the parade for a profession in which almost everyone has answered to the description "sore-armed" at some point. Even atypically durable right-handers like Nolan Ryan (405 days, or 2.5 seasons) and Roger Clemens (202 days, 1.25 seasons) have been shelved for extended periods. Our hypothetical superstaff's superb depth would undoubtedly come in handy over the course of the long season. While Lidge worked out the kinks in his hamstrings, Rivera could close; if Santana's labrum shredded itself, Willis could step into the breach. Further, given the variability of even the best pitchers, the team's depth would allow it to minimize the negative impact of any one or two pitchers having an off year.

In this example, our hypothetical Astros team wouldn't have to spend any money or give up any players in trade; Houston general manager Tim Purpura could sneak up behind the other GMs, hit them over the head with a club, and make off with their players. In the real world, baseball teams must consider how best to allocate finite resources. Pitching costs money, and sometimes good players in trade or sacrificed draft picks, and room must be left in the budget for position players. Satchel Paige's grandstanding exhibitions aside, most pitchers aren't so certain of getting strikeouts that they don't need fielders to help them retire the hitters. The real question then is not whether you can have too much pitching but what percentage of a team's resources should be devoted to pitching. The answer proves to be quite simple: As Albert Einstein might have said, it's all relative.

Conventional wisdom says that a team can only benefit from overbalancing its efforts on the pitching side.

The only thing that matters is what happens on that little lump out in the middle of the field.
—Earl Weaver, Hall of Fame manager

The pitcher is the most important player in the field, and on his skills and judgment depends half the battle in a match.
—Henry Chadwick, *Henry Chadwick: Father of Baseball* (1824–1908)

Pitching is 75 percent of baseball—or 70 percent, or 90, or any other high number that pops into the mind of the speaker. . . . There is no disagreement about the point itself; pitching is the most important element in the game. As a rule, the team with better pitching wins the game, and the team with a heavy-hitting lineup winds up nowhere because its pitching is poor.

—Leonard Koppett, *All About Baseball*

Pitching is 70 percent of baseball, said Connie Mack. Pitching is 50 percent of baseball, said Branch Rickey. Pitching is 35 percent of baseball, said George Weiss. More recent guesstimates . . . have ranged from a high of 80 percent, by Herman Franks when he managed the Cubs, to a low of 15 percent, by Joe McDonald when he was G.M. of the Mets. . . . As far as we're concerned, the best answer to this confusing if not downright silly question is [pitching is 44 percent of baseball].

—John Thorn and Pete Palmer, *The Hidden Game of Baseball*

Taking these formulations to their logical end, in an efficient market for talent, pitchers would be compensated at a far higher level than hitters, and team payrolls would reflect this disparity. Tellingly, teams of recent vintage do not reflect this valuation of pitching. The 180 teams since 1999 have devoted an average of 41 percent of player payroll to pitching. Only 31 teams (17 percent) have accorded 50 percent or more of their player payrolls to pitching. The most extreme of these was the 2002 Minnesota Twins, with nearly 74 percent of player compensation going to pitchers. This team went 94-67 and advanced to the ALCS, where the Twins lost to the Anaheim Angels. This was the greatest success of the top ten teams within the 50 percent and above group, where only one other team made the playoffs (Table 8-1.1).

The overall winning percentage of the teams in the 50 percent and over group was .525, equivalent to 85 wins over a full season. Ten of the thirty-one teams (32 percent) made the playoffs. Just squeaking in at the bottom of the list, with 50.7 percent of payroll devoted to pitching, is the 2005 champion Chicago White Sox. The 2001 champion Diamondbacks, with 52 percent, also make this group. Of the four other champions crowned during this period, the 2000 Yankees devoted just 46.2 percent of their payroll to pitching, the 2002 Angels 43.7 percent, the 2003 Marlins 30.8 percent and the 2004 Red Sox 46.2 percent. The ten teams with the most regular-season wins during the period—from the 2001 Mariners (116) to the 2003 Giants (100)—devoted about 40

TABLE 8-1.1 Teams with Highest Percentage of Player Payroll Devoted to Pitching, with Results, 2000–2005

Year	Teams	Total Player Salaries	Pitcher %	W	L	Finish
2002	Minnesota Twins	40,225,000	73.9	94	67	Lost ALCS
2003	Minnesota Twins	55,505,000	65.6	90	72	Lost ALDS
2001	Minnesota Twins	24,130,000	65.6	85	77	2nd, AL C
2005	Cleveland Indians	41,502,500	64.9	93	69	2nd AL C
2005	Los Angeles Dodgers	83,039,000	64.8	71	91	4th, NL W
2001	Los Angeles Dodgers	109,105,953	57.0	86	76	3rd, NL W
2004	Texas Rangers	55,050,417	56.6	89	73	3rd AL W
2000	Florida Marlins	19,870,000	56.3	79	82	3rd, NL E
2003	Los Angeles Dodgers	105,872,620	56.1	85	77	2nd, NL W
2000	Minnesota Twins	15,654,500	55.5	69	93	5th, AL C

percent of expenditures to pitching, with a low of 33.3 percent by the 2002 Athletics, winners of 102 games.

On the opposite side of the spectrum, there were thirty-three teams that devoted less than a third of their player expenditures to pitching. These teams had an overall winning percentage of .459, or 74 wins over a full season. This group includes only two playoff teams: the champion Marlins of 2003 and the 2004 Houston Astros, losers of the NLCS. It is in the vast middle—the teams that devoted a third or more of their player budget but less than 50 percent—that the budgetary sweet spot emerges. Thirty-eight of these teams (one-third of them) won 90 or more games, with an overall winning percentage of .596, as compared to .579 for the 90-game winners in the greater than 50 percent group. These teams devoted an average of 42 percent of player payroll to pitching.

This doesn't mean that teams with pitching payrolls of greater than 50 percent of overall expenditure have incorrectly valued pitching; in fact, run prevention is slightly more valuable than run scoring. A team that adds hitting to a strong offense will eventually see diminishing returns because the marginal value of each additional run to a high-powered offense is increasingly small (see Fig. 8-1.1). The reverse is also true, though not quite to the same extent: Adding pitching to a team already good at preventing runs brings diminishing returns at the extremes, but the extremes are further off.

In the purest sense, then, you *can't* have too much pitching. The fewer runs allowed, the greater the benefit to the team (Fig. 8.1-2). This doesn't require statistics to see, just common sense; a team

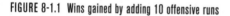

FIGURE 8-1.1 Wins gained by adding 10 offensive runs

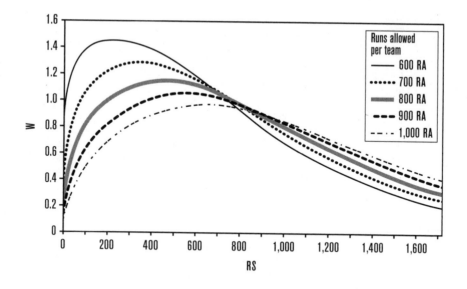

FIGURE 8-1.2 Wins Gained by reducing RA by 10 runs

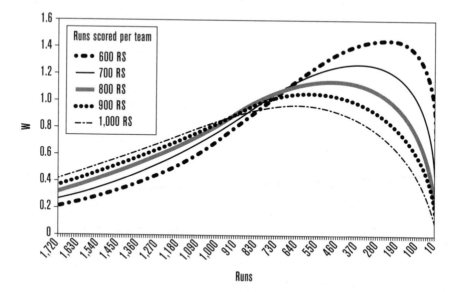

whose pitchers allow no runs is going to win no matter how many runs the offense scores. A team that allows just 1 run still stands a very good chance of winning. In 2005, major league teams went 446-40 (.918) in games in which they allowed only 1 run. Eight teams were undefeated in such games.

Unfortunately, in the modern, home-run-centric era of baseball, holding teams to 1 run is exceedingly difficult; there were 747 1- or no-run games pitched in 2005, representing just 15 percent of the schedule. Building a pitching staff good enough to allow 1 or no runs on a regular basis is impossible under current conditions. No team has had an ERA under 3.00 since 1989; no team has had an ERA under 2.50 since 1968; and only two teams have hit 2.50 or lower since 1919. Thus, no matter how good a team's pitching is, it is impossible for it to be so dominant that it can make up for a completely ineffective offense. A team that loses every game 1-0 or 2-1 is no better off than a team that loses 5-0 or 10-1. Since 1901, ninety-eight teams have led their leagues in runs prevented (the least total runs allowed, rather than earned runs) but had offenses so poor that they failed to make the postseason, while teams with weaker pitching staffs but more robust hitters played on into the fall. During that same period, ninety-seven teams have led their leagues in runs scored and failed to make the playoffs, another testament to the need for proportionality (Table 8-1.2).

TABLE 8-1.2 Where League-Leading Teams Finished in the Standings, 1901–2005

Led League in Runs Scored							Led League in Runs Allowed						
1	2	3	4	5	6	7	1	2	3	4	5	6	7
111	35	29	18	11	6	1	113	47	31	14	5	3	1
53	17	14	9	5	3	0.4	53	22	14	7	2	1	0.4

Note: The numbers 1 through 7 in the top row refer to the position in the standings where each finished. The second row refers to the number of teams that finished in that position. The third row refers to the frequency at which those results occurred, measured by percentage.

Being a dominant offensive team or run-prevention team is no guarantor of success. The only surefire recipe for winning is to dominate the league in both categories. With the exception of the 1902 Pirates and 1904 Giants (neither team had any playoffs to go to) none of the thirty-five teams that were both offensive and pitching leaders failed to play on into October. Twenty of thirty-three won the World Series.

Teams with an imbalance will usually not win, no matter how strong they are on one side of the equation. For the ultimate example of the risks of having a lopsided team, look no further than the Los Angeles Dodgers of 2003, the National League run-prevention leader for that season. The rotation had Kevin Brown and Hideo Nomo throwing as well as they ever did. In the bullpen, Eric Gagne had one of the best relief seasons in history. Setup men Guillermo Mota and

Paul Quantrill supported Gagne's successful run at the Cy Young Award. All three posted ERAs under 2.00. Frequently injured southpaw Wilson Alvarez was also dominant in 95 innings. The Dodgers allowed 3.43 runs per 9 innings, the league 4.64. Adjusted for park and league, the 2003 Los Angeles Dodgers posted a team ERA nearly 30 percent better than the league average. Historically, this is one of the biggest gaps between a team's performance and the league's.

On offense, the Dodgers were as weak as the pitching was strong. The hitters pulled off a special kind of Triple Crown, finishing last in batting average, on-base percentage, and slugging average. Overall, the team hit .243/.303/.368 in a league that batted .262/.332/.417. The best hitter, outfielder Shawn Green, batted just .280/.355/.460 with 23 home runs (36.6 Value Over Replacement Player [VORP], the forty-fourth-best player in the league in that category; VORP measures the number of runs a player contributes above what a fringe bench-warmer would offer). Shortstop Cesar Izturis was more typical, batting .251/.278/.315 (–2.2 VORP) while consuming 10 percent of the team's total offensive playing time. The Dodgers finished sixteenth of sixteen teams in runs scored, trailing the fifteenth-best offense by 68 runs. Dodger Stadium is one of the toughest hitter's parks in baseball, mitigating the Dodgers' woes a bit. Still, after adjusting for their home park and league, the Dodgers' team on-base percentage plus slugging average (OPS) was 17 percent worse than league average. Despite the great performance of the pitching staff, the team scored just 18 more runs than it allowed.

Despite this imbalance, the Dodgers did post a winning record, landing in second place in the National League West with an 85-77 record. They finished 15.5 games behind a San Francisco Giants team whose pitching, though strong, was not nearly as good as the Dodgers' at 3.43 runs allowed per game. The difference was in the offense. Though the Giants tallied only a few more runs than the typical team, their average of 4.69 runs scored per game gave them enough separation from the pitching staff to give them a chance to win on most nights. The Dodgers' average of 3.54 runs scored per game did not offer them the same benefit. They were shut out 13 times, the most in the National League, and were limited to 1 run a major league–leading 27 times. The Dodgers pitched 17 shutouts that year, but those shutouts didn't necessarily coincide with the nights the offense had only 1 run in it—the Dodgers were only 2-25 when scoring just once.

Measured by VORP, the 2003 Dodgers had the most pitching-heavy team (315.8 VORP from the pitchers, 62.9 from the hitters) in major league history, a condition that does not lead to happy outcomes (Table 8-1.3).

TABLE 8-1.3 Teams with the Greatest Difference Between Pitching and Hitting VORP

Year	Team	Pitching VORP	Hitting VORP	Record/Finish
2003	Dodgers	315.8	62.9	85-77, 2nd
1997	Blue Jays	285.4	18.2	76-86, 5th
1941	White Sox	243.9	14.4	77-77, 3rd
1933	Indians	256.8	26.2	75-76, 4th
1936	Red Sox	404.2	100.6	74-80, 6th
1925	Reds	325.7	63.4	80-73, 3rd
1998	Devil Rays	269.1	36.4	63-99, 7th
1996	Royals	325.1	66.6	75-86, 5th
1983	Rangers	310.6	60.5	77-85, 3rd
1996	Blue Jays	384.5	102.2	74-88, 4th

With three exceptions, these "all pitching" teams did not dramatically improve in the years immediately following their extreme seasons, and none won pennants until at least a few years later. Those teams' lack of hitting was so pronounced that they simply could not change at enough positions before the pitching decayed from its lofty position.

Winning does not depend solely upon pitching, or even 70 percent upon pitching, but is a product of the interplay of runs scored and allowed. A team needs both enough hitting and enough pitching to excel at both run scoring and run prevention. This can be further demonstrated by experimenting with the Pythagorean Formula. In his 1980 *Baseball Abstract,* Bill James demonstrated that a team's total runs scored and runs allowed had a predictable relationship to wins and losses. This equation:

$$\frac{(\text{runs scored})^2}{(\text{runs scored})^2 + (\text{runs allowed})^2} = \text{winning percentage}$$

invariably produced a result that almost exactly matched a team's actual record. The equation's three squares reminded James of the Pythagorean theorem, so he called the result of this equation the Pythagorean Record.

Using James's formulation, we can approximate results for a hypothetical team that hews even closer to the "pitching-is-everything" school than did the 2003 Dodgers. Let's assume that since we've successfully signed all of the best pitchers available, our pitching staff will allow an unprecedented 40 percent fewer runs than the typical team in its league. Since we've spent all our money on pitching, we'll have to play replacement-level players—defined as Triple-A lifers or players regularly on waivers, such as Gerald Williams—on offense. The 1922 Boston Braves hit .263/.317/.341 and scored 596 runs in a league in which the average team hit .292/.348/.404 and scored 774. It's hard to imagine a modern, racially integrated offense in the current era's offense-friendly parks doing much worse, so the '22 Braves will be our model.

Translating all of this to a 2005 National League offensive environment, our hypothetical team would allow just 547 runs in the season. Unfortunately, the pathetic offense, in which the typical player would resemble current Pittsburgh shortstop Jack Wilson (2005 edition), would score just a few runs more, 554. Without even running through the Pythagorean calculations, it is apparent at a glance that this team isn't going to be a world-beater. The only way to win games is to score more runs than your opponent, and with a runs scored/allowed differential of just +7, there's no way this team did that very often. The Pythagorean Formula predicts that this team would have a winning percentage of .506, or an 82-80 record over a full season. The Mets won the NL East with an 82-79 record in 1973 and the 2005 San Diego Padres won their division with a record of 82-80. But those are rare exceptions; in just about any other year, 82-80 is good for no better than third place.

Give the Pythagorean Formula a reversed version of the above, with the best offense of all time and the worst pitching staff, and the results are similar. The 1931 Yankees are a strong choice for greatest offense of all time; with Babe Ruth, Lou Gehrig, and the rest they scored the most runs ever, 1,067, and batted .297/.383/.457 in a league that hit .278/.344/.396. On a per-game basis they scored about 35 percent more runs than the average team. In a 2005 context, that would mean a season total of about 1,034 runs. There are many candidates for the worst pitching staff ever, including the 1911 Boston Braves and 1930 Philadelphia Phillies. But the 1996 Detroit Tigers have stronger qualifications, including playing in a neutral ballpark decades after integration and in the era of the amateur draft. Despite these advantages, they posted a 6.38 ERA in a league that averaged 4.99; when adjusted for context, their ERA was 21 percent below average. In 2005 terms, this is equivalent to 973 runs allowed. Thus, this highly imbalanced team's Pythagorean won-lost record is .530, or 86-76 over a full season. That's not bad, but in most years it's not good enough to make the playoffs.

As this suggests, a team can score 1,000 runs, but if the pitching isn't of some quality, it still won't win. Since 1901, seven teams have scored 1,000 runs in a season. It didn't guarantee them a page in the annals of great ballclubs (Table 8-1.4).

TABLE 8-1.4 The 1,000-Run Offenses

Team	Year	R	RA	DIFF	W-L	Finish	Postseason
Yankees	1931	1,067	760	307	94-59	2nd-AL	
Yankees	1936	1,065	731	334	102-51	1st-AL	Won WS
Yankees	1930	1,062	886	176	86-68	3rd-AL	
Red Sox	1950	1,027	804	223	94-60	3rd-AL	
Indians	1999	1,009	860	149	97-65	1st-ALC	Lost ALDS
Cardinals	1930	1,004	784	220	92-62	1st-NL	Lost WS
Yankees	1932	1,002	724	278	107-47	1st-AL	Won WS

Nineteen teams have scored between 950 and 998 runs in a season. Of these:

◆ Six won the World Series.
◆ Three lost the World Series.
◆ One lost the League Championship Series.
◆ Two lost the Divisional Series.
◆ Four finished second in the league or division but did not make the playoffs.
◆ Two finished third.
◆ One finished fourth.

To win, a team must accurately assess its assets in both the pitching and hitting department. It must also evaluate its defense, the invisible hand that affects much of what we perceive as pitching. The team then needs to project all these elements as accurately as possible and add or subtract as needed, dealing from strength to improve weaknesses wherever possible. Of course, this is not as easy as it sounds. Projecting hitters from year to year can be done with a certain broad accuracy. But a pitcher's results are subject to so much external noise that trying to define their future in narrow terms is quite difficult (see

Chapter 2-1, "Why Are Pitchers So Unpredictable?" for more on this topic).

What is predictable is the relationship of runs scored and runs allowed to wins. In 2005, the average National League club allowed 4.45 runs per game. A team striving to build a winning roster needs to keep such figures in mind as it assesses what it needs to do to win. If we assume that the scoring environment will stay the same the next season, an NL team looking ahead to 2006 that expects to allow the league-average figure of 4.45 runs a game (720 total runs) would need to score about 860 runs if it wants a solid chance to win 95 games, as shown in Figure 8-1.3.

FIGURE 8-1.3 Pythagorean runs allowed as a function of runs scored

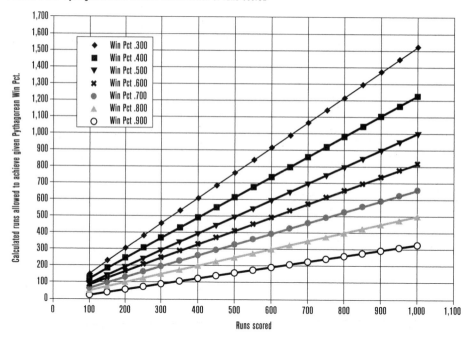

Note that if we use the Pythagorean method for a team that both scores and allows 750 runs, we expect a .500 team. If we add 100 more runs scored (850:750), we expect a .560 team. If we add 200 runs (950:750), we expect a .613 winning percentage. However, if we start at 750:750 and *subtract* 100 runs allowed (750:650), we get a .566 winning percentage. If 200 runs are subtracted (750:550), we get a .637 winning percentage. The runs prevented are worth more than the runs scored, if the Pythagorean model holds (Fig. 8-1.4).

FIGURE 8-1.4 Pythagorean record as a function of runs scored

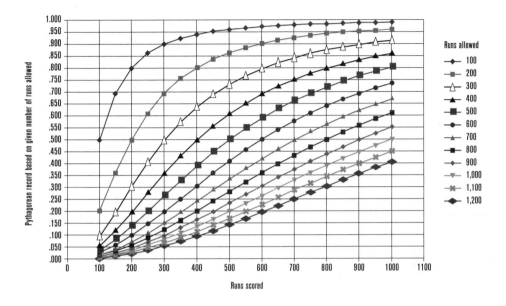

The consistent relationship among runs scored, runs allowed, and wins allowed for a variety of approaches to team building besides adding pitchers. History offers a number of useful case studies of teams trying to adjust their runs scored/allowed mix, including the mediocre 2003 Dodgers, who transformed into the division-winning 2004 Dodgers. Following the '03 season, the Dodgers made a series of moves intended to balance the team's pitching-heavy mix. On December 13, General Manager Dan Evans made an astute trade, dealing his best starting pitcher, Kevin Brown, to the Yankees for three pitchers— Jeff Weaver, Yhency Brazoban, and Brandon Weeden. Brown's age and injury history made it unlikely that he would repeat his great performance, and his annual salary of nearly $16 million made him an albatross on the team's payroll. Weaver had flopped in New York, but a Los Angeles resurgence would somewhat offset Brown's loss. Meanwhile, the Dodgers gained payroll flexibility to add hitting.

That same day, Evans dealt minor league outfielder Travis Ezi to the Florida Marlins in exchange for veteran outfielder Juan Encarnacion. Ezi was not a prospect, but the transparent futility of adding Encarnacion, a corner outfielder who did not hit like one, may have doomed Evans with the new ownership group that was taking over the team. Partly because of the slow transition to the new owners, Evans never did take full advantage of the Brown trade. By the time new GM

Paul DePodesta was installed in February, it was too late for the team to sign any premier free agents. DePodesta did find help elsewhere, though, parlaying Milton Bradley's off-field conflict with Indians management into a deal that sent two prospects to Cleveland for the talented center fielder.

The pitching declined tremendously. Brown was gone, Nomo was injured, and Weaver was just average. The bullpen, while still good, was neither as effective nor as deep as it had been before. While league offense rose only slightly, the Dodgers' runs allowed jumped to 4.24. But the offense picked up the slack, surging from 3.54 runs scored per game to 4.70. Bradley replaced Punch-and-Judy hitter Dave Roberts in the lineup, improving the center-field position's contribution from 4.9 VORP to 25.2 VORP. The rest of the offensive improvement came from the holdovers rebounding from abnormally poor years. Third baseman Adrian Beltre led the way, zooming from a rock-bottom .240/.289/.424 with 23 home runs (17.7 VORP) to .334/.388/.629 with a league-leading 48 home runs (89.1 VORP). Though the Dodgers went from allowing 26 percent fewer runs than the average team to 9 percent fewer, the team's runs scored jumped from 27 percent below average to just 4 percent below average. The Dodgers scored 77 more runs than they allowed, and with a little luck (they exceeded their Pythagorean projection by 3 games) improved their record by 8 games and won their division with a record of 93-69.

Two of the other most pitching-heavy teams experienced short-term turnarounds. The 1997 Toronto Blue Jays lacked even one notable offensive star. The team's best hitter, Carlos Delgado, batted .262/.350/.538 with 30 home runs, a solid but unspectacular season given the quality of first basemen at the time. Meanwhile, outfielder and designated hitter Joe Carter was allowed to consume 11 percent of the team's offensive playing time despite batting a horrific .234/.284/.399 (–2.4 VORP). He drove in 102 runs, yet another bullet point in the "RBIs are not a measure of quality" brief. (See Chapter 1-1 for more on the vastly overrated RBI statistic and the vastly overrated Joe Carter.)

The Blue Jays pitching staff, which featured defending Cy Young Award winner Pat Hentgen and the other sub-2.00 ERA season of Paul Quantrill's career (1.94 in 88 innings) would have been merely decent had it not been for the presence of Roger Clemens. In one of the greatest seasons in baseball history, Clemens pitched 264 innings, amassing an earned run average of 2.05—in a league where the average ERA was 4.57. Adjusted for park and league, the league ERA was 125 percent higher than Clemens's average. Overall, the team allowed 15 percent fewer runs than the average team, yet the team scored 40 fewer runs than it allowed and finished last in the American League East with a 76-86 record.

That off-season, the Blue Jays went heavily into the free-agent market. They signed catcher Darrin Fletcher to share time with incumbent Benito Santiago. They nabbed righty slugger Mike Stanley away from the Yankees to share time at designated hitter and first base. Free agent Tony Fernandez would take second base from the execrable Carlos Garcia, who had posted a .208 EqA. Carter was allowed to leave as a free agent, replaced by Jose Canseco. Simultaneously, the club planned to promote young players Shawn Green and Shannon Stewart to everyday status. General Manager Gord Ash made only one move on behalf of the pitching staff, signing lefty reliever Randy Myers, who had just saved 45 games for the Orioles.

These moves had the desired effect. All the new players hit, and the team's adjusted OPS improved from 19 percent below league average to 3 percent above, with runs scored showing a similar improvement. Simultaneously, the pitching staff declined. Clemens was again great but not historic, Hentgen's arm gave out, and Myers was a bust. Runs allowed declined from 15 percent better than average to just 7 percent, while the team's adjusted ERA suffered a proportionate decline. Yet the team scored 816 runs and allowed just 768, improving by 12 games to 88-74. Unfortunately, the team had the misfortune to play in the same division as one of the teams on the short list for greatest of all time, the 1998 Yankees, so they actually finished further out than they had the year before.

The third on the list of most-pitching-heavy teams to show quick improvement was the 1925 and 1926 Cincinnati Reds. The 1925 edition had an offense that scored 127 runs fewer than the average team, a deficit that was not completely offset by the dominance of the pitching staff, which was 142 runs better than average. The Reds finished in third place with an 80-73 record.

The team didn't make any dramatic moves in the off-season. One of its main problems had been that first baseman Jake Daubert had died, leaving it without a regular at the position, so Wally Pipp was purchased from the Yankees to replace him. The club also made a good signing in minor league outfielder Walter "Cuckoo" Christensen, a professional eccentric who would bat .350/.426/.438 in 114 games. Holdover catcher Bubbles Hargrave unexpectedly batted .353 and won the batting title. The Reds also added pitching. They signed righty prospect Red Lucas, who would prove to be a solid control artist and an excellent hitter. Meanwhile, ace submariner Carl Mays recovered from a shoulder injury to pitch 281 strong innings. Nonetheless, the pitching staff declined, the team's adjusted ERA changing from 21 percent better than average to only 8 percent better. The offense covered the difference, the batters scoring 4 more runs on the season than the average team. While the 1925 Reds scored just 47 more runs than they allowed, in 1926 they scored 96 more. Consequently they jumped from an 80-73, third-place finish to 87-67 and a very close second-place finish (2 games behind the pennant-winning St. Louis Cardinals). Less pitching plus more hitting led to a more favorable outcome than strong pitching and no hitting.

The 2000 and 2001 Houston Astros offer an example of a team working from the other side of the spectrum, trying to add pitching to a strong offense. The 2000 Astros were one of the most hitting-unbalanced teams in history, receiving 408.0 VORP from the hitters and just 63.8 VORP from the pitchers. The best pitcher ("best" perhaps being a misnomer) was the immortal Joe Slusarski. Despite scoring 938 runs, the Astros couldn't overcome a pitching staff that allowed 6 runs per game—they went 72-90. In 2001, Houston enjoyed the return of starter Shane Reynolds and closer Billy Wagner, both of whom had been sidelined by arm injuries. The Astros also promoted two young pitchers, Roy Oswalt and Wade Miller, into the rotation. Both would prove effective. The offense was constant relative to the league, but the pitching staff improved from 10 percent below league average to 4 percent above. The Astros more than reversed their record, going 93-69 and claiming the NL Central title. Again, success is all in the mix.

Teams that were both pitching- and hitting-neutral provide special insight into the "too much pitching" question, since they could make changes to either side of the operation and hope to improve. Not counting World War II–era clubs, there have been eighteen teams that were between +15 and –15 runs above or below average on both runs scored and runs allowed in the same season. These teams had an aggregate winning percentage of .532, equivalent to a record of about 86-78 over a full season.

In the next season, ten of these teams declined, while eight improved. Tables 8-1.5, 8-1.6, and 8-1.7 contain brief summaries of how these teams tried to undo their average profiles. If a team can never have too much pitching, then the approach taken should have been to add pitching in all cases. Instead, these teams found that their problems required a variety of solutions. Caveat lector: Just because these teams changed does not mean that a rational or measured approach was used to fix their problems. Indeed, as with many of today's managers and general managers, for most of these teams there was no plan, just day-to-day improvisation in the face of changing circumstances and in some cases neglect. Assuming a controlling intelligence at work would in many cases be giving too much credit to the teams for these results. Numbers in the "Runs" and "Runs Allowed" columns represent the percentage above or below average the team was in those two categories. Teams that improved are in bold.

TABLE 8.1-5 Neutral Teams, Group One

	Year One			Year Two		
Team	R	RA	Result	R	RA	Result
1928 Browns	5	0	82-72, 3rd	-4	8	79-73, 4th
1932 Giants	6	-1	72-82, 7th	1	22	92-61, 1st
1936 Tigers	6	0	83-71, 2nd	15	-3	89-65, 2nd
1936 White Sox	5	0	81-70, 3rd	-2	10	86-68, 3rd

TABLE 8.1-6 Neutral Teams, Group Two

	Year One			Year Two		
Team	R	RA	Result	R	RA	Result
1949 Giants	5	1	72-81, 5th	3	12	86-68, 3rd
1961 Dodgers	6	1	89-65, 2nd	15	7	102-63, 2nd
1968 A's	4	2	82-80, 6th	9	-1	88-74, 2W
1972 White Sox	7	0	87-67, 2W	-6	-1	77-85, 5W
1972 Yankees	5	1	79-76, 4E	-6	12	80-82, 4E

TABLE 8.1-7 Neutral Teams, Group Three

	Year One			Year Two		
Team	R	RA	Result	R	RA	Result
1974 Twins	1	-1	82-80, 3W	6	-7	76-83, 4W
1978 Pirates	7	1	88-73, 2E	12	9	98-64, 1E
1979 Cardinals	5	1	86-73, 3E	13	-9	74-88, 4E
1988 Pirates	6	1	85-75, 2E	-3	-4	74-88, 5W

Of the four clubs listed in Table 8-1.5, only one, the 1932–1933 New York Giants, made a concerted effort to change the team's hitting-pitching balance. Manager Bill Terry made an affirmative decision to exchange offense for defense. Terry's 1932 pitching staff included two dominant starters, Carl Hubbell (77-52, 3.13 ERA to that point in his career) and Freddie Fitzsimmons (120-72, 3.68), as well as two promising prospects in Hal Schumacher (twenty-one years old) and Roy Parmelee (twenty-five). As such, Terry felt little need to add pitchers; rather, he correctly intuited that he could improve the pitchers he had by giving them better support in the field. "The managerial policy which I have adopted is built upon defense rather than offense," he said. "The Giants do not usually need to score many runs. All that we must do is score more than the other fellow. Our system is built upon airtight pitching. We commonly play for one run. I have said to the players many times, 'If we can hold them to the seventh inning, we can win.'"

The 1932 Giants were not only error-prone (they made 191 errors, 3 behind the league-worst Phillies), they were also handicapped by players who lacked range. Since 1923, the starting shortstop had been two-way standout Travis Jackson. He was just twenty-eight, but when his already balky right knee was joined by a broken left knee early in the season, his ability to play the position effectively was destroyed. His replacement, Eddie "Doc" Marshall, had been compared to Coleridge's Ancient Mariner because "he stoppeth one of three." Catcher Shanty Hogan could not block low pitches because he was overweight, a big problem on a staff with screwball pitcher Hubbell and knuckleballer Fitzsimmons. Left fielder Freddie Lindstrom was playing out of position in center field. Terry became the Giants' manager on June 2, 1932, taking over from thirty-year incumbent John McGraw. He was so concerned with defense that his very first move was to bench McGraw's left fielders, Len Koenecke and Chick Fullis, and call up Jo-Jo Moore, a rookie defensive standout, from Jersey City.

That winter, pure fielder Blondy Ryan replaced the hard-hitting Jackson. The Giants acquired all-glove, no-bat catcher Gus Mancuso from the Cardinals to start behind the plate. Due to personal issues, Terry also dealt away Lindstrom, throwing Fullis into the trade and bringing back defense-first center fielder Kiddo Davis. "The changes we've made," said Terry, "should give us more power than any club in the circuit next to Philadelphia, and we have them stopped, because we'll have the better defense." In fact, all of the changes involved trading offense for defense.

Terry got exactly what he was looking for. National League scoring dropped dramatically from 1932 to 1933, shrinking from 4.6 runs per game to 4.0. The Giants went even further, allowing 3.28 runs per game, down from 4.62 the year before. Hubbell's ERA improved from 2.50 to 1.66, while Fitzsimmons's dropped from 4.42 to 2.89. Schumacher had posted a 3.56 ERA in a 101-inning audition in 1932. A full-time starter in 1933, he posted a 2.15 ERA in 259 innings. With one of the tightest defenses in the league, the Giants improved their percentage of balls in play converted into outs from 69.4 percent in 1932 to 71.2 percent in 1933; that's a huge jump, the equivalent of winning eight more games thanks solely to defensive improvement. The Giants played 45 1-run games and won 28 of them, up from a 17-31 record the year before. The Giants became so dependent on their defense that when Blondy Ryan missed time in early July with a minor injury, the Giants lost seven straight games. Hastening to join them on the road, Ryan wired to Terry, "THEY CAN'T BEAT US! AM ON MY WAY!"

Indeed, with Ryan back, they couldn't lose. The Giants won the pennant and the World Series. In this case, the Giants "didn't have enough pitching" to win but solved the problem via an indirect route.

After 1949, Giants' manager Leo Durocher was generally focused on making his team faster and more athletic, specifically aiming to upgrade his double-play combination. He got the opportunity when the Braves traded him their starting double-play combo, Eddie Stanky and Alvin Dark. In 1949, the Giants turned 144 double plays; the league average was 152. A year later, the Giants turned 181 double plays, 2 short of the league lead and 18 above the league average. The improved defense helped make important players of two pitching acquisitions: Sal Maglie, a thirty-three-year-old journeyman who had been brought back to the States after having jumped to the Mexican League, and Jim Hearn, a May purchase from the Cardinals who won the league ERA title with a 1.91 mark as a Giant.

It is important to note that Durocher's valuation of pitching and defense over offense probably cost the team the 1950 pennant, when it finished just 5 games behind the Phillies. The Giants had had a lot of power—in 1947 they had set the record for home runs in a season—but to Durocher, this meant that they weren't a dynamic offense. One of Durocher's first moves in pursuit of a speedier offense with which to hit and run and bunt was to sell slow but powerful first baseman Johnny Mize to the Yankees. This led to the installation of punchless rookie Tookie Gilbert at first base. Gilbert batted .220/.314/.307 in 113 games (.226 EqA). Mize, playing part time for the Yankees, batted

.277/.351/.595, worth about 3 wins more than a replacement-level first baseman. National League home-run production increased between 1947 and 1950, but the Giants headed in the other direction. By 1950, the team had shed 88 home runs from its record 1947 total and finished fifth in the league, despite playing in a good home-run park. In 1951, Durocher installed Whitey Lockman, an average hitter but not much of a fielder, at first, and the Giants won the National League pennant. Durocher had debilitated his offense. It was only when the team started scoring again (the Giants were second in the National League in both runs and home runs in 1951) that winning the pennant became possible. This was a victory of bolstering the offense rather than the pitching staff.

The 1979 Pirates, who would go on to win the World Series, added a little bit of everything. It took General Manager Harding "Pete" Peterson some time to figure out that they had to do anything at all. After a quiet winter, the Pirates remade their team with two April deals, dealing lefty starting pitcher Jerry Reuss (who had been buried in the bullpen) to the Dodgers for twenty-five-year-old righty starter Rick Rhoden (42-24, 3.40 in his career). This proved to be a minor upgrade because shoulder problems would end Rhoden's season after one start. Twelve days after the Rhoden deal, the Pirates addressed their defense, which had been characterized as "inept . . . a nuisance they perform to get to bat again." The Bucs dealt their shortstop of six years, the speedy Frank Taveras, to the Mets for shortstop Tim Foli. Not only was Foli a better fielder than Taveras, but he batted .291, making 1979 the one year that he wasn't completely impotent with the bat.

The Pirates were prepared to endure the second comeback of second baseman Rennie Stennett, at least for a time. Stennett had broken his leg while sliding in 1978 and had lost his batting stroke as a result. At the time of the injury, he was batting .336/.376/.430, but in his first return he slumped to .243/.274/.309. When June 28, 1979, rolled around and Stennett was still hitting as he had the year before (.238/.289./292), the team benched him. The Pirates then moved third baseman Phil Garner to second and traded three pitchers to the Giants for third baseman Bill Madlock, a career .319/.380/.461 hitter. The realigned defense was a benefit to the pitchers, while the offense scored 5 runs a game over the rest of the season. The Pirates improved by addressing weak points other than the pitching staff.

As these neutral teams demonstrate, it never hurts to have pitching, but fielding and hitting pay dividends as well. This is an important factor in assessing a team's needs, because position players are more consistent at their jobs—both in the field and at the plate—than are pitchers. They are also less likely to become injured. While in the purest sense adding pitching can have the most dramatic impact on a team's won-lost record, building around pitchers means that a team is subject to a greater chance of suffering a crippling injury or injuries (as the defending champion 1986 Mets found when four of their five starting pitchers spent time on the disabled list in 1987, dropping the team from 108 to 92 wins).

In team building, ballclubs try to collect scarce resources (hitters, pitchers, fielders) using scarce resources (money). Pitching is a bit like oil: Nothing happens without it, and you'd like to get as much of it as money will allow, but if you don't buy food you will have a more immediate problem than whether or not your car will run. In strictest mathematical terms, a team can only benefit by adding pitching. But in the absence of available pitching, making other changes will work just as well.

Which is to say that you can't have too much pitching—except when you don't have enough of everything else.

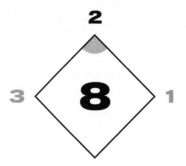

2

3   8   1

How Much Does Coors Field Really Matter?

KEITH WOOLNER

In 1993, Major League Baseball expanded for the first time since 1977. Two teams joined the National League: the Florida Marlins and the Colorado Rockies. The Rockies were the first to reach the playoffs, winning the Wild Card in 1995. But twelve years after joining the league, the Marlins have two World Championships and the Rockies have only that one brief postseason appearance under their belts. In fact, the Rockies haven't managed to win more than 83 games in any year of their existence (Table 8-2.1).

The signature characteristic of the Rockies hasn't been any individual player, their 1995 Wild Card–winning team, or even their stellar attendance record (they led MLB in attendance for each of their first seven years and didn't drop below three million fans in a season until 2002). Instead, it's the

TABLE 8-2.1 Rockies Year-by-Year Won-Lost Record and Finish

Year	W	L	Win %	Finish	Postseason
1993	67	95	.414	6	
1994	53	64	.453	3	
1995	77	67	.535	2	Wild Card
1996	83	79	.512	3	
1997	83	79	.512	3	
1998	77	85	.475	4	
1999	72	90	.444	5	
2000	82	80	.506	4	
2001	73	89	.451	5	
2002	73	89	.451	4	
2003	74	88	.457	4	
2004	68	94	.420	4	
2005	67	95	.414	5	

ballparks in which they've played, Coors Field and Mile High Stadium—or to be more precise, those parks' legendary effects on offense and run production. In the baseball community, it's taken for granted that playing at high altitude wreaks havoc with the game. Yet most fans and sportswriters don't really know how to account for it.

How do we know that Coors Field causes massive spikes in offense, rather than the Rockies simply having terrible pitching and great hitting for a decade? If playing at a mile-high altitude affects the game, which elements are most affected, and by how much? In short, how does a player's home park affect his value?

A quick glance at the statistical record is enough to raise suspicions. Since 1993 the Rockies have had only two pitchers post a Run Average below 4.00 in at least 100 innings: Marvin Freeman's 3.11 RA in 112.2 innings in 1994, and Joe Kennedy's 3.77 RA in 162.1 innings in 2004. No other team has fielded so few stingy pitchers during that time. In fact, only three other teams have fewer than *seven* such seasons over that span: the Rangers and Brewers with four each and the Tigers with three. The Rockies' expansion counterparts, the Marlins, have fifteen such seasons.

During the same period, Rockies batters have hit .300 or better in at least 500 PA 34 times, tops in the majors by a wide margin (27 percent more than the #2 team, the Cleveland Indians). Even by a more sabermetrically friendly measure of hitting such as OPS (on-base percentage plus slugging average), the Rockies have had thirty-six players top an 850 OPS, 20 percent more than the next-best teams (Red Sox and Yankees). Of all the 500-PA seasons posted by Rockies batters since 1993, an amazing 62 percent of those topped an 850 OPS, easily the highest ratio in the majors. No other team topped 50 percent (Yankees and Rangers were at 48 percent), and the median was 33 percent.

That combination of stellar hitting and feeble pitching is enough to raise eyebrows, but it alone can't prove that the Rockies play in an unusual environment. It could very well be that the Rockies have had studly hitters and girly-men pitchers for over a decade. Indeed, the Rockies have never ranked lower than fourth in runs scored per game, often leading the league in that category. Meanwhile, they've dominated the top of the list in most runs allowed per game (Table 8-2.2).

To show that it's the ballpark, not the quality of the team's players that are most to blame, we have to find a way isolate the park's influence and keep the quality of players constant. The way to do this is to use just the games played by the team at its home park. So to see the effect of Coors Field, compare the results from Rockies' home games

TABLE 8-2.2 Colorado's League Rank in Best Offense and Worst Defense, by Year

Year	Runs per Game	Rank	RA per Game	Rank
1993	4.68	4	5.97	1
1994	4.90	4	5.45	1
1995	5.45	1	5.44	1
1996	5.93	1	5.95	1
1997	5.70	1	5.60	1
1998	5.10	3	5.28	2
1999	5.59	2	6.35	1
2000	5.98	1	5.54	4
2001	5.70	1	5.59	1
2002	4.80	4	5.54	1
2003	5.27	3	5.51	1
2004	5.14	4	5.70	1
2005	4.57	5	5.32	2

to their away games. Since a team plays roughly the same mix of opponents at home and on the road, the overall quality of players in the two sets of games are approximately the same. Both sets of data contain Rockies hitters facing opposing pitchers, and opposing hitters facing Rockies pitchers. Even if the Rockies hitters are exceptionally good as a group, they are equally represented and weighted in both Rockies home games and Rockies away games, so overall they balance out. The same is true of the Rockies pitchers: Regardless of their actual quality, the fact that they contribute half the innings in both the home and away totals means that the overall quality of each pitcher is constant between the two sets of totals.

For example, in 2004, the Rockies and their opponents combined for 1,752 hits in 5,739 at-bats over 81 games in Colorado. In the Rockies' 81 road games, there were 1,413 hits in 5,467 at-bats. Here are the batting averages for both sets of games:

COL Home: 1,752 H/5,739 AB = .30528 AVG
COL Road: 1,413 H/5,467 AB = .25846 AVG

With the same hitters and pitchers, the games in Colorado yielded a .305 batting average, while the games away from Colorado produced a .258 batting average. That 47-point difference can be attributed in large part to the effect of Coors Field. Usually the effect of a park on a particular statistic is expressed as a ratio, as shown below:

.30528/.25846 = 1.18 COL park factor for batting average

Coors Field increases batting averages by 18 percent in the aggregate, compared to the league average (or more accurately, the weighted average of opposing parks the Rockies played in, which are usually close to the overall league average).

However, it's not quite that easy.

One difficulty in looking at the statistical record is that things don't even out perfectly over 162 games. Even if parks and environmental conditions were identical, we'd expect to see some random differential between two halves of the season (such as home and road games). Similarly, if you flip a coin 100 times, you are unlikely to have the same number of heads as tails, even if the expected value is 50-50. Also, just because there's a difference between stats in home and road games doesn't automatically mean that the differences are due entirely to the influence of the home park itself.

In fact, we can determine mathematically how much variability to expect just from taking a small sample of games. For a single season of stats, the expected standard deviation in an observed park factor due just to chance is about 5 percent. (Standard deviation measures the spread around the mean. Very few, if any, of the data points are exactly at the overall average—each point is some distance away, either higher or lower. The standard deviation is a way to average those distances to find out how far the typical data point is from the average.) So with the +18 percent park factor for batting average being more than three standard deviations away, we can be relatively sure that we're seeing something real. This is less of a problem for Coors Field than for most other parks in the majors that are less extreme, where it's harder to distinguish true park effects from other factors influencing the results. To become more confident about what effect a park has on hitters, we look at more players, over more games and plate appearances, spanning more years. Since one-year park factors fluctuate quite a bit for a given park (due to simple random chance as we've seen, but also due to actual environmental changes like temperature, humidity, and wind), we usually use three-year or five-year park factors to yield a more stable, reliable result.

The most commonly used park factor is the one employed to measure overall run scoring. A neutral park factor is commonly printed as 100. A 110 park factor thus indicates that a park inflates run scoring by 10 percent (110 = 1.10 = 10 percent above average). A park factor of 85 indicates that a park deflates run scoring by 15 percent (85 = 0.85 = 15 percent below average). The park factor for runs summarizes the overall effect the park has on hitters. We'll discuss how to properly use the park factor for runs later on.

What Causes Coors Field's Park Effect?

The underlying causes of park effects are surprisingly varied. There are the obvious ones, such as different outfield dimensions. But there are also subtle ones, such as differences in the quality of hitting backgrounds, lighting and shadows, amount of foul territory, quality of grounds maintenance, height of walls, prevailing wind direction and speed, average temperature, humidity, shape and area of the outfield, grass versus turf, and the proportion of day versus night games. And, of course, altitude, which is one of the key factors that makes Coors Field unique. Robert K. Adair, a professor of physics at Yale, has written an entire book titled *The Physics of Baseball* in which he explains the underlying physical reasons that a high-altitude ballpark like Coors creates a favorable offensive environment. We'll let him do the heavy lifting on explaining the science behind the park effect:

Offense

Since the retarding force on a ball is proportional to the density of the air, a baseball will travel farther in ball parks at high altitude. A 400-foot drive . . . near sea level could [be expected] to travel about 430 feet at mile-high Denver. And if the Major Leagues are further internationalized some day with a team in Mexico City, at 7800 feet, [that] blow could be expected to sail nearly 450 feet. . . . Old home run records will be swept away unless the fences are moved out in high parks.

The air in Denver is thinner than at sea level, offering less resistance to a ball in flight. Balls travel farther and faster. This is most apparent with flyballs, which carry farther, and line drives, which are more likely to fall for hits because of both the thin air and the huge expanse of grass in Coors Field's outfield. The result is an increase in offensive totals (home runs, hits) and rate statistics (batting average, on-base percentage, slugging average) for Rockies players.

Furthermore, swings themselves are more likely to produce a ball in play than a strike at Coors. Looking at the percentage of pitches swung at and not put into play, we see that Coors Field has shown a definite, albeit slight, tendency to help batters miss or foul a pitch off less often. This could be because of the hitting background or the thin air lessening the movement on pitches, thus making them less effective (Table 8-2.3).

Pitching

The pitchers will also be hurt at high altitude. A mile high at Denver, the fast ball will take a little less time to cross the plate—and gain about 6 inches—but the curve will break about 25 percent less.

A curve that will break left-right about 8 inches and drop an extra 8 inches (due to the overspin component) at sea level will break about 1 5/8 inches less and drop about 4 inches less in Denver. The ball breaks less because it crosses the plate faster, and thus has a little less time to break; in addition, the Magnus force is smaller. Similarly, the knuckle ball will dance perhaps 25 percent less.

In 2001, Colorado General Manager Dan O'Dowd undertook a bold (and expensive) experiment. He signed two starting pitchers, Mike Hampton and Denny Neagle, who rely primarily on changing speeds to fool hitters, for a combined $170 million. The rationale was that if breaking pitches break less at Coors than at sea level, then breaking-ball pitchers should be hampered disproportionately by the altitude. Adair's commentary supports this notion. Pitchers with exceptional change-ups, the Rockies thought, wouldn't be affected by the thin air and thus could succeed in Denver.

TABLE 8-2.3 Percentage of Swings That Were Misses or Fouled Off

Year	COL Home (%)	COL Away (%)	Park Factor for Swings Missed or Fouled Off
1993	54.8	56.9	0.965
1994	55.9	58.6	0.954
1995	56.4	58.0	0.972
1996	55.2	58.9	0.938
1997	54.0	56.9	0.949
1998	53.7	57.6	0.932
1999	54.1	56.6	0.955
2000	54.6	57.0	0.958
2001	56.7	58.3	0.973
2002	55.8	57.5	0.969
2003	56.4	57.7	0.978
2004	57.7	59.1	0.976
2005	56.6	58.6	0.967
Total	55.5	57.8	0.961

Hindsight being twenty-twenty, we can see now that neither Hampton nor Neagle had dominant strikeout rates, which meant that they were relying on getting outs on balls in play—balls that at Coors carry farther and go faster, as we've seen. Neagle was already prone to giving up home runs, a problem that was exacerbated by pitching in Coors. Hampton's HR rate tripled in his first season with the Rockies. Adair comments that fastballs seem to be a little bit faster, and change-ups lose less velocity during flight than they would at sea level for the very same reason. The batter's timing is less disrupted because the velocity difference between a good change-up and what he's used to seeing is reduced. What was a dominating change-up in most parks turns into a third-rate fastball at Coors. Both pitchers were considered massive disappointments, and their ERAs soared after they landed in Colorado. The team's record regressed by 9 games in the first Rockies season for Hampton and Neagle.

TABLE 8-2.4 Colorado Park Factors for Groundball Percentage (of balls in play)

Year	Home %	Away %	PF_GB %
1993	51.3	48.6	1.056
1994	56.3	50.1	1.125
1995	50.7	53.3	0.951
1996	53.4	53.4	0.999
1997	52.9	52.2	1.013
1998	50.2	52.1	0.963
1999	53.3	53.2	1.002
2000	57.6	52.6	1.095
2001	54.2	51.7	1.049
2002	56.7	54.9	1.032
2003	56.1	55.1	1.019
2004	56.7	57.3	0.989
2005	46.0	45.4	1.012
Total	53.0	52.1	1.018

Note: The 2005 numbers were much lower than preceding years–this is a known data issue because in previous years GB/FB data were recorded only for outs, not for hits. In 2005, we have data for all such batted balls. For the less accurate but more consistent treatment between 2005 and prior years, these are the 2005 and total numbers:

Year	Home %	Away %	PF_GB%
2005	54.2	52.0	1.042
Total	53.8	52.7	1.020

One explanation sometimes cited for the increase in hitting at Coors is that, even after home runs are accounted for, Coors plays as a "flyball" park—it increases the tendency of batters to hit the ball in the air, resulting in more doubles and triples than would be expected. That turns out not to be the case, though. Looking at the number of batted balls that stay in the park, broken down by groundballs or flyballs, the percentage of groundballs is actually slightly higher at Coors than in Rockies road games—although the park factor is less than 2 percent, well within the margin for error (Table 8-2.4).

Another effect of the higher overall offense at Coors is that it takes more pitches to get through a game. Because it's harder to get batters out, more of them come to the plate in a typical game. Each game averages 6.5 percent more pitches when played in Colorado—that equates to an extra 5 or 6 games' worth of pitches per year that the Rockies have to get out of their staff. Just about all that difference is a direct result of there being more batters; there's virtually no difference in the number of pitches each batter sees per plate appearance between Coors and the rest of the league (Table 8-2.5).

In an effort to weigh other factors that might make the ball travel farther, the Rockies have experimented with keeping baseballs in a humidor prior to games at Coors, believing that higher humidity will make it easier for pitchers to keep the ball in the park. There is some scientific basis for that belief. Adair says that "long flies hit with balls stored under conditions of extreme humidity could be expected to fall as much as 30 feet short of the distance expected for normal balls."

After the Rockies' experiment became public, there were attempts to experimentally determine the effect of humidity on a baseball's "coefficient of restitution," which measures how elastic, or lively, a ball is.

TABLE 8-2.5 Colorado Park Factors for PA per Game and Number of Pitches per Game

	PA/G			NP/G		
Year	COL	Away	Park Factor	COL	Away	Park Factor
1993	39.9	37.5	1.062	132.8	127.5	1.042
1994	39.8	38.4	1.036	131.0	140.5	0.933
1995	40.7	38.1	1.069	136.5	123.0	1.109
1996	41.3	37.3	1.108	149.2	117.6	1.269
1997	40.5	38.3	1.058	137.9	130.0	1.061
1998	40.3	37.2	1.083	140.2	126.8	1.106
1999	41.8	38.1	1.099	149.9	138.8	1.080
2000	41.3	37.7	1.095	150.0	141.3	1.061
2001	40.2	38.2	1.054	146.4	141.4	1.035
2002	39.4	37.8	1.041	143.8	141.1	1.019
2003	39.7	38.4	1.034	147.4	145.3	1.015
2004	40.9	38.5	1.063	152.9	145.0	1.055
2005	40.2	37.7	1.066	147.9	141.7	1.044
Total	40.5	37.9	1.067	143.9	135.4	1.063

One such experiment was done by David Kagan (CSU Chico Department of Physics) and David Atkinson. Their results (documented at http://phys.csuchico.edu:16080/kagan/profdev/COR.pdf) agree with Adair's findings. High humidity results in a less lively baseball.

However, the effect of the humidor is overstated. The Rockies were keeping the humidor at about 40 percent humidity, versus the Denver air, which can often be 10 percent or lower. While the difference between zero and 100 percent humidity can produce an effect of 30 feet distance on a batted baseball, the 30 percent difference between the humidor and the ambient air would produce an effect of only about a nine-foot reduction in distance. But even more importantly, the Rockies claimed they were keeping the balls in the humidor at around 90 degrees Fahrenheit, which turns out to be self-defeating. A warmer ball is more elastic than a colder ball, and thus will travel farther. The effect from temperature would completely counteract the effect of the wetter air. So other than providing a little physics lesson on the sports pages, the great humidor experiment really didn't amount to much.

Fielding

But even if the fences are adjusted, the high-altitude stadiums will still be a batter's boon, and a pitcher's bane. With fences moved back, there will be acres of ground for balls to fall in for base hits. . . .

With the smaller drag, the ball will also get to the outfielder faster in Denver than at Fenway Park in Boston. Indeed, a hard-hit "gapper" hit between the outfielders will reach the 300-foot mark about 0.3 second sooner in Denver than at sea level, thus cutting down the range of the pursuing outfielder 8 or 9 feet, a not inconsiderable amount in this game of inches. Even the range of a shortstop covering a line drive or one-hopper will be cut by nearly a foot in Denver.

Here we see that Coors alters the game for everyone on the field. Hitters feast on pitches with less movement, driving them farther than at sea level. Those batted balls move faster, so fielders have less time to react and catch the ball. The result is that more balls hit in play will fall for base hits. We can measure the batting average on balls in play (often abbreviated BABIP) against a team as well as Defensive Efficiency (created by Bill James), which measures the percentage of batted balls turned into outs as a measure of overall team defense. Defensive Efficiency is just 1 minus BABIP—thus, we'll speak of either a .700 Defensive Efficiency or a .300 BABIP. We'll stick with the batting average representation (BABIP), as its scale is more familiar to most readers:

$$BABIP = (H - HR)/(AB - HR - SO)$$

The vast majority of home runs are hit out of the field of play, so removing them from the hit total leaves us with just the hits where the defense had at least a fighting chance of retiring the batter. Similarly, strikeouts end at-bats without putting the ball into play, so they, along with home runs, are removed from the denominator. By calculating the park factor for BABIP, we can see how much harder Coors Field is on fielders (Table 8-2.6).

We saw before that Coors does not really change the mixture of groundballs and flyballs that are produced, so we

TABLE 8-2.6 Colorado Park Effect for Defensive Efficiency

Batting Average on Balls in Play (BABIP)

Year	Home	Away	Park Factor
1993	.339	.293	1.155
1994	.340	.301	1.131
1995	.343	.290	1.182
1996	.351	.283	1.240
1997	.343	.301	1.137
1998	.342	.299	1.145
1999	.346	.291	1.188
2000	.346	.289	1.199
2001	.338	.289	1.170
2002	.325	.287	1.132
2003	.318	.300	1.062
2004	.340	.296	1.149
2005	.336	.294	1.145
Total	.339	.293	1.157

can't attribute the change in BABIP to a shift in distribution. In fact, the effect is pronounced and roughly the same magnitude regardless of the type of batted ball. Whether a groundball that scoots by a diving shortstop or a line drive hit past a sprinting right fielder, balls fall for hits roughly 15 percent more often (Table 8-2.7).

TABLE 8-2.7 Colorado Park Effects for Different Types of Batted Balls in Play

Batted Ball Type	Park Factor for Batting Average
Groundball	1.19
Flyball	1.17
Pop-up	1.19
Line drive	1.12

The Proper Use and Interpretation of Park Effects

Since we now know that Coors Field has genuine and pronounced effects on player statistics and team offense, the next question to consider is this: How can we make use of that knowledge to better understand player value in an extreme environment like that of the Rockies' home field?

Consider the 1997 National League MVP race, where Larry Walker beat out Mike Piazza, getting 22 first-place votes to Piazza's 3 (Jeff Bagwell, who finished third overall, also got 3 first-place votes). Walker had more home runs (49 to 40), hits (208 to 201), runs (143 to 104), and RBI (130 to 124). He also posted a higher batting average (.366 to .362), on-base percentage (.452 to .431), and slugging average (.720 to .638). Seems like a clear case for Walker, at least offensively. However, Piazza played for the Dodgers in pitcher-friendly Dodger Stadium, while Walker played half his games in Coors Field. The two players' aggregate park factors were almost 15 percent different, in Walker's favor. If we make the proper adjustments, we can see what a performance in a neutral park that's equivalent to each hitter's stats would be (Table 8-2.8).

TABLE 8-2.8 Mike Piazza vs. Larry Walker Park-Adjusted Statistics, 1997

Year	Name	PA	AVG	OBP	SLG	Park Factor	Adjusted AVG	Adjusted OBP	Adjusted SLG
1997	Mike Piazza	633	.362	.431	.638	0.965	.368	.439	.650
1997	Larry Walker	664	.366	.452	.720	1.113	.347	.428	.682

Taking park effects into account to put both hitters on a level playing field, Piazza and Walker are now much closer. Piazza has a 21-point advantage in adjusted batting average, an 11-point advantage in adjusted on-base percentage, and has narrowed the gap to 32 points in adjusted slugging average. Taking into account the difficulty in finding good-hitting catchers compared to good-hitting right fielders, there's a compelling argument that Piazza should have won the MVP in '97 in a landslide, given that he and Walker were almost equivalent in value as hitters before considering their positions.

The careful reader will note that we didn't rely upon Walker's home-versus-road stats and Piazza's home-versus-road stats to determine whether to adjust their stats or not. Rather, we used the park factor observed for all players aggregated together. Walker actually posted comparable or better numbers on the road in 1997 (.346/.443/.733 on the road versus .384/.460/.709 at home). Yet we penalized him for his home park, even though his personal stats were not better at home. Is this fair?

Whether or not it's fair depends on what you are trying to accomplish. As we've seen, park factors are calculated using the league-wide change in offensive production for the park in question. For an MVP discussion, which is centered on player value, the average park adjustment is exactly what we want.

Park factors are used to adjust for the value of a player's performance, not to project how a particular player's stats would change in another park. The entire league got a huge boost from playing in Coors. As a result, each individual run was less valuable in Colorado than it was elsewhere in the NL, because it takes more runs to win a game there.

Think of it as a currency exchange between runs and wins. Suppose I get paid for doing some kind of work at two different parks (Coors Field, and let's pick Busch Stadium in St. Louis, which not only played as a roughly neutral park but also has a beer-related name) and get paid in the form of a voucher that I can convert into cash. I earn both 10 Coors vouchers and 10 Busch vouchers. I'm able to convert 10 Coors vouchers into a dollar, but it takes only 8 Busch vouchers to get a dollar. Which is worth more? The 10 Coors vouchers are worth $1, but the 10 Busch vouchers are worth $1.25. I can't say 10 vouchers = 10 vouchers, because one voucher buys less than the other. To normalize this discrepancy, we use a currency converter, or a park factor, to say that 10 Coors vouchers and 8 Busch vouchers have equivalent purchasing power.

The run-park factor is a currency conversion from Coors runs to NL league-average runs because the typical number of runs to earn a win is different in those environments. Walker spent half his games producing Coors runs, the other half producing NL runs. Even if he was more productive on the road, we still need to deflate the value of the home stats because the rest of the world cares about wins, and Coors runs purchase fewer wins than NL runs do. The fact that Walker did not perform better at Coors, relative to the league-wide improvement at Coors, means that his production was worth relatively less at home than away.

Suppose I buy the most expensive house on the block with a market value of $80,000 in a neighborhood where the average price is $50,000—then I have the most valuable asset of any of the houses. But if that house appreciates at a slower rate than the rest of the homes over the next ten years (say 4 percent instead of 10 percent annually), then my house will eventually be worth less than the average: $118,419 to $129,687. My house's value didn't get the same economic boost from my environment as those of other homeowners, so now that asset is worth less than other assets even though it started as the most valuable.

Similarly, Walker's observed offensive production didn't appreciate as much at Coors as most players' hitting did, so his relative value compared to those players drops. He was still tremendously valuable at Coors and overall, but not quite as valuable as the raw numbers might have you think.

Trying to project what that particular player would do in another park or league, rather than estimating the value of his performance, requires a different type of analysis because each park can have a different specific effect on players. A park may influence right-handed and left-handed batters differently. A park may have the most effect on an aspect of the game that isn't part of a player's repertoire; on the other hand, the player's skill set may be uniquely positioned to take better advantage of a park's quirks than average.

Consider Dante Bichette, an extreme flyball hitter whose statistics soared when he got to Colorado. If because of his tendencies to loft the ball he gained more in batting average and power than usual, he was more valuable in Coors than elsewhere. Suppose Bichette had hit .310/.380/.600 in raw stats, and that a clairvoyant was able to tell us that if Bichette had played in a neutral park, such as Busch Stadium, he would have hit .250/.310/.440. That's an 80 percent boost in offense, compared to the typical 20 percent to 40 percent jump. That extra run-creating ability above and beyond what's typical has real value at Coors. When we apply the regular park adjustment to Bichette's production, we might find that his park-neutral value of his Coors-enhanced performance may in fact be .280/.350/.510—higher than what the clairvoyant told us he would actually hit at sea level, reflecting the value of his taking extra advantage of Coors.

On the other hand, consider Walt Weiss, who posted OBPs of .375 or higher for several years in Colorado but had no power. Would he have done much worse at sea level? His batting average at Coors would be expected to go up because more of his groundballs would go for hits (as we showed earlier). But groundballs rarely turn into doubles and triples, so Weiss's slugging average was likely not enhanced as much as Bichette's (or indeed, an average hitter's).

The run-based park effect that we've been discussing can give you only a rough approximation, based on how the average player gained (or lost) in a particular park. It's imprecise to project those general adjustments down to specific players and say, "This is what they would have done if it weren't for the home park." It's difficult to answer that question with any certainty without a much deeper analysis of specific types of hitters. These include contact hitter versus free-swinger, righty versus lefty, and groundball versus flyball in different kinds of parks.

Since it takes more runs on average to win in a high-offense ballpark than in a low-offense ballpark, the value of a run is proportionally lessened. If a player at Coors, such as Walker, produces at the same level at home and away, then his bat is worth less at home than it is on the road. When the value of a run is taken into account, Piazza's bat was comparable in value to Walker's.

How much does Coors Field matter? It's critically important for a variety of reasons:

- For not overrating hitters with superficially superior statistics.
- For planning for how taxing it will be on a pitching staff.
- For evaluating fielding, recognizing that reaction times are lessened.
- For understanding the value of hitters and pitchers contributing toward winning.

And for Mike Piazza, it might matter even more than that. Coors Field probably cost him the 1997 NL MVP Award.

Consistent, but Not in a Good Way

Of the teams in existence during the Rockies' inaugural season, there's only one sub-.500 team that has been more consistent (defined by the standard deviation in seasonal winning percentage) than the Rockies year after year.

Most Consistent Teams Since 1993, Ranked by Lowest Standard Deviation

Team	W	L	Win %	Standard Deviation
PIT	69.4	87.4	.443	.03147
ATL	95.3	61.5	.608	.03342
LAN	82.2	74.8	.524	.03749
COL	73.0	84.2	.465	.04034
MIL	69.7	87.1	.445	.04080
NYA	93.7	62.8	.599	.04514
HOU	85.3	71.7	.543	.04660
BOS	85.9	71.0	.548	.04725
CHA	82.6	73.9	.528	.04821
TEX	78.2	78.7	.498	.05122
TOR	77.1	79.8	.491	.05209
PHI	76.8	80.2	.489	.05761
CHN	75.6	81.3	.482	.05859
BAL	76.2	80.6	.486	.05989
CIN	77.0	80.0	.490	.06063
ANA	78.8	78.1	.502	.06452
KCA	69.0	87.5	.441	.06516
SFN	85.1	71.8	.542	.06620
FLO	74.1	82.8	.472	.06675
NYN	76.8	80.0	.490	.06722
MIN	74.7	81.7	.478	.06732
SLN	84.3	72.5	.538	.06807
SDN	74.7	82.5	.475	.06826
DET	65.4	91.4	.417	.07191
CLE	85.2	71.3	.544	.07350
OAK	81.5	75.2	.520	.07813
MON	75.1	81.4	.480	.07824
SEA	81.9	74.7	.523	.08352

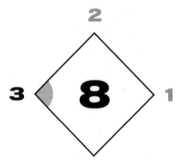

Is Wayne Huizenga a Genius?

JONAH KERI

The 1996 Florida Marlins featured an interesting blend of talent. Young, promising players such as Edgar Renteria and Charles Johnson combined with veterans Devon White, Kevin Brown, and Al Leiter to form a promising core. Just entering their prime, Gary Sheffield and Robb Nen provided power in the middle of the lineup and the back of the bullpen. Still, the team wasn't quite ready for prime time, ending the season with an 80-82 record and a third-place showing in the National League East.

Conservative tactics suggested patience. Let Renteria, Johnson, and the other kids improve gradually. Let Sheffield carry the offense, with Brown and Leiter anchoring the pitching staff. Make an opportunistic trade here or there, ideally trading high-priced older talent in exchange for younger players who could complement the team's nucleus. With a modest revenue stream from sketchy attendance and media deals, the Marlins would need to bide their time, keep stockpiling talent, then maybe look to make a run a couple years down the road.

Wayne Huizenga was having none of that. Four years removed from the team's expansion 1993 season, the Marlins owner decided the time was right to damn the torpedoes and go for it all. To bolster the pitching staff, the Marlins—led by Huizenga and General Manager Dave Dombrowski—lured Alex Fernandez to Miami with a big free-agent contract. Seeking an offensive boost, they paid big bucks for another free agent, slugging third baseman Bobby Bonilla. Three weeks later, Florida reeled another big free-agent fish, top-flight outfielder Moises Alou. In a flurry of smaller moves, the Marlins signed reliever Dennis Cook and outfielders John Cangelosi and Jim Eisenreich, adding depth to a roster that had lacked secondary talent. In all, Huizenga and the Marlins shelled out more than $89 million in the 1996–1997 off-season, a startling total for any team in that era, let alone a franchise with one of the smallest revenue streams in Major League Baseball.

Spending orgies often fail in baseball. In recent years, the Baltimore Orioles and New York Mets have spent huge sums in futile attempts to recapture past glory. After a dominant run from the mid-1990s to 2000 that included four World Series titles, the New York Yankees have remained perennial contenders the last five years but have fallen short of winning it all each time, despite payrolls that rival the gross domestic product of many third-world countries.

But for the Marlins, it worked like a charm. With strong performances from their hired guns and the emergence of several young players, they compiled a 92-70 record, making the playoffs for the first time in franchise history. When the twenty-two-year-old Renteria delivered the winning hit in Game 7 of the World Series against the Cleveland Indians, the Marlins found themselves on top of the baseball world. With young talent such as Cliff Floyd, Mark Kotsay, and Luis Castillo joining a deep team stacked with elite talent, the Marlins looked like a dynasty in the making.

And then Huizenga blew it all up. At the owner's behest, the Marlins unloaded Fernandez, Bonilla, Alou, Sheffield, Nen—virtually every veteran on the club making any kind of significant money. Not since Connie Mack sold off his top Athletics players following a stretch of three World Series titles and four AL pennants in five seasons more than eighty years earlier could anyone remember a fire sale of this magnitude under similar circumstances. The backlash across baseball was intense. Marlins fans and sportswriters across the country ripped Huizenga for being a cheapskate, claiming he was only in it for the money and didn't care about the fans or the integrity of the game.

But maybe, just maybe, Wayne Huizenga was a genius. Seeing an opening others may have missed, he made an all-out run at the sport's biggest prize and won, causing euphoria in South Florida. Then with his eye on the bottom line, he unloaded his hefty financial commitments and saved himself tens of millions of dollars in contracts. If the twin goals of baseball ownership are to win it all and turn a profit (not necessarily in that order), who's to say Huizenga did anything wrong?

The Marlins' coup raises a key question: Is there an optimal time for a team to make a run at the World Series? At first glance, the answer would appear to be a resounding yes. Winning a World Series is an arduous task fraught with uncertainty and requiring high levels of both talent and luck. Of the twenty-six World Series played since 1979, there have been nineteen different winning teams, a tribute to baseball's parity that belies Bud Selig's "hope and faith" sermon of a few years ago. Two of those nineteen waited more than eighty years before finally grabbing the brass ring.

One theory that gained traction in sabermetric circles is the notion of a success cycle. My first article for Baseball Prospectus explored this topic in detail: "The [success] cycle is a baseball continuum on which every team resides. To measure a team's place in the cycle, assess its talent in the majors and minors. Can the players in the organization, mixed with a few trade acquisitions and free agents the team could reasonably sign, yield a competitive team? More precisely, can the team expect to compete while its current core of major-league players remain productive and under contract?"

The article's main subject was the 2002 Pittsburgh Pirates. A cash-strapped team with only three solidly above-average players (Brian Giles, Jason Kendall, and Aramis Ramirez—though Kip Wells enjoyed a strong 2002 season), coming off a 100-loss season and a decade removed from their last winning record, the Pirates couldn't simply snap their fingers and make a run at winning it all. Instead, the article argued, the team needed to conserve its limited financial resources, both by avoiding big-ticket free-agent signings and by trading Giles and Kendall for a passel of young talent, major league–ready but low on service time and thus millions cheaper.

Other teams—especially those lacking top-shelf talent and in similar revenue-challenged positions—would do well to take the same advice, the article argued. Eschew desperate runs at a .500 record, since the financial returns would fall well short of the midlevel veteran salaries paid to try and reach that mark. Instead, ship out expensive parts for young, high-upside talent, build through a strong farm system, and take their shot at glory a few years down the road when all the pieces were in place.

More broadly, teams were slotted into three categories within the success cycle: rebuilding, building, and competing. *Rebuilding* teams needed to unload all their veteran stars, hoard draft picks and young players, and look down the road to their next shot at contending. Teams often call this the five-year plan, a window that gives the front office a chance to implement its plan and (presumably) deliver results later.

Building teams were one step more advanced, having gone back to square one and begun to reap dividends from their improving young core. The importance of knowing where you are in the success cycle looms large at this stage. In a follow-up to "The Success Cycle," I looked at the negative events that can occur when teams misinterpret where they are in the continuum—especially when they break the bank before their talent base merits that kind of risk. The delicate balance between a general manager's job security and the need to have a long-term vision comes into play here. It's one thing to say you have a five-year plan. It's another thing for your team to lose 90 games three years in a row, with ownership breathing down your neck, the fans getting restless, and your job at stake if the team doesn't start winning soon.

Finally, *contending* teams were those that had gone through all the necessary growing pains and were now poised to take their shot at the playoffs and (if things broke right) the World Series. At this juncture they have enough talent and trade chits available to make aggressive deals, spend money, and try to get to the promised land.

Why go through this whole painstaking cycle to reach the final goal? Because achieving that goal can have far-reaching effects for a club. Beyond the intangible glow and a World Series flag flapping in the breeze for eternity, there are real, substantial gains to be had from winning a championship. Attendance shows a marked improvement immediately following a World Series title, often lasting several years. Merchandise sales rise, and future media contracts become more lucrative. Marketing studies suggest that brand awareness, though harder to measure, increases when a team wins it all—there's no denying that Los Angeles–area residents viewed the Angels differently after the team won the World Series in 2002. Increased revenue from multiple sources coupled with a new, aggressive owner in Arte Moreno has in turn enabled the Angels to build on their success, signing stars like Vladimir Guerrero to stay atop the standings. If a contending team can understand the virtue of signing one superstar (like Pedro Martinez) instead of two overpriced second-tier players (like Carl Pavano and Jaret Wright), the chances for prolonged success rise.

A year after the initial success-cycle article came out, Derek Zumsteg wrote a follow-up article for Baseball Prospectus that refuted the theory. Teams rarely follow any kind of smooth progression in their winning and losing, he noted. History is littered with examples of teams that have remained contenders long after their rosters have aged, their payrolls have become bloated, and their farm systems have dried up. Conversely, an array of sad-sack teams have failed to progress for years—even decades—at a time, having tried and failed to assemble the young talent needed to win. While the concept of the success cycle seemed to make sense, Zumsteg's research of thirty seasons showed little discernible pattern in how teams built championship rosters: "The idea of the success cycle is seductive, like the concept of biorhythms. It appeals to our sense of larger order, and intuitively we think that teams go up and come down. But as we looked more closely for actual evidence of its existence in baseball, we found only that if there is such a thing, it is lost in the much larger forces of organizational quality, team strength, and luck."

Several teams of recent vintage have driven this point home. After years of bungling under George Steinbrenner's meddling command, the Yankees returned to their winning ways in the mid-'90s, when a nucleus of strong up-the-middle players emerged from the farm system. Those top prospects mixed with the Yankees' ability to spend for top free agents, a combination that has propelled the club to four World Series titles and several near misses in the past decade. Though the Bombers have made numerous suspect moves in recent years—including huge contracts for injury-prone pitchers Pavano and Wright—they haven't suffered much for their misdeeds. Sure, they haven't won a World Series since 2000. But they have made the playoffs in each of the past eleven seasons, a feat only one other team has managed.

That team, the Atlanta Braves, has done more to challenge the notion of a success cycle than perhaps any other ballclub. Like the Yankees of the 1950s, the Braves have proven adept at introducing one prospect into their starting lineup just about every season, ensuring that the team does not fall victim to complacency or old age. As old stars like Ron Gant, David Justice, and Terry Pendleton faded, new faces like Andruw Jones, Marcus Giles, and Rafael Furcal emerged to fill the breach. As Casey Stengel said of his Yankees in 1955, "That's a lot of bunk about them five-year building plans. Look at us. We build and win all the time." Braves GM John Schuerholz or Manager Bobby Cox could have easily said the same thing, albeit with a little less Stengelese mixed in.

When the Braves started their dynasty, they owned one of the best starting rotations in the history of the game. Like the Yankees of the

1990s, the Braves supplemented a core of exciting young talent with well-placed free agents, including the best one of all, Greg Maddux. Yet the Braves also differed from the Yankees in many ways. For one, the team's spending leveled off after AOL Time Warner assumed control of the team from maverick owner Ted Turner. The team's media revenue still allowed the Braves to retain their best players and make occasional forays into the off-season talent market. But their payroll made them an upper-middle-class team, several rungs below the Yankees' stratospheric $200-million-a-year level. The Braves also found different ways to win, going from a pitching-dominated roster to one with merely above-average pitching and an elite offense.

The Braves' coup de grace came in 2005. With Greg Maddux and Tom Glavine gone and injuries felling holdovers Chipper Jones, Johnny Estrada, and others, the Braves unleashed the full fury of their farm system on the National League. Jeff Francoeur, Ryan Langerhans, and Kelly Johnson bolstered the depleted outfield. Wilson Betemit solidified the infield. Brian McCann picked up the slack behind the plate. Shrewd trades for Jorge Sosa and Kyle Farnsworth gave the pitching staff a big lift. Pegged by many to finally cede their dominance of the division to the Phillies, Marlins, or Mets, the Braves rolled to yet another NL East crown.

What about teams dwelling in the same low-rent district as the Pirates? Several have been perennial contenders in recent years.

Though they failed to make the playoffs in 2005, the Oakland A's hung in the pennant race down to the season's final days, winning 88 games. That marked the seventh straight season the A's had won 87 games or more, with four straight playoff appearances from 2000 to 2003. As made famous in Michael Lewis's book *Moneyball,* the A's turned the trick while operating with one of the tightest budgets in the game. It took abundant creativity from A's GM Billy Beane. Taking a page from the build-and-win playbook, Beane engineered a swapfest at the 1999 trading deadline that saw Kenny Rogers, Jason Isringhausen, and Billy Taylor change teams, with the A's getting better and younger without adding significant payroll. Capitalizing on market inefficiencies, Beane grabbed freely available talent for next to nothing, gaining solid production from scrap-heap survivors. All the while, the A's got the bulk of their production from one of the best farm systems in the game. Tim Hudson, Barry Zito, Mark Mulder, Jason Giambi, Miguel Tejada, and Eric Chavez headed the list of homegrown stars who allowed the A's to win on the cheap, keep winning, and in the process flout the conventions of the success-cycle theory.

The Twins of recent vintage have done the same. Minnesota won three straight division titles from 2002 to 2004, despite being shackled by a below-average revenue stream and the skinflint spending of billionaire Carl Pohlad. General Manager Terry Ryan and his scouting and player development staff have shuttled in an army of homegrown talent. Brad Radke, Torii Hunter, and Corey Koskie played pivotal roles in the Twins' sustained success. The team found talent in other ways too: It snagged Johan Santana—the best pitcher in the American League in 2004 and 2005—through the Rule 5 draft, an avenue largely ignored by many other clubs. Though the Twins haven't sold off their stars en masse as part of any kind of rebuilding process, they have gotten younger and cheaper when needed. In dealing veterans for prospects, though, they've focused on securing top talent in return. With #1 draft pick Joe Mauer primed to take over behind the plate, the Twins nabbed a king's ransom for A. J. Pierzynski, shipping the catcher to the Giants for Joe Nathan, Boof Bonser, and Francisco Liriano. Bonser's star has dimmed a bit since then, but he remains a candidate for a future spot in the Twins' starting rotation. Meanwhile, Nathan has become an ace closer and Liriano has grown into arguably the best pitching prospect in the game.

Just as teams can challenge the notion of a success cycle through prolonged success, so too can the dogs of baseball challenge it through prolonged incompetence. Some teams talk about "building for the future," then take intelligent steps to do just that, adopting more effective methods for evaluating players, using a combination of astute scouting and skillful statistical analysis. But for others, supposed long-term plans are just an excuse to make cheap, counterproductive player moves. Building for a championship a number of years down the road is a tremendously difficult task that tends to work only if everything goes perfectly. Countless unexpected events—both positive and negative—can happen along the way. Having the flexibility to adjust to opportunities, as the Braves have done, tends to work better than X-year plans, no matter what number X represents. Like Stengel, maverick baseball owner Bill Veeck looked down on the ubiquitous five-year plan: "It has been my experience that the Youth Plans and Five-Year Plans lead not to pennants but only to new Five-Year Plans. For further details, please consult the Philadelphia Phillies." (The Phillies went thirty-five years between National League pennants from 1915 to 1950, including a thirty-one-year stretch where the team finished over .500 just once, putting up several historically awful seasons in the process.)

More recently, the Pirates haven't cleared .500 since opting to re-sign Andy Van Slyke instead of Barry Bonds after their third straight division title in 1992. When the Milwaukee Brewers went 81-81 in 2005, that marked the first time they'd reached the break-even point since '92; they haven't made the playoffs in twenty-three years. Tampa Bay Devil Rays fans haven't suffered as much—mostly because the team hasn't been around as long. Still, whether building with young talent or foolishly breaking the bank for washed-up veterans like Greg Vaughn, the Rays have been awful throughout their eight-year history, their best season a 70-91 stinker in 2004.

Few teams of this generation have had their plans foiled more than the Tigers. Detroit has gone twelve seasons without a .500 record, eighteen without a playoff berth. In an August 2004 article published on the BaseballProspectus.com Web site, Nate Silver argued that the Tigers had made positive moves to help their bottom line. In the 2003–2004 off-season, the Tigers signed midlevel free agents Rondell White and Fernando Vina, along with the top free-agent catcher on the market, Ivan Rodriguez. The moves helped the team improve by 29 games, hoisting itself up from a 43-119 season that ranked among the worst in MLB history to a 72-win campaign that saw the Tigers contend until the dog days of summer. Those signings also played a big part in boosting attendance by 40 percent, ending a sharp three-year slide after the team drew 30,000-plus fans a game in its first sea-son at newly built Comerica Park in 2000. If a team intentionally goes through a down period and fan support evaporates in the process, Sil-ver argued, attendance, concessions, merchandising, and other rev-enue streams could quickly dry up. Thus, when the rebuilding team finally wants to mount a playoff challenge, it may lack the resources to do so. The Tigers did the right thing in making moves to revive fan interest, Silver claimed, even if they had too far to go to make a legiti-mate playoff push.

A year later, in doing research for Chapter 5-2 of this book, Silver discovered some findings that contradicted his work in "The Tiger Plan." Those findings also underscored one of the key points outlined in the success-cycle concept: Teams benefit a lot more in jumping from 85 to 95 wins (and a playoff berth) than they do in going from 65 to 75. As he explained in a follow-up article called "The Tiger Plan, Re-visited": "There is a very substantial, and very non-linear, increase in local revenues that a team can expect as a result of making the play-offs. More specifically, this increase is felt over the longer term. A sin-gle playoff appearance can result in a meaningful increase in both attendance revenues and local broadcasting revenues for as many as 10 years."

If making the playoffs carries such big benefits—both psychic and financial—it should be instructive to examine how teams reach that goal. Since winning the World Series marks the pinnacle of that goal, we'll look at all the World Series winners of the Wild-Card era to see how they built their ballclubs and if we can draw any lasting lessons from their efforts. (We'll examine the 1997 Marlins last.)

1995 Atlanta Braves

Opening Day payroll, year before World Series victory (to nearest million): $40 million

Opening Day payroll, year of World Series victory: $47 million (18 percent increase)

Record, year before World Series victory: 68-46 (.596)

Key additions: Marquis Grissom

More playing time, big results: Chipper Jones, Mark Wohlers

The Braves went 68-46 in 1994. They owned the second-best record in the National League behind the division-leading Expos, leading the Wild-Card race. The labor stoppage and cancellation of the World Series marked the only time in the fifteen-year 1991-to-2005 stretch that the Braves failed to make the playoffs. A dominating pitching staff headed by Greg Maddux and Tom Glavine got stronger as John Smoltz lowered his ERA nearly a full run to 3.18, a mark that was 33 percent better than the league average. GM John Schuerholz showed his typically deft player acquisition skills, grabbing Marquis Grissom from the Expos in the off-season for 75 cents on the dollar (a.k.a. Roberto Kelly, Tony Tarasco, and Esteban Yan) when Montreal went into fire-sale mode. As usual, the farm system also played a big role: Mark Wohlers excelled in his first season as the team's closer, while Chipper Jones launched his superstar career with a great rookie season, seamlessly replacing departed former MVP Terry Pendleton. As was their wont, the Braves won not by breaking the bank for a slew of big-name free agents but by making less-heralded, intelligent deals and bringing up top prospects at the right time.

1996 New York Yankees

Opening Day payroll, year before World Series victory: $58 million

Opening Day payroll, year of World Series victory: $62 million (7 percent increase)

Record, year before World Series victory: 79-65 (.549)
Key additions: Tino Martinez, Kenny Rogers
More playing time, big results: Derek Jeter, Mariano Rivera

That paltry 7 percent boost in team payroll looks like a misprint compared to the annual bacchanalia that is today's Yankees spending. This was another team that was on the cusp, made a series of smart if not eye-catching moves, and got over the hump. The big-ticket deal saw the Yankees trade Russ Davis and Sterling Hitchcock to the Mariners for Tino Martinez, Jim Mecir, and Jeff Nelson. Though both Nelson and Martinez regressed from their huge 1995 seasons in Seattle, both provided upgrades over incumbent players and would go on to become integral parts of the 1996–2000 Yankees dynasty.

Meanwhile, Manager Joe Torre, in his first season at the helm, bestowed huge responsibility on a talented core of young players. Twenty-two-year-old rookie shortstop Derek Jeter hit .314/.370/.430, winning the AL Rookie of the Year award; twenty-four-year-old sophomore Andy Pettitte went 21-8, amassing a 3.87 ERA that was 31 percent better than league average; and Mariano Rivera put up one of the greatest seasons ever recorded by a relief pitcher, logging 107.2 innings, 130 strikeouts, and a 2.09 ERA that was a ridiculous 142 percent better than league average while setting up closer John Wetteland. The Yankees' deep stable of prospects and their willingness to give key roles to young talent while ridding themselves of older, past-their-prime players (including the beloved Don Mattingly) paved the way for the team's first World Series title in eighteen years. The erosion of their farm system would eventually catch up to the Yankees, exposing a flawed team that couldn't paper over its faults no matter how much money it spent. Luck played a role in '96 too: The Yankees barely improved their record compared to 1995 (a .569 winning percentage vs. 1995's .548) but won it all anyway after going 92-70 in the regular season, a mark that would have left them playing October golf in many other years.

1998 New York Yankees

Opening Day payroll year before World Series victory: $64 million
Opening Day payroll year of World Series victory: $68 million
    (6 percent increase)
Record year before World Series victory: 96-66 (.593)
Key additions: Chuck Knoblauch, Scott Brosius, Orlando
    Hernandez
More playing time, big results: Jorge Posada, Darryl Strawberry

The Yankees started aggressively using the fruits of their farm system to acquire key players around this time. The trade of Eric Milton, Cristian Guzman, Brian Buchanan, Danny Mota, and cash to the Twins for Chuck Knoblauch was one of the biggest deals of that ilk. The Yankees received some criticism from prospect mavens for passing on Milton (at the time regarded as one of the top pitching prospects in the game) and Guzman (a promising young shortstop prospect). Both became major league regulars, but neither came close to stardom. Meanwhile Knoblauch gave the Yankees an upper-echelon second baseman, something they'd lacked on a consistent basis since the Willie Randolph era. The trade of Kenny Rogers to the A's for Scott Brosius added great defense at third base. Though his offense would soon fade, Brosius's .300/.371/.472 line earned him a berth in the All-Star Game; his postseason heroics earned him the World Series MVP award and a permanent spot in Yankees fans' hearts. Knoblauch and Brosius added to an offensive core that used exceptional plate discipline to draw more walks than the competition, compile higher on-base percentages, get into more hitters' counts, and wear down pitchers, reaching the soft underbelly of the opposing teams' bullpens. The Yankees also used their bucks and their renown to lure Orlando "El Duque" Hernandez to the Bronx, netting a 12-4 record and a staff-best 3.13 ERA as their reward. Meanwhile, Jorge Posada wrested the starting catcher job from Joe Girardi, launching the career of a perennial All-Star and occasional MVP candidate. With Jeter and Bernie Williams in their prime; balance throughout the lineup; a starting rotation headed by Pettitte, David Cone, and David Wells; and a strong bullpen with Rivera now the closer, this was every bit the 114-win powerhouse that steamrolled all comers to claim the big prize.

1999 New York Yankees

Opening Day payroll, year before World Series victory: $68 million
Opening Day payroll, year of World Series victory: $90 million
  (32 percent increase)
Record, year before World Series victory: 114-48 (.704)
Key additions: Roger Clemens
More playing time, big results: None

Take the winningest team in decades, add the best pitcher of all time, and what do you get? Well, 16 fewer wins, but also a repeat championship, the Yankees' second in four years. This was one of Roger

Clemens's worst seasons, following two dominant years in Toronto: His 90 walks tied Cone's for most on the staff, and his 4.60 ERA was 3 percent worse than league average, the only time other than his rookie season that Clemens has ever posted an above-average ERA. Still, the team's strong nucleus remained completely intact—Jeter (.349/.438/.552) and Williams (.342/.435/.536) destroyed opposing pitchers while Rivera rode his unhittable cut fastball to another sub-2.00 ERA and playoff invincibility. That 32 percent bump in payroll suggests that the Yankees loaded up on free agents and big-ticket trades. Other than Clemens, though, the team didn't absorb any big new salaries. Instead, Williams, Cone, and others saw their salaries rise, either through advancing service time or escalating long-term contracts. This was a natural progression for a team whose core players were entering their prime or in the middle of it. Of course, smaller-revenue teams don't usually have the luxury of signing all their best players to big long-term deals, as the Yankees would do throughout this period with Williams, Jeter, Posada, and others.

2000 New York Yankees

Opening Day payroll, year before World Series victory: $90 million
Opening Day payroll, year of World Series victory: $101 million
  (12 percent increase)
Record, year before World Series victory: 98-64 (.605)
Key additions: Denny Neagle (wait—does a 5.81 ERA count as a
  key addition?)
More playing time, big results: None

The Yankees saw more salary appreciation as escalating contracts propelled total payroll over the $100 million mark. Many of the teams on this list sport an average age that fits into the twenty-five to twenty-nine peak range, as found by Bill James in his work in the annual *Baseball Abstract* books of the 1980s. Though there's some argument that better medical treatment, nutrition, and exercise programs have lately skewed that peak range a little older, that doesn't explain the Yankees' average age during their 2000 title run: 31.6 years. Brosius (age thirty-three, .230/.299/.374) and Paul O'Neill (age thirty-seven, .283/.336/.424) were fading fast, while Cone (age thirty-seven, 6.91 ERA!) was nothing short of horrific. No team in baseball history has ever won a World Series in the same year that one of its starters has pitched that poorly while starting that many games—let alone giving another 15 starts to a pitcher with a 5.81 ERA, as the Yankees did with Neagle. Few *last-place* teams hand that much playing time to two such abysmal players.

This was by far the luckiest of the World Series–winning teams of the last decade and one of the luckiest of all time. The Yankees went just 87-74 that year. The team's .540 winning percentage was the second-worst in major league history for a championship club, ahead of only the 1987 Twins at .525. Going by Pythagorean formula—a gauge developed by Bill James that measures a team's runs scored and runs allowed and provides a more reliable look at a team's true ability than its won-lost record by stripping out much of the effects of luck and 1-run games—the Yankees were even worse, at 85-76. This was a far cry from the 1998 team, which cruised to the fourth-best regular-season record of any World Series winner, thanks to a solid mix of young stars and veteran (but not yet old) talent. That the Yankees regressed so much, so fast—even while upping their payroll by 49 percent over two years—shows the precarious road even the best teams must travel to win and then keep winning. If not for a terribly weak AL East that year, the last of the Yankees' titles would never have happened.

2001 Arizona Diamondbacks

Opening Day payroll, year before World Series victory: $87 million
Opening Day payroll, year of World Series victory: $76 million
    (13 percent *decrease*)
Record, year before World Series victory: 85-77 (.525)
Key additions: Reggie Sanders, Mark Grace
More playing time, big results: Curt Schilling

This was another old team, but one whose over-thirty players—Randy Johnson, Curt Schilling, Luis Gonzalez, Steve Finley, and Reggie Sanders—were their stars, not their over-the-hill gang. Even more remarkably, the Diamondbacks reduced their Opening Day payroll by 13 percent from 2000 to 2001, one of only two teams on this list to cut salary and win it all. This wasn't the result of some fire sale or rebuilding effort but rather was due to a bunch of painful contracts expiring for chaff like Todd Stottlemyre and Bernard Gilkey. The Diamondbacks had finished third in a strong NL West in 2000, with Johnson and Gonzalez heading a talented but shallow roster. Though a lot of things went right in '01, Arizona can mostly thank two factors for the leap: Luis Gonzalez's season for the ages at age thirty-three (.325/ .429/.688, 57 homers) and a full year of Schilling after coming over midseason in 2000 from the Phillies (Schilling finished second to

Johnson in the 2001 Cy Young voting; led the league in wins, innings pitched, and complete games; finished second in ERA, strikeouts, and fewest walks per 9 innings; and shared World Series MVP honors with Johnson). Even with three of the best single-season performances of the last twenty years by Gonzalez, Schilling, and Johnson, it took a bloop single in the bottom of the ninth inning of Game 7 of the World Series against the Yankees for the Diamondbacks to claim their first championship. Yup, more luck.

2002 Anaheim Angels
Opening Day payroll, year before World Series victory: $34 million
Opening Day payroll, year of World Series victory: $61 million
   (79 percent increase)
Record, year before World Series victory: 75-87 (.463)
Key additions: Brad Fullmer, Kevin Appier
More playing time, big results: John Lackey, Francisco Rodriguez,
   Brendan Donnelly

While people often dwell on Huizenga's spending spree that led to the 1997 Marlins' title, the '02 Angels actually saw a bigger jump in their payroll. The Angels would pay the mediocre (or worse) Aaron Sele $25 million from 2002 to 2004. Sele aside, there were extenuating circumstances hiking the team's payroll—the salary shell game played out in the team's acquisition of starting pitcher Kevin Appier for lap-dance connoisseur Mo Vaughn and the big progression in salaries for players like Tim Salmon, Troy Glaus, and Troy Percival.

Any team that improves by 24 games in one season—winning a World Series in the process—has to have some luck. But the Angels deserve a world of credit for some terrific moves too. Brad Fullmer proved a bargain at $4 million, giving the club a potent .289/.357/.531 performance in the DH slot. Skipper Mike Scioscia eschewed the usual mindless, veteran-obsessed managerial protocol in favor of a true meritocracy, handing jobs to unknowns like minor league lifer Brendan Donnelly and reaping great results (2.17 ERA as a setup man). Scioscia also gave key roles to top prospects, resulting in huge late-season and playoff performances by call-ups John Lackey and Francisco Rodriguez. Coupled with near across-the-board improvement by incumbents, the Angels piled up a seemingly endless string of singles and doubles all year long and into the playoffs, winning it all while harkening back to a different era of . . . not quite Smallball but maybe Mediumball.

2003 Florida Marlins

Opening Day payroll, year before World Series victory: $48 million
Opening Day payroll, year of World Series victory: $50 million
   (4 percent increase)
Record, year before World Series victory: 79-83 (.488)
Key additions: Ivan Rodriguez, Juan Pierre, Mark Redman,
   Ugueth Urbina
More playing time, big results: Dontrelle Willis, Miguel Cabrera

In *Baseball Prospectus 2004*, I cataloged the long run of good fortune that helped the Marlins win the 2003 World Series. Among those strokes of luck:

◆ Getting Dontrelle Willis in a trade from the Cubs when he was the team's third or fourth choice for a pitching prospect;

◆ Making the team's one high-priced, off-season acquisition Ivan Rodriguez after failing to land Mike Hampton and Bartolo Colon;

◆ Changing its mind at the last moment about hoping to acquire Rondell White or Reggie Sanders at the trade deadline and going with rookie Miguel Cabrera instead;

◆ Getting stunning, lights-out performances from Ugueth Urbina, Chad Fox, and Rick Helling after acquiring them in late-season deals.

But General Manager Larry Beinfest also made a series of terrific moves: Rodriguez and Juan Pierre gave the team strong two-way threats up the middle; Mark Redman was a low-cost coup for the starting rotation; and Manager Jack McKeon, hired in-season after the team's slow start under Jeff Torborg, struck just the right tone with the young Marlins while also handling the talented young pitching staff with aplomb. The team shunned risky multiyear contracts in favor of higher-salaried, shorter-term deals like the one given to Rodriguez. It took full advantage of a strong farm system, headed by twin jewels Cabrera and Willis. In short, after that lousy start, the Marlins did just about everything right.

2004 Boston Red Sox

Opening Day payroll, year before World Series victory: $100 million
Opening Day payroll, year of World Series victory: $133 million
   (33 percent increase)
Record, year before World Series victory: 95-67 (.586)

Key additions: Curt Schilling, Keith Foulke, Mark Bellhorn,
   Orlando Cabrera
More playing time, big results: Bronson Arroyo

You'll find more details on this team than you could ever imagine by reading *Mind Game,* Baseball Prospectus's look at the 2004 Red Sox and the lessons they taught the baseball world (given some of the head-scratching moves made by several teams more recently, those lessons apparently didn't stick for long). As much as it may pain Red Sox fans to hear it, this team resembled the dominant Yankees teams of the 1990s in many ways, including a high team payroll and a terrific offense driven by a high on-base percentage. The 2003 Sox actually scored more runs than the championship team of a year later. The additions of ace starter Curt Schilling (there he is again) and ace reliever Keith Foulke played a huge role in Boston's success, further underscoring the findings in Chapter 9-3. As has become legend, though, all the Red Sox' talent and all the front office's machinations would have gone for naught if Dave Roberts had been thrown out on that fateful steal attempt in Game 4 of the ALCS.

2005 Chicago White Sox
   Opening Day payroll, year before World Series victory: $81 million
   Opening Day payroll, year of World Series victory: $75 million
      (7 percent *decrease*)
   Record, year before World Series victory: 83-79 (.512)
   Key additions: A. J. Pierzynski, Tadahito Iguchi, Jermaine Dye,
      Dustin Hermanson, Scott Podsednik
   More playing time, big results: Freddy Garcia, Jose Contreras,
      Neal Cotts, Bobby Jenks

This was arguably the best job by a general manager heading into a championship year of any on this list. The White Sox saw huge roster turnover between the 2004 and 2005 seasons—of the starting lineup's nine most frequent batters in '05, five weren't on the roster in '04. Far from some go-for-broke spending explosion, though, GM Kenny Williams actually reduced the total payroll in 2005, letting Magglio Ordonez walk as a free agent and trading the expensive (and hugely productive) Carlos Lee. The team's replacements included catcher A. J. Pierzynski and second baseman Tadahito Iguchi, who combined made just $4.5 million in '05 while posting a collective Value Over Replacement Player (VORP) of 48.6 (in other words they were worth about five wins above what fringe players would have delivered, while getting paid salaries not far above fringe levels). Jermaine Dye—who made a staggering $32 million over three years as an oft-injured free-agent bust in Oakland—finished second on the Sox and fourth among AL right fielders with a 35.6 VORP. He made just $4 million and is signed for a reasonable $5 million in 2006. Williams also nabbed the troubled but talented Bobby Jenks off the scrap heap for a song, then watched as he blossomed into a devastating closer and postseason hero.

Though the team parted ways with power hitters Ordonez and Lee, the White Sox continued to rely heavily on the longball in homer-friendly U.S. Cellular Field, finishing fifth in MLB in home runs. The emergence of Jon Garland and a full season of Freddy Garcia and Jose Contreras upgraded the starting rotation to elite status, while Jenks, young lefty Neal Cotts, and veterans Dustin Hermanson and Cliff Politte carried the load at various times for a dominant bullpen. Add the excellent defense of Podsednik, Joe Crede, and company, and this was a quintessential Earl Weaver team—one that wins with pitching, defense, and homers.

◆

At first glance, the eleven winning teams on this list would seem to share little in common. Some relied on dominant pitching (1995 Braves), others on devastating hitting (2004 Red Sox). There were younger teams (2002 Angels) and older teams (2001 Diamondbacks). There were patient teams (all the Yankees entries) and clubs filled with hackers (2005 White Sox). Most of the teams looked to be a player or two from a possible title run, with records solidly over .500 the year before their World Series wins—but the 2002 Angels as well as the '97 and '03 Marlins turned the trick following sub-.500 seasons, when no one thought they had a chance.

There may have been one common trait: luck. If, as Branch Rickey once said, luck is the residue of design, then these World Series winners must have hired some all-world design teams. From the Yankees squeaking by with 87 wins in 2000 to the Diamondbacks' World Series–winning blooper in '01 to the unremarkable Ugueth Urbina suddenly pitching for the 2003 Marlins like vintage Dennis Eckersley down the stretch, these teams all benefited from healthy doses of good fortune. Teams with a handful of top-flight pitchers may give themselves the best chance to win in the postseason (see Chapter 9-3). But when it comes to combined regular-season and playoff success, there's

no one surefire way to win it. The teams with the best chance to succeed simply start with a strong talent base, make well-placed additions, then put themselves in position to benefit from luck.

Which brings us back to our friend Wayne Huizenga and the 1997
Marlins.

1997 Florida Marlins
Opening Day payroll year before World Series victory: $31 million
Opening Day payroll year of World Series victory: $52 million
(68 percent increase)
Record, year before World Series victory: 80-82
Key additions: Alex Fernandez, Bobby Bonilla, Moises Alou
More playing time, big results: Livan Hernandez

It seems impossible that the small-revenue Marlins bought a World
Series while the big, bad Yankees barely opened their checkbooks a
year earlier, winning largely by promoting young talent, but it's the
truth. The Marlins did hand the starting second-base job to Luis
Castillo in 1997, but Castillo slugged just .270 and wasn't nearly the
on-base demon he later became. Some young players did take a step
up, notably Charles Johnson, whose 19 homers and .454 slugging average in pitcher-friendly Joe Robbie Stadium made him one of the
best offensive catchers in the league. Still, the Marlins did the deed by
adding Fernandez, Bonilla, and Alou to a core that included elite
starter Kevin Brown and star slugger Gary Sheffield. One of the
biggest challenges for a team striving to take the next step is to know
when the talent is there to warrant opening the checkbook and going
for it all. While the Marlins definitely had some top-flight talent on
board, few statistical indicators suggested greatness for the 1997
squad. The Marlins' 1996 Pythagorean record was 79-83. This was
worse than the team's actual record of 80-82, hardly portending a title-
worthy team. But just as Luis Gonzalez did four years later, Edgar
Renteria waited until the bottom of the ninth in Game 7 of the World
Series, then slapped a single that could have landed in someone's
glove if hit a little harder, or softer. More luck.

Wayne Huizenga had something extra at stake. Hoping to gain public support for a publicly financed new stadium that would boost the
team's revenue (and line his own pockets), Huizenga loaded up for
1997 to gain attention in South Florida. The ploy worked in one
sense—attendance surged 35 percent during the 1997 season, with additional revenue gains during the playoffs. Having failed to gain the

necessary assurances from local and state government even after winning it all, Huizenga dismantled the team, sending the Marlins from first to worst and paving the way for the owner to sell his controlling interest to commodities trader (and later owner of the 2004 champion Boston Red Sox) John Henry a year later.

Even without the surrounding stadium intrigue, it may have made sense for the Marlins to cut payroll—if not quite so dramatically. A lower-revenue team like the Marlins can stay competitive over a period of several years with a strong farm system and intelligent roster construction. But it's still much tougher for the Marlins and their ilk to be championship contenders for half a decade or more, as the Braves and Yankees have been since the early to mid-1990s. Teams like the A's and Twins have shown it's possible. But a few missteps—a payroll-wrecking Jermaine Dye signing here, a David Ortiz non-tender there—can have far-reaching effects on lower-revenue teams that richer clubs can more easily overcome.

The Marlins reached the pinnacle, traded away their veteran stars, and went back to building through scouting and player development. Huizenga's actions ushered in an era of fiscal conservatism in South Florida that in some ways helped the Marlins avoid the pitfalls that felled so many other teams. General Manager Dave Dombrowski would continue to build the farm system in later years, setting the stage for the Marlins to contend when new owner Jeffrey Loria rolled into town. With the help of several shrewd moves by GM Larry Beinfest and a healthy dose of luck, the Marlins improbably won another World Series just six years later.

Meanwhile, Huizenga profited from the Marlins even after he sold the team. After making his fortune as the head of Blockbuster Video, Huizenga had bought the NFL's Miami Dolphins and 50 percent of Joe Robbie Stadium in 1990. He secured the rest of the park's ownership rights four years later, after spending $10 million in renovations to allow the expansion Marlins—another Huizenga property—to play there. When Henry bought the Marlins in 1998, he inherited the highly unfavorable stadium lease Huizenga had negotiated with himself for the Marlins. Huizenga has continued to collect rent as the Marlins' landlord in renamed Pro Player Stadium. New owner, new championship team, new stadium name, same guy reaping the benefits.

Philadelphia Athletics owner and manager Connie Mack was the Huizenga prototype—he didn't mince words about it either. "What I like to do is to keep my ballclub in contention from first to fourth place until the first of July. By that time we have made enough money that we can tail off, and with a last-place ball club you don't have to raise anybody's salary. With a first-place ball club everybody wants a raise, so I can make more money finishing last than I can first." Mack was a master at building championship clubs, then cashing in. In his fifty years at the helm, the A's won nine American League pennants and five World Series titles, alternating Hall-of-Fame rosters with sandlot ensembles as Mack built and tore down teams at will.

Wayne Huizenga is in many ways the modern-day Connie Mack. But unlike Mack, Huizenga needed only five years to get his World Series. Despite claiming heavy losses, he made more from the team in 1998 after selling off his best players than he did when the Marlins won the World Series a year earlier. He then sold his team for a staggering $63.5 million profit. On top of all the money he rakes in from parking, concessions, and luxury suites at Pro Player Stadium, to this day he still receives $2 million a year from the state of Florida as part of a tax rebate he obtained when he acquired the Marlins as an expansion franchise.

So is Wayne Huizenga a genius? With apologies to sentimental types, the twin goals of a baseball team are: (a) to seize the opportunity when it arises and win the World Series and (b) to make money. Huizenga recognized that winners and losers are often separated by mere inches, the bat of an eyelash. He also saw a moneymaking opportunity, with a winning team likely to rake in the bucks and a dismantled winner likely to make more. He spent the right amount of money at the right time for the right team, with the right results. Mensa has reserved a spot for Wayne Huizenga at the head of the table.

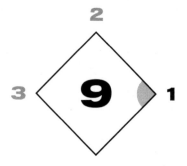

What Do Statistics Tell Us
About Steroids?

NATE SILVER

In December of 2004, with the frenzy over the BALCO investigation at its peak, Alan Schwarz of the *New York Times* asked Baseball Prospectus to assist him with an analysis of Barry Bonds and Jason Giambi. The idea was to use BP's projection system, Player Empirical Comparison and Optimization Test Algorithm (PECOTA), to compare how Bonds and Giambi might have been expected to perform based on their statistics up through 2000, against what actually happened to their careers from that point forward.

To retell the story: Entering the 2000 season, each of these players was at a career crossroads. Bonds would turn thirty-five that year— the age at which even great players can begin to struggle—and was coming off an injury-plagued season in 1999. Giambi was a slow-footed first baseman about to enter his thirties; he'd had a good season in 1999, but it looked like a career year. Instead of withering, however, both players blossomed. Giambi won the MVP Award in 2000, and Bonds set a career high in home runs, launching an upward trajectory that would see him rewrite baseball's record books. Needless to say, PECOTA found that Bonds and Giambi had far outperformed reasonable expectations. Bonds produced 142 more home runs between 2000 and 2004 than PECOTA would have guessed and hit .339 rather than the projected .272. Giambi produced 60 percent more home runs and 50 percent more RBI than PECOTA expected.

It doesn't take a fancy projection system, of course, to tell us that Bonds and Giambi had unusual career paths. Still, Schwarz's article was written fairly and thoughtfully, and he let people draw their own conclusions about Bonds, Giambi, and steroids.

Upon reflection, PECOTA's analysis may have done the sabermetric community a disservice. The analysis *seemed* to lend credibility to everyone's worst fears: Players like Giambi and Bonds have benefited from steroids, not just incrementally but by a huge margin. With 142 fewer home runs, Bonds would be chasing Jimmie Foxx and Willie McCovey, not Babe Ruth and Hank Aaron. Without those extra RBI, Giambi wouldn't have won the MVP, and the A's wouldn't have made the playoffs. *Moneyball* might never have been written.

On the other hand, lots of players have had unusual career paths, back from the days when ballplayers' drugs of choice were Schaefer Beer and Vitalis Hair Tonic. Starting in 1953, a twenty-eight-year-old Ted Kluszewski, who had averaged just 15 home runs a season to that point in his big-league career, reeled off consecutive seasons of 40, 49, and 47. In 1973, Davey Johnson, who had just turned thirty, hit 43 home runs; he had never hit more than 18 before (and would never hit more than 15 thereafter). Even Hank Aaron defied expectations. In 1971, a season in which he missed more than twenty games, he set a career high in home runs with 47. Aaron was thirty-seven years old at the time.

It is natural to tie together cause and effect. These days, it has become just as natural to attribute any unexpected change in performance to ulterior motives. Eric Gagne adds 5 mph to his fastball? He's juicing. Albert Pujols, who was considered a second-tier prospect, bursts onto the scene with a performance worthy of Joe DiMaggio? He's juicing—unless he faked his birth certificate. Sammy Sosa? Not only was he juicing, he was also corking his bat, using a laser-eye mechanism in his batting helmet, and bribing the opposing pitcher to throw him hanging sliders.

This reaction is understandable. Steroids upset a lot of people— steroids ought to upset a lot of people. They ought to upset baseball researchers as much as anybody, since we make our bread and butter out of the integrity of baseball's numbers. Nevertheless, this is one reason why sabermetricians have been reluctant to address the question of steroids. We might insist on a measured conclusion, informed by baseball's history. But steroid use is an emotional issue, and we can't guarantee that everyone will heed that warning.

Still, it seems likely that sabermetricians would have addressed the steroids question more aggressively if more statistical evidence existed. We know that Jason Giambi took steroids for some period of time, but we don't know precisely when he started or precisely when he stopped. Some reports have speculated that Giambi had used steroids prior to his MVP season in 2000. But in his testimony to the BALCO grand jury, Giambi said that he had begun using the steroid Duca Durabolin in 2001. This problem has corrected itself to some degree with the significant number of minor league players (and the much smaller number of major league players) suspended for use of steroids and other banned substances during the 2005 season. In these cases, we have a specific date associated with recent steroid use and can probably assume that the player discontinued using steroids after his positive finding, which would subject him to more frequent testing and harsher penalties for a repeat violation. These data too have their imperfections. But the information is worth examining.

We can look at the steroids question by examining the *indirect* statistical evidence. I am very much against the notion that a sudden improvement in performance by any one particular player is necessarily indicative of steroid use. In fact, such "inexplicable" performance jumps are common enough throughout baseball's history that it is safe to conclude that the vast majority of them have nothing to do with steroids. However, if on a macroscopic level there are more performance jumps than there used to be, that might tell us that something is amiss.

The Indirect Evidence

One way to examine this question is by looking at what I'll call a Power Spike. A Power Spike occurs when a player "suddenly" starts hitting home runs more frequently than he used to. More specifically, we can define a Power Spike as follows:

- ◆ A player is an established major league veteran, at least twenty-eight years old, with at least 1,000 plate appearances (PA) accumulated among his previous three seasons; and
- ◆ The player improves upon his established home-run rate by at least 10 HR per 650 PA, in a season in which he had at least 500 PA.

We can look at the frequency of Power Spikes throughout different eras in baseball's recent history. Although there are many permutations in how we might define such eras, I prefer the following:

- *Golden Age (1949–1957).* Runs from the complete reestablishment of baseball following World War II until the movement of the Giants and Dodgers from New York to California in the 1958 season. A last period of stability featuring relatively high levels of offense.
- *Expansion Era (1958–1969).* Coincides with the westward expansion of baseball, the expansion in the number of franchises (from sixteen to twenty-four during this period), and the full racial expansion of the sport. The instability off the field is paralleled by instability in offensive levels, which varied maniacally from year to year.
- *Dynasty Era (1970–1976).* The period immediately preceding the implementation of full-blown free agency in 1977. Three great dynasties—those of the Cincinnati Reds, Oakland A's, and Baltimore Orioles—accounted for six of the seven World Series championships during the period and nine of the sixteen league pennants. Offense was relatively low, prompting the American League to implement the DH in 1973.
- *Balanced Era (1977–1985).* The 1977 season was marked by a sharp increase in offense as a result of the expansion to twenty-six clubs and a new manufacturer of baseballs. The offensive improvement brought the game back into balance, and the era is remembered for the wide variety of styles that prospered during the period.
- *Canseco Era (1986–1993).* Begins with Jose Canseco's Rookie of the Year award in 1986 and ends with the last full season before the 1994 strike. The Canseco Era saw the resumption of large year-to-year fluctuations in offensive levels. The 1987 season, in particular, featured the highest levels of run scoring seen in either league since the 1950s.
- *Juiced Era (1994–2004).* One of the great boom periods in baseball history, along with the Roaring '20s. Offensive levels improved sharply between 1993 and 1995, escalated further in 1999, and have remained high since then. Associated with small ballparks, small strike zones, and the allegation of widespread steroid usage.

Table 9-1.1 provides the average number of runs and home runs produced per game in each era.

TABLE 9-1.1 Average Number of Runs and Home Runs Produced per Game in Different Eras

Era	American League		National League	
	R/G	HR/G	R/G	HR/G
Golden Age (1949–1957)	4.50	0.73	4.48	0.89
Expansion Era (1958–1969)	4.09	0.86	4.11	0.81
Dynasty Era (1970–1976)	4.03	0.73	4.11	0.71
Balanced Era (1977–1985)	4.44	0.85	4.10	0.69
Canseco Era (1986–1993)	4.50	0.89	4.15	0.77
Juiced Era (1994–2004)	5.06	1.12	4.68	1.04

Tracking the number of Power Spikes is relatively simple, once we have these definitions in place. Figure 9-1.1 presents the frequency of Power Spikes per 100 eligible hitters in each of our six eras. The dashed line in Figure 9-1.1 indicates the average frequency of Power Spikes between 1949 and 1993—about 5.8 per 100 hitters. Since 1994, the frequency has increased to 9.1 per 100 hitters. Just how much emphasis you want to place on the increase is a matter of perspective. Power Spikes have been 57 percent more common during the Juiced Era than they had been previously, which is certainly statistically significant. On the other hand, some number of Power Spikes has always occurred, and the difference amounts to only a handful of "extra" Power Spikes per season.

In some sense, however, Figure 9-1.1 is telling us something that we already knew. We know that there has been an increase in home runs in recent seasons, and that somebody has to be responsible for providing those extra home runs. If home runs have become easier to hit for some reason *other* than steroids, be it smaller ballparks, inferior pitching, juiced baseballs, or something else, then Power Spikes will be easier to come by.

In fact, if we rerun the numbers to account for macroscopic changes to the offensive environment, then the increase in Power Spikes disappears. Figure 9-1.2 presents the same information but incorporates an adjustment for league and park effects rather than using raw totals. More specifically, all the historical home run numbers are adjusted to the standards of the 2004 American League. There were about 20 percent more home runs hit per game in the 2004 AL,

FIGURE 9-1.1 Power Spikes per 100 hitters in different eras

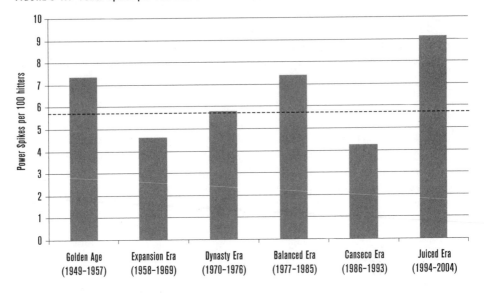

FIGURE 9-1.2 Power Spikes per 100 hitters in different eras, adjusted for park and league effects

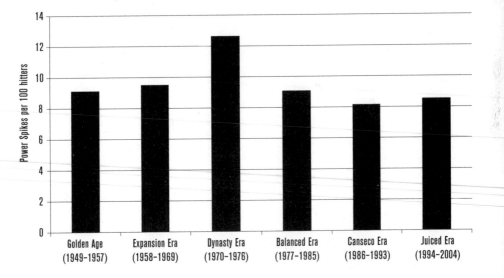

for example, than there were in 1986. So a player who hit 30 home runs in 1986 is credited with 36 adjusted home runs (20 percent more). An identical technique is applied to account for park effects (Figure 9-1.2).

By this definition, Power Spikes have been neither any more nor any less frequent in the Juiced Era than in previous periods. Instead, the period that stands out is the Dynasty Era of the early and mid-'70s, which interestingly enough corresponds with the widespread introduction of "greenies" (amphetamines) into major league clubhouses.

Then again, perhaps the league adjustment is not the right thing to do after all. This gets to what I call a "chicken-and-egg" problem: Are there more home runs hit because there are more Power Spikes? Or are there more Power Spikes because there are more home runs?

One way to refocus the question is to look at which hitters are responsible for the increase in home runs. Are home runs up because shortstops who look like Bugs Bunny are suddenly turning in 20-homer seasons? Because players like Barry Bonds and Mark McGwire, who were already very good, have taken their power output to unprecedented levels? Or is the difference felt universally—a rising tide lifts all boats?

Figure 9-1.3 returns to the unadjusted data set but breaks the frequency of Power Spikes down based on the number of home runs that the player had hit previously. We call this his "established" home-run rate—his frequency of home runs per 650 PA in the three seasons before the Power Spike occurred. The figure is further broken down between the Juiced Era and the "Pre-Juiced" years of 1949–1993.

FIGURE 9-1.3 Power Spikes per 100 hitters, compared to established home-run rates, 1949–1993 and post-1993

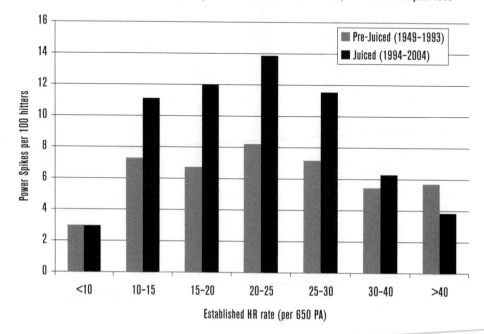

This figure reveals something very interesting: Power Spikes have occurred more frequently in the Juiced Era, but the increase in frequency is almost entirely attributable to *certain types* of hitters. In particular, Power Spikes have become more frequent among hitters with average power—those guys who will hit more than 10 home runs but fewer than 30 in a typical season. Power Spikes have *not* become more frequent among hitters who have no power at all. It has never been very common for a hitter who has a weak, slap-hitting swing to transform into a power threat, and it is no more common today.

But there is also no increase in Power Spikes among players who were already very good power hitters, capable of hitting at least 30 home runs per year. Sometimes a very good power hitter will turn into an insanely great one, as Bonds and McGwire did. But this is no more common today than it had been previously. The players who have been most responsible for the Juiced Era home-run boom are the middle-of-the-road players: those guys who used to hit 15 or 20 homers a season and are now hitting 25 or 30.

The typical steroid user might not be the prima donna slugger who endorses Budweiser between innings but the "hardworking late bloomer" who is struggling to maintain his spot in the lineup or is trying to leverage a good season into a big free-agent contract.

Certainly these players might have more economic incentive to enhance their performance, as compared to their counterparts who have already signed multiyear, guaranteed major league contracts. Among professional athletes, the decision about whether to use steroids is not a result of locker-room peer pressure but rather a relatively rational calculation about the medical, moral, and financial costs and the risk of getting caught as compared to the potential upside. In that sense, it is just like any other form of cheating. The anonymous minor leaguer profiled in Will Carroll's book *The Juice*, who used steroids at a time when he was struggling to maintain his status as a credible major league prospect, expressed this calculation succinctly: "Look, if you told me shooting bull piss was going to get me ten more home runs, fine."

It may also be that, whether or not they are more inclined to use steroids, marginal players have the most to gain from them. Steroids are used to help a player develop his musculature and physique. It is conceivably easier for steroids to turn a relatively weaker, smaller player into a bigger, stronger player than it is for steroids to turn a player who is already very big and very strong into some sort of super-hero.

The Direct Evidence

At least seventy-six players in professional baseball were suspended for testing positive for the use of steroids or other performance-enhancing drugs during the 2005 season, including sixty-five minor leaguers and eleven major leaguers. The list of suspended players is revealing:

- The players are generally not an impressive lot. Of the sixty-five minor leaguers suspended, none made the Baseball Prospectus Top 50 prospects list prior to the 2005 season, and only one made the *Baseball America* Top 100 prospects list (Oakland A's outfielder Javier Herrera, who ranked sixty-eighth). Of the eleven players suspended under the major league policy, only one—Rafael Palmeiro—has ever appeared in the All-Star game.
- Although most people assume that hitters stand the most to gain from steroids, nearly half of the suspended players (36 of 76) were pitchers.

We'll return to the pitchers in a moment, but let's first compare the performances of the position players before and after their suspensions. In particular, we'll use a tool called the Davenport Translations (DTs), which convert minor league performances into their major league equivalents. For example, in 2004, Milwaukee Brewers prospect Rickie Weeks spent most of the season at Huntsville in the Double-A Southern League, where he posted a raw batting line (AVG/OBP/SLG) of .259/.366/.407. The DT associated with these statistics, which adjusts for the comparative difficulty of the Southern League relative to the majors, as well as league and park effects associated with playing in Huntsville, was .240/.330/.382. Weeks made the majors as a regular in 2005, where he put up a .239/.331/.394 batting line in Milwaukee—a dead match for his DT from the previous season. (The DTs are explained in more detail in Chapter 7-2.)

The DTs do not ordinarily incorporate an adjustment for player age, but I have included one here. The reason is that most of the suspended players were young prospects, and we'd ordinarily expect a young prospect to improve his performance from season to season. If a prospect posted the same DT batting line as a twenty-two-year-old that he did as a twenty-one-year-old, he'd be losing ground relative to other players at his age, and his prospect status would dim. Thus, the DTs displayed here include an additional adjustment for the average improvement (or decline) for a player of his given age.

Table 9-1.2 (on the following page) presents the before-and-after comparison of the suspended players. The "before" category consists of a player's translated batting statistics in 2004, and in any games he played in 2005 prior to his suspension, while the "after" category includes his 2005 statistics after his suspension. Note that the vast majority of players were suspended at or near the start of the season for a positive steroid test in spring training. Note also that a sizable minority of players were released after their positive tests and did not appear in organized baseball at all in 2005; these players are not included in the table. The statistics presented are equivalent AVG, OBP, and SLG as well as their companion summary statistic, Equivalent Average (EqA), which is designed to operate on the same scale as batting average but account for all facets of offensive performance (for example, a .300 EqA is a very good one, a .260 EqA is average, and a .220 EqA is poor by major league standards).

There is no immediately obvious trend here. Certainly, a few players like Herrera and Cubs third-base prospect Matt Craig posted dramatically worse numbers after their steroid suspensions. But other players actually saw their performances improve—the Devil Rays' Alex Sanchez and White Sox' Jorge Toca are some obvious examples. A summary of the average change in EqBA, EqOBP, EqSLG, and EqA is presented in Table 9-1.3. These results are weighted by plate appearances—more specifically, the minimum number of plate appearances between the "before" and "after" categories. For example, although Rafael Palmeiro performed terribly after his suspension, he also received only a handful of at-bats, and so his performance is not accounted for heavily in the average.

TABLE 9-1.3 Weighted Average Change in Performance Among Suspended Position Players

Batting average	−.010
On-base percentage	−.014
Slugging average	−.006
Equivalent average	−.009

The players did exhibit a decline in performance after their suspensions; the change is just on the verge of being statistically significant. Interestingly, the players' on-base percentages suffered more than their slugging averages, suggesting that steroids may affect a batter's overall game rather than just his power output. In certain ways, this is an impressive finding.

Nevertheless, we don't see a systematic, large-scale change. If you subtracted 14 points of OBP and 6 points of SLG from Barry Bonds's batting statistics during his 2001–2004 seasons, he'd still have been far and away the best player in the league. That doesn't rule out the

TABLE 9-1.2 Performance of Players Suspended for Substance Abuse, Before and After Suspensions

Player	Organization	Date of Suspension	Before Suspension (incl. 2004)					After Suspension				
			PA	EqAVG	EqOBP	EqSLG	EqA	PA	EqAVG	EqOBP	EqSLG	EqA
Alex Sanchez	Devil Rays	4/3/05	349	.324	.340	.386	.257	194	.321	.359	.424	.270
Baltazar Lopez	Angels	4/4/05	252	.266	.314	.436	.258	202	.197	.249	.229	.177
David Castillo	A's	4/4/05	463	.200	.290	.312	.217	98	.135	.197	.190	.146
Javier Herrera	A's	4/4/05	280	.276	.316	.434	.263	392	.219	.288	.356	.229
Jesus Guzman	Mariners	4/4/05	484	.269	.339	.376	.251	494	.235	.298	.361	.228
Justin Hatcher	Rangers	4/4/05	222	.228	.297	.312	.220	319	.206	.243	.232	.176
Lizahio Baez	Rangers	4/4/05	89	.200	.242	.319	.198	338	.194	.227	.348	.199
Luis Perez	A's	4/4/05	341	.233	.288	.317	.219	369	.235	.264	.365	.215
Matthew Craig	Cubs	4/4/05	424	.257	.338	.478	.277	349	.235	.289	.408	.239
Neil Wilson	Rockies	4/4/05	358	.183	.243	.297	.196	313	.194	.240	.333	.200
Omar Falcon	Mariners	4/4/05	175	.162	.228	.260	.175	156	.210	.301	.340	.223
Oscar Bernard	Cubs	4/4/05	131	.191	.208	.253	.172	234	.184	.216	.251	.165
Robinson Chirinos	Cubs	4/4/05	347	.215	.271	.356	.221	245	.227	.271	.335	.209
Ryan Christianson	Mariners	4/4/05	303	.251	.305	.372	.239	313	.223	.295	.336	.225
Ryan Leahy	Angels	4/4/05	199	.210	.261	.237	.187	283	.209	.270	.274	.197
Jon Nunnally	Pirates	4/6/05	274	.171	.263	.270	.201	226	.169	.243	.266	.191
Tom Evans	Pirates	4/6/05	134	.245	.315	.368	.242	379	.218	.291	.355	.230
Jorge Piedra	Rockies	4/11/05	478	.275	.314	.443	.260	314	.270	.328	.470	.270
Adam Seuss	Astros	4/22/05	458	.233	.300	.335	.229	93	.119	.194	.177	.142
Eider Torres	Indians	4/22/05	530	.274	.304	.367	.247	395	.257	.285	.373	.238
Gary Cates Jr.	Orioles*	4/22/05	499	.242	.276	.321	.218	373	.236	.287	.302	.215

Name	Team	Date										
James Jurries	Braves	4/22/05	465	.251	.316	.478	.266	357	.253	.326	.480	.274
Rafael Diaz	Orioles	4/22/05	305	.185	.207	.212	.163	146	.148	.166	.169	.126
Jamal Strong	Mariners	4/26/05	325	.288	.374	.358	.270	378	.283	.344	.370	.263
Darnell McDonald	Indians	5/6/05	523	.206	.267	.312	.212	326	.253	.301	.413	.250
Guillermo Rodriguez	Giants	5/12/05	271	.166	.217	.283	.184	192	.207	.240	.316	.200
Jonathan Herrera	Rockies	5/12/05	434	.225	.271	.308	.211	367	.208	.249	.251	.183
Jorge Toca	White Sox	5/12/05	350	.240	.256	.365	.215	331	.265	.305	.428	.251
Robert Valido	White Sox	5/12/05	627	.223	.267	.302	.213	375	.228	.244	.337	.214
Josh Pressley	Royals	5/13/05	513	.255	.334	.364	.250	354	.254	.321	.415	.255
Luis Ugueto	Royals	5/13/05	483	.237	.299	.361	.238	194	.178	.259	.327	.214
Wilson Delgado	Marlins	5/13/05	645	.234	.287	.317	.217	235	.223	.263	.313	.205
Rafael Palmeiro	Orioles	8/1/05	650	.271	.369	.465	.290	28	.079	.145	.117	.109
Michael Morse	Mariners	9/7/05	650	.269	.327	.434	.261	21	.186	.223	.186	.151

possibility that steroids have made a much larger difference in some isolated cases, which in turn might depend on the type and quality of the steroid employed and the duration of use. But there are also probably cases in which steroids had the opposite of their desired effect: The player lost reflex speed with increased musculature, he got a "bad batch" of his drug, or the side effects outweighed the performance-enhancing benefits. For every Jason Giambi, there is also a Jeremy Giambi—the brother of the fallen superstar who also admitted to steroid use, and whose performance fell far short of expectations.

We perform the same study for the suspended pitchers in Table 9-1.4. As in the case of the position players, all statistics are based on our DT system and include an additional adjustment for player age. The categories evaluated are ERA as well as a pitcher's key peripheral statistics: his strikeout, walk, and home-run rates per 9 innings pitched.

As for the position players, there are a wide variety of outcomes following the suspension. Padres prospect Clay Hensley, suspended in spring training, had a spectacular season in 2005, going from a second-tier prospect to one of the better relievers in the National League. On the other hand, pitchers like the Braves' Ricardo Rodriguez went from being legitimate prospects to complete washouts. The average change in performance, weighted based on the minimum number of innings pitched between the "before" and "after" time periods, is included in Table 9-1.5.

TABLE 9-1.5 Weighted Average Change in Performance Among Suspended Pitchers

Walk rate	+0.3 per 9 IP
Strikeout rate	−0.1 per 9 IP
Home-run rate	+0.2 per 9 IP
Earned run average	+0.13

The pitchers' performance changed in the "right" direction—they gave up a few more walks, runs, and homers while striking out slightly fewer batters after their suspension. But the effect is tiny and would not be considered statistically significant by any standard test. It also may be that we're looking in the wrong category for a performance change. According to Baseball Prospectus's Will Carroll, the primary benefit of steroid use for pitchers is in stamina and recovery time, meaning that the pitchers might be able to go fewer days between relief appearances or start a game on shorter rest. Thus, it might not be that steroids allow the pitcher to pitch better but that they allow him to pitch more often. It is worth noting that most of the suspended pitchers were relievers.

What We Know and What We Don't

It is still very early in the life cycle of the steroids question. I am writing this in October 2005, just after the first season in which major

TABLE 9-1.4 Performance of Pitchers Suspended for Substance Abuse, Before and After Suspensions

Pitcher	Organization	Date of Suspension	Before Suspension (incl. 2004)					After Suspension				
			IP	EqBB9	EqK9	EqHR9	EqERA	IP	EqBB9	EqK9	EqHR9	EqERA
Clay Hensley	Padres	4/4/05	148.7	2.9	4.8	1.2	5.39	127.3	2.5	5.4	0.7	3.64
Damian Moss	Mariners	4/4/05	114.3	6.7	5.1	1.1	6.85	128.7	5.0	4.6	0.8	5.06
Darwin Soto	Mariners	4/4/05	63.7	4.0	4.7	0.4	4.81	22.7	4.8	5.1	0.4	6.27
Elvis Avendano	A's	4/4/05	67.7	3.1	3.9	0.9	5.05	54.3	3.2	4.8	1.6	5.97
Francisco Cordova	Angels	4/4/05	48.0	5.8	2.4	1.7	7.88	81.7	4.3	4.3	1.8	6.06
Jason Diangelo	Rockies	4/4/05	50.7	4.3	5.7	1.4	5.51	69.3	4.4	5.2	2.5	7.35
Nathan Sevier	Padres	4/4/05	65.7	3.0	4.8	0.5	4.39	47.3	2.3	5.1	1.3	5.27
Renee Cortez	Mariners	4/4/05	50.7	4.3	5.9	1.8	5.68	60.3	3.8	6.5	0.8	4.87
Troy Cate	Mariners	4/4/05	74.0	3.4	4.6	1.8	6.39	40.0	6.5	6.9	0.2	4.92
William Collazo	Angels	4/4/05	140.3	2.6	4.2	1.1	5.23	88.3	4.3	4.9	3.0	7.83
Brian Mallette	Pirates	4/6/05	41.0	2.9	5.9	0.2	3.18	34.7	5.6	5.9	1.8	5.82
Agustin Montero	Rangers	4/20/05	89.3	5.4	6.7	1.7	6.35	43.0	7.0	6.1	1.7	6.55
Grant Roberts	Mets	4/22/05	5.0	9.0	1.8	3.6	13.50	22.0	8.1	4.9	1.2	6.51
Ricardo Rodriguez	Braves	4/22/05	56.3	3.0	7.0	1.1	4.55	68.3	6.2	4.6	2.2	7.59
Richard Salazar	Orioles	4/22/05	3.0	18.0	9.0	6.0	15.00	41.3	6.1	5.1	1.5	5.96
Juan Rincon	Twins	5/2/05	91.3	3.4	10.9	0.4	2.66	63.3	3.4	9.2	0.3	3.06
Brian Mazone	Giants	5/12/05	43.7	2.5	4.9	1.0	4.95	95.7	3.1	4.0	1.2	5.29
Christian Parker	Rockies	5/12/05	68.7	3.5	4.1	0.8	5.31	88.7	3.6	2.9	0.9	5.58
Oscar Montero	Giants	5/12/05	14.7	1.8	8.0	0.0	3.07	34.0	7.8	7.4	2.6	6.84
Steve Smyth	A's	5/12/05	96.3	7.4	4.8	2.0	7.57	40.3	6.8	3.6	1.8	7.99
Jeremy Cummings	Cardinals	5/13/05	102.3	3.7	4.6	1.9	5.89	96.3	3.4	5.1	1.8	5.53
Rafael Betancourt	Indians	7/8/05	103.0	2.4	9.3	0.7	3.28	30.3	4.6	10.0	0.9	3.71
Ryan Franklin	Mariners	8/2/05	320.7	2.8	4.4	1.3	4.98	65.3	2.0	3.9	1.3	5.01

leaguers were subject to suspensions for steroid use and the first season in which the names of minor league violators were disclosed publicly. Perhaps more than any other issue we've explored in this book, the effect of steroids is a subject that we should understand far better in ten years' time than we do now.

Nevertheless, it is worth accounting for what we can say objectively about steroids and their effects on player performance, based on the information we've been able to gather to date.

Unexplained Changes in Performance Are the Norm, Not the Exception

This might seem outside the scope of the steroids issue itself, but it is a tremendously important point of context. As I describe in Chapter 7-3 on player forecasting, both statheads and "ordinary" fans tend to underestimate the haphazardness of player performance from season to season. "Inexplicable" changes in performance have always been relatively common and may be the result of anything from a new batting stance to LASIK eye surgery to a tippling player finding Jesus and cutting out his drinking and carousing. More often, they may be the result of simple luck. This same caution applies at a league-wide level. While present levels of offense are high, they are not materially higher than they have been during other sustained periods in baseball history, such as the 1920s and the early 1950s.

Relatively Few Players Are Steroid Users

Eleven major league players tested positive for steroids in 2005 out of approximately 750 on major league rosters, or somewhere between 1 and 2 percent. A similarly small fraction of minor league players tested positive. This low figure may partly be the result of the deterrent effect of the existing steroids testing program and the public "outing" of violators. However, even during the 2003 major league season, when steroid tests were anonymous and there were no suspensions associated with steroid use, only about 6 percent of major leaguers tested positive. Similarly, an analysis of power breakouts during recent seasons suggests that they have become only slightly more common than in years past—no more than three or four "extra" Power Spikes per season among major league veterans. One steroid user, of course, is one too many. But there is no evidence that points to an epidemic of steroid use, as former players such as Jose Canseco and the late Ken Caminiti have alleged.

Marginal Players Are More Inclined Than Star Performers to Use Steroids

On this point, we have both direct and indirect evidence. The list of players suspended during the 2005 season contains few elite prospects and even fewer elite major leaguers. Meanwhile, the increase in home-run output in recent seasons has been almost entirely attributable to average players, who would ordinarily hit between 10 and 30 home runs per season, and not players who were already outstanding power hitters.

The reason that marginal players are more inclined to use steroids is because they stand more to gain from doing so. Baseball, like any other modern economy, is characterized by a large gap between rich and comparatively poor players. In 2004, for example, a majority of major league payroll was allocated to fewer than one hundred players, and most of this money was tied up in guaranteed, long-term contracts. Players have tremendous incentive to break into this economic elite by receiving a lucrative free-agent contract, by whatever means may be at their disposal. There is a similarly important gap in compensation between the major and minor leagues. In 2005, the minimum salary for a major leaguer was $317,000, while the minimum salary for a Triple-A player was $12,900. A player who is considered a fringe prospect will have more incentive to use steroids than one who is good enough to be essentially guaranteed a major league job.

The Average Performance Improvement from Steroid Use Is Detectable but Small

Our study of performance for confirmed steroid users during the 2005 season suggests that the effects of steroid use are small—perhaps an average gain of 10 points of AVG, OBP, and SLG for a position player. The gains for pitchers were even smaller and fell below the threshold of statistical significance. Although the effects may be much larger in isolated instances, they are negligible in most cases and may be negative in others.

◆

Anything beyond these points is speculation. Frustratingly, this includes the question of exactly how much benefit players like Giambi, Palmeiro, and Bonds have derived from using steroids. We cannot rule out the possibility that these players have gained tremendously from steroids. There may be a few players for whom steroids represent a "tipping point," allowing a relatively minor gain in muscle strength, bat speed, or recovery time to translate into a dramatically improved performance.

However, it is best to reserve judgment on these players. Not in the "innocent until proven guilty" spirit; the evidence that Giambi, Palmeiro, and Bonds have used steroids would hold up in a court of law (though Bonds has testified that he used one such substance contrary to how a player seeking performance enhancement would use it). Rather, I mean it in the conservative sense of the scientific method: We cannot reject the null hypothesis that the spectacular performances of players like Barry Bonds is the result of something far different than steroid use, such as good, old-fashioned determination and hard work. One of the beauties of baseball is its unpredictability. Every time we thought we'd seen everything, we see something else, whether it's the Red Sox and White Sox winning the World Series in consecutive seasons or a thirty-six-year-old shattering the home run record. In the Juiced Era, we have the right to be skeptical, but it would be a shame if we've become so cynical that we can no longer enjoy these achievements.

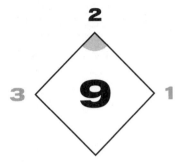

What Does Mike Redmond Know About Tom Glavine?

JAMES CLICK

Every time a television or radio crew talks about how a player is "10 for his last 25" or has "3 hits in 5 career at-bats against this pitcher," the immediate reaction shouldn't be awe of his success or mastery over the pitcher but rather skepticism because of the sample size. Five at-bats tell us virtually nothing about a player's true abilities. Consider the case of Mike Redmond versus Tom Glavine. The elastic backup catcher (often stuck in that role even though he was better than the ostensibly superior starter) Redmond had batted .285/.347/.362 (AVG/OBP/SLG) over parts of seven seasons from 1998 to 2004. The most at-bats he had gotten in any season was 256 in 2002.

Tom Glavine is one of the great left-handed pitchers of the last twenty years. Through 2004, he had amassed an ERA under 3.50 in nearly 4,000 career innings despite pitching in one of baseball's most offensively bloated eras. He had won two Cy Young Awards, made nine All-Star appearances, and earned nearly 300 wins. Yet Redmond, the unworthy backup, has somehow hit .438/.471/.604 against Glavine in 48 career at-bats. Does Mike Redmond *own* Tom Glavine? If he could hit against Glavine all the time, would Redmond be in the Hall of Fame?

Twenty-five at-bats, or the 48 Redmond has against Glavine, tell us very little about a player's actual abilities. In 2004, Barry Bonds had one stretch of 48 at-bats in which he hit .074 and slugged .111. Matchups like Redmond-Glavine, with results so out of line with our expectations, are simply the result of the small sample size. "Sample size" is a phrase statisticians use to describe the amount of information upon which one is basing a conclusion. The smaller the sample size, the more likely it reflects nothing more than random chance. The larger the sample size, the more it reflects reality. For example, we could conduct a survey of chain smokers to determine how great the incidence of lung cancer is among them. If we surveyed only three smokers, we might find that they were all perfectly healthy despite inhaling four packs a day. Should we then conclude that heavy smoking poses no danger to our health? If we expanded the survey to include one hundred or one thousand such smokers, we might find that our original three nicotine addicts are part of a tiny minority. Likewise in baseball, if a batter is 2-for-4 in a game, is he a .500 hitter? In that game he is, but none of us believe he will maintain that performance. Twenty-five or 50 at-bats tell us little more.

Through 2004, Redmond was a career .284 hitter, while Glavine had allowed all opposing batters a .254 average. Based on those two numbers, we should expect Redmond to hit about .275 against Glavine. The probability of Redmond's hitting .438 or better against Glavine in 48 at-bats is only 0.5 percent. Does this mean that Redmond's performance is *not* the random result of a small sample size? Does Redmond have some particular advantage? Has he spotted something in Glavine's motion that no one else sees, or is Glavine's best pitch Redmond's best pitch to hit? It would seem that there's a 99.5 percent chance that the answers are yes, but we still haven't answered these questions for sure.

Let's examine all batters that Glavine has faced at least 50 times, a group of seventy-three hitters who've hit a composite .287 against him. (Note that this batting average is higher than Glavine's career AVG allowed, most likely because the group of players who've stayed in the National League long enough to collect 50 plate appearances against Glavine [or anyone] includes a disproportionate number of very good hitters.) Of those seventy-three hitters, Redmond leads the pack with a .438 batting average (though he only has 48 at-bats, Redmond has exceeded 50 plate appearances against Glavine), while Mariano Duncan, out of the big leagues since 1997, brings up the rear at .145. Notable hitters such as Bobby Abreu (.172) and Sammy Sosa (.234) also trail well behind the pack, outplayed by the likes of Robby Thompson (.393) and Tim Wallach (.367). While it's clear that some very good hitters have struggled and some very bad hitters have succeeded against Glavine in the past, we have yet to confirm whether a trend like Redmond's will continue, as it should if he truly has some special ability to hit Glavine.

To help us answer this question, we can use a statistical tool called standard deviation. "Standard deviation" is a term statisticians use to indicate the average spread of a bunch of data points—how far any one measurement is likely to be from the midpoint. While the formula is complicated and involves many Greek letters, one simple rule of thumb is that in a randomly distributed sample—a bell curve, to normal humans—a little over two-thirds of the measurements will fall within one standard deviation of the mean. To put this in baseball terms, if the league batting average is .270, and your team's standard deviation in batting average is .030, then about two-thirds of your players can be expected to finish between .240 and .300. If the standard deviation suddenly soars to .060, then the bulk of your players are spread out between .210 and .330—in other words, you're the San Francisco Giants.

Normally standard deviation is taken by sampling the data, but a stat like batting average is a special case because it's a binomial distribution. A binomial distribution involves values that can be only one of two values, hence "binomial." With batting average, an at-bat ends in a hit or it doesn't. (If the player walks, the plate appearance doesn't count as an at-bat.) With statistics like batting average, the standard deviation can be found using a formula based on individual batting average and the number of at-bats.

What does it tell us if the batter is within one standard deviation of his batting average? Standard deviation gives us a range of likely values and tells us how likely each value is. In the case of a 50-at-bat sample, the standard deviation is going to be around 60–65 points of batting average. That means that a batter who bats .438 in 50 at-bats is 68 percent likely to bat between .378 and .498 over his next 50 at-bats. In the case of Glavine versus those 73 batters whom he faced at least 50 times in his career, standard deviation tells us that we should expect about 68 percent of the values to fall within one standard deviation of Glavine's overall .287 average allowed and 95 percent of the values to fall within two standard deviations. Inside that range, any differences in batter performance against Glavine are most likely the result of the small sample sizes, *not* any batter's particular skill. The same rule applies for 100, 200, or any number of at-bats, but as the at-bats increase, the standard deviation decreases. If Redmond hits .438

against Glavine in 50 at-bats, that's more than likely the result of sample size. If he does it over 500 at-bats, then the chance that Redmond is actually a .285 hitter who just got lucky is virtually nil.

This distribution of batting averages isn't unique to Glavine; it is a result of the natural distribution inherent in a binomial distribution. This is not unlike flipping a coin. If we flip a coin 50 times, we cannot be certain that it's going to end up heads 25 times. The standard deviation formula tells us that in any set of 50 tosses, we should expect it to land on heads 21 to 29 times 68 percent of the time and between 18 and 32 times 95 percent of the time. If we don't get 25 heads every 50 flips, that doesn't mean the coin isn't a fair coin; it's just a result of not having a large enough sample size. Runs of 35, 40, or even 45 heads in 50 tosses do occasionally happen. If they didn't, flipping a coin would not be a random process.

Of Glavine's 73 hitters, 50 of them (68.5 percent) fall within one standard deviation of .287, and 71 of them (97.3 percent) fall within two. (On-base percentage—another binomial distribution—has a similar distribution.) Because this distribution matches the expected range so closely, it means that even the statistical outliers—averages like Redmond that fall way outside the expected range—are probably random. They are the result of sample size, not skill. Going forward, there is no statistical reason to expect Redmond to hit any better against Glavine than Mariano Duncan did.

Other batter-pitcher matchups follow a similar pattern, but we must acknowledge that there is a bit of a selection bias: Only pitchers who have long careers face a single batter as many as 50 times. Unfortunately for our study, the longer the career, the better the pitcher. Therefore, the randomness in batting performance may simply be a result of the best pitchers pitching consistently well against everyone. Perhaps mediocre pitchers have weaknesses that make the opposing batters' success rates against them less random. To check this, we can reduce the minimum plate appearances to 25 and look at Glavine and other great pitchers' distributions again, as well as some of the lesser luminaries of the 1990s. The results are in Table 9-2.1.

This list is restricted to pitchers who faced at least ten thousand batters, but their ability levels vary greatly, from Roger Clemens and Greg Maddux down to Bobby Witt and Terry Mulholland. In general, while every player has his demons—Tony Gwynn hit .429/.485/.538 against Maddux; Greg Gagne never got a hit off Roger Clemens—the variety of performance of the batters closely resembles that of a random binomial distribution. Because of this distribution, the statistical

TABLE 9-2.1 Batter Performances Within Given Standard Deviations for Notable Pitchers (minimum 25 plate appearances)

Pitcher	1 SD (%)	2 SD (%)	Batters	Low	High
John Burkett	59.2	95.2	125	.033	.487
Roger Clemens	64.8	92.4	173	.000	.435
Tom Glavine	67.5	94.8	125	.032	.480
Randy Johnson	70.5	94.9	173	.000	.452
Greg Maddux	68.8	94.5	173	.059	.500
Terry Mulholland	65.7	94.1	102	.103	.486
Kenny Rogers	73.7	97.1	137	.087	.511
David Wells	72.4	97.8	134	.121	.455
Bobby Witt	66.4	96.0	125	.108	.542

evidence can't prove that the difference in individual batter-pitcher matchups is not random. Almost certainly, Mike Redmond doesn't own Tom Glavine. He was just lucky.

Does this mean that all batter-pitcher matchups are random, and success in baseball is just the luck of the draw? Absolutely not. Batters and pitchers display a variety of talent levels over their careers. The difference in the performance of a list of batters against a particular pitcher centers on that pitcher's talent level. For example, while our sample group of batters hit .287 off Tom Glavine, the same sample group—who hit for a .282 average overall—would likely hit for a much higher batting average against a worse pitcher. But the variation in any one batter's performance against any one pitcher is more randomly distributed than is commonly assumed. When we look at the problem from the batter's perspective—for example, how Barry Bonds (or a hitter of similar longevity) performs against a variety of pitchers—the results are the same.

This doesn't mean that players cannot abuse their opponents' weaknesses. While the divergences from expected performance in individual batter-pitcher matchups are largely the result of the randomness inherent in small sample sizes, there are characteristics of batters and pitchers that can help predict future performance. The most common is the handedness of players, which leads many managers to divide playing time between two or more players, usually deploying left-handed batters against right-handed pitchers and vice versa. Originally referred to as a "shift" or "two-platoon," the idea of platooning has been around since the game's early days. Though many managers—including Earl Weaver, author of the managerial bible *Weaver on Strategy*—cite Casey Stengel as the inventor of platooning, the technique was employed by earlier managers such as George Stallings and John McGraw. These and other managers realized they could improve a player's overall performance by playing him only in situations in which he was more likely to succeed.

Among recent players, A's third baseman Eric Chavez is one of the more notorious specimens of the effect of handedness on performance. A four-time Gold Glove winner, Chavez earned a six-year, $66 million contract in the spring of 2004 after slugging over .500 for three straight seasons and showing consistent improvement at getting on base. But he had a glaring hole in his game: he couldn't hit left-handed pitching at all. In 2002, Chavez hit .301/.379/.571 against righties and .209/.261/.362 against lefties. In 2003, it was .312/.387/.567 and .220/.271/.403. Any southpaw could turn one of the game's great young hitters into Neifi Perez just by striding to the mound with a ball in his hand.

Will Chavez's struggles against left-handers continue? We've already seen that a particular batter-pitcher matchup yields no predictive information, but perhaps if we view players on a more general basis—grouping by handedness rather than by individual player—we can see some trends emerge. For example, in 2004, left-handed batters hit .259/.334/.406 against left-handed pitchers but .273/.354/.451 against righties. Righties hit .262/.320/.417 against right-handed pitchers and .269/.340/.443 against southpaws. Table 9-2.2 shows how batters perform against pitchers, broken down by their handedness. For example, in 2004, lefty batters hit 14 points higher against right-handed pitchers than they did against southpaws. Likewise, they hit 20 points higher in OBP and 45 points higher in SLG. Conversely, right-handed batters hit for 7 fewer points in AVG, 20 fewer points in OBP, and 26 fewer points in SLG. In every case, batters perform significantly better against pitchers of the opposite handedness.

TABLE 9-2.2 Difference in Batter Performance Against Right-Handed Pitchers

Year	Left-Handed Batters			Right-Handed Batters		
	AVG	OBP	SLG	AVG	OBP	SLG
2004	.014	.020	.045	−.007	−.020	−.026
2003	.022	.032	.056	−.017	−.027	−.038
2002	.026	.034	.052	−.005	−.015	−.016
2001	.016	.022	.049	−.012	−.022	−.030

This should surprise no one; managers have long exploited these tendencies in attempts to win games. New relievers may be brought in several times in an inning because of their handedness; batters get days off against particularly tough pitchers of the same handedness in favor of opposite-handed batters of inferior talent. On the whole, handedness is highly predictive, but there has been some debate about how predictive it is for individual batters. When the A's signed Eric Karros in 2004, GM Billy Beane justified the move by saying that Karros "has been very, very good against lefties." The numbers supported Oakland's decision: Karros had hit .310/.391/.450 and .369/.444/.550 against southpaws in 2002 and 2003, respectively. But he tanked with the A's, hitting only .210/.265/.339 in 62 at-bats in 2004 before they released him.

Could Beane have seen this coming? In a 2004 column, ESPN.com's Rob Neyer cited two studies—one from Bill James's *Historical Baseball Abstracts* and another by independent statistical analyst Mitchel Lichtman—demonstrating that while individual left-handed batters show consistent platoon splits from year to year, right-handed batters show a significantly stronger regression to the mean. Neyer concluded, "In fact, if every [right-handed] player played enough games—thousands and thousands of games, I mean—eventually all of them would have roughly the same platoon split. There is some evidence that some types of hitters will have slightly larger platoon splits than others, but essentially they're all the same." If this theory is correct, then the A's should have expected Karros's split to return to the league average—.017/.027/.038 in 2003 (see Table 9-2.1)—rather than the .125/.159/.154 difference Karros displayed in 2003.

Previous methods of checking for consistency in platoon splits have separated right-handed batters into two groups—those that have exceeded the league average platoon split and those that haven't—and then followed how those groups do in subsequent seasons. This method doesn't quite answer the question surrounding Beane's signing of Karros because it placed very similar hitters—those just above or below the average—in two distinct groups, while the A's believed they were signing a batter who showed a distinct skill so far removed from the average that it could be expected to continue. The problem, once again, is small sample size. Not only are there significantly fewer lefty pitchers in baseball generally, they are also pitching fewer innings than in past decades. As a result, right-handed batters total fewer PAs against lefties than ever before. Just as we cannot read anything into 50 at-bats between Glavine and Redmond, we cannot place much faith in Karros's 100 PAs against left-handers in 2003.

To combat this problem, we can instead break a player's career into two halves, yielding much larger sample sizes. But, because many factors change over a career—for instance, a player's skills, his competition, and his park—taking first and second halves of a career could give us skewed data. Instead, we'll employ a technique used by Keith Woolner and break a player's career into even- and odd-numbered years. Then, restricting the list to batters with at least 1,000 career at-bats in both even and odd years, we can compare the platoon splits in each half of a batter's career. For example, in odd numbered years, Karros's platoon advantage was .028/.038/.031; in even years, it was .030/.054/.019. This is a very consistent difference. But is Karros the rule or the exception?

To compare large groups of data, a statistical tool called the coefficient of determination—commonly referred to as R-squared—provides a handy measure of how much one group of data explains another. R-squared is on a scale of 0 to 1; an R-squared of zero means the two groups of data are completely unrelated, while 1 indicates a perfect correlation. For example, a player's performance compared to his uniform number would have an R-squared of 0.

In the case of our right-handed batters, the correlation of their batting averages from one half of their careers to the other is .0053, almost completely random. In OBP and SLG, R-squared is .0171 and .0302, meaning that even over an entire career, righties show no consistent platoon split from year to year. For left-handed batters, the story is slightly different. Lefty batters have correlations of .0587, .0693, and .0943 in average, on-base percentage, and slugging. These are still quite low. While we can say that left-handed batters show significantly more consistent platoon splits from year to year than right-handed batters, their splits still involve a high degree of randomness.

As Neyer and others have pointed out, if Beane signed Karros based on the assumption that his platoon splits from the previous two seasons would continue, Beane made a critical error. Any general manager who signs a player based on his individual platoon splits is crediting him with a skill no batter has definitively possessed. This is not to say that no batter shows platoon splits, only that the league-average platoon splits are a better predictor of performance than an individual player's splits. Over the years, left-handed batters have shown significantly larger platoon splits than right-handed batters (theories about this discrepancy abound, but few are even theoretically testable), but any one hitter's variation from year to year must be random.

Meaningless numbers abound. TV announcers can hardly get through a tight late-inning situation these days without remarking that a certain batter is 6-for-11 against the relief pitcher and wondering why the manager isn't striding to the mound to rescue the poor schlub from certain disaster. Viewers are left to wonder whether the manager has picked the worst possible moment to show some tough love or is simply an ignoramus. But in fact, he should stay in the dugout: 6-for-11 tells you nothing.

By the same token, a left-handed hitter who has never hit lefty pitchers very well but is suddenly on a season-long tear against them will often explain that he is seeing the ball better or the hitting coach has fixed some minor flaw in his swing. But next season, his vision will almost certainly get worse or his swing will pick up a new flaw. Platoon splits are consistent on a league-wide basis but highly unpredictable for individual players.

The future of platooning lies in using player characteristics that aren't already part of traditional assumptions about player performance. Rather than simple left-right platooning, teams should look into other differences like groundball-flyball, speed-power, or, as Stengel suggested long ago, different pitches. For example, Stengel would substitute a batter of the same handedness as the pitcher if he knew that batter's particular hitting ability—for instance, being able to hit a curveball or changeup—was a better predictor of performance than handedness. As he said, "If [the opposition has] a right-handed hitter who can't hit an overhanded curve ball [at bat], and you've got a right-handed pitcher in there who hasn't got an overhand curve, don't you think you might be better off with a left-hander who has?"

Baseball has never absorbed this insight, but the data to perform such analysis is now becoming available. Once it does, rather than seeing managers shuttle in an endless series of alternate-handed relievers, teams may take advantage of other platoon characteristics. Platooning and matchups are all about maximizing the resources at a team's and manager's disposal in order to gain the incremental advantages that over a long season bring a few more wins.

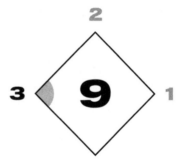

Why Doesn't Billy Beane's Shit Work in the Playoffs?

NATE SILVER AND DAYN PERRY

In 1963—with wars ongoing in Vietnam, Sudan, Tibet, Malaysia, Angola, and the Congo and relations between the United States and the USSR deteriorating in the wake of the Cuban Missile Crisis—J. David Singer, a professor of political science at the University of Michigan, embarked on an important effort. Singer's endeavor, the Correlates of War Project, was designed to collect as much data as possible about different types of wars and the states that fought them. The data Singer and his colleagues collected were to be distributed freely, available for research scientists worldwide.

Singer's rationale was as follows: War, while perhaps the most fundamental and persistent problem in political science, is notoriously difficult to predict and even more difficult to prevent. What's more, quantifiable data on war was hard to come by, especially in the days before the Internet. There was no census of wars before Singer came along. There wasn't even any consensus about what constituted a war and what didn't. Setting up a standardized database, Singer hoped, would enable researchers to focus their efforts on studying the causes of war rather than spending their time collecting data. It would be a Manhattan Project for social scientists.

Singer's project quickly gained traction within the research community and has by any definition been a tremendous success. The

Correlates of War data set has been used, among other things, to show that democracies rarely go to war with one another and that nations that are trading partners are unlikely to engage in armed conflict. The project is still ongoing today, and its massive collection of data can be downloaded by anyone with an Internet connection.

What does any of this have to do with Billy Beane?

With Beane as their general manager, the Oakland A's have earned the lavish praise of the statistically inclined for succeeding through the use of quantitative analysis and despite tightly constrained budgets. From 2000 through 2003, the A's averaged 98 wins per season and made four consecutive postseason appearances despite annual payrolls that ranked twenty-fifth, twenty-ninth, twenty-eighth, and twenty-sixth in the major leagues, respectively.

Yet Beane's teams have been pilloried for flopping year after year in the postseason. Not only have they never advanced past the first round of the playoffs, but they've lost all of their series in galling fashion. In 2000, defensively challenged center fielder Terrence Long lost a flyball in the sun, allowing the Yankees to score a critical run; the A's lost the series 3 games to 2. In 2001, Jeremy Giambi infamously failed to slide and was tagged out at the plate after a Derek Jeter no-look relay flip. In 2002, Billy Koch gave up a home run to the Twins' A. J. Pierzynski in the ninth inning that provided the margin of defeat in the deciding game of the American League Division Series. The following year, Oakland allowed the Red Sox to come back from down 2 games to none to win in 5, taking the final 3 games of the series by a total of 4 runs.

To hear some tell it, the A's have been serial victims of bad luck. Others argue that recent A's teams have been improperly constructed for success in the postseason. Beane himself seems flummoxed over their failures. As he said in the best-selling book *Moneyball*, "My shit doesn't work in the playoffs." Baseball analysts have had a similar reaction. While we have exhausted a lot of energy debating what *doesn't* work in the playoffs, we have thrown up our hands when it comes to explaining what *does* work.

As seriously as we might take the game, it is many degrees less important than armed conflict. But baseball, particularly postseason baseball, has one thing in common with war: It's very hard to predict. Every supposed rule—"defense wins championships," "you have to play Smallball to win," "an experienced team performs better in the playoffs"—has far too many exceptions. (For counterexamples, we need look no further than the last three World Champions. The 2003 Marlins rated as a below-average defensive club, the 2004 Red Sox disdained Smallball, and the 2005 White Sox had almost no post-season experience.)

The strategy that we'll use in our statistical dig borrows from Singer. We will collect every variable about postseason teams that we can think of and see what relates to postseason success and what doesn't. When trying to explain a phenomenon with so many moving parts—like postseason baseball—it helps to have as much information as possible at our disposal.

That there is a great deal of luck involved in the playoffs is an incontrovertible mathematical fact. While it takes 162 games to sort out who is the better team in the regular season, a playoff series can be decided in as few as 3 games. Moreover, while there are both good and bad teams in the regular season, those teams that reach the playoffs are closely bunched together in ability level.

We can estimate the probability of one team's beating another using something known as the log-5 method, introduced by Bill James in the 1981 *Baseball Abstract*. The log-5 method has been demonstrated empirically to be a highly accurate method of predicting the likelihood of one team's beating another. Log-5 estimates, for example, that a great team that goes 100-62 in the regular season (.617 winning percentage) will beat a good team that goes 90-72 (.556) about 56 percent of the time. This is before accounting for home-field advantage. The home-field advantage in baseball is small as compared with other sports but is very consistent throughout time. Historically, the home team has won roughly an extra 4 percent of the time; about 54 percent of all baseball games are won by the home team. Thus, we add 4 percent to the win probability of whichever team is playing at home.

It is relatively easy to extrapolate this method to determine which team is likely to prevail in a postseason series. For example, a 100-win team with the home-field advantage should win a 5-game series against a 90-win team 63.1 percent of the time; it should win a 7-game series 64.5 percent of the time. This is a discernible advantage, but the lesser team will still prevail more than one-third of the time as a result of luck alone. The overall short-series win probabilities, given teams of various ability levels, are shown in Table 9-3.1.

Although the advantage can become more substantial when a particularly good team faces a particularly mediocre one—the 2005 Cardinals-Padres series comes to mind—there are few big upsets in postseason play. We can also evaluate the various permutations to estimate a team's odds of winning the World Series. Table 9-3.2 presents these estimates for the 2005 postseason.

TABLE 9-3.1 Win Probabilities of Different Team's in Playoff Series

Five-Game Series: Probability of Home Team Winning (%)

| | | Away Team | | | |
	.700	.650	.600	.550	.500
.700 (113-49)	51.5	62.1	71.2	78.7	84.8
.650 (105-57)	40.9	51.5	61.4	70.2	77.8
.600 (97-65)	31.6	41.5	51.5	61.0	69.7
.550 (89-73)	23.7	32.5	42.0	51.5	60.8
.500 (81-81)	17.3	24.7	33.1	42.1	51.5

(Home Team)

Seven-Game Series: Probability of Home Team Winning (%)

| | | Away Team | | | |
	.700	.650	.600	.550	.500
.700 (113-49)	51.3	63.5	73.8	82.0	88.2
.650 (105-57)	38.9	51.3	62.7	72.8	81.0
.600 (97-65)	28.3	39.7	51.3	62.3	72.2
.550 (89-73)	19.8	29.4	40.1	51.3	62.1
.500 (81-81)	13.3	20.9	30.0	40.4	51.3

(Home Team)

TABLE 9-3.2 Team Odds at End of Regular Season of Winning 2005 World Series

	Regular Season W-L	Win LDS (%)	Win LCS (%)	Win WS (%)
Cardinals	100-62 (.617)	71.7	46.9	25.3
White Sox	99-63 (.611)	56.3	32.0	18.7
Angels	95-67 (.586)	51.5	24.0	12.7
Red Sox	95-67 (.586)	43.7	21.3	11.3
Yankees	95-67 (.586)	48.5	22.6	12.0
Braves	90-72 (.556)	52.7	21.5	8.6
Astros	89-73 (.549)	47.3	20.2	7.9
Padres	82-80 (.506)	28.3	11.4	3.4

Under the current playoff format—which requires three series wins to claim the World Series title—it is rare for any team to have more than a 25 or 30 percent chance of winning the whole enchilada. This is something that first-place-or-bust owners like George Steinbrenner would do well to keep in mind. Billy Beane's A's didn't merely fail to win it all—they lost four straight times in the ALDS. While none of their opponents were pushovers, the A's were favored based on regular-season winning percentage on all four occasions (Table 9-3.3).

TABLE 9-3.3 Oakland A's Playoff Odds, 2000–2003

Year	W-L	Opponent	A's Win %
2000	91-70	vs. Yankees (87-74)	56.2
2001	102-60	at Yankees (95-65)	55.7
2002	103-59	vs. Twins (94-67)	61.6
2003	96-66	vs. Red Sox (95-67)	52.7

The probability of the A's losing all four of these series consecutively is 3.5 percent, or odds of about 27-to-1 against. Since we're only talking about four playoff series, we've got a small sample size that limits our ability to extrapolate meaning from these losses. But a 27-to-1 shot is unlikely enough that it's still worth exploring whether there was something in particular about the A's that made them less equipped for postseason play than their regular-season record would suggest.

First, however, we need to settle on a definition of postseason success. Ideally, we'd want to give the highest scores to teams that win the World Series but also give partial credit to teams that win a series or two before bowing out. Similarly, it would be useful to account for the margin of victory; the 2005 White Sox, who lost just 1 game in their postseason run, should get more credit than the 1985 Royals, who managed to squeak by the Blue Jays and the Cardinals by a 4-3 margin. The metric that we'll use is Playoff Success Points (PSP), a handy invention that assigns credit to teams as follows:

- ◆ 3 points for making the playoffs
- ◆ 3 points for winning the LDS
- ◆ 4 points for winning the LCS
- ◆ 4 points for winning the World Series
- ◆ 1 point for each postseason win
- ◆ −1 point for each postseason loss

The highest possible PSP is 25, for a team that sweeps through all 11 postseason games. The lowest is 0, for a team that gets its 3-point spot for making the playoffs, but fritters it away by being swept out of the LDS in 3 games. The system is intuitively consistent. The "worst" possible World Series team, a team that plays the maximum number of games in each of its postseason series, receives 17 points. Meanwhile, a team that sweeps through the LDS and LCS but loses the World Series in 7 games receives a PSP of 16. Playoff Success Points for the teams in the memorable 2003 postseason are listed in Table 9-3.4.

Let's start our study of the Correlates of Playoff Success by looking at the most fundamental of all measures: wins and losses, and runs scored and allowed during the regular season. (Runs scored and allowed are normalized for league and park effects. The 1972 A's, who scored 3.9 runs per game in a league that averaged 3.5 runs per game, had a better offense than the 2005 White Sox, who scored 4.6 runs a game in a league that averaged 4.8.) Our study covers the 180 teams that made the postseason between 1972 and 1995. The correlations between these statistics and Playoff Success Points are as follows:

TABLE 9-3.4 Team Playoff Success Points, 2003

Team	PSP
Marlins	19
Yankees	11
Red Sox	6
Cubs	6
A's	2
Braves	2
Giants	1
Twins	1

W-L percentage	.22
Runs scored/game	.00
Runs allowed/game	.22

We've introduced correlation coefficient to you already. It is a measure of the correspondence between two variables, and runs on a scale from –1.0 to 1.0, where 1.0 represents a perfectly linear relationship, –1.0 represents a perfect *inverse* relationship, and zero represents no relationship at all (randomness). The first thing to notice is that the relationship between regular-season and playoff success is not very strong. The correlation between winning percentage and PSP is .22, which is a lot closer to zero than it is to 1. However, this should not be a surprise given the high degree of luck that the structure of postseason play introduces. Still, we shouldn't be too quick to discard small but positive statistical relationships, given all the possible variables that could be in play.

Besides, there is something far more interesting going on here. While *preventing* runs correlates with postseason success, *scoring* them does not. There is literally no relationship between regular-season offense and postseason success in our data set; the correlation is 0.0014—in other words, it doesn't exist.

As far as we're aware, this finding has never been reported before. What's strange is that it isn't that hard to detect, even without the sophisticated math:

◆ Since 1972, there have been twenty-seven teams that made the postseason in spite of having below-average offenses. Of these, seven won the World Series: the 1985 Royals, 1987 Twins, 1990 Reds, 1995 Braves, 1996 Yankees, 2000 Yankees, and 2005 White Sox. All of these teams, except the 1987 Twins, had excellent pitching staffs; it's hard to make the playoffs with a below-average offense *unless* you have an excellent pitching staff.

◆ Conversely, twenty teams have made the postseason with below-average run prevention. *None* of them won the World Series, and only two (the 1982 Brewers and 1993 Phillies) even played for the championship. Sixteen of the twenty lost the first playoff series in which they played.

Does this mean that defense really does win championships after all? The short answer is yes, probably.

The long answer requires a bit of qualification. First, we don't buy that the quality of an offense is of *no* importance in the playoffs. If the World Series were played tomorrow between a team that scored 6 runs a game in the regular season and a team that scored 4, it would take an awful lot of pitching to get us to bet on the Little Engine That Could. What has probably happened is that offense was swallowed up by the myriad other factors that come into play in the playoffs.

What does seem clear is the *diminished* importance of offense in the playoffs. When we first came across this finding, that run prevention tends to prevail in the postseason, several of us at Baseball Prospectus discussed its implications. The consensus was that the playoff schedule provides for extra off days, since teams get a day off any time they travel from city to city. These off days then tip the balance in favor of pitching, since the staff is better rested and the team can assign more innings to its best pitchers. You'll hear this explanation pretty often, both from statheads and in the mainstream press.

Unfortunately, it doesn't really help us. It's true that the extra off days are an important structural element of the playoffs. However, that should reward top-heavy pitching staffs like that of the 2005 Astros, as opposed to well-balanced ones. It shouldn't make Roy Oswalt pitch any better against Paul Konerko in October than he would in July.

What else is different between the regular season and the playoffs? Well, the weather is cooler in October. That should lower run scoring a bit, since hitters like hot, humid days. But that ought to affect everyone just about evenly. It shouldn't reward good run-prevention teams at the expense of good offenses.

In fact, the most important structural difference between the playoffs and the regular season is so obvious that people often fail to consider it: *There aren't any bad teams in the playoffs.* There are teams with average offenses but great pitching and teams with average pitching but great offenses. But you'll almost never see a legitimately bad offense or a legitimately bad pitching staff in the playoffs; those teams don't make the cut.

The question we should ask is what happens when great pitching faces off against great hitting in the *regular* season. Does run prevention tend to dominate then too? We ran a search through our databases for teams that had great pitching but average offenses and a parallel search for teams that had great offenses but average pitching. The idea is to see what happened when these teams played against one another. This isn't as easy as you might think; you need to find a "great pitching, average offense" team in the same year and the same league as a "great offense, average pitching" team. Still, we were able to identify twenty-eight pitching-versus-hitting pairings from the birth of modern baseball in 1901 through 2005. The pairings are listed in Table 9-3.5, along with the regular-season records of the teams in question. The table compares what actually happened in the season series against what we would have expected based on the log-5 method. For example, we would have expected the 1924 Pirates, a great pitching team, to go 11-11 against the New York Giants, an evenly matched great hitting team. Instead, the Pirates won the season series 13-9.

All told, we would have expected the great pitching teams to go 230-238 against the great offenses (the offense-oriented teams in our sample were slightly stronger on average). Instead, they went 241-227. That represents a swing of 11 games, or an extra win 2 to 3 percent of the time. That isn't a large advantage, but it's consistent with what we'd expect based on our study of the postseason.

The difference probably has to do with the nonlinear nature of run scoring. Scoring runs in baseball requires stringing together singles, walks, and extra-base hits; it doesn't do any good to draw a leadoff walk if you get stuck at first base. Research has indicated that good pitchers do allow their fair share of extra hits and walks when they're facing good hitters. However, the pitchers may be able to distribute those hits evenly enough to mitigate the damage and avoid their translating into increased run scoring; they can render the hitters less than the sum of their parts. It isn't that good pitchers have a structural

TABLE 9-3.5 Pitching-Heavy vs. Offense-Heavy Regular-Season Team Matchups, 1901-2005

	Great Pitching, Average Offense			Great Offense, Average Pitching		
Year	Team (W-L)	Expected Wins	Actual Wins	Team (W-L)	Expected Wins	Actual Wins
1905	Cubs (92-61)	12	12	Phillies (83-69)	9	9
1907	Cubs (107-44)	14	12	Pirates (91-63)	8	10
1908	Indians (90-64)	11	13	Tigers (90-63)	11	9
1912	Senators (91-61)	10	7	A's (90-62)	10	13
1913	Indians (86-66)	10	9	A's (96-57)	12	13
1916	Dodgers (94-60)	11	15	Giants (94-59)	11	7
1921	Pirates (90-63)	11	10	Browns (87-66)	10	11
1924	Pirates (90-63)	11	13	Giants (93-60)	11	9
1931	A's (107-45)	13	11	Yankees (94-59)	9	11
1943	Tigers (78-76)	10	13	Senators (84-69)	12	9
1953	Braves (92-62)	9	9	Dodgers (105-49)	13	13
1955	White Sox (91-63)	13	14	Tigers (79-75)	9	8
1956	Indians (88-66)	10	10	Yankees (97-57)	12	12
1962	Pirates (93-68)	8	7	Giants (103-62)	10	11
1962	Pirates (93-68)	8	8	Dodgers (102-63)	10	10
1962	Cardinals (84-78)	7	9	Giants (103-62)	11	9
1962	Cardinals (84-78)	7	11	Dodgers (102-63)	11	7
1965	Dodgers (97-65)	10	12	Reds (89-73)	8	6
1972	Cubs (85-70)	5	8	Reds (95-59)	7	4
1976	Dodgers (92-70)	8	5	Reds (102-60)	10	13
1987	Blue Jays (96-66)	6	6	Tigers (98-64)	7	7
1993	Braves (104-58)	7	6	Phillies (97-65)	5	6
1994	Braves (68-46)	3	3	Astros (66-49)	3	3
1994	Orioles (63-49)	4	4	Yankees (70-43)	6	6
2002	Braves (101-59)	3	5	Cardinals (97-65)	3	1
2003	Mariners (93-69)	3	2	Red Sox (95-67)	4	5
2003	Giants (100-61)	3	4	Braves (101-61)	3	2
2005	White Sox (99-63)	3	3	Yankees (95-67)	3	3
	Total	**230**	**241**	**Total**	**238**	**227**

advantage against good *hitters,* but that good pitchers have a structural advantage against good-hitting *teams.* That advantage comes to the forefront in the playoffs, when all the teams can hit pretty well.

Perhaps offense as a whole isn't quite as important in the playoffs, but some particular offensive statistics are? For that matter, which pitching statistics are the greatest drivers of playoff success? Figure 9-

3.1 presents the correlations between PSP and twenty-six different measures of team quality. All statistics are normalized for league and park effects.

FIGURE 9-3.1 Correlations between Playoff Success Points and twenty-six different measures of team quality

Summary Measures	Correlation
W-L %	.22
Pythagorean W-L %	.20
Runs Scored	.00
Runs Allowed	.22
Offense	
Batting Average	.04
Isolated Power	.01
Unintentional Walk Rate	.02
Strikeout Rate	-.01
Speed Score	-.01
Stolen Base Attempts	.13
Sacrifice Hits	-.07
% of Runs Scored on HR	.04
VORP for Top 3 Hitters	-.01
Clutch Hitting Wins (Chapter 1-2)	.00
Pitching and Defense	
VORP for All Starting Pitchers	.20
VORP for Top 3 Starters	.18
VORP for #1 Starter	.15
Reliever WXRL (Chapter 2-2)	.13
Closer WXRL	.22
Opponents' Batting Average	.23
Pitcher Strikeout Rate	.13
Pitcher Walk Rate	-.06
Home Runs Allowed	.09
Fielding Runs Above Average	.16
Unearned Runs/Game	.16
Miscellaneous	
W-L % After August 31	-.09
W-L % in 1-Run Games	.04
Team Age	.04
Team Playoff Experience	.12

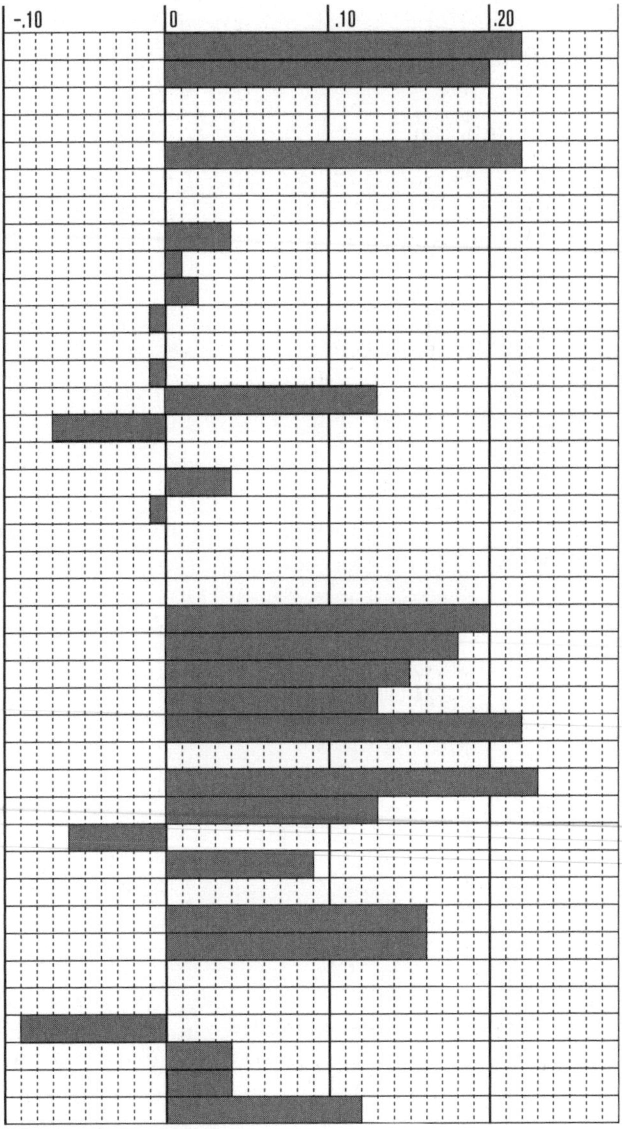

Summary Measures of Team Quality

We've already discussed the summary metrics. The only new thing to look at is Pythagorean won-lost record, an estimate of what a team's winning percentage "should" be based on its runs scored and runs allowed. Pythagorean record doesn't correlate any better with PSP than regular old winning percentage does. This might be considered surprising, since Pythagorean record has been demonstrated to be a slightly more accurate predictor of *regular-season* performance than straight won-lost record. But we should not make too much of this, as the difference between the two figures is small. Also, teams that outperform their Pythagorean record tend to have good bullpens, while teams that underperform it have poor ones. If the bullpen takes on extra importance in the playoffs, then Pythagorean record may be misleading.

Offensive Measures

Just as run production as a whole hasn't had much relationship with playoff success, neither have any of the individual offensive metrics. The A's postseason struggles have sometimes been attributed to their tendency to rely on walks and home runs, but there is no evidence that teams that play Smallball instead fare better in the postseason. Although stolen-base attempts have a slight (but statistically insignificant) positive relationship with PSP, sacrifice-hit attempts have a slight negative one. Speed Score, a composite of five different offensive statistics that provides evidence about a player's wheels, has no relationship with PSP at all. Nor do teams that hit well in the clutch in the regular season see that advantage carry forward into the playoffs.

Pitching and Defense

There is a lot more to look at here. We can first try to test the proposition that it's especially important to have three great starters in the postseason, since the extra off days the schedule provides will allow those three to make a disproportionate number of starts. Indeed, the top three starters are relatively more important in the playoffs, but we still do a little bit better if we look at the starting pitching as a whole:

- Correlation between top-three starting pitcher VORP and PSP: .18
- Correlation between non-top-three starting pitcher VORP and PSP: .11
- Correlation between all starting pitcher VORP and PSP: .20

It's worth remembering that the "other" starting pitchers do pitch some in the playoffs. Most of today's playoff teams prefer a four-man rotation to trotting pitchers out on short rest, and extraneous starters may be useful out of the bullpen.

Where we see a stronger effect is in the bullpen. The relationship between the closer's Win Expectancy, adjusted for replacement level and the opposing lineup (WXRL, also known as the increase in the probability of a pitcher's team's going on to win the game given the game situation; see Chapter 2-2) and PSP is quite strong—stronger in fact than when we look at the bullpen as a whole. Put differently, the performance of *non-closer* relievers is of very little importance in the postseason; the correlation between non-closer WXRL and PSP is just .02. Between the absence of fourth and fifth starters who often require bullpen help and the willingness of managers to stretch their closers into multiple-inning stints, it is the secondary relief pitchers who get squeezed in the playoffs.

Of all the statistics in our study, the one with the highest correlation to postseason success is opponents' batting average. Certainly, preventing hits is very important in the playoffs—when you're matched up against good offensive clubs, it's vital to stop them from stringing together hits and starting rallies. But we also need to think about how a team can go about preventing hits. The best ways to prevent hits are: (1) to strike the batter out, so that he doesn't put the ball into play in the first place and (2) to catch the ball when it is put into play. As we describe in Chapter 3-1, the relationship between strikeouts, defense, and hit prevention is complicated. It takes a more sophisticated type of analysis to sort everything out, which we will get to in a moment.

The other interesting finding is that avoiding walks doesn't seem to have much relationship with playoff success. A good rule of thumb for pitchers is: Let bad hitters beat themselves, but don't let good hitters beat you. While walking a hitter who can't hit the ball out of the infield is tragic, pitching around a guy who can slam the ball 450 feet can be advisable. Pitchers encounter a lot more of the latter kind of hitter than the former in the playoffs. Finally, we see that the two defensive metrics examined here—Fielding Runs Above Average (FRAA) and unearned runs—show a promising correlation with PSP. We'll get back to that in a moment too.

Miscellaneous Metrics

The final section is reserved for testing some commonly held precepts about the playoffs. Finishing the year hot doesn't matter at all. In fact, there is a slight inverse relationship between W-L record from September 1 onward and playoff success. This may be because the best teams can afford to rest their starters late in the season, while merely good teams will be scratching and clawing for every victory and may come into the postseason tired. Playing well in 1-run games, meanwhile, has no particular effect on how a team fares in the postseason.

We also looked at two measures of experience: chronological age and the average number of lifetime postseason at-bats or innings pitched for the players on the roster. Although age made no difference, there was a slight relationship between playoff experience and PSP. A good deal of the correlation was the result of the recent Yankees dynasty, a team that was both very experienced (especially in its last couple of years) and very successful. Although we don't think the "experience counts" hypothesis can be dismissed out of hand, the relationship isn't statistically significant, especially if we consider that those who have accumulated a lot of postseason experience tend to be better players.

You've probably heard the axiom, "Correlation does not imply causation." For example, we might find that the stock market is closed on days beginning with the letter S; there is a correlation between these two things. However, it is not because Saturday and Sunday begin with an S that the stock market it closed on those days but rather because the stock market is closed on weekends. This axiom isn't quite correct; correlation can *imply* causation, but it doesn't *prove* causation. Nevertheless, to get a better sense for causation, we need to use a more sophisticated tool: regression analysis. Regression analysis is designed precisely for assessing causation; its goal is to see which independent variables can explain a resultant one (in our case, Playoff Success Points).

Regression analysis is particularly helpful when evaluating a number of interrelated variables, as we're doing in our study of the postseason. For example, we notice that both opponents' batting average and pitcher strikeout rate are correlated with postseason success, but they are also correlated with one another. Which variable is the real driver of good postseason pitching? Although not as widely appreciated as landscape painting or playing electric guitar, regression analysis can be an art form, especially when it comes to complicated analyses such as we have here. One favored technique is as follows: Avoid redundant variables and use the most fundamental statistic where possible. For example, we'd rather look at runs allowed than winning percentage, since winning games results in part from allowing fewer runs. But we'd rather still look at strikeout rate, since preventing runs results in part from striking batters out.

After any number of permutations of the twenty-six variables in our database, we identified three factors that have the most fundamental and direct relationship with Playoff Success Points. These variables are as follows:

- Closer WXRL
- Pitcher strikeout rate
- FRAA

Striking batters out, catching the ball, and having a good closer wins championships. It makes a good deal of sense why each of these variables is so important in the postseason.

Closer WXRL

Since 1972, the average closer (the pitcher who received the most save opportunities of anyone on his team during the regular season) has had a WXRL of 2.7. Of the 180 teams in our sample, 53 managed to reach the playoffs with a below-average closer. However, only five of those teams went on to win the World Series. The reason for the importance of the closer is simple: Postseason games are usually close contests between evenly matched teams, and that provides many more opportunities for the closer to pitch in high-Leverage situations. Between 1996 and 2004, Mariano Rivera pitched 5.1 percent of the Yankees' regular-season innings. Over the same period, he pitched 10.4 percent of their postseason innings, more than twice as many.

It's also worth noting that managers use closers more optimally in the playoffs than they do in the regular season. They'll have them enter the game in the seventh or eighth inning, pitch for multiple innings at a time, and come into a tie game or even one in which their team is trailing. If any managers are reading this book, this would be a good bit for them to read: *We've seen over the past thirty years how important a good closer can be in the playoffs. So let's pay attention and start using them that way in the regular season.*

In any event, this particular conjecture about postseason play is true: It's very difficult to win close games against good offensive teams if you don't have an ace reliever to finish things off.

Pitcher Strikeout Rate

Strikeout rate is always very important for a pitcher. If you strike a batter out, you'll prevent him from doing any harm. He can't put the ball in play and get a hit, can't draw a walk, and can't hit a home run. (He might be able to reach first base, however, if the home-plate umpire is Doug Eddings.) Striking hitters out becomes particularly important, however, when facing good offenses like the ones seen in postseason play. The reason—which Baseball Prospectus details in the book *Mind Game*—is because good hitters tend to tee off against finesse pitchers while losing some of their advantage against power pitchers who can throw an unhittable pitch.

Fielding Runs Above Average

In general, there is an inverse relationship between FRAA and pitcher strikeout rate. This makes a certain amount of sense: The defense becomes more important when you have a staff of finesse pitchers that like to put the ball in play, so you're liable to pay more attention. That's less true when you have strikeout pitchers who can get the job done all by themselves. (It's also possible that pitchers feel more comfortable challenging hitters when they have a good defense to back them up.)

However, when a team has both a strikeout-heavy pitching staff and a great defense at its disposal, it can become nearly impossible for its opponents to get hits and generate rallies. There are two layers of security—the hitter first has to find a pitch to hit; then he has to hope that the defense won't catch it. It's not that defense is inherently more important in close games, but it almost certainly is more important against good offenses, since good offenses put hard-hit balls in play and test the defense far more frequently. Of the thirty-three teams to win the World Series since 1972, only five had a below-average defense and none had an FRAA worse than –10.

It would be misleading to suggest that this is some kind of secret sauce. Collectively, these three factors—the quality of the closer, the defense, and the strikeout rate of the pitching staff—account for only about 11 percent of playoff success. The majority of the time, it's plain old luck that prevails. But when these three elements are aligned together, they can become quite powerful. We can rank the 180 playoff teams from first to worst in each of these categories, then average the ranking into a composite score. Table 9-3.6 lists the 10 teams with the best and worst composite rankings.

Of the ten teams with the highest composite rankings, nine played in the World Series and seven of them won it. That one World Series–losing team was the 1979 Orioles, who lost in seven games to the Pirates—who also appear in the top-ten list. Some of these teams, like the 1984 Tigers and 1998 Yankees, were powerful clubs that had a lot going for them anyway. But this helps to explain the success of teams

TABLE 9-3.6 Ten Teams with Best and Worst Composite Rankings

Composite Rankings	Rank out of 180 Teams				Result
	Closer	FRAA	K Rate	Average	
Highest Composite Ranking					
1. 1979 Orioles	31	9	48	29.3	Lost in World Series
2. 1990 Reds	38	15	49	34.0	Won World Series
3. 2001 D'Backs	37	61	10	36.0	Won World Series
4. 1998 Yankees	23	17	72	37.3	Won World Series
5. 1984 Tigers	1	63	51	38.3	Won World Series
6. 1979 Pirates	20	29	70	39.7	Won World Series
7. 1979 Mets	36	32	63	43.7	Lost in NLCS
8. 2002 Angels	24	5	106	45.0	Won World Series
9. 1995 Indians	12	62	67	47.0	Lost in World Series
10. 1978 Yankees	53	47	47	49.0	Won World Series
Lowest Composite Ranking					
180. 1997 Giants	167	152	167	162.0	Lost in NLDS
179. 2005 Red Sox	164	141	131	145.3	Lost in ALDS
178. 1989 Blue Jays	120	166	144	143.3	Lost in ALCS
177. 2000 A's	155	107	150	137.3	Lost in ALDS
176. 1974 Orioles	66	168	173	135.7	Lost in ALCS
175. 1995 Rockies	161	109	136	135.3	Lost in NLDS
174. 1981 Expos	118	173	111	134.0	Lost in NLCS
173. 1996 Orioles	160	138	102	133.3	Lost in ALCS
172. 1981 Brewers	143	83	172	132.7	Lost in ALCS
171. 1979 Reds	91	150	151	130.7	Lost in NLCS

like the 1990 Reds, an unimpressive squad that happened to have the perfect combination of talents for postseason play, including their fine defense and the Nasty Boys bullpen of Randy Myers, Norm Charlton, and Rob Dibble.

On the other hand, none of the ten *worst* composite teams so much as played in the World Series. Collectively, they compiled a postseason record of just 16-35.

What does this mean for Billy Beane's A's? We see that one of his clubs, the 2000 version, ranked fourth from the bottom in composite ranking. This team featured a young offense with budding stars like Eric Chavez, Miguel Tejada, and Jason Giambi, coupled with a cheap veteran pitching staff that had been cobbled together from the waiver wire. The starter in the decisive ALDS Game 5 was Gil Heredia, a finesse pitcher who treaded water by avoiding mistakes and doing just enough to give his offense a chance. However, he was no match for the Yankees, who crushed him for 6 runs in one-third of an inning in Game 5. Meanwhile, A's closer Jason Isringhausen had yet to really establish himself. And while the infield defense was reasonable, the outfield of Ben Grieve, Terrence Long, and Matt Stairs was one of the worst defensive groups in recent memory. Things got a little bit better in the seasons thereafter, as we see in Table 9-3.7. The Big Three of Barry Zito, Tim Hudson, and Mark Mulder established themselves, and Billy Beane, learning from his experience, began to pay more attention to relief pitching and outfield defense.

TABLE 9-3.7 Oakland A's Composite Rankings by Category, 2000–2003

Composite Ranking	Rank out of 180 Teams				
	Closer	FRAA	K Rate	Average	Result
177. 2000 A's	155	107	150	137.3	Lost in ALDS
97. 2001 A's	81	148	62	97.0	Lost in ALDS
57. 2002 A's	111	19	103	77.7	Lost in ALDS
30. 2003 A's	92	17	80	63.0	Lost in ALDS

By 2003, the A's had become a legitimately strong postseason club, but they still succumbed in 5 heartbreaking games to the Red Sox. It was neither bad luck nor a design ill suited for postseason play that did the Athletics in but a combination of the two. Miguel Tejada and Keith Foulke left after 2003, and Tim Hudson and Mark Mulder the year after. Young shortstop Bobby Crosby and 2005 Rookie of the Year closer Huston Street have since emerged. But in 2004 and 2005 at least, Billy Beane's window of opportunity had closed.

Extra Innings

Can Stats and Scouts Get Along?

DAYN PERRY

If you've followed baseball at all over the last few seasons, you've probably been privy to a deliriously tiresome debate over the proper way to build a winning team. Some say an organization is best guided by the emergent principles of statistical analysis, particularly those found at places like Baseball Prospectus. Meanwhile, those of a traditional bent insist that bricks-and-mortar scouting is the best approach. So are the numbers the best organizational sextant, or should the instincts of scouts inform the decisions of the front office? There's really only one correct answer to this question: both. To argue otherwise betrays either ignorance or one's own agenda.

Former Oakland A's owner Charlie Finley, a notorious skinflint, once fired all his scouts and then attempted to run a successful major league organization without any semblance of a scouting department. The immediate result was that Finley, in the next two amateur drafts (1979 and 1980), would fritter away top-five picks on shortstop Juan Bustabad and pitcher Mike King, neither of whom would ever make the majors (a "feat" matched only by the top picks of the Montreal Expos in 1971 and 1972 and the Toronto Blue Jays, also in '79 and '80). This from an organization renowned for its homegrown talent base for much of the 1970s. Until recently, the Tampa Bay Devil Rays operated with an almost gleeful ignorance of basic statistical principles. The result was a club that finished in last place in seven of the eight seasons it's been in existence. With cautionary tales such as these, why would an organization *not* seek a way to reconcile stopwatches and spreadsheets?

At Baseball Prospectus, we likened this false dichotomy to choosing between beer and tacos. Why make an either-or quandary out of two options that can coexist and be equally embraced? Beer or tacos? Nope: beer *and* tacos. Stats *and* scouts. After all, when it comes to evaluating baseball talent, stats and scouts are complementary, not contradictory approaches.

The weaknesses of one are, if properly utilized, papered over by the other. For instance, one of the problems with scouting is the issue of sample size. Scouts often draw conclusions about a player based on a few isolated plate appearances or a handful of innings pitched. Catch a player on an off night, and you're likely to be left with a faulty impression of his genuine abilities. The statistical approach, meanwhile, isn't as prone to this weakness, provided it's employed properly. Another weakness of scouting shows up when a scout grows overly fond of a player because of his raw baseball abilities, or "tools," in scouting parlance. Are those tools helping his team win games? The numbers can better answer such a question.

Conversely, crunching numbers doesn't yield information such as whether a pitching prospect is getting by with average stuff in the lower rungs of the minors. It doesn't warn of an injury time bomb about to go off due to a pitcher's flawed mechanics. It doesn't reveal whether a hitter has natural loft to his swing or is getting consistently fooled by quality breaking balls.

In other words, the two approaches to evaluating talent make the perfect organizational tandem. So why in the world would an organization focus on one and neglect the other? If it's guided by a capable front office, such narrowness of focus will be avoided.

The "both, please" position makes perfect horse sense and hardly sounds radical. In the heart of hearts of even the shrillest advocates on both sides, they probably know this to be true. However, the occasional bomb throwing from both sides has caused positions to become entrenched and prompted those in both camps to venture the snidest ways to dismiss their opponents. Keep a tight perimeter and all that. Asking who started it may be a rather juvenile indulgence. But, well, who started it?

Ask this question of anyone even vaguely familiar with the debate, and that person might blame Michael Lewis's best-selling book *Moneyball*. In *Moneyball*, which detailed the prevailing theories and machinations of the Oakland A's front office under General Manager Billy Beane, Lewis seemed to delight in dismissing the importance of the traditional grizzled "baseball man." If you didn't know better, it'd be easy to come away from a reading of the book with the notion that scouts were little more than bumbling fossils with a grumpy disdain for all things innovative or empirical.

After the tenor of Lewis's book raised enough hackles, those in the other camp trotted out a string of withering rejoinders. Longtime baseball scribe and co-founder of Baseball America (which is, in some senses, the scouting house organ) Tracy Ringolsby sniffed in a column that Lewis "has a limited knowledge of baseball and a total infatuation with Billy Beane." Gerry Fraley of the *Dallas Morning News* wrote in response to *Moneyball*, "One good scout is worth more than 100 numbers-crunchers." Hall-of-Fame second baseman and ESPN announcer Joe Morgan on two occasions decried the book and cited Beane as its author. (In a *Sports Illustrated* counterpunch, Lewis quipped, "It was, in a perverse way, an author's dream: The people most upset about my book were the ones unable to divine that I had written it.") Statistical adherents were cast as dwelling in an insulated world of abstraction, far removed from the true viscera of the game.

Not surprisingly, it took quite a while for relations between the two sides to thaw. The debate is still with us, but at the very least, a reasonable sense of decorum has been restored. Of course, let none of this give you the impression that such hostilities are a recent phenomenon. Canadian-born Allan Roth was the first professional statistician employed by a major league team, starting in the first half of the twentieth century. Like many other of the game's innovations, this one was brought about by the inestimable Branch Rickey. While Rickey was running the St. Louis Cardinals in the 1920s and 1930s, he once hired a man by the name of Travis Hoke to perform some statistical evaluations of the team's offense. Not long after Rickey took over the Brooklyn Dodgers, Roth approached him, shoved reams of hand-compiled stats at him, and agitated for a job. Rickey, who made a career out of defying convention, hired Roth as the team's statistician in 1947—the same year the great Jackie Robinson would begin a more vital and more grossly overdue revolution in Brooklyn.

As Alan Schwarz explains in his outstanding book, *The Numbers Game*, Roth's work went on to inform many of Rickey's bolder decisions with the Dodgers—to wit, trading away Dixie Walker and moving Jackie Robinson to the cleanup spot prior to the 1949 season. "Baseball is a game of percentages," Roth himself once said. "I try to find the actual percentage."

If Roth's prominence in the Dodgers' front office served as an augury of industry-wide changes to come, so did his quasi-pariah status portend the resistance to statistical analysis in later years. Roth stayed on after Rickey left the Dodgers for Pittsburgh, but he saw his role with the team whittled down. Manager Charlie Dressen eschewed Roth's work almost entirely, and Roth eventually found himself exiled to the press box, where his numbers were used mostly to fill the column inches and dead air of writers and broadcasters.

Even so, the seeds of upheaval had been planted. Scouts had been an indelible part of the game since the turn of the twentieth century (and as entrenched as they are, they're still not a part of baseball's Hall of Fame), so there was certainly a head start to work against. However, the biggest steps toward reconciling the established scouting approach and the underpinnings of quantitative analysis were not taken by Billy Beane or even Branch Rickey or Allan Roth; rather, it was a scout by the name of Jim McLaughlin who introduced early innovations.

McLaughlin for many years served as scouting director for the Orioles and Reds during their dynastic runs of the 1960s and 1970s. Needless to say, those two organizations cultivated a number of excellent prospects during that era. And it was McLaughlin at the switch. In *Dollar Sign on the Muscle*, Kevin Kerrane's seminal and brilliant book on the scouting profession, McLaughlin recounts his struggle to change the ways organizations went about scouting talent. "I said, 'I don't have the time to reeducate you guys diplomatically,'" McLaughlin said. "I was dictatorial. I was opinionated. I said, 'This is the way it's gonna be.' I wanted to inculcate basic principles. . . . I wanted rationality. I wanted science."

McLaughlin wanted to steer scouting away from its dearly held reliance on subjectivity and superstition—no more "the good face" and the like. And, according to *Dollar Sign*, he had a three-pronged approach for doing this:

1. Computerize player data, rationalize draft procedures, and develop consistency in the hiring, training, and grading of scouts.
2. Utilize professional psychological testing methods to assess the makeup of each prospect.
3. Utilize physical testing to evaluate eyesight, general health, bat speed, reflexes, and ratios of physical strength.

Sounds like something a notionally progressive organization such as the A's might come up with these days, yet this was McLaughlin's vision almost forty years ago. As Kerrane puts it, McLaughlin used "doubt as a method." It's this brand of healthy, informed skepticism that drives successful approaches to talent evaluation in the here and now.

The Boston Red Sox have populated their front office with everyone from iconoclasts like Bill James to salt-cured purveyors of old-school wisdom like Bill Lajoie. The A's, famously, lean heavily on statistical analysis but also pay serious mind to a player's makeup and mental fitness (a fact not lost on those who bothered to read and remember Chapter 3 of *Moneyball*). The Braves, baseball's contemporary dynasty nonpareil, employ a unique "division of labor" setup with their scouts. That system entails having those with a ken for say, spotting pitchers, focus on—novelty of novelties—pitchers. The Padres, Indians, Yankees, Angels, and Cardinals have all, to varying degrees, succeeded by dint of the scouts-stats hybrid approach. In other words, winning, successful organizations these days take their tacos with beer, and even when they hew more closely to one side or the other, as the Braves and A's do, they seek ways to distinguish their approach from that of the competition.

Not surprisingly, it's catching on. More and more organizations are employing statistical consultants and seeking to nudge their scouting departments toward the "new-school" end of the continuum. And, hey, we even seem to be getting along better these days. At Major League Baseball's 2004 winter meetings, Alan Schwarz, writing for Baseball America, had a sit-down with Baseball Prospectus founder and current Oakland A's consultant Gary Huckabay, noted statistical analyst and onetime Boston Red Sox consultant Voros McCracken, Angels scouting director Eddie Bane, and Cubs assistant general manager (and longtime scout) Gary Hughes. As you might expect, the former two beat the drum for the "stathead" approach, while the latter two defended the traditional approach. Presumably, it would be a veritable Yalta Conference of mixed motives and tenuous alliances, but, for the most part, diplomacy carried the day. As Bane himself concluded, "I want them [statistical analysts] to realize that we're not spitting tobacco on the draft board to make our picks. As far as *Moneyball* goes, I didn't like it. But the respect I have for these two guys today [Huckabay and McCracken], just hearing them talk, I'm going to get their phone numbers and find out what Boston and Oakland's paying them. I can't tamper, but maybe get permission. This is good stuff. We use it. Maybe we don't acknowledge it enough."

Thankfully, attitudes like those of Bane are becoming more common these days: What can we learn from each other? How can we work together to improve the game? The statistical revolution—at least in its more rational corners—has never been about replacing scouts or rendering them obsolete; it's about striking a balance between the two approaches and making front-office work a more collaborative endeavor. The grousing and sniping is just a natural outgrowth of change, and it's a temporary condition. After all, only a fool would deny the native and vital acuities of good scouts, just as only a fool would pooh-pooh the value of sound statistical analysis. So, you know, don't be a fool.

Notes

Batting Practice

xvii   "one player at a time, until just one remained": http://survivor.dmlco.com/about.html.

xx   "its cozy dimensions down the lines and large center field": Tiger Stadium and Minute Maid Park, two modern fields that fit this description, have tended to have the same effect on offense.

xx   "The lifetime park factors for Ruth and Bonds are listed in Table BP.2": Historical home-road splits, which form the basis for park adjustments, are available going back to Ruth's time in the specific categories of runs and home runs but not for other categories such as singles or doubles. Thus, the park factors as listed in Table BP.2 for those categories are extrapolated based on a regression analysis. The key thing to recognize is that if a park rates as average or worse for run scoring but is favorable to home runs, it must necessarily diminish base hits. Note also that ballparks have very little effect on walk or strikeout rates, which occur before the ball is hit into play.

xx   "The mechanics behind normalization are somewhat involved": The normalization process applied here is to evaluate a player's performance in terms of standard deviations above the league average in a particular category, after adjusting for park effects. This figure is then translated back to standard deviations above league average in the 1985 AL. For example, Babe Ruth hit .356 in the 1927 AL, which we adjust upward to .360 after accounting for park effects. The 1927 AL had a league-wide batting average of .293, with a standard deviation on batting average of .044. Thus, a .360 AVG is 1.52 standard deviations better than average. Conversely, the 1985 AL had a league-wide batting average of .261, with a standard deviation of .036. It would require a batting average of .316 to be 1.52 standard deviations above average in this league. Thus, Ruth's 1927 batting average, normalized to the 1985 AL, is .316.

    League averages and standard deviations are weighted based on playing time. Note further that pitchers' batting statistics are excluded from the league averages. Pitchers are not paid to hit, and their presence in the data set artificially increases the standard deviation by a large margin. Finally, note that the league averages and standard deviations do not include the performances of Babe Ruth and Barry Bonds specifically; it would be unfair to dock Bonds or Ruth because they bring the entire league average up.

xxii   "gold medal–winning times in the men's 100-meter freestyle swimming competition": www.infoplease.com/ipsa/A0114975.html.

xxiii   "about an inch and a half taller than he was fifty years ago": www.base ballprospectus.com/article.php?articleid=3979.

xxiii   "players aged thirty-five or older": It is not as though the thirty-five-and-over set has been kept around just to provide a veteran presence in the clubhouse. These players combined to hit for a .344 OBP and a .434 SLG; both figures are better than their under-thirty-five counterparts managed.

xxiv   "Tommy John surgery": en.wikipedia.org/wiki/Tommy_John_surgery.

xxiv   "Foreign-born players . . . major league rosters": www.baseballprospectus .com/article.php?articleid=4194.

xxiv   "at least five active major leaguers from that nation": Although the countries of England and Ireland would have qualified in the early days of professional baseball under this standard, we have not included them here. The 1890s and 1910s were a time of massive immigration into the United States, and essentially all of the English and Irish players had emigrated in childhood and learned the game after they came to the States. It is misleading to suggest that baseball was actively drawing from those countries, as it does now from Latin America or Asia. Some readers may also be surprised by the relatively early date associated with Cuba. This timing is a product of two things: the modest degree of acceptance in baseball, before integration, for "light-skinned" Latinos and American colonial endeavors in Cuba at the turn of the twentieth century, including the Spanish-American War.

xxiv   "The resulting effect on baseball's population is seen in Figure BP.1": "Commonwealth" designates Canada plus Australia. Population estimates in Figure BP.1 are contemporaneous with the years listed on the graph. The population estimates are compiled from three Internet sources: the U.S. Census Bureau (all U.S. population estimates), the Globalis database from United Nations University (foreign country population estimates from 1950 onward), and the Populstat database from Utrecht University in Germany (foreign country population estimates before 1950).

xxv   "900,000 people per baseball player": This assumes a standard of twenty-five players per major league team. In 1930, the effective baseball playing population was 124.15 million, and there were 16 teams, representing 400 roster spots. In 2005, the effective baseball playing population was 687.66 million, and there were 30 teams, representing 750 roster spots.

xxv   "when debating back-in-the-day types": We also recommend carrying a copy of *The Onion* article "In My Day, Ballplayers Were for Shit," www. theonion.com/content/node/33402.

xxvii   "The figure is calibrated so that the 1975 AL is assigned a difficulty rating of 1.0": The method used here is similar to one applied in John Thorn and Pete Palmer, *The Hidden Game of Baseball: A Revolutionary Approach to Baseball and Its Statistics*, rev. ed. (New York: Doubleday, 1985). This method has come in for some criticism because it does not account for the effects of player aging, which conceivably could be responsible for some decline in skill level from season to season. However, we have studied our version of the Timeline Adjustment both with and without an adjustment for player age and found that it does not make a material difference. Applying the Occam's Razor principle, we present the original version without an age adjustment herein. It should be noted that many sabermetricians (as well as many casual fans) tend to overstate the importance of the predictive relationship between age and player performance, particularly for players in the middle portions of their playing careers (as most major leaguers are).

xxvii "an even sharper decrease in the early 1900s after the American League was established": Another interesting finding is that the American League was actually stronger than the National League in the early part of the twentieth century. Conventional wisdom has held the opposite, frequently citing the strength of the early Giants, Cubs, and Pirates dynasties. As we see it, the gaudy winning percentages these franchises posted in the decade of the 1900s is a reflection of the relative weakness of their league rather than its strength.

xxxvi "EqAs for all players in . . . 2004": Minimum of 250 plate appearances. Minor leaguers have their EqAs translated to their major league equivalents. We do not translate statistics for minor leaguers in rookie ball, and they are not included in the analysis.

xxxvii "EqA is a 'rate statistic'": A rate statistic evaluates a player's production on a per-plate-appearance or per-innings-pitched basis; batting average and ERA are rate statistics. A counting statistic, as the name implies, simply counts up a player's contribution in a particular statistical area over time. Thus, it will be sensitive to the amount of playing time that a player accumulates. Home runs and saves are classic counting statistics.

xxxviii "more playing time than Ruth": It should also be pointed out that Bonds played in the era of the 162-game schedule, while Ruth's teams played 154 games. On the other hand, Bonds lost about 75 games due to the strike in 1994–1995. The differences approximately cancel out.

xxxviii "'eyesight, good teaching, and perfect coordination made him a natural'": All quotations in this and the next paragraph are taken from Marshall Smelser, *The Life That Ruth Built*, reprint (Lincoln: University of Nebraska Press, 1993), pp. 172, 451.

xlii "Ruth's statistics in his ten World Series were even more impressive": Ruth hit .326/.467/.744 for his career against tough World Series pitching, versus .342/.474/.690 against average competition in the regular season.

Chapter 1-1

2 *"The Hidden Game of Baseball"*: John Thorn and Pete Palmer, *The Hidden Game of Baseball: A Revolutionary Approach to Baseball and Its Statistics*, rev. ed. (New York: Doubleday, 1985), p. 20.

3   "RBI Opportunities Report": Baseball Prospectus RBI Opportunities Report: www.baseballprospectus.com/statistics/sortable/index.php?cid= 4564.

6   "Most teams have difficulty": Steven Goldman, "Truly One of the Greatest Yankees," *New York Sun,* September 26, 2005.

9   "Studies have shown that a player who strikes out a lot": See these BaseballProspectus.com articles: www.baseballprospectus.com/article .php?articleid=3857; www.baseballprospectus.com/article.php?articleid =2617.

Chapter 1-2

15   "dozens, if not hundreds, of studies on clutch hitting": see, for example, www.geocities.com/cyrilmorong@sbcglobal.net/ClutchLinks2.htm.

15   "Most of these studies": There are exceptions. Cramer's 1977 study, for example, applied a method that was similar in spirit to that which I describe here, although he was able to analyze only two seasons of play-by-play data.

16   "'In the 7th inning or later . . . with the potential tying run at least on deck'": ESPN.com player cards.

16   "making the first out of the inning is more than twice as costly as making the last out of the inning": With no runners on base, making the first out of the inning reduced a team's run expectation by about .24 runs in 2005, versus .11 runs for the third out with no runners on.

16   "considerably reducing his team's run expectation": In 2005, teams scored an average of .98 runs with a runner on third and one out, versus .37 runs with a runner on third and two outs, a difference of .61 runs. The difference is comparatively larger than analogous situations; striking out with one out and a runner on second reduces run expectation by only about .35 runs.

17   "a walk is virtually as good as a home run": A home run is very slightly better because the runner on base is a liability—he may be the victim of a double play, a pickoff, a baserunning blunder, and so forth.

17   "a strikeout is preferable to a groundout": With runners on first base and less than two outs, groundouts result in double plays approximately 50 percent of the time. This risk is easy enough to attain that it outweighs any gains from baserunner advancement, even if the runner moved up to second base half the time that there was *not* a double play, which is less than the actual figure.

17   "48 percent of the time when this new situation occurred": The number is slightly less than 50 percent because of the home field advantage.

19   "the probability of a team's going on to victory at any point in a given game": Keith Woolner, "An Analytical Framework for Win Expectancy," *Baseball Prospectus 2005* (New York: Workman, 2005), pp. 520–533.

19   "smooth over issues related to small sample sizes": Some situations simply haven't occurred frequently enough to provide a reliable estimate of

their associated win expectation based on the historical record alone, particularly those involving lopsided scoring margins. For example, the situation "home team ahead by five runs in the bottom of the second with one out and the bases loaded" has occurred just a handful of times during the past decade.

19   "an example of the procedure in action": This example was originally used in a column by James Click for the Baseball Prospectus Web site, available at www.baseballprospectus.com/article.php?articleid=4463.

19   "the player's Win Expectancy (WinEx)": WinEx is not intended to account for a player's contributions on defense or from his baserunning.

22   "'He's the best clutch hitter . . . ,' said . . . Sparky Anderson": www.latino sportslegends.com/tonyperez.htm.

22   "Perez's most comparable players": Per Bill James's similarity scores. See www.baseball-reference.com/p/perezto01.shtml.

23   "MLV operates by comparing the number of runs . . . specific player": A fuller description of the MLV method is available at www.stathead.com/bbeng/woolner/mlvdesc.htm.

24   "I placed the player in the lineup of his actual team": Because run scoring is nonlinear, a player's MLV is sensitive to the lineup that he is placed in; players in a better lineup produce more runs with the same batting statistics because they will have a better chance of having runners on base in front of them and will have good hitters to drive them in behind them. Ordinarily, this is not a desirable characteristic because it removes the context neutrality of the statistic; the same player will look better in a good lineup than in a bad one, making comparisons between different players less reliable. In this particular case, however, the context sensitivity is helpful because a player in a good lineup will have more opportunity to hit in clutch situations with runners on base, thereby increasing his WinEx if he performs well.

24   "with Guerrero replaced by an average hitter": More specifically, a league average hitter in the player's home ballpark.

24   "the Angels would score 737 runs with Guerrero": The Angels scored 760 runs in 2005, outperforming their expected runs total by 23. Teams can outperform their expected runs total through lineup constriction; luck; and situational, or "clutch," hitting.

24   "for a marginal contribution of 37 runs": I also made one other, more technical modification to the formula, based on a regression analysis that compared the number of runs per game (RPG) estimated by the MLV formula versus the actual number of RPG scored by major league teams between 1972 and 2004. The equation associated with this regression is: RPG(Actual) = RPG(MLV) × .891 + .426. The slope term of .891 implies that run scoring might be very slightly "flatter"—less responsive to the inputs of batting average (AVG), on-base percentage (OBP), and slugging average (SLG)—than the original MLV formula implies. The intercept term of .426, interestingly, implies that teams would score a few runs even if they had AVG, OBP, and SLG of zero. This is not as ridicu-

lous as it might seem; teams score a certain number of runs by virtue of reaching base on errors, with the runners coming around to score as a result of a combination of events such as sacrifices, stolen bases, wild pitches, and additional errors, none of which are reflected in AVG, OBP, or SLG.

24   "a variation of the Bill James Pythagorean Formula": Specifically, I use the so-called Pythagenpat formula, which varies the exponent used to estimate winning percentage based on the run-scoring environment. A description of the Pythagenpat formula, and its close relative, the Pythagenport formula, can be found in the Glossary and in more detail at www.baseballprospectus.com/glossary/index.php?search=pythagenport.

24   "about 3.7 additional wins to the 2005 Angels": One interesting property of this method is that players are naturally credited with more wins for teams that had a close run-scoring differential. For example, on a team that scored 800 runs and allowed 800 runs, a player who contributed 50 marginal runs is credited with 4.97 wins. However, for a team that scored 800 runs but allowed 600 runs, the player would be credited with 4.74 wins, and for a team that scored 800 runs but allowed 1,000 runs, the player would be credited with 4.70 wins. This property is helpful here because WinEx will reflect the fact that teams with small run-scoring differentials play a large number of close games, in which clutch plate appearances will occur more frequently.

24   "a favorable effect on his WinEx": Of course, if a player failed in those opportunities, it would especially hurt his WinEx.

25   "stay close to the 1.00 benchmark": The average Leverage score is actually 1.03.

25   "the range of Leverage scores among regular hitters": Minimum 500 PA.

25   "the model can explain about 70 percent of WinEx": As measured by the regression's R-squared. R-squared is a statistic that measures the percentage of variance in the dependant variable (WinEx) that the independent variables can explain.

The regression analysis was specified as follows:

$$\text{WinEx} = \left(\frac{\text{MLVWins}^2}{\text{MLVRuns}} \right) \times (6.63 + 2.29 \times \text{Leverage})$$

The regression was weighted by plate appearances. The constant term was statistically insignificant and was dropped.

This specification may appear complicated at first glance, but it's important to keep in mind what it is doing. The term

$$\left(\frac{\text{MLVWins}^2}{\text{MLVRuns}} \right)$$

is equivalent to

$$MLVWins \times \left(\frac{MLVWins}{MLVRuns} \right)$$

or the player's MLVWins multiplied by the ratio of wins to runs in his run-scoring environment. Typically, this ratio is about 1/9, or 9 runs to a win. On the other hand, the right side of the equation also resolves to about 9. That is, we have:

$$WinEx = MLVWins \times \left(\frac{MLVWins}{MLVRuns} \right) \times (6.63 + 2.29 \times Leverage) \sim MLVWins \times \left(\frac{1}{9} \right) \times (9)$$

Or WinEx is approximately equal to MLVWins. The more complicated specification, however, does allow us to account more precisely for the effects of run-scoring environment and Leverage on a player's WinEx, which materially improves the R-squared. Note also that the equation is specified such that the intercept with MLVWins is zero. Hitters with positive MLVWins totals have a positive predicted WinEx, but the WinEx is relatively greater if he hits in higher-Leverage situations (as measured explicitly by Leverage and implicitly by the wins/runs ratio). Conversely, hitters with negative MLVWins have negative predicted WinEx scores, but WinEx is relatively more negative if he hits in high-Leverage situations.

25   "his run-scoring environment": Including both MLV Runs and MLV Wins is implicitly a way to account for a hitter's run-scoring environment; see the earlier discussion.

25   "the Red Sox would likely have lost the Wild Card to the Cleveland Indians": The Red Sox finished at 95-67 and the Indians at 93-69.

33   "walk rate and strikeout rate": The other statistics I tested were batting average, Isolated Slugging, and speed score. Isolated Slugging and speed score had no relationship whatsoever with clutch hitting. There is some relationship between batting average and clutch hitting—players with higher AVGs have slightly better clutch ratings—but it does not rate as statistically significant if we put it into a regression analysis with batting eye, recognizing that there is a strong correlation between batting eye and AVG.

34   "his clutch scores over his previous three seasons": For purposes of this experiment, I considered only hitters who had at least 1,000 PA over their three previous seasons.

34   "instead of explaining 70 percent of WinEx, the model now explains 71 percent or 72 percent of WinEx": In spite of the small increase in R-squared, the difference is statistically significant.

34   "perhaps 2 percent clutch- or situational-hitting skill": There may be some confusion in sorting between this conclusion and the statistic I presented earlier that clutch-hitting performance is about 10 percent explained by clutch-hitting skill. Although a player's clutch-hitting track record can predict about 10 percent of his *clutch*-hitting performance, it

explains a much smaller fraction—between 1 and 2 percent—of his *overall* performance as measured by WinEx. As important as clutch situations might be when they arise, hitting in regular situations is plenty important too; a team doesn't need to worry about how it performs in the clutch if it takes a six-run lead by the third inning.

Chapter 1-3

36   "the key to scoring . . . is getting the first batter on base": James noted: "The largest determination of how many runs are likely to be scored in an inning is whether or not the lead-off man reaches base. If the lead-off man reaches base, the number of runs that will probably be scored in an inning is about three times as high as if the lead-off man is put out. . . . The one player who is least likely to lead off the second inning is the number-three hitter. . . . Thus, the one player who is most likely to start a successful inning and the one player who is least likely to start the second inning are the same player." http://baseballanalysts.com/archives/2005/01/abstracts_from_23.php.

36   "an article originally appearing at BaseballProspectus.com": www.baseballprospectus.com/article.php?articleid=3766.

37   "26 runs . . . may seem like a big difference": A team's won-lost record can be estimated with a great deal of accuracy based solely on its runs scored and runs allowed. While certain events may win a few more close games than others, over a full season, runs scored and runs allowed provide a very accurate measure of a team's quality and thus its won-lost record. Bill James discovered this in his early *Baseball Abstracts* using a team's runs scored squared divided by its runs scored squared plus its runs allowed squared. Given modern run-scoring environments and this formula, 10 runs are enough to sway the pendulum by one game, so many baseball analysts equate 10 runs with one win. It's a rough scale that's slightly different for some teams on the extreme ends of the run-scoring environments, but it's a good rule of thumb.

38   "a follow-up article": www.baseballprospectus.com/article.php?articleid=3779.

41   "three classes of subsequent batters": In this case, a batter's class is determined by his Marginal Lineup Value Rate (MLVr). MLVr is a measure of how many runs a player contributed per game over a league-average player, as measured by his AVG, OBP, and SLG.

43   "As Palmer and Thorn pointed out in *The Hidden Game of Baseball*": John Thorn and Pete Palmer, *The Hidden Game of Baseball: A Revolutionary Approach to Baseball and Its Statistics,* rev. ed. (New York: Doubleday, 1985), p. 64.

Chapter 2-1

54   "Voros McCracken took the baseball analysis world by storm": Voros

McCracken's Baseball Prospectus article: www.baseballprospectus.com/article.php?articleid=878.

55   "his conclusions were scrutinized thoroughly and were largely confirmed": Follow-up Keith Woolner and Mailbag articles: www.baseball prospectus.com/article.php?articleid=883; www.baseballprospectus .com/article.php?articleid=890.

Chapter 2-3

76   "Mathewson described his methods for staying fresh": Christy Mathewson, *Pitching in a Pinch: Baseball from the Inside,* reprint (Lincoln: University of Nebraska Press, 1994), pp. 64–66.

77   "One of the earliest analyses of historical trends in pitcher usage": Craig Wright and Tom House, *The Diamond Appraised* (New York: Simon and Schuster, 1989).

77   "Rany Jazayerli was one of the first researchers": "Pitcher Abuse Points: A New Way to Measure Pitcher Abuse," www.bbp.cx/article.php?article id=148.

77   "In *Baseball Prospectus 2001,* we showed evidence": "Analyzing PAP," *Baseball Prospectus 2001* (Dulles, VA: Potomac Books, 2001).

77   "We found that pitchers throw fewer innings per start": "Analyzing PAP, Part 1," www.baseballprospectus.com/article.php?articleid=1477.

80   "Biomechanical studies by people like Dr. Glenn Fleisig at the American Sports Medicine Institute": www.baseballprospectus.com/chat/chat. php?chatId=48.

     For more information, see "Analyzing PAP, Part 2,": www.baseball prospectus.com/article.php?articleid=1480; "PAP Frequently Asked Questions," www.baseballprospectus.com/article.php?articleid=1480; "BP Basics: How We Measure Pitcher Usage," www.baseballprospectus. com/article.php?articleid=2633; and "PAP: A Historical Perspective," www.baseballprospectus.com/article.php?articleid=383.

Chapter 3-1

88   "Michael Wolverton satirized the twisted logic": "Not Earning Its Keep: Why the 'Earned' Run Needs to Go," www.baseballprospectus.com/article.php?articleid=2753; see also "Not Earning Its Keep, Part II: More on the Unearned Run," www.baseballprospectus.com/article.php?article id=2846.

90   "In *Baseball Prospectus 2000,* we wrote": Keith Woolner, "Baseball Hilbert Problems," *Baseball Prospectus 2000* (Dulles, VA: Potomac Books, 2000), p. 280.

90   "In a 2001 article . . . McCracken posited": Voros McCracken, "Pitching and Defense: How Much Control Do Hurlers Have?" www.baseball prospectus.com/article.php?articleid=878.

91   "Subsequent research by Baseball Prospectus's Keith Woolner": Keith

Woolner, "Counterpoint: Pitching and Defense: Another Look at Pitchers Preventing Hits," www.baseballprospectus.com/article.php?articleid=883.

92 "and Clay Davenport": Clay Davenport, "Minor League Batting Averages on Balls in Play: Does Voros' Theory Work on the Farm?" www.baseball prospectus.com/article.php?articleid=3946.

92 "Tom Tippett . . . revealed several problems": "Can Pitchers Prevent Hits on Balls in Play?" Tom Tippett, www.diamond-mind.com/articles/ipavg 2.htm.

Chapter 3-2

95 "J. P. Ricciardi . . . summed things up": Jonah Keri, "Prospectus Q&A: J. P. Ricciardi, Part III," www.baseballprospectus.com/article.php? articleid=3415.

96 "an error is not always an error": Equally important, using a metric that includes "ordinary effort" as criteria effectively caps the achievement level of the participants at "ordinary." Even if official scorers were completely accurate and consistent—an impossible task with the limited direction they are given—a player who fields every ordinary play perfectly will look exactly the same in the stat sheets as a player who fields every ordinary play as well as all of the extraordinary ones perfectly. Errors, by their very name, provide no upside to the fielders; the best they can be is perfectly ordinary.

96 "Thomas Gilovich noted the many problems . . .": Thomas Gilovich, *How We Know What Isn't So* (New York: The Free Press, 1991).

97 "FR provides a handy way to compare . . . performance . . . before play-by-play data were available": With the availability of new play-by-play data, several new metrics have been developed, using these new data to eliminate some of the assumptions involved in FR. However, data are not available prior to 1972, and many of the new metrics have their own assumptions or blind spots. While none of these defensive metrics is perfect, FR provides the opportunity to compare modern defensive players to their historical counterparts. Most notable among the new defensive metrics are Ultimate Zone Rating (UZR), developed by independent analyst Mitchel Lichtman (www.baseballthinkfactory.org/files/main/article/lichtman_2003-03-14_0/) and the Probabilistic Model of Range (PMR), developed by David Pinto, the author of Baseball Musings (www.baseballmusings.com/).

98 "costing the Yankees a total of 140 runs, or about 1.5 games per season": See Chapter 1-3 for a discussion of the relationship between runs and wins.

98 "Clay Davenport could find no single change that clearly explained it": www.baseballprospectus.com/article.php?articleid=3600.

100 "'slow reaction time and poor footwork'": www.baseballprospectus.com/article.php?articleid=2535.

100 "Bill James's idea of a defensive spectrum": James elaborated: "As a

player grows older . . . he tends to be shifted leftward along this spectrum. Sometimes he moves in dramatic leaps, like Ernie Banks, a shortstop one year and a first baseman the next, or Rod Carew, from second to first. Sometimes he crawls unevenly along the spectrum, like Pete Rose. Sometimes, like Willie Mays, the only movement in a player's career is within the area covered by one position; that is, the player moves gradually from being a center fielder who has outstanding range to being a center fielder with very little range. But always he moves leftward, never right. Can you name one aging first baseman who has been shifted to second base or shortstop to keep his bat in the lineup?" (www .baseballanalysts.com/archives/2004/08/abstracts_from_17.php).

Chapter 3-3

104 "Pierzynski 'was not, to put it mildly, a particular favorite of the pitching staff'": Mike Bauman, Baseball Perspectives at MLB.com, http://san francisco.giants.mlb.com/NASApp/mlb/news/article_perspectives.jsp? ymd=20050321&content_id=973267&vkey=perspectives&fext=.jsp.

106 "the book by Craig Wright and Tom House": Craig Wright and Tom House, *The Diamond Appraised* (New York: Simon and Schuster, 1989).

106 "every qualifying pitcher-catcher battery over a seventeen-year span": Keith Woolner, "Field General or Backstop: Evaluating the Catcher's Influence on Pitcher Performance," *Baseball Prospectus 1999* (Dulles, VA: Potomac Books, 1999), pp. 466–474, reprinted at www.baseball prospectus.com/article.php?articleid=432.

Chapter 4-1

113 "John Thorn and Pete Palmer . . . *The Hidden Game of Baseball*": John Thorn and Pete Palmer, *The Hidden Game of Baseball: A Revolutionary Approach to Baseball and Its Statistics*, rev. ed. (New York: Doubleday, 1985), pp. 153, 158–159.

116 "In an essay in *Baseball Prospectus 2005*": James Click, "Station to Station: The Expensive Art of Baserunning," *Baseball Prospectus 2005* (New York: Workman, 2005), pp. 511–515.

Chapter 4-2

128 "run-expectation tables popularized by John Thorn and Pete Palmer in *The Hidden Game of Baseball*": John Thorn and Pete Palmer, *The Hidden Game of Baseball: A Revolutionary Approach to Baseball and Its Statistics*, rev. ed. (New York: Doubleday, 1985).

128 "George Lindsey, in his article "An Investigation of Strategies in Baseball": *Operations Research* (Summer 1963): www-math.bgsu.edu/ ~albert/papers/saber.html; Earnshaw Cook, *Percentage Baseball* (Baltimore, MD: Waverly Press, 1964).

129 "'my home games in Coors Field . . . my home games in PETCO Park or Dodger Stadium'": Quoted in Bill Shaikin, "They Won't Sacrifice Beliefs; Angels' Scioscia, Dodgers' Tracy Continue to Use Strategy of the Bunt," *Los Angeles Times*, June 24, 2005, p. D8.

130 "Dodger Stadium and Kauffman Stadium had overall park factors of 95 in 2004": These park factors are centered around 100. Factors above 100 indicate that the park increases the likelihood of the event. In this particular case, both Kauffman Stadium and Dodger Stadium decrease run scoring by 5 percent compared to the league average. However, Dodger Stadium's 103 HR park factor indicates that a league-average team would hit 3 percent more home runs if it played all its games in Dodger Stadium.

132 "Bill James noted . . . that even he 'would certainly signal a bunt . . .' . . . advance of a baserunner": Dave Sheinin, "Too Much of a Sacrifice? While Old Guard Stands by Bunt, 'Moneyball' Crowd Says It Comes Up Short," *Washington Post*, August 28, 2005, p. E01.

132 "A series of articles at Baseball Prospectus titled 'Taking One for the Team: When Does It Make Sense to Sacrifice?'": www.baseballprospectus .com/article.php?articleid=2844.

134 "The results are listed in Table 4-2.4": When applying the information given in the table, the thresholds in OBP and SLG are far more important than AVG. Additionally, the "1 run" situations assume that the opposing manager intentionally walks the following batter when appropriate to keep the double play in order. Without a subsequent double play, the thresholds rise slightly in the final two situations. For full results, see www.baseballprospectus.com/article.php?articleid=2869.

135 "Nate Silver introduced One-Run Value Yield . . . at Baseball Prospectus": www.baseballprospectus.com/article.php?articleid=4003.

135 "the Indians have a 32.7 percent chance to win the game": This value is different from the 49.6 percent cited earlier because that was the win expectation after Broussard's double.

Chapter 4-3

140 "'very well-paid and very perturbed adviser'": Jack Curry, "Psst . . . Showalter Had Second Chance," *New York Times*, December 3, 1995, p. S1.

142 "the results of any managerial Win-Expectancy analysis": In Tables 4.2–4.5, the SH column only includes sacrifice attempts by non-pitchers. Pitcher bunts were excluded for a few reasons. Primarily, managers in the AL don't have the opportunity to bunt with pitchers, so it would be unfair to judge them against their NL counterparts in that aspect. Second, as discussed in the previous chapter, bunting with pitchers is almost always a good idea because they're such terrible hitters. More important, Win Expectancy would unduly punish managers for bunting with pitchers because it does not consider the hitting abilities of the spe-

cific batters involved. Thus, every time a pitcher bunts, Win Expectancy would reduce a manager's wins added. When quantifying bunts by position players, Win Expectancy works well because most position players hit within a very small range of AVG, OBP, and SLG. It is only with outliers as bad as pitchers that Win Expectancy is drastically in error. Finally, virtually no managers deviate from the conventional wisdom with regards to sacrifice hits by pitchers. By removing pitcher sacrifices from the measure of managers, virtually no distinguishing information is lost.

145 "sets of even- or odd-numbered years to simulate randomly selected career halves": For more on this analytical technique, see www.baseball prospectus.com/article.php?articleid=883.

146 "Baseball Prospectus's defensive measure 'Rate'": "Rate" is discussed in detail in Chapter 3-2.

151 "ability to manage their bullpen better than the rest of the league": Specifically, relievers were ranked within the team bullpen, and situations in which a reliever was used more than one rank from his ideal position were considered. For example, because Duchscherer was the fourth-best reliever for the A's but was used in their highest-Leverage situations, Macha was credited with one misappropriation. Overlooking single-spot differences allows managers some leeway to take advantage of platoon matchups and other advantages not accounted for in FRA and also overlooks situations in which two relievers may fall very close in FRA, making their rankings less significant.

155 "'He could take kids out of the coal mines'": *Baseball's Greatest Quotations*, Paul Dickson (New York: HarperCollins, 1991), p. 64.

155 "'You're a Yankee. Act like one'": David Halberstam, *Summer of '49* (New York: Avon, 1989), p. 21.

Chapter 5-1

157 "Mario Mendoza wasn't the kind of player you'd expect to achieve immortality": http://en.wikipedia.org/wiki/Mario_Mendoza.

157 "It gave rise to the term 'Mendoza Line'": http://en.wikipedia.org/wiki/Mendoza_Line.

172 "Is it possible to link Mendoza to the Babe?": www.baseball-reference .com/m/mendoma01.shtml.

Chapter 5-2

174 "it promised Rodriguez more than $500 per pitch": http://espn.go.com/columns/ratto_ray/938042.html.

174 "the annual salaries of 530 . . . teachers, or 660 . . . firefighters": Estimates provided by Salary.com.

175 "he's a supremely talented baseball player who makes his team more competitive and more fun to watch": The value of goods and services is also highly associated with scarcity, and there are few baseball players

around who perform as well as Rodriguez. A common problem put to Economics 101 students is the "diamond-water paradox." Water is essential to human life, while diamonds are a luxury, but diamonds are extraordinarily expensive, while water is cheap. Why? The answer to the riddle is twofold: first, diamonds are scarce, while water is plentiful. Second, value is subjective: Although diamonds have little practical use, people desire them tremendously, which drives up their price. We might think of Alex Rodriguez as a diamond.

175 "the baseball club is just one tiny part of a huge business": Large companies sometimes break down profits and losses by business segments in their public filings. However, Generally Accepted Accounting Principles (GAAP) rules limit their responsibility for doing so, and baseball team operations would generally not be considered material enough to require a segmented disclosure. In 2004, for example, the Atlanta Braves accounted for $162 million in revenue to Time-Warner, according to estimates by *Forbes* magazine. This represents only 0.4 percent of the $42.1 billion that Time-Warner reported as its overall revenue in its fiscal year 2004.

175 "One exception is the Cleveland Indians": See www.sec.gov/Archives/edgar/data/1059019/0000950152-98-003022.txt.

176 "collected annually since 1993 by Team Marketing Report": See, for example, www.teammarketing.com/fci.cfm?page=fci_mlb2005.cfm.

177 "more people will buy 2007 season tickets as a result": I did not evaluate different levels of postseason performance specifically (e.g., winning the World Series versus losing in the Wild-Card round) because of the large number of highly correlated variables that this evaluation would introduce.

177 "ESPN.com . . . assigned ratings . . . to each of the . . . ballparks": http://sports.espn.go.com/mlb/stadiums.

177 "The lowest-rated park was Olympic Stadium, . . . the highest was PNC Park in Pittsburgh": I filled in ratings for ballparks that did not exist in 2003 or underwent significant renovations over the period 1997–2004. Three Rivers Stadium in Pittsburgh, for example, where the Pirates played before moving into PNC, was assigned a rating (57.5) similar to Veterans Stadium in Philadelphia (53.5), which is included in the ESPN analysis. The park ratings that I entered were as follows:

Angels (Angel Stadium of Anaheim/Edison Field): Rating of 84 in 2003 ESPN survey. Substantial renovations were made to Anaheim Stadium between 1997 and 1998. I rated the stadium as a 70 in 1997, a 77 in 1998, and an 84 thereafter, consistent with the ESPN.com rating.

Astros (Astrodome): Astros' home field before opening of Minute Maid Park (originally Enron Field) in 2000. The Astrodome was assigned a rating of 55.

Brewers (County Stadium): Brewers' home field before opening of Miller Park in 2001. County Stadium was assigned a rating of 70.

Giants (Candlestick Park): Giants' home field before opening of SBC

Park (originally Pac Bell Park) in 2000. Candlestick Park was assigned a rating of 55.

Mariners (Kingdome): Mariners' home field before opening of Safeco Field in the middle of the 1999 season. The Kingdome was assigned a rating of 57.5 in 1997 and 1998. In 1999, the Mariners were assigned a stadium rating of 69.5, representing the average between the Kingdome rating and ESPN's 81.5 rating for Safeco Field.

Padres (PETCO Park): PETCO Park was opened for the 2004 season, replacing Qualcomm Stadium, and assigned a rating of 82.5.

Phillies (Citizens Bank Park): Citizens Bank Park was opened for the 2004 season, replacing Veterans Stadium, and assigned a rating of 82.5.

Pirates (Three Rivers Stadium): Pirates' home field before opening of PNC Park in 2001. Three Rivers Stadium was assigned a rating of 57.5.

Reds (Cinergy Field): Reds' home field before opening of Great American Ballpark in 2003. Cinergy Field was assigned a rating of 57.5.

Tigers (Tiger Stadium): Tigers' home field before opening of Comerica Park in 2000. Tiger Stadium was assigned a rating of 75.

White Sox (Comiskey Park/U.S. Cellular Field): Rating of 74 in 2003 ESPN survey. A series of renovations was made between 2002 and 2004. I rated the park as a 70 in 1997–2001, a 72 in 2002, a 74 in 2003 (consistent with the ESPN.com rating), and a 76 in 2004.

178   "The honeymoon effect is a well-documented phenomenon": See, for example, www.baseballprospectus.com/article.php?articleid=2009.

178   "the honeymoon effect variable": One team—the Seattle Mariners—opened its new ballpark, Safeco Field, in the middle of the 1999 season. In this case, Safeco Field was assigned a honeymoon variable of 2.5 for each of 1999 and 2000, 1.5 for 2001, and 0.5 for 2002.

178   "Mike Jones . . . evaluated the top-fifty Nielsen TV markets": http://home.nycap.rr.com/nickandaj/marketsize.html.

178   "Per-capita income . . . based on 2001 Bureau of Economic Analysis estimates": More specifically, per-capita personal income by metropolitan area. See www.bea.gov/bea/newsrel/MPINewsRelease.htm. Because the BEA does not provide data on foreign cities, and because the Canadian government reports per-capita income metrics that are not directly comparable to those used by the BEA, per-capita income estimates for Toronto and Montreal were extrapolated based on evaluating the per capita income of a comparable U.S. city—Detroit—and adjusting downward to reflect the relatively lower purchasing power of the Canadian dollar.

178   "seven . . . variables had a statistically significant impact": The regression also included an independent variable for calendar year, as baseball attendance revenue increased notably faster than inflation over the period 1997–2004. Specifically, the variable "Year" was defined as the number of years since 1997.

The coefficients, standard errors, and t-scores for the regression analysis are as follows:

Variable	Coefficient	Standard Error	T-Score
Stadium rating	754,394	79,359	9.51
Market size	127,389	18,561	6.86
Honeymoon effect dummy	5,624,264	1,280,211	4.39
Wins in previous season	415,468	95,802	4.34
Playoff appearances in past 10 years	1,925,551	581,249	3.31
Wins in current season	289,149	90,076	3.21
Years elapsed since 1997	1,014,522	406,404	2.50
Per-capita income	366	197	1.86
Constant	−102,000,000	10,500,000	−9.74

The R-squared of the regression was .67.

178 "A team . . . that has a small stadium can still capture increased demand": Indeed, essentially all of the new stadiums that have opened in the past 15 years have been "small" facilities of about 40,000 seats, as teams have found that distant, upper-deck seats potentially dilute from the premium experience they'd like fans to associate with their new stadiums, while smaller capacities create some pent-up demand for tickets.

179 "no statistically significant effect after other, similar variables were accounted for": Regression analysis seeks to isolate those independent variables that most directly drive changes in the dependent variable, excluding redundant variables where possible. It should be noted that some of these excluded variables would turn up as statistically significant if the similar variables were excluded.

179 "upgrading to a new ballpark is potentially a highly profitable endeavor": A team that receives $19 million in additional gate receipts a year by upgrading its facility, plus a "bonus" of $17 million associated with the honeymoon effect, could expect to recoup the cost of a new, $250 million stadium in just twelve to thirteen seasons before accounting for the favorable treatment of new-stadium debt under baseball's revenue-sharing rules. Although major league teams certainly have an incentive to get the public to pick up a share of the new-stadium tab, substantially private investments, such as those made by the Giants and the Cardinals, should also provide for a healthy return.

179 "The largest market . . . the New York Yankees . . . the smallest market . . . the Kansas City Royals": Put differently, if the size of the Yankees' market is assessed at about eighteen million (75 percent of the metropolitan population of New York City, plus some provision for markets like Hartford), and the Royals' market at about two million (the approximate size of the Kansas City metroplex), each additional citizen in the metropolitan area can be said to provide about $1.78 in additional income to the local baseball club. Such an analysis could presumably be applied to provide a more equitable basis for profit sharing among pro baseball clubs. See, for example, www.baseballprospectus.com/news/20020815zumsteg.shtml.

180 "should probably not be considered a luxury good": Something like

luxury-box rentals, on the other hand, might be more dependent on both individual and corporate wealth within the metropolitan area.

180 "its on-field quality probably makes the largest difference": If the team-quality, stadium-quality, and market-quality metrics are considered in the regression analysis one group at a time, excluding the other factors, team quality goes the longest way toward explaining differences in attendance revenue.

180 "an additional playoff appearance is worth about $14.9 million": As our model suggests that the benefit of a playoff appearance is felt for ten years going forward, we can calculate the total present value of a playoff appearance by assigning a $1.9 million increase in revenue in each of the next ten seasons and discounting future revenue at a rate of 5 percent per year to account for the time value of money.

181 "number of games . . . an individual player season is worth": See the discussion on Wins Above Replacement Player (WARP) in Chapter 1-1.

181 "if we take playoff appearances out of the regression equation": If the playoff variable is removed from the analysis, the regression results are as follows:

Variable	Coefficient	Standard Error	T-Score
Stadium rating	780,241	80,684	9.67
Market size	133,181	18,878	7.05
Wins in previous season	531,270	91,127	5.83
Honeymoon effect dummy	5,326,002	1,304,676	4.08
Wins in current season	349,002	90,155	3.87
Years elapsed since 1997	1,225,560	410,067	2.99
Per-capita income	386	201	1.92
Constant	-111,700,000	9,768,479	-11.93

The R-squared of the regression was .65.

182 "a ratio of about 30 percent": This revenue represents "pure" profits without regard to the direct costs of producing such concessions items because the Indians' licensed concessions operator, Sportservice, was responsible for procuring those items. This accounting treatment is helpful for a couple of reasons. First, not all concessions revenue flows through directly to the team. Rather, profits are shared between the team; a catering company that is licensed to operate the concessions facilities; and, in some cases, the municipality that leases the stadium to the club. Finally, there are some direct costs associated with preparing concessions items; it's more costly to produce twenty thousand Dodger Dogs than ten thousand Dodger Dogs. (Admittedly, the margins on these items are likely to be very high—compare the price of a hot dog at a baseball game with what you'd pay at a supermarket.) This is not the case with gate receipts—apart from a few immaterial costs like printing extra tickets and perhaps hiring additional ushers, it costs no more to have a full seat at a baseball stadium than an empty one.

182 "Loews Cineplex . . . reported profits on concessions items": Loews reported gross concessions as averaging $238 million over the period. It

operated these concessions itself and reported the direct costs of the concessions items as averaging $38 million per year, for a $200 million annual profit. See www.sec.gov/Archives/edgar/data/1054588/0000940 180-00-000662-index.html.

182 "data on luxury suites and club seats . . . at . . . sportsvenues.com": www.sportsvenues.com/info.htm.

183 "an average of about $52 million in gate receipts": As estimated from 2004 attendance and ticket-price data, adjusted to 2005 dollars.

184 "$45.5 million in postseason revenue": See http://roadsidephotos.sabr .org/baseball/mlbsez.htm. Although there have been some questions about the validity of the MLB financial disclosures, most have concerned items like media revenue and operating expenses that are larger in scope and easier to manipulate; there is no reason to doubt the accuracy of the postseason revenue figures.

185 "profits of slightly less than $4 million per year on merchandise sales": Unlike the case of selling additional seats or low-grade hot dogs, the cost of producing this merchandise and operating the retail stores may be substantial. The Indians reported an average of $16 million in merchandise revenue between 1996 and 1997, but the cost of selling the goods was $12 million per season, for an annual profit of $4 million.

185 "merchandise sales . . . operate as a multiplier on gate receipts": There is also some solid anecdotal evidence, such as the vast bounty of Red Sox merchandise sold following their 2004 World Series championship, that merchandise sales are quite sensitive to team success.

185 "In 2003 . . . the Expos earned nothing": In 2003, the Expos had no local TV deal and could not find a station willing to carry their games in English. The Expos licensed their French-language radio broadcasts in 2003 but did not charge for these rights.

185 "may be subject to manipulation": Because some teams own their media outlets—the Yankees and the YES Network, or the Cubs (Tribune Corp.) and WGN—they have some leeway to regulate the rights fees associated with their media deals as a matter of intercompany transfer pricing. Because teams incur MLB revenue-sharing payments on their local media deals, there may be some incentive to underreport media revenue accruing to the club in a case where a related party owns these rights. Suppose, for example, that the Cubs report $30 million in revenue from their deal with WGN, when in fact these media rights are worth $40 million to WGN. From the standpoint of Tribune Corp.'s bottom line, since it owns both entities, the price paid from the Cubs to WGN will not matter—if there is $10 million too little on the Cubs' income statement, there will be $10 million extra on the WGN income statement to make up for it. However, Cubs revenue is subject to MLB revenue sharing, whereas WGN revenue is not, producing some savings for the mother company.

185 "as reported in . . . *Broadcasting & Cable* magazine": Teams can accrue broadcasting revenue in one of two ways—they can license their rights to a third party in exchange for royalty payments, or they can operate

their own networks and receive money from advertising or subscription fees. Although *Broadcasting & Cable* distinguished between these two revenue models in its reports, I considered them one and the same for purposes of this analysis. Similarly, while *Broadcasting & Cable* itemizes broadcast TV, cable TV, and radio revenue, I lumped them into one category for this study.

185 "The independent variables . . . in the regression analysis": In addition, as in the case of the attendance revenue regression, I included an additional explanatory variable for calendar year. However, this variable did not prove to have a statistically significant effect on local media revenue and was dropped from the analysis.

185 "average number of games won in the *previous three seasons* proved to be more reliable": This measure proved to be preferable because: (1) broadcast royalty fees are established prior to the start of the season, meaning that the current season's performance is irrelevant, and (2) some fraction of broadcast deals is made for multiple years at a time, meaning that looking at just the preceding season may be misleading.

186 "the vast bulk of differences . . . can be explained by evaluating just three variables": Complete regression results were:

Variable	Coefficient	Standard Error	T-Score
Superstation dummy	35,300,000	2,615,799	13.50
Market size	135,273	11,970	11.30
Playoff appearances in past ten years	1,825,069	371,905	4.91
Constant	2,314,510	1,343,092	1.72

The R-squared of the regression was .77.

186 "Market size is also a highly significant predictor of local media revenue": Indeed, market size is a relatively more important determinant of broadcast revenue than of attendance revenue. Although teams are limited in the number of high-quality seats that they can make available to their ballgames, broadcasts of their games can be made available to anyone owning a TV antenna or radio receiver in their local markets, without any deterioration in quality.

186 "baseball games can become an important part of a . . . network's brand and . . . schedule": The latter point is illustrated in my home market, Chicago. Until 2004, Fox Sports Net owned cable rights to the Cubs, White Sox, NBA Bulls, and NHL Blackhawks, providing it with programming on about three hundred nights per season. At that time, Comcast pursued an aggressive strategy and purchased the cable rights to all four clubs over a span of several months for its own local sports network. As a result, Fox Sports Net's programming schedule in the Chicago market has been devastated, featuring a mix of beach volleyball, poker tournaments, and arena football.

187 "If the playoff appearances variable is removed": With the playoff appearances variable removed, the regression results are as follows:

Variable	Coefficient	Standard Error	T-Score
Superstation dummy	38,800,000	2,589,982	14.99
Market size	137,177	13,266	10.34
Average number of wins			
in past three years	243,228	78,162	3.11
Constant	–14,500,000	5,932,584	–2.44

The R-squared of the regression was .76.

187 "teams earning below-average local revenue gain from it": Revenue sharing is sometimes referred to as a "tax." In practice, however, it operates differently than a normal corporate tax. Whereas federal and state taxes are assessed to corporations at the operating income (profit) level, MLB revenue-sharing obligations are assessed at the revenue (sales) level. This distinction has some material consequences for team behavior. Consider, for example, a team that pays $20 million to a group of free agents and has a successful season as a result, generating an extra $25 million in local revenue for a $5 million profit. If the 34 percent fee was assessed at the profit level, the team would pay a tax of $1.7 million, providing for a healthy after-tax profit. If, however, the tax is assessed at the revenue level, a team now must pay taxes of 34 percent on revenue of $25 million, or $8.5 million. When combined with the $20 million the team pays out in salaries, it now must pay $28.5 million to earn $25 million, turning a winning transaction into a losing one.

This is, of course, the intent of revenue sharing. Revenue sharing is intended to discourage teams from spending money on free agents by reducing the financial upside these free agents provide. This is why the players' union, which has an interest in promoting higher salaries for its members, is so opposed to revenue sharing. I will not describe the strategic implications of revenue sharing further, as this topic is addressed in detail in Chapter 6-3, other than to reiterate that revenue sharing discourages spending among all teams, not just "rich" teams. If the Devil Rays earn an extra $10 million as a result of signing a good free agent, they are responsible for $3.4 million in revenue-sharing payments, just as the Yankees would be if they earned the same $10 million.

187 "Economist Andrew Zimbalist estimates that in 2005": Andrew Zimbalist, *May the Best Team Win: Baseball Economics and Public Policy*, updated ed. (Washington, DC: Brookings Institution Press, 2004), p. 103. The "paradox" arises from the fact that the total amount redistributed under the "split pool" portion of the system is fixed as a proportion of base plan revenue sharing. The mathematics behind this are not entirely intuitive, but I have confirmed Zimbalist's findings thorough my own simulations.

188 "you wouldn't pay a player $6 million if you expect him to earn you only $5 million": In fact, since MLB contracts are guaranteed, the amount a team should be willing to pay for a free agent should be somewhat less than the anticipated revenue in order to compensate for the risk a team takes when committing millions of dollars to a player who might get injured or see his performance decline.

188   "an analysis of the winter 2005 free-agent market": Specifically, the following procedures were applied on the salary side:

1. Salary payments were spread out evenly over the number of guaranteed contract years. For example, a player who was signed to a $15 million, three-year contract is assumed to be paid $5 million in each of 2005, 2006, and 2007.

2. The major league–minimum salary of $317,000 was subtracted from each year of the contract. Because teams are obligated to pay at least $317,000 for each of the players who make up their twenty-five-man major league roster, this cannot be considered a part of the marginal cost associated with signing a player to a more expensive contract.

3. Future contract payments were discounted at a rate of 5 percent annually to reflect the time value of money.

4. An additional luxury-tax payment, equal to 40 percent of contract value, was assessed to the four players signed by the Yankees (Jaret Wright, Carl Pavano, Tino Martinez, and Tony Womack). Although the luxury tax, implemented under baseball's 2002 Collective Bargaining Agreement, has been the subject of much discussion, in practice its application has been limited. The payroll thresholds applied to the luxury tax are quite high by the standards of any team other than the Yankees. The only teams other than the Yankees to have incurred the luxury tax are the Red Sox and the Angels in the 2004 season, and the payments those clubs made were minor. No team, other than the Yankees, is projected to trigger the luxury tax in 2005. On the other hand, the Yankees certainly will trigger the luxury tax in 2005 and in any other years in which the luxury tax is in place for the foreseeable future. The luxury-tax system is progressive, meaning that the tax rate increases with each violation. As the Yankees have already violated the luxury tax twice, their tax rate now stands at 40 percent.

Applying these adjustments resulted in allocations of $101.3 million and $56.8 million in payments to Carlos Beltran and Adrian Beltre, respectively, versus reported figures of $119 million and $64 million. On the other hand, Carl Pavano will actually cost $50.4 million, rather than the official figure of $39.95 million, because of the luxury-tax payments the Yankees will be making on his contract. The total present value of the salaries guaranteed to the 2005 free-agent class under this method was $1.08 billion.

The projection method applied to assess the free agents' expected output was as follows. I took the weighted average of each player's WARP score over the previous three seasons, weighted 50 percent based on his 2004 performance, 30 percent on his 2003 performance, and 20 percent on his 2002 performance. I applied this weighted average to each year of the contract but reduced it by 5 percent for each year of the contract in which the player will be at least twenty-nine years old, and an additional 5 percent for each year in which he will be at least thirty-two years old. This method projects, for example, that Jason Varitek, who signed a four-year contract with the Red Sox, will be worth 5.3 wins in 2005, 4.7 wins in 2006, 4.3 wins in 2007, and 3.8 wins in 2008. The total number of wins for the free agents projected by this method was 612.

A version of this analysis was originally performed for the Baseball Prospectus Web site. See www.baseballprospectus.com/article.php?articleid=3910.

189   "Teams are willing to pay about $1.75 million per additional win": This implies that the relationship between salary and wins is linear: a 6-win player will cost exactly twice as much as a 3-win player. In practice, however, teams are willing to pay a "premium" for scarce, premium talent: the 6-win player will cost more than twice as much as the 3-win player. There is some legitimate economic rationale for this behavior; see www.baseballprospectus.com/article.php?articleid=4535 for a discussion.

189   "Are baseball teams . . . incapable of performing a rational cost-benefit analysis?": The answer, by the way, is not that the projection method used is too pessimistic. If a more rigorous projection system like Player Empirical Comparison and Optimization Test Algorithm is used, the total output in wins associated with the free agents turns out to be smaller. This implies that teams are actually paying more than $1.75 million per additional win, and perhaps more than $2 million.

191   "which won the NL Central with an 84-78 record": This analysis was originally conducted prior to the completion of the 2005 season. In 2005, the San Diego Padres reached the playoffs by winning the NL West with an 82-80 record,

194   "As described at a popular Web site": http://en.wikipedia.org/wiki/Winner%27s_curse.

194   "triggering claims of collusion": Whether the sharing of information between teams on free-agent negotiations constitutes collusion is a matter of some debate. MLB teams, however, have tended to err on the side of caution in these matters since they were required to pay more than $280 million in damages as a result of successful collusion claims made by the player's union between 1986 and 1988.

195   "With five bidders . . . $6.7 million, and with seven bidders, $6.9 million": If the player instead was paid according to the second-highest bid (or $1 higher than the second-highest bid), his advantage would be much less. This is the procedure, for example, that eBay uses: The winner of the auction isn't responsible for paying the seller in accordance with the winner's highest possible bid but rather, in accordance with the highest losing bid. Baseball teams can't employ this advantage (unless they're colluding). If the Rangers make a binding offer to Alex Rodriguez of $252 million, it is of no comfort to them that the next-highest bid on Rodriguez might have been "just" $170 million.

195   "the player should wind up doing very well": The problem has no doubt been exacerbated by the introduction of the Wild Card in 1995, which

places many more teams on the playoff bubble. If it seems that Wild-Card races are becoming more and more competitive each season, with many teams gravitating around the 90-win mark, this is no accident, since this is the point at which the returns on signing free agents is highest, and which many teams implicitly or explicitly plan around.

196 "the value of an additional win is greater in a larger market than a smaller one": See, for example, John D. Burger and Stephen J.K. Walters, "Market Size, Pay and Performance: A General Model and Application to Major League Baseball," *Journal of Sports Economics* (May 2003). Burger and Walters, who studied local revenue among MLB clubs from 1995 to 1999, found an interaction effect between wins and market size in predicting local revenue. That is, an extra win produces more revenue in New York than it does in Kansas City.

I tested for this interaction effect but did not find evidence of it on a statistically significant level. While market size and team success each have a profound effect on local revenue, my analysis implies that it is proper to treat these effects separately: The Mets make more money than the Royals because they play in a larger market, but the *marginal* effect of a win is about the same between the two teams.

That I did not find evidence of the interaction effect does not mean that it does not exist. Such an interaction effect, indeed, would tend to support my argument that the value of a win can vary significantly from situation to situation.

196 "the revenue-sharing plan in place": Prior to the new Collective Bargaining Agreement going into place for the 2003 season, teams were required to pay 20 percent of their locally generated revenue into the revenue-sharing pool, rather than 34 percent. If Tom Hicks did not anticipate an increase in revenue-sharing payment, this might excuse some of his overpayment of Rodriguez.

197 "the Yankees would likely have made the playoffs even without him": WARP evaluates Rodriguez as having been worth about 8 wins in 2004, a year in which the Yankees went 101-61. With a replacement-level player in Rodriguez' place, the Yankees would have finished at 93-69, good enough to edge out the 91-71 Oakland A's for the Wild Card, although they would have lost the AL East to the Red Sox.

198 "the evaluation would have been much harsher": Of course, it is not Rodriguez's fault that the rest of the Rangers played so poorly around him. However, the traditional notion that players are most valuable when they catapult their teams into playoff contention has a strong basis in economic reality and makes it hard to make the case that Rodriguez has provided a good return on investment to his employers. In fact, these estimates may be too generous. The Rangers had agreed to a long-term contract with Fox Sports Net Southwest for broadcast and cable TV rights prior to the 2000 season, a year before Rodriguez was signed, meaning that they could not use their new star as leverage in broadcasting negotiations.

Chapter 6-1

207 "baseball's 'biggest problem'": Will Lester, Associated Press, "Fans Fret High Wages More than Steroids," April 4, 2005.

208 "'We may do something nobody else has ever done'": Mike Lopresti, *USA Today*, "Reds Listen to Fans and Pay the Price: Larkin Stays in Cincinnati, But Ticket Prices Might Be Going Up," July 25, 2000, p. 5C.

208 "'We finished last with you'": Marvin Miller, *A Whole Different Ball Game* (New York: Birch Lane Press, 1991), p. 6.

210 "'Nobody has to force an owner to raise ticket prices:'" James Quirk and Rodney Fort, *Pay Dirt: The Business of Professional Team Sports* (Princeton, NJ: Princeton University Press, 1992), pp. 219–220.

211 "'You take the suites, the signage, throw the media on top'": John Helyar, *Lords of the Realm: The* Real *History of Baseball* (New York: Ballantine Books, 1995), p. 478.

213 "'Ticket prices have also gone up rather dramatically'": Allen Sanderson, personal communication, July 2005.

213 "'Certainly people in the upper half of the income distribution'": Sanderson, ibid.

213 "'Just as we trade up from Sears or Penney's to Nordstrom's'": Sanderson, ibid.

Chapter 6-2

217 "'Professional sports generally have no significant impact on a metropolitan economy'": Robert A. Baade, "Stadiums, Professional Sports, and Economic Development: Assessing the Reality," *A Heartland Policy Study*, Heartland Institute, April 4, 1994, www.heartland.org/Article.cfm ?artId=8828.

219 "'In every case, the conclusions are the same'": Roger G. Noll and Andrew Zimbalist, "Sports, Jobs, & Taxes: Are New Stadiums Worth the Cost?" *The Brookings Review* 15, no. 3 (Summer 1997), pp. 35–39.

219 "'if the hockey players sat out the whole season too'": CBC News, August 26, 1994, http://archives.cbc.ca/IDCC-1-41-1430-9217/sports/sports_ disputes/.

219 "'The strike had little, if any, economic impact on host cities'": John F. Zipp, "The Economic Impact of the Baseball Strike of 1994," *Urban Affairs Review* 32 (November 1996), pp. 157–185.

220 "'The stadium may have served as little more than an economic conduit'": Robert A. Baade, "The Impact of Sports Teams and Facilities on Neighborhood Economies: What Is the Score?" in William S. Kern, ed., *The Economics of Sports* (Kalamazoo, MI: W. E. Upjohn Institute for Employment Research, 2000), p. 33.

220 "'If you want to inject money into the local economy'": Michael O'Keeffe and T. J. Quinn, "The House That You Built: Owners, Pols Play Games with Billions of Taxpayer Dollars," *New York Daily News*, October 12, 2002, www.nydailynews.com/sports/baseball/story/26446p-25057c.html.

223 "'The streets are often empty on nights when there are no sporting events or shows'": Alan Achkar and Bill Lubinger, "Gateway's Scorecard: Sports Complex Still Trying for Home Run," *Plain Dealer* (Cleveland, OH), September 10, 2000, p. 1A.

223 "'three or four blocks walking distance from the stadium'": Baade, "The Impact of Sports Teams and Facilities on Neighborhood Economies," p. 40.

223 "'nobody was willing to pay anywhere near what cities were routinely spending'": John T. Davis, "Centre Professor Breaks New Ground in Sports Economics," *Advocate-Messenger* (Danville, KY), June 13, 2005, www.amnews.com/public_html/?module=displaystory&story_id=14265 &format=html.

Chapter 6-3

229 "gets to keep about 60 cents on every new dollar it earns": It's actually 61 percent at the top, 53 percent at the bottom—that's right, MLB has managed to devise a system where the more money you make, the more of it you get to keep.

233 "Doug Pappas suggested a simple progressive revenue-sharing rate": www.baseballprospectus.com/article.php?articleid=1600.

233 "One such revenue-sharing plan, devised by Baseball Prospectus's Keith Woolner": www.baseballprospectus.com/article.php?articleid=1432.

234 "In his book *May the Best Team Win*": Andrew Zimbalist, *May The Best Team Win* (Washington, DC: Brookings Institution Press, 2004).

Chapter 7-1

237 "Rany Jazayerli, in a 2005 series of articles": Rany Jazayerli, "Doctoring the Numbers: The Draft," www.baseballprospectus.com/article.php? articleid=4026; www.baseballprospectus.com/article.php?articleid=4042; www.baseballprospectus.com/article.php?articleid=4064; www.baseball prospectus.com/article.php?articleid=4090; www.baseballprospectus .com/article.php?articleid=4113; www.baseballprospectus.com/article .php?articleid=4291; www.baseballprospectus.com/article.php?articleid =4429.

Chapter 7-3

254 "Mattingly compared Maas to Will Clark": Some background in this section is adapted from Steven Goldman, "Before He Was King," *Yankees Magazine,* October 1999.

256 "age-twenty-five season": Baseball ages are traditionally defined by the age of the player as of July 1 of the season in question.

256 "speed score": Speed score is another Bill James invention. We use a variation of speed score that incorporates five measures associated with

speed: stolen-base attempts, stolen-base success rate, triples, double plays grounded into, and runs scored as a percentage of time reaching first base.

256　"isolated power": Isolated power is traditionally defined as slugging percentage less batting average and evaluates the frequency with which a player hits for extra bases. I use a slight variation of the traditional formula here, which treats triples as doubles, since triples are primarily the result of additional speed rather than additional power.

257　"Equivalent Runs": See the discussion of Equivalent Average and other offensive metrics in Chapter 1-1.

257　"a control group . . . in their age-twenty-five seasons": Players who dropped out of the big leagues entirely are averaged in as zeroes. The exception is players who are too young to have played at the age in question. Eric Munson, for example, has yet to complete his age-twenty-seven season as of this writing, so his results are not figured into the average at all for his age-twenty-seven year and onward.

258　"PECOTA": The first version of PECOTA that I developed was for pitchers, rather than position players, and so PECOTA is an acronym for Pitcher Empirical Comparison and Optimization Test Algorithm. We mention this for the sake of completeness; it is our hope that PECOTA will be remembered.

258　"Establish a player's 'baseline' level of performance": Most projection systems, including PECOTA, figure the weighted average based on the three most recent seasons of performance.

258　"such a system can provide some competent projections": See, for example, the "Marcel the Monkey" forecasting system at www.tangotiger .net/marcel/.

258　"adjustments that make its forecasts materially more accurate": After its debut season in 2003, we compared PECOTA to six other projection systems and found that it substantially outperformed all of them. See www .baseballprospectus.com/article.php?articleid=2515.

259　"key offensive statistics across consecutive seasons": These figures account for all major league players from 1946 to 2004 who had at least 300 plate appearances in consecutive seasons.

261　"players who hit between .250 and .260": The players also had to qualify for the batting title in the subsequent season to be included in the analysis. Only players from 1946 onward were considered.

261　"an average improvement of almost 30 points": A small portion of this improvement is the regression to the mean concept discussed above. If all players in the database who hit between .250 and .260 and qualified for the batting title in consecutive seasons are considered—not just those with low strikeout rates—the average improvement in batting average is 13 points.

262　"including Baseball Prospectus's own Keith Woolner": www.stathead .com/bbeng/woolner/peakage.htm.

262　"all post–World War II hitters at a given age": The batting statistics of pitchers were excluded from the analysis.

262 "average number of Equivalent Runs produced by those players in their next season": The average was weighted by the *minimum* number of plate appearances that the player had between the two consecutive seasons. This represents a compromise of sorts. We could use a "rate" statistic such as EqR produced per PA, but this would understate the impact of playing-time decrease as a result of injuries or unacceptably bad performances, which become more of a concern as a player ages. On the other hand, without this weighting scheme, a young player might be rewarded too significantly for breaking into the lineup as a rookie and seeing his EqR increase dramatically as a result of his receiving more playing time.

265 "PECOTA's Similarity Scores involve . . . differences from James's version": See *Baseball Prospectus 2003* for additional details on the difference between the PECOTA and James versions of Similarity Scores.

265 "PECOTA's Similarity Scores are meant to be applied *prospectively*": PECOTA's similarity factors are determined based on a technique known as analysis of variance (ANOVA). ANOVA is a sort of first cousin of regression analysis that measures which factors are most responsible for differences in a dependent variable—in PECOTA's case, the dependent variable is the number of Equivalent Runs produced per plate appearance in the upcoming season.

266 "Playing time": As measured by plate appearances in the past three seasons. This serves partly as a proxy for injury history, as detailed information on player injuries is not available to the public.

266 "Defensive ability": As measured by Clay Davenport's Fielding Runs.

267 "three different categories based on . . . their age-twenty-five seasons": Players must have had at least 300 PA in their age-twenty-five season in order to qualify. All performances are adjusted for park and league characteristics. As elsewhere in this analysis, only players from 1946 onward are included in the study.

267 "The Speed + Power players . . . in their age-twenty-six peak season": Note that, while players were classified into groups based on their performances at age twenty-five, the first year in which we assess their performance is one season later, at age twenty-six. This is necessary in order to avoid biasing the analysis. Since players are classified based on their performances in categories like isolated power that are highly correlated with run production, it is necessarily the case that players who received more favorable classifications would have produced more EqR in their age-twenty-five season. Delaying our analysis of the player's performance by one season, on the other hand, allows us to place the emphasis on using these characteristics to predict how the players are going to perform in the future. This is highly analogous to the process employed by PECOTA.

268 "As seen in Figures 7-3.6 and 7-3.7": I have defined batting eye here as twice a player's unintentional walk rate, less his strikeout rate. The interaction between walk rate, strikeout rate, and other player attributes can be a complicated one. For example, players who hit for power and

draw walks but also strike out frequently don't tend to age particularly well, while players with power and walks but more moderate strikeout rates age more gracefully. The invention of the "batting eye" statistic is intended to work around this problem, but it is better to consider strikeout rate and walk rate as separate attributes, as PECOTA does.

Chapter 8-1

273 "The all-time leader in days spent on the disabled list": Pete Palmer and Gary Gillette, eds., *The 2005 ESPN Baseball Encyclopedia* (New York: Sterling, 2005), p. 1167.

273 "'The only thing that matters'": Paul Dickson, *Baseball's Greatest Quotations* (New York: HarperCollins, 1991), p. 466.

273 "'The pitcher is the most important'": Jonathan Fraser Light, *The Cultural Encyclopedia of Baseball* (Jefferson, NC: McFarland, 1997), p. 562.

274 "'Pitching is 75 percent of baseball'": Leonard Koppett, *All About Baseball* (New York: New York Times, 1974), p. 36.

274 "'Pitching is 70 percent of baseball'": John Thorn and Pete Palmer, *The Hidden Game of Baseball: A Revolutionary Approach to Baseball and Its Statistics*, rev. ed. (New York: Doubleday, 1985), p. 177.

278 "Despite this imbalance": Ryan Wilkins, *Baseball Prospectus 2004* (New York: Workman, 2004), pp. 142–143.

279 "In his 1980 *Baseball Abstract,* Bill James demonstrated": Bill James, *The New Bill James Historical Baseball Abstract* (New York: Free Press, 2001), p. 674. See also Jim Baker and Clifford Corcoran, "A Streak of Insignificance," in The Writers of Baseball Prospectus, *Mind Game: How the Boston Red Sox Got Smart, Won a World Series, and Created a New Blueprint for Winning* (New York: Workman, 2005), p. 132.

279 Pythagorean tables: Dr. Richard Mohring, unpublished data, 2005.

288 "'The managerial policy which I have adopted'": Peter Williams, *When the Giants Were Giants* (Chapel Hill, NC: Algonquin, 1994), p. 136.

288 "His replacement, Eddie 'Doc' Marshall": ibid., p. 119.

288 "'The changes we've made'": ibid., pp. 138–139.

288 "his very first move was to bench McGraw's left fielders": Frank Graham, *The New York Giants* (New York: Putnam, 1952), p. 200. Joe Vila, "Ruppert Reserves Enthusiasm," *Sporting News*, July 7, 1932, p. 1.

289 "'THEY CAN'T BEAT US'": Graham, *The New York Giants*, p. 206. Noel Hynd, *The Giants of the Polo Grounds* (Dallas, TX: Taylor, 1995), p. 285.

289 "After 1949, Giants' manager Leo Durocher": Leo Durocher, *Nice Guys Finish Last* (New York: Simon and Schuster, 1975), pp. 255–256.

290 "'inept . . . a nuisance'": Zander Hollander, ed., *The Complete Handbook of Baseball, 1979* (New York: New American Library, 1979), p. 204.

Chapter 8-2

293 "Since 1993 the Rockies have had only two pitchers post a Run Average below 4.00": Run Average is similar to ERA except it accounts for all runs allowed by a pitcher. See Chapters 2-1 and 3-1 for more details.

296 "Robert K. Adair . . . has written an entire book titled *The Physics of Baseball*": quotations from Robert K. Adair, Sterling Professor of Physics, Yale University, *The Physics of Baseball*, 2nd ed. (New York: HarperCollins, 1994).

296 "Since the retarding force": ibid., pp. 18–19.

296 "The pitchers will also be hurt": ibid., pp. 43–44.

298 "long flies hit with balls stored under conditions of extreme humidity": ibid., pp. 19–20.

299 "But even if the fences are adjusted": ibid., pp. 19–20.

Chapter 8-3

308 "My first article for Baseball Prospectus": Jonah Keri, "The Success Cycle," BaseballProspectus.com, www.baseballprospectus.com/article.php ?articleid=1357.

309 "In a follow-up to 'The Success Cycle'": Jonah Keri, "Avoiding Dissonance," BaseballProspectus.com,www.baseballprospectus.com/article .php?articleid=1439

309 "Derek Zumsteg wrote a follow-up article": Derek Zumsteg, "Success Cycles Revisited," BaseballProspectus.com, www.baseballprospectus.com/ article.php?articleid=1707.

310 "That's a lot of bunk about them five-year building plans": Casey Stengel, *Sporting News*, April 6, 1955; quoted in The Writers of Baseball Prospectus, *Mind Game: How the Boston Red Sox Got Smart, Won a World Series, and Created a New Blueprint for Winning* (New York: Workman, 2005), p. 288.

312 "'It has been my experience'": Bill Veeck, *Veeck as in Wreck* (Chicago: University of Chicago Press, 1962), p. 143.

313 "In an August 2004 article . . . Nate Silver argued": Nate Silver, "The Tiger Plan," BaseballProspectus.com, www.baseballprospectus.com/ article.php?articleid=3382.

313 "Silver discovered some findings that contradicted his work in 'The Tiger Plan'": Nate Silver, "The Tiger Plan, Revisited," BaseballProspectus .com, www.baseballprospectus.com/article.php?articleid=4412.

320 "In *Baseball Prospectus 2004*, I cataloged": Jonah Keri, "Florida Marlins," *Baseball Prospectus 2004* (New York: Workman, 2004), pp. 104–105.

321 "You'll find more details on this team": The Writers of Baseball Prospectus, *Mind Game*.

324 "'What I like to do is ... than I can first'": Quoted in David Kaiser, *Epic Season: The 1948 American League Pennant Race* (reprint Amherst: University of Massachusetts Press, 1998), p. 32.

325 "Despite claiming heavy losses, he made more from the team in 1998": Andrew Zimbalist, "A Miami Fish Story," *New York Times*, October 18, 1998, www.ssc.uwo.ca/economics/faculty/jpalmer/Eco182/marlins.html.

Chapter 9-1

326 "Alan Schwarz . . . asked Baseball Prospectus to assist him": Alan Schwarz, "Finding a Power Stroke When Most Hitters Start to Fade," *New York Times*, December 12, 2004, www.nytimes.com/2004/12/12/sports/baseball/12score.html.

327 "he let people draw their own conclusions about Bonds, Giambi, and steroids": Throughout this chapter, I have used the popular and generic term "steroids." A more precise term, preferred by my colleague Will Carroll, is performance-enhancing drug (PED). Not all PEDs are pharmacologically classified as steroids, including some PEDs that are banned by the major league and minor league testing policies. For example, a sufficiently large quantity of caffeine is classified as a PED under the minor league testing policy, but caffeine is not a steroid. My usage of "steroid" differs from the proper medical usage and is intended to be inclusive of nonsteroid PEDs.

328 "Giambi said that he had begun using . . . Duca Durabolin in 2001": Mark Fainaru-Wada, Lance Williams, "Giambi Admitted Using Steroids," *San Francisco Chronicle*, December 2, 2004, http://sfgate.com/cgi-bin/article.cgi?file=/c/a/2004/12/02/MNG80A523H1.DTL.

328 "minor league players . . . suspended . . . during the 2005 season": Major League Baseball instituted a more stringent steroids-testing policy for the minor leagues in 2001, but the 2005 season was the first in which the names of violators were made public.

328 "an established major league veteran, at least twenty-eight years old": The age minimum of twenty-eight is put in place because power is a skill that can continue to develop throughout a player's early and mid twenties. Not all young players (nor anywhere near a majority) benefit from a Power Spike. Nevertheless, Power Spikes are common enough among young players that it would be facetious to classify them as "unexpected."

328 "by at least 10 HR per 650 PA": A player playing the vast majority of a 162-game season will usually accumulate about 650 PA.

329 "a new manufacturer of baseballs": Rawlings replaced Spalding as the official supplier of major league baseballs prior to the 1977 season. Observers were convinced that the new baseballs were manufactured differently than they had been in the past. See Will Carroll, *The Juice: The Real Story of Baseball's Drug Problems* (Chicago: Ivan R. Dee Publisher, 2005), pp. 220–221.

329 "the wide variety of styles that prospered during the period": For example, the World Series champion in 1982, the Cardinals, hit just 67 home runs while stealing 200 bases. The World Series champion in 1983, the Orioles, hit a league-leading 168 home runs but stole just 61 bases.

330 "the frequency of Power Spikes per 100 eligible hitters": An "eligible hit-ter" is one who was at least twenty-eight years old, had at least 500 PA in the season in question, and had at least 1,000 PA over his three previous seasons.

333 "'Look, if you told me shooting bull piss . . . fine'": Carroll, *The Juice*, p. 18.

334 "At least seventy-six players": As of this writing, there is no centralized database of players who were identified as testing positive for steroids. We were able to identify seventy-six after a thorough search of online re-sources. However, the number may be moderately higher, and some re-ports have described as many as eighty-one minor league steroid violators (but not listed them by name). Note also that this figure in-cludes two players, pitchers Carlos Almanzar and Felix Heredia, who were suspended in October 2005 after the regular season had already been completed.

Players on the forty-man roster of major league clubs are subject to the major league steroids testing policy, even if they are not on the active (twenty-five-man) roster at the time. This can be considered a privilege of being on the forty-man roster, as the minor league policy is more comprehensive than the major league one.

334 "Davenport Translations (DTs)": We also employ DTs for major league players, which essentially just account for park effects and any small dif-ferences in difficulty between the AL and NL.

335 "the vast majority of players were suspended . . . for a positive steroid test in spring training": In some cases, the date of the suspension may postdate the steroid use by a significant margin. For example, the Pi-rates claimed that Tom Evans's suspension in April 2005 was a result of a positive test in the 2004 season, when he was not in their organization. However, most of the suspensions came just before the start of the sea-son as a result of a positive test in spring training and so should be rea-sonably contemporaneous.

335 "the change is just on the verge of being statistically significant": A t-test on change in EqA among players who had at least 200 PA in both "be-fore" and "after" categories confirms statistical significance at the ninety-fifth percentile level.

335 "this is an impressive finding": By this I mean it is impressive to find some evidence of statistical significance given a relatively small data set, and one in which we'd naturally expect to see a lot of "noise."

338 "the type and quality of the steroid employed": Since many steroids are fabricated in illegal laboratories, they are subject to the same lack of "quality control" as are illicit recreational drugs. Higher-quality steroids are also more expensive and may be out of the financial reach of minor league players. See Carroll, *The Juice*, ch. 12, for a fuller discussion.

338 "whose performance fell far short of expectations": We wrote the follow-ing of Jeremy Giambi in *Baseball Prospectus 2002*, after he posted a .307/.413/.491 equivalent batting line with the Oakland A's in 2001: "He

showed flashes of the offensive brilliance that was expected of him after punishing the ball in the minors. He's going to break out in a big way sooner rather than later." Instead Giambi's career fell apart, and he found himself out of a major league job at the age of twenty-eight after putting up numbers of .197/.342/.352 with the Boston Red Sox in 2003.

340 "not materially higher than . . . during other sustained periods in baseball history": A particularly comprehensive and interesting treatment of this issue was conducted by Arthur De Vany of the Institute for Mathematical Behavioral Sciences at the University of California, Irvine. De Vany concludes that the current boom in home runs is well within the realm of normal, statistical fluctuation. His work can be found at www.arthurdevany.com/webstuff/images/HomeRunHitting.pdf.

340 "A similarly small fraction of minor league players": A typical major league organization includes about 150 players in its minor league system. Thus, among the thirty major league clubs, there are about 4,500 minor league players. We identified sixty-five minor leaguers who tested positive, which works out to 1.4 percent. If we use the higher estimate of eighty-one minor league suspensions as reported in some other accounts, that works out to about 2 percent of minor leaguers.

341 "guaranteed, long-term contracts": Doug Pappas salary database, http://roadsidephotos.sabr.org/baseball/data.htm.

341 "receiving a lucrative free-agent contract": It is my belief that the "contract year" phenomenon is related to steroid use. As we document in Chapter 5-3, players really do perform better in seasons in which they are up for a new contract. Major league teams could help to mitigate the problem by focusing on a player's longer-term track record when bidding on a free agent rather than just his most recent season of performance.

341 "the minimum salary for a Triple-A player was $12,900": Or $2,150/ month, assuming a six-month season. See www.minorleaguebaseball .com/app/milb/info/faq.jsp.

341 "a fringe prospect will have more incentive to use steroids": If this seems too Machiavellian, keep in mind the good news: If the decision to use steroids is essentially a rational one based on the player's personal cost-benefit analysis, then negative incentives like stricter punishments or more rigorous testing policies ought to work just as powerfully as positive ones.

342 "a few players for whom steroids represent a 'tipping point'": I suspect that if this "tipping point" effect exists, it probably appears most frequently among players who already have very effective workout and training regimens and are able to leverage the effects of steroids in the gym. In this sense, steroids are much like another performance-enhancing drug, Viagra. Sitting on your couch and watching *Bambi* after injecting steroids won't give you muscles, any more than sitting on your couch and watching *Bambi* after taking Viagra will give you an erection.

Chapter 9-2

344 "the probability of Redmond's hitting .438 or better . . . is only 0.5 percent": A handy tool in this situation is a measure called the cumulative distribution function. What this function tells us is the probability that a certain binomial event—an event with only two possible outcomes—will occur x times in y trials given a theoretical probability of success. For example, if we have a coin and we flip it 100 times, we can determine the probability of the coin's coming up heads 40 or fewer times using the cumulative distribution function, assuming the true probability of a heads flip is .5, or 50 percent. As the successes (in this case, a heads flip) move further and further away from the "true" probability of the coin (50 percent), the probability of achieving that many successes or fewer falls dramatically. In the case of Redmond versus Glavine, we simply assume that our "coin" will come up heads 27.5 percent of the time (Redmond's assumed .275 batting average against Glavine). The odds of that coin's landing on heads 43.8 percent of the time in 48 trials—the odds of Redmond's hitting .438 in 48 at-bats—is 0.5 percent.

345 "the standard deviation is going to be around 60–65 points of batting average": In a binomial distribution, the standard deviation can be calculated using the formula

$$\sqrt{\text{trials} \times \text{AVG} \times (1 - \text{AVG})}.$$

Thus, in the case of a hitter with a .287 average in 50 at-bats against Tom Glavine, the standard deviation would be

$$\sqrt{50 \times .287 \times (1 - .287)},$$

or 3.20 hits. Since we would expect a batter hitting .287 to have 14.35 hits in 50 at-bats, the range of hits that are within one standard deviation of the theoretical mean (.287) is 11.15 to 17.55, or about .223 to .351. The closer a batter's average is to .500, the higher the standard deviation. Thus, while we can conclude that a batter hitting .287 has a standard deviation of 64 points of batting average, players batting higher will have higher standard deviations and those faring worse at the plate will have lower standard deviations. As a result, we can say that 50 at-bats has a standard deviation of roughly 60–65 points of batting average for an average batter.

347 "the managerial bible *Weaver on Strategy*": Earl Weaver with Terry Pluto, *Weaver on Strategy: A Guide for Armchair Managers by Baseball's Master Tactician* (New York: Collier Books, 1984).

349 "Karros 'has been very, very good against lefties'": Susan Slusser, "Right-Thinking A's Excited to Have Karros," *San Francisco Chronicle*, February 3, 2004, www.sfgate.com/cgi-bin/article.cgi?file=/chronicle/archive/2004/02/03/SPGS74NJE31.DTL.

349 "'In fact . . . essentially they're all the same'": Rob Neyer, "A's Rating of Karros a Bit Too High," ESPN.com, February 6, 2004, http://proxy.espn .go.com/mlb/columns/story?columnist=neyer_rob&id=1728907.

350 "break a player's career into even- and odd-numbered years": For more on this analysis technique, see www.baseballprospectus.com/article.php ?articleid=883.

351 "'don't you think you might be better off with a left-hander who has?'": Quoted in Ed Linn, *The Great Rivalry: The Yankees and Red Sox, 1901– 1990* (Boston: Ticknor and Fields, 1991).

Chapter 9-3

353 "democracies rarely go to war with one another": There is some degree of debate about this point, known as "democratic peace theory," but the scholarly consensus is in its favor. See James Lee Ray, *Annual Review of Political Science* 1 (1998), www.mtholyoke.edu/acad/intrel/ray.htm. Note that democratic peace theory applies to democracy-versus-democracy wars specifically, and sometimes to civil wars within democracies. It does not claim that democracies are less likely to fight wars against autocracies.

353 "its massive collection of data can be downloaded": www.correlates ofwar.org.

353 "The 2003 Marlins rated": The 2003 Marlins were 10 fielding runs worse than average using our Fielding Runs Above Average (FRAA) system.

354 "log-5 . . . introduced by Bill James": A good description of log-5 and the method used herein for estimating series win probabilities can be found at www.diamond-mind.com/articles/playoff2002.htm.

354 "the likelihood of one team beating another": www.diamond-mind .com/articles/playoff.htm

356 "a team that sweeps through all 11 postseason games": Our study considers teams from 1972 onward, for which we have play-by-play data. It might be thought that those teams from 1972 through 1993, before the Wild-Card round was introduced, are at a disadvantage under the PSP system, since they can't collect points in the LDS. However, this isn't really the case because these teams had the advantage of not playing an additional playoff round in which they might have faced elimination. The average PSP is exactly 6 in all seasons since the introduction of the divisional play in 1969.

356 "The lowest is 0": This is a slight misstatement. The lowest plausible PSP under today's playoff format is 0. However, it was possible to receive a PSP of –1 in the years between 1985 and 1993, when the League Championship was a 7-game series, but the Wild-Card round had not yet been introduced. Two teams in our study, the 1988 and 1990 Boston Red Sox, have a PSP of –1 as a result of being swept in 4 games in the LCS.

357 "Runs allowed/game": Technically, the correlation between runs allowed and PSP is negative (–.22), since teams that allow *fewer* runs do better in

the postseason, as we should expect. However, we find it more intuitive to list the "favorable" attribute on the positive axis: it is favorable to allow fewer runs, and allowing fewer runs is associated with postseason success, so we call this a positive correlation. We've used this convention throughout this chapter.

358   "seven won the World Series . . . 1996 Yankees, 2000 Yankees": The modern Yankees dynasty is usually thought of as having a very good offense, but this wasn't the case for the 1996 and 2000 clubs. The 1996 Yankees scored 871 runs, in a league in which the average team scored 872; Yankee Stadium rated as a slight hitters' park in that season. The 2000 Yankees also scored 871 runs, in a league that averaged 857. However, Yankee Stadium boosted run scoring by 4 percent in 2000. If we take this 4 percent off the Yankees' run total, we come up with 838 runs, which qualifies as below average.

359   "great pitching but average offenses . . . great offenses but average pitching": "Average" hitting or pitching is defined as being within 6 percent of the league average in runs scored per game or runs allowed per game, respectively, after adjusting for park effects. This represents a span of roughly ±.25 RS/G from the average. "Great" hitting is defined as scoring at least 15 percent more runs per game than the league average, while great pitching is defined as allowing 15 percent runs fewer than the league average.

359   "in the same year and the same league": We searched only for teams within the same league, without considering interleague matchups. However, there are probably only a handful of interleague games that have met the criteria.

359   "good pitchers . . . when they're facing good hitters": www.baseball thinkfactory.org/btf/scholars/levitt/articles/batter_pitcher_matchup.htm.

360   "good pitchers have a structural advantage against good-hitting *teams*": It is possible to demonstrate this theory mathematically. Suppose that we have two teams, the Sharks and the Jets, in a league that averages 4.5 runs per team per game. The Sharks have an average offense that scores 4.5 runs per game but a great pitching staff that allows 3.0. The Jets are the opposite; they score 6.0 runs per game but allow 4.5. According to the Pythagenpat formula (a refined version of Clay Davenport's Pythagenport, which is itself a take-off on Bill James' original Pythagorean Formula) the teams will perform almost identically in the regular season: The Sharks will win 70.4 percent of their games and the Jets 70.3 percent.

But what happens when the Sharks and the Jets play one another? It should be clear that the Sharks will score 4.5 runs per game, since they have an exactly league average offense and are facing an exactly league average pitching staff.

How many runs the Jets will score is less evident. It is tempting to take the average of the Jets' RS/G figure of 6.0 and the Sharks' RA/G figure of 3.0, which works out to 4.5 runs per game. However, this is probably not mathematically correct. Imagine that the Jets are facing another team, the Giants, who have an average offense but a below-average pitching staff that allows 5.0 runs per game. If we average the Jets' 6.0 RS/G and the Giants' 5.0 RA/G, we come up with 5.5 runs per game. But this is not a satisfactory result: The Jets score 6.0 runs per game against an *average* pitching staff, so they should certainly score *at least* 6.0 runs per game against a below-average pitching staff.

An alternative formula is as follows:

$$\text{JetsRS} = \left(\frac{\text{JetsRS}}{\text{LeagueRS}}\right) \times \left(\frac{\text{SharksRS}}{\text{LeagueRS}}\right) \times \text{LeagueRS} = \frac{\text{JetsRS} \times \text{JetsRA}}{\text{LeagueRS}}$$

That is, we figure out how many runs the Jets score relative to league average, and how many runs the Sharks allow relative to league average, then combine the two figures. The formula predicts that the Jets will score 4.0 runs per game against the Sharks, as compared with the Sharks' 4.5 runs. The Pythagenpat formula predicts that the Sharks would win this matchup 57.1 percent of the time.

What happens to the Jets' "disappearing" wins? They make them up against the Giants, against whom they'll score 6.7 runs per game, enough to win some 77.8 percent of the time according to Pythagenpat. Conversely, the Sharks will not win quite as often as they "should" against poor offensive teams, against whom they encounter diminishing returns.

362   "teams that outperform their Pythagorean record . . . teams that underperform it": www.baseballprospectus.com/article.php?articleid=347.

362   "stolen-base attempts have a slight . . . positive relationship": Even the small correlation of .13 between stolen-base attempts and PSP overstates the case because stolen-base attempts are correlated reasonably strongly with FRAA, which has a relatively strong effect on PSP.

363   "extraneous starters may be useful out of the bullpen": Also, one of the top-three pitchers may be injured by the time the postseason rolls around, or a team may disagree with VORP about just who its best starters are.

363   "the closer's Win Expectancy": A "closer" is defined as the pitcher who has the most save opportunities in the regular season.

364   "the average number of lifetime . . . innings pitched ": Innings pitched were taken to be equivalent to 4 at-bats to create parity between pitchers and hitters.

364   "tend to be better players": The correlation between postseason experience and regular-season winning percentage was .19. A regression analysis suggests that accounting for playoff experience does not materially improve our ability to predict postseason success, once we have accounted for regular-season wins.

364   "they are also correlated with one another": The correlation between opponents' batting average and strikeout rate is .44 for the teams in our sample.

365   "we identified three factors": The key ideas behind the variable selection are as follows:

1. Each of these three variables has a highly statistically significant relationship with postseason success.
2. There are no other variables, or combinations of variables, that would materially improve the predictive ability of the regression equation, once these three variables have been accounted for.
3. The three variables are not especially redundant with one another.
4. Each of the three variables is a "fundamental" measure and does not derive from another, simpler metric.

The results of the regression on Playoff Success Points are as follows:

Variable	Coefficient	Standard Error	T-Score
FRAA	0.073	0.022	3.32
Normalized Pitcher Strikeout Rate (strikeouts per batter faced)	92.76	32.40	2.86
Closer WXRL	0.628	0.226	2.78
Constant	–12.67	5.47	–2.32

The R-squared of the regression was .11.

365   "only five of those teams went on to win the World Series": The exceptions were the 1981 Dodgers, 1987 Twins, 1988 Dodgers, 1991 Twins, and 1997 Marlins.

366   "Baseball Prospectus details in the book *Mind Game*": *Mind Game: How the Boston Red Sox Got Smart, Won a World Series, and Created a New Blueprint for Winning* (New York: Workman, 2005), ch. 24, "The Substance of Style."

366   "power pitchers who can throw an unhittable pitch": Conversely, finesse pitchers do especially well against poor, undisciplined hitters, while power pitchers sometimes beat themselves by trying to make a perfect pitch when it isn't necessary and delivering a walk.

366   "an inverse relationship between FRAA and pitcher strikeout rate": This tends to obscure the correlation of these statistics with PSP because they are often working against one another; the regression analysis can sort around this problem.

366   "11 percent of playoff success": As measured by the regression's R-squared.

Glossary

Throughout this book we introduce and define various statistical terms. There are also many terms not mentioned in this book that are relevant to baseball analysis. In an effort to consolidate all these concepts in one place, we've compiled this wide-ranging glossary.

Age-twenty-seven peak: In studying baseball players' peak age, Bill James found that for players with significantly long careers, the most common peak age was twenty-seven. More broadly, the peak age range for players with long careers has been pegged at twenty-five to twenty-eight and twenty-five to twenty-nine by various researchers. Improved medical care, nutrition, and exercise regimens have helped the current generation of players—including future Hall-of-Famers Roger Clemens and Randy Johnson—perform at peak levels well into their thirties and early forties, leading to speculation that peak age may be older than it once was. To date, though, no study has conclusively refuted James's findings, suggesting that the Rocket and the Big Unit remain outliers. (Chapter 7-3)

APR: Adjusted Pitching Runs. Measures the number of runs a pitcher prevented as compared to a league-average pitcher in a neutral park in the same number of innings. Derived from the pitching component of Linear Weights (Pitching Runs), APR includes an adjustment for ballpark and is based on all runs allowed, not just earned runs (*see* RA). The formula is $APR = L \times IP - R/PF$, where L is the league average of runs per inning and PF is the park factor for the player's home park. (Chapter 2-1)

ARP: Adjusted Runs Prevented. A measure of the number of runs a relief pitcher prevented as compared to an average pitcher, given the Base/Out state (the combination of outs and bases occupied) in which he entered and left each game, adjusted for league and park. Runners on base when a pitcher enters the game are called Inherited Runners. Runners on base when a pitcher exits the game are called Bequeathed Runners. (Chapter 2-2)

AVG/OBP/SLG: The holy trinity of batting stats, meant to convey a more accurate gauge of hitting ability than the traditional AVG/HR/RBI. AVG is the familiar batting average: hits per at-bat, not counting walks, hit by pitches, or sacrifices. OBP is on-base percentage: total number of times on base (hits plus walks plus hit by pitches) divided by the total of at-bats, walks, hit by pitches, and sacrifice flies (often called total plate appearances, although in fact sacrifice bunts and catcher's interference are excluded). SLG is slugging average: total bases on hits (one for a single, two for a double, etc.) divided by at-bats.

Together, the three provide an excellent snapshot of offensive prowess, combining the ability to get on base and to hit for power. (Chapter 1-1)

BABIP: Batting average on balls in play. A hitter's average or pitcher's average allowed on batted balls ending a plate appearance, excluding home runs. In the case of pitchers, BABIP for the most part is a function of luck and defense. The flip side of BABIP is Defensive Efficiency. (Chapters 2-1, 3-1, 3-2)

Base-Out Matrix: *See* Run Expectancy Table

Base-Out state: Also called Base-Out situation. For a given point during an inning, the combination of the number of outs and the bases occupied represents the "state" of the inning. This summary of the game situation is used to determine the expected number of runs that will score during the rest of the inning, to evaluate relief pitching effectiveness, and to help compute the expected win probability for the game. (Chapter 4-2)

Bequeathed Runs Prevented: Given the Base/Out state (the combination of outs and bases occupied) left by a pitcher exiting the game, the number of runs subsequent relievers allowed to score as compared to a park-adjusted league-average performance. A positive figure means the subsequent relievers kept more of the bequeathed runners from scoring than expected. A negative figure means more of the runners scored than expected. (Chapter 2-2)

BFP: Batters Faced Pitching, the total number of plate appearances against a given pitcher. Teams sometimes track BFP in addition to pitch counts to measure a pitcher's workload and make decisions on leaving him in or lifting him based on those factors. (Chapter 2-3)

BRAA: Batting Runs Above Average, the difference between the Equivalent Runs that this player produced and the Equivalent Runs that an average player would have produced in the same number of outs. An "average player" by definition, has an Equivalent Average of .260. (Chapter 1-1)

BRAR: Batting Runs Above Replacement, the difference between the Equivalent Runs that this player produced and the Equivalent Runs that a replacement player would have produced in the same number of outs. A "replacement player" in EqA terms, has an Equivalent Average of .230; players who hit for a .230 EqA rarely remain in the major leagues for long unless they are seen as good defensive players. (Chapter 1-1)

Category I–V starts: Starting-pitcher outings are divided into five categories based on how many pitches were thrown and the associated risk of short-term decline in pitching performance. Derived from Baseball Prospectus's Pitcher Abuse Points (PAP) research. (Chapter 2-3)

Category	Pitch Range	Risk of Short-Term Decline
I	0–100	smallest
II	101–109	minimal
III	110–121	moderate
IV	122–132	significant
V	133+	high

CERA: Catcher ERA. Invented by Craig Wright for his book *The Diamond Appraised*, Catcher ERA is an attempt to measure a catcher's defensive ability, in particular his ability to work with pitchers and call a good game. Subsequent studies suggest that catchers' game-calling ability is nearly impossible to measure and that CERA isn't a reliable stat. CERA = (Earned Runs while catching)/(Innings Caught) × 9. (Chapter 3-3)

Competitive balance: A somewhat nebulous term used to indicate the degree to which every team has a shot at competing for a postseason berth. Whether this means having a shot in a given year or being assured of a pennant race at least once every few years generally depends on who is making the argument. Commissioner Bud Selig has frequently argued for a drag on salaries (whether a salary cap, a luxury tax, or another mechanism) to provide more teams with "hope and faith" and improve competitive balance. This despite Major League Baseball's producing nineteen different World Champions in the past twenty-six years, a record of parity unmatched by any other major professional sport. (Chapter 6-3)

Complete game percentage: The percentage of games completed by the starting pitcher, a number that has fallen drastically in recent times due to a variety of reasons including specialized relief roles, increased scoring, higher salaries, and the understanding that high pitch counts increase the risk of injury and ineffectiveness. In 2005, starters pitched complete games 3.9 percent of the time. In 1985, the percentage was 14.9 percent, in 1955 it was 30.3 percent, and a century ago it was 79.9 percent. (Chapter 2-3)

Correlation: A measure of how closely aligned two statistics are, on a scale of 1 to –1. A correlation of 1 means that the two move in lockstep (if statistic X goes up, so does statistic Y); –1 means they move in opposition (if X goes up, Y goes down); 0 means they bear no statistical relationship (X tells you nothing about what Y does, and vice versa).

Counting statistic/rate statistic: A counting statistic evaluates a player's performance based on the total number of times he achieved a certain event. For example, home runs are a counting stat. A rate statistic looks at a player's performance based on the rate at which he achieves a certain event. For example, batting average, which divides the number of hits a player produces by the number of at-bats he sees, is a rate stat. Both counting stats and rate stats can in some cases present a skewed view of a player's achievements. A leadoff hitter, for instance, is more likely to accumulate 200 hits in a season than a cleanup hitter because he gets more chances at bat over the course of a season. On the other hand, a batter who hits .400 may seem like a superstar. But if he achieved that .400 average by collecting 4 hits in 10 at-bats, his feat is all but meaningless, since it's skewed by a small sample size. (Chapter 1-1)

Defensive Efficiency: A thumbnail measure of the team's defense that's also the flip side of BABIP. Defensive Efficiency measures the percentage of balls in play (i.e., non-home-run batted balls ending a plate appearance) that a defense converts into outs. As is the case with all other statistics, Defensive Efficiency works best when adjusted to reflect the tendencies of the park in question. For instance, in Boston, balls that bang off the Green Monster thirty feet in the air count against the defense, even though such a ball is impossible to turn into an out. (Chapter 3-2)

Defensive Spectrum: An observation by Bill James that talent is unequally distributed across the range of defensive positions: The harder the position, the fewer players capable of handling it at a major league level. The spectrum runs 1B-LF-RF-3B-CF-2B-SS, with catchers something of a special case but toward the right end as well. As players age, they tend to drift leftward on the defensive spectrum, toward positions requiring less defensive skill; think of an outfielder moving to first base as he gets older and slows down. The result is a greater pool of talent available to play those left-of-spectrum positions, enabling teams to find better hitters to take those jobs. Shifts to the left happen frequently, sometimes in the low minor leagues just after a player is drafted. Shifts to the right rarely take place with any success; an exception would be Cal Ripken Jr. moving from third base to shortstop as a rookie. (Chapter 3-2)

DERA: Derived from Pitching Runs Above Average (PRAA), it is simply the ERA a pitcher would need to have that many PRAA in this many innings, given that an average pitcher has an EqERA of 4.50. Like PRAA, DERA has been adjusted for park effects, league offensive level, and the team's fielding level. (Chapter 2-1)

DIPS: Stands for Defense-Independent Pitching Statistics. Developed by analyst Voros McCracken, DIPS attempts to isolate a pitcher's performance from that of the fielders supporting him. To do this, DIPS focuses on the elements of the game most under the pitcher's direct control: strikeouts, walks, hit batsmen, and home runs allowed. (Chapter 3-1)

DIPS ERA: An adjusted version of a pitcher's traditional ERA in keeping with the tenets of Voros McCracken's Defense-Independent Pitching Statistics. DIPS ERA differs from ERA in that the former uses as its components the elements of the game directly controlled by the pitcher (strikeouts, walks, hit batsmen, and home runs allowed). (Chapter 3-1)

DT: Davenport Translations, a process for converting a player's statistical line from one league into a line of statistics for a different league without changing the underlying value of those statistics when it comes to wins and losses. Players' statistics are a combination of their own skills and a background level of play that is unique to their league and park. DTs isolate the league and park effects from the stat line, allowing us to add the park and league effects we want—most often to give everybody the same effects and thus to project all players onto a common background. They are often used to compare players across eras (what would Ty Cobb hit if he played now?). They can also be used to convert minor league performances into an equally valuable major league line. In that context, they are conceptually similar to Bill James's Major League Equivalencies, although the procedure itself is totally different. (Batting Practice, Chapter 7-2)

DW: Delta Wins, the difference between actual wins and expected wins based on a Pythagorean Formula that uses runs or run components (hits, walks, total bases, hit by pitches, stolen bases, etc.). A positive number indicates a team that has won more games than expected from its statistics.

EqA: Equivalent Average, a rate statistic designed to do two things: measure the offensive performance of a player and make the result easy to understand.

EqA combines a player's abilities to hit for average, hit for power, draw walks, get hit by pitches, and steal bases. It adjusts for the offensive level of the league and of the park; it can also adjust for the difficulty level of the league or for not facing your own team's pitchers. It is basically Equivalent Runs per out, with some extra math included to make the answer look like a batting average. An average player in any league has, by definition, an EqA of .260 (unless league difficulty adjustments are made). The historical distribution between career EqAs and career batting averages is extremely close. Because of that, it is easy for even a casual fan to recognize the difference between a good EqA (.300), a really good EqA (.350), and a historically good EqA (.400) as well a really bad one (like Mario Mendoza's career .191 EqA). (Chapter 1-1, others)

EqBR: Equivalent Base Runs. A player's number of runs gained by baserunning (not including stolen bases) over league average, given his home park and the situations in which he ran the bases. The estimated number of runs gained is based on the Expected Runs Matrix (*see* Expected Runs) for the given season and the number of times the player took the extra base or was thrown out on the basepaths. (Chapter 4-1)

EqERA: Equivalent ERA, calibrated to an ideal major league where EqERA = 4.50. While a major league pitcher's equivalent stats should not differ substantially from his actual numbers, a minor league pitcher's equivalent stats undergo translation and may differ significantly. Equivalent stats are adjusted for park effects. (Chapters 2-1, 7-2)

EqR: Equivalent Runs, an estimate of how many runs a player produced for his team. EqR combines the abilities to hit for average, hit for power, draw walks, and steal bases—as well as playing time—into an estimate of runs added to an average team. When applied to teams throughout baseball history, EqR is a better estimator of how many runs they've scored than any other similar statistic (runs created, linear weights, etc.) we have tested. EqR is normally adjusted for park and league effects so that all players can be compared evenly (an EqR without those adjustments is called UEqR, for Unadjusted). A fan looking at EqR should think of them like runs or RBI; 100 in a season are a reasonable standard for excellence. (Chapter 1-1)

Expected Runs: The number of runs an average team will score in the remainder of the inning after a given number of outs and baserunners. For example, in 2005, with a man on first and no one out, teams scored an average of .90 runs in the rest of the inning. With a man on second and one out, they scored .69 runs. Expected Runs are extremely useful for testing the efficacy of 1-run strategies and analyzing the performance of relief pitchers. (Chapter 4-2)

Expected Wins: Like Expected Runs, Expected Wins show a team's odds of winning the game given the inning, score, outs, and baserunners. Expected Wins are expressed as a percentage. For example, in 2005, visiting teams leading by 1 run in the top of the ninth inning won the game 87.6 percent of the time; if the game was tied, they won only 47.9 percent of the time. Expected Wins has many of the same practical applications as Expected Runs, but the Win Expectancy framework has largely replaced it in practical application. The primary reason for this is because some situations happen very infrequently in a season, and thus there is no Expected Wins number associated with that situation for a given season. In 2005, no visiting team ever loaded the bases with no one out while trailing by 1 run in the eighth inning; no home team faced a tie game in the ninth with a man on third and no one out. The absence of data points for these situations makes the theoretical Win Expectancy Framework a more robust tool for analyzing questions involving Expected Wins. (Chapter 4-2)

FRA: Fair Run Average, which measures a pitcher's runs allowed per nine innings—adjusted to reflect the presence of inherited or bequeathed runners. (FRA also differs from the more traditional ERA in that it doesn't unfairly distinguish between earned and unearned runs.) For instance, if a starter leaves the game with the bases loaded and no outs and the subsequent reliever manages to polish off the inning without allowing a run, then that starter's "fair" runs allowed will exceed his actual runs allowed. After all, he deserved to give up more runs than he did in the frame, but thanks to the fine work of his bullpen, those three bequeathed runners didn't score. (Chapters 2-1, 3-1)

FRAA: Fielding Runs Above Average, the number of runs a fielder has saved his team compared to an average player at the same position. Fielding Runs are determined through a complicated process that begins by separating the team's defensive performance into pitching and fielding components. The team fielding is separated into catching, infield, and outfield portions; each of those is then split into separate positions; finally, each position is split into all of the players who played there during the season. At each step, the player's defensive statistics are compared to standards defined by the league and modified by the team's pitching (strikeouts, baserunners allowed, groundball/flyball ratios). The best player at any position in a given year is usually around 20 runs—typically a little higher for skill positions like shortstop and catcher and a little lower for first basemen and corner outfielders. (Chapter 3-2)

FRAR: Fielding Runs Above Replacement, similar to FRAA except that instead of being compared to an average player at his position, a player is compared to a replacement-level player at his position—roughly, the worst semiregular player in the league at that position. In general, the more important the position, the more runs the worst player costs you, so that FRAR works as a positional adjustment. In today's game, an average shortstop or catcher is about 30 runs better than replacement level over the course of a season, while an average first baseman is only about 10 runs better (and a designated hitter, of course, is worth no runs, defensively). In the past, with fewer strikeouts and more balls in play, fielders had a higher share of total team pitching plus fielding; this is reflected in higher FRAR for players from other eras. (Chapter 3-2)

G/F: The ratio of groundballs to flyballs hit by a batter or produced by a pitcher. Depending on the data source, sometimes this ratio includes all batted balls or just balls converted into outs (many systems now strip out line drives and popouts as well). Either way, it's a useful indicator for pitchers and one that correlates very well from year to year. Pitchers with a G/F ratio of 1.5 or greater are generally considered groundball pitchers. They tend to give up more base hits but fewer extra-base hits and home runs. Pitchers with G/F less than 1.5 are considered flyball pitchers. They tend to give up fewer base hits but more extra-base hits and home runs. Among pitchers who qualified for the ERA title in 2005 were Brandon Webb (4.58), Derek Lowe (3.69), and Jake Westbrook (3.61). The lowest G/F ratios were by John Patterson (0.90), Scott Elarton (0.90), and Chris Young (0.96). Among the ninety-two pitchers who qualified, the median G/F was 1.67. (Chapter 2-1)

Inherited runners: Baserunners still on base who are the responsibility of a previous pitcher when a relief pitcher comes into the game in the middle of an inning. We look at the percentage of inherited runners a relief pitcher allows to score in determining how well he's pitched when brought into jams. Provides a useful measure of a relief pitcher's value to the team. (Chapter 2-2)

ISO: Isolated Slugging, a measure used to evaluate a player's pure power. It's calculated by subtracting batting average from slugging average, i.e., SLG – AVG = ISO. Isolated Slugging is one of the most powerful predictors of a hitting prospect's future success. (Chapter 1-1)

League adjustments: A fundamental principle of statistical analysis in baseball is that environment must be accounted for. Most often, this takes the form of park adjustments, but league context is also critical. Because of factors like rule changes, playing styles, training and nutrition breakthroughs, trends in park construction, and even equipment, different eras can affect run scoring in different ways. For instance, in 1968, when the strike zone stretched from the hitter's shins to his shoulders, runs were hard to come by. But in, say, 1998, when the strike zone was much more compact and a number of hitter-friendly parks had been built, scoring levels were much, much higher. As a result, a run scored in one era may mean more or less than one scored in another era. (Batting Practice)

Leverage: Measures how important a given situation during a game is, relative to the start of the game. The start of the game is defined as a Leverage of 1.0. As the game progresses, the Leverage goes up and down, based on the inning, the number of outs, the runners on base, and the difference between the two teams' runs scored thus far. More specifically, Leverage is the ratio between how much a single run scored changes the expected probability of winning in the current situation and how much a run would have changed the expected probability of winning at the very beginning of the game. For example, if a run scored in the seventh inning increases the probability of winning by 10 percent, while a run at the start of the game increases it by 5 percent, the Leverage of the situation in the seventh inning is 10 percent/5 percent = 2.00 Leverage. (Chapter 2-2)

Linear Weights: Created by Pete Palmer for Total Baseball, a system of estimating runs by assigning a weight to each event (via Batting Runs, Pitching Runs, and Fielding Runs) and adding up the sums. The total represents the number of runs contributed or saved beyond those of a league-average player or team.

Line drive percentage: The percentage of those batted balls ending a plate appearance that are classified as a line drive, as opposed to a groundball, a flyball, or a pop-up. Can be used as a predictor of future batting average gains or losses. (Chapter 8-2)

Log-5: A method introduced by Bill James in the 1981 *Baseball Abstract* to predict the probability of victory when two teams of a given winning percentage play against one another. The formula for Log-5 is as follows:

$$\text{WPct} = \frac{A - A \times B}{A + B - 2 \times A \times B}$$

. . . where A is team A's winning percentage, and B is team B's winning percentage. The result of the formula indicates how often Team A should beat Team B. For example, if Team A wins 60 percent of its games and Team B wins 45 percent of its games, Team A should beat Team B 64.7 percent of the time. Researcher Tom Ruane has verified the log-5 method as an accurate predictor of team-versus-team matchups throughout baseball's history. (Chapter 9-3)

Luck: The number of extra wins or losses a pitcher totaled compared to his expected record. That expected record, also known as a Support-Neutral Won-Lost record, is the mark a pitcher "should" have reached given his own performance and park-adjusted, league-average support from his offense and his bullpen. (Chapter 2-1)

Also, an element that helps explain the gap between actual performance and expected performance. In baseball the role of luck, or perhaps more accurately randomness, cannot be overstated. From a performance-analysis standpoint, it rears its head to varying degrees in the rates of hits on batted balls in play, in a team's record in 1-run games, in the outcome of a short series, in the amount of offensive and bullpen support a pitcher gets, and in the season-to-season variations in player performance. All of these are generally the results of limited sample sizes, measured by imperfect tools. *See also* Delta Wins, DIPS, Regression to the mean, SNW. (Chapters 3-1, 5-3, 9-2)

Marginal cost: The additional cost occasioned by a certain move. For example, signing a $10 million a year player represents a marginal cost of $10 million, while trading a $7 million player for a $10 million one is a marginal cost of $3 million. Often compared with "marginal revenue," which is how much more income is generated by a given move (from added ticket sales, a free-agent signing, a new stadium). (Chapter 5-2)

Marginal Wins/Marginal Dollars: A statistic first devised by the late Baseball Prospectus author Doug Pappas that measures efficiency in team spending. Marginal Wins are the number of wins above what a team making the major league minimum could reasonably accumulate (set by Pappas at 49); Marginal Dollars are how much actual payroll exceeds the minimum for a forty-man roster ($13 million in 2003). Dividing the two provides a number ranging from under $500,000 per added win (extremely efficient) to more than $4 million per added win (extremely inefficient). (Chapter 5-2)

Mendoza Line: A hypothetical line representing a .200 batting average. The term is named after weak-hitting shortstop Mario Mendoza, who played nine otherwise unremarkable seasons from 1974 to 1982 for three teams. The idea behind the term holds that if you can't hit for a higher average than a popgun threat like Mendoza (though Mendoza's lifetime batting average was actually .215), you don't deserve a major league job. The concept has broader implications: It establishes a major league "replacement level," the bare-minimum skill level that allows teams to make intelligent spending decisions based on how much a player contributes above that threshold. (Chapter 5-1)

MLEs: Major League Equivalencies, a system developed by Bill James for translating minor league performances into their major league equivalents by adjusting not only for scoring environment and park effects but also for the quality of competition. By correcting for these often-drastic distortions (such as the inflated hitting stats of the Pacific Coast League), past minor league performances become as useful for predicting future major league performances as past major league performances. Thus, it becomes possible to compare the production of a Triple-A player with that of a marginal major leaguer in considering personnel decisions. James held that in terms of using his sabermetric findings to help a baseball team, MLEs were the most important research he had ever done. (Chapter 7-2)

MLV: Marginal Lineup Value, a statistic measuring offensive production, expressed in runs above an average offensive player. Conceptually, MLV takes a theoretical team of nine average hitters, then replaces one of them with the player we want to measure, gives him the same percentage of the team's total plate appearances as he had on his real team, and computes how many more (or fewer) runs the team would score as a result of the change. A positive MLV indicates that the player is above average. MLV can be negative, indicating the player is a below-average hitter. MLV is park-adjusted and calibrated to league average. Jason Giambi had a 41.0 MLV in 2005, meaning that his offense would have produced 41 more runs for an average team than a league-average hitter would have had in the same amount of playing time. (Chapter 1-1)

MLVr: Whereas MLV is a counting statistic like hits, home runs, or RBI, MLVr is a rate statistic like batting average or ERA. MLVr measures the rate of offensive production, expressed as runs per game. An MLVr of 0.000 is exactly league average (say, 4.50 runs per game). An MLVr of 0.100 means that an average team would score 0.1 more runs per game by replacing one of its hitters with this player (from 4.50 to 4.60 R/G). An MLVr of –0.050 means that an average team would score 0.05 R/G fewer with this player (from 4.50 to 4.45 R/G). (Chapter 1-1)

Normalization: As applied to baseball, the process of adjusting player statistics for a variety of contexts to allow better comparison without corrupting influences. For example, players compete in a variety of parks, leagues, and even historical eras that influence their performance. Normalization allows player performance from any league—minor leagues, foreign leagues, independent leagues—in any era to be compared to other players in different settings by removing extraneous factors and leveling the playing field. (Batting Practice)

NRA: Normalized Runs Allowed, used primarily in Davenport Translations to compare pitchers across different eras. Because some eras have vastly different averages—the 1960s were notoriously pitcher-friendly, while the late 1990s saw a massive increase in offense—pitchers with the same runs allowed (RA) in two different seasons may have different values to their teams. An RA of 4.00 in 2000 is very good; an RA of 4.00 in 1968 is very bad. NRA removes those differences and allows for an apples-to-apples comparison of pitchers from different eras. (Batting Practice)

Old player's skills: Hitters who walk a lot and strike out a lot without showing meaningful speed on the bases and while playing a noncritical defensive position are said to have "old-player skills." Players who show old-player skills early in their careers tend not to age well. In contrast, hitters who don't strike out much and run the bases well tend to hold up better over time. (Chapters 7-2, 7-3)

1-run strategy: In-game decisions that attempt to exchange the possibility of a big inning for the increased probability of scoring a single run. The most popular of these strategies are stolen bases, sacrifice bunts, and intentional walks, typically employed late in close games when the value of a single run is nearly as valuable as that of many runs. (Chapter 4-2)

OPS or PRO: The sum of on-base percentage plus slugging average (a.k.a. Production from Total Baseball). While math purists cringe at the notion of adding what are in essence two fractions with different denominators (OBP is based on plate appearances, SLG on at-bats), OPS is a quick-and-dirty stat for gauging offensive productivity. It's useful because it correlates better with run scoring than batting average, on-base percentage, or slugging average alone. However, OPS has its limitations. First, it assumes that OBP and SLG are of equal value while steamrolling the nuances preserved by keeping OBP and SLG separate. A hitter with a .350 OBP and a .350 SLG is very different from a hitter with a .250 OBP/.450 SLG; when considering how to build a lineup, those two players offer distinct pluses and minuses. OPS also ignores the context of ballpark effects and league scoring levels, both of which can greatly influence its two components. A .700 OPS in 1905 means something very different from a .700 OPS in 2005. The first limitation makes it more desirable to consider the trinity of AVG/OBP/SLG as a unit, with all of those nuances intact. The second limitation can be overcome by using a statistic such as Equivalent Average, which links the abilities to get on base and to advance runners with the run-scoring context. (Chapter 1-1)

OPS+ or PRO+: A comparison of a player's OPS (on-base percentage plus slugging average) to the park-adjusted league average, providing a good deal more context than OPS itself. The formula is:

$$100 \times [(\text{Player OBP})/(\text{Park-Adjusted League OBP}) + (\text{Player SLG})/(\text{Park-Adjusted League SLG}) - 1]$$

An OPS+ of 100 is average. Thus, an OPS+ greater than 100 is better than league average; less than 100 is worse than league average. (Chapter 1-1)

PADE: Park-Adjusted Defensive Efficiency. Based on Defensive Efficiency, PADE measures team defense by determining the percentage of balls in play a defense converted into outs and adjusting for the team's home park. For example, the Colorado Rockies face an inherent disadvantage in Defensive Efficiency because their park is so much larger than the league average. By adjusting for parks such as Coors Field, PADE shows how well each team's defense would have performed in a league-average ballpark.

PAP: Pitcher Abuse Points, a measure developed by Baseball Prospectus to quantify starting pitcher usage and the risk of ineffectiveness and injury associated with overuse. PAP is computed for each game started as PAP = (# pitches – 100)^3, if # pitches = more than 100, or 0 otherwise. (Chapter 2-3)

Park adjustments: Adjustments made to player statistics to reflect the playing environment. For example, a hitter slugging .500 in Coors Field, which drastically inflates run scoring, is showing less power than one slugging .475 in PETCO Park, which drastically deflates run scoring. Adjustments are made by comparing the numbers produced by a team and its opponents in home games versus what they produce in road games. Ideally, park adjustments will span at least three seasons so that a sizable data sample is used. (Batting Practice, Chapters 1-1, 8-2, others)

PECOTA: Short for Player Empirical Comparison and Optimization Test Algorithm (though the spelled-out version is not commonly used), a system used to forecast a player's future performance based not only on his own past statistics but on the statistics of players similar to him. Age, position, and body type are all taken into account, along with the adjustment of the player's statistics for ballpark, league, and quality of competition. Thus, a slow, slugging first baseman who walks a lot will be compared with the career progression of other slow, slugging first basemen who walked a lot, while a speedy center fielder will be compared to the progression of other speedy center fielders. PECOTA forecasts are expressed as a range of possible outcomes at the ninetieth, seventy-fifth, sixtieth, fiftieth, fortieth, twenty-fifth, and tenth percentiles, along with a weighted mean projection that accounts for the likelihood that performances in the lower percentiles will reduce his playing time. (Chapter 7-3)

PERA: A pitcher's ERA as estimated from his peripheral statistics—including homers, walks, and strikeouts per 9 innings—adjusted for ballpark, league, and level of competition (abbreviated as EqHR9, EqBB9, EqK9). Because it's not sensitive to the timing of batting events, PERA is less subject to luck than ERA and a better predictor of ERA going forward than actual ERA itself. PERA and its component peripherals are calibrated to an ideal league with an average PERA of 4.50. (Chapter 2-1)

Peripherals: The underlying pitching statistics that carry more predictive value (and thus offer more insight into a pitcher's true ability) than other stats more readily embraced by the mainstream. Key peripherals include strikeout rate, walk rate, groundball-to-flyball ratio, and home-run rate. Studies of pitcher performance show that those peripheral stats allow teams to better gauge a pitcher's future than won-lost record or even ERA. (Chapter 2-1)

Pitch counts: The number of pitches thrown by a pitcher in a game. The stat has gone from obscure to ubiquitous in the last decade, thanks to more advanced studies of pitcher usage and injuries. Studies of pitcher abuse—including those conducted by Baseball Prospectus—have shown that high-pitch-count starts can lead to future injuries and ineffectiveness for pitchers. Those findings remain controversial, though, given the multitude of variables associated with pitching performance and the numerous different types of pitchers. (Chapter 2-3)

Playoff Success Points (PSP): A measure designed by Nate Silver to indicate a team's degree of success in the postseason in the era of divisional play. PSP assigns points to playoff teams as follows:

- 3 points for making the playoffs
- 3 points for winning the LDS
- 4 points for winning the LCS
- 4 points for winning the World Series
- 1 point for each postseason win
- –1 point for each postseason loss

The highest possible PSP is 25, for a team that sweeps through all eleven postseason games, while the lowest is 0, for a team that is swept in the first round. (Chapter 9-3)

Plexiglas Principle: The tendency of players or teams to alternate seasons of improvement with those of decline. Bill James introduced this term in the 1982 *Baseball Abstract* by likening that proclivity to a piece of Plexiglas, which, once bent, tends to return to form. It's really just a colorful, nonmathematical term for describing the concept of regression to the mean.

PMLV/PMLVr: Positional MLV (PMLV) is like MLV, except instead of comparing a batter to a league-average hitter, he is compared to an average hitter at the position he plays. First basemen are compared to an average first baseman; shortstops are compared to average-hitting shortstops. PMLVr is the rate statistic version, measuring the runs per game the batter produced above an average hitter at the same position. (Chapter 1-1)

PRAA: Pitching Runs Above Average, the number of runs that a pitcher saved his team compared to what an average pitcher would have allowed in the same number of innings. Pitchers are rated primarily by the number of runs (all runs, not just earned runs) they allow. We make adjustments for park effects and for league offensive level, just as we do for batting stats. However, pitchers also receive an adjustment for the quality of the fielders working behind them, who can have an enormous influence on the pitcher's statistics (*see* FRAA and FRAR). Strikeout pitchers are somewhat less dependent on their defensive support than finesse pitchers, and this is also reflected in PRAA. (Chapter 2-1)

PRAR: Pitching Runs Above Replacement, like PRAA except that we compare a pitcher's adjusted runs allowed to a replacement pitcher rather than an average pitcher. The level of a replacement pitcher has changed dramatically over time, increasing as the pitcher's share of total defense (pitching plus fielding) has increased—as indicated by higher strikeout, walk, and home-run rates over time. The WARP system considers replacement-level defense—a replacement-level pitcher combined with a full set of replacement-level fielders—to be worth a little more than 3 runs a game. The pitcher's share of those 3 or more runs has increased from about 15 percent in the 1800s to about 70 percent today. Thus, the RA of a replacement-level pitcher has risen from about 5.00 in the 1880s to about 6.75 today (on a scale where 4.50 = league average). (Chapter 2-1)

Pythagenport: The general name given to certain versions of the Pythagorean formula. Instead of using a fixed exponent, like "2" or "1.83," Pythagenport versions use a variable exponent based on runs scored and allowed per game—the more runs, the higher the exponent. The first such formula, developed by Clay Davenport, used a logarithmic formula to estimate the exponent; later versions by other researchers, notably David Smyth and a blogger known as "Patriot," developed simpler and better versions (sometimes called "Pythagenpat"). (pp. 308, 309)

Pythagorean Formula: Developed by Bill James around 1980, in answer to the question: Can you tell how many games a team will win, based on its runs scored and runs allowed? James found that there was a simple relationship between them, namely, that winning percentage was roughly equal to runs scored, squared, divided by the square of runs scored plus the square of runs allowed; writing it out reminded him of $C^2 = A^2 + B^2$, the equation credited to the Greek mathematician Pythagoras describing the sides of a right triangle. James subsequently claimed that using an exponent of 1.83 in the formula worked better than 2; later researchers found that the formula could be adjusted for even more accuracy (*see* Pythagenport). (Chapter 8-1)

RA: Run Average, the number of runs (earned and unearned) allowed by a pitcher or team per 9 innings. Many measures of pitcher success focus on earned runs, but the arbitrary nature of official scoring and error attribution, the problems of reconstructing an inning to determine unearned runs, and the relatively small number of errors nowadays compared to a century ago (before gloves were used) make considering *all* runs allowed by a pitcher more desirable from a predictive standpoint. Pitchers good at preventing earned runs tend to be good at preventing unearned runs. (Chapters 2-1, 3-1)

RA: Runs allowed, the total number of runs allowed by a team (most often used as a component in calculating a team's expected winning percentage via the Pythagorean formula); or the total number of runs, including unearned runs, allowed by a pitcher, to be used in calculating Run Average, which is useful for the reasons stated previously. (Chapters 2-1, 3-1)

RA+: A comparison of the number of runs per 9 innings (both earned and unearned) allowed by a particular pitcher to the performance of a league-average pitcher in the same ballpark. RA+ is calculated by taking the league RA (Run Average) per 9 innings, multiplying it by a park factor (which expresses the percentage by which a player's home ballpark inflates or deflates scoring), dividing that by the pitcher's RA, and multiplying the result by 100. An RA+ of 100 is league average, an RA+ of 110 is 10 percent better than league average, and an RA+ of 90 is 10 percent worse than league average.

RA+ is thus ideally suited to compare pitchers across contexts and eras. If we compare the relative quality of Bob Gibson's 1968 (in which he posted an

ERA of 1.12 and an RA of 1.45 in a league that averaged 3.43 runs per game) and Pedro Martinez's 2000 (an ERA of 1.74 and an RA of 1.82 in a league that averaged 5.30 runs per game), we find that once the league context is taken into account, Martinez's 293 RA+ (in fact the top single-season RA+ since 1890) is better than Gibson's 236 (which ranks eighth). (Batting Practice, Chapter 2-1)

RBI Opportunities: The total number of runners on base during a player's at-bats, as defined by Baseball Prospectus's RBI Opportunities report at BaseballProspectus.com. The report also shows which bases those runners occupied. Different hitters will get different numbers of RBI Opportunities depending on multiple factors, including the on-base percentage of batters in front of them and total number of plate appearances. This can cause observers to label certain high-RBI hitters as "clutch," when in fact they're benefiting from greater opportunities. (Chapters 1-1, 1-2)

RCAA: Runs Created Above Average, an offensive statistic created by Lee Sinins that determines how many runs a hitter contributes relative to the league-average hitter.

Regression analysis: A statistical technique for estimating the value of one variable based on another. Visually, this can easily be represented on a scatter-plot graph with the independent variable on one axis and the dependent variable on the other. Viewed this way, the relationship between the two variables often appears as a line or trend on the graph. Determining the relationship—or "line of best fit," as it is sometimes called—involves the technique of Least Squares.

Regression to the mean: Baseball statistics are imperfect tools for measuring player performance. Given enough at-bats or innings pitched, the performance of a given player will reflect his actual skills. But the number of opportunities in a single season—to say nothing of a month, or a best-of-seven playoff series—generally isn't enough for the performance and skill levels to converge perfectly. A good deal of randomness or luck comes into play, exaggerating the difference between players. Players whose performances tend toward the extremes—say, a batter hitting .450 or .150 for a couple of weeks, or a reliever allowing a 5.00 ERA one year and a 2.00 ERA the next—are almost always benefiting from a run of simple random luck (good or bad) beyond their inherent level of ability. Since randomness is, well, random, you don't expect to see it continue, so the observed performance more likely will be closer to the player's actual level than continue on a very lucky (or unlucky) streak. This statistical phenomenon, known as regression to the mean, has been observed in venues far beyond baseball stats. It's the great equalizer, the reason streaks and slumps don't last forever. (Chapter 9-2)

Replacement level: The expected level of performance a major league team will receive from one or more of the best available players who substitute for a suddenly unavailable starting player at the same position, who can be obtained with minimal expenditure of team resources. Measuring player value, the difference from replacement level, instead of the difference from average, more properly accounts for the value of durability and better reflects the distribution of talent that major league teams are able to draw from. (Chapter 5-1)

Baseball Prospectus uses the following formulas as replacement level, based on research presented in *Baseball Prospectus 2002*. For position players, replacement level is set at a percentage of the average production for the position, measured in runs per out.

Position	Replacement Level %
1B, DH	75
2B, 3B, SS, OF	80
Catcher	85
Pitcher	100 (applies to pitcher's hitting only; see below)

For pitchers, replacement-level Run Average (RA) is defined as:

Starting pitchers: RepLvlRA = 1.38 × LeagueRA – 0.66
Relief pitchers: RepLvlRA = 1.70 × LeagueRA – 2.27

R-squared: The common name for the "coefficient of determination," a statistical measure that indicates the proportion of variance explained by a variable, expressed on a scale of zero to 1. (An R-squared of zero represents complete randomness, while 1 indicates a perfect determination.) In English, that means that when two variables are used in a regression, R-squared shows how much of the change in the second variable is a result of changes in the first. For example, batter strikeout rate and Isolated Slugging (ISO) usually have a high R-squared because players swinging for the fences have a propensity to strike out. Likewise, of the three major rate stats—AVG, OBP, and SLG—OBP has the highest R-squared when correlated to run scoring, meaning the team with the highest OBP will score the most runs more often than the team with the highest AVG or SLG. The high R-squared between OBP and team run scoring is one of the major reasons the Oakland Athletics determined that OBP was undervalued in the late 1990s, one of the main points of Michael Lewis's best-selling book *Moneyball*.

Run environment: A term used to describe how park and league factors affect run-scoring levels. For example, Dodger Stadium in 1968 was much more hostile to hitters than Coors Field in 2000. (Chapter 8-2)

Run Expectancy Table (a.k.a. Base-Out Matrix State, a.k.a. Expected Run Matrix): A table showing the twenty-four combinations of outs and bases occupied and the number of runs a team can expect to score in the rest of that inning given that situation. For example, in 2005, teams in bases-loaded, no-out situations averaged 2.31 runs scored, while teams with two outs and nobody on averaged 0.11 runs. A Run Expectancy Table is often based on several seasons' worth of data. It can be used to estimate the value of a given strategy, such as sacrificing a runner on second base over to third with nobody out. It's important to remember that such outcomes are based on average hitters and pitchers and that different skill levels need to be taken into account as well. (Chapter 4-2)

Runs Created: A seminal modern offensive statistic created by Bill James, one of a number of statistics that attempts to account for multiple offensive events in one number. Its basic formula is OBP × TB, or (Hits + Walks) × total bases/plate appearances. More complicated forms include stolen bases, intentional walks, grounded into double plays, etc.

Sabermetrics: Popular name for advanced baseball statistical analysis, coined by Bill James after the acronym for the Society for Advanced Baseball Research (SABR, pronounced "saber"), where much of the early work was done. James defined the field simply as "the search for objective knowledge about baseball."

SNL: Support-Neutral Loss(es), the expected number of losses a pitcher would accumulate given his performance plus park-adjusted, league-average offensive and bullpen support. (Chapter 2-1)

SNLVA: Support-Neutral Lineup-adjusted Value Added, the number of wins above average added by a pitcher's performance, given league-average offensive and bullpen support and adjusted for the Marginal Lineup Value rate of each batter a pitcher faced. (Chapter 2-1)

SNLVAR: Support-Neutral Lineup-adjusted Value Added above Replacement, the number of wins above replacement level (as opposed to average) added by a pitcher's performance, given league-average offensive and bullpen support and adjusted for the Marginal Lineup Value rate of each batter a pitcher faced. (Chapter 2-1)

SNVAR: Support-Neutral Value Above Replacement, the number of wins above replacement level added by a pitcher's performance, given league-average offensive and bullpen support. (Chapter 2-1)

SNW: Support-Neutral Win(s), the expected number of wins a pitcher would accumulate given his performance plus park-adjusted, league-average offensive and bullpen support. The Support-Neutral stats, created by Baseball Prospectus author Michael Wolverton and updated by Keith Woolner, are a way to measure a starting pitcher's performance in the familiar terms of wins and losses but without the distortions that make actual won-lost records extremely flawed. (Chapter 2-1)

Speed Score: One of five metrics used in the PECOTA projection system to identify players comparable to a given hitter. Speed Scores include five components: stolen-base percentage, stolen-base attempts as a percentage of times on first base, triples, double plays grounded into, and runs scored as a percentage of times on base. (Chapters 4-1, 7-3)

Statistical significance: An expression of the certainty that the result of an analysis is not random. Statistical significance is sometimes referred to as if there is a hard-and-fast level of significance, but in reality, significance is expressed in levels, or percentages. (It may also be referred to as the observed significance level, or p-value.) Results of statistical analysis can be significant at any percentage, allowing the certainty of the results of an analysis to be quantified. For example, if you wanted to determine the average walk rate in the National League, sampling a smaller number of players will yield an estimate of the overall league average. Depending on the number of players sampled, the statistical significance may be any number of values, expressing the certainty that the walk rates of the small group of players sampled matches the overall league average. As that sample size grows, the statistical significance of the result increases as well because you can be surer that the observed average is very close to the overall average. (Chapter 9-2)

Stress: A characterization of how much of a pitcher's workload has been compressed into high pitch count outings. Higher stress ratings over the course of a career are associated with a higher likelihood of arm injuries. Stress = PAP/# pitches. (Chapter 2-3)

Support (bullpen): A cousin of run support, bullpen support measures the contributions relievers make in a given pitcher's games. In addition to won-lost record, bullpen support can also skew a pitcher's ERA. If a reliever replaces the starter with two outs and two on and gives up a 3-run homer to the worst hitter in baseball, the starter bears the brunt of that lousy performance by adding 2 earned runs to his ledger. (Chapters 2-1, 3-1)

Support (run): The number of runs a team scores when a given pitcher is on the mound. This can have a significant effect on a pitcher's won-lost record that's beyond his control. In 1987, Nolan Ryan led the league with a sparkling 2.76 ERA (and 270 strikeouts) for the Houston Astros but still finished with an ugly 8-16 record, thanks largely to poor run support. Meanwhile, Aaron Sele posted an 18-9 record in 1999, thanks to strong run support from the Texas Rangers—despite a 4.79 ERA that even after adjusting for his hitter-friendly home park was still just a tick better than average. Baseball Prospectus's Support-Neutral statistics strip out run support to evaluate pitchers based on their own achievements rather than their teammates'. (Chapter 2-1)

Talent Pyramid: Baseball ability is not distributed equally. Rather, the distribution of talent is more like that of a pyramid. The largest number of players—say, those unable to make the jump from amateur baseball to the pros—form the base. Somewhere above that level are those capable of a replacement-level performance in the major leagues, a smaller subset of the remaining population. Above those are major league starters. Above that level are major league stars. The elite superstars of the game reside at the tip of the pyramid. If there are ten players currently playing who will wind up in the Hall of Fame, there may be one hundred capable of making an All-Star team, three hundred capable of holding down a regular job, one thousand who might appear in a major league game in a single year, and six thousand playing professional baseball. The pyramid helps to explain why the superstars make the salaries they do. Elite talent is truly scarce, whereas average to good players are comparatively plentiful and players worth the league minimum abound.

Three True Outcomes: Another term for strikeouts, walks, and home runs, Three True Outcomes are those events that occur independent of the defense. Three True Outcome hitters have often been underrated and underpaid, with teams underrating the value of walks and overrating the impact of a batter's strikeout. Baseball Prospectus celebrates the Three True Outcomes by recognizing the hitter who had the highest percentage of his plate appearances result in a strikeout, walk, or home run. On the flip side, a pitcher who racks up a lot of strikeouts while yielding few walks and homers is said to possess good peripherals and is a candidate for future success. The term "Three True Outcomes" is derived from a tongue-in-cheek cult called the "Rob Deer Fan Club" whose eponymous slugger excelled at producing all three outcomes.

TINSTAAPP: A term coined by Baseball Prospectus founder Gary Huckabay that stands for "There Is No Such Thing As A Pitching Prospect." TINSTAAPP is meant to be a warning to teams not to overinvest in young pitchers—especially high school pitchers—due to their high attrition rates. The term shouldn't be taken absolutely literally, as some pitching prospects do beat the odds and become successful major leaguers. Inspired by TANSTAAFL, an acronym for "There Ain't No Such Thing As A Free Lunch" from Robert Heinlein's classic book *The Moon Is a Harsh Mistress.*

UZR: An individual defensive statistic developed by independent statistician Mitchel Lichtman, Ultimate Zone Rating uses a similar technique to Zone Rating but makes adjustments such as comparing players to the league-average fielder, then expresses its results in the number of runs each fielder saved his team. The results of UZR are very similar to FRAA, but whereas FRAA estimates the fielder's total chances based on commonly available statistics, UZR does so with newly available play-by-play data.

Variance/standard deviation: Variance measures the dispersion of values around their average. If a set of values are widely scattered around the average, the variance will be high. If the values are close to the average, the value will be low. The standard deviation is simply the square root of the variance. For many kinds of statistical analyses in baseball, the standard deviation is a useful measure to include because it helps quantify the amount of statistical noise we would expect to see. Approximately two-thirds of all observed values will fall within plus or minus one standard deviation, and about 95 percent of all observed values will fall within two standard deviations of the mean due just to randomness and a limited sample size.

Suppose a player is a "true" .300 hitter, and thus has exactly a 30 percent chance of getting a hit in each at-bat. Over the course of 600 at-bats, we'd expect him to have 180 hits (the average, or mean, number). The standard deviation is 11.22 hits, meaning that about two seasons out of three, we'd expect him to have between 168.78 (180 – 11.22) and 191.22 hits (180 + 11.22), which corresponds to an observed batting average of between .281 and .319.

VORP: Value Over Replacement Player captures most aspects of a player's value. It is like MLV, except instead of comparing a batter to a league-average hitter, he is compared to a replacement-level hitter at the position he plays. First basemen are compared to a replacement-level first baseman; shortstops are compared to replacement hitting shortstops. (Chapter 1-1, others)

VORPr: The rate statistic version of VORP, measuring the runs per game the batter produced above a replacement hitter at the same position. *See* MLV, Replacement Level, VORP. (Chapter 1-1)

WARP (WARP-1, WARP-2, WARP-3): Wins Above Replacement Player. WARP combines a player's BRAR, PRAR, and FRAR into a single estimate of how many wins that player was worth to his team, compared to a replacement-level player. Note that the replacement-level player used in WARP is substantially worse than the replacement-level player used by other statistics, such as VORP. The traditional definition of replacement level considers the hitting level of an average defensive player, while the WARP replacement player is both a bad hitter and a bad fielder (and a bad pitcher, if he did that too). As a result, a team composed entirely of replacement-level players would be really, really bad, only winning about 25 games in a full season. The different flavors of WARP reflect different applications of the system. In WARP-1, players are compared only to the rest of their league. WARP-2 adds two adjustments: It uses a rating of the league's quality of play to adjust all players in a league up or down, and it normalizes fielding totals across time. WARP-3 is exactly like WARP-2, except that it expands the rating to a 162-game schedule. This allows nineteenth-century stars, who played with short schedules and difficulty ratings stacked against them, to shine a little more brightly. (multiple chapters)

WinEx: Win-Expectancy framework, a theoretical framework introduced in *Baseball Prospectus 2005*. WinEx determines the probability that a team will win the game based on the overall offensive tendencies of the two teams involved, the number of outs, the inning, the score, and the runners on base. As opposed to observed win expectation (*see* Expected Wins), WinEx's theoretical framework does not suffer small sample-size issues, allowing win expectations to be calculated for hypothetical situations and games that have not actually occurred yet and making it a more complete and intuitive measure of a team's chances of winning a game. (Chapter 4-2)

Winning percentage: A team's wins divided by its total games played (or, for pitchers, wins divided by total decisions). This is written as a decimal but is easily understood as a percentage: A team with a .600 winning percentage has won 60 percent of its games—excellent in baseball. (Chapter 8-3)

W-L record: For a team, the total number of wins and losses (won-lost) accumulated to date in a season. For a pitcher, the total number of wins and losses credited to that pitcher. (In either case, wins are always listed first, so that "20-10" indicates 20 wins and 10 losses.) Since the rules governing pitcher wins and losses can be somewhat arbitrary—the winning pitcher is the one who was in the game when his team took the lead for good, regardless of who pitched the most effectively—W-L record is considered by most sabermetricians to be a poor gauge of a pitcher's actual performance level. (Chapter 2-1)

WX: Win expectation is the increase in the probability of a pitcher's team going on to win the game given the game situation (inning, number of outs, runners on base, run differential) from when the pitcher entered the game until his exit, and how many runs the pitcher allowed to score, assuming that the pitcher's team has a league average distribution of run scoring, and that all other pitchers on his team who follow are average. For example, Chad Orvella came into a game on July 22, 2005, with no outs in the sixth, a runner on first base, and a 2-run lead. He pitched two innings, stranding the runner, and allowing no additional runs to score. That performance increased Tampa Bay's expected probability of winning from 73.0 to 90.8 percent. So Orvella is credited with $0.908 - 0.730 = 0.178$ WX. (Chapter 2-2)

WXRL: Win expectation, adjusted for replacement level and lineup faced. WXRL is like WX but also adjusts the expected probability of winning during the pitcher's appearances for how strong the opposing batters he faced have been during the season. It also compares the pitcher's performance to how a replacement-level pitcher would have done in the same situation and number of innings. (Chapter 2-2)

ZR: Zone Rating, an individual defensive statistic developed by STATS, Inc., divides the field into zones. ZR assigns each player a specific part of the field—his "zone"—and determines the percentage of balls hit into that zone that he fielded. (Chapter 3-2)

Acknowledgments

A man I greatly respect once said that an editor's job is much like a tailor's: His work can be no better than the fabric he gets to work with. In the case of *Baseball Between the Numbers,* my seven coauthors contributed the finest cloth imaginable. I'm humbled by their hard work and tremendous insight and hope this book fits you well.

Nate Silver played a key role from day one. As Baseball Prospectus's executive vice president, he helped cultivate the group's relationship with our publisher, Basic Books. Nate fleshed out numerous chapter ideas, developing much of the template on which the book rests. He introduced thought-provoking new research in his writing, uncovering findings that often—I was thrilled to find—countered previously held beliefs. He helped refine topics near the end of the process that gave the book a needed lift in crunch time.

Before I can thank Keith Woolner for his huge contributions to this book, I should first point to the many contributions he'd previously made to the field of baseball analysis. Over the years, Keith has taken on both conventional wisdom and conventional sabermetric wisdom, changing the way we think about the game. His advances in such areas as identifying a replacement level for major league players informs the work of countless budding baseball analysts while also offering more casual fans new ways to appreciate the game. Keith's tremendous work extends from his enlightening writing to his vetting and polishing of various parts of this book, including the glossary.

Many Baseball Prospectus authors wear multiple hats, as their talents are in demand for many different roles. James Click was one of the book's most prolific authors during one of the busiest and most successful years of his life. His constant professionalism and patience, despite my endless e-mails and instant messages asking for "just one more thing," won't soon be forgotten. Another jack-of-many-trades, Dayn Perry, is one of Baseball Prospectus's most popular and prolific Web columnists and a key contributor to *Baseball Prospectus 2006* as well as a vital component of the *Baseball Between the Numbers* team. Oh, and he also recently added a book of his own to his impressive résumé. Neil deMause has proven a worthy successor to the late Doug Pappas; although Neil himself would quickly note that Doug could never truly be replaced, Baseball Prospectus is fortunate to have an accomplished and savvy writer such as Neil to cover the business of baseball, both for the BP Web site and in this book.

Clay Davenport and Steven Goldman stepped into this project at just the right time, employing their unique talents with aplomb. Many of the book's chapters that don't include his byline nonetheless owe a debt to Clay's work. It's the rare analyst who can take concepts as complex as defensive statistics or an all-in-one offensive measure and make them as simple to understand as Clay has. Steven's hand has also touched many aspects of this book, often quietly and behind the scenes. Need a pithy Casey Stengel quote to make a point? Steven's your man. Want to know the skinny on the 1912 St. Louis Browns? Steven's got it covered. He was also there whenever I needed editorial guidance or good humor during difficult times, having turned challenging deadlines and the writing of a massive group of authors into excellence with his work on the 2005 book *Mind Game*. Merci, mon ami.

Steven sang the praises of Jason Karegeannes for Jason's tireless efforts on *Mind Game;* now Jason gets to hear it from me too: Thanks for being there throughout this project, often on incredibly short notice. Mike Groopman's research skills likewise lent a big hand to the facts and figures you'll read in these pages. Baseball Prospectus authors Jay Jaffe and Will Carroll were also valuable contributors: Will for his guidance in assembling the chapter on steroids, Jay for his excellence under the gun when the glossary turned into a far more ambitious effort than first expected.

A number of outside parties—friends, colleagues, spouses, respected peers—played important roles at various times. My ridiculously supportive and wonderful wife, Angèle Fauchier, offered constant warmth and good wishes from start to finish. As if that weren't enough, she also provided a key piece of statistical analysis at a critical juncture. She'll become Dr. Fauchier soon after this book is published, and I couldn't be prouder.

Our agent and trusted adviser, Sydelle Kramer, helped make this book happen, then provided valuable counsel well into extra innings. Rod Fort, Andrew Ross, Thomas Hubbard, Frank Rashid, Tom Goldstein, and Andy Gefen get big thanks for their help on the business-of-baseball side. Steven Walters helped us answer the seminal question, "Is A-Rod Overpaid?" Mindy Nass chipped in with some valuable pre-editing editing. We can't thank all our media friends who supported this book after this note was written, so we'll extend a blanket thank-you to all those fine folks. Alan Schwarz, Ken Rosenthal, Allen Barra, and Rob Neyer get big thanks for their help earlier in the process. Thanks also to David Leonhardt and Lee Froelich.

This book borrows from and expands upon the analytical groundwork laid by Baseball Prospectus's forefathers as well as its contemporaries. For their groundbreaking research and on-field tactics that have led to many of the topics discussed here, we're grateful to, among others, Bill James, Pete Palmer, John Thorn, Dick Cramer, Craig Wright, George Lindsey, Earnshaw Cook, Henry Chadwick, David Tate, Branch Rickey, Allan Roth, Earl Weaver, Casey Stengel, Billy Martin, and Voros McCracken.

When the Baseball Prospectus name appears on any project, that stamp represents the collective work of scores of contributors over the last decade. Though you won't see their bylines within these pages, we'd have never arrived at this point without their tireless work. Sacrifices have been made; gracious spouses have had their endless patience tested and retested; grand plans to win world hang-gliding championships have been placed on hold. Sincere thanks go to present and past Baseball Prospectus contributors not already mentioned in these acknowledgments, including Gary Huckabay, Dave Pease, Christina Kahrl, Joe Sheehan, Michael Wolverton, Rany Jazayerli, Derek Zumsteg, Jim Baker, Ben Murphy, Keith Law, Doug Pappas, Chris Schofield, Mike Rice, John Erhardt, Mark McClusky, Tom Fontaine, Bill Burke, Dave Metz, Ryan Wilkins, David Cameron, Jeff Bower, Mark Armour, Jeff Hildebrand, Greg Spira, Tom Gorman, and Gary Gillette. Also, thanks to every Baseball Prospectus intern who's ever slaved away multiple hours on a weekend when they could have been sitting by a pool somewhere, doing keg stands and all the other wholesome activities available to exuberant college students. We're grateful that you chose to funnel some of that exuberance into largely anonymous work that makes the rest of us look good.

It was Bill Frucht who used the tailor analogy to describe the role of an editor, and it was Bill who provided a steadying influence throughout the book process. Never overzealous but always seeking to improve the final product, his approach was perfect for a group of talented authors with strong convictions, plus one occasionally harried Canadian. We also give thanks to John Sherer, David Shoemaker, Jamie Brickhouse, Liz Maguire, Will Morrison Garland, Vince Wladika, Connie Oehring, and many others at Basic Books.

Finally, thanks to you, the readers. Nothing makes us happier than hearing from people who boast of their dog-eared copy of *Baseball Prospectus 1996*, one of less than two hundred sold. From those humble beginnings, we've been fortunate to have many more readers follow us through our annual book, on the Web at BaseballProspectus.com and elsewhere, into new projects such as *Baseball Between the Numbers*. We sincerely hope this book reaches well beyond that core group of Baseball Prospectus enthusiasts, making a new generation of baseball fans think—and smile, and laugh.

Index

The Baseball Prospectus
Team of Experts

Editor

Jonah Keri is a stock market writer and editor for *Investor's Business Daily*. He writes the "Keeping Score" column on college basketball for *The New York Times*, covers baseball for YESNetwork.com and everything from hockey to cricket and all sports in between for ESPN.com's Page 2.

Authors

James Click left Baseball Prospectus shortly after the completion of this book and is now the Coordinator of Baseball Operations for the Tampa Bay Devil Rays, where he spends his time doing proprietary statistical research not unlike that contained in the book you're holding.

Clay Davenport is a meteorologist, so you could say that he has plenty of forecasting experience. His contributions to the field of baseball analysis include the Davenport Translations, Equivalent Average, and other seminal concepts and statistics.

Neil deMause is the co-author of *Field of Schemes: How the Great Stadium Swindle Turns Public Money Into Private Profit*, and he runs the stadium news Web site fieldofschemes.com. In addition to his work for Baseball Prospectus, he has written regularly for the *Village Voice* sports section, SportsJones.com, and other publications.

Steven Goldman writes the "Pinstriped Bible" and companion blog at YESNetwork.com, the "You Could Look It Up" history column for baseball prospectus.com, and he is a columnist for *The New York Sun*. He's the author of *Forging Genius: The Making of Casey Stengel*, the editor of Baseball Prospectus's *Mind Game*, and co-editor of the best-selling Baseball Prospectus annual.

Dayn Perry is a regular contributor to FOXSports.com. He's written for Baseball Prospectus, ESPN.com, the *Washington Monthly*, the *Montreal Gazette*, the *Miami Herald*, and *The New York Sun*, among others. He is the author of *Winners: How Good Baseball Teams Become Great Ones*.

Nate Silver is the Executive Vice President of Baseball Prospectus and the creator of the PECOTA projection system. He has also written on behalf of *Sports Illustrated*, ESPN.com, and *Slate*.

Keith Woolner works in the software industry. He has been analyzing and writing about baseball for more than ten years. He earned undergraduate degrees from M.I.T. in mathematics, computer science, and management and a master's degree from Stanford University in decision analysis.